Classical Rhetorics and Rhetoricians

CLASSICAL RHETORICS AND RHETORICIANS

Critical Studies and Sources

Edited by

Michelle Ballif

and

Michael G. Moran

Westport, Connecticut
London

Library of Congress Cataloging-in-Publication Data

Classical rhetorics and rhetoricians : critical studies and sources / edited by Michelle Ballif
and Michael G. Moran.
    p. cm.
Includes bibliographical references and index.
ISBN 0-313-32178-7 (alk. paper)
    1. Classical literature—History and criticism—Theory, etc. 2. Rhetoric, Ancient.
I. Ballif, Michelle, 1964– II. Moran, Michael G.
PA3013.C58 2005
880'.09—dc22   2004062806

British Library Cataloguing in Publication Data is available.

Library of Congress Catalog Card Number: 2004062806
ISBN: 0-313-32178-7

First published in 2005

Praeger Publishers, 88 Post Road West, Westport, CT 06881
An imprint of Greenwood Publishing Group, Inc.
www.praeger.com

Printed in the United States of America

The paper used in this book complies with the
Permanent Paper Standard issued by the National
Information Standards Organization (Z39.48-1984).

10 9 8 7 6 5 4 3 2 1

CONTENTS

Introduction

Michelle Ballif and Michael G. Moran

Although classical rhetoric has survived a multiple-millennia history, at times subject to slander as well as praise, it has only recently, within the last century, been historicized more generally within the history of rhetoric. Writing in 1983, James J. Murphy noted that it "is indeed ironic" that rhetoric—"one of the very oldest and most truly international human disciplines"—"should even today suffer from the lack of a complete historical account of its development" (1). Although this volume cannot claim to provide a "complete historical account," it seeks to contribute to the project of writing, specifically rewriting, the history of rhetoric in the Western tradition by refiguring classical rhetorics and rhetoricians.

Since the time of Murphy's lament, rhetoric scholars have produced a generous number of important contributions to the history of rhetoric. This is not to say that the historiography of rhetoric was altogether neglected prior to the past few decades; indeed, classical authors themselves historicized the rhetorical tradition. However, the history of rhetoric has certainly garnered the recent attention of a multitude of researchers—George Kennedy, Richard Enos, Jeffrey Walker, Sharon Crowley, and Edward Schiappa, to name only a handful—resulting in a rich body of historical work, which informs the theory and practice of contemporary rhetoric and composition studies.

In exciting and interesting ways, much of this current work challenges our historical understanding, calling into question the authorship of rhetorical texts as well as the very existence of some rhetorical figures, such as the infamous "Tisias," one of the supposed inventors of rhetoric. Additionally, scholars pose an even greater challenge to the history of rhetoric: alongside this proliferation of new histories is a concern for revising the historical tradition by exposing its prejudices and its blind spots, and for composing more inclusive histories. Specifically, scholars of rhetoric have challenged the rhetorical tradition and the histories thereof for their exclusions of women and of sophistry.

That is, scholars have cast a gendered lens on the rhetorical tradition, inquiring how classical rhetoric has been theorized as a practice—as "public, deliberative discourse"—which by its very definition excluded women as participants, as Kennedy notes: "Classical rhetoric was largely a male phenomenon [. . . .] Women were not allowed to speak in the law courts or political assemblies in Greece or Rome; public speaking by women was largely restricted to a few queens ruling in their own right in Greek-speaking portions of Asia Minor or in Egypt" ("Classical Rhetoric" 93). In response, Cheryl Glenn writes, "Rhetoric always inscribes the relation of language and power at a particular moment (including who may speak, who may listen or who will agree to listen, and what can be said); therefore, canonical rhetorical history has represented the experience of males, powerful males, with no provision or allowance for females" (1–2). Glenn continues with a call for "inclusionary rhetorics of the future, rhetorics that will account for the regendered rhetorical terrain on which feminist archaeologists and researchers have already begun to identify women's bodies" (2). Examples of such inclusionary rhetorics would include the work of Andrea Lunsford, Susan C. Jarratt, and Patricia Bizzell, and would employ a variety of methodological strategies. According to Bizzell, there are at least three such strategies for regendering the history of rhetoric. One is to be a "resisting reader," to "notice aspects of the canonical texts that the reader is not supposed to notice, but that disturb, when the reader is a woman, and create resistance to the view of reality the work seems to want to purvey" (51). Another strategy is to recover women who were practicing rhetoric as traditionally defined, to include them alongside the already canonized male rhetors. A third is to redefine what rhetoric is by including in the history of rhetoric discursive practices of women (51).

Likewise, and often adopting similar revisionary strategies, rhetorical scholars have interrogated the rhetorical tradition to reveal how its exclusionary practices result in what Victor J. Vitanza calls the repression or even the extermination of sophistry (*Negation* 27–56). That is, although the older Sophists played a determining role in the "invention" of rhetoric—in theory, practice, and education—they have historically suffered from a bad reputation, denounced as flippant stylists, manipulative liars, and vulgar relativists, as Plato's infamous case against the Sophists in the *Gorgias* details. Scholars have attempted to reread—if not to redeem—the Sophists by resisting the Platonic—that is, philosophic—condemnation by examining the Sophists firsthand, by investigating sophistic practices and individual Sophists, insofar as possible with what textual evidence remains, and thereby to work against the tradition's hegemony of what Kennedy has characterized as the "philosophic" rhetoric of Aristotle in particular. "In most histories," Susan C. Jarratt notes, "the sophists are buried under the sweep of 'philosophy' in its progress toward the fully 'rational' mind" (48) and its demand for logical, rational communication. Because, Jarratt continues, "of the traces of oral, poetic," and even magical language in sophistic discourse, the Sophists—in the philosopher's estimation—will always "fall short" (48). That is, the rhetorical tradition has privileged logical and deliberative language games in an attempt to control what one might call the tropic: the seductive, poetic, or magical element of language, which, in

the words of Paul de Man, "radically suspends logic and opens up vertiginous pos-
sibilites of referential aberration" (10).

Such efforts at revisionary histories of rhetoric have been motivated by the
presumption that the history of rhetoric is itself a rhetorical construction, as James
Berlin et al. noted: "The difficulty for the historian is that, even when evidence is
available and extensive, the writing of history is itself a rhetorical act" (11) and
indeed a political act: "The historian is herself underwriting a version of the normal,
of the proper arrangement of classes, races, and genders. History does not write
itself, having in itself no inherent pattern of development. Historians cannot escape
this play of power, inherent in all signifying practices" (11). Such acknowledgments
have prompted rhetorical historians to examine not only the ideological formation
of history in terms of who gets included and who does not—but also in terms of
the ideological nature of historical narrativization, as a process of reifying the
individual by perpetuating the "great man" idea of history, which obscures the
material conditions of possibility for anyone to do anything. History, then, becomes
the history of "great actors" (Poulakos, "Nietzsche and Histories of Rhetoric" 86),
the tracing of "one great individual to another" (88). Such linkages—those that
stress the continuity or progress of such linkages—serve, according to Carole Blair,
to "preserve the 'politics of preservation' and the 'tracing of influence'" (405),
resulting in what Poulakos characterizes as an "uncritical acceptance of the past as
the reservoir of all meaning for human existence" (89). For our purposes, we could
rewrite Poulakos to add that some histories adopt an uncritical acceptance of
classical rhetoric as the basis for contemporary rhetorical practices. Revisionary
histories, on the contrary, critically reexamine the rhetorical tradition, querying its
exclusions, investigating its presuppositions.

ROTATING THE TROPES

Thomas Sloane's edited *Encyclopedia of Rhetoric* abstracts rhetoric as a set of principles
and practices, divorcing it from individual rhetoricians. And so, he tells us, "Although rhetoric is a people art, not one person is listed among the entries of this
encyclopedia—not even Aristotle, not even Nietzsche. That decision was based on
our effort to abstract rhetoric as far as we could, not only from this or that
discipline but also from this or that theorist, time, place, culture, and to endeavor
to search for its principles" (xi). The editors of this volume wished to navigate
between the Scylla and Charybdis of historiography. That is, our focus on individual
figures of rhetoric could be viewed as traditional "great man" canonizing. Yet,
unlike Sloane (although he acknowledges the paradoxical nature of his attempt), we
did not want to divorce rhetoric from the history of rhetoric: that is, we wanted to
acknowledge that rhetoric is a historical construct as well: a function of particular
times, places, cultures, and political influences. Hence, each figure is situated in his
or her historical and political moment to stress the material conditions of possibility
for the figure's rhetorical theorization.

However, lest we reify the politics of the individual with our focus on individual rhetorical figures, we invite the reader to think of these entries as, indeed, rhetorical figures, as tropes to be turned, which we have attempted to do. If, according to Steven Mailloux, one mobilizes tropes in order to rotate the troops (299), we have—through our selection process of featured figures—attempted just that. That is, we have attempted to rotate the canon by:

1. Including figures not traditionally included in the history of rhetoric—women, poets, historians, pre-Socratic philosophers, lesser-known figures, and, indeed, figures for whom there are no extant rhetorical works
2. Shifting, ever so slightly, the relative importance of the traditionally canonized figures by, for example, granting Gorgias as much coverage as Aristotle, Aspasia as much as Socrates, in an attempt to reshuffle the deck of future influence
3. Encouraging our contributors to focus on contemporary uses for and significances of the figures

Our attempt to rotate the tropes/troops of classical rhetoric is an attempt " 'to break up and dissolve a part of the past' [. . .], specifically that part that interferes with present living" (Poulakos, "Nietzsche" 90). As John Poulakos argues, "I assume that one studies the past not in order to become familiar with it, and thus learned, but in order to make sense out of it and come to terms with some of the irresolutions of the present. At the same time, I assume that one looks at the past futuristically, so as to go beyond it, to forget it even temporarily, to work against its burdens, and thus to become able to express the hitherto unexpressed" (*Sophistical Rhetoric* 3). This volume, then, will—by featuring specific figures—participate in the traditional historiography of classical rhetoric, but it will also—by including figures heretofore neglected—contribute to the demand to revise the history of rhetoric in order to contribute to the future invention of the history of rhetoric or, in a revision of Roland Barthes, to invent the history of rhetoric that does not yet exist ("The Old Rhetoric" 11).

Of course, our selection of figures constructs not only a particular history but a particular definition of rhetoric. According to Barthes, rhetoric has been defined variously as a technique, a teaching, a science, an ethic, and a social practice, as well as a ludic practice (13–14). Within this volume, you will encounter such variety of definition. We have attempted to include figures whose rhetorics instantiate the traditional definition of rhetoric as "the art of persuasive communication" and "the systematization of natural eloquence" (Vickers 1), as well as those that expand and even belie traditional definitions.

Additionally, our selection of figures defines—or redefines—the classical period. That is, we have included figures who may be viewed by some as predating as well as postdating the classical period, "historically defined," according to Kennedy, as "the total record [. . .] of Greek and Roman rhetorical teaching and practice from the time of the Homeric and Hesiodic epics to that of the Sophists, orators, dramatists, and philosophers of the fifth and fourth centuries BCE; to Roman speakers and writers beginning in the second century BCE; to speeches, sermons, rhetorical poetry, and handbooks of composition dating from the time of the Roman Empire" ("Classical Rhetoric" 92–93). That is, if one presupposes, as many historicans do, that rhetoric, proper—as systematized eloquence—did not come into being until roughly the time of Plato, then the classical period of rhetoric would not, likewise, begin until the time of Plato. As you will see, however, we have included figures predating Plato, predating traditional definitions of rhetoric. Likewise, we have included figures that some may view as belonging to the medieval period, such as St. Augustine or Boethius. We do so because we view such figures as transitional, cohabiting—despite their years—several periods of rhetorical practice and theorization. Murphy identifies St. Augustine as the "clearest bridge to the Middle Ages," and notes that he "is sometimes called 'the last classical man and the first medieval man'" ("The End of the Ancient World" 211), and Kennedy identifies Boethius as "the major figure in transmitting Aristotle's logical works to the medieval West" (*A New History* 282). And Corbett and Connors define classical rhetoric not as rhetoric of the classical period but as rhetoric practiced in the classical tradition, and this period "covers more than two thousand years, from the fifth century BCE, until the first quarter of the nineteenth century" ("A Survey of Rhetoric" 489). The reader of *Classical Rhetorics and Rhetoricians*, then, will encounter a variety of rhetorics of the classical tradition.

An Overview of the History of Classical Rhetorics

In addition to the book-length histories of rhetoric currently available, there are many shorter surveys that can provide the interested reader with a more detailed survey of the history of classical rhetoric in the Western tradition (see the bibliographic essay in this volume for sources). For the purposes of this volume, the following brief overview—a generalized "standard story" of classical rhetoric—will serve to contextualize and historicize the various figures featured in this collection. This traditional account is, of course, subject to reinterpretation and challenge, which current research continues to maintain and demonstrate.

Of course, where to begin the history of rhetoric depends on one's definition of rhetoric. If one defines rhetoric as simply persuasion or eloquence, then the history of rhetoric begins with the proverbial dawn of time or at least since humans began communicating with each other. Many scholars, however, prefer to locate the coming into being of rhetoric—as the "art" of rhetoric—with the dawn of democracy, when political reforms necessitated a civic body equipped to determine itself by deliberating past, present, and future fact. Or so the story goes.

Prior to the "invention" of rhetoric, the practice of persuasion, "conceived of as persuasive oratory," according to Corbett and Connors, "figured prominently in the speeches and debates in the Homeric epics, in the plays of the Greek dramatists, in the histories of Herodotus and Thucydides, and in the philosophical treatises of Hesiod" (490). Kennedy refers to such persuasion as "rhetoric before rhetoric" ("Historical Survey" 7), whereas Cole characterizes it as "arhetorical" (x). Cole argues,

"Rhetoric is to poetry and eloquence what science is to magic, or philosophy to mythology, or politics and jurisprudence to the rule of ancestral tradition" (1). That is, rhetoric is not reducible to natural eloquence or persuasively performed orations; rhetoric, according to Cole and others, is the systematization of such persuasion, the codification of eloquence, and the development of handbooks of rhetorical techniques. "These include," Kennedy notes, "techniques of logical, ethical, and emotional appeal; the arrangement of formal speeches into logical parts; the use of different styles by different speakers or on different occasions; and the ornamentation of speech by tropes and figures" ("Classical Rhetoric" 94).

Theorists speculate that the "invention" of rhetoric as a codifiable practice—as *technē*—was a function of the "literate revolution" of fifth-century Greece, a period of transition from a largely oral society to an increasingly literate one, from the mythic world dominated by poetic thought and expression to a world dominated by rational thought and expression (see Connors, "Greek Rhetoric and the Transition from Orality"). Scholars such as Eric Havelock, most notably in his *Preface to Plato*, have speculated that the shift to literacy affects particular kinds of cognitive developments, specifically the ability to think abstractly; indeed, Havelock suggests, the "linguistic task of the presocratics" was to think thoughts about thought: to theorize in a meta-analytical way. Likewise, it may be said that the rhetorical task of the prerhetoricians was to compose rhetoric about rhetoric: to construct a systematization of practices and render it a codified discipline, which is precisely what the early handbook writers accomplished in the second half of the fifth century BCE. Although this is the standard account—that persuasion does not become rhetoric until it has transmogrified from unself-conscious acts of eloquence (characteristic of the "verbal virtuosity" of the lyric poets and Homeric heroes [Cole ix]) to self-conscious acts of systematized persuasion—scholars are questioning it. Susan C. Jarratt's *Rereading the Sophists* challenges the assumption "that certain mental operations, specifically an elaborated syllogistic logic and the introspection or critical distance presumed necessary for such logic, are not possible within an 'oral' or 'mythic consciousness'" (31). Jeffrey Walker's *Rhetoric and Poetics in Antiquity* revises this traditional historical account, which privileges rhetoric by subordinating poetry, by demonstrating "'poetry' and 'poetics' as essential, central parts of 'rhetoric's' domain" (ix); (*see* Heraclitus, Homer, Pythagorean Women, Sappho).

Scholars also contest the standard narrative of rhetoric's "invention," traditionally dated at 467 BCE and attributed to a pair of Sicilians, Corax and his student, Tisias, who offered systematic rhetorical instruction as well as a handbook to aid those who wished to reclaim their property, which had been previously seized by tyrants, now deposed. Although ancient sources, including Aristotle and Plato, speak of Corax and/or Tisias's art of rhetoric, current scholars cast doubt on this originary tale, most by challenging the details, some by calling it apocryphal (see Schiappa, "The Standard Account of Rhetoric's Beginnings"). Most scholars agree, however, that rhetoric, as an art, flourished in the fifth century BCE in response to newly formed democracies in Syracuse and Athens (see Katula, "Greek Democracy," for a discussion of the political and historical context). Kennedy explains, "Under democracies citizens were expected to participate in political debate, and they were expected to speak on their own behalf in courts of law" (*A New History* 3).

Capitalizing on this new need, Sophists—traveling teachers or "wisdom-bearers"—instructed citizens in a variety of subjects, including the art of public speaking, for a fee; additionally, the Sophists composed handbooks of rhetorical precepts. Although we are wisely cautioned against attributing a common, unifying sophistic pedagogical or practical art, we can acknowledge some approaches or practices that may be fairly characterized as sophistic. One such practice is the argumentative strategy of arguing from probability. Especially in litigious arguments concerning property ownership, where no certain evidence existed to definitively prove one's case, claimants found it necessary to make claims based on probability. "Argument from probability," Katula and Murphy explain, "is based upon the precept that one of two propositions is *more likely* to be true than the other one. In the ancient tradition, the classic example of probability is that of the little man accused of beating a larger man: 'It is not likely (probable) that I would do so,' he would reply, 'for the bigger man is stronger than I am and would defeat me. Since I would know that, I would not anger him by hitting him'" (19). Also attributed to the Sophists is the argumentative aim of "making the weaker case the stronger," based on the ability to see the same issue from two different vantage points. Attributed to the Sophist Protagoras, the art of "antilogic," is, as Conley explains, "the method of resolving disputes by examining the arguments on both sides of the question, without recourse to some objective criterion of truth or to some traditional standard of behavior" (5; *see also Dissoi Logoi*).

This art, this approach to argument, has been characterized as rhetorical as opposed to philosophical. That is, the sophistic, rhetorical approach to disputation is to assert that there is no objective (and/or accessible) standard of truth to which one can appeal to determine the truthfulness of claims; rather, one appeals to probability, to conventional values, and to the judgment of public opinion, which will determine the "truth" of any case. Philosophers and philosophically prone rhetoricians, such as Plato, however, fiercely denounced the Sophists, with their rhetorical strategies and presuppositions, as liars, as flatterers, as word stylists without substance, and as lovers of the appearance (of truth) rather than of the reality (of truth). Even more rhetorically oriented philosophers, such as Aristotle, condemned sophistry as fallacious argument, as illogical. Regardless, argue Katula and Murphy, sophistry

proved a useful and effective art in the courts and assemblies of Athens. In such situations, truth is elusive. People see past [and present] events differently, each according to their interests and their recollections, and decisions about policies that will shape the future can only be based on what is "probably" going to be the best course of action. In such public affairs, where exigencies of the situation make each decision unique, rhetoric was an effective method for deciding the appropriate course of action; that is, each person with a position on the matter at hand gave his speech and decisions were based upon which speech seemed most accurate, persuasive, appropriate at the time. In an uncertain world, there is no better way. (20)

Although distancing himself and his practice from the Sophists, Isocrates agreed that philosophic truths were not available; hence, Isocrates aimed to provide the kind of instruction that would help his students be effective—if not virtuous— citizens and leaders of the civic body.

In any event, sophistic handbooks contributed to the formation and future history of rhetoric by

> divid[ing] a judicial speech into a series of parts, each performing a specific function. [. . .] The minimum number of parts of a judicial speech was considered to be four (some authorities identified more): a prooemion, to secure the attention, interest, and good will of the jury; a narration, to provide the facts of the case as the speaker wanted them to be understood; a proof of the speaker's contention, drawing on any witnesses, evidence, and probabilities; and an epilogue, recapitulating the speech and stirring the emotions of the jury to vote in the speaker's favor. (Kennedy, "Classical Rhetoric" 95)

Aristotle's *Rhetoric* serves as a historical mediator between Plato and the Sophists by claiming rhetoric as the counterpart of philosophic inquiry. And "by concentrating in the first two books of his *Rhetoric* on the discovery of arguments," Corbett and Connors suggest, Aristotle

> sought to answer those who accused rhetoricians of being more concerned with words than with matter. And by extracting first principles from the practice of oratory, he hoped to show that rhetoric was not, as Plato had accused it of being, a mere "knack," but was a true art [a faculty, even], a teachable and systematic discipline that could guide men in adapting means to an end. (493)

Aristotle's *Rhetoric* also enumerated three kinds of rhetoric or speech occasions: "legal or forensic speech, which takes place in the courtroom and concerns judgment about a past action; the political or deliberative speech in the legislative assembly, concerned with moving people to future action; and the ceremonial or epideictic speech in a public forum, intended to strengthen shared beliefs about the present state of affairs" (Bizzell and Herzberg 3). Aristotle also articulated the three major forms of "persuasive appeal: to reason (*logos*), to emotion (*pathos*), and to the speaker's authority (*ethos*)" (4). So great is Aristotle's lasting influence that, according to Bizzell and Herzberg, "To speak of classical rhetoric is thus to speak of Aristotle's system and its elaboration by Cicero and Quintilian" (2).

Scholars challenge, however, Aristotelian foundations of rhetoric, which have a continued influence. Jasper Neel, for example, argues that Aristotle's rhetoric is haunted by sexism, racism, and classism; others argue that classical rhetoric so defined not only excludes sophistic rhetorics but also delimits rhetorical practice to public, civic, deliberative address. As Jane Sutton has wryly noted, the word "civic" is a palindrome—a two-way street, to be sure, but one without an exit or an on-ramp: it is a language game based on and determined by exclusionary practices (*see* Alcidamas, Anaximenes, Antiphon, Aristotle, Aspasia, Attic Orators, Corax and

Tisias, Diogenes, Diotima, *Dissoi Logoi*, Gorgias, Hippias, Isocrates, Pericles, Plato, Prodicus, Protagoras, Socrates, Thrasymachus).

Hellenistic and Roman rhetorics between the fourth and first centuries BCE continued to be taught as the art of public address, but rhetorical education at this time had an additional function: to civilize and to initiate "young men into the Greek way of life" (Conley 30). The colonizing conquests of Alexander the Great necessitated hellenizing efforts: to turn non-Greeks into Greeks. Although, as Kennedy reminds us, "these centuries were the time when classical rhetoric and rhetorical education assumed the form that it largely retained [some may say up to the eighteenth or nineteenth centuries], primary sources are lacking for reconstruction of these developments" ("Classical Rhetoric" 101). We learn from Cicero and others, however, what the rhetorical *paideia* attempted. Conley explains: "The teaching of rhetoric centered on an analysis of the art into five component parts: invention, the modes of discovering arguments; arrangement; expression, which included the study of style in argumentation; memory; and delivery, including both pronunciation and gesture" (30). These five parts or canons of rhetoric "recapitulated the actions of planning, composing, and delivering a speech" (Kennedy, "Classical Rhetoric" 101). The product of this process, the speech, was to include the following elements: a prologue, narration, argument, rebuttal, and conclusion (Conley 30). A reader of Plato's *Phaedrus* might infer that this period contributed little to earlier theories of rhetoric; however, the inventional theory of *stasis*, which allows a rhetor to establish the grounds of dispute, "the state of the argument," and thereby to appropriately and effectively argue is considered to be one of the contributions of this period (although some readers of Aristotle's *Rhetoric* may disagree; *see* Hermagoras of Temnos). The codification of the figures is another. The educational program, or series of stepped exercises, known as the progymnasmata is a pedagogical innovation, which had continuing influence (*see* Progymnasmata). Declamation, another rhetorical exercise, as practiced by the Romans, took two forms, the *controversiae* and the *suasoriae*. The more popular *controversiae* were elaborate set speeches that dealt with a point of law using outlandish characters, such as pirates and tyrants, and striking situations, such as poisonings or abductions. The less popular *suasoriae* mirrored legislative discourse by giving advice to historical and mythological figures. These practice speeches developed in response to the diminution of freedoms due to the fall of the Roman Republic, which drove oratory out of the legislature and into the schools. There ingenuity and verbal display was valued over serious argument.

Although "opportunities for political oratory declined somewhat under the Hellenistic monarchies and later Roman rule" (Kennedy, "Classical Rhetoric" 100), the foundation of the necessity for rhetorical training, the necessity for rhetorical deliberation on political issues, evidenced itself in the writings of Cicero and Quintilian but with a definitively Isocratean twist: such rhetorical training cannot replace natural talent nor goodness. According to Conley, "the history of rhetoric in Hellenistic Greek and Roman settings is the history of the continuing influence of Isocrates" (46).

The fall of the Roman Republic and the rise of dictatorial emperors resulted in, according to Murphy, the "casualty" of public, political discourse ("The End of the Ancient World" 205). "Imperial power," Murphy explains, "produced a political climate that for several centuries virtually eliminated any serious deliberate debate in the Roman society. Roman orators were therefore effectively denied the safe exercise of the first major type of speaking, the deliberative or political speech" (206). Rhetors of this time—hailed as "the Second Sophistic" by Philostratus—practiced, then, epideictic orations, largely given at "imperial functions," and served, according to Conley, to communicate "to the public the ideas and values of the rulers, thus performing many of the functions of a state-controlled press in a society without newspapers" (61). Historians typically characterize these orations as examples of "oratorical excess in which subject matter became less important" than issues of "style and delivery" (Murphy, "The End of the Ancient World" 205). Because of classical rhetoric's bias against style and against epideictic discourse, this period has received relatively little attention, typically dismissed as a time of mere sophistry. Conley, for one, however, attempts to reassess the contributions of these Sophists. He writes, "Rhetoric, it is true, seems to retreat from courtrooms and assemblies into a scholastic setting, as it had in Hellenistic times. This should not, however, be taken to suggest that rhetoric was no longer considered relevant in the 'real' world. [. . .] 'Sophistry' was a profession, not just a literary indulgence, that enabled a successful student to enter public life in one of the many municipal assemblies that were active in the provinces" (59, 60; see *Anonymous Seguerianus*, Apsines of Gadara, Marcus Tullius Cicero, Cornelia, Demetrius of Phaleron, Demetrius, Dio [Chrysostom] Cocceianus, Dionysius of Halicarnassus, The Elder Seneca, Favorinus, Marcus Cornelius Fronto, *On Style*, Hermagoras of Temnos, Hermogenes of Tarsus, Herodes Atticus, Himerius, Hortensia, Hypatia, Libanius, Longinus, Menander of Laodicea, Philodemus, Philostratus, Pliny the Younger, Plutarch, Verginius Flavus, Marcus Antonius Polemo, *Progymnasmata*, Fabius Quintilianus, *Rhetorica ad Herennium*, Seneca the Younger, Sextus Empiricus, Cornelius Tacitus, Theophrastus).

Classical rhetoric exerted a strong influence on the Christian writers of late antiquity and the early medieval periods. New Testament writers wrote in Greek, and therefore were forced to accept some conventions of classical rhetoric. The New Testament, for instance, is filled with the major speech types from the classical system (Kennedy, *A New History* 258–59). But many Christian writers questioned the value of the kind of ornamental style popular among the Romans. Most Christian writers emphasized content (the Word of God) over expression, and we see this tendency in the self-conscious simplicity of many of Christ's parables in the Gospels. As the Catholic Church expanded, however, rhetoric played important roles in three particular contexts. First, in order to convert the heathen, proselytizers such as Paul and others had to write and speak effectively, often drawing on many of the principles of the classical system. Second, in the internecine battles within the church over questions of dogma, church leaders argued among themselves and used classical methods to make their positions convincing. Third, in order to keep their Christian flocks on the paths of righteousness, the clergy had to write and give sermons that persuaded them to keep the faith. Generally considered the first "manual of Christian eloquence" (Conley 77), book 4 of Augustine's *De doctrina christiana* outlines the principles of Christian eloquence, and this work remained the central text of its kind well into the Middle Ages (*see* Aurelius Augustinus, Anicius Manlius Severinus Boethius, John Chrysostom, Gregory of Nazianzus).

While this collection is designed primarily to provide an introduction to the major statements in the classical system, we want to emphasize that the rhetoric that developed in classical Greece and Rome is not only of antiquarian interest. Instantiations of this 2,500-year-old system have remained viable since rhetoric's inception. The issues that theorists such as Plato, Aristotle, Cicero, and Quintilian, and practitioners such as the Sophists, raised remain central to the issues of how to write, speak, and communicate thoughtfully and effectively. An indication of the system's continued viability is that every age has restated at least parts of the classical system to meet its own needs. Augustine restated Cicero in book 4 of *De doctrina christiana* for Christian sermons; John Lawson restated much of Aristotle in *Lectures Concerning Oratory* for his eighteenth-century students at Trinity College; and, more recently, the late Edward P. J. Corbett produced a composition text-book for contemporary American students with the telling title *Classical Rhetoric for the Modern Student* that has remained in print for forty years. An additional sign of classical rhetoric's perpetuity and pervasive influence is the flood of publications by recent scholars, who have begun to question contemporary communicative and pedagogical practices, querying, for example, if classical rhetoric has constructed deliberation as agonistic or public address—written or spoken—as masculine. We hope that this volume contributes to the continued interest in classical rhetoric as a scholarly subject and as a system for teaching students to communicate effectively.

BIBLIOGRAPHY

Barthes, Roland. "The Old Rhetoric: An Aide-Mémoire." *The Semiotic Challenge*. New York: Hill and Wang, 1988. 11–93.

Berlin, James A., Robert J. Connors, Sharon Crowley, Richard Leo Enos, Victor J. Vitanza, Susan C. Jarratt, Nan Johnson, and Jan Swearingen with James J. Murphy. "The Politics of Historiography." *Rhetoric Review* 7.1 (1988): 5–49.

Bizzell, Patricia. "Opportunities for Feminist Research in the History of Rhetoric." *Rhetoric Review* 11.1 (1992–93): 50–58.

Bizzell, Patricia, and Bruce Herzberg, eds. *The Rhetorical Tradition*. 2nd ed. Boston: Bedford/ St. Martin's, 2001.

Blair, Carole. "Contested Histories of Rhetoric: The Politics of Preservation, Progress, and Change." *Quarterly Journal of Speech* 78.4 (1992): 403–28.

Brody, Miriam. *Manly Writing: Gender, Rhetoric, and the Rise of Composition*. Carbondale: Southern Illinois UP, 1993.

Cole, Thomas. *The Origins of Rhetoric in Ancient Greece.* Baltimore: Johns Hopkins UP, 1991.

Conley, Thomas M. *Rhetoric in the European Tradition.* Chicago: U of Chicago P, 1994.

Connors, Robert J. "Greek Rhetoric and the Transition from Orality." *Philosophy and Rhetoric* 19.1 (1986): 38–65.

Corbett, Edward P. J. and Robert J. Connors. "A Survey of Rhetoric." *Classical Rhetoric for the Modern Student.* New York: Oxford UP, 1999. 489–543.

de Man, Paul. *Allegories of Reading: Figural Language in Rousseau, Nietzsche, Rilke, and Proust.* New Haven, CT: Yale UP, 1979.

Glenn, Cheryl. *Rhetoric Retold: Regendering the Tradition from Antiquity through the Renaissance.* Carbondale: Southern Illinois UP, 1997.

Havelock, Eric A. *Preface to Plato.* Cambridge: Harvard UP, 1963.

Jarratt, Susan C. *Rereading the Sophists: Classical Rhetoric Refigured.* Carbondale: Southern Illinois UP, 1991.

Katula, Richard A. "Greek Democracy and the Study of Rhetoric." Ed. James J. Murphy and Richard A. Katula. *A Synoptic History of Classical Rhetoric.* 2nd ed. Davis, CA: Hermagoras P, 1995. 3–16.

Katula, Richard A., and James J. Murphy. "The Sophists and Rhetorical Consciousness." Ed. James J. Murphy and Richard A. Katula. *A Synoptic History of Classical Rhetoric.* 2nd ed. Davis, CA: Hermagoras P, 1995. 17–50.

Kennedy, George A. "Classical Rhetoric." Ed. Thomas O. Sloane. *Encyclopedia of Rhetoric.* New York: Oxford UP, 2001. 92–115.

———. "Historical Survey of Rhetoric." *Handbook of Classical Rhetoric in the Hellenistic Period 330 B.C.–A.D. 400.* Ed. Stanley E. Porter. Leiden, Netherlands: Brill, 1997. 3–42.

———. *A New History of Classical Rhetoric.* Princeton: Princeton UP, 1994.

Mailloux, Steven. "Afterward: A Pretext for Rhetoric: Dancing 'Round the Revolution." *Pre/Text: The First Decade.* Ed. Victor J. Vitanza. Pittsburgh: U of Pittsburgh P, 1993. 299–314.

Murphy, James J. "The End of the Ancient World: The Second Sophistic and Saint Augustine." *A Synoptic History of Classical Rhetoric.* Ed. James J. Murphy and Richard A. Katula. 2nd ed. Davis, CA: Hermagoras P, 1995. 205–14.

———. "The Historiography of Rhetoric: Challenges and Opportunities." *Rhetorica* 1.1 (1983): 1–8.

Murphy, James J., and Richard A. Katula, eds. *A Synoptic History of Classical Rhetoric.* 2nd ed. Davis, CA: Hermagoras P, 1995.

Neel, Jasper. *Aristotle's Voice.* Carbondale: Southern Illinois UP, 1994.

Porter, Stanley E., ed. *Handbook of Classical Rhetoric in the Hellenistic Period 330 B.C.–A.D. 400.* Leiden, Netherlands: Brill, 1997.

Poulakos, John. "Nietzsche and Histories of Rhetoric." *Writing Histories of Rhetoric.* Ed. Victor J. Vitanza. Carbondale: Southern Illinois UP, 1994. 81–97.

———. *Sophistical Rhetoric in Classical Greece.* Columbia: U of South Carolina P, 1995.

Schiappa, Edward. "The Standard Account of Rhetoric's Beginnings." *The Beginnings of Rhetorical Theory in Classical Greece.* New Haven, CT: Yale UP, 1999. 3–13.

Sloane, Thomas O., ed. *Encyclopedia of Rhetoric.* New York: Oxford UP, 2001.

Sutton, Jane. "On the Structure of Rhetoric in Aristotle: The Space of Speech, Self and Other." *The Philosophy of Communication.* Vol. II. Eds. Konstantine Boudouris and Takis Poulakos. Athens: Ionia, 2002. 204–12.

Vickers, Brian. *In Defence of Rhetoric*. Oxford: Clarendon, 1988.

Vitanza, Victor J. *Negation, Subjectivity, and the History of Rhetoric*. Albany: State U of New York P, 1997.

———. "Some Rudiments of Histories of Rhetorics and Rhetorics of Histories." *Rethinking the History of Rhetoric*. Ed. Takis Poulakos. Boulder, CO: Westview P, 1993. 193–239.

Walker, Jeffrey. *Rhetoric and Poetics in Antiquity*. Oxford: Oxford UP, 2000.

ALCIDAMAS

(fifth century–after 369 BCE)

Neil O'Sullivan

Alcidamas was born in Elaia, a Greek colony on the central coast of Asia Minor (Avezzù, *Testimonia* [T] 1–3). His father is named as Diocles (T 2), concerning whom we are told only that he wrote on music and/or poetry. No firm dates exist for Alcidamas's birth or death, but information about one of his writings and about his teachers and pupils allows us to say that he was born in the second half of the fifth century BCE and continued working until at least 369. He was a pupil of Gorgias (TT 1–3, 5, 13) and certainly shared many of his stylistic habits; in fact he is supposed to have taken over his master's school (i.e., program of teaching) (T 3). Gorgias came from Leontini in Sicily, on the other side of the Greek world, but was drawn to Athens not only to teach but also to represent his city in political negotiations, famously in 427 BCE; it is reasonable to assume that Alcidamas made his acquaintance there, as Elaia (like Leontini) was an Athenian subject city, and Alcidamas may have gone to the metropolis in search of teachers or perhaps pupils. Further evidence for an Athenian sojourn exists in the ancient reports of his influence on two of the greatest Attic orators, Demosthenes and Aeschines (TT 4–8); instruction of the latter is linked to Aeschines' stylistic grandeur and prowess in extemporary speech, of which we know Alcidamas was a keen proponent.

Very late testimony (Tzetzes, *Chiliades* 11.382.663, 11.385.739 Leone) explicitly tells us that he was a contemporary and antagonist of Isocrates, whose laborious, written method of composition and avoidance of public delivery suggest a natural point of difference. Alcidamas's *Messenian Speech* (Avezzù, *Fragments* [FF] 3–4) was written in the wake of the successful revolt of Messenia from Sparta in 369 BCE, which provides a *terminus post quem* for Alcidamas's active life.

Numerous similarities have been detected between Plato's *Phaedrus* and Alcidamas's work, but it seems impossible to establish priority, and in any case the lack of an absolute chronology for any of Plato's works before *Laws* renders them essentially useless for dating purposes. Although the chronology of Isocrates' work is clearer, its points of contact with Alcidamas are no more helpful, as it has proved impossible to demonstrate priority on any particular point. That Alcidamas has convincing points of contact with his great contemporaries allows us to see that he was a mainstream figure in his own time, but his generally low profile in the rhetorical tradition indicates that his contribution to its history was not a long-lasting one, since the tradition developed in ways that were essentially opposed to his interests.

ALCIDAMAS'S RHETORICAL THEORY AND PRACTICE

Writings

Two complete short works ascribed by their medieval MSS to Alcidamas survive; otherwise we have only a few fragments of his writings or else their bare titles. The two complete works are *On those writing written speeches* or *On Sophists* (henceforth *Soph.*) and *Odysseus (Against the Treason of Palamedes)*. The authenticity of the first, a speech devoted essentially to championing the claims of extemporaneous speech over those of written eloquence, seems universally accepted now, showing as it does strong similarities to the stylistic quirks of Alcidamas criticized by Aristotle. Many have thought, however, that the second speech, a rhetorical exercise based on a mythological episode from the Trojan War, is spurious. But its authenticity was strongly maintained in Hubert Auer's 1913 dissertation, the conclusions of which are yet to be refuted and have been accepted by the two most recent editors of Alcidamas. More work, however, remains to be done on the question, and linguistic research in progress at the time of writing may yet confirm the skeptics' doubts.

The lost works included similar jeux d'esprit: an encomium of death, of a prostitute, and perhaps also of poverty and a dog (T T 1, 14). But there was also more serious material. His *Messenian Speech* contained the only recorded condemnation of the institution of slavery from the ancient world (F 3: "God set all men free; nature has made no one a slave"). He also left behind a *Physicon* ("Book of Natural Science"), of which the only certain fragment (F 8) tells of the lives of famous philosophers. He wrote a rhetorical handbook (T 15), to which must belong a number of technical fragments about language; other fragments may have come from a broader discussion of literature (passages of Homer are paraphrased) and persuasion. Most controversial has proved to be his *Mouseion* (FF 5–7). Two fragments explicitly quoted from it occur in the late (Hadrianic era) work the *Contest of Homer and Hesiod*, and papyrus discoveries have strengthened the hypothesis (originally Nietzsche's) that Alcidamas's work contained an earlier version of the *Contest*, but the nature of the *Mouseion* remains disputed. Various conjectures have been made about his possible authorship of other works, but the above are the only ones attested by the ancient evidence.

Style

In chapter 3 of the third book of his *Rhetoric*, Aristotle criticized the style of both Alcidamas and his teacher Gorgias on the grounds that it was "too poetic"; in particular, he specified the use of compound words, of noncurrent words, of inappropriate or too many adjectives, and of far-fetched metaphors as faults in prose style to be avoided, and he quoted instances for each category from now lost works of Alcidamas. Studies have shown that the same characteristics are to be found in his surviving writings (especially in *Soph.*). Influential though Aristotle's censure has been, it should be seen as an essentially subjective aesthetic judgment that has its roots in the polemics of Alcidamas's generation about the nature of poetry and prose; Isocrates (see esp. 9.9–10), Alcidamas's rival, clearly influenced Aristotle's definition of "the poetic" in prose. In any case, some of Aristotle's censures were at best idiosyncratic: his condemnation of Alcidamas's description of the *Odyssey* as "a fine mirror of human life" (F 34) is clearly out of step with the popularity of the image in the ancient, medieval, and modern worlds. That said, it cannot be claimed that Alcidamas is a great advertisement for Greek eloquence; compared with the most obvious benchmarks, Gorgias and Isocrates, in the surviving pieces he lacks his teacher's audacious brilliance and his rival's careful if somewhat monotonous polish. But this may well be because most of his energies were devoted to developing an improvised "agonistic style," one keyed to immediate delivery rather than to careful later study: even his great critic Aristotle (*Rhetoric* 1413b16) acknowledged that successfully delivered speeches could appear amateurish when privately read later.

Doctrines

Our knowledge of Alcidamas's rhetorical theories depends chiefly on the comparatively extensive and explicit arguments in his *Soph.*; a few fragments also convey some information. To start with the latter: like Aristotle, he saw a close link between dialectic and rhetoric (the former is "the capacity for persuasion" (F 13), but contrary that philosopher (*Rhetoric* 1414a20), he thought that "magnificence" (*megaloprepeia*) should be reckoned a virtue of style (along with clarity, concision, and persuasiveness) (F 15). Following the example of the earlier sophist Protagoras, Alcidamas also sought to make a comprehensive classification of language in general, dividing up discourse into four categories: assertion, denial, interrogation, and address (F 12). Finally, he also shared with the other Sophists a love of technical vocabulary and mentioned the use of "subsidiary narrative" (*paradiēgēsis*) (F 14).

   In the context of fifth- and early fourth-century BCE rhetorical theory, *Soph.* is quite significant in terms of its length and detail. Alcidamas's pamphlet is not tightly structured, but in the course of defending the practice of extemporary speech he makes some important points: that even speechwriters aim at the "unwritten" style of extemporary eloquence; that speakers need to rehearse the arguments, but not the words, of their speeches; that extemporary speakers are much better able to exploit the emotions of their audiences and the right opportunity (*kairos*) in general. At one point, he likens written speeches to statues in terms of their greater beauty but practical uselessness in comparison with living bodies, and similar is his idea that written speeches are closer to poetry than to real speech. Nevertheless, the pamphlet ends with a grudging acceptance of the benefits of written speeches for keeping a record of one's progress and for achieving a certain immortality. As mentioned above, Alcidamas's contribution to the *Contest of Homer and Hesiod* remains obscure, but it has been plausibly argued that the virtues of extemporary speech are expressed in that document by the presentation of Homer's great skill at producing spontaneous poetic replies to Hesiod's questions, and it is possible that further echoes of Alcidamas's views are to be found in the work.

Influence

In retrospect, it is easy to conclude that, as a recent study has put it, Alcidamas was engaged in a "rear-guard action in the face of developments in literacy and rhetoric which were already becoming unstoppable" (Muir 66). Living in an age of transition, he followed up both the "poetic" prose and the extemporary practical eloquence of his master Gorgias, but the time for both of these was soon to pass. Aristotle's *Rhetoric* memorably condemned Alcidamas's prose style as essentially not proper prose at all, and it would be hard to overestimate the influence that this condemnation had on subsequent generations. At the same time, Alcidamas was living in an age of increasing literacy but also in the twilight of Greek democracy, that very development which, as Aristotle was to point out (recorded by Cicero, *Brutus* 46), and as he himself hinted at in *Soph.* 11, was intimately tied up with the birth and practice of formal rhetoric. But the end of democracy in Greece meant an end to the sort of public speaking that Alcidamas championed: no longer the urgent business of arousing strong emotions of big crowds for vital decisions, oratory was on its way to becoming an ancient form of infotainment, for which the study of other authors was much more useful.

But, remembered for his influence on Aeschines and also Demosthenes, Alcidamas emerges as a name again during the rise of Atticism in the mid-first century BCE. Cicero had read some of his work, and later he is mentioned by Quintilian and other educationalists. Even as late as the twelfth century there was much more of his work available than there is now, and he was apparently read keenly by at least one Byzantine scholar.

BIBLIOGRAPHY

Primary Sources and Translations

Avezzù, Guido, ed. *Alcidamante. Orazioni e frammenti.* Roma: L'Erma di Bretschneider, 1982.

Leone, P. A. M. *Ioannis Tzetzae historiae.* Napoli: Libreria Scientifica Editrice, 1968.

Muir, J. V., ed. *Alcidamas: The Works and Fragments.* London: Bristol Classical P (Duckworth), 2001.

Radermacher, L., ed. *Artium scriptores (Reste der voraristotelischen Rhetorik).* Wien: Rudolf M. Rohrer, 1951.

Critical Sources

Auer, H. "De Alcidamantis declamatione quae inscribitur Ὀδυσσεὺς κατὰ Παλαμήδους προδοσίας." Diss. Münster, 1913.

Liebersohn, Yosef Z. "Alcidamas' *On the Sophists*: A Reappraisal." *Eranos* 97 (1999): 108–24.

Milne, M. J. "A Study in Alcidamas and His Relation to Contemporary Sophistic." Diss. Bryn Mawr, 1924.

O'Sullivan, Neil. *Alcidamas, Aristophanes and the Beginnings of Greek Stylistic Theory*. Hermes Einzelschriften 60. Stuttgart: Franz Steiner Verlag, 1992.

Richardson, N. J. "The Contest of Homer and Hesiod and Alcidamas' *Mouseion*." *Classical Quarterly* 31 (1981): 1–10.

Walberer, G. "Isokrates und Alkidamas." Diss. Hamburg, 1938.

West, M. L. "The Contest of Homer and Hesiod." *Classical Quarterly* 17 (1967): 433–50.

ANAXIMENES, *RHETORICA AD ALEXANDRUM*

(ca. 341–300 BCE)

Sean Patrick O'Rourke

The *Rhetoric to Alexander*, so named because of a spurious introductory letter purporting to be from Aristotle to his student Alexander, was preserved on that basis among the works of Aristotle. Although some scholars have thought to date the text as late as the third century BCE, consensus now assumes that it was roughly contemporaneous with Aristotle's *Rhetoric*, and dates from the second half of the fourth century. The treatise is in thirty-eight chapters, treats many of the important themes in Greek rhetoric, and is now attributed to Anaximenes.

Of Anaximenes we know little. He was from Lampsacus, on the Hellespont in Thrace (in what is now Turkey), and flourished between 380 and 320 BCE. He studied under Zoilus and perhaps Diogenes of Sinope and, like Aristotle, tutored Alexander; according to one account, he accompanied Alexander on his Persian campaigns. A historian and a biographer, Anaximenes wrote treatises on Greece, Philip of Macedon, and Alexander, only fragments of which exist. He was also an orator, a logographer, and a teacher of rhetoric. And we know, on good authority (e.g., Quintilian III.iv.9), that he also wrote a rhetoric.

Whether that rhetoric is the text known as the *Rhetorica ad Alexandrum* is a matter of dispute. It covers, as does Quintilian, seven species of rhetoric found in three general types of speech. Although Quintilian attributes only two of the three types (deliberative and forensic) to Anaximenes, and despite Vinzenz Buchheit's arguments to the contrary, most scholars now consider the treatise, with George A. Kennedy, "basically the work of Anaximenes" (*Art of Persuasion* 115).

The *Rhetorica ad Alexandrum* is significant not because it influenced or was influenced by Aristotle or because later rhetoricians felt required to wrestle with its legacy, but rather because it is the best surviving example of a full-length sophistic or practical handbook from the period. As such, it provides a rare glimpse of the rhetorical tradition Aristotle responded to and, in so doing, reformed.

COMPARISON TO ARISTOTLE'S *RHETORIC*

Given the roughly contemporaneous composition and the early Aristotelian attribution, a good deal of the scholarship on the *Rhetorica ad Alexandrum* is devoted to the similarities and differences between it and Aristotle's *Rhetoric*.

Scholars note both structural and substantive similarities. Kennedy, for example, notes that the *Rhetorica ad Alexandrum* consists of three parts which "correspond [. . .] roughly" to the three main parts of Aristotle's treatise (*Art of Persuasion* 117). In his first five chapters, Anaximenes outlines the qualities of the genera and species of oratory, the subject Aristotle treats in book I. Chapters six through twenty-two of the *Rhetorica ad Alexandrum* consider, broadly, common topics and proofs, which Aristotle treats in lengthy sections of books I and II. And Anaximenes' discussion of style, found from chapters twenty-three through twenty-eight, corresponds (again roughly) with Aristotle's coverage in the first half of book III.

The chief difference between the two might be described, in modern terms, as the difference between a theoretical treatise concerned with advancing our understanding of the art and a practical handbook concerned with imparting skills to the practitioner. The *Rhetoric to Alexander* offers no definition of rhetoric (indeed, apart from the title, there is no use of the term *rhētorikē*), provides no psychological or ethical depth to its treatment of emotion and character, and offers no theoretical rigor in its discussions of enthymeme, example, and style. Moreover, Anaximenes really discusses only two of Aristotle's three kinds of rhetoric and makes no use of Aristotle's three modes of proof or means of persuasion.

Late nineteenth-century critics found the *Rhetorica ad Alexandrum* inferior to Aristotle's work, different and somehow diminished in tone and tenor. As E. M. Cope notes, our text shows a "marked inferiority in subtlety and spirit, power and interest," an absence of the "logical element" and "style," and a distinct lack of Aristotle's "higher moral tone" (402).

It is clear, then, that the *Rhetorica ad Alexandrum* is not Aristotle's work. It is probably safe to say that neither directly influenced the other. The best evidence seems to be that the two works emanate from a shared rhetorical and cultural tradition (not, as was once believed, a common textual source), one Anaximenes perpetuates with his *Rhetorica ad Alexandrum* and Aristotle reacts against and responds to with his *Rhetoric*.

THEORY OF RHETORIC

Taken on its own terms, however, Anaximenes' treatise is of considerable interest for, as indicated above, it offers the only full-length sophistic account of rhetoric. The work is a "preceptual" treatise, in that it functions by offering precepts of persuasive speaking.

The *Rhetorica ad Alexandrum* divides rhetoric into three genera, the familiar deliberative, epideictic, and forensic, and seven species: persuasion and dissuasion in deliberative speeches, eulogy and vituperation in epideictic speeches, accusation and defense in forensic speeches, and inquiry or investigation, which may stand alone or participate in any of the genera. The first and last chapters of the treatise also appear to make the rules contained therein applicable not only to oratory but to private conversation as well. This application, however, is not taken up elsewhere in the work.

Each of the genera is concerned with its own subject matter. Deliberative speeches support or oppose legislative, constitutional, or foreign policy proposals, or consider matters of public religious ritual. Epideictic speeches generally have to do with a person's character and conduct. Forensic speeches involve error, crime, and punishment. Inquiry or investigation concerns the contradictions in a person's words or between the words and the person's actions and may therefore be used in each of the three genera.

The *Rhetorica ad Alexandrum* treats common topics diffusely. Our author first lists as topics "common" to all the various kinds of oratory: the just, the lawful, the expedient, the honorable, the facile, the practical, and the necessary. These, however, are said to be more often found in deliberative oratory. He then notes that the methods of amplifying or minimizing the traits of a person's conduct or character, elaborated in chapter 3 and more often found in epideictic oratory, are also "common" topics insofar as they are useful in all types of oratory. Finally, and in addition to the above, "common" topics include direct and supplementary proofs (most useful in forensic speech), anticipation of contrary arguments, postulates, recapitulation, length of speech, and explanation. In the course of this discussion, the author also discusses aspects of style, including word choice, sentence forms, irony, and "elegancies" of style.

In chapters 29 through 37, our author discusses various schemes of arrangement, as well as the tactics to be employed in each section. The discussion is, again, by type of speech. Deliberative speeches include an introduction, a narration or exposition of past, present, or future events, confirmation by proof, anticipation and refutation of objections, and conclusion by an appeal to appropriate feelings. Epideictic and investigative speeches are organized by topics and modes of proof. Forensic speeches differ according to whether one is prosecuting or defending. The chief difference appears to be when to refute one's opponent's proof (early if one is defending).

Overall, then, the *Rhetorica ad Alexandrum* offers a set of guidelines or rules for effective speech. The precepts are defined and illustrated, but rarely investigated with any theoretical rigor.

CONCLUSION

While by no means a fully developed theory of rhetoric with the philosophical depth of Aristotle's, the *Rhetorica ad Alexandrum* is nonetheless an important work in the discipline's history. The early handbook tradition it represents was a vibrant part of fourth-century Greek culture. Whether studied on its own terms or as representative of the rhetorical and cultural tradition to which Aristotle responds, Anaximenes' work is the most complete surviving text from a tradition we are only now coming to fully understand.

BIBLIOGRAPHY

Primary Sources and Translations

Bekker, Immanuel, ed. *Aristotelis Opera.* 2 vols. Berlin: G. Reimer, 1831. II: 1420–47.

C., H. "Aristotle's Rhetoric to King Alexander." *Aristotle's Rhetoric: Or, The True Grounds and Principles of Oratory; Shewing, the Right Art of Pleading and Speaking in Full Assemblies and Courts of Judicature.* London: T. B. for Randall Taylor, 1686. Book 4.

Forster, E. S. "De Rhetorica ad Alexandrum." *The Works of Aristotle Translated into English.* Ed. W. D. Ross. 12 vols. Oxford: Oxford UP, 1924. XI. Rev. ed., "Rhetoric to Alexander." *The Complete Works of Aristotle: The Revised Oxford Translation.* Ed. Jonathan Barnes. 2 vols. Bollingen Series 71. Princeton: Princeton UP, 1984. II: 2270–2315.

Free, B[eckwith] D[odwell]. "Collections from Aristotle's Rhetorick, Addressed to His Pupil Alexander the Great." *Rhetorick; or, the Art of Persuasion.* London: Brown, 1782. 2–22.

Fuhrmann, Manfred, ed. *Anaximenes Ars rhetorica quae vulgo fertur Aristotelis ad Alexandrum.* Leipzig: Teubner, 1966. 2nd ed. Munich: K. G. Saur Verlag, 2000.

Hammer, Caspar, ed. *Rhetores Graeci.* Leipzig: Teubner, 1894, 8–104.

Manutius, Aldus, ed. *Rhetores Graeci.* 2 vols. Venice: Aldine, 1508–09. I: 253–68.

Rackham, H. "Aristotle's Rhetoric to Alexander." *Aristotle: Problems II: Rhetorica ad Alexandrum.* Loeb Classical Library 317. Cambridge: Harvard UP, 1937. 257–49, 456.

Spengel, Leonard, ed. *Rhetores Graeci.* 3 vols. Leipzig: Teubner, 1853–56. Rpt. Frankfurt: Minerva, 1966. I: 169–242.

Biographical Sources

Arnott, Peter D. "Anaximenes of Lampsacus." *Ancient Greek and Roman Rhetoricians: A Biographical Dictionary.* Ed. Donald C. Bryant, et al. Columbia, MO: Artcraft P, 1968. 3.

Weissenberger, Michael. "Anaximenes of Lampsacus." *Brill's New Pauly.* Leiden: Brill, 2002. I: 662–63.

Critical Sources

Barwick, K. "Die 'Rhetorik ad Alexandrum' und Anaximenes, Isokrates, Aristoteles, und die Theodektia." *Philologus* 110 (1966): 212–45; 110 (1967): 47–55.

Buchheit, Vinzenz. *Untersuchungen zur Theorie des Genos epideiktikon von Gorgias bis Aristoteles.* Munich: Huber, 1960.

Carey, C. "*Nomos* in Attic Rhetoric and Oratory." *Journal of Hellenic Studies* 116 (1996): 33–46.

Cope, E. M. *An Introduction to Aristotle's Rhetoric.* London: Macmillan, 1867. 401–64.

Fuhrmann, M. *Untersuchungen zur Textgeschichte der pseudoaristotelischen Alexander-Rhetorik.* Wiesbaden: Steiner, 1965.

Grube, G. M. A. "The *Rhetorica ad Alexandrum* and Its Language." *A Greek Critic: Demetrius on Style.* Toronto: U of Toronto P, 1961. 156–63.

Havet, Ernest. *De la rhétorique connue sous le nom de Rhétorique à Alexandre.* Paris: N.p., 1852.

Ipfelkopfer, Adalbert. *Die Rhetorik des Anaximenes unter den Werken des Aristoteles.* Diss. Erlangen, 1889.

Kennedy, George A. "The *Rhetorica ad Alexandrum.*" *The Art of Persuasion in Greece.* Princeton: Princeton UP, 1963. 114–23.

———. "The *Rhetoric for Alexander.*" *A New History of Classical Rhetoric.* Princeton: Princeton UP, 1994. 49–51.

Marsh, David. "Francesco Filelfo's Translation of the *Rhetorica ad Alexandrum.*" *Peripatetic Rhetoric after Aristotle.* Ed. William W. Fortenbaugh and David C. Mirhady. Rutgers University Studies in Classical Humanities 6. New Brunswick: Transaction Publishers, 1994. 349–64.

Mirhady, David C. "Aristotle, the *Rhetorica ad Alexandrum* and the *tria genera causarum.*" *Peripatetic Rhetoric after Aristotle.* 54–65.

———. "Non-Technical *Pisteis* in Aristotle and Anaximenes." *American Journal of Philology* 112 (1991): 5–28.

Reeve, M. D. "Notes on Anaximenes' *Technē Rhētorikē.*" *Classical Quarterly* 20 (1970): 237–41.

Wendland, Paul. *Anaximenes von Lampsakos.* Berlin: Weidmann, 1905.

———. "Die Schriftstellerei des Anaximenes von Lampsakos." *Hermes* 39 (1904): 499–509.

ANONYMOUS SEGUERIANUS

(ca. 170–230? CE)

J. E. Parker Middleton

The *Anonymous Seguerianus* is a late second- or early third-century Greek handbook on the parts of a speech that was named for the text's discoverer and first editor, the French baron Seguier, Marquis de St. Brison, who found the work on a twelfth-century manuscript in the royal library in Paris in 1838 (Dilts and Kennedy x). The treatise (hereafter *AS*) collects and summarizes second-century advice on invention and arrangement, dramatizing debates between the rival Apollodorean and Theodorean schools, the latter holding the more flexible view of rhetoric that the *AS* arguably favors. Titled *The Art of Political Speech*, the handbook was probably written by a student, who recorded the contrasting views of his teachers on civic speeches for his own use. He could have lived in Athens, the main site for rhetorical study in Greece of the Roman Empire, in a Greek city of Asia, in Egypt, or in other places with flourishing rhetoric schools (Dilts and Kennedy xiii).

Mervin Dilts and George Kennedy provide the first modern language edition of the handbook in *Two Greek Rhetorical Treatises from the Roman Empire: Introduction, Text, Translation of the Arts of Rhetoric Attributed to Anonymous Seguerianus and to Apsines of Gadara* (1997).[1] Prior to Dilts and Kennedy, Hammer's *Rhetores Graeci* (1894) provided the most useful edition of *AS*, while Johannes Graeven's *Cornuti Artis Rhetoricae Epitome* (1891) supplied the most controversial. In view now discredited, Graeven argued that the *AS* was an epitome of a lost work by third-century rhetorician Cornutus; however, "use of a common source" probably explains similarities that sparked Graeven's attribution (Dilts and Kennedy x–xi).

The significance of the *AS* is that the handbook shows how rhetoric was taught in the Greek-speaking world at the time of the Second Sophistic. According to Kennedy, who has long championed the text's importance, the handbook, together with Apsines, provides "probably the best surviving" example of the content of rhetorical education in most Greek schools in the period (Dilts and Kennedy ix). Primarily interested in theory, the *AS* delivers the rhetoric of Aristotle filtered through second-century sources, and it preserves sharp debates about invention between the doctrinaire Apollodoreans and the more moderate Theodoreans. The *AS* remains "the best source we have in Greek" for these early empire debates and adds to accounts from Quintilian (Dilts and Kennedy x). Polarizing theoretical concerns of *AS*, the debates underscore the relevance of the handbook to issues about rhetoric's character and function (science/art; *tuchē/technē*; rigid rules/flexible heuristics; practical/productive) that have long engaged rhetoricians and that continue to influence rhetoric's status.[2]

RHETORICAL THEORY IN *ANONYMOUS SEGUERIANUS*

The theory and teaching tradition of *AS* are recognizably Aristotelian. Aristotle's influence is clear in the handbook's interest in invention, its approach to proof, and the weight it gives to a flexible, pragmatic, and contingent understanding of rhetorical advice. Compiled before Hermogenes' rise, the *AS* touches on *stasis* only briefly, preferring to list ways of thinking about rhetoric and approaching the parts of a speech.

Following Aristotle, the *AS* distinguishes between artistic and inartistic persuasion, divides *pisteis* into *ēthos, logos*, and *pathos*, underscores the enthymeme and paradigm as tools of logical proof, explains that even inartistic proofs may be put to artistic purposes, and emphasizes the flexibility of the topics (Dilts and Kennedy ix). Furthermore, the *AS* continues Aristotle's interest in the psychological processes of rhetoric, elaborating, for instance, the need to consider audience emotions in order to make key parts of a speech, especially presentation of proofs, successful.

The *Anonymous* author, however, ventures no original ideas about rhetoric, recording instead the views of his teachers. The text's main named sources are Alexander Numenius and Neocles, second-century rhetoricians whose views infuse *AS* with an Aristotelian flexibility and align loosely with the Theodoreans. Alexander, whose father was a Roman official under Hadrian (117–138 CE), wrote a rhetoric handbook with "a marked anti-Apollodorean view" on which the *AS* draws (Kennedy 224; Smith 2–3). The *AS* supplies "virtually the only source" for the rhetoric of Neocles. According to *AS*, Neocles advises the rhetor to "always assess the moods and views of the court," adapting "classroom rules and definitions accordingly" (Stewart 78–79). Neocles thus opposes "those who believe that theory is inviolable," since "he is willing [. . .] to place Narration anywhere in a speech, or to omit it entirely, always considering the immediate needs of the case at hand." A clear contribution of the handbook is that it preserves the teachings of Alexander, Neocles, and Aelius Harpocration, another named second-century source, whose ideas are not cited by other writers of the period (Dilts and Kennedy xiii).

The *AS* organizes its material according to the *moria logou* tradition, which means that it orders and develops content according to the parts of a speech, from *prooemion*, to narration, to *pisteis*, to epilogue, the parts of a speech providing a guide through the rhetorical process, as well as "a fair skeletal outline of the treatise" (Kirby 336). The handbook then treats the four parts of a speech by listing views on invention, arrangement, and style for each. The *AS* mentions declamation themes, such as whether the old should be cast out during a siege, to support theoretical points, rather than to supply exercises.

A sampling of advice demonstrates the handbook's continuity with Aristotle, interest in the rhetorical process, and engagement with theory quarrels of the day. For example, characteristic of its interest in the preparatory persuasive role of all material that comes before the proof, the *AS* opens with a definition of *prooemion*, likely from Neocles, that "is found in no earlier writer": "A *prooemion* is speech that arouses or calms the emotions of the hearer; for it is impossible to prepare the hearer without arousing or soothing his emotions" (*AS* 5; Dilts and Kennedy 3n). Readers will recognize Aristotle (*Nichomachean Ethics* 2.5; *Rhetoric* 2.11) and Quintilian (6.2.8) in the framings of *ēthos* and *pathos* that follow, which, as Dilts and Kennedy point out (3n), also emerge in Byzantine rhetorical writings that draw on *AS*:

> *Pathos* is the contemporary condition of the soul arousing a rather strong positive or negative impulse such as pity, anger, fear, hate, desire. It differs from *ēthos* in that the latter is hard to affect, the former easy to affect; for *ēthos* is a permanent state of the soul and hard to wipe out, such as the feelings of fathers toward sons. (*AS* 6)

To emphasize how the parts of a speech serve the larger rhetorical process, the *AS* advises via Harpocration that "The *skopos* [goal or function] of the *prooemion* is to prepare the hearer to be of a certain sort, and its *telos* [end or purpose] is to create attention and receptivity and goodwill" (*AS* 9; Dilts and Kennedy 5n). Consonant with the advice of most rhetoricians, the handbook explains that "if the hearers know what the speeches are about, they will become more receptive" (*AS* 10).

However, the handbook's interest in competing ways of thinking about rhetoric provides its rhetorical piquancy. Setting up one of the quarrels that punctuate the treatise, the handbook takes its characteristically flexible theoretical turn—in which the occasion rules the rhetor—by citing the caveat that "One should understand that often *prooemia* should be omitted" (*AS* 21). After adducing such occasions, the handbook outlines the more rigid position of the Apollodoreans, who argue that *prooemia* are always necessary, since by definition a speech "not composed of all parts is neither complete nor sound" (*AS* 26). "No part of a speech" the Apollodoreans maintain, "should be left out, and especially the *prooemion* [. . .]" (*AS* 26).

The *AS* countervails with Theodorean appeals to rhetoric's higher mission, as Alexander charges that the Apollodoreans "have not rightly perceived the nature of rhetoric, which is 'stochastic' [that is, 'it aims at a different effect in each speech,' Dilts and Kennedy 11n]; for it has escaped their attention [. . .] as though they were discussing a science" (*AS* 30).[3] Defending rhetoric's dynamic character, Alexander teaches a principled adaptability that echoes Aristotelian and Isocratean ideals:

> Since rhetoric is an art and its theorems ["*theoremata*, the rules of rhetoric," Dilts and Kennedy 36n] are adapted to occasions, the Apollodoreans err in stating theorems scientifically and saying that it is always necessary to use a *proomeion*. 32. But we say that since at different times we are involved in different subjects, and since our art is

adapted to what is useful in the existing circumstances, one should use a *prooemion* if it is advantageous, and if not one should omit it; for things appropriately omitted will do no harm. (*AS* 31–32)

Consistent with its format for presenting the sticking points in these debates, in general, the handbook appears to give final say to the more resonantly modern—and distantly Aristotelian—teachings of Alexander and Neocles, whose more pragmatic rhetoric is an art in which circumstances and contingencies rule persuasive choices.

Readings of the *AS* made possible by the Dilts and Kennedy edition make the handbook's continuities with and contributions to the tradition of rhetoric more clear. Heretofore, the lack of a modern translation, plus the fact that scholarly commentary was for the most part "scattered in nineteenth-century publications" not only obscured the importance of the treatise but also hindered critical discussion (Yunis). "That should now change," according to Harvey Yunis, as scholars of "rhetoric, literature, and education" investigate the handbook's relations to "the rest of the rhetorical tradition." In short, the *AS* shows how a student of early empire might have learned about and regarded rhetoric and who he thought were its best teachers.

NOTES

1. The *Anonymous Seguerianus* survives in one manuscript only, codex Parisinus graecus 1874, which also contains Apsines' *De problematis*, Minucianus, Apsines' *Rhetoric*, and *Menander Rhetor* (Dilts and Kennedy xxii).

2. Apollodorus of Pergamum (ca. 105–23 BCE) saw rhetoric as a science with every speech always having four parts "always in the exact order" (Smith 6–7). The Theodoreans, led by Theodorus of Gadara, a first-century BCE rhetorician, saw rhetoric as a more flexible art and held that the parts of a speech, except proofs, might be left out or changed as the occasion asked (Smith 6–7; Arnott 97). In general, the Theodoreans, with which the main sources of the *AS* are "loosely identified," saw "the 'rules' of rhetoric as flexible generalities, in contradistinction to the dogmatism of their adversaries" (Stewart 78).

3. Harvey Yunis notes that when Alexander calls rhetoric "a stochastic art," it "does not mean that rhetoric aims at a particular effect in each speech" but refers, more consonant with the view favored by *AS*, to the idea that "rhetoric is a conjectural art, one that involves flexibility and approximation, as opposed to an exact art of episteme that never varies." According to Yunis, "This sense of rhetoric as a stochastic art, which goes back at least to Chrysippus [. . .] is precisely what allows Alexander to argue that the rules of rhetoric are not invariable but must be bent according to the demands of the occasion."

BIBLIOGRAPHY

Primary Sources and Translations

Dilts, Mervin R., and George Kennedy, eds. *Two Greek Rhetorical Treatises from the Roman Empire: Introduction, Text, and Translation of The Arts of Rhetoric Attributed to Anonymous*

Seguerianus and Apsines of Gadara. Mnemosyne Supplement 168. Leiden, Netherlands: Brill, 1997.

Graeven, Johannes, ed. *Comuti Artis Rhetoricae Epitome.* Berlin 1891; rpt. Zurich: Weidmann, 1973.

Hammer, Caspar, ed. *Rhetores Graeci,* Vol. I *ex recognitione Leonardi Spengel.* Leipzig: Teubner, 1894.

Seguier, Nicholas Maximilien Sidoine, Marquis de St. Brison. "*Editio princeps of* Anonymous Seguerianus," monograph. Paris, 1840.

———, ed. *Notices et extraits des manuscrits de la bibliotheque du roi* 14.2 (Paris 1843): 183–212.

Critical Sources

Angermann, O. *De Aristotle retorum auctore.* Diss. Leipzig, 1904: 28–45.

Arnott, Peter D. "Theodoras of Gadara." *Ancient Greek and Roman Rhetoricians.* Ed. Donald C. Bryant et al. Columbia, MO: Artcraft P, 1968: 97.

Bryant, Donald C. et al., eds. *Ancient Greek and Roman Rhetoricians.* Columbia, MO: Artcraft P, 1968.

Egenoff, P. Review of Graeven. *Berliner Philogische Wochenscrift* 13 (24 March 1894): 389–95.

Kennedy, George A. *A New History of Classical Rhetoric.* Princeton: Princeton UP, 1994.

Kirby, John T. Review of *Two Greek Rhetorical Treatises from the Roman Empire: Introduction, Text, Translation of The Arts of Rhetoric Attributed to Anonymous Seguerianus and to Apsines of Gadara. Rhetorica* 17.3 (1999): 336–38.

Marx, Friedrich. Review of Graeven. *Berliner Philogische Wochenscrift* 25 (18 June 1892): 778–72.

Solmsen, Freidrich. "The Aristotelian Tradition in Ancient Rhetoric." *American Journal of Philology* 62 (1941): 169–90.

Stewart, Donald J. "Neocles." *Ancient Greek and Roman Rhetoricians.* Ed. Donald C. Bryant et al. Columbia, MO: Artcraft P, 1968. 78–79.

Volkmann, Richard. *Die rhetorik der griechen und romer im systematischer ubersicht dargestellt.* Leipzig, 1972.

Yunis, Harvey. Review of *Two Greek Rhetorical Treatises. Byrn Mawr Critical Review,* posted 8 August 1998, accessed 1 December 2004. <http://omega.cohums.ohio-state.edu/mailing_lists/BMCR-L/1998/0048.php>.

ANTIPHON

(ca. 480–411 BCE)

Michael Gagarin

Antiphon was born to an old and wealthy Athenian family. His father, Sophilus, reportedly had a school and was considered by some a Sophist. Thus Antiphon was undoubtedly well educated and would have been exposed from a young age to the intellectual and cultural elite from all over the Greek world, and in particular to the current ideas and activities of the new intellectuals, who as a group would later be labeled Sophists. Combining these advantages of family and background with strong intellectual powers—as his younger contemporary, the historian Thucydides, observed, "of all the Athenians of his day he was the best at thinking and at expressing what he knew"—he soon became a leading intellectual himself. Issues of law and justice were of special interest to him, but he also expressed views, often provocatively, on many of the other issues of the day, including geometry (he proposed a method for squaring the circle), cosmology, and the pseudoscience of dream interpretation (which he seems to have made fun of). Indeed, his interests were so wide ranging that many scholars (including some in antiquity) have divided him into two (or even three) Antiphons, an orator and a Sophist (and sometimes a dream interpreter). But this view has been steadily losing ground in recent decades, and a majority of scholars now agree that there was just one fifth-century Antiphon who was interested in and wrote on all these subjects, while at the same time composing speeches for delivery in court.

Antiphon may have also been a teacher during the period after 450, as some ancient sources report (Thucydides is said to have been a pupil of his); but if he was, he probably did not have a school in any formal sense. Moreover, by around 450 the reforms enacted in Athens by Ephialtes and Pericles had resulted in a considerable expansion of the power and activity of the popular law courts, where cases were decided by large juries composed of ordinary Athenians, who reached their verdict entirely on the basis of the speeches of the two litigants. Antiphon must have followed these developments closely, and even if he himself stayed in the background, he may have attended sessions of the courts as a spectator, and he had

friends who were public figures and undoubtedly found themselves in court regularly. Despite his continuing desire to remain behind the scenes, Antiphon's intelligence and ability to express himself well, together with his interests in the nature
of justice and the practical workings of the Athenian legal system, made him a
sought-after adviser by others who were involved in litigation. He continued this
practice until sometime after 430, when at some point the work of advising others
about their litigation gave him the idea of writing an entire speech for a litigant to
memorize and deliver in court. He was thus the first to put a speech in writing, and
from this practice developed a new art of prose discourse, forensic oratory, and a
new type of career, "logography" or writing speeches for others. Antiphon soon
built a reputation for expertise in this field, and he earned a great deal of money by
this career until his death in 411. After that, the practice of logography grew rapidly,
and in the fourth century it became the leading form of public discourse in Athens.

During this same period, the ongoing war with Sparta, which began in 431, was
the main political issue in Athens. Many of the cases for which Antiphon composed
speeches were political in nature, and his clients included cities allied with Athens in
the war and prominent public individuals. Thus, his legal consulting would have
overlapped considerably with political consulting. Finally, after the Athenian forces
suffered a crushing defeat in Sicily in 413, Antiphon and others took the step from
political consulting to political action. In 411 they engineered a coup, installing a
group of Four Hundred as leaders of the city. This government rapidly fell apart,
however, and the previous democratic institutions were soon reinstated. Almost all
the members of the Four Hundred left Athens, but Antiphon remained to face trial.
In his speech in his own defense (which no longer survives), he apparently refused
to admit any wrong, claiming that his aim was to preserve the democracy under
which he had prospered, not to overthrow it. Although the speech was one of his
most highly regarded throughout antiquity, it failed to win him acquittal, and he was
executed, his property confiscated, and his family sent into exile.

The only contemporary witness to Antiphon's life, Thucydides, wrote a tribute
to the man he clearly admired:

> The one who planned the course of the entire affair and who gave it the most thought
> was Antiphon; of all the Athenians of his day he was second to none in valor (*aretē*)
> and was the best at thinking and at expressing what he knew. He did not come
> forward in public or enter any dispute willingly, but was regarded with suspicion by
> the multitude because of his reputation for cleverness. However, for those involved in
> a dispute in court or in the Assembly, he was the one man most able to help whoever
> consulted him for advice. [. . .] Of all the men up to my time [. . .] he seems to me to
> have made the best defense in a capital case. (8.68)

As the first person to compose a full speech in writing for delivery in a court of
law, Antiphon can justly be called the father of Athenian oratory, which flourished
for about a century (420–320 BCE) and culminated in the work of Demosthenes
and Isocrates. Antiphon pioneered not only the practice of writing speeches for

others, but also of writing down one's own speech for later circulation. In addition, as an intellectual (sometimes called a Sophist), he theorized not only about law and justice but also about the nature of *logos* (speech, argument, language), the nature of truth (like Protagoras, he titled one of his most important works *Truth*), and the relation of language to reality. In this way he, together with his slightly older contemporaries Gorgias and Protagoras, made important contributions to the theory of public speaking as well as to its practice.

ANTIPHON'S RHETORICAL THEORY AND PRACTICE

Antiphon's first written works were probably the Tetralogies, most likely written between 450 and 430. These were inspired by the practice, attributed to Protagoras, of composing opposing speeches on the same issue (*Antilogiae*). Antiphon expanded this format from two to four speeches on the model of some Athenian trials, where the main speeches of the plaintiff and the defendant were each followed by a second, rebuttal speech. Three Tetralogies have come down to us (confusingly numbered 2, 3, and 4 among his six surviving speeches). Each is concerned with a hypothetical case of homicide. In the First Tetralogy (2), a man is accused of murdering another man who, together with his dying attendant, was found dead in the street late one night. The four individual speeches deploy a wide variety of arguments from likelihood (*eikos*) in support of each side (the defendant is the likely killer; others are more likely to have killed him than I, etc.). The Second Tetralogy (3) concerns a boy who was killed by a javelin thrown by a young man during javelin practice. The plaintiff argues that the thrower is obviously guilty (of unintentional homicide, which in Athens was punishable by perhaps a year in exile), but the defense counters with a complex and sophisticated argument that the guilty party is the one who made a mistake and that, since the boy mistakenly ran out to pick up javelins at the wrong time whereas the youth threw the javelin at the same time as everyone else and thus made no mistake, the boy is (as it were) guilty of killing himself. Finally, the Third Tetralogy concerns a drunken fight, started by one man but resulting in his own death after the other strikes back. The plaintiff argues that the man who struck the lethal blow is guilty. The defense counters that the man who started the fight caused the other to strike back and is thus guilty. Another link in the causal chain is later introduced, namely the doctor who treated the victim after he was struck and allegedly caused his death.

None of the Tetralogies has a conclusion or verdict; their apparent aim is to explore issues and forms of argument, such as the argument from likelihood (or probability) that reportedly so interested Corax and Tisias. In addition to displaying many examples of this type of argument, in the First Tetralogy Antiphon also suggests views about the value of such arguments relative to more direct, factual arguments. In the Second Tetralogy he raises questions about the relationship of *logos* (speech, argument) and reality, the relationship of opposed arguments to one another when each claims (with some justification) to present the truth, and the relationship of both of the opposed speeches to the overall truth that the jurors are supposed to ascertain. Given that so little remains of the original words of Protagoras, or of Corax and Tisias, Antiphon's Tetralogies stand with Gorgias's *Helen* as the major fifth-century explorations of the nature and function of *logos*. The Tetralogies are full of experimental and provocative arguments concerning law, justice, language, and argumentation. Although they may have been read by students hoping to learn to argue actual cases in court, they were clearly not primarily written for that purpose, since many of the arguments would appear suspiciously clever ("sophistic") to ordinary Athenian jurors. Thus these works were probably intended for general intellectual stimulation and pleasure and perhaps for public performance, but not for specific training in the techniques of litigation.

Perhaps a bit later, in the 420s, Antiphon composed two treatises, *Truth* (in two books) and *Concord*. Both exist now only in fragments, but it is clear that *Truth*, in particular, explored a wider range of issues than the Tetralogies while still maintaining the experimental and provocative attitude of those works. *Truth* also appears to continue to employ the technique of juxtaposing opposing viewpoints. The largest surviving fragments show Antiphon putting his own stamp on the discussion of *nomos* (law, convention) and *physis* (nature), which was one of the major issues of the sophistic period. For Antiphon, the importance of this issue lay in its implications for understanding law and justice. Does law have any grounding in nature or is it purely a matter of convention that one obeys only in order not to be caught and punished? Questions such as these were hotly debated in the last third of the fifth century, and though speakers in court generally avoided such arguments as being overly intellectual for the large popular juries they were addressing, the intellectual discussion undoubtedly informed forensic rhetoric in more indirect ways.

The third group of works written by Antiphon are the speeches intended for delivery in court. Many of these speeches were preserved in antiquity, and they cover a variety of types of cases, many of them with political ramifications. Today only three complete speeches survive, all concerned with homicide and probably all written in the last decade of his life. *Against the Stepmother* (1) was written for a young man who is prosecuting his stepmother for poisoning her husband (his father). Apparently the victim, on his deathbed, summoned his son, who was still a young boy, accused his wife of murdering him, and entreated the boy to bring her to justice when he came of age. The young man has very little other evidence, but relies on a vivid narrative that recreates a treacherous plot whereby his stepmother tricked a servant girl into adding poison to the man's drink (under the impression it was a love potion). *The Murder of Herodes* (5) is a defense speech, written for a man from Mytilene (a city on the island of Lesbos) who is accused of murdering an Athenian named Herodes. He complains about the specific form of procedure used by the prosecution (which was not the normal homicide procedure), accuses them of prosecuting only for financial gain, and alleges many inconsistencies and illegalities in their handling of the case, especially in their treatment of a slave on whose testimony they seem to have relied. *On the Chorus Boy* (6) is another defense speech written for a man who was in charge of training a chorus of young boys for a public competition and is now accused of being responsible for the accidental death of one of the boys during the training period. The accused denies he was even present during the fatal incident (and has witnesses to prove it), and then alleges that he is victim of a conspiracy, engineered by his political opponents, who have bribed the plaintiff to bring this case in order to prevent the defendant from prosecuting them on charges of public corruption.

In none of these cases do we know the verdict, nor do any of the opposing speeches survive, so that we can only guess at the outcome. Antiphon was famous in antiquity, however, for helping others win their cases, and especially for helping defendants whose situations seemed hopeless. So the chances are that he was successful in at least some of these three cases. The only case that we know he lost was his last, the speech in his own defense.

These three groups of works that have survived—the Tetralogies, the sophistic works *Truth* and *Concord*, and the court speeches—all share an interest in law and justice, and in the nature of truth and of language. Perhaps even more important is a common approach or attitude that challenges traditional views and explores novel ideas and methods of argument. This attitude, which Antiphon shares with the other Sophists, especially Gorgias and Protagoras, is naturally more evident in the Tetralogies and sophistic treatises than in the court speeches, which were written for delivery to an audience of ordinary Athenian jurors; but even these show clear traces of it, and it is especially evident in his last speech in his own defense.

There are also, of course, important differences among these three groups (and even between the two sophistic treatises), which can be attributed in large part to their different forms and purposes. The Tetralogies and *Truth* were clearly intended to be read by the intellectual elite—other Sophists, students of Antiphon and of others, and other educated Greeks (not just Athenians) who took an interest in current intellectual issues. The Tetralogies were an attempt to use the new form of opposed speeches, or *Antilogiae*, to explore legal and philosophical issues. *Truth*, on the other hand, has the form of an intellectual treatise, but its method seems to be heuristic and skeptical, not dogmatic, though its fragmentary state makes it impossible to be certain in many instances. *Concord* may have been intended for oral presentation to a larger, less intellectual audience, and the surviving fragments (which may not be representative of the whole) have a more anecdotal style replete with moralizing tendencies. They may challenge common views but they do so in a more constructive and moralistic fashion. Finally, the court speeches were composed for oral delivery to a group of ordinary citizens, and thus are written in a simpler, more direct style. However, it is likely that Antiphon's last speech, in his own defense, which was written down and later circulated, was also aimed at a wider audience, and this may account for what appears to be a more intellectual or sophistic tone to the arguments that survive.

CONCLUSION

If one examines simply the doctrines Antiphon developed or the positions he took on the various intellectual issues of his day, it is relatively easy to divide him into two different figures. One was a radical believer in nature as opposed to law, who dismissed truth and traditional morality as relative or subjective or both, and who valued rhetoric as having the power to overturn any traditionally approved or commonsensical views or standards; as a wealthy aristocrat, he opposed the mainstream democratic position of most Athenians, a position he finally acted on at the end of his life. The other Antiphon recognized human weaknesses but sought to improve people, criticized the divisions that separate people from one another, and spoke directly in his forensic speeches about the sanctity of the laws and the importance of human justice. But if we accept that Antiphon's specific positions, as well as the form of his arguments and the style of his writing, may have varied according to the specific context in which and the audience to which they were expressed, and if we concentrate instead on his methods, his attitudes, and his areas of interest, we find a more consistent picture. From this perspective, we can observe a broad interest in challenging tradition and questioning received views, in suggesting innovative, paradoxical, often deliberately shocking positions, and in tolerating ambiguous, even contradictory conclusions, but ultimately in drawing on these methods to construct more positive views and communicate more directly with a popular audience.

Antiphon's career was thus an unusual mixture: a political leader who for most of his life avoided public prominence and an elite sophistic thinker whose main influence was not so much on later philosophy as on a new genre of public discourse, forensic oratory. We can only speculate what personal qualities caused him to remain in the background politically, but his intellectual qualities are more evident. Although he was broadly interested in almost all the major sophistic issues of the day, from the beginning his main interest centered on issues of law and justice. In this area, his intellectual and practical interests were combined and led him to create innovative intellectual studies that took the dramatic form of trials, to give practical advice about litigation and forensic strategies, and finally, to compose full forensic discourses for practical use. His renowned skill in this practice drew on both his long experience in observing the courts and his theoretical work on law, justice, and language.

This last accomplishment is his main legacy, for logography and other forms of oratory became a major cultural institution in the fourth century and afterward. It is traditionally (though probably misleadingly) said that rhetoric was invented in Sicily several decades before Antiphon began writing speeches. But the theoretical work of Corax, Tisias, Gorgias, and others had a relatively narrow impact on Greek intellectual life until Antiphon turned it to practical use and created an institution (forensic oratory) and a profession (logography) that in the fourth century played a significant role in the lives of many Athenians. Later critics, interested primarily in prose style, valued Antiphon less highly than his successors like Lysias and Demosthenes, who took the practice he created and carried it to greater heights. Most of Antiphon's works were lost before the modern era, and so we can only glimpse the full range and quality of his intellectual and rhetorical work. But he clearly deserves credit for being the pivotal link between the intellectual activity of fifth-century Sophists and the public oratory of fourth-century politicians and logographers. The Western rhetorical tradition began with a small group of theorists and practitioners in the fifth century BCE—Corax, Tisias, Gorgias, Protagoras, and Antiphon. Antiphon may be the least known of these but he was in some ways the most important.

BIBLIOGRAPHY

Primary Sources and Translations

Decleva Caizzi, Fernanda. *Antiphontis, tetralogiae.* Milan: Cisalpino, 1969.

———. "Antipho." *Corpus dei papiri filosofici greci e latini.* Ed. Francesco Adorno et al. Florence: Leo S. Olschki, 1989. 176–236.

Diels, Hermann, and Walther Kranz. *Die Fragmente der Vorsokratiker.* 6th ed. Berlin: Weidmann, 1951.

Edwards, Michael, and Stephen Usher. *Greek Orators I: Antiphon and Lysias.* Warminster: Aris and Phillips, 1985.

Gagarin, Michael, ed. *Antiphon, the Speeches.* Cambridge: Cambridge UP, 1997.

Gagarin, Michael, and Douglas MacDowell, trans. *Antiphon and Andocides.* Austin: U of Texas P, 1998.

Gernet, Louis. *Antiphon, discours.* Paris: Belles Lettres, 1923.

Morrison, J. S., trans. "Antiphon." *The Older Sophists.* Ed. Rosamond K. Sprague. Columbia: U of South Carolina P, 1972. 106–240.

Pendrick, Gerard J., ed. *Antiphon the Sophist: The Fragments.* Cambridge: Cambridge UP, 2002.

Thalheim, Theodore, and Friedrich Blass, eds. *Antiphon, orationes et fragmenta,* Leipzig: Teubner, 1914.

Biographical Sources

Anonymous. "Life of Antiphon." Thalheim and Blass xvi–xvii.

Plutarch. *Life of Antiphon. Lives of the Ten Orators (Moralia* 832b–834b).

Thucydides. *History of the Peloponnesian War.* 8.68.

Critical Sources

Carawan, Edwin. *Rhetoric and the Law of Draco.* Oxford: Oxford UP, 1998.

Cassin, Barbara. "Histoire d'une identité: Les Antiphons." *L'écrit du temps* 10 (1985): 65–77.

Cole, Thomas. *The Origins of Rhetoric in Ancient Greece.* Baltimore: Johns Hopkins UP, 1991.

Dover, Kenneth J. "The Chronology of Antiphon's Speeches." *Classical Quarterly* 44 (1950): 44–60.

Due, Bodil. *Antiphon: A Study in Argumentation.* Copenhagen: Museum Tusculanum, 1980.

Gagarin, Michael. "The Nature of Proofs in Antiphon." *Classical Philology* 85 (1990): 22–32.

———. *Antiphon the Athenian: Oratory, Law and Justice in the Age of the Sophists.* Austin: U of Texas P, 2002.

Kennedy, George A. *The Art of Persuasion in Greece.* Princeton: Princeton UP, 1963.

Ostwald, Martin. "*Nomos and Phusis* in Antiphon's *Peri Aletheias*." *Cabinet of the Muses: Essays on Classical and Comparative Literature in Honor of Thomas G. Rosenmeyer*. Ed. Mark Griffith and D. J. Mastronarde. Atlanta: Scholars P, 1990. 293–306.

Schiappa, Edward. *The Beginnings of Rhetorical Theory in Classical Greece*. New Haven: Yale UP, 1999.

Solmsen, Friedrich. *Antiphonstudien*. Berlin: Weidmann, 1931.

Zinsmaier, Thomas. "Wahrheit, Gerechtigkeit und Rhetorik in den Reden Antiphons: Zur Genese einiger Topoi der Gerichtsrede." *Hermes* 126 (1998): 398–422.

Apsines of Gadara

(ca. 190–ca. 250 CE)

Sean Patrick O'Rourke

Of the several "Apsines" who taught rhetoric and declaimed during the Roman imperial period, Valerius Apsines of Gadara is the most important. Unfortunately, little is known of his life, and what is known hangs on rather slim evidence. He was born in Coele Syria, probably around 190 CE. On the basis of a single Athenian inscription, we assume that his family name was indeed Valerius. Scholarly consensus now holds that he married into an important family but not that, as was earlier assumed, he was related to the later Sophists Onasimus and Apsines of Sparta.

He studied rhetoric at a young age, first in Smyrna under Heracleides of Lycia and then in Nicomedia with Basilicus. Apparently he excelled, for, when he moved to Athens around 225, he gave public declamations and taught rhetoric. His declamations were highly regarded, as much for the memory and accuracy they demonstrated as for any of the standard stylistic criteria of the age. He was also a popular teacher and may even have held one of the official Athenian chairs of rhetoric. The Emperor Maximinus (235–238) awarded him the *ornamenta consularia*, an honorary title. Apsines died around 250.

Few of Apsines' works survive. His chief theoretical work, the *Art of Rhetoric*, exists in twenty-one manuscripts, five modern editions, and two English translations, but its attribution to Apsines has recently been questioned. Also surviving (usually appended to the manuscripts of the *Art of Rhetoric*) are portions of an essay, "On Figured Problems," though this too may not be Apsines'. He published some of his declamations, fragments of which, according to Mervin R. Dilts and George A. Kennedy, seem to survive as interpolations in the text of his chief work. No longer extant are a work on figures of speech and a commentary on at least one of Demosthenes' speeches.

Apsines' modest significance in the history of rhetoric, then, rests almost exclusively on the *Art of Rhetoric*. Its importance is both theoretical and historical. Theoretically, Apsines offers a distinctive account of *prokatastasis* (preparation of the proof), a thorough treatment of refutation, and a detailed analysis of pity. Historically, Apsines' *Technē* is one of the few complete rhetoric texts from the second and third centuries of the Common Era, and therefore provides rare insight into the rhetoric taught in the Greek schools during the so-called Second Sophistic.

TEXT AND THE ATTRIBUTION CONTROVERSY

Apsines' popularity may in part account for some of the textual problems associated with his chief work, the *Art of Rhetoric*. Editors and translators agree that the text received considerable posthumous editing from students and later transcribers, who almost certainly added examples and other illustrations to some sections, abridged others, inserted material from Apsines' declamations, and played with key technical terms.

Recently Malcolm Heath has argued that there are grounds for doubting the traditional attribution of the text to Apsines. Heath notes the unusual references to "Apsines" by name as the author of speeches used to illustrate key points, references indistinguishable in form from citations to authors of other illustrative speeches. Such "third-person self-citation" is, Heath urges, not common in rhetorical treatises of the period ("Apsines" 92). While modern editors of the text have explained the problem as one of interpolation by later transcribers, Heath notes that there are no independent text-critical grounds for doing so. Moreover, he argues, if the attribution to Apsines is doubted, the pseudo-Hermogenean treatise *On Invention*, also attributed to Apsines in some manuscripts but discounted as his because of inconsistencies between that text and the *Art of Rhetoric*, can be reconsidered. Heath suggests the possibility that, under this hypothesis, the *Art of Rhetoric* and the fragment on figured speeches are works of Aspasius, a pupil of Apsines.

As Heath notes, however, his hypothesis is provisional and there is currently no basis for a clear resolution of the problem. Dilts and Kennedy, suggesting that a student may have added chapter 10 and references to Apsines' declamations, assume the traditional attribution.

APSINES' RHETORICAL THEORY

The authorship controversy notwithstanding, the text is theoretically and historically interesting. In their translation, Dilts and Kennedy add the subtitle "On the Parts of a Political Speech," indicating that the text is organized by the parts of the oration and that it deals mainly with deliberative and judicial, and not epideictic, themes. It does not directly consider purely organizational problems. Rather, in keeping with many of the treatises of antiquity, it merely uses the parts of the traditional oration as a convenient scheme to arrange the treatment of inventional and tactical issues. The text has ten chapters of unequal length. A chapter apiece is devoted to *prooemium*, *prokatastasis*, narration, paradigms, enthymemes, "headings," and the epilogue, while refutation is treated over the course of three chapters.

In the first chapter, Apsines offers a way for speakers to devise a *prooemium* efficiently. He divides the sources of the *prooemium* into generic categories he calls *theōrēma*, an unusual term found only in chapter 1. The *prooemium* can be derived from praise of the hearers after persuading them of something or after they have performed an action, from what follows from a previous decision, from the weightiness of the matter, from a slanderous attack against the speaker, from the circumstances of repeated accusations, from the result of something that has been said or written, and the like. Each option is posed as a tactical opportunity to introduce arguments, often with an accompanying appropriate approach such as invective, deprecation, or "injured tone."

The second chapter sets forth Apsines' theory of *prokatastasis*, the preparation of the proof. The discussion stands in lieu of (but also hints at) the familiar treatments of the "statement of the case" or "the partition." Apsines indicates nine ways to create a *prokatastasis*, including "scrutiny of intention," "removal of objection," contrasting circumstances of the past and the present, and so forth. He subdivides scrutiny of intention into three sets—speaker, audience, and opponent—and details the circumstances when each is appropriate. The theory here is both interesting and distinctive. As Dilts and Kennedy observe, only the pseudo-Hermogenean *On Invention* (noted above) contains a similarly extended discussion.

After an uninspiring but coherent treatment of narration in chapter 3, the text provides an extended treatment of refutation. Refutation, Apsines claims, is accomplished in two general ways, by reversal and by method. By "reversal" he seems to mean denying the opponent's claim directly, while by "method" he seems to mean granting the opponent's claim but providing a plausible explanation in one's favor. Apsines connects these refutational modes to types of arguments and kinds of evidence. This general treatment in chapter 5 is supplemented by brief but specific applications to "objections" (chapter 4) and "paradigms" (chapter 7). Taken as a whole, Apsines' handling of refutation is detailed if not exhaustive, and remains in large part useful today.

Apsines' alignment with Aristotle is most apparent in his treatment of paradigms, enthymemes, and "headings" in chapters 6, 8, and 9, respectively. Paradigms (examples) and enthymemes are treated as the two forms of rational argument. Apsines is concerned primarily with paradigms taken from "persons of the past" or historical examples, and outlines when and how they should be employed. He treats enthymemes, again consistent with Aristotle, as rhetorical syllogisms. He notes the chief characteristics of enthymemes (they are "agonistic" and "refutative") and, as with examples, suggests how they may appropriately be employed. He chooses not to provide a treatment of stasis theory, noting that such matters "have been sufficiently discussed," and opts instead for a treatment of the "headings" or topics. He describes and explains the legal, the customary, the just, the advantageous, the honorable, and the possible.

Finally, in chapter 10, Apsines treats epilogues. After noting the general characteristics and functions of epilogues, Apsines discusses pity and *pathos*. The treatment of *pathos* is a bit thin; the handling of pity is full, with richly detailed explanations of the applicable *topoi*. In keeping with his general approach, Apsines' discussion of pity is tactical, concerned with winning persuasive cases.

CONCLUSION

Theoretically, then, Apsines' *Art of Rhetoric* offers little that is innovative or controversial. On the other hand, the sections on refutation are copious and still relevant, while the treatments of *prokatastasis* and pity are two of the more extensive treatments of their subjects in antiquity.

Historically, however, Apsines' text offers considerable insight. First, the interposed excerpts from Apsines' declamations provide evidence that at least some declamations of the period stressed reasoned argument and deliberation. Second, because most scholars agree that Apsines' *Art of Rhetoric* shows little influence from Hermogenes (though Douglas J. Stewart finds similar technical vocabulary), the text also helps us to see that the Hermogenean restructuring of rhetoric, so obvious after the fourth century, was yet to take hold. Finally, the orientation toward invention, the treatment of the topics, the brief mention of stasis, and the pairing of paradigms and enthymemes all suggest the continued influence of the Aristotelian tradition.

As Stewart has said, in an age "frequently dismissed as decadent and intellectually listless," Apsines' rhetoric stands out as one of "shrewdness and ingenuous confidence" ("Apsines of Gadara" 10). To these qualities we might also add, without too much hesitation, historical and theoretical importance.

BIBLIOGRAPHY

Primary Sources and Translations

Bakius, John, ed. *Apsinis et Longini Rhetorica: e Codicibus MSS., adhibita supellectili Ruhnkeniana.* Oxford: Typographus Academicus, 1849.

Dilts, Mervin R., and George A. Kennedy, eds. and trans. "Apsines' Art of Rhetoric (On the Parts of Political Speech)." *Two Greek Rhetorical Treatises from the Roman Empire: Introduction, Text, and Translation of the Arts of Rhetoric Attributed to Anonymous Seguerianus and to Apsines of Gadara.* Leiden: Brill, 1997. 75–239.

Hammer, Caspar, ed. *Rhetores Graeci.* Leipzig: Teubner, 1894. 217–329.

Manutius, Aldus, ed. *Rhetores Graeci.* 2 vols. Venice: Aldine, 1508–09. II: 682–730.

Spengel, Leonard, ed. *Rhetores Graeci.* 3 vols. Leipzig: Teubner, 1853–56. Rpt. Frankfurt: Minerva, 1966. I: 331–414.

Stewart, Douglas J., trans. "Apsines' The Art of Rhetoric." MA thesis. Cornell U, 1959.

Walz, Christian, ed. *Rhetores Graeci.* 9 vols. London and elsewhere, 1832–36. Rpt. Osnabrück: Zeller, 1968. IX: 467–96.

Biographical Sources

Bowie, Ewan. "Apsines." *Brill's New Pauly*. Leiden: Brill, 2002. I: 914.

Brzoska, Julius. "Apsines." *Paulys Real-Encyclopädie der classischen Altertumswissenschaft*. Stuttgart: J. B. Metzler, 1896. II: 277–83.

Dilts, Mervin R., and George A. Kennedy. "Introduction." *Two Greek Rhetorical Treatises from the Roman Empire: Introduction, Text, and Translation of the Arts of Rhetoric Attributed to Anonymous Seguerianus and to Apsines of Gadara*. Leiden: Brill, 1997. xv–xix.

Stewart, Douglas J. "Apsines of Gadara." *Ancient Greek and Roman Rhetoricians: A Biographical Dictionary*. Ed. Donald C. Bryant et al. Columbia, MO: Artcraft P, 1968. 8–10.

Critical Sources

Aulitzky, Karl. "Apsines *peri eleou*." *Wiener Studien* 39 (1917): 26–47.

Dilts, Mervin R., and George A. Kennedy. "Textual History of the Treatises." *Two Greek Rhetorical Treatises from the Roman Empire: Introduction, Text, and Translation of the Arts of Rhetoric Attributed to Anonymous Seguerianus and to Apsines of Gadara*. Leiden: Brill, 1997. xxii–xxvii.

Geiger, Joseph. "Notes on the Second Sophistic in Palestine." *Illinois Classical Studies* 19 (1994): 221–30.

Heath, Malcolm. "Apsines and Pseudo-Apsines." *American Journal of Philology* 119 (1998): 89–111.

———. "Notes on Pseudo-Apsines." *Mnemosyne* 55.6 (2002): 657–68.

Volkmann, Richard. "Zu Apsines." *Neue Jahrbücher für Philologie und Pädogogik* 109 (1875): 593–96.

AELIUS ARISTIDES

(117–ca. 180 CE)

Jeffrey Walker

Publius Aelius Aristides Theodorus originated from Mysia (a region in what is now northwestern Turkey, just below the Hellespont and opposite the Greek island of Lesbos); he was educated at Pergamum and Athens but for most of his career was associated with the city of Smyrna (modern Izmir). He became one of the most illustrious Sophists of his day—he appears as a major figure in Philostratus's *Lives of the Sophists*—and today is the best surviving example of a practicing *rhētōr* during the Second Sophistic at its peak in the second century CE. Aristides is also one of the quirkier personalities in ancient literature, and, thanks to what he tells us about himself, one of the best known. A large number of his writings have been preserved—fifty-three "orations" in all (though two seem spurious)—comprising speeches, tracts, "prose hymns," declamations, and the strange autobiographical texts known as the *Sacred Tales*, plus a scattering of fragments and a handful of inscriptions. This preservation is due, in part, to the fact that Aristides is one of the few late antique orators to be regarded in the Byzantine period as an equal of the Attic orators of early antiquity, and studied as a classical, canonic figure for rhetorical studies in the schools of medieval Constantinople. There is also a rhetoric manual that in the Middle Ages was ascribed to Aristides (the "Aristides Rhetoric"), though that identification is now regarded as erroneous.

Aristides' significance for modern rhetorical studies lies in his status as an exemplary (if eccentric) embodiment of the version of sophistic rhetoric that runs from Isocrates through such figures as Dionysius of Halicarnassus to later antiquity, and that becomes dominant in the Second Sophistic and sets the stage for Patristic and Byzantine rhetoric. His Isocrateanism is most explicitly evident in his lengthy tract *Against Plato in Defense of Rhetoric*, and implicit in his other orations and the general pattern of his career. This Isocrateanism inheres, on one hand, in an understanding of rhetoric as a mode of political "philosophy" whose primary functions are the cultivation of the shared ideals that make civil community possible, and the maintenance and guiding of that community through reasoned speech, particularly symbouleutic or "advisory" discourse (*sumbouleutikon*, which often is translated as "deliberative"). On the other hand, and as a consequence of this first understanding, this Isocratean, "philosophical" rhetoric tends to regard the various types of "panegyric" or epideictic discourse as the primary modalities for high eloquence: in the case of Aristides' surviving texts, these range from public declamations on symbouleutic themes to public panegyric, "prose hymns," and advisory discourses to city councils and, on at least one occasion, to the common council of the whole province of Roman "Asia" (roughly, today's western Turkey). Aristides plays a cultural role that, in later centuries, will be taken over by the Christian homiletic tradition. At the same time—though this is less visible, or less obvious in his extant orations—he also plays the practical civic roles that, from the earliest beginnings of the rhetorical tradition, have always inhered in rhetoric's application to the discourses of judicial and political decision making. He thus gives us some representation of the actual political functions of sophistic rhetoric in the Roman Empire.

Perhaps equally significantly, Aristides is really more of a practitioner than a theorist—though he did have students, whom he probably taught through a process of rhetorical critique (of canonic texts), modeling (in the Sophist's own performances), and imitation and practice. Thus the best way to approach an understanding of "Isocratean, Second Sophistic rhetoric" as exemplified by Aristides is to consider his rhetorical practices over the span of his career. (In what follows, I refer to Aristides' extant orations by the numbering used in the editions of Behr/Lentz and Keil, and also in Behr's translation of Aristides' complete works.)

ARISTIDES' RHETORICAL CAREER

The main features of Aristides' life and career have been worked out in some detail by his chief modern editor and commentator in English, Charles Behr (see *Aelius Aristides and the Sacred Tales*, from which most of the biographical information here is drawn). Aristides was born in 117 CE, at his family's ancestral estate in Mysia, at Hadriani, not far east from Hadrianutherae (modern Balikesir). The family had substantial agricultural holdings and was wealthy, but not extremely rich. They were, however, important enough to have citizenship not only in Hadriani but also Smyrna, which with Pergamum and Ephesus was one of the three chief cities of Roman Asia. Aristides' father, Eudaemon, was sufficiently prominent and well-connected to be appointed to a priesthood (a civic honor) and granted Roman citizenship by Hadrian, during that emperor's tour of Mysia in 123.

Aristides received an exceptionally fine education. After his elementary studies, he went to Smyrna to study literature under the *grammatikos* Alexander of Cotiaeum, who would later go to Rome as tutor to Marcus Aurelius. Aristides then went on to study rhetoric under some of the most distinguished *rhētōres* of the day: first under Polemo at Smyrna; then under Aristocles at Pergamum; and finally, at Athens, under the celebrated Sophist Herodes Atticus. (Philostratus discusses each of these in *Lives of the Sophists*, and devotes an especially long chapter to Herodes; unfortunately

Herodes' writings have not survived, except for a single declamation.) Aristides' rhetorical training was supplemented with philosophical studies at both Pergamum and Athens, through which he seems to have acquired considerable familiarity with Plato.

Around 141, at the age of twenty-four, Aristides embarked on his rhetorical career. He toured through Cos, Cnidus, Rhodes, and Egypt, declaiming with great success. Orations 5–16 in Behr's edition and translation of Aristides provide a representative sample of his declamations, though most of these cannot be precisely dated, and some clearly belong, at least in their extant form, to later periods in his career. All of these declamations are "deliberative" or symbouleutic themes, and all but one are historical pieces set at fateful moments in the glory days of Athens, from the Peloponnesian War to the coming of Philip of Macedon: whether the Athenians should make peace with Sparta, when the Spartans have asked for a truce after the Athenian victory at Sphacteria (two speeches, for and against, Or. 7–8); whether the Athenians should send reinforcements to rescue their Sicilian expedition, when things have gone badly wrong (two speeches, for and against, Or. 5–6); whether the Athenians, after the Theban victory over Sparta at Leuctra, should form an alliance with Thebes, Sparta, or neither (five speeches, consisting of a tetralogy of two speeches each for Thebes and Sparta, and the fifth for neither, Or. 11–15); and whether, in the circumstances preceding the battle of Chaeronea, the Thebans should ally with the Athenians against Philip of Macedon (two ambassadorial speeches to the Thebans, spoken presumably by Demosthenes [whose actual speeches from that embassy were not preserved], with an assumed counterspeech by Philip's ambassadors between them, Or. 9–10). The one nonhistorical declamation is an embassy speech to Achilles, set in the circumstances of *Iliad* book 9 (Or. 16). These declamations, in their rehearsal of themes from Athenian history and their re-creation of Attic oratory, show Aristides as a participant in the Atticist revival then underway. At the same time, in featuring symbouleutic rather than judicial discourse the declamations reveal a preference for an Isocratean ideal of rhetoric as a medium of political thought, and present a model of the *rhētōr* as an advisor (*sumboulos*) to the civil community, or to a council (*boulē*). Further, in featuring ambassadorial speeches, the declamations also model what was in fact one of the most important practical functions of a sophist-*rhētōr* in the Roman empire.

While in Egypt, Aristides traveled south as far as the first cataract of the Nile (modern Aswan) but then fell ill and decided to return to Smyrna. This intervention by illness would prove to be a hallmark of his career. The sea journey home was difficult, and back in Smyrna, in 142, he delivered his oration *Regarding Sarapis* (Or. 45 in Behr) in thanksgiving to the Egyptian savior-god for his safe return, and in prayer for the protection of his life and health; this appears to be his earliest datable oration. Notably, the prologue of *Regarding Sarapis* proposes that prose oratory (*logos*, "speech") should be a suitable medium for "hymns," and treats poetry (meaning verse) as an antiquated, artificial form of expression. Prose hymns—featuring short, rhythmic, almost songlike cola, in the manner of Hellenistic "Asianism," or Gorgias's *Epitaphios*—would later become a prominent and distinctive part of Aristides' repertoire, beginning with *Sarapis*, and culminating with *Monody for Smyrna* (Or. 18) in 177.

In 143 Aristides launched a new tour, with the ambition of declaiming at the imperial court in Rome. An appearance before the emperor was more than just a show: a Sophist who had built up a reputation through his touring performances, and who made a favorable impression on the emperor, had a good chance of being appointed to a significant post in the imperial administration; there are many such cases in Philostratus's *Lives of the Sophists*. Shortly before his departure, Aristides caught a severe cold but set out anyway. By the time he reached Rome he was too sick to continue, gave up on his plans, and sailed back to Smyrna, finally reaching home in a state of almost total collapse. This was the beginning of a chronic, recurring illness (or set of illnesses) that would dog him for the rest of his life. He seems to have suffered a number of problems, mostly respiratory and digestive, some real and some psychosomatic. Aristides also seems, in spite of his problems and his constant fretting over his condition, to have had a resilient constitution; he always recovered (if temporarily), and later in life would suffer and survive even smallpox. But in 143–144, after his miserable return from Rome, the twenty-seven-year-old Aristides seemed to have no hope of continuing his oratorical career: he was too sick.

Around 144–145, Aristides had two dream visions of the healing god Asclepius, which persuaded him to become an "incubant" at the famous shrine of Asclepius at Pergamum. An incubant slept in the temple precinct, in hopes of receiving a dream vision in which the god would reveal a cure for the incubant's illness. The Asclepieion also had facilities for physical exercise and therapy, baths, a library, a theater that could seat 3,500, and other amenities: it was a religious health spa. Aristides remained there until 147, and was visited by Asclepius many times (and, afterward, throughout his life).

During his incubation period, which Aristides later called his "Cathedra" (*kathedra*, "sitting, inactivity" or "seat"), he began the dream diaries that eventually would form the basis of his *Sacred Tales* (*Hieroi Logoi*; Or. 47–52), which he composed around 170. In the *Sacred Tales*, he celebrates the god's care for him by describing 130 dreams and the fortunes of his health over a period of about twenty-five years. This odd set of texts—a short selection from the more than 300,000 lines Aristides says he compiled in his parchment notebooks over the years—is one of the most extraordinary documents in ancient literature. The *Sacred Tales* provide fertile ground for the psychoanalytic study of a remarkable ancient personality; they also provide ground, along with some of Aristides' orations (especially his "prose hymns"), for the study of Aristides as an eclectic, pagan religious thinker contemporary with early Christianity.

Aristides' "Cathedra" period also saw the revival of his rhetorical ambitions. This resulted partly from certain dreams sent by Asclepius, and partly from the encouragement of his friends at the Asclepieion—a circle of wealthy, neurasthenic intellectuals like himself—who helped him to interpret these dreams as the god's injunction to practice rhetoric as part of his cure. This would lead him, for the rest of his life, to regard rhetoric as a holy calling. Aristides resumed declaiming, probably to small audiences of his friends. He also wrote poetry during this time, including choral hymns that he arranged to have performed in the theater of the Asclepieion (none of this poetry has been preserved); and he delivered at least two prose hymns, to Dionysus (Or. 41) and Athena (not preserved).

These activities led to others: a remark in his prose hymn to Athena provoked a criticism, to which he responded with *Concerning a Remark in Passing* (Or. 28). More important, philosophical critiques of rhetoric based on Plato's *Gorgias* seem to have been current among the Platonist and Cynic philosophers at Pergamum, and these prompted Aristides' most important programmatic statement on rhetoric, *Against Plato in Defense of Rhetoric* (Or. 2). The Greek title of this lengthy tract, *Pros Platōna Huper Rhētorikēs*, is translated by Behr as "To Plato: In Defence of Oratory"; but by *rhētorikē* Aristides means something more expansive than "oratory," and more akin to Isocrates' notion of *logōn technē* ("discursive art"). The basic argument is an extended refutation of the *Gorgias*'s charges that rhetoric is not an "art" (*technē*) and is merely a form of "flattery." This refutation leads to further arguments that resonate with Isocrates' myth of *logos* ("discourse") as the medium through which civil communities are formed and sustained, and without which there is only savagery (the absence of community, the war of all against all), or tyranny enforced by violence and coercion. Rhetoric, as Aristides defines it, is an "amulet of justice" (*Defense* 210): it works toward the creation and maintenance of a civil community based on a shared sense of what is right; it is "a kind of philosophy" (305) whose goal is to produce "right thinking" and "right action" in oneself and others (392); and, as such, it is a gift from the gods to humankind. Ultimately, as Aristides contends—and thinking no doubt of himself—any person engaged in the pursuit of an eloquent, virtuous, practical wisdom, even if he does not orate in the public forum, is a true devotee and practitioner of rhetoric (429–30).

After the *Defense*, Aristides composed *To Capito* (Or. 3), a relatively short reply to Platonist objections, especially to the *Defense*'s critique of Plato's behavior (e.g., his ineffectual political adventure in Sicily) and his treatment of the Athenian statesmen Pericles, Cimon, Miltiades, and Themistocles as orators who "flattered" and corrupted the Athenians—an argument that Aristides treats as an outrage. Much later in his career, Aristides would still be responding to this debate with his *Defense of the Four* (Or. 3, composed ca. 161–165), in essence an expanded version of the arguments of *To Capito*. The debate would not end there; more than a century later the Neoplatonist philosopher Porphyry replied with a seven-book tract *Against Aristides* (of which only a few fragments now survive). Aristides' *Defense of Rhetoric* is a significant document in the ancient intellectual debate over the nature and status of rhetoric.

The last known works of Aristides' "Cathedra" period are a birthday speech for the son of a Roman magistrate at Pergamum (Or. 30) and *The Sons of Asclepius*, a prose hymn for the priests at the Asclepieion (Or. 38), which seems to have been delivered in conjunction with a choral performance that Aristides produced. These are minor pieces, but they show Aristides feeling well enough to resume something like the typical performance work of an itinerant Sophist, which was physically demanding (it required physical abilities comparable to those required by opera today). Sometime between 147 and 149, after his return to Smyrna (or his estates), Aristides composed his *Egyptian Discourse* (Or. 36), a treatise on the Nile based on what he had learned during his travels there.

In the next period of his life, from 147 to 153, Aristides was preoccupied with lawsuits. On several occasions, provincial magistrates appointed him to "liturgies," civic duties that typically were seen as honors, but that also involved significant expenses (and thus were a form of taxation). Aristides was appointed high priest of the imperial cult in Asia, tax collector at Smyrna, and eirenarch (*eirēnarchēs*, roughly "chief of police"). In each case he successfully fought the appointment in the courts, and eventually was granted a permanent exemption, in view of his status as a practicing *rhētōr*. (This had a legal basis: the *rhētōr* through his speaking performed civic services, especially in embassies to the emperor on behalf of cities.) While these courthouse speeches have not been preserved—probably because he thought them too mundane, or beneath the dignity of literature—Aristides' lawsuits indicate a dimension of Second Sophistic rhetorical activity that often is not visible to us now. The courts were busy. The *Sacred Tales* report a dream of February 12, 166 that involved one of Aristides' "adversaries in a lawsuit at Hadrianutherae" (1.52), thereby showing that he was, indeed, still engaging in lawsuits (apparently over private matters) fairly late in his career.

During the years while he was fighting off liturgies in the courts, Aristides, also produced a number of orations that he thought worthy of preservation. These include *To the Rhodians Concerning Concord* (Or. 24), a symbouleutic ("advisory") letter to the Rhodian assembly on resolving problems of class conflict that had emerged during the rebuilding of their city after an earthquake; prose hymns to Zeus and Athena (Or. 43, 37); and a funeral encomium for his old *grammatikos*, Alexander of Cotiaeum (Or. 32).

By 155, Aristides felt well enough to attempt another speaking tour and to accept students. This tour took him to Athens, where he delivered his *Panathenaicus* (Or. 1), a grand panegyric of Athens's deeds and gifts to civilization, at the Panathenaic festival; and to Rome, where he delivered before the imperial court his equally grand panegyric *Regarding Rome* (Or. 26), celebrating Rome's administrative wisdom. These two speeches have traditionally been regarded as Aristides' greatest orations; they are certainly, along with the *Defense of Rhetoric*, his longest. They follow what already were deeply traditional genre conventions, and for the modern reader can seem tedious. Their excellence, however, lies in their management of the conventional headings, the fullness of their treatment, their stylistic grace and copiousness (which is less perceptible in translation), and, last but not least, the nobility of their political ideals (though this has to be judged from within the standards appropriate to their time). It might be said that these two speeches are Aristides' fullest realizations of the Atticist ideal, both thematically and stylistically, in actual orations. While the *Defense* should be compared with Isocrates' *Antidosis*, these should be compared with Isocrates' *Panegyricus*.

During this same tour, Aristides delivered two prose hymns, *Regarding the Aegean Sea* (Or. 44) at Delos, and *Regarding Poseidon* (Or. 46) at Corinth for the

Isthmian games. Back at Smyrna, between 157 and 165, he delivered his first *Smyrnaean Oration* (Or. 17), a panegyric of the city; and a symbouleutic speech, *On the Prohibition of Comedy* (Or. 29), in rather prudish opposition to the inclusion of satirical (and often obscene) comedy performances at the city's Dionysia festival. He also delivered a funeral oration for one of his students (Or. 31) and composed his *Defense of the Four* (Or. 3), the last installment in his dispute with Plato.

In 165, at the age of forty-eight, during a plague, Aristides contracted smallpox. It apparently was a somewhat less virulent variety, and he survived; but he seems to have reduced his oratorical activities—there were no more grand tours abroad. In 166, not long after his illness, while resting at his favorite estate at Laneion (about fifteen miles northeast of Hadrianutherae, modern Balikesir), he composed a discourse, *To Those Who Criticize Him Because He Does Not Declaim* (Or. 33). But his activities did not entirely cease: between 166 and 170 he delivered a prose hymn to Heracles (Or. 40); a panegyric celebrating the restoration of an earthquake-damaged temple in Cyzicus (Or. 27); a prose hymn, *The Well in the Temple of Asclepius* at Pergamum (Or. 39); a speech to the Smyrnaean council, *Against Those Who Burlesque the Mysteries* (Or. 34), a critique of orators who abuse the art of rhetoric, comparable to Isocrates' *Against the Sophists*; and a symbouleutic speech to the general assembly of Asia (the *koinon*) at Pergamum, *Concerning Concord* (Or. 23), in which he urges Pergamum, Ephesus, and Smyrna to patch up their endless disputes with each other. During 170–171, Aristides wrote the *Sacred Tales* at his Laneion estate; and in 171 he delivered before the Smyrnaean council his *Eleusinian Oration* (Or. 22), on the barbarian sack of the great shrine at Eleusis near Athens.

In 176, according to Philostratus (*Lives* 2.9, 582–83), the emperor Marcus Aurelius visited Smyrna. Aristides delayed making an appearance before the emperor, and stayed at Laneion, until the emperor began to ask about him. At that point he appeared, and Marcus asked him to declaim. Aristides asked to be given a day to prepare—he never was particularly good at extempore speaking, and made his penchant for detailed preparation a boasting point—and in addition he requested permission to bring his own students and followers with him to applaud. Marcus gave permission, but said that the applause would be up to the listeners; and so the performance was given before the imperial entourage. This little episode tells us much about the relationship between Greek Sophists and Roman authority in the later empire. It also may be the last occasion on which Aristides declaimed; he was now fifty-nine or sixty years old. In 177 he delivered a prose hymn, *Regarding Asclepius* (Or. 42), at the Pergamene Asclepieion, and (perhaps somewhat later) composed *Panegyric on the Water in Pergamum* at his Laneion estate. After 177 he no longer performed in public, and sent written discourses to his recipients instead.

In 177–178 the city of Smyrna was destroyed by an earthquake; Aristides was at his Laneion estate at the time. When he received the news, he immediately (so he says) wrote his plangent *Monody for Smyrna* (Or. 18). The next day, he wrote his *Letter to the Emperors Concerning Smyrna* (Or. 19), urging Marcus Aurelius and his coemperor Commodus to undertake the rebuilding of the city. The *Monody* is purely a lament, in the rhythmic style of a prose hymn. The *Letter* begins by reminding Marcus of his recent visit to Smyrna—conducting the emperor on a memory tour of the city, in the order that he had seen things (the approach, the arrival, etc.)—and then describes the devastation, and presents a series of appeals for imperial intervention. It was extremely effective. Philostratus was present at the imperial court when Aristides' message arrived (*Lives* 2.9, 582): he describes Marcus as reading the *Monody* but quotes the *Letter*; it seems likely that both were sent together. According to Philostratus, when the emperor came to the words "the west wind blows through desolation" (in the *Letter*, Or. 19.3), he broke down and wept, and granted Aristides' request. Like the anecdote of Marcus and Aristides at Smyrna, this episode also tells us much about the relation between Greek Sophists and Roman imperial power, and about the very real political functions of sophistic rhetoric in the later empire.

In the year following this episode, Aristides wrote two more Smyrnaean "orations" (Or. 20, 21) while in retirement at Laneion, celebrating the progress and swift completion of the rebuilding of Smyrna. There is no evidence of Aristides' activities after 179–180, suggesting that he died at this time or shortly after, in his mid-sixties.

In the Vatican Library, there is a portrait statue of Aelius Aristides that dates to the reign of Septimius Severus (Richter vol. 3, 287 and fig. 2051). The identification of the statue is somewhat doubtful, but on balance it seems reasonably likely that it is indeed a portrait of Aristides. If so, it would have been completed very near his own lifetime, since Septimius Severus ruled from 193 to 211. It shows Aristides in later age: he is bald, with a broad face, large eyes, and a full beard; and for a man plagued all his life by illness, he looks surprisingly robust. He is in a sitting posture, as if about to rise and speak. The expression on his face is serious, dignified, and thoughtful—but also somewhat queasy.

BIBLIOGRAPHY

Primary Sources and Translations

Behr, Charles A., trans. *P. Aelius Aristides: The Complete Works*. 2 vols. Leiden: Brill, 1981–86.
———, ed. and trans. *Aristides*. Loeb Classical Library (Greek and English). Vol. 1 of 4. Cambridge: Harvard UP, 1973.
Behr, Charles A., and Freidrich W. Lentz, eds. *P. Aelii Aristidis Opera Quae Extsant Omnia*. Vol. 1 of 2. Leiden: Brill, 1976–80.
Dindorf, Wilhelm, ed. *Aristides*. Leipzig, 1829. 3 vols. Rpt. Hildesheim: Olms, 1964.
Keil, Bruno, ed. *Aelii Aristidis Smyrnaei Quae Supersunt*. Vol. 2 of 2. Berlin, 1898. Rpt. Berlin: Weidmann, 1958.

Critical Sources

Behr, Charles A. *Aelius Aristides and the Sacred Tales*. Amsterdam: Hakkert, 1968.
Bowie, Ewen L. "Greek Sophists and Greek Poetry in the Second Sophistic." *Aufstieg und Niedergang der römischen Welt* 2.33.1. Berlin: De Gruyter, 1989.

Day, Joseph W. *The Glory of Athens: The Popular Tradition as Reflected in the Panathenaicus of Aelius Aristides.* Chicago: Ares, 1980.

Gasco, F. "The Meeting between Aelius Aristides and Marcus Aurelius in Smyrna." *American Journal of Philology* 110.3 (1989): 471–78.

Horst, Pieter Willem van der. *Aelius Aristides and the New Testament.* Leiden: Brill, 1980.

Kennedy, George A. *The Art of Rhetoric in the Roman World.* Princeton: Princeton UP, 1972. 582–85.

———. *A New History of Classical Rhetoric.* Princeton: Princeton UP, 1994. 239–41.

Lentz, Friedrich W., ed. *The Aristeides Prolegomena.* Leiden: Brill, 1959.

Martin, L. H. "Aelius Aristides and the Technology of Oracular Dreams." *Historical Reflections/ Réflexions Historiques* 14.1 (1987): 63–72.

Oliver, James H. *The Civilizing Power: A Study of the Panathenaic Discourse of Aelius Aristides.* Philadelphia: American Philosophical Society, 1968.

———. *The Ruling Power: A Study of the Roman Empire in the Second Century after Christ through the Roman Oration of Aelius Aristides.* Philadelphia: American Philosophical Society, 1953.

Philostratus. *Lives of the Sophists.* Trans. W. C. Wright. Loeb Classical Library (Greek and English). Cambridge: Harvard UP, 1921.

Richter, Gisela M. A. *The Portraits of the Greeks.* London: Phaidon, 1965. 3 vols.

Russell, D. A. "Aristides and the Prose Hymn." In *Antonine Literature*, ed. D. A. Russell. Oxford: Oxford UP, 1990. 199–219.

Walker, Jeffrey. *Rhetoric and Poetics in Antiquity.* New York: Oxford UP, 2000. 111–13.

ARISTOTLE

(384–322 BCE)

Janet M. Atwill

Aristotle was born in 384 BCE in the city of Stagira, a disputed territory in northern Greece that bordered Macedonia. His father, a member of the Asclepiadae medical guild, was a physician in the court of the Macedonian king Amyntas III; and these ties to Macedonia, which were political as well as familial, followed Aristotle throughout his life. At the age of seventeen Aristotle left Stagira for Athens. Though he certainly left to study with Plato, his departure also coincided with political turmoil that followed the death of Amyntas III.

For twenty years, Aristotle studied and taught at Plato's Academy, leaving after Plato's death sometime in 348–347. Some traditions suggest that Aristotle departed in anger over Plato's decision to appoint his nephew Speusippus to lead the school. Again, however, it is likely that anti-Macedonian sentiments in Athens also influenced his decision to leave, for Philip II of Macedon had attacked the Greek city of Olynthus in 349 and by 348 had enslaved its population. From Athens, Aristotle went to the court of the tyrant Hermias in Assos, an area of Asia Minor then allied with Persia. Historians generally agree that Aristotle was serving as an emissary for Philip since a secret agreement was soon made that shifted Assos's allegiance from Persia to Macedon. While in Assos, Aristotle married Hermias's adopted daughter Pythias. It was also in Assos that Aristotle began his biological research. He left in 345–344 and returned to Macedon some two years later after a brief stay in Mytilene.

In Macedon, Aristotle became a tutor to Philip's son Alexander. Historians speculate that during this time Aristotle was also being groomed to build Athenian support for Philip. Aristotle returned to Athens in 335 and opened his school, the Lyceum, with the financial support of the Macedonian court. Pythias died not long after Aristotle's return to Athens, leaving him with a daughter. Aristotle spent the rest of his life with Herpyllis, an enslaved woman, whom Aristotle freed only in his will. Together they had a son, Nicomachus.

Aristotle's ties to Macedonia followed him to his death. Athenian hatred of Macedonia was reignited when Alexander died in 323. According to Diogenes

Laertius, Aristotle was charged with sacrilege but left Athens before he could be tried, turning over the Lyceum to his longtime assistant Theophrastus. Aristotle spent his last year in Macedonian territory on the island of Euboea and died one year after Alexander in 322. Aristotle's Lyceum became identified with the Peripatetic School of philosophy and remained a center of learning in the Hellenistic period.

Aristotle may be one of the most forceful and enduring influences on rhetoric in dominant Western traditions. The nature of that influence, however, has been debated, literally, for millennia. Those debates have turned on a number of questions. How relevant is Aristotle's *Rhetoric* for contemporary rhetorical theory and practice? Should Aristotle's theory of rhetoric be interpreted in light of his larger philosophical system? Does Aristotle's contribution to rhetoric reside in his explanation of why rhetoric is an ethical practice, a form of philosophical knowledge, or a productive art? Underlying each of these questions are whole sets of assumptions not only about rhetoric, but also about knowledge, truth, and ethics. Indeed, one might argue that Aristotle's richest legacy to the rhetorical tradition is this broad set of debates, rather than their definitive resolutions.

ARISTOTLE'S PHILOSOPHICAL SYSTEM AND CONCEPT OF ART

The corpus of texts on which we depend for our understanding of Aristotle's thought was organized and edited by the Peripatetic Andronicus Rhodius in the first century BCE. Though Aristotle, like Plato, originally presented his work in dialogue form, this corpus is a combination of notes and records of lectures. Scholars speculate that the corpus does not include all of the texts that survived at the time and that the texts of other Peripatetic philosophers may have been included.[1]

Aristotle's rhetorical theory is really a very small part of his thought as a whole. Since many of the debates concerning Aristotelian rhetoric are based on selective readings of the broader corpus, it is useful to outline the elements of Aristotle's thought that bear on its relationship to rhetoric.

Aristotle's theory of four causes structures his division of knowledge into the theoretical, practical, and productive, which shapes, in turn, his depiction of rhetoric's identity and province. The four causes theory suggests that in order to understand something, one must look at it from a number of perspectives, specifically its formal, final, efficient, and material causes. Formal causality is one of the most complex causes, referring to the essence, definition, formula, or principle (*archē*) of a thing. As definition, formal causality plays a role in Aristotelian logic; as "form" or formula, it invokes Plato's theory of forms. This identification with Platonic forms is likely the reason some have construed Aristotle's thought as offering a model of formalism, whereby an artistic product is judged according to the harmonious subordination of parts to the whole. These interpretations generally fail to acknowledge the way the other three causes complicate this static notion of "form." Final causality refers to the *telos* or "end" of a thing. As such, it is closely tied to formal causality, which determines that end. Efficient causality is frequently described as a thing's "source of motion" because it is responsible for the change that moves a formal cause to its *telos* or end. Material cause simply refers to that out of which a thing is made. Though the four causes have been depicted as a closed, determinate system, throughout the corpus Aristotle acknowledges the roles of two other causes, the spontaneous (*to automaton*) and chance (*tychē*).[2]

The four causes are at the heart of Aristotle's concept of art. Standard interpretations of Aristotle point out that the philosopher's depiction of nature is tied to his theory of art; one cannot be explained without reference to the other.[3] Nature provides the example of the convergence of all four causes. Formal causality explains why an acorn grows into a tree; and, as with all natural elements, the tree contains within itself its own source of motion (efficient cause) and that out of which it is made (material cause). The four causes operate very differently in art, as Aristotle explains in the *Physics*, using the art of house building as an example. The formal cause of a house is the knowledge in the mind of the artist/architect who designs the structure. The house's material cause may be wood and stone, and builders are its efficient cause. The *telos* of this art, however, is not the house itself, but rather the usefulness of the house to the person who lives in it. These same principles apply to such arts as medicine, poetics, and rhetoric. The formal causes of these arts reside, respectively, within the doctor, artist, and rhetor. Their material and efficient causes are somewhat more ambiguous. In various places, Aristotle suggests that the material cause of a speech is discourse (or words), while the rhetor may perform the function of efficient cause. In each case, however, art's *telos* clearly resides in those who receive or experience the art. The *telos* of medicine is health in the patient; the *telos* of poetics, catharsis in the audience; and the *telos* of rhetoric, belief (or *pistis*) in the audience.[4]

Other discussions of art in the corpus are also important for understanding Aristotle's concept of rhetoric. One of the most important definitions of art is found in the *Metaphysics*, where the art of medicine serves as an example:

> [A]rt arises, when from many notions gained by experience one universal judgement about similar objects is produced. For to have a judgement that when Callias was ill of this disease this did him good, and similarly in the case of Socrates and in many individual cases, is a matter of experience; but to judge that it has done good to all persons of a certain constitution, marked off in one class, when they were ill of this disease [...]—this is a matter of art. (*Metaphysics* 981a4–10)

In the case of rhetoric, art is the product of observing the features that characterize a successful rhetorical performance. The *Rhetoric* defines and classifies a number of these features: appeals for creating *ēthos*, appeals to *pathos*, enthymemic argument, premises for political, forensic, and ceremonial discourse, and principles of style and arrangement. What is important about this definition, however, is that it suggests that an art can never be static since it must be based on observations of successful performance; and what constitutes success will change across time and situations. Moreover, this definition of art does not restrict rhetoric to the three Athenian contexts invoked by Aristotle since one can observe the principles of performance in any context.

Finally, debates concerning rhetoric's identity and province frequently turn on its classification in Aristotle's three domains of theoretical, practical, and productive knowledge, which correspond respectively to *epistēmē*, *praxis*, and *poēsis*. Each category is defined by the four causes and each encompasses specific domains of inquiry, disciplines, or arts.[5]

Theoretical knowledge, which encompasses philosophy, mathematics, and the natural sciences, is concerned with what "holds always" (or what cannot be "otherwise"), things that are "universal and necessary" (*Nicomachean Ethics* 1140b31). In relation to the four causes, theoretical knowledge is concerned with determining *archai*, or first principles, which to Aristotle is knowledge that cannot be "applied." In contrast to the principles of an art, which are aimed at enabling production or intervention, theoretical knowledge can have no earthly use. Aristotle explains: "For it was when almost all the necessities of life and the things that make for comfort and recreation were present, that such knowledge began to be sought. Evidently then we do not seek it for the sake of any other advantage, but as the man is free, we say who exists for himself and not for another, so we pursue this as the only free science, for it alone exists for itself" (*Metaphysics* 982b23–28). The idea that theoretical knowledge can never be utilitarian draws on the ancient sense of *theoria* as observation rather than participation.

Practical knowledge, identified with practical reasoning (*phronēsis*), practical wisdom, and prudence, is concerned with action (*praxis*) toward the end of *eudaimonia*—translated as either happiness or "the good life." Practical knowledge encompasses politics and ethics; and, in contrast to the subjects of theoretical knowledge, it is concerned with "what can be otherwise":

> Practical wisdom on the other hand is concerned with things human and things about which it is possible to deliberate [...] no one deliberates about things that cannot be otherwise, nor about things which have not an end. (*Nicomachean Ethics* 1141b8–10)

Aristotle describes *phronēsis* as "a reasoned and true state of capacity to act with regard to human goods" (*Nicomachean Ethics* 1140b20).

Productive knowledge encompasses all the arts and is defined as "identical with a state of capacity to make, involving a true course of reasoning" (*Nicomachean Ethics* 1140a10–11). As we have noted, the "origin" or formal cause of art resides "in the maker and not in the thing made" (*Nicomachean Ethics* 1140a13–14). Like practical knowledge, productive knowledge deals with what can be "otherwise": it is "concerned neither with things that are, or come into being, by necessity, nor with things that do so in accordance with nature (since these have their origin in themselves)" (*Nicomachean Ethics* 1140a14–16). However, practical and productive knowledge have different ends. Ethics and politics are directed toward the end of *eudaimonia*, while arts have as their end those toward whom the art is aimed; in the case of rhetoric, as we have noted, art's end is in the audience.

As we shall see, Aristotle's theory of causes and categories of knowledge play significant roles in his depiction of rhetorical art.

ARISTOTLE'S CONCEPT OF ART AND THE *RHETORIC*

Perhaps the most important thing to bear in mind in exploring Aristotle's *Rhetoric* is that he was not a practicing rhetor. As received histories have it, he only included the subject in his curriculum because he was forced to compete with Isocrates for students. Aristotle's political treatises suggest that he believed that the best state was, like Plato's, crafted by the philosopher. For the most part, Aristotle identifies democratic forms of government, deliberation, and public rhetoric with either the ignorant masses or the somewhat hapless middle class; he doubts that either group could understand the ideals of "the good" that drive a state governed by an aristocracy. However, Aristotle's relative indifference to the subject—neither declared enemy nor blind advocate—may be at the heart of the *Rhetoric*'s usefulness. Unlike Plato, who saw rhetoric as philosophy's adversary, Aristotle makes a place for the art in his taxonomy of knowledge, according rhetoric epistemological legitimacy, while at the same time exempting it from the requirements of truth that define the "highest" knowledge (theoretical knowledge or philosophy). Aristotle also distinguishes himself from Isocrates, who called his rhetorical education *philosophia*, despite the fact that it contained little (perhaps nothing) that Aristotle would place in the domain of theoretical knowledge. Ironically, the penchant for classification for which Aristotle is sometimes criticized is likely the product of his effort to create a kind of epistemological tolerance that would never allow him to insist that either philosophy (e.g., Plato) or rhetoric (e.g., Isocrates) were the only game in town. The most useful way to view Aristotle's relationship to rhetoric may be to see him as a philosopher who systematized many of the existing artistic precepts of the time and then provided a theory (or account) of that system. For Aristotle, however, providing a theory of art is not the same thing as placing that art in the domain of theoretical knowledge.

The *Rhetoric* consists of three books. Book I begins by outlining Aristotle's theory (or account) of rhetoric, which includes definitions of the art and its species (deliberative, judicial, and epideictic), as well as types of proof (*ēthos, pathos*, and *logos*). Book I then offers topics useful for each species, as well as topics related to specific types of proof (e.g., ethical topics in deliberative rhetoric). Book II offers a more detailed treatment of the rhetorical topics, including Aristotle's discussion of logical proof and the enthymeme. Book III focuses on style and arrangement. The *Rhetoric* remains one of the most exhaustive treatments of classical Western rhetoric, defining in explicit terms three of the five traditional canons of rhetoric: invention, arrangement, and style.

Book I begins with a discussion of the character and province of rhetoric as an art. Chapter 1 invokes the *Metaphysics'* description of art by defining rhetoric as "an ability, in each [particular] case, to see the available means of persuasion" (Kennedy 36; 1355b26–27).[6] The significance of Aristotle's opening assertion that "[r]hetoric is an *antistrophos* to dialectic" has been debated for centuries (Kennedy 28; 1354a1). Dialectic was the art of philosophical disputation, a formal practice of question and answer used to debate philosophical theses.[7] Kennedy suggests that this statement was intended to elevate the practice of rhetoric in the minds of his students, who regularly practiced dialectic in the Lyceum (26–27). More important, this assertion defines the limits of rhetoric's subject matter and, thus, the province of the art. Training in dialectic focused on strategies for argument and refutation, not the substance of philosophical questions (e.g., the character of virtue). Similarly, rhetoric "does not belong to a single defined genus of subject" (Kennedy, 35; *Rhet.* 1355b8). The commonplaces of argument would necessarily incorporate, for example, political and legal knowledge; however, the art of rhetoric is neither restricted nor identical to that special subject matter. Aristotle maintains that if the propositions of an argument are too specific, the argument has moved outside the province of rhetoric: "The more [speakers] fasten upon [the subject matter] in its proper sense, [the more] they depart from rhetoric or dialectic" (Kennedy 44–45; 1358a24–25). Aristotle asserts that the subjects of rhetorical deliberation are those things that "seem to be capable of admitting two possibilities" (Kennedy 41; *Rhet.* 1357a4–5). Thus, rhetoric is concerned with probable, not certain, knowledge.

Much like the sophists, Aristotle insists that the rhetor "should be able to argue persuasively on either side of a question" (Kennedy 34; 1355a29–30). To be sure, Aristotle does not define rhetoric, as did some Sophists, in terms of the capacity to reason "in opposite directions." Indeed, he asserts that "the underlying facts are not equally good in each case; but true and better ones are by nature always more productive of good syllogisms, and in a word, more persuasive" (Kennedy 35; 1355a36–38). However, Aristotle suggests that rhetoric's character is not defined by truth or falsity but rather the contingency of its subject matter. Even the significance of Aristotle's description of "true and better" facts asserts that their value resides in their being "more persuasive," not more "true." On the whole, the opening discussion of rhetoric's identity is consistent with the principles that distinguish productive knowledge from theoretical and practical knowledge. Rhetoric as a productive art is distinct from the certainty identified with theoretical knowledge and the specific subject matter of ethics and politics, which comprise practical knowledge.

Aristotle's theory of causes structures the *Rhetoric*'s treatment of the three "species" of rhetoric (deliberative, judicial, and epideictic), as well as the rhetorical appeals. The *Rhetoric*'s system of discourse classification is grounded in the time with which discourse is concerned and its *telos* in the audience: deliberative discourse (the political discourse of the assembly) deals with the future and is concerned with exhortation or dissuasion toward the *telos* of either the advantageous or the harmful; judicial or forensic discourse (legal arguments in the courts) deals with acts in the past and is concerned with accusation or defense directed toward the *telos* of either justice or injustice; and demonstrative or epideictic discourse (public

ceremonial discourse in such contexts as funerals and the Olympic games) focuses neither on the past nor the present but is concerned with praise and blame to the end of conferring on its object either honor or shame. Aristotle's teleology also appears in his description of the rhetorical situation: "A speech [situation] consists of three things: a speaker and a subject on which he speaks and someone addressed, and the objective [*telos*] of the speech relates to the last (I mean the hearer)" (Kennedy 47; 1358a37–b2).

Aristotle begins his discussion of invention and the enthymeme in book I. Chapter 2 outlines two broad types of proof as artistic and nonartistic. The non-artistic encompasses given elements, such as witnesses, that are not supplied by the rhetor. Artistic proofs are those that are invented. Here Aristotle uses the verb *heurein*, meaning "to find out" or "to discover"; the noun form, *heuresis*, becomes, as Kennedy notes, the standard term for rhetorical invention (37n39).[8] Aristotle also describes three modes of persuasion: through the character, *ēthos*, the rhetor's self-construction in the speech; through emotion, *pathos*, which the rhetor elicits in the audience, and through argument, *logos*, when the rhetor "show[s] the truth or the apparent truth from whatever is persuasive in each case" (Kennedy 39, 1356a18–20). The enthymeme, which is distinguished from proof through example (*paradeigma*), is described as a rhetorical syllogism that differs from the syllogism discussed in Aristotle's treatises on logic in two important ways. First, an enthymeme is generally based on premises that are "true [only] for the most part" (Kennedy 42–43; 1357a30–31); these premises relate to the things about which people deliberate, the doxa associated with probable knowledge. Second, a rhetorical enthymeme is less complex than a syllogism, making it easier for an audience to follow (Kennedy 42; 1357a7–11; see also book II, chapter 2).[9]

The major portion of the *Rhetoric* is concerned with the lines of arguments and common knowledge that can be used in enthymemes for deliberative, forensic, and epideictic rhetoric. Though these are sometimes loosely referred to as Aristotle's "topics" or topical system, they are divided into three categories: *koina*, *topoi*, and *idiai*. Aristotle distinguishes these types according to their range of applicability, which broadly corresponds to their place on a continuum ranging from the most general to the most specific. The *koina* refer to three lines of argument that can be used in all types of speeches: the possible/impossible, past fact/future fact, and degree of magnitude (see book I, chapters 3, 7, 14 and book II, chapter 19). The *topoi*, also known as the twenty-eight "common topics" outlined in book II, chapter 23, are less abstract, but they can similarly be used in all types of speeches. An example of the common topics is the "argument from opposites," for which Aristotle gives the following explanation: "one should look to see if the opposite [predicate] is true of the opposite subject [...] for example [saying] that to be temperate is a good thing, for to lack self-control is harmful" (Kennedy 190; 1397a8–10). The common topics also include arguments based on definition and cause and effect. Finally, the *idiai*, which constitute much of the *Rhetoric*, refer to topics specific to certain bodies of knowledge and rhetorical contexts; thus, they are called "special topics." While these topics are related to such well-defined bodies of

knowledge as politics, they are still "popular" or accessible versions of that knowledge. Aristotle offers a broad range of *idiai* in the *Rhetoric*. Book I includes topics specific to each type of rhetoric (deliberative, epideictic, and judicial). Special topics for political discourse are further subdivided into topics related to finances and war. The special topics are not, in the strictest sense, readymade arguments; rather, in the ancient sense of *topos* as "place," they refer to sites the rhetor might explore in order to invent (*heurein*) useful arguments. As such, the special topics, at times, sound more like advice. For example, the following discussion is offered concerning special topics for war and peace that are useful in deliberative rhetoric: "On war and peace, [it is necessary] to know the power of the city, both how great it is already and how great it is capable of becoming, and what form the existing power takes and what else might be added and, further, what wars it has waged [. . .] and with whom there is probability of war" (Kennedy 54; 1359b33–37).

The *Rhetoric* classifies special topics in a number of ways. For example, book II, chapters 2–11 detail topics about the emotions that can be used in all types of rhetoric. Some of the special topics, however, have raised questions about Aristotle's intentions. Scholars have observed that some of these topics appear to be far more useful in argument than others. The discussion of the emotions in book II, for example, is generally viewed as a brilliant work of early psychology; however, it is difficult to see how parts of the discussion could serve as resources for public arguments. Though this treatment of the emotions would give the rhetor insights into human response, many scholars suspect that Aristotle may have composed this section for another context and audience.[10]

Whereas books I and II focus on the rhetorical canon of invention (*heuresis*), book III is concerned with the canons of style (*lexis*) and arrangement (*taxis*), offering only the briefest account of delivery (*hypokrisis*) in the opening chapter. Aristotle observes that there is no extant treatment of delivery and simply raises three things the rhetor should consider in delivery: volume, pitch, and rhythm. The first part of book III discusses such characteristics of good prose style as clarity and appropriateness, both qualities Aristotle found lacking in such Sophists as Gorgias. He explains that language should be clear in order to "perform its function": it should be "neither flat nor above the dignity of the subject, but appropriate [*prepon*]" (Kennedy 221; 1404b3–4). The doctrine of *to prepon* is taken up again in book III, chapter 7, where Aristotle extends the notion of appropriateness to include the character of the speaker: "If, then, a person speaks words appropriate to his moral state, he will create a sense of character" (Kennedy 235–36; 1408a30–31). Aristotle describes four means of breaching clarity and appropriateness: (1) "double words" or awkward compounds, such as Gorgias's "beggar-mused flatterers"; (2) "glosses" or unusual words that an audience would not recognize; (3) "long or untimely or crowded" epithets; and (4) inappropriate metaphors (Kennedy 226–28; 1405b35–1406b19). Chapters 5 and 6 raise the importance of grammatical correctness and conciseness; chapters 8 and 9 warn against excessive meter in prose and overly complex periodic style. Chapter 10 includes a discussion of *aesteia*, translated "urbanities," as a desirable feature of style. These expressions, which avoid being

obscure, may be achieved through metaphor, antithesis, and two other stylistic features. The first feature, *energeia,* is translated as "actualization" and generally refers to what we now might call "vividness." The second feature is translated as "bringing-before-the eyes" and refers to language that goes beyond word-level metaphor to "signify things engaged in an activity" (Kennedy 248; 1411b24–25).[11] Aristotle discusses simile, but metaphor receives the most treatment. Metaphor would seem to have a special status in Aristotle's thought. Metaphors are important in effective prose style because they can be at the same time "unfamiliar"—or distinctive—and clear (Kennedy 223; 1404b34–36). An effective metaphor is distinguished by "clarity and sweetness and strangeness, and its use cannot be learned from someone else" (Kennedy 223; 1405a8–9). Aristotle's concludes with a discussion of the stylistic differences between different types of rhetoric (deliberative, forensic, and epideictic) and between written and oral discourse.[12] He observes that written style is more exact, while oral delivery may require repetition. Referring specifically to *asyndeta,* he observes that such repetition would be "criticized in writing but not in speaking" (Kennedy 225; 1413b19–21). Thus, as with the enthymeme, Aristotle is sensitive to audiences' needs in following and remembering oral arguments.

The *Rhetoric* closes with a discussion of arrangement. Though Aristotle explains that a speech has two necessary parts, statement of the subject (proposition or thesis) and proof, he also give a brief treatment of conclusions in the text's last chapter. He criticizes discussions of arrangement in existing handbooks, noting that they describe such parts of a text as *diēgēsis* (narration of facts), which would be used in only judicial discourse (Kennedy 258; 1414a38–40). Chapter 15 includes a discussion of rhetorical categories that will develop into *stasis* theory, terms that aid in determining what is at issue in a legal case. Historically, these categories have taken a number of forms. Kennedy defines them as "fact, law, quality of the act, or jurisdiction of the court" (265). Aristotle calls them *topoi.* "Another topic is to make a denial in regard to what is at issue: either that it is not true or not harmful or not to this person" (Kennedy 266; 1416a6–9).

DEBATES CONCERNING THE *RHETORIC*

Debates concerning Aristotle's *Rhetoric* have taken place at a number of levels. Interpretations of Aristotelian invention have frequently turned on the broad question of the usefulness of classical rhetoric for contemporary practice. Those who view Aristotle's topics as static commonplaces cite them as proof that the classical tradition was more concerned with recycling the known than discovering the new.[13] As Janice Lauer observes, one of the basic issues in this debate turns on the purpose of classical systems of invention. Did they serve only to help the rhetor prove a thesis already in hand or were they also intended to aid the rhetor in discovering new perspectives? Those who defend the usefulness of the classical tradition maintain that Aristotle's topics have an inventional (or heuristic) function that can enable the discovery of alternative perspectives and the creation of "new" knowledge. These arguments have generally paid special attention to the distinction between the specific (*idiai*) and common topics. By these accounts, because the common (28) topics are at a higher level of generality than the *idiai*, they have special potential for enabling the kind of inferencing that can lead to new knowledge. The twentieth-century revival of composition studies frequently drew on this heuristic interpretation of classical invention. Richard Young, for example, gives the name "new classicists" to those who accord a heuristic function to topical invention. Young points out that if one accepts Aristotle's definition of art as principles drawn from the observation of expert performance, these principles would never constitute a closed system, for they would always be in the process of being determined and revised. Sharon Crowley and Debra Hawhee offer such a revision in *Ancient Rhetorics for Contemporary Students*. However, other scholars, such as Michelle Ballif, have argued against this recuperation of the classical tradition, maintaining that its gendered and logocentric character undermines its usefulness in heterogeneous, postmodern cultures.

Aristotle's divisions of knowledge into the theoretical, practical, and productive have provided the framework for a number of debates concerning rhetoric's ethical, political, and epistemological status. Many of these debates have engaged the issue of instrumentalism. If rhetoric is an art whose *telos* is in the audience, does this mean that it is only instrumental knowledge with no intellectual or ethical constraints? The two English-language commentators on the *Rhetoric* offer the most detailed treatments of these questions, though neither scholar concludes that Aristotle restricted rhetoric to the domain of productive knowledge. Edward M. Cope's nineteenth-century scholarship and commentaries on the *Rhetoric* reflect the utilitarian orientation of its British cultural milieu. Cope acknowledges the art's relationship to the category of productive knowledge. In the end, however, he draws on book I, chapter 2 of the *Nicomachean Ethics* to argue that rhetoric should be allied with politics since both are concerned with probable knowledge.[14] Thus, rhetoric has the same end and model of reasoning as practical knowledge. William M. A. Grimaldi provides the most rigorous argument for viewing Aristotle's rhetoric as a form of philosophical knowledge, though he redefines this domain to encompass the concern with ethics, which characterizes practical knowledge. Strongly influenced by the structural linguistics of the mid-twentieth century, Grimaldi argues that both Aristotle's enthymeme and his three modes of proof (*ēthos, logos, pathos*) define rhetoric as philosophy and ethics because they mirror natural forms of intellection and moral reasoning: "Rhetoric is the art which presents man with the structure for language, and by way of structure, enables language to become an effective medium whereby man apprehends reality" (*Studies* 8). Grimaldi maintains that the enthymeme plays a special role in this relationship between language and reality because it serves as a mode of inferencing that mirrors the "natural ways in which the mind thinks" (*Studies* 130).[15]

The end of the twentieth century refocused attention on Aristotle's domain of practical knowledge as scholars probed rhetoric's identity as a civic art. Gerard

Hauser, for example, maintains that "Aristotle's argument on *phronēsis* firmly situated rhetoric within a politics based on the ideal of civic virtue" (19). More in the tradition of E. M. Cope, Arthur Walzer contends that the *Nicomachean Ethics* places "rhetoric under the direction of politics" (51). Others scholars, such as Eugene Garver and Thomas Farrell, emphasize the ethical dimensions of Aristotle's practical knowledge, arguing that rhetoric is identified more with the practical reasoning associated with *phronēsis* than the calculation involved in acts of *poēsis*, or making.[16] I have argued that the resistance to placing rhetoric in Aristotle's domain of productive knowledge is the result of modernist distinctions between subjects, objects, and value. Productive knowledge, I contend, is more consistent with the epistemology and ethics of postmodernism as articulated by Barbara Herrnstein Smith and Pierre Bourdieu.[17] From a different perspective, Alan Gross has also argued for rhetoric's classification as a productive *technē*. Similar debates concerning rhetoric's ethical constraints have been played out in discussions of Aristotle's ethical, pathetic, and logical proofs. Eckart Schutrumpf and Jacob Wisse, for example, have confronted Aristotle's challenging statement in the *Rhetoric* that sometimes an artistically crafted *ēthos* is more rhetorically effective than real character, while Jeffrey Walker has probed Aristotle's concept of *pathos*.

Though I have offered a perspective on Aristotle's concept of rhetoric, it may be that extracting a conceptual orthodoxy from the corpus would certainly be the worst use of Aristotle's texts. The texts are, themselves, both records and products of conflicts and compromises. It is, perhaps, to Aristotle's credit and ours that his thought has better served as a touchstone for questions and debates than as a repository of answers and conclusions.

NOTES

1. For more on the textual history of the *Rhetoric*, see George Kennedy's "The Composition and Influence of Aristotle's *Rhetoric*" in Amelie Oksenberg Rorty's *Essays on Aristotle's Rhetoric*.

2. Spontaneity and chance play a role in earlier accounts of the art of ancient medicine, where they refer either to physical symptoms or to instances of recovery that cannot be predicted or explained. Spontaneity is generally defined as the "self-acting," and Aristotle specifically describes chance as a cause that is "inscrutable to human intelligence" (*Physics* 196b7). Both spontaneity and chance are concerned with things that are not predictable—in contrast to things that "happen always" or "for the most part" (*Physics* 196b10–11). Consequently, spontaneity and chance belong in what Aristotle describes as a special "class"—the domain of the *paralogos*, translated as the "unaccountable" or "incalculable." The *paralogos* escapes the kind of *logos*, or account, identified with art, whether it is due to the temporary limits of understanding or the phenomenon itself.

3. See Abraham Edel's *Aristotle and His Philosophy*.

4. Aristotle's concepts of potentiality (*dynamis*) and actuality (*energeia*) are closely related to the four causes and provide some explanation for the close relationship between formal and final causality. *Dynamis* refers to the capacity of something to act (or develop) and to be

acted upon; *energeia* refers to movement toward fulfillment (*entelechaia*). In the *Physics*, Aristotle explains that a house is a potentiality in the process of building. Once completed, the potentiality is no longer there. Thus, actuality is the process by which a potentiality is fulfilled.

5. For a detailed discussion of the domains of knowledge, see Janet M. Atwill's *Rhetoric Reclaimed: Aristotle and the Liberal Arts Tradition*.

6. Since many students of rhetoric use George Kennedy's translation in *Aristotle: On Rhetoric*, I reference the text by providing, first, the page numbers from Kennedy's translation and, second, the standard Bekker line numbers used in most translations of Aristotle's corpus.

7. Kennedy suggests the terms "counterpart," "correlative," and "coordinate" as fair translations of *antistrophos* (26n2). Lawrence Green's "Aristotelian Rhetoric, Dialectic, and the Tradition of *Antistrophos*" offers another perspective.

8. See Janice M. Lauer and Richard Enos, "The Meaning of *Heuristic* in Aristotle's *Rhetoric* and Its Implications for Contemporary Rhetorical Theory."

9. The character of Aristotle's enthymeme has been another subject of debate. For several treatments of this subject, see Lawrence Green, "Enthymematic Invention and Structural Prediction"; M. F. Burnyeat, "Enthymeme: The Logic of Persuasion," in Furley and Nehamas; and T/Ed Dyck, "Topos and Enthymeme." For a survey and critique of interpretations of the enthymeme in pedagogical traditions, see Robert N. Gaines, "Aristotle's *Rhetoric* and the Contemporary Arts of Practical Discourse" in Gross and Walzer.

10. See Kennedy's discussion on pp. 122–23.

11. See Sarah Newman's "Aristotle's Notion of 'Bringing-Before-the-Eyes': Its Contributions to Aristotelian and Contemporary Conceptualization of Style and Audience."

12. See Richard Graff, "Reading and the 'Written Style' in Aristotle's *Rhetoric*."

13. For an early discussion, see Andrea Lunsford and Lisa Ede, "On Distinctions between Classical and Modern Rhetoric." For feminist accounts and critiques of Aristotle, see Cynthia A. Freeland, ed., *Feminist Interpretations of Aristotle*.

14. For a brief discussion of these commentary traditions, see Atwill, "Instituting the Art of Rhetoric."

15. See Green, "Enthymematic Invention and Structural Prediction."

16. For more interpretations of practical knowledge, see Robert Hariman's edited collection *Prudence: Classical Virtue, Postmodern Practice*.

17. See Atwill, *Rhetoric Reclaimed*.

BIBLIOGRAPHY

Atwill, Janet M. "Aristotle." *Encyclopedia of Rhetoric and Composition*. Ed. Theresa Enos. New York: Garland, 1996. 26–30.

———. "Instituting the Art of Rhetoric: Theory, Practice, and Productive Knowledge in Interpretations of Aristotle's Rhetoric." *New Perspectives on the Histories of the Rhetorical Tradition*. Ed. Takis Poulakos. Boulder: Westview, 1993. 91–117.

———. *Rhetoric Reclaimed: Aristotle and the Liberal Arts Tradition*. Ithaca and London: Cornell UP, 1998.

Ballif, Michelle. *Seduction, Sophistry, and the Woman with the Rhetorical Figure*. Carbondale: Southern Illinois UP, 2001.

Barnes, Jonathan. *Aristotle: A Very Short Introduction*. Oxford: Oxford UP, 2000.

Cope, Edward M. *An Introduction to Aristotle's* Rhetoric. London: Macmillan, 1867.

———. *The* Rhetoric *of Aristotle, with a Commentary.* Ed. John Sandys. 3 vols. Cambridge: Cambridge UP, 1877.

Crowley, Sharon, and Debra Hawhee. *Ancient Rhetorics for Contemporary Students*, 3rd ed. Needham Heights: Allyn and Bacon, 2003.

Dyck, T/Ed. "Topos and Enthymeme." *Rhetorica* 20.2 (2002): 105–17.

Farrell, Thomas. *Norms of Rhetorical Culture.* New Haven: Yale UP, 1993.

Edel, Abraham. *Aristotle and His Philosophy.* Chapel Hill: U of North Carolina P, 1982.

Farrell, Thomas. *Norms of Rhetorical Culture.* New Haven: Yale UP, 1993.

Freeland, Cynthia A. *Feminist Interpretations of Aristotle.* University Park: Penn State UP, 1998.

Furley, David J., and Alexander Nehamas, eds. *Aristotle's Rhetoric: Philosophical Essays.* Princeton: Princeton UP, 1994.

Garver, Eugene. *Aristotle's Rhetoric: An Art of Character.* Chicago: Chicago UP, 1994.

Graff, Richard. "Reading and the 'Written Style' in Aristotle's *Rhetoric*." *Rhetoric Society Quarterly* 31 (Fall 2001): 19–44.

Green, Lawrence. "Aristotelian Rhetoric, Dialectic, and the Tradition of *Antistrophos*." *Rhetorica* 8.1 (1990): 5–27.

———. "Enthymematic Invention and Structural Prediction." *College English* 41 (1980): 623–34.

Grimaldi, William M. A. *Aristotle*, Rhetoric I: *A Commentary.* New York: Fordham UP, 1980.

———. *Studies in the Philosophy of Aristotle's* Rhetoric. Wiesbaden: Franz Steiner Verlag GMBH, 1972.

Gross, Alan G. "What Aristotle Meant by Rhetoric." *Rereading Aristotle's Rhetoric.* Ed. Alan G. Gross and Arthur E. Walzer. Carbondale: Southern Illinois UP, 2000. 24–37.

Gross, Alan G., and Arthur E. Walzer, eds. *Rereading Aristotle's Rhetoric.* Carbondale: Southern Illinois UP, 2000.

Hariman, Robert, ed. *Prudence: Classical Virtue, Postmodern Practice.* University Park: Penn State UP, 2002.

Hauser, Gerard. *Vernacular Voices: The Rhetoric of Publics and Public Spheres.* Columbia: U of South Carolina P, 1999.

Kennedy, George A., trans. *Aristotle on Rhetoric: A Theory of Civic Discourse.* New York: Oxford UP, 1994.

Kraut, Richard. *Aristotle.* Founders of Modern Political and Social Thought. Oxford: Oxford UP, 2002.

Lauer, Janice. "Issues in Rhetorical Invention." *Essays on Classical Rhetoric and Modern Discourse.* Ed. Robert J. Connors, Lisa S. Ede, and Andrea A. Lunsford. Carbondale: Southern Illinois UP, 1994. 127–139.

Enos, Richard Leo, and Janice M. Lauer. "The Meaning of *Heuristic* in Aristotle's *Rhetoric* and Its Implications for Contemporary Rhetorical Theory." *A Rhetoric of Doing: Essays on Written Discourse in Honor of James L. Kinneavy.* Ed. Stephen Witte, Roger Cherry, and Neil Nakodate. Newbury Park, CA: Sage, 1992. 79–87.

Lunsford, Andrea A., and Lisa S. Ede. "On Distinctions between Classical and Modern Rhetoric." *Essays on Classical Rhetoric and Modern Discourse.* Ed. Robert J. Connors, Lisa S. Ede, and Andrea A. Lunsford. Carbondale: Southern Illinois UP, 1994. 37–49.

Newman, Sarah. "Aristotle's Notion of 'Bringing-Before-the-Eyes': Its Contributions to Aristotelian and Contemporary Conceptualization of Style and Audience." *Rhetorica* 20 (2002): 1–23.

Rorty, Amélie Oksenberg, ed. *Essays on Aristotle's Rhetoric.* Berkeley: U of California P, 1996.

Schutrumpf, Eckart. "The Meaning of ἤθοσ in the Poetics—A Reply." *Hermes* 115 (1987): 175–81.

Walker, Jeffrey. *"Pathos and Katharsis* in 'Aristotelian' Rhetoric: Some Implications." *Rereading Aristotle's Rhetoric.* Ed. Alan G. Gross and Arthur E. Walzer. Carbondale: Southern Illinois UP, 2000. 74–92.

Walzer, Arthur. "Aristotle on Speaking 'Outside the Subject': The Special Topics and Rhetorical Forums." *Rereading Aristotle's Rhetoric.* Ed. Alan G. Gross and Arthur E. Walzer. Carbondale: Southern Illinois UP, 2000. 38–54.

Wisse, Jakob. *Ethos and Pathos from Aristotle to Cicero.* Amsterdam: Adolf M. Hakkert, 1989.

Young, Richard. "Arts, Crafts, Gifts, and Knacks: Some Disharmonies in the New Rhetoric." *Reinventing the Rhetorical Tradition.* Ed. Ian Pringle and Aviva Freedman. Conway, AR: L&S Books, 1981.

Aspasia of Miletus

(fifth century BCE)

Kathleen Ethel Welch and Karen D. Jobe

An educated Milesian, Aspasia distinguished herself as a rhetorician, political theorist, and teacher in Pericles' innermost group in the fifth century BCE. These three roles enabled Aspasia to publicly speak and act. Aspasia likely collaborated with and perhaps taught the most powerful men and some girls and women on subjects ranging from what later came to be called philosophy (*philosophia*) to various writing practices. Her school for young women doubled as a meeting place for the intellectual circle that she and Pericles worked to achieve. A free foreigner, with all that implied for her new Greek milieu, she probably arrived in Athens sometime between 450 and the mid-440s BCE, having emigrated from Miletus (present-day Turkey), a wealthy Greek colony on the coast of Asia Minor known at the time for its large number of literate citizens. Aspasia may have been educated in a literate Milesian family or in a school for *hetaerai*, or upper-class courtesans (Keuls 194). Her status as a free foreigner remained important to her ability to work in political circles, even as her gender complicated her status. She was able to avoid the usual constraints of Athenian women of her social class, most of whom were unable to move about in society at will or to speak in public.

Aspasia became Pericles' companion or spouse equivalent, and she remained his companion until his death from the plague in 429 BCE. Plutarch, writing in Greek during the Roman Empire, reports that she modeled herself on Thargelia, an Ionian courtesan "who was a resourceful woman as well as being beautiful and charming [and who] cohabited with a great many Greek men and won all her partners over to the Persian cause" (165). Plutarch writes of Aspasia's "political expertise" (165) that made politicians such as Pericles think highly of her. He further describes her as a woman who "controlled the leading public figures of the day and got the philosophers to write about her in [. . .] glowing terms" (165). Other ancient sources indicate that she opened a school for young women that later became a popular meeting place for influential men as well. Consistently recognized for her intelligence, training, and political judgment, Aspasia made important contributions that remain notable partly because she appears to have gone beyond the domestic sphere and functioned as an influential intellectual in the public arena. She was one of the most important women of fifth-century Athens and an important rhetorician and political theorist.

ASPASIA'S RHETORICAL PRACTICE AND THEORY

Aspasia's writing practices and rhetorical theory can be gleaned from classical sources. A central aspect of her rhetorical practice, presumably based on the rhetorical theory that was developing rapidly during this period, concerns the issue of who is allowed to speak in public venues. Her apparent commitment to epideictic rhetoric can be seen in Plato's fictional rendition of her work in *Menexenus*, where he suggests that she composed a funeral oration for Pericles to deliver. While she has had substantial influence on the rhetorical theorizing of post-1970 second wave feminism, it is difficult to know if she had a similar effect in the fifth century. It appears likely that she did influence the men of that era, and that her rhetorical theory, her practice of oratory in public places, and her writing practices all intertwined with many of the theories and practices of Pericles. Her commitment to writing as a rhetorical practice would set her apart from her contemporary Socrates, who (in Plato's version) is well known for having disparaged the technology of writing as a destroyer of memory.

ASPASIA'S CONTRIBUTIONS AND RECEPTION

Just as we have nothing written by Socrates, so we have no written trace of Aspasia's thought (Jarratt and Ong 10). Many scholars avoid commentary on Aspasia because of the absence of primary sources (Welch). Her life and work can be inferred from secondary sources such as Plato, Xenophon, and Plutarch and from historical receptions of these writers. From these sources, we can see that Aspasia influenced Pericles, Socrates, Xenophon, and other major thinkers of the time. Plutarch reports that Socrates "occasionally came to visit her with his disciples, and his closest friends brought their wives to her to listen to her speak" (165)—a point that would indicate the inclusion of more women in the rhetorical realm. Xenophon's Socrates repeatedly mentions that he has followed her advice in marriage (e.g., in *Memorabilia*). In Plato's *Menexenus*, Plato's Socrates states that Aspasia was his teacher in enacting rhetoric, and he offers an account of the way in which Aspasia composes a funeral oration. Much later, Plutarch writes that "even though the beginning of Plato's *Menexenus* is not entirely serious, it still contains an element of historical fact when it states that it was Aspasia's rhetorical skill which was commonly supposed to be the reason why a number of Athenians spent time with her" (165). Significantly, many scholars continue to exclude her altogether, contributing to an erasure typical of many women in rhetoric as well as in other fields of the West.

The classical Greek reception of Aspasia was typically influenced by attitudes toward public women. Writers who would have resisted the ideas of a public intellectual and woman such as Aspasia portrayed her almost exclusively as a *hetaera*, and, as Henry notes, she was always sexualized. For example, Aristophanes mentions "Aspasia's whores" in *The Acharnians*, his earliest extant comedy.

In the twentieth century, Aspasia was constructed as both a *hetaera* and as an intellectual (Glenn; Henry 117). Late twentieth-century feminists focused on Aspasia the rhetorician and intellectual, and how she has been historicized according to her presumed erotic and reproductive roles. The focus of late twentieth-century scholars in rhetoric-composition studies, and in different ways in classics, was on the unusual nature of Aspasia's activities in public among male intellectuals at a time when women ordinarily were confined to the household. Alternative ways of historicizing her contribution have tried to make that contribution visible. Cheryl Glenn writes,

> Aspasia's appearance among the educated, accomplished, and powerful was unprecedented at a time when the construction of gender ensured that women would be praised only for such attitudes as their inherent modesty, their inborn reluctance to join males (even kinsmen) for society or dining, and their absolute incapacity to participate as educated beings within the polis. (38)

Twenty-first-century rhetoric-composition scholars continue to rewrite Aspasia's place in rhetorical, political, and intellectual history as well as to examine the historiographies that construct her as a *hetaera* rather than as an intellectual.

BIBLIOGRAPHY

Biographical Sources

Blundell, Sue. *Women in Ancient Greece*. Cambridge: Harvard UP, 1995.

Henry, Madeleine M. *Prisoner of History: Aspasia of Miletus and Her Biographical Tradition*. New York: Oxford UP, 1997.

Plutarch. "Life of Pericles." *Greek Lives*. Trans. Robin Waterfield. Oxford: Oxford UP, 1998. 140–78.

Waithe, Mary Ellen, ed. *A History of Women Philosophers: Volume 1: 600 B.C.–500 A.D.* Dordrecht: Kluwer Academic Publishers, 1987.

Critical Sources

Aristophanes. *Four Comedies by Aristophanes: Lysistrata, The Acharnians, The Congresswomen, and The Frogs*. Trans. Douglass Parker. Ann Arbor: U of Michigan P, 1969.

DuBois, Page. *Sowing the Body: Psychoanalysis and Ancient Literary Representations of Women*. Chicago: U of Chicago P, 1988.

Fantham, Elaine, Helene Peet Foley, Natalie Boymel Kampen, Sarah B. Pomeroy, and H. Alan Shapiro. *Women in the Classical World: Image and Text*. New York: Oxford UP, 1994.

Glenn, Cheryl. *Rhetoric Retold: Regendering the Tradition from Antiquity through the Renaissance.* Carbondale: Southern Illinois UP, 1997.

Jarratt, Susan, and Rory Ong. "Aspasia: Rhetoric, Gender, and Colonial Ideology." *Reclaiming Rhetorica: Women in the Rhetorical Tradition.* Ed. Andrea A. Lunsford. Pittsburgh: U of Pittsburgh P, 1995. 9–24.

Keuls, Eva C. *The Reign of the Phallus: Sexual Politics in Ancient Athens.* Berkeley: U of California P, 1985.

Plato. *Menexenus.* In *Euthypro, Apology, Crito, Meno, Gorgias, Menexenus: The Dialogues of Plato, Volume I.* Trans. R. D. Allen. New Haven: Yale UP, 1984.

Welch, Kathleen E. "Writing Instruction in Ancient Athens after 450 B.C." *A Short History of Writing Instruction: From Ancient Greece to Twentieth-Century America.* Ed. James J. Murphy. Davis, CA: Hermagoras P, 1990. 1–17.

Xenophon. *The Anabasis and the Memorabilia of Socrates.* Trans. J. S. Watson. London, 1883.

———. *Oeconomicus: A Social and Historical Commentary with a New English Translation by Sarah B. Pomeroy.* Oxford: Clarendon, 1994.

Attic Orators: Demosthenes, Aeschines, and Lysias

(ca. early fifth century–late fourth century BCE)

David Christopher Ryan

Revered for their oratorical prowess and studied for their literary style, the Attic Orators were the heralds of rhetorical excellence in the fifth and fourth century BCE. Demosthenes, Aeschines, and Lysias were the most influential orators of their era, and they were among the first canonized stylists who exemplified the finest writers of Attic Greek. Their canonization represents one of the first attempts to establish a taxonomy on the varying nature of classical rhetoric. This effort gave shape and scope to the development of a prose genre used to distinguish the excellence and propriety of Atticized literature from the speech of demotic Greek and the amplified rhetoric of Asia Minor.

In this era, speech was the living memory of the *polis*, the supreme instrument of power—*the* epistemic paradigm. Though Athens held considerable faith in the power and authority of teaching, the dominance of sophistic education was challenged by Plato, Aristotle, and Isocrates. In particular, Isocrates revolutionized rhetoric education when he established literacy as part of his curriculum. Though scholars are unsure when literacy became commonplace, Isocrates' decisive mutation from the orality of sophistic education helped rhetoric shift to a literacy-based epistemology. However, his argument for establishing a literary *paideia* never would have gained any credence without the literary efforts of the Attic Orators, who were probably the first to respond to his teachings. By using writing as an epistemic tool, they further legitimized literacy as an instrument for rhetoric education.

Praised as a great orator and prose stylist yet characterized as a tragic figure who perished by his own hands, Demosthenes (384–322) was Athens's most powerful orator. At seventeen, he argued against the executors who grossly mismanaged or plundered his family's estate. His success heightened his interest in the mechanics of civic culture, and he progressed to writing epideictic speeches. After the Peloponnesian War, he emerged from private practice to influence Athenian policy for three decades in its confrontations with Philip II of Macedonia. For his accomplishments, he was twice awarded a golden crown. Approximately fifty-nine orations exist, though scholars are unsure if all were delivered publicly.

Demosthenes' most bitter rival, Aeschines (390–315?), was a hoplite and assembly secretary before becoming a statesman. Blessed with natural talent, broad aptitude, and easy charm, he used his training as a scribe and actor to lead Athens's Macedonian political party. Demosthenes and Aeschines served as ambassadors to Macedonia, but Aeschines grew disenchanted with the resistance to Philip II and advocated improved relations. Although Aeschines enjoyed a productive career as a politician, his prosecution of Ctesiphon for his decree that Demosthenes receive a golden crown in *Against Ctesiphon* ended in political disaster and ruined reputation. Unable to pay a heavy fine, he was exiled to Rhodes, where he ended his career as a teacher.

With the exception of Isocrates, the most well-known Attic Orator is Lysias (458?–380). The son of a Syracusean who was a friend of Pericles, Lysias studied under Protagoras and became an influential speechwriter and orator. Praised by rhetoricians yet scorned by Plato in the *Phaedrus*, Lysias is known for his plain yet lucid style, a style contrasted with the middle style of Isocrates and the grandeur of Thucydides. Approximately thirty-four orations exist.

RHETORICAL CONTRIBUTION

In their writings, the Attic Orators capture the exigency of rhetorical combat. They were active theorists who battled in the courts, agora, and assembly. In this era, the boiling caldron of Athenian politics created a *kairos* steaming with personal jealousies, partisan politics, and out-and-out treachery. Political leadership had become a complex rhetorical art in which arguments often combined candor with deception—where fact was woven with fiction. Consequently, scholars have struggled with the historical veracity of their orations as they try to comprehend rhetoric's relationship with political power.

Though they distinguished themselves as speakers, one of their most important contributions was fostering the literate revolution of *Hellas*. Demosthenes, Aeschines, and Lysias were orators who used writing in a time when most Athenians were suspicious of and hostile to literacy. As an orator, Demosthenes was the most powerful; he stirred not only the spirit of Athenians better than his rivals, but he defined persuasively that spirit as well. In Demosthenes, we understand that the art of leadership is best explained in rhetorical terms. As a speaker and writer, he confronted the tension between orality and literacy by synthesizing their respective styles of composition.

Though Demosthenes used subordination frequently to compose his orations—a style associated with writing—his *Erotic Essay* uses a coordinative style employing apothegms as transitions, a style often identified with speechmaking. In *Letters*, he combined coordination and subordination, achieving an oral-literate synthesis. In his finest work, *De Corona*, his elaborate argument reveals an exemplary process of *ēthos* building: models of concession, modesty, planned digressions, public concern, and personal strength are coupled with appeals to the historical, communal, and personal memories of his audience. His scathing yet graceful synthesis of epideictic and forensic rhetoric was aimed at rescuing the integrity of Ctesiphon, sinking the position of Aeschines, and clarifying his own public standing. His varied use of parallelism and antithesis achieves a syntactic control that juxtaposed the poisonous follies of Aeschines with the thundering truisms of his testimony.

In *De Corona*, his stylistic orchestrations reveal a careful effort at controlling language in a dangerous debate, so he may instruct, persuade, and entertain his audience. For Demosthenes and Aeschines, their prose rhythm exudes a euphonic elegance faithful to the poetic tenets of *psychagogia*, an approach meant to satisfy an audience educated in an oral tradition. Their effort at governing written language was meant to evoke an intellectual and aesthetic response by controlling the sound of written words. A carefully crafted prose rhythm created a quality of expressive sound meant to satisfy solitary readers who read prose works aloud. This aesthetic complexity is connected closely to a tension created by a confluence of characteristics flowing from the paradigms of orality and literacy. For instance, in *De Corona*, Demosthenes' oral testimony utilizes official decrees and letters as forensic evidence. Using written documents was risky given the unpredictable nature of an audience suspicious of writing, but a modern audience may view this intertextuality as an effort to create a symbiosis between orality and literacy.

This tension is seen with less frequency in the work of Aeschines. In his orations, he covets a coordinated style using lengthy clauses connected by conjunctions. Aeschines strives for fluency but often achieves unevenness because his prose sags under the weight of numerous prepositional and infinitive phrases, especially in *On the Embassy*, an approach that deflates his prose and defers his points. However, *Against Ctesiphon* achieves an improved balance and cadence because his attack is framed within the schemes of antithesis and parallelism. Unfortunately for Aeschines, his charge that Demosthenes was corrupt and cowardly collapsed, and a cogent criticism of Ctesiphon and Demosthenes failed to emerge.

Though scholars have praised Demothenes at the expense of Aeschines, most ancient and modern critics have treated Lysias with reverence. Lysias's style excels at concision and clarity. His approach to the tension created by orality and literacy was to graft features of the oral style (frequent uses of coordination) onto his writing, a tactic meant to align yet subordinate literacy within the dominance of orality. Ancient and modern scholarship, however, have placed Lysias in a taxonomic stasis—ossified in our literary records as a purveyor of one style. Modern audiences are left to ponder if Lysias used his plain style for all occasions, an approach that violates the maxims of *ethopoeia*. Since the primacy of our literary records often dissuades us from exploring other possibilities for Lysias, scholars have categorized him as a speechwriter instead of a speechmaker.

In this era, the varying uses of style raise some interesting pedagogical theories. Lysias and Isocrates probably viewed style as a fundamental part of their *ēthos*. Demosthenes and Aeschines, however, saw style as an important tool of civic discourse. For instance, Lysias used writing as an extension of oral discourse to maintain his identity as an orator, but Isocrates used writing to create a model literary rhetor contrary to the orators who, from his perspective, corrupted education and polluted civic discourse. Most interestingly, Demosthenes internalized the tensions of orality and literacy in order to maximize his public influence and affirm the rhetorical nature of writing.

RECEPTION, THEN AND NOW

The Alexandrines and Romans, particularly Cicero and Quintilian, used the orations of the Attic Orators as heuristics for mimesis in their respective Greek language and rhetoric studies. Unfortunately, many modern scholars have obscured these rhetors in favor of studying the conflict between Plato, Aristotle, and the Sophists, but recent scholarship into Isocrates' rhetorical theory may arouse interest in these rhetors as well as the rhetorical scholarship of Werner Jaeger, R. C. Jebb, and James Murphy. These scholars have urged us to understand the boldness of these orators in giving expression to a post-Peloponnesian Athenian *ēthos* that was plagued by tension yet struggled resiliently for resurrection.

Scholars such as Jaeger, Jebb, and Murphy have studied the speeches of the Attic Orators for their rhetorical significance and literary merit, but classicists such as Ian Worthington and Michael Edwards have cautioned readers on the methodological problems of determining the historical authenticity of the information in these orations. One useful way to approach this problem is to examine these orations rhetorically. This approach can help readers better comprehend the nature and purpose of literacy in relation to the complex needs of their audience. Furthermore, a careful extension of Tony Lentz's work on the orality and literacy of Isocrates may help us further understand the Attic Orators' role in transforming rhetoric from an art that governed speech to an art that transformed the purpose of writing into a vital means of communication.

BIBLIOGRAPHY

Primary Sources and Translations

Aeschines. *The Speeches of Aeschines*. Trans. Charles Darwin Adams. Cambridge: Harvard UP, 1919.
Demosthenes. *Demosthenes II*. Ed. E. H. Warmington. Trans. C. A. Vince and J. H. Vince. Cambridge: Harvard UP, 1926.
Lysias. *Lysias*. Trans. W. R. M. Lamb. Cambridge: Harvard UP, 1960.

Biographical Sources

Dionysius. *Ancient Orators. Vol. I.* Trans. Stephen Usher. Cambridge: Harvard UP, 1974.

Critical Sources

Edwards, Michael. *The Attic Orators.* London: Bristol Classic P, 1994.

Jaeger, Werner. *Paideia: The Ideals of Greek Culture. Vol. III.* Trans. Gilbert Highet. Oxford: Oxford UP, 1984.

Jebb, R. C. *The Attic Orators from Antiphon to Isaeos.* London: Macmillan, 1876.

Lentz, Tony. *Orality and Literacy in Hellenic Greece.* Carbondale: Southern Illinois UP, 1989.

Murphy, James J. *Demosthenes' On the Crown: A Critical Study of a Masterpiece of Ancient Oratory.* New York: Random House, 1967.

Wooten, Cecil W. *Cicero's Philipics and Their Demosthenic Model: The Rhetoric of Crisis.* Chapel Hill: U of North Carolina P, 1983.

Worthington, Ian, ed. *Demosthenes: Statesman and Orator.* New York: Routledge, 2000.

AURELIUS AUGUSTINUS

(354–430 CE)

Roxanne Mountford

Aurelius Augustinus, also known as St. Augustine of Hippo, was born in North Africa on November 13, 354 CE. His town of birth, Thagaste (now Souk Ahras, Algeria), lay 200 miles south and west of the ancient Mediterranean port city of Carthage, in territory that had been colonized by the Roman Empire for more than 300 years. His father, Patricius, struggled to provide Augustine with a classical education and connections so that he could rise above his family's social and economic status. His mother, Monica, whose devotion and Christian influence is famously portrayed in the *Confessions*, believed that Augustine's pagan education would not only aid his advancement but also lead him closer to God (*Confessions* 2.3.8). After his initial education in Thagaste, Augustine traveled to Carthage to study at the university. While not atypical, his overall education was surprisingly limited (for example, Augustine is one of the few Latin fathers without a strong knowledge of Greek), but in one area his education was rich: rhetoric (Brown 24). Augustine was trained as an orator and began his career as a teacher of rhetoric. He taught in Thagaste (375–376), Carthage (376–383), Rome (383–384), and finally in Milan, where he was named professor of rhetoric.

In Milan, Augustine's career as a rhetoric teacher would not last long. While there, Augustine met Ambrose, then Bishop of Milan, and through his influence began to replace his beliefs in Manichaeism (a dualistic religion that conceived of the body as evil and the soul as good) with Catholicism, a process recounted in the *Confessions*. His conversion to Christianity in some form was probably inevitable since he was committed to respectable public life, and under Theodosius (in 380), Christianity had become the state religion of the Roman Empire. Indeed, we know that Augustine held such commitments because of his rejection of a concubine (unnamed) whom he met in Carthage and with whom he had had a son (he dismissed her so that he might marry an heiress). However, what was to be a pro forma conversion became instead a great intellectual and spiritual struggle for Augustine, a man devoted to the pursuit of truth and an admirer of Greek and

Roman philosophers (particularly Plato and Cicero). His mother, Monica, who joined him in Milan after the death of Patricius, rejoiced when Augustine's struggle resulted not only in his conversion to Christianity at thirty-two, but also in the fulfillment of her wish that his intellectual pursuits would lead to a life of religious devotion.

Following his conversion in 386, Augustine retired from teaching, never to return. Baptized by Ambrose in 387, Augustine devoted the rest of his life to religious contemplation, education, and leadership. In 391 he founded a monastery at Hippo and was ordained by Valerius, then Bishop of Hippo; in 395 he succeeded Valerius as Bishop of Hippo, a position he held until the end of his life. Throughout that period, Augustine worked to uphold the institutional authority of the Catholic Church, focusing his writing, both formal and informal, on this task (Brown 445). Indeed, as scholar Claude Lepelley has suggested, Augustine's world—at the outskirts of the Roman Empire—was still largely pagan and secular, providing him sufficient exigency for a lifetime of institutional defense against other religious and philosophical traditions. Augustine's extant writing, which includes letters, sermons, and treatises on a wide range of religious subjects, is vast, and includes *On Christian Doctrine* and *The City of God*, which, along with the *Confessions*, are his greatest works. He died in 430, having set the course for Christianity in the West and placed his mark on many academic subjects, including philosophy and rhetoric.

Largely preserved and widely read by scholars during the Middle Ages, Augustine's approach to Christian rhetoric was immediately recognized as important. His *On Christian Doctrine* was used to train preachers for hundreds of years and influenced such medieval writers as Thomas Aquinas, Alan of Lille, Humbert of Romans, and Robert of Basevorn (Kennedy 182). Like Ambrose and other Christians of the fourth century, Augustine was a Neoplatonist who favored wisdom over eloquence, contemplation over civic action. So wary was he of rhetoric that he confined his discussion of eloquence primarily to style, drawing heavily from Cicero. However, Augustine connects hermeneutics with rhetoric in a rich and fruitful way, offering a model of the recursive role of interpretation, inspiration, and annunciation in the Christian life. Augustine demonstrates this process in the *Confessions* and teaches it to preachers in *On Christian Doctrine*.

AUGUSTINIAN HERMENEUTICS

Any discussion of Augustine's perspectives on rhetoric must begin with an understanding of his intellectual orientation. Augustine and many of his contemporaries were trained as rhetoricians, but they were Neoplatonists to the core: they elevated the study of truth over the practice of oratory and were drawn inexorably to a life of philosophy, which meant withdrawal from worldly pursuits, devotion to reading, and commitment to self-contemplation. In his writing, Augustine drew on Plotinus to anchor his thinking on such theological projects as understanding the nature and origin of beauty (Steinhauser 26), and states his admiration for Platonic philosophy above all other pagan systems of thought in *The City of God*. As a result of his Neoplatonic orientation, Augustine appears to place more value on dialectic than rhetoric, devoting only one book of *On Christian Doctrine* to preaching, a book he delayed writing until the end of his life (books 1 through 3 were completed around 397; book 4, devoted to preaching, was not completed until 427, three years before his death).

Therefore, to understand Augustine's contributions to rhetoric, one must begin with an exploration of his hermeneutics. Hermeneutics concerns interpretation of texts, while rhetoric concerns public expression of ideas. While hermeneutics and rhetoric "both keep in the center of their attention the close connection between language and practical life in human affairs" and aim to affect the understanding (Marshall 276), hermeneutics is more closely associated with private study and the pursuit of truth than rhetoric. Augustine begins *On Christian Doctrine* with the observation that "there are two things necessary to the treatment of the Scriptures: a way of discovering those things which are to be understood, and a way of teaching what we have learned" (1.1.1). But of greater importance is the development of the understanding. In book 4, quoting Cicero, Augustine argues that wisdom is more important than eloquence, for an audience profits from the words of an orator who is wise but not eloquent, but may be harmed by an orator who is eloquent but not wise (4.5.122). Therefore, a preacher's time is better served studying the Scripture than studying rhetoric. In books 1 through 3, Augustine takes up the task of teaching a hermeneutics designed to reveal the truths of Scripture.

Augustine explains that doctrine always "concerns either signs or things," but things are mediated through the study of signs (1.2.4). In the Scripture, a "thing" can be a natural object like a stone, but it can also be a "sign" of something else, as when Jacob places a stone on his head in Genesis 28:11. Book 1 is devoted to the study of things. Some things are to be "enjoyed," some are to be "used," and some are to both used and enjoyed. Things that are enjoyed directly benefit a Christian, such as the Father, Son, and Holy Spirit. Things that are used help the Christian on the way to a love of God, and include love of those above us, love of ourselves, love of those like us, and love of those below us. At the end of book 1, Augustine sets this discussion in the context of the interpretation of Scripture. Any reading of Scripture that does not encourage love of God and neighbor is in error (1.36.40). Right interpretation will never violate the golden rule (Marshall 282).

In books 2 and 3, Augustine tackles the problem with interpreting obscure passages in Scripture through an analysis of signs. In book 2, he identifies two kinds of signs: natural signs and conventional signs. A natural sign occurs in nature without the intervention of conscious agency; for example, when one sees a track in the woods, one thinks of the animal that made it. A conventional sign occurs when humans or animals use language to convey "something they have sensed or understood" (2.2.3). Continuing a theme of book 1, Augustine distinguishes between right interpretation and "errors" by arguing that signs drawn from systems of thought that are antithetical to Christian life, such as the practice of astrology, should be strenuously avoided. Augustine then turns to problems with interpreting

Scripture. Readers who are careful, have good knowledge of all Scripture, and have a good memory will be rewarded in their efforts. Augustine proposes that some passages of Scripture are to be understood as literal (signs used in a familiar way), while others are to be understood as figural (signs that include a sense beyond the familiar). Problems of interpretation occur when passages are either unknown or ambiguous. In book 3, Augustine continues to discuss the problems with the interpretation of Scripture by focusing on ambiguous signs. In the case of ambiguous literal signs, he suggests study of different translations. For ambiguous figurative signs, Augustine suggests that a first step is recognizing that the sign in question is figurative and not literal. Inexperienced readers are more apt to miss the figurative nature of signs than mature readers.

But finding the right interpretation sometimes requires study beyond the Scriptures. In book 2, Augustine recommends study of languages, things (because figural signs often rely on knowledge of the natural world), dialectic logic, pagan philosophy (particularly the Platonists), and rhetoric. To defend the use of pagan learning for Christian purposes, Augustine suggests that the true source of all knowledge and the facility for learning is God: the philosopher discovers the divine order of things, and the rhetorician recognizes that God has made human beings receptive to eloquence. He then offers a metaphor for this process: drawing on pagan learning for the glory of God, he argues, is like the Israelites taking the gold and silver of their captors out of Egypt for use in the Promised Land. Through this metaphor, Augustine allowed secular disciplines "to find a new life in medieval Christianity and, through medieval Christians, in the late twentieth century in the West" (Tracy 270). However, because Augustine believed that the most fundamental sign of truth was its manifestation in love of God and neighbor, he also argued that one could live rightly without Scripture or any other books, in total solitude (1.34). The most important principle in Augustine's hermeneutics, then, is interpretation and lived experience that exhibit faith, hope, and charity.

Augustine's insistence that "love of God and neighbor" is the touchstone for right interpretation presupposes that, finally, the audience (a community of believers) will be the judge of good Christian teaching. It is for this reason that some scholars consider Augustine's perspective on interpretation to be rhetorical in nature. As Donald G. Marshall puts it, Augustine's "conception of language as firmly rooted in community and thus saturated implicitly in the values of the life that discourse sustains is profoundly rhetorical. It is far from those philosophical, epistemologically formulated anxieties over how to guarantee a proper relation of word to thing" (283). Indeed, Augustine's overall "defense of the spiritual, allegorical sense of Scripture" places him in a far more rhetorical relationship with hermeneutics than Thomas Aquinas and Martin Luther, who, though indebted to Augustine, advocated a more literal and restricted hermeneutics (Tracy 261). Books 1 through 3 form the *inventio* of Augustine's rhetorical vision of Christian teaching, for as he suggests in book 1 and repeats at the beginning of book 4, the first task for the teacher is "a way of discovering those things which are to be understood" (1.1.1; 4.1.1). While Augustine's *inventio* is infused with a moral/spiritual imperative, it is still part of the larger process of discovering that which will edify (and therefore persuade) an audience.

AUGUSTINIAN RHETORIC

As students of rhetoric are often reminded, importing pagan precepts into Christian life was considered heretical by the early church fathers. Of the significance of Greek philosophy to Christianity, Tertullian (160–225 CE) wrote, "What has Athens to do with Jerusalem? What concord is there between the Academy and the Church?" (*De praescriptione haereticorum* 7). Augustine's contemporary Jerome (348–420 CE) reaffirmed this suspicion, writing in a letter to Eustochium in 384, "What has Horace to do with the psalter, Virgil with the gospels, Cicero with the apostle? [. . .] [W]e ought not to drink the cup of Christ, and, at the same time, the cup of devils" (*Epistulae* 22:29). In the same letter, Jerome reports having scourged himself for his love of reading Cicero (*Epistulae* 22:30). Nevertheless, the early Latin and Greek fathers of the Catholic Church—including Tertullian and Jerome—had secular training in rhetoric and many, including Gregory of Nazianzus, gave sermons replete with the complex figures and tropes that secular and Christian audiences had come to expect from their orators.

Augustine was unimpressed by his predecessors' critiques of secular learning. Instead, he adopted a perspective that recognized what other church fathers had put into practice despite protestations to the contrary: eloquence was useful. In book 4 of *On Christian Doctrine*, he writes,

> For since by means of the art of rhetoric both truth and falsehood are urged, who would dare to say that truth should stand in the person of its defenders unarmed against lying, so that they who wish to urge falsehoods may know how to make their listeners benevolent, or attentive, or docile in their presentation, while the defenders of truth are ignorant of that art? [. . .] Who is so foolish as to think this is wisdom? While the faculty of eloquence, which is of great value in urging either evil or justice, is in itself indifferent, why should it not be obtained for the uses of the good in the service of truth if the evil usurp it for the winning of perverse and vain causes in defense of iniquity and error? (4.2.3)

Thus, whereas the other Latin and Greek fathers maintained a strict line between Christian and pagan learning, Augustine brought all learning useful to the propagation of the faith into the Christian arena. In the Western tradition of preaching theory, this trend continued almost unbroken to the present age.

The first element of the art of preaching Augustine addresses is the training of the preacher. Augustine suggests that the preacher learn the art of rhetoric in secular schools at an appropriate age (4.1.2, 4.3.4). Following the sophistic *paideia*, Augustine urges those who wish to learn eloquence to listen to, read, and study those who are eloquent and to gain practice by rehearsing through writing, dictating, and speaking all that they have learned in their study of the Scriptures (4.3.4–5).

The second subject of book 4 is the nature and function of style. According to Augustine, the goal of eloquence is clarity, which should always be chosen above grace. However, when the purpose of the sermon favors enlightenment over understanding, then the style can be changed to suit these purposes. Augustine writes that an orator should desire to speak both wisely and eloquently, and to do so he "should so speak that he is heard intelligently, willingly, and obediently" in every sermon (4.25.55). Drawing on Cicero, Augustine distinguishes among the plain, moderate, and grand styles. The plain style is suited for moving the understanding, the moderate style for moving the will, the grand style for inspiring obedience. To illustrate these three styles, Augustine draws on Scripture and the preaching of the early church fathers. For instance, in order to illustrate an appropriate time to use the grand style, which is "forceful with the emotions of the spirit" (4.20.42), Augustine draws from Cyprian and Ambrose, both of whom sought to persuade women to refrain from excessive attention to their appearance (4.21.49–50). Like other ancients, Augustine notes human characteristics among audiences that affect their receptiveness; for example, no one can listen to the grand style for a protracted period of time (4.22.51). Therefore, if right interpretation is the first step in Christian teaching, choosing the right amplification of the material is the second step: the style must fit the subject matter.

Augustine's approach to *ēthos* is in keeping with his hermeneutics. The preacher's role is to heal the sinner through application of the Wisdom of God, a divine medicine. His ability to do so depends much on his piety but also on divine grace. Augustine writes that the church, whose "malady arose through the corrupted spirit of a woman" is cured by Christ (1.14.13). God in Christ is the Great Physician, and the minister, as the deliverer of God's wisdom, is God's physician on earth. The orator is fundamentally active, the congregation, fundamentally passive and distant in this formulation. Preachers do not win over their congregations through personal appeal except through their piety and the right interpretation of Scripture (the preacher must only speak of "the just and holy and good" so "he may be willingly and obediently heard") (4.25.32). But despite all human intention, divine grace is active in persuasion. God can even speak through those who live falsely; Augustine quotes Matthew 23.3: "'All things therefore whatsoever they shall say to you, observe and do: but according to their works do ye not; for they say, and do not,' thus they may hear usefully those who do not act usefully" (4.27.59). For this reason, the best preparation for the preacher is to pray for God's intervention in the sermon, for through divine grace, even a wicked speaker can benefit the audience. Therefore, in the end of book 4, Augustine circles back to his hermeneutics: good preaching will inspire love of God and neighbor, and this goal transcends all other rhetorical principles, including eloquence itself.

Most scholars of rhetoric have focused on Augustine's contributions to rhetorical theory but not his own practice of preaching. In his early extant sermons, Augustine's style is highly ornamented and heavy with obscure biblical references (Oberhelman 110). However, early in his career Augustine abandoned his Second Sophistic training and adopted the style of his mentor Ambrose, which can be recognized by "a direct, simple, and familiar tone; very straightforward, though often fragmented syntax; parataxis, parallelism, and antithesis; questions; short clauses; and elements of oral speech" (Oberhelman 110–11). Indeed, while Augustine offers examples of the grand style in book 4 of *On Christian Doctrine*, he seems to have reserved the plain or moderate style for his own pulpit. John D. Schaeffer argues that Augustine opposed the elaborate performances of the Second Sophistic because he believed in the extemporaneous utterance, which meant a sermon that was carefully prepared but not memorized or rehearsed (1143 fn. 3).

AUGUSTINE AND INNER PERSUASION

Although most historians of rhetoric focus on Augustine's contributions to the art of preaching in *On Christian Doctrine*, the *Confessions* also contribute to the history of rhetoric. *On Christian Doctrine* has been called the first Christian treatment of rhetoric (C. S. Baldwin asserts that *On Christian Doctrine* "begins rhetoric anew") (51). But as Kenneth Burke notes, both the *Confessions* and *On Christian Doctrine* concern the movement of the pagan word to the Christian Word (49), or, put another way, the "conversion" of pagan perspectives to Christian ones through the mediation of language. Both works also include Augustine's theory of hermeneutics. But in rhetorical terms, the *Confessions* demonstrate the internal process through which the secular and sacred worlds are bridged through intellectual persuasion.[1]

Written around 397, shortly after Augustine was ordained Bishop of Hippo, the *Confessions* include thirteen books—ten autobiographical/philosophical and three exegetical in nature. The thirteen books are written as a conversation with God that the reader "overhears." Scholars agree that the *Confessions* would have been recognized by Augustine's contemporaries as a Neoplatonic intellectual exercise, common in the ancient world, in which a philosopher engages in self-examination and introspection, using the form of a prayer to God (Brown; Stock). The idea of such a meditation is to engage an entity whose ethics and knowledge of the universe are far above the philosopher's, thus elevating thought to a new level (Stock 29).

The *Confessions* detail Augustine's intellectual journey "from one philosophical or religious school to another without finding the answer to the moral problems with which he was preoccupied" (Stock 32). Augustine embarks on this exploration of his thirty-year journey to reveal his "errors" and to uncover his true identity. In book 4 he writes, "Allow me, I beseech You, grant me to wind round and round in my present memory the spiral of my errors [. . .]" (4.1.1). In book 10, he asserts, "I would know you, my knower; I would know you as I am known" (10.1.1). Books 1 through 8 detail Augustine's intellectual and spiritual conversion to Christianity; book 9 focuses on the death of his mother, Monica; books 10 through 13 are an exegesis of Genesis. Because of the inclusion of the last four books, scholars conclude that Augustine's treatise cannot be reduced to mere autobiography; instead, the *Confessions* are a teaching document, intended to lead others through the inner process of persuasion that led Augustine to God (Brown 151–75; Steinhauser 25). Indeed, in the *Retractationes*, Augustine himself states that the *Confessions* are intended to "lift up the understanding and affection of men to Him" (2.6.32).

In the *Confessions*, Augustine writes that his transformation began with his search for the truth of his existence. Among the significant events of his quest, Augustine recounts his discovery of Cicero's *Hortensius* at age nineteen and later, after arriving in Milan, the work of Plotinus and other Neoplatonist writers. Brown writes that in 386, the year of Augustine's conversion, Augustine was embarked on "a spell of long and patient reading, apparently aided by some discussions" (86). By the time Augustine met Ambrose, this reading had caused in Augustine an "inner turmoil that was to characterize [his] days for many months, even years, to come" (5.99). Caught up in philosophical contemplation, he writes that at first his primary concern upon meeting Ambrose was not the conversion of his soul; rather, he listened carefully to Ambrose in order to study his style of speaking, which he had heard was extraordinary. However, he reports the rhetoric affected him and admits that Ambrose's "meaning, which I tried to ignore, found its way into my mind together with his words, [and . . .] I also began to sense the truth of what he said, though only gradually" (5.14.25).

True to the Neoplatonic tradition from which the *Confessions* descend, Augustine relates the search for truth as a great intellectual struggle. Caught between secular and Christian philosophy, Augustine's attempt to deal with the contradictions between his beliefs and identity and Ambrose's is consuming, even as a wound (6.6.9). Augustine and Ambrose are both rhetoricians, yet Ambrose is a proponent of God's Word, while Augustine is a proponent of the secular world. In rhetorical terms, Augustine details his recognition of an internal *stasis* in his beliefs: there was the truth of the Academics, whose God was remote, but whose intellectual riches were great, and there was the truth of the Christians, whose God was near, but whose intellectual tradition was poor. In Augustine's struggle to connect, to identify with Ambrose and subsequently with Christ, he had to move beyond *stasis*. In the end, the internal process of persuasion came about through language. At the height of his internal struggle, Augustine recounts what is now a famous scene in the *Confessions*:

> I was asking myself these questions, weeping all the while with the most bitter sorrow in my heart, when all at once I heard the sing-song voice of a child in a nearby house. Whether it was the voice of a boy or a girl I cannot say, but again and again it repeated the refrain, "Take it and read, take it and read." [. . .] I stemmed my flood of tears and stood up, telling myself that this could only be a divine command [. . .] (8.12.29)

Augustine opens Paul's letters and reads, " 'Not in revelling and drunkenness, not in lust and wantonness, not in quarrels and rivalries. Rather arm yourselves with the Lord Jesus Christ; spend no more thought on nature and nature's appetites' " (8.12.29). It is at this point he realizes that through a life of contemplation and total devotion to God, the contradictions in his beliefs would be overcome.

The prize in this struggle is the same one for which secular Neoplatonists struggled: knowledge of God, who was thought to be the source of all truth and beauty. And indeed, in the end, the *Confessions* turn out to be a celebration of the beauty of the Christian God as revealed, finally, through Genesis. Augustine's conversion ended his career, because the contemplative life meant rejecting a career, marriage, and family; only through quiet study and contemplation could he find the God he sought. He was baptized by Ambrose, which in the early church normally meant conversion to an ascetic lifestyle (Christians who lived "in the world" were often baptized on their deathbed). He moved his mother and circle of friends out of town and began to write polemics against secular philosophy. Not long after, Augustine founded a monastery at Hippo, his transformation of lifestyle and belief complete. The *Confessions* serve as the *testimonio* to *On Christian Doctrine's paideia*: one's reading and interpretation of texts and one's devotion to teaching are worthless if they do not ultimately lead to love of God and neighbor.

The impact of the *Confessions* on literary and religious history is profound. His exploration of the inner life has influenced the modern concept of the self (Cary), leading Northrop Frye to regard Augustine as the progenitor of the autobiography (307). Other critics credit the *Confessions* with beginning a long history of "confessional autobiographies" (Gusdorf; Fleishmann). Of course, the word "autobiography" is relatively modern in origin, dating to the turn of the nineteenth century (Scott 34); nevertheless, Augustine's impact on contemplative literature and contemporary understandings of conversion is undenied. Indeed, the form of Augustine's inner persuasion continues to inspire great thinkers. At the end of his life, Jean-François Lyotard was working on *The Confessions of Augustine*, published incomplete in 1998 just after his death. In it, Augustine's and Lyotard's language mixes poetically, and God is addressed by both. It is, in a sense, a postmodern extension of the *Confessions*.

AUGUSTINIAN INFLUENCE AND CURRENT SCHOLARSHIP

Augustine's influence on the Western world cannot be underestimated. Augustine's sermons, letters, and treatises were enthusiastically copied and distributed throughout the medieval period, even during periods in which other ancient works were lost. *On Christian Doctrine* was the most important treatise on Christian preaching until the Renaissance, copied by monks more often than the works of Cicero (Schaeffer 1134). Augustine has been linked to the Carolingian renaissance (Amos 23), the rise of humanistic education (Johnson), the founding of homiletics (Murphy), and the establishment of a reading culture (Stock). He is credited with ensuring the dominance of Neoplatonism in the medieval period. Finally, his theological views on grace and free will influenced important successors, including Thomas Aquinas and Martin Luther,[2] considered two of Christianity's greatest thinkers.

Augustine's contributions to rhetoric are recounted in many histories, including Murphy's *Rhetoric in the Middle Ages* and Kennedy's *Classical Rhetoric*. Most rhetoricians focus their attention on the influence of *On Christian Doctrine*. Two recent anthologies focus on this important treatise: *Reading and Wisdom*, edited by Edward English, and *De doctrina christiana: A Classic of Western Culture*, edited by Duane W. H. Arnold and Pamela Bright. Other important treatments of *On Christian Doctrine* not mentioned above include Fortin's study of Ciceronian influence on Augustine and Sutherland's study of style. Scholars interested in rhetorical study of the *Confessions* will be interested in *Augustine: From Rhetor to Theologian*, edited by Joanne McWilliam and, of course, Burke's *The Rhetoric of Religion*. Perhaps the greatest testament to Augustine's enduring influence is that he continues to inspire international scholarship in such a wide range of disciplines and among scholars with such different theoretical and historical temperaments.

Although Augustine was a philosopher (see Copleston; Johansen) and theologian (see Dodaro, Lawless, and Bonner), he was, above all, a rhetorician, and he remained committed to the importance of secular training in rhetoric to the end of his life. In one of the newly discovered Divjak letters,[3] Augustine asks Firmus to pass along a message to his son, reminding him of his Cicero. "Eloquence combined with wisdom has proved to be of the greatest benefit to states," he writes, "but eloquence without wisdom, harmful and of no good to anyone" (12.379.90). It was among the last letters Augustine would ever write. He died two years later, the last of the great ancient rhetoricians and the first of many to intermingle Christian and secular perspectives on this important art.

NOTES

1. I am grateful to Jennifer Walker for her generous feedback on the rhetorical implications of Augustine's *Confessions*.

2. Although, as John Monfasani points out, Luther was selective in his use of Augustine's ideas (174).

3. See *Letters VI*. The Fathers of the Church series offers English translations of most of Augustine's works, including translations of these newly found Divjak letters. Throughout its history, this series has been published by several presses, most recently Catholic University of America Press. The most recent volume on Augustine at the time of this writing was released in 2004.

BIBLIOGRAPHY

Primary Sources and Translations

Augustine. *Confessions*. Trans. R. S. Pine-Coffin. London: Penguin Books, 1961.

———. *De doctrina christiana* (On Christian Doctrine). Trans. R. P. H. Green. Oxford: Clarendon, 1995.

———. *De doctrina christiana* (On Christian Doctrine). Trans. D. W. Robertson, Jr. Indianapolis: Bobbs-Merrill, 1958.

————. *Letters VI (1–29)*. Trans. Robert B. Eno. Fathers of the Church 81. Washington, DC: Catholic U of America P, 1989.

————. *Retractationes* (The Retractions). Fathers of the Church 60. Washington, DC: Catholic U of America P, 1968.

————. *Sermones de Tempore* (Sermons on the Liturgical Seasons). Fathers of the Church 38. New York: Fathers of the Church, 1959.

————. *Solliques; and the Immortality of the Soul*. Trans. Gerard Watson. Warminster, UK: Aris and Phillips, 1990.

Biographical Sources

Brown, Peter. *Augustine of Hippo: A Biography*. 2nd ed. Berkeley: U of California P, 2000.

Van der Meer, Frederick. *Augustine the Bishop: The Life and Work of a Church Father*. Trans. Brian Battershaw and G. R. Lamb. London: Sheed and Ward, 1961.

Wills, Garry. *Saint Augustine*. Penguin Lives Series. New York: Viking, 1999.

Critical Sources

Amos, Thomas L. "Augustine and the Education of the Early Medieval Preacher." *Reading and Wisdom: The* De doctrina christiana *of Augustine in the Middle Ages*. Ed. Edward English. Notre Dame: U of Notre Dame P, 1995. 23–40.

Arnold, Duane W. H., and Pamela Bright, eds. *De doctrina christiana: A Classic of Western Culture*. Christianity and Judaism in Antiquity 9. Notre Dame: U of Notre Dame P, 1995.

Baldwin, Charles S. *Medieval Rhetoric and Poetic*. New York: Macmillan, 1928.

Burke, Kenneth. *The Rhetoric of Religion: Studies in Logology*. Berkeley: U of California P, 1961.

Cary, Phillip. *Augustine's Invention of the Inner Self: The Legacy of a Christian Platonist*. New York: Oxford UP, 2000.

Copleston, Frederick. *A History of Philosophy*. Vol. 2. 1950. New York: Doubleday, 1993.

Dodaro, Robert, George Lawless, and Gerald Bonner, eds. *Augustine and His Critics: Essays in Honour of Gerald Bonner*. New York: Routledge, 2000.

Fleishmann, Avrom. *Figures of Autobiography*. Berkeley: U of California P, 1983.

Fortin, Ernest L. "Augustine and the Problem of Christian Rhetoric." *Augustine Studies* 5 (1974): 85–100.

Frye, Northrop. *Anatomy of Criticism: Four Essays*. Princeton: Princeton UP, 1957.

Gusdorf, Georges. "Conditions and Limits of Autobiography." Trans. James Olney. *Autobiography: Essays Theoretical and Critical*. Ed. James Olney. Princeton: Princeton UP, 1980. 28–48.

Johansen, Karsten Friis. *A History of Ancient Philosophy: From the Beginnings to Augustine*. Trans. Henrik Rosenmeier. London: Routledge, 1998.

Johnson, W. R. "Isocrates Flowering: The Rhetoric of Augustine." *Philosophy and Rhetoric* 9.4 (1976): 217–31.

Kennedy, George A. *Classical Rhetoric and Its Christian and Secular Tradition from Ancient to Modern Times*. 2nd ed. Chapel Hill: U of North Carolina P, 1999.

Lepelley, Claude. *Les Cités de l' Afrique romaine au Bas-Empire*. 2 vols. Paris: Études augustiniennes, 1979, 1981.

Lyotard, Jean-François. *The Confessions of Augustine*. Stanford: Stanford UP, 2000.

Marshall, Donald G. "Rhetoric, Hermeneutic, and the Interpretation of Scripture: Augustine to Robert of Basevorn." *Rhetoric and Hermeneutics in Our Time: A Reader*. Ed. Walter Jost and Michael J. Hyde. New Haven: Yale UP, 1997. 275–89.

McWilliam, Joanne, ed. *Augustine: From Rhetor to Theologian*. Waterloo, Ontario: Wilfrid Laurier UP, 1992.

Monfasani, John. "The *De doctrina christiana* and Renaissance Rhetoric." *Reading and Wisdom: The* De doctrina christiana *of Augustine in the Middle Ages*. Ed. Edward English. Notre Dame: U of Notre Dame P, 1995. 172–88.

Murphy, James J. *Rhetoric in the Middle Ages: A History of Rhetorical Theory from St. Augustine to the Renaissance*. Berkeley: U of California P, 1974.

Oberhelman, Steven M. *Rhetoric and Homiletics in Fourth-Century Christian Literature*. American Classical Studies 26. Atlanta: Scholars P, 1991.

Press, Gerald A. "*Doctrina* in Augustine's *De doctrina christiana*." *Philosophy and Rhetoric* 17.2 (1984): 98–120.

Schaeffer, John D. "The Dialectic of Orality and Literacy: The Case of Book 4 of Augustine's *De doctrina christiana*." *PMLA* 111.5 (1996): 1133–44.

Scott, Jamie. "From Literal Self-Sacrifice to Literary Self-Sacrifice: Augustine's *Confessions* and the Rhetoric of Testimony." McWilliam. 31–49.

Steinhauser, Kenneth B. "The Literary Unity of the *Confessions*." McWilliam 15–30.

Stock, Brian. *After Augustine: The Meditative Reader and the Text*. Philadelphia: U of Pennsylvania P, 2001.

Sutherland, Christine M. "Reforms of Style: St. Augustine and the Seventeenth Century." *Rhetoric Society Quarterly* 21.1 (1991): 26–37.

Tracy, David. "Charity, Obscurity, Clarity: Augustine's Search for Rhetoric and Hermeneutics." *Rhetoric and Hermeneutics in Our Time: A Reader*. Ed. Walter Jost and Michael J. Hyde. New Haven: Yale UP, 1997. 254–74.

Anicius Manlius Severinus Boethius

(ca. 475–ca. 524 CE)

Beth S. Bennett

Called "the last of the Roman philosophers, and the first of the Scholastic theologians,"[1] Anicius Manlius Severinus Boethius was born around 476 CE, the year that the last Roman emperor in Italy, Romulus, was deposed by an East German chieftain named Odoacer.[2] To secure his dominance over Italy, Odoacer offered the Roman imperial insignia to the eastern emperor Zeno, in Constantinople, a gesture that would eliminate the two-emperor system that had been operating for nearly two centuries, in order to obtain Zeno's endorsement for his position as *Patricius*. Zeno's response was ambiguous, and Odoacer served as king to his followers and as an imperial official to Roman citizens and the rest of Italy for about a dozen years before Zeno took action. In 488, Zeno decided to send a barbarian leader named Theodoric with his Ostrogoth people to invade Italy. By 493, Theodoric had defeated Odoacer and established his own court in the imperial capital, Ravenna. Boethius, thus, was born and reared in an era when Roman citizens were under the political control of outsiders and when religious allegiances could conflict with political alliances and have serious consequences.

Boethius came from an old, aristocratic Roman family, the Anicii, faithful Christians for nearly one hundred years. When his father died, shortly after becoming consul in 487, Boethius was orphaned and subsequently raised by Quintus Aurelius Memmius Symmachus, one of the most venerable aristocrats of the time and a pillar in the Catholic Church. In Symmachus's home, Boethius "thought of himself as a Roman, spoke Latin as a native language, was fluent in Greek, and had access (unlike any Latin thinker after him) to a living tradition of Greek philosophy based on the study of Plato, Aristotle, and their commentators" (Marenbon 3). Although scholars have disagreed about the specific details of Boethius's education,[3] they agree that his knowledge and skills were exceptional for an age in which "veneration for Roman traditions, knowledge of Greek culture, and Christian beliefs were unproblematically combined" (Marenbon 10). Around 495, Boethius married the daughter of Symmachus, a woman named Rusticiana, and they had two sons, who would serve as joint consuls in 522.

Boethius chose to situate himself and his family in Rome, where a person of his social ranking could have a successful public career without the political risks inherent in Theodoric's court in Ravenna. Boethius served as consul in 510, but seems to have spent most of his time devoted to his own scholarly pursuits. His chief project aimed to translate all of the works and commentaries of Plato and Aristotle, in order to demonstrate the logical coherence of the two philosophers, but he also translated works on mathematics and music, wrote theological essays, and composed several works of his own. John Marenbon divides the Boethian corpus into four groups: (1) books on the *quadrivium*, a word Boethius invented, including two on mathematics and one on music; (2) five short theological tractates, *Opuscula sacra*; (3) numerous translations, commentaries, and textbooks on logic and areas of rhetoric pertaining to logic,[4] and (4) his final and best known work, the *De consolatione philosophiae* (14).

For the most part, Boethius was able to pursue his ambitious project on Aristotle and Plato, but his erudition caught the attention of Theodoric. As a ruler, Theodoric seems to have functioned essentially as an independent monarch, while officially a representative of the eastern emperor.[5] Despite having spent some ten years of his youth in Constantinople, under the auspices of Emperor Leo, Theodoric was not literate, reportedly unable to sign his own name,[6] which is why he relied upon rhetorically educated Romans to compose official documents for him. Over the course of his thirty-three year reign, Theodoric seems to have recognized the value in having his own people and the Romans serve different functions for the state: the Ostrogoths he employed as defenders of the country, the Romans as civil administrators (Barrett 27). In the *Variae*, a collection of official documents written on behalf of Theodoric by Cassiodorus Senator, is the following request:

> Exert yourself therefore, oh Boetius, to get this thing put in hand. You have thoroughly imbued yourself with Greek philosphy. You have translated Pythagoras the musician, Ptolemy the astronomer, Nicomachus the arithmetician, Euclid the geometer, Plato the theologian, Aristotle the logician, and have given back the mechanician Archimedes to his own Sicilian countrymen (who now speak Latin). (Hodgkin, *Variae* I.45, 169)

Around 523, Boethius left Rome and his unfinished work on Aristotle and Plato to accept Theodoric's position as *Magister officiorum*, head of all government and court offices.[7]

In this capacity, Boethius became involved in efforts initiated in 519, by the new eastern emperor, Justin I, to mend the religious rift between orthodox Christians in Rome and those in Constantinople. Theodoric had long been aware that his status as an Arian Christian could be a political liability and had cultivated a climate of religious tolerance during his reign.[8] By 523, though, under considerable political pressure, an aging Theodoric apparently came to suspect the Roman senate of plotting treason with Constantinople against him (Barrett 50–52). When the senator Albinus was accused by court official Cyprian of having written treasonous letters to Emperor Justin, Boethius took Albinus's defense. Rather than dropping the charges, Cyprian turned on Boethius, accusing him of writing letters hoping for "Roman liberty," of suppressing evidence against Albinus, and of engaging in magic.[9] For reasons of their own, members of the Roman Senate did not defend Boethius against the charges; he was found guilty and imprisoned at Ticenum, now Pavia, until his execution.[10] There, while enduring physical torture and awaiting execution, Boethius wrote his most famous work, *De consolatione philosophiae*, one of the most popular books in the Middle Ages.

CONTRIBUTIONS TO THE RHETORICAL TRADITION

Through his various works, Boethius had a profound impact on medieval thinking and rhetorical practice. As Howard Patch summarizes,

> [H]is books were indispensable in European education for centuries; his *Consolatio* was translated by important poets and even by monarchs; and his influence has undeniably given an impulse to artistic creation which we cannot fully trace to-day. "The blessed soul that exposes the deceptive world to anyone who gives ear to him," is how Dante characterized his genius. (1)

Marenbon emphasizes that medieval scholastics, examining faith and classifying knowledge, relied upon the logical works of Boethius to learn about Aristotelian ideas on logic and dialectical argumentation (165). In addition, though Boethius only dealt with rhetoric as it pertained to logic, his analysis of rhetoric in *De topicis differentiis* had a significant effect on how medieval rhetoric was conceptualized and transmitted into the Renaissance.

De consolatione philosophiae

While imprisoned before his death, convinced that evil and corruption were being rewarded with his suffering, Boethius found himself questioning his Christian faith. As he sought to find some comfort and understanding for his fate, he wrote a five-book treatise that transmitted key tenets of Neoplatonism to medieval and Renaissance Christians. Combining Plato with Plotinus and other Neoplatonists, along with Aristotelian logic, Boethius composed a literary dialogue between a character, not unlike himself, and a beautiful woman named Philosophy.[11] Unlike his other writings, this work draws from literary traditions, such as the philosophical dialogues of Plato and Cicero, the *consolatio* genre, and the Roman tradition of Menippean satire, alternating between prose and poetry, and was influenced by the allegorical *De nuptiis Philologiae et Mercurii* of Martianus Capella.[12]

As the dialogue begins, the Boethian character is despairing over his misfortune; he has been wrongly condemned to death, has had all of his possessions seized, and has been thrown into prison. He asks Philosophy how one can believe in divine providence amid such wickedness and oppression. Philosophy responds, "Do you think that this is the first time that Wisdom has been attacked and endangered by a wicked society?"[13] With her guidance, he learns that the only true sources of happiness are the pursuit of Wisdom, which protects us from "crazed ignorance" and "raging stupidity" (I.3.42–48), and the love of God. His mistake, says Philosophy, has been in assuming that pleasure can be derived from transitory possessions, political power or position, or material comforts, all of which she dismisses as "useless baggage" (*inutiles sarcinulas*). Finally, she assures him that wickedness is always punished and virtue always rewarded because "that regard of providence which looks forth on all things from eternity, sees this and disposes all that is predestined to each according to his desserts" (V.2.27–29).

Widely read throughout the Middle Ages, *De consolatione philosophiae* was also translated by King Alfred the Great, in the ninth century; by Notker Labeo, an eleventh-century German monk; by Jean de Meun, a thirteenth-century French poet; by Geoffrey Chaucer in the fourteenth century; even by Elizabeth I, in the sixteenth century. As Patch concludes, its popularity may be explained by its ability to appeal to different audiences:

> To writers of imaginative works it offered inspiration as a work of art through its allegory and through its lyric interludes; on the other hand, to the intellectual it raised interesting questions in an informal and easy manner through its philosophical discussion. The debate on the subject of fate and free will, the treatment of the problem of fortune, the attempt to explain adversity in a universe ruled by a loving God, all show the matter and the manner that were adopted by numerous books in the ages that came after. (Patch 5–6)

De topicis differentiis

Written around 522, this treatise, perhaps more than any other in the Boethian corpus, influenced the development of rhetoric in the Middle Ages.[14] The *Topica Boeti*, as it was known in that era, begins by acknowledging that what Boethius calls the "whole science of discourse (*ratio disserendi*)," or the study of logic (λογική), is comprised of discovery (invention) and judgment (analysis).[15] Boethius aims to show that topics used for discovery or invention (τοπική, *loci*) can all be systematized by the same basic set of distinctions (1173C.9–D.21). While his chief interest is in analyzing topical invention for the field of logic, he cautions against treating only dialectical topics or ignoring the ways in which rhetorical topics are different (1173D.29–1174.C). Nonetheless, as Michael Leff notes, "His concern for rhetoric is purely intellectual and schematic. He has no interest in practical application" ("Boethius's" 22). As a result, the theory of rhetorical topics presented in

De topicis differentiis subordinates rhetoric, which Boethius treats only as rhetorical argumentation, under dialectical theory.

In book 1, Boethius explains that topics assist the discovery of ideas, functioning as seats of argument (*sedes argumentorum*), in four kinds of discourse, dialectic, oratory, philosophy, and sophistic (Murphy 68). As such, topics serve either (1) as abstract premises that express a basic mode of inference (*propositio maxima*) or (2) as headings for classes of arguments (*maximae propositionis differentia*). What Boethius wants to develop is a method for analyzing the second group, topic differences, within a coherent theory of topical argumentation (Leff, "Boethius's" 6–8).

In books 2 and 3, Boethius outlines and explicates Aristotelian and Ciceronian theories of topics and compares Cicero's system with that of Themistius, a fourth-century teacher of Aristotle in Constantinople (see Murphy 69, n. 93). Boethius concludes that topic differences may be classified based on the relationship between the nature of the logical inference and the terms of the proposition in question. Specifically, he identifies three sets of dialectical topic differences (*maximae propositionis differentia*): those intrinsic to the subject, substance, or consequence; those extrinsic to the subject, making comparisons; and those intermediate topics, based on the form of the word. (cf. Leff, "Boethius's" 8).

In book 4, Boethius turns his attention to rhetorical topics and argumentation. He claims that, to distinguish between rhetoric and dialectic, we must consider the nature of each as a faculty (*facultatum*, 1205C.9). Accordingly, in 1205C.14–1207A, Boethius discusses how the two faculties, or disciplines, differ in substance, method, and goals. Dialectic deals with thesis, proceeding through interrogation to examine syllogisms in order to extract the conclusion from the adversary. Rhetoric, on the other hand, deals with hypothesis, proceeding through discourse by means of enthymemes to persuade the judge. Boethius asserts that he also must present an account of the whole art of rhetoric, "a great and difficult task" because "[w]e have received no tradition from the ancient authors on this subject, for they taught the particulars but did not work at the whole at all" (1207A.21–28). In his brief summary of the art of rhetoric, Boethius says the three rhetorical genera are its species; its subject matter is usually a political question; its five parts are all necessary to the oratorical discipline; its instrument is the speech, which has six parts; its work is to teach and to move; the function of its orator is to speak appropriately for persuasion; and its end is to have spoken well or to persuade (1207B–1209A). Boethius then provides a rather conventional discussion of the doctrine of *status*, based largely on Cicero's *De inventione* (Leff, "Boethius's" 11). Noticeably absent from his treatment of rhetoric is any discussion of style, memory, or delivery, as well as any audience-centered topics. In *Rhetoric in the Middle Ages*, James J. Murphy comments, "his total concern with rhetoric as an art is with its function of *inventio*" (71).

Boethius's purpose for book 4 is to demonstrate how rhetorical topics fall under the same categories of topic differences that operate in dialectical theory. The difference, as far as he is concerned, is that rhetorical topics are drawn from circumstances linked to the particular case and draw their proof from that material, unlike dialectical topics, which are independent of circumstances and deal with forms of inference. Similar to dialectical topics, though, rhetorical topical differences may be divided into three logical sets: (1) those intrinsic to the case, including attributes both of the person and of the act itself; (2) those extrinsic to the case, namely, consequences; and (3) those intermediate to the case, that is, adjuncts of the act. As a result, Boethius concludes:

> [T]he rhetorician always proceeds from dialectical Topics, but the dialectician can be content with his own Topics. For since a rhetorician draws cases from circumstances, he takes arguments from the same circumstances; but these must be confirmed by the universal and simple, namely, the dialectical [Topics]. (1215D.21–26)

The *De topicis differentiis* was quite popular during the Middle Ages. Books 1 through 3 served as the major source for dialectical theory in European universities, as part of the "Old Logic." Despite its narrow focus, book 4, or *Topica IV*, came to be used separately as a standard reference text on rhetoric at Paris and Oxford and was cited as late as the fifteenth century by Traversagni (Leff, "Boethius's" 4). Its popularity had far-reaching consequences for the classical rhetorical tradition. Not only did rhetoric become reduced to a subcategory of logical argumentation, but also it was removed from its classical foundations in public practice. Leff explains, "Boethius could view the topics of rhetoric as special instances of dialectical topics, emphasizing their logical form and ignoring their function in relation to the audience" ("Boethius's" 23). As a result, the conception of rhetoric and how it should function changed significantly, and medieval scholars tended to view it as a preceptive art to be applied to other types of discursive action, such as preaching and letter or poetry writing, and recognized for its diverse uses rather than by any single body of theoretical doctrine.

HISTORICAL SIGNIFICANCE

Apart from the intellectual and literary influence he exerted on the rhetorical tradition, Boethius is considered a significant historical figure in at least two other respects. From the time of his death until the eighteenth century, he was regarded as a martyr to the Catholic faith by those who viewed his execution as religious persecution. His theological tractates helped support this view, and he came to be revered by some as "Saint Severinus." In 1883, Pope Leo XIII approved of him as a saint for the diocese of Pavia (Barrett 3).

Boethius also had considerable impact on the development of medieval logic and philosophy. Although there is no evidence that his logical writings, especially Porphyry's *Isagoge* and Aristotle's *Organon*, were read significantly before the eleventh century (Grabmann 10; Marenbon 165), his translations and commentaries came to be the basic texts for medieval Scholasticism, dominating the training of medieval clergy and those in the court schools. Before the thirteenth century,

Western Europe knew about Greek philosophy only through Boethius's translations. Stump claims, "he was one of the main influences on the early scholastics and was an authority for them second perhaps only to Augustine among Christian philosophers" (15). Brian Davies is even more emphatic: "Nobody seriously concerned with medieval philosophy and theology, whether from the historical or evaluative perspective, can afford to ignore him" (Marenbon xi). Nonetheless, the impact Boethius made on medieval Latin culture was not only for serving as an intellectual conduit for others, but also for the imprint he left with his own original ideas.

NOTES

1. H. F. Stewart and E. K. Rand, "Life of Boethius," in Boethius's *Tractates, De consolatione philosophiae* xii. Cf. Eleonore Stump ("Introduction" to her translation of *De topicis differentiis* 13), who adds her own "and the tutor of the Middle Ages"; and Howard Patch (*The Tradition of Boethius* 2), who attributes the first part to Henry Osborn Taylor and the second to Arturo Graf.

2. His name is also spelled "Odovacar." Helen Barrett argues that in terms of the political impact upon the people of that time, this act was more symbolic than substantive. The Roman Empire had been largely unstable politically throughout the fifth century. See her discussion, *Boethius* 9–17.

3. See Stump's discussion of this debate in "Introduction," 13–14. Cf. Barrett, *Boethius* 35.

4. A detailed study of the chronology of Boethius's logical works has been made by L. M. de Rijk. Cf. Stump's short summary, "Introduction," 15.

5. Technically, Theodoric was king of the Ostrogoths; his Roman citizens and he himself remained subjects of the emperor in Constantinople (Barrett 26).

6. Refer to Barrett's account of his life, 18–32.

7. In his *De consolatione philosophiae*, Boethius claims that he made this decision based on Plato's teaching in the *Republic*: "You, through that same Plato, told us that this was why philosophers must involve themselves in political affairs, lest the rule of nations be left to the base and wicked" (I.4.21–25).

8. Most of the Teutonic people of this time were recognized as Arian Christians because their conversion from heathenism had resulted from the teachings of Bishop Ulfilas, the "Apostle of the Goths," rather than the ministry of the Catholic Church. See Barrett 30–32.

9. Marenbon 9. This last charge was based on Boethius's work in mathematics and astrology.

10. The evidence against Boethius now seems doubtful, the alleged motivation for treason is inconsistent with his character, and he maintained to the end that his accusers were lying. Refer to Barrett's review of the trial, 57–74.

11. On the originality of this composition and its use of Neoplatonic doctrine, see Patch, who argues that "Neoplatonists led men to the worship of intellect; Boethius brought them to God," 4–5.

12. For an extensive analysis of this treatise, see Marenbon 96–163.

13. *De consolatione philosophiae* I.3.15–17, trans. Stewart et al.

14. Michael Leff offers different reasons why this work on topical invention, not rhetoric, was so attractive to medieval scholars in "Boethius and the History of Medieval Rhetoric" 140.

15. *De topicis differentiis* 1173C.3, trans. Stump.

Bibliography

Primary Sources and Translations

Boetii, Anicii Manlii Severini. *Opera.* Ed. Ludovicus Bieler. Corpus Christianorum, Series Latina, vol. 94. Turnholt: Brepols, 1957.

———. *Opera.* Ed. Samuel Brandt. Corpus Scriptorum Ecclesiasticorum Latinorum, vol. 48. Vindobonae: Tempsky, 1906.

———. *Opera omnia.* Ed. J.-P. Migne. Patrologiae latinae, Vol. 64. Paris: Migne and his Successors, 1891.

Boethius. *De topicis differentiis.* Trans. Eleonore Stump. Ithaca: Cornell UP, 1978.

———. *In Ciceronis topica.* Trans. Eleonore Stump. Ithaca: Cornell UP, 1988.

———. *Tractates, De consolatione philosophiae.* Trans. H. F. Stewart, E. K. Rand, and S. J. Tester. Cambridge: Harvard UP, 1973.

Cassiodori Senatoris. *Variae.* Ed. Theodore Mommsen. Berlin: Weidmann, 1894.

Cassiodorus. *Institutiones.* Ed. R. A. B. Mynors. Oxford: Clarendon, 1937.

———. *The Letters of Cassiodorus: A Condensed Translation of the* Variae Epistolae *of Magnus Aurelius Cassiodorus Senator.* Ed. Thomas Hodgkin. London: Henry Frowde, 1886.

Notker Labeo. *Boethius, De Consolatione Philosophiae.* Ed. Petrus W. Tax. Altdeusche Textbibliothek 94, 100, 101. Tübingen: M. Niermeyer, 1986.

Radulphus, Brito. *Commentary on Boethius'* De differentiis topicis *and the Sophism* "Omnis homo est omnis homo." Ed. Niels Jørgen Green-Pedersen and Jan Pinborg. Copenhague: Université de Copenhague, 1978.

Biographical Sources

Barrett, Helen Marjorie. *Boethius: Some Aspects of His Times and Work.* Cambridge: Cambridge UP, 1940.

Bury, John Bagnell. *History of the Later Roman Empire from the Death of Theodosius I. to the Death of Justinian (A.D. 395 to A.D. 565).* Vol. 2. New York: Dover, 1958. Ch. 18.

Chadwick, Henry. *Boethius: The Consolations of Music, Logic, Theology, and Philosophy.* Oxford: Clarendon, 1981.

Fuhrmann, Manfred, and Joachim Gruber. *Boethius.* Wege der Forschung 483. Darmstadt: Wissenschafliche Buchgesellschaft, 1984.

Gibson, Margaret T., ed. *Boethius: His Life, Thought and Influence.* Oxford: Basil Blackwell, 1981.

Marenbon, John. *Boethius.* Oxford and New York: Oxford UP, 2003.

Masi, Michael, ed. *Boethius and the Liberal Arts.* Barne: Peter Lang, 1981.

McInerny, Ralph. *Boethius and Aquinas.* Washington, DC: Catholic U of America P, 1990.

Obertello, Luca. *Severino Boezio.* I and II. Collana de monografie, 1. Genoa: Accademia ligure di scienze e lettere, 1974.

Patch, Howard Rollin. *The Tradition of Boethius: A Study of His Importance in Medieval Culture.* New York: Oxford UP, 1935.

Reiss, Edmund. *Boethius.* Boston: Twayne, 1982.

Stewart, Hugh Fraser. *Boethius, An Essay.* London: W. Blackwood, 1891.

Critical Sources

Alfonsi, Luigi. "Studi Boeziani." *Aevum* 19 (1945): 142–57.

———. "Studi Boeziani (continua)." *Aevum* 25 (1951): 132–46, 210–29.

Brandt, Samuel. "Entstehungszeit und zeitliche Folge der Werke von Boethius." *Philologus* 62 (1903): 141–54; 234–75.

Conley, Thomas M. *Rhetoric in the European Tradition.* Chicago and London: U of Chicago P, 1990.

Courcelle, Pierre-Paul. *"La Consolation de Philosophie" dans la tradition littéraire, antecedents et posterité de Boèce.* Paris: Études augustinienne, 1967.

———. *Late Latin Writers and Their Greek Sources.* Trans. Harry E. Wedeck. Cambridge: Harvard UP, 1969 [1948].

de Rijk, Lambertus Marie. "On the Chronology of Boethius' Works on Logic." I and II. *Vivarium* 2 (1964): 1–49, 122–62.

De Vogel, Cornelia J. "Boethiana." I and II. *Vivarium* 9 (1971): 49–66, and 10 (1972): 1–40.

Frakes, Jerold C. *The Fate of Fortune in the Early Middle Ages: The Boethian Tradition.* Studien und Texte zur Geistesgeschichte des Mittelalters 23. Leiden and New York: E. J. Brill, 1988.

Gibson, Margaret, and L. Smith. *Codices Boethiani. A Conspectus of the Manuscripts of the Works of Boethius.* Surveys and Texts 25. London: Warburg Institute, 1996.

Grabmann, Martin. *Die Geschichte der scholastischen Methode.* 2 vols. Freiburg im Bresgau and St. Louis, MO, 1909–11.

Green-Pedersen, Niels Jørgen. *The Tradition of the Topics in the Middle Ages: The Commentaries on Aristotle's and Boethius' Topics.* München: Philosophia Verlag, 1984.

Hoenen, Maarten J. F. M., and Lodi Nanta, eds. *Boethius in the Middle Ages: Latin and Vernacular Traditions of the* Consolatio philosophiae. Studien und Texte zur Geistesgeschichte des Mittelalters 58. Leiden and New York: Brill, 1997.

Leff, Michael C. "Boethius and the History of Medieval Rhetoric." *Central State Speech Journal* 25 (1974): 135–41.

———. "Boethius's *De differentiis topicis*, Book IV." *Medieval Eloquence: Studies in the Theory and Practice of Medieval Rhetoric.* Ed. James J. Murphy. Berkeley and Los Angeles: U of California P, 1978. 3–24.

Lerer, Seth. *Boethius and Dialogue: Literary Method in* The Consolation of Philosophy. Princeton: Princeton UP, 1985.

Magee, John. *Boethius on Signification and Mind.* Philosophia Antiqua 52. London and New York: Brill, 1989.

McKeon, Richard. "The Methods of Rhetoric and Philosophy: Invention and Judgment." *The Classical Tradition: Literary and Historical Studies in Honor of Harry Caplan.* Ed. Luitpold Wallach. Ithaca: Cornell UP, 1966. 365–73.

McKinlay, Arthur Patch. "Stylistic Tests and the Chronology of the Works of Boethius." *Harvard Studies in Classical Philology* 18 (1907): 123–56.

Minnis, Alastair J., ed. *The Medieval Boethius: Studies in the Vernacular Translations of* "De Consolatione Philosophie." Cambridge: Brewer, 1987.

Murphy, James J. *Rhetoric in the Middle Ages: A History of Rhetorical Theory from Saint Augustine to the Renaissance*. Berkeley: U of California P, 1974.

Nietzsche, Friedrich. *Das System des Boethius*. Berlin: Wiegandt und Grieben, 1860.

O'Daly, Gerald J. P. *The Poetry of Boethius*. Chapel Hill: U of North Carolina P, 1991.

Shanzer, Danuta. "The Death of Boethius and the 'Consolation of Philosophy.' " *Hermes* 117 (1984): 352–66.

Shiel, James. "Boethius' Commentaries on Aristotle." *Medieval and Renaissance Studies* 4 (1958): 217–44.

Solmsen, Friedrich. "Boethius and the History of the *Organon*." *American Journal of Philology* 65 (1944): 69–74.

Stump, Eleonore. "Boethius's Works on the Topics." *Vivarium* 12 (1974): 77–93.

———. "Dialectic and Boethius's *De topicis differentiis*." In *Dialectic and Its Place in the Development of Medieval Logic*. Ithaca: Cornell UP, 1989. 31–56.

JOHN CHRYSOSTOM

(349–407 CE)

Justin Killian and David M. Timmerman

John of Antioch (John Chrysostom) represents one of the most animated orators of the early Christian church. He has been referred to as "Chrysostom" (meaning golden mouthed) since the fifth century CE. In 349 CE, Chrysostom was born into an upper-class family. He was trained in rhetoric and then baptized into the church in the early 370s. Soon after his conversion, there was a movement to have him ordained. Chrysostom resisted and instead joined a vigorous and ascetically severe Syrian monastic movement, living in the mountains outside Antioch. His monastic life began in a semicommunal form, but he ultimately adopted isolationism and stern asceticism. During this time he wrote "Against those who Oppose the Monastic Life," an essay encouraging wealthy parents to persuade their young sons to become monks.

Chrysostom returned to Antioch in the late 370s in failing health due to his monastic practices. He was ordained a deacon in 381 and spent the next two decades preaching as bishop and archbishop in both Antioch and Constantinople. He provoked resentment by ending many of the excesses of his predecessors. For example, he refused to hold the lavish dinner parties that they customarily had. In addition, he sold many expensive furnishings from the bishop's residence and donated the proceeds to the poor.

Chrysostom eventually transformed his knowledge of rhetoric to the benefit of his liturgical career. His sermons illustrate the blending of rhetorical style and Christian theology into a powerful public voice. He is regarded to this day as the greatest preacher of the Greek church. He explicitly notes the influence of Isocrates, Demosthenes, Thucydides, and Plato in his development. While Augustine developed what was to become the dominant understanding of the relationship between Christianity and its surrounding culture through his writings in the West, Chrysostom implemented an approach that at the level of praxis was very close to Augustine's through his preaching in the East.

John Chrysostom was a virulent, outspoken critic of what he took to be the failings of the social, political, and religious leaders of his day. He railed against the paganism of the city and the church. His exposition of biblical texts demonstrates his deep commitment to the faith and his passion for urging Christians to dedicate their lives to the teachings of Christianity. His legacy to the rhetorical tradition lies most prominently in the manner in which he united the classical rhetorical tradition with Christian homiletical practice. He is the practitioner closest to his contemporary Augustine, the theologian and theoretician. He died in the fall of 407 CE, in exile from Antioch.

CHRYSOSTOM'S RHETORICAL PRACTICE

Chrysostom was educated in the traditional, classical style. He studied rhetoric with Libanius, a famous Hellenist and essential figure in the Second Sophistic movement. Libanius encouraged pupils to use their rhetorical training not simply to speak well or persuade, but to evoke a sense of zeal and conviction within an audience. He believed that *paideia*, or the use of classical texts to promote virtue, was the true purpose of rhetoric. Libanius's style stressed *logoi*, the use of classical writings to add validity to a work. Thus, Chrysostom learned to use myths as allegorical examples that could inspire and persuade an audience and to encourage adherence as an ethically laudable and virtuous decision.

After finishing with Libanius, Chrysostom quickly became a master of rhetorical style. He claimed that sermon writing, like preparation for a banquet or feast, must be diverse and extensive. To hold the attention of the audience, both the chef and the orator must keep their production interesting and diverse. Chrysostom states, "We must not set before them a meal prepared haphazardly, but a variety of dishes so the patient may choose which suits his taste. We should proceed in the same way in spiritual banquets. Since we are weak the sermon must be varied and embellished; it must contain comparisons, examples, elaborations, digressions, and the like so that we may select what will profit our soul" (*Proph. Obscur I*: 56.165, in Wilken, *John Chrysostom* 106–07). If his public discourse was to help Christianity in its quest for religious superiority, then his sermons had to be brilliantly composed and utilize the full range of persuasive techniques from the classical tradition.

As an early church father, Chrysostom sought to persuade listeners to abandon paganism and to follow Christianity, which he considered the true religion. Because Christianity and state-sponsored paganism were rivals, he could not use pagan literature as inspiration from the Christian pulpit. He was, however, able to use rhetorical technique to great effect. He simply relied on Christianity, not paganism, for his source of virtue. Through this means he crafted a Christian *logoi* rooted in biblical texts and Christian theology. His *logoi* replaced Hellenism with Christianity, and it solved the central paradox of the church during this period; how the Christian church would relate to its surrounding culture. Chrysostom guided the church down a path that is followed by the vast majority of churches to this day: mimicking the form of the surrounding culture while propagating a different content. Chrysostom crafted a technique that combined ancient practice and biblical belief, bridging the gap between rhetorical style and Christian theology.

Ultimately, Chrysostom's rhetorical transformation crafted a new set of rules from which he conveyed his religious agenda. In transforming rhetorical practice to suit the Christian tradition, Chrysostom enabled Christianity to absorb the tools necessary to win the hearts and minds of the masses. Rhetoric allowed for the promotion of Christian theology within the Roman Empire and eventually the majority of the Western world.

The extant works of Chrysostom consist of a number of essays (e.g., "On the Priesthood," "On Monasticism," "On Baptism"), a number of letters, and a larger number of sermons on biblical texts. This last category includes homilies on the entire gospel of Matthew, the book of Acts, and most of the epistles. These sermons are marked by the consistent use of a clear expository style that powerfully presses the audience with the principles of specific biblical texts. Chrysostom typically takes the passages line by line, explaining the grammatical details and historical and cultural contexts. His rhetorical practice is marked by a high degree of authoritativeness and demonstrativeness and, always, a direct call to virtuous, Christian living.

CHRYSOSTOM'S RECEPTION

Chrysostom understandably has come under attack because several of his writings were anti-Semitic treatises. These are typically given the disputed title, "Against the Jews." These writings cannot be excused, but scholarly investigations must consider the historical and religious circumstances in which these ten sermons were written (Bloch; Jones; Wilken, *John Chrysostom*). During this period, the Emperor Julian, a friend of Libanius, had a short-lived yet influential reign from 361 to 363 CE. During this time, he revived Hellenistic religious practices and sought to reduce the influence of Christianity. Julian made plans to rebuild the temple in Jerusalem, and he offered state support for Judaism in an attempt to reduce the influence of Christianity. Even after his reign, the Roman governmental structure played a role in the resurgence of both Judaism and Judaizing Christians in the Near East.

It seems clear from his sermons that many in Chrysostom's church were following Jewish practices while keeping their Christian traditions. Chrysostom's sermons were delivered before Christian audiences in an attempt to stop the adherence to two religions simultaneously. If Christianity was to become the dominant religion of the empire, as Chrysostom clearly hoped, it had to deter its followers from visiting the synagogue and participating in Jewish festivities. Chrysostom's sermons attacked the movement by comparing Jews to a sickness and equating the synagogue to a place of sin. Sadly, Chrysostom tried to end Judaizing by painting Jews and their practices as less than human. As such, Chrysostom's anti-Jewish homilies are errant and dangerous. They are a prime example of the misuse of the rhetorical tradition in that they exaggerate for the purpose of falsely attacking a class of individuals and failing to respect either audience or subject.

Rhetorical scholars continue to examine Chrysostom's contribution to rhetorical theory and practice (Mitchell), as well as his contribution to the development of homiletics during this period (Kelly). Chrysostom's most significant rhetorical contribution was in the creation of a public discourse for Christianity. In the fourth century, early church leaders, as well as the imperial government of Rome, actively sought a way to bolster the growth of Christianity. Both church and government leaders wanted Christianity to triumph as the main religion of the empire, and it was Chrysostom who blended Christian belief and rhetoric for this purpose.

BIBLIOGRAPHY

Primary Sources and Translations

Chrysostom, John. *A Select Library of the Nicene and Post-Nicene Fathers of the Christian Church.* Ed. Philip Schaff. New York: Christian Literature, 1886–90.

Schatkin, Margaret, ed. "St. John Chrysostom's Homily on the Protopaschites." *Orientalia Christiana Analecta* 195 (1973): 167–86.

Biographical Sources

Bauer, Chrysostomus. 1870. *John Chrysostom and His Time.* 2 vols. Trans. M. Gonzaga. Westminster, MD: Newman P, 1959–60.

Jones, A. H. M. "St. John Chrysostom's Parentage and Education." *Harvard Theological Review* 46 (1953): 171–73.

Critical Sources

Bloch, Herbert. "The Pagan Revival in the West at the End of the Fourth Century." *The Conflict between Paganism and Christianity in the Fourth Century.* Ed. A. Momigliano. Oxford: Oxford UP, 1963. 193–218.

Burger, Douglas C. *Complete Bibliography of Scholarship on the Life and Works of Saint John Chrysostom.* Diss. Ann Arbor: U Microfilms, 1967.

Burns, Mary A. *Saint John Chrysostom's Homilies on the Statues: A Study of Their Rhetorical Qualities and Forms.* Washington, DC: Catholic U of America P, 1930.

Goodall, Blake. *The Homilies of St. John Chrysostom on the Letters of Paul to Titus and Philemon.* Berkeley: U of California P, 1979.

Hubbell, Harry M. "Chrysostom and Rhetoric." *Classical Philology* 19 (1924): 261–76.

Jones, A. H. M. "The Social Background of the Struggle between Paganism and Christianity." *The Conflict between Paganism and Christianity in the Fourth Century.* Ed. A. Momigliano. Oxford: Oxford UP, 1964.

Kelly, John N. D. *Golden Mouth: The Story of John Chrysostom—Ascetic, Preacher, Bishop.* Ithaca: Cornell UP, 1995.

Maat, William A. *A Rhetorical Study of St. John Chrysostom's De Sacerdotio*. Washington, DC: Catholic U of America P, 1944.

Mitchell, Margaret. *The Heavenly Trumpet: John Chrysostom and the Art of Pauline Interpretation*. Louisville, KY: Westminster John Knox P, 2002.

Stephens, William R. W. *Saint Chrysostom. His Life and Times: A Sketch of the Church and the Empire in the Fourth Century*. London: J. Murray, 1872.

Wilken, Robert L. *John Chrysostom and the Jews: Rhetoric and Reality in the Late 4th Century*. Berkeley: U of California P, 1983.

———. "Pagan Criticism of Christianity: Greek Religion and Christian Faith." *Early Christian Literature and the Classical Intellectual Tradition*. Ed. Robert L. Wilken and William R. Schoedel. Paris: Editions Beauchesne, 1979. 117–34.

Marcus Tullius Cicero

(106–43 BCE)

Richard Leo Enos

Marcus Tullius Cicero was a prominent Roman politician whose career as a senator and consul was inextricably bound with the most significant events of the late Republic. Cicero is also recognized as a preeminent advocate, and his forensic arguments have become a standard for effective legal argument. In both politics and law, the source for Cicero's impact came principally from his rhetorical ability. Through his eloquence, Cicero was able to persuade his colleagues in ways that shaped the legal and political history of Rome. As such, Cicero has become a paradigm for the importance of eloquence in civic affairs and a central figure in the history of rhetoric. What makes Cicero unique for our discipline is that he was not only an exemplary model of rhetoric but also an astute theoretician. Through his orations, his theories of rhetoric, and his other numerous writings, we have the most complete picture of any figure in ancient rhetoric. There is a tremendous advantage in having this repository of information available for the study of such a preeminent figure in our history. Because of our extensive knowledge of Cicero, we have been able to contextualize both his theory and practice of rhetoric to a much greater degree than those of any other figure in ancient rhetoric and therefore advance more sensitive and detailed observations than for other individuals of the classical period.

Cicero has had an enduring impact in the history of rhetoric. In the last several decades, historians of ancient rhetoric have emphasized the importance of Aristotle and his volume, *The Art of Rhetoric*, to such an extent that current students may well be inclined to infer that Aristotelian rhetoric dominated the history of rhetoric in the West. The principle reasons for the current popularity of Aristotelian rhetoric center on its applicability as a theory and its relevance to the modern teaching of rhetoric. Aristotle's rhetoric is contained in a coherent and unified offering. The heuristics derived from Aristotle's *Rhetoric* are readily transferred to a semester's worth of instruction in both oral and written rhetoric. Cicero's rhetorical theory, however, is dispersed throughout several works and is oriented toward both a curriculum of study and a broad-based application in civic affairs. As such, it is much more difficult to synthesize the heuristics from Ciceronian rhetoric that can be applied in the classroom. Yet Cicero, along with his model Isocrates, are the pillars upon which the curriculum for humanistic education in the West was constructed.

In point of fact, and only until the twentieth century, Ciceronian rhetoric was the dominant paradigm of our discipline's history. A prolific writer and practitioner of rhetoric, Cicero's theories about effective expression as well as his orations became standards for artistic expression. His speeches and rhetorical theory not only were models but also say much about the social and cultural climate of the Roman Republic and, of equal importance, offer lessons for our own times. Cicero's other writings in philosophy and ethics, as well as his hundreds of personal letters to friends and influential political figures, provide the most extensive information for study of any individual in classical rhetoric. So profound and enduring was Cicero's impact that the demarcation for many of the subsequent periods of the history of rhetoric in the West is defined by how the principles of Ciceronian rhetoric were discovered, applied, modified, or even abandoned.

CICERO'S EDUCATION AND CAREER AS AN ADVOCATE

Because Cicero's rhetoric is grounded in his education and practical experience, it is therefore necessary to understand the forces that helped to shape his theory. Unlike many of his prominent colleagues, Cicero was not born into an affluent, patrician Roman family, but rather came from the small village of Arpinum, which is approximately sixty miles from Rome. Cicero was born a Roman citizen, but his family ranked only as members of the equestrian class, an order that we best understand as upper middle class and far below the elite patrician class of Roman "aristocracy." Even at the earliest age, as Plutarch's account reveals, Cicero's abilities as a student were apparent (*Parallel Lives*). Coming from a family of moderate wealth, Cicero had the opportunity for higher education; his native talent made the advanced study of rhetoric a natural fit. Rome was predominantly an oral society and, correspondingly, much of the study of rhetoric focused on oral argument through declamation. Yet, as we shall see, it was also Cicero's ability as a writer that distinguished him from other rhetoricians. In fact, just as Isocrates is recognized by H. I. Marrou as the first literate rhetorician in Greece (79–81), we may extend that point and say that Cicero was, if not the first, certainly the most preeminent literate rhetorician of the Roman Republic.

In order to seize the advantages of education, Cicero was required to go to Rome. At this point in the Republic, Rome was a center for rhetorical education. The military and commercial achievements that Romans gained in the preceding generations not only resulted in the city's immense new wealth, but also reinforced the success of the republican system of government. That is, stunning political and military gains underscored for Romans the belief that the republican system provided an atmosphere whereby merit was rewarded. Moreover, and as noted above, much of the political and legal affairs of the Republic were deliberated orally. The judgments that were made in republican Rome were shaped by effective argument in both the Senate and courts. The environment for open deliberation was important for, in an oral society, Cicero's ability in rhetoric could be utilized.

Through his own accounts and our knowledge of Roman history, it is clear that Cicero benefited from the advantage of distinguished educators. Cicero's early remarks in *De Amicitia* offer his own account of those early years, as do his retrospective comments in his *Brutus* and *Tusculanae Disputationes*. As was typical of many aspiring Romans, Cicero's early training in declamation focused on legal and deliberative argument with an eye toward a political career. Along with his training in Rome, Cicero studied abroad from 79 to 77 BCE and was educated in ethics, philosophy, and rhetoric by some of the most prominent Sophists in Athens, Rhodes, and Asia Minor. There is little doubt, however, that Cicero had been introduced to Greek education in Rome prior to his study abroad. Many prominent Hellenic educators, from the mainland as well as from the Greek cities of southern Italy, came to Rome. Yet, as his later works reveal, Cicero believed his Hellenic training abroad was invaluable and his mastery of Greek gave him access to knowledge that was beyond the limits of many of his Roman contemporaries.

PARTY POLITICS AND CIVIC VIRTUE

We can better understand the merits of Ciceronian rhetoric if we realize that the standards for judgment in Roman rhetoric were not determined by the rigors of philosophical logic but rather the norms of rationality determined by the Republic in which he lived. For Cicero, rhetoric was studied for its instrumental value: the study of rhetoric helped to secure agreement through suasory eloquence in civic matters. Cicero began his political career shortly after his return from study in Greece and steadily rose through the *cursus honorum*, or normal course of offices for political advancement. Why would Romans choose to enter a life of politics? Many doubtlessly were attracted to the dynamics, power, and glory that are associated with being a social force. If we are to believe his own words, Cicero's personal motivation was amazingly consistent throughout his life. Throughout his works, Cicero stresses his obligation to serve Rome by using his ability in rhetoric to maintain the best that the republican form of government could offer. Involvement in politics is a natural condition of Ciceronian rhetoric.

Cicero believed that his best and earliest opportunity for political recognition came when he served as quaestor in Sicily, Rome's oldest colony, in 75 BCE. Much of Sicily was populated by earlier-formed Greek colonies, and Cicero's familiarity with Greek and his intimacy with Hellenic culture were understandable assets to his position. At that time, Rome was undergoing a famine and Cicero's diligence in supplying Rome with Sicilian grain was (he thought) a notable accomplishment. It was Cicero's belief that his efforts would be widely acknowledged and appreciated when he completed his duties and returned to Rome. After his office was completed, however, Cicero returned to Rome to discover that his efforts were all but unnoticed; it is from this point that Cicero concentrated on building his political career through his ability as an advocate.

The Republic had very clear avenues for success. The famous Roman "dynasts" who were Cicero's contemporaries achieved their status through the conventional paths of success. Lucius Licinius Crassus was influential because of his immense wealth and ancestry. Gaius Pompey rose to power because of his military accomplishments. Julius Caesar emerged as the dominant force because of his military genius and astute sense of party politics. Ancestry, wealth, and military triumphs were the dominant routes to power in the Republic. Yet, to a degree, Cicero helped to create yet another source of power: the power of rhetoric. Lacking enormous wealth, denied patrician status, and wanting in military brilliance, Cicero realized that his ability in rhetoric could be a source of power. Recognized as brilliant in both oral and written argument, Cicero applied his rhetorical training to become one of Rome's most powerful advocates and eloquent politicians.

Cicero achieved his status as Rome's preeminent advocate when he successfully prosecuted Gaius Verres in 70 BCE for the many crimes Verres committed as governor of Sicily. Cicero's triumph in Verres' case came by defeating the opposing advocate, Quintus Hortensius Hortalus, who was then recognized as Rome's leading forensic orator. As mentioned above, Cicero's familiarity with Sicily, exhaustive preparation for the case, and excellent opening arguments secured a decisive victory. The recognition that Cicero earned continued to grow with subsequent court victories. Cicero used his career as an advocate to gain support through the successful defense of many influential *clientelae*, and through their influence established a basis of patronage that enabled him to become consul in 63 BCE; in fact, Cicero became the first *novus homo*, or "new man," to be so elected in approximately thirty years. Cicero's rise in politics came about because of his ability in rhetoric. Cicero demonstrated that rhetoric could be not only an instrument for regulating the norms of civic virtue, but also a source of political power in the Republic.

Cicero's ability in rhetoric was also his primary political weapon. During his consulship, Cicero successfully suppressed a reactionary conspiracy to overthrow the government led by Catiline. While his rhetoric against Catiline thwarted a conservative revolution—thus resolving an imminent, pragmatic problem—the subsequent publication of his *In Catilinam* transcended the moment and became a classic statement for the ideals of a free and just government. An unabashed champion of republicanism during a period of sycophancy, duplicity, and opportunism, Cicero alienated many powerful Romans and was, for a brief period, exiled. Although his return from exile was widely hailed, Cicero was disenchanted with the rampant pettiness of party politics in Rome and turned away from an active political career to writing. Many of Cicero's most important works on rhetoric were composed from 56 to 44 BCE, and we can see in these writings not only a well-trained theoretical mind but also a well-practiced, experience authority. It is this unique combination of talent, practice, and experience that make Cicero's works on rhetoric so influential.

Cicero opened his most influential work on rhetoric, *De Oratore*, with his desire to have "*otium cum dignitatae*" or "retirement with dignity" from politics. In point of fact, however, Cicero never really was allowed to retire from politics and remained a visible political figure. His eloquent diatribes against those who threatened the harmony and welfare of the Republic (the *concordia ordinum*) became both the subjects and the targets of his civic orations. So adamant was Cicero's belief in the Republic that he used his rhetorical force to oppose the political career and plans of his lifelong associate Caesar and even sided with Brutus in his efforts to save the Republic. Cicero's most vitriolic orations were against Mark Antony. Cicero's orations against Antony, called the *Philippicae* because they were intended to complement the speeches of Demosthenes against Philip of Macedonia, largely contributed to his own death. Even those who disagreed with Cicero's political philosophy respected the intent of his civic virtue. A longtime admirer of Cicero's contributions to the Republic, Augustus (then Octavius) sought to keep Cicero's name off Antony's death list. Antony eventually succeeded in having Cicero murdered and had Cicero's dismembered head and hands mounted on the Rostra for public display. Antony's vitriolic remark was that he wished to have the hands that wrote the *Philippicae*. In the earlier-mentioned account of Cicero's life, Plutarch records that the animosity toward Cicero was so bitter that Antony's wife, Fluvia, stuck a pin in Cicero's tongue. Ever the moralist, Plutarch wrote that when viewers saw this despicable sight, they viewed not the disgrace of Cicero but rather the darkness of Antony's own soul. Augustus, however, maintained his affection and appreciation for Cicero long after the Republic had given way to the Empire. By Suetonius's account (*Divius Iulius*), Augustus provided the best view of Cicero, for when he found his grandsons hiding the works of Cicero that they had been reading for fear of being "caught," he rebuked them not because they were reading the words of a republican but rather that they had not appreciated how and why Cicero gave his life for Rome. Augustus explained that Cicero was a champion of liberty and returned the books to the boys so that they might learn from a true lover of Rome.

CICERO'S *RHETORICA*

Cicero wrote several works on rhetoric throughout his life, which are collectively known as his *Rhetorica*. Although the *De Inventione* (ca. 86 BCE) dates back to his youth, the majority of his *Rhetorica* were written after his consulship and return from exile. That is, the body of work on rhetoric that we have from Cicero comes after considerable experience in politics and law and thus offers views that are not only theoretically sophisticated but also grounded in practical experience. Despite the availability of Cicero's rhetorical theory, much of the scholarship on Cicero has been directed toward his orations. His speeches did serve as models throughout the history of rhetoric, and it is not uncommon for historians of rhetoric to extract principles of rhetoric from his addresses. John Kirby's rhetorical analysis of Cicero's *Pro Cluentio* is an excellent example of what we can learn from Cicero's application of theory into practice. In a sense, Cicero's oratory has become ancient literature. The enduring attractiveness of his lively orations, the timelessness of the issues that he faced, and the general romanticism of this tumultuous period have all contributed to the enduring popularity of his speeches. The popularity of Cicero's oratory overshadows the study of his insightful rhetorical theory. Scholarly editions of Cicero's *Rhetorica*, letters, and orations are available from Oxford University Press and B. G. Teubner (Classical) Texts. Augustus S. Wilkins's edition of *De Oratore* (Georg Olms, 1965) is an excellent example of such scholarship, particularly the introduction, which is dated but thorough. The Loeb Classical Library of Harvard University Press offers English translations along with the Latin text and includes all the major rhetorical works, letters, and orations of Cicero. Secondary scholarship on Cicero's oratory is extensive but, as indicated above, much less research has been done on his rhetorical theory.

There are reasons why Cicero's theoretical works, the focus of this essay, have received far less scholarly attention than his oratory. Not only, as mentioned above, did Cicero write on rhetoric in several volumes and across several decades, but he modified his views across time. These modifications, however, are very important to note since they are frequently based on direct experiences in the courts and Senate. One further item to note in Cicero's *Rhetorica* is that he frequently discussed principles of rhetoric in works that are considered to be nonrhetorical. Often these principles are mentioned in his philosophical treatises, but examples of comments on rhetorical theory can even be found in many other works, including his private letters. This eclectic habit makes Cicero's "rhetoric" difficult to synthesize into a single, unified theory and makes virtually every point subject to qualification. Yet, there are persistent tenets that serve as the foundation for his views and reveal a coherent theoretical view.

As mentioned above, Cicero's earliest treatise, *De Inventione*, was written ca. 86 BCE and endured through the Middle Ages as one of the most important works on rhetoric in the Latin-speaking West. There is good reason to believe, however, that *De Inventione* was largely Cicero's adaptation of existing manuals. A clear Greek influence is evident in both his concepts and his obvious homage to Isocrates when discussing the social importance of rhetoric and oratory. Despite the title, a large part of this (fragmentary) treatise is devoted to arrangement and how invention is "localized" within the disposition of rhetorical composition. In this work, Cicero reveals the close ties between the creation of argument and how argument is situated within discourse. In this respect, Cicero provides us with an early illustration of what he consistently stressed throughout his later works, that the canons of rhetoric— invention, arrangement, style, memory, and delivery—should be best understood as coordinated and interactive. As insightful as Cicero's youthful observations were, Cicero later exhorted his readers to ignore this work. In the opening passages of his *De Oratore*, Cicero devalued his youthful *De Inventione* as nothing more than the notes of a schoolboy. Ironically, however, *De Inventione* was enduringly popular, becoming one of his few treatises to survive until the eventual rediscovery of many of his other works on rhetoric in the Middle Ages and Renaissance.

There is little question that *De Oratore* (55 BCE) is Cicero's major treatise on rhetoric and remains one of the most important statements on the place of rhetoric in society. *De Oratore* is best understood not as a *ratio*, or manual packed with prescriptive schemes, but rather as a philosophical justification for the importance of studying rhetoric as a humanistic discipline in a society valuing free expression. The dialogue format of *De Oratore* allows Cicero to create powerfully charged and pointed exchanges on the relative merits of rhetoric specifically and a liberal education generally. Cicero doubtlessly selected this orientation because the study of rhetoric, he believed, had been largely misunderstood by the Roman intelligentsia and even disparaged by some of his powerful contemporaries. A lively and well-argued debate among his dialogue characters provided a compelling justification for its civic and pedagogical value.

Departing from the more technical treatments of the subject, Cicero has his main dialogue characters Lucius Licinius Crassus and Marcus Antonius discuss the place of rhetoric and oratory in Roman society. Other dialogue characters are brought into the discussion to underscore the relative merits of such specific subjects as ethics and dialectic. However, it is primarily Crassus and Antonius who treat such important topics as the importance of rhetoric and philosophy in education and civic affairs, the relationship between orality and literacy, the interaction between natural talent and rigorous training, and the implications of creativity and wit in the invention of discourse. In synthesis, these topics make for a well-rounded justification for the value of humanistic education as a route to forming not only a liberal temperament but also the ability to express views eloquently. The enduring attractiveness of this appeal is obvious, and the rediscovery of *De Oratore* in the Renaissance was heralded as nothing less than a major achievement. In fact, so popular was *De Oratore* that it became the next major work printed after the Gutenberg Bible. *De Oratore* has since enjoyed uninterrupted popularity both for its insights into rhetoric and indirectly as a standard for humanistic education.

Despite the enduring popularity of *De Oratore*, it was severely criticized by Cicero's contemporaries, many of who favored a terser, plain style of rhetoric than what they believed Cicero presented in this influential work. In response to this criticism, Cicero wrote a number of works devoted to rhetoric, many of which elaborate (and justify) points made in *De Oratore*. Often, these technical treatises were put forth under the pretense that they were written at the request of specific individuals. In actuality, these rhetorical treatises were public works that were widely known and circulated. *Partitiones Oratoriae* (50 BCE), for example, is a brief statement on the compositional structure of discourse and a later view on the canon of arrangement. This work is doubtlessly a revision of the overly schematized treatment of arrangement found in his juvenile *De Inventione*. In a similar mode of defense, his *De Optimo Genera Oratorum* (46 BCE) was presented as a preface to his own Latin translation of Demosthenes' *On the Crown* and Aeschines' *Against Ctesiphon*. We do not have these translations, and it is doubtful that they were ever done, but Cicero uses this work to discuss the qualifications for the best type of orator. The *Brutus* (46 BCE) is a fascinating work that indirectly justifies the views of his *De Oratore*. Cicero states that his intent in writing the *Brutus* is to reveal that Roman eloquence compares favorably with its Greek counterpart in both quality and history. In actuality, Cicero puts forth this "history" of Roman rhetoric to demonstrate to his contemporaries that his own view of rhetoric is not only compatible with the best of Roman tradition, but also that his view is derived from the principles of expression that have long been practiced. From this perspective, Cicero was able not only to distance himself from the claims that he was little more than a "Greekling," but also to justify the historical grounding of his rhetoric as distinctly Roman. For historians of rhetoric as well as theoreticians, the *Brutus* is one of the most important treatises in Cicero's *Rhetorica*. Cicero uses the *Brutus* to discuss the qualifications of rhetors by mentioning scores of prominent Romans about whom we would otherwise know little or nothing. Although the *Brutus* is fragmentary, it is nonetheless clear that without this treatise, much of what we know about rhetoric and oratory prior to Cicero would be limited or lost.

It is reasonable to infer that the debate about the appropriateness of the study of rhetoric, the nature and civic function of eloquence, and the direction of education remained contested for some time. Cicero's *Orator* (46 BCE) continued the "discussion" of the qualifications of the rhetor. In the *Orator*, Cicero examines the nature of the ideal rhetor. In the process of discussing the ideal qualifications of effective rhetoric, Cicero makes reference to prominent models, including Demosthenes, as well as extending his discussion to the abstract qualities of effective expression. As with *De Oratore*, Cicero underscores the importance of viewing the ideal rhetor not as an individual who possesses mastery of only one specific style, but rather as an individual who has the capacity to adapt to rhetorical situations. For Cicero, the capacity to be versatile, to adapt one's rhetoric to the appropriateness of the audience and situation, persists as the trait to be sought after and learned. From this perspective, it is clear why Cicero would not select any one style of rhetoric as the best, but rather portray the ideal rhetor as one who has mastery of all features of rhetoric and can compose effective discourse in accordance to the constraints of the context.

There are other works by Cicero that arguably can be included in his *Rhetorica*. Although Cicero's *Topica* (44 BCE) is often considered to be a treatise on the study of philosophical argument, Cicero reveals (in the process) his continued belief in the close ties between rhetoric and philosophy. The link between rhetoric and philosophy in the *Topica* is invention, specifically the process of creating and using argument. But, unlike Aristotle's work of the same name, Cicero develops much closer ties between rhetorical and logical argumentation, especially in the discussion of commonplaces (*loci communes*). Those interested in the discussion of argumentative *loci*, particularly as it compares with Aristotle's treatment of *topoi* in the *Rhetoric*, will find this a valuable statement. Cicero's *Hortensius* can also be considered a bridge treatise, because he also discusses the relationship between rhetoric and philosophy. Unfortunately, we have only a patchwork collection of fragments of the

Hortensius. From the extant material, however, we can also infer that Cicero wrote the treatise because prominent contemporaries—in this case his longtime associate Quintus Hortensius Hortalus—did not agree with him on the merits of uniting philosophy with rhetoric. We do know that Cicero's *Hortensius* did survive intact until at least the early Middle Ages, because St. Augustine makes favorable reference to the influence of the *Hortensius* on his life in the *Confessions*. Such works as the *Topica* and *Hortensius* reveal the view that Cicero stressed in his *De Oratore*: effectiveness in the study of rhetoric can only be attained when it is integrated with such other related subjects as philosophy.

Similar to the philosophical works mentioned above, Cicero's speeches and personal letters normally are not included in the corpus of his *Rhetorica*. Yet, in order to appreciate fully Cicero's rhetoric, we must again qualify the standard practice of cataloguing Cicero's works. For a good part of the history of rhetoric in the West, the study of rhetoric has been the study of models. That is, rather than abstract theory or even prescriptive heuristics, rhetoric has been taught by a critical study of Cicero's oratory. This practice is not unlike the way that literature was once taught as a route to effective writing. That is, just as teachers of literature hoped that the personal writing traits of readers would improve by reading and emulating great authors of fiction, so also did teachers of declamation believe that modeling Cicero's oratory would improve their students' expression. Cicero's numerous speeches—about fifty-eight survive in various form of completion and approximately forty-eight are known but lost—served as paradigms of effective expression and were used to illustrate principles of rhetoric. In our own research, Cicero's orations are often cited to illustrate his application of rhetorical techniques. Cicero's *In Verrem*, *In Catilinam*, and *Philippicae* are frequently modeled for their respective merits in forensic, deliberative, and epideictic rhetoric. These, as well as other orations, have been extensively studied both for their use of rhetorical strategies and as cultural statements. Despite how we label his works, studying Cicero's *Rhetorica* requires that we examine not only treatises that directly deal with rhetorical theory, but also those artifacts that indirectly complement our understanding of his rhetorical theory by either example or in relationship with other topics.

Bibliography

Primary Sources and Translations

Cicero, Marcus Tullius. *Brutus*. Trans. G. L. Hendrickson. *Orator*. Trans. H. M. Hubbell. The Loeb Classical Library. Cambridge: Harvard UP, 1952.

———. *De Inventione—De Optimo Genere Oratorum—Topica*. Trans. H. M. Hubbell. The Loeb Classical Library. Cambridge: Harvard UP, 1949.

———. *De Oratore: I–II*. Trans. E. W. Sutton and H. Rackham. The Loeb Classical Library. Cambridge: Harvard UP, 1942. Rev. ed. 1948.

————. *De Oratore: III—De Fato—Paradoxa Stoicorum—De Partitione Oratoria.* Trans. H. Rackham. The Loeb Classical Library. Cambridge: Harvard UP, 1942.

————. *Hortensius, M. Tulli Ciceronis.* Ed. Albertus Grilli. Milano: Institutio Editoriale Cisalpino, 1962.

————. *M. Tulli Ciceronis De Oratore Libri Tres.* Ed. Augustus S. Wilkins. Hildesheim: Georg Olms Verlangsbuchhandlung, 1965.

————. *On Oratory and Orators.* Trans. J. S. Watson. Landmarks in Rhetoric and Public Address. Carbondale: Southern Illinois UP, 1986.

Plutarch. *Parallel Lives. Demosthenes and Cicero, Alexander and Caesar.* Trans. Bernadotte Perrin. Vol. 7. The Loeb Classical Library. Cambridge, MA: Harvard UP, 1919.

Critical Sources

Enos, Richard Leo. *The Literate Mode of Cicero's Legal Rhetoric.* Carbondale: Southern Illinois UP, 1988.

————. *Roman Rhetoric: Revolution and the Greek Influence.* Prospect Heights, IL: Waveland P, 1995.

Horner, Winifred Bryan, ed. *The Present State of Scholarship in Historical and Contemporary Rhetoric.* Rev. ed. Columbia: U of Missouri P, 1990.

Kennedy, George A. *The Art of Rhetoric in the Roman World: 300 B.C.–A.D. 300.* Princeton: Princeton UP, 1972.

Kirby, John T. *The Rhetoric of Cicero's* Pro Cluentio. London Studies in Classical Philology 23. Amsterdam: J. C. Gieben, 1990.

Marrou, H. I. *A History of Education in Antiquity.* Trans. George Lamb. Madison: U of Wisconsin P, 1956. Rpt. 1974.

May, James M. *Trials of Character: The Eloquence of Ciceronian Ethos.* Chapel Hill: U of North Carolina P, 1988.

Murphy, James J., ed. *A Short History of Writing Instruction: From Ancient Greece to Twentieth-Century America.* Rev. ed. Mahwah, NJ: Lawrence Erlbaum Associates, 2001.

Ochs, Donovan J. "Cicero's Rhetorical Theory. With Synopses of Cicero's Seven Rhetorical Works." *A Synoptic History of Classical Rhetoric.* Ed. James J. Murphy, Richard A. Katula, et al. 2nd ed. Davis, CA: Hermagoras P, 1994. 129–76.

CORAX AND TISIAS

(mid-fifth century BCE)

Wilfred E. Major

Almost no reliable biographical information survives about Corax and Tisias other than that they lived in the middle of the fifth century BCE in Syracuse, then a wealthy, powerful city on the island of Sicily. More important, within the next few hundred years they acquired the reputation of being founders of rhetoric in ancient Greece (and consequently for much of the Western tradition), and the reputation has endured largely for the more than two thousand years since. Unfortunately, the validity and importance of every single scrap of information about these two figures are open to sharp criticism and vigorous debate.

The traditional story holds that Gorgias of Leontini brought the teachings of the new rhetoric to Athens, and it was in classical Athens that the legacy of Corax and Tisias blossomed. By the end of the fourth century BCE, the sophisticated discipline of classical rhetoric was well established, as exemplified in the *Rhetoric* of Aristotle and the *Rhetoric to Alexander* attributed to Anaximenes.

Not a word written by Corax or Tisias survives, but other authors from antiquity do mention them. Plato, who wrote several generations later than Corax and Tisias supposedly lived, is the first source to mention either man. He speaks of Tisias in the context of rhetoric and arguments based on *eikos*, probability (*Phaedrus* 273a). A generation later, Aristotle is the first to mention Corax, again about arguments from probability (*Rhetoric* 2.24.1402a). He elsewhere mentions Tisias as an early pioneer of rhetoric (*De Sophisticis Elenchis* 32.183b). Aristotle's great anthology of rhetorical writings (the *Synagoge Technon*), which started with Tisias, has been lost. Over the next several hundred years, a handful of Greek and Roman sources refer to Corax and Tisias as the founders of rhetoric, with little additional information. Cicero, in the first century BCE, quotes Aristotle as saying Corax and Tisias were involved in legal disputes over property in Syracuse after the tyranny ended and a democracy was formed.

In the fifth through the thirteenth centuries CE, more detailed stories appear in the writings of Byzantine scholars. With only slight variations, the story runs as follows: Corax invented and defined rhetoric as the "art of persuasion" in the fifth century BCE at Syracuse. He taught Tisias his new discovery and Gorgias brought their new ideas to Athens. Corax developed rhetoric in response to the needs of the new democratic society, where individuals needed skill in public debate. Toward the end of systematizing this skill and making it teachable, he devised the canonical division and order of parts of a formal speech. A fable also accompanies these stories, wherein Corax sued his student Tisias for failure to pay tuition for learning the new art of rhetoric. In court, however, the student used his new training against his own teacher. Tisias argued that if he failed to defend himself successfully in the suit, he was not obligated to pay, since clearly his training had not been adequate. Corax, however, countered that if Tisias did defend himself successfully in the case, payment should be made since clearly the student had learned his lessons well. By this point, the jury apparently became disgusted with both of them, shouting out "bad crow [Greek *corax*], bad egg," and the case was thrown out. Because of the late date for these sources and the known creative predilections of Byzantine writers, scholars generally agree that both the anecdote and the biographical narrative are fiction. Overall, the best we can say is that Corax and Tisias became synonymous with the creation of rhetorical studies in fifth-century Greece.

THE RHETORICAL THEORY OF CORAX AND TISIAS

The problem then becomes sorting out, from the meager evidence available, what Corax and Tisias did in fact do, say, or theorize about rhetoric. Modern scholarship has mostly, though not exclusively, pursued this question by attempting to sift out what theoretical and practical precepts Corax or Tisias promulgated, which then provided the foundation for later developments and accretions, most notably the work of Aristotle.

Plato and Aristotle mention the only device that can still be reasonably traced back to Corax or Tisias, the argument from probability (*eikos*). This is a rationalizing argument, usually illustrated by the example of a defendant persuading a jury that he did not start a fight. A smaller man can argue that it is less likely he attacked a larger man, since he would not be able to defeat a stronger opponent. Conversely, a larger man can argue that he would not likely attack a smaller man, for he knows a large man automatically draws the suspicion of guilt. Such *eikos* arguments do in fact appear in some early court speeches from the fifth and fourth centuries and thus provide our closest look at what might have been the legacy of Corax and Tisias for early rhetorical speech making. Claims about any other theoretical precepts originating with Corax or Tisias range from implausible to highly speculative.

In recent years, however, the whole problem of rhetoric as Corax and Tisias knew it has been recast in a fundamentally new way. Two scholars, Edward Schiappa and Thomas Cole, have radically overhauled our understanding of rhetorical teaching and theorizing in the period prior to Plato and Aristotle, with concomitant revision of the role of Corax and Tisias during that time. Both Cole and Schiappa have established that in the fifth century BCE (embracing the time of Corax and Tisias) and even the early fourth century, the formal discipline of rhetorical studies did not exist, and at most we can characterize discussion of persuasive language prior to Plato as "protorhetorical." Over the course of the fourth century, Plato, Aristotle, and others formulated and institutionalized a discipline and pursuit that we can properly identify as rhetoric. Cole further makes a compelling case that Corax ("crow") is merely a nickname for Tisias, who became a separate, mythical inventor as stories developed. He also argues that Tisias's writings consisted of pragmatic examples for use in speeches, but not theoretical precepts or the scientific breakdown of parts of speeches and types of argumentation as described in detail later by Aristotle. Schiappa emphasizes how Plato actively formulated the intellectual discipline in his writings (including coining the word *rhetorike*) and how Aristotle retroactively injected an evolutionary history into the tradition. The historical reality of Tisias is all but unrecoverable, and therefore could not have included "inventing" rhetoric in any meaningful way.

In sum, Corax and Tisias are best regarded as legendary figures associated with the beginnings of rhetorical study in fifth-century Greece. Using arguments from probability to persuade listeners is the only technique that can be plausibly attributed to their work. In general, they also stand at the very beginning of the process of analytically studying formal speeches, which paves the way later for the professional discipline of rhetoric.

BIBLIOGRAPHY

Primary Sources and Translations

Radermacher, Ludwig. *Artium Scriptores: Reste der voraristotelischen Rhetorik*. Österreichische Akademie der Wissenschafte, Philosophisch-historische Klasse 227.3. Vienna: Rudolf M. Rohrer, 1951.

Biographical Sources

Cole, Thomas. "Who Was Corax?" *Illinois Classical Studies* 16 (1991): 65–84.

Critical Sources

Cole, Thomas. *The Origins of Rhetoric in Ancient Greece*. Baltimore: Johns Hopkins UP, 1991.
Schiappa, Edward. *The Beginnings of Rhetorical Theory in Classical Greece*. New Haven: Yale UP, 1999.

CORNELIA

(ca. 190s–100s BCE)

D. Alexis Hart

Cornelia was the second daughter of Aemila Tertia and General Publius Cornelius Scipio Africanus Major, the conqueror of Hannibal. Most likely born in the 190s BCE, she had a long life and died sometime in the last two decades of the century. Her family was wealthy, and Cornelia received a bilingual education in Latin and Greek. Her proficiency in Greek literature and philosophy was widely known, particularly since it was so rare among women. In her late teens, she married Tiberius Sempronius Gracchus, a politician many years her senior, to solidify a political alliance. She bore twelve children and was widowed in 154. She never remarried, although she had many suitors including King Ptolemy VIII of Egypt, preferring instead to remain a widow in order to dedicate her time to the education of her children and the management of her estates. Only three of her children survived to adulthood: her daughter Sempronia and her sons Tiberius and Gaius. Her sons were influential liberal reformers in the Roman Republic. Both were murdered for political reasons. Her daughter Sempronia once broke with tradition by speaking in court. As the controller of her own wealth after her husband's death, Cornelia maintained a powerful profile in public life and became a well-known literary patron. After the death of her elder son Tiberius, Cornelia retired to her estate at Misenum. Upon her death, a bronze statue was made in her likeness and placed in a public portico, the first known instance of a statue of a secular Roman woman being displayed in public.

CORNELIA'S INFLUENCE

Although Cornelia was associated with numerous powerful men throughout her life, she was most closely associated with her powerful sons, and thus was best known as the "mother of the Gracchi." Unable to participate directly in politics and public affairs herself, the principal way Cornelia exerted her influence was by using her own education and her associations with political and scholarly men to train her sons for public activism. Both Tiberius and Gaius were elected to public office and praised for their oratorical skills, successes for which Cornelia received much credit. Plutarch acknowledges that Cornelia brought up her boys "with such care and such ambitious hopes that [. . .] they were considered to owe their virtues even more to their education than to their heredity" ("Tiberius Gracchus" 1). Cicero commends Cornelia for taking pains to ensure Tiberius had a thorough education in Greek, the culture and literature from which many political and heroic examples were expected to be drawn during public speeches. In their treatises on the education of orators, both Cicero and Quintilian emphasize the important formative influence a mother's speech has on her sons' eloquence and extol Cornelia as a model for other mothers to emulate.

The extant classical honoraria of Cornelia clearly emphasize her traditionally female domestic roles as dedicated mother and *univira* (married only once), thereby diminishing her personal achievements in education and her substantial impact on society and politics in her own right. In addition to educating her sons and consistently counseling them on their political affairs, she extended her influence by hosting literary gatherings at her retreat in Misenum. In the tradition of Sappho, the men of this scholarly circle engaged Cornelia as an equal in their literary, philosophical, and political debates and certainly were moved by her opinions and patronage. She maintained written correspondence with many of these literary personalities and other powerful public figures. Several of her letters were published.

CORNELIA'S RHETORICAL PRACTICE

Cornelia's letters were commended for their elegant style and educated content. Cicero describes how he read the letters of Cornelia, from which he concluded that her speech must have been equally eloquent. Quintilian remarks that Cornelia's "highly cultivated style is known also to posterity from her letters" (1.1.6). The only surviving letter is a set of fragments purportedly from Cornelia to her son Gaius found in Nepos's *On the Latin Historians*, in which she admonishes her younger son for attempting to destroy the Republic by supporting the Tribunate:

> I would venture to take a solemn oath that, except for the men who killed Tiberius
> Gracchus, no enemy has given me so much trouble and toil as you have done because
> of these matters. You should rather have borne the part of all those children whom
> I had before and taken care that I should have the least possible anxiety in old age,
> that, whatever you did, you wanted it above all to meet my approval and that you
> thought it sinful to do anything of major importance against my views, especially since
> so little of my life remains. Cannot even the brevity of that period do anything to stop
> you opposing me and destroying the state? What respite will there ever be? Will our
> family ever desist from madness? (Cornelia 43)

Some scholars doubt the authenticity of the letter because they do not believe Cornelia, a typically active supporter of her sons' politics, would have so strongly disapproved of Gaius's actions.[1] Others theorize that the letter may have been forged by anti-Gracchan forces in an effort to bring the brothers discredit by showing them at odds with their mother.[2] Regardless of whether the fragments are authentic or not, Cornelia undoubtedly was capable of writing such a letter. She was highly educated and was familiar with the rhetorical conventions of the time, which can be seen in the series of rhetorical questions, the appeal to emotions, and the letter's speechlike quality. As stated earlier, as a young girl she received a thorough grounding in Greek and Latin literature, and in her later life as a matron she engaged in correspondence and debate with educated writers and political orators.

Since sisters and brothers were trained at home by the same grammarians, and since women were not expected to pursue public speaking careers, no formal differentiation was made between men's and women's rhetorical education. Consequently, Cornelia's rhetoric is not markedly "feminine." Her surviving letter could just as easily have been an appeal from a father to his son. She emphasizes Gaius's duties to his family and the state, which are proper masculine concerns, and gives no indication that she is sitting at home weaving or wailing or that it is not proper for her, as a woman, to get involved in political affairs. It is unclear whether Cornelia was consciously adopting a more traditionally masculine role in an effort to gain authority or not, but her letters may have been admired and circulated expressly because they could have been written by a man. They also may have served as examples to other educated and wealthy mothers of the proper eloquence to employ when speaking to their sons.

CORNELIA'S SIGNIFICANCE

Cornelia cannot be credited with inventing a unique feminine rhetorical style. Her letters were most likely published because they were illustrative of well-crafted, stylistically elegant, and appropriate rhetorical arguments in general. Likewise, today's composition students are not specifically trained in masculine or feminine rhetorical styles, but are taught instead to write in a manner fitting the audience and situation. As a rhetorician who mastered the conventions of persuasion and eloquence and put them to practical use, Cornelia clearly deserves a place in history alongside her male counterparts.

NOTES

1. See Fantham et al. 264 and Hemelrijk 196.
2. See Fraschetti 55–56; "Cornelia," *Biographical Dictionary* 78; and "Cornelia," *Encyclopedia of Women* 70.

BIBLIOGRAPHY

Primary Sources and Translations

Cornelia. "Letter of Cornelia." *Cornelius Nepos: A Selection.* Ed. and Trans. Nicholas Horsfall. Oxford: Oxford UP, 1989. 43.

Biographical Sources

"Cornelia." *Biographical Dictionary of Ancient Greek and Roman Women: Women from Sappho to Helena.* Ed. Majorie Lightman and Benjamin Lightman. New York: Facts on File, 2000. 78–79.

"Cornelia" and "Motherhood, Roman." *Encyclopedia of Women in the Ancient World.* Ed. Joyce E. Salisbury. Santa Barbara: ABC CLIO, 2001. 70–71, 236–308.

"Cornelia." *The Oxford Classical Dictionary.* 3rd ed. Ed. Simon Hornblower and Antony Spawforth. Oxford: Oxford UP, 1996.

Dixon, Suzanne. *The Roman Mother.* Norman: Oklahoma UP, 1988.

Critical Sources

Bauman, Richard A. *Women and Politics in Ancient Rome.* London: Routledge, 1992.

Best, Edward E. "Cicero, Livy and Educated Roman Women." *Classical Journal* 65.5 (1970): 199–204.

Cape, Robert W., Jr. "Roman Women in the History of Rhetoric and Oratory." *Listening to Their Voices: The Rhetorical Activities of Historical Women.* Ed. Molly Meijer Wertheimer. Columbia: U of South Carolina P, 1997. 112–32.

Cicero. *Brutus.* Trans. G. L. Hendrickson. Cambridge: Harvard UP, 1939.

Fantham, Elaine, Helene Peet Foley, Natalie Boymel Kampen, Sarah B. Pomeroy, and H. A. Shapiro. *Women in the Classical World: Image and Text.* New York: Oxford UP, 1994.

Fraschetti, Augusto. *Roman Women.* Trans. Linda Lappin. Chicago: U of Chicago P, 2001.

Glenn, Cheryl. *Rhetoric Retold: Regendering the Tradition from Antiquity through the Renaissance.* Carbondale: Southern Illinois UP, 1997.

Hemelrijk, Emily. *Matrona Docta: Educated Women in the Roman Élite from Cornelia to Julia Domna.* London: Routledge, 1999.

Livy. *Book XXXVIII.* Trans. P. G. Walsh. Warminster: Aris and Phillips, 1993.

Plinius Secundus. *The Natural History of Pliny.* 6 vols. Trans. John Bostock and H. T. Riley. London: Henry G. Bohn, 1855–1857.

Plutarch. "Gaius Gracchus." *Makers of Rome: Nine Lives by Plutarch.* Trans. Ian Scott-Kilvert. New York: Dorset P, 1965. 175–93.

———. "Tiberius Gracchus." *Makers of Rome: Nine Lives by Plutarch.* Trans. Ian Scott-Kilvert. New York: Dorset P, 1965. 153–74.

Pomeroy, Sarah B. *Goddesses, Whores, Wives, and Slaves: Women in Classical Antiquity.* New York: Schocken Books, 1975.

Quintilian. *Institutio Oratoria. Quintilian: The Orator's Education.* Trans. Donald A. Russell. Cambridge: Harvard UP, 2001.

Tacitus. *Dialogue on Oratory, Agricola, Germania.* Trans. William Peterson. Cambridge: Harvard-Heinemann, 1963.

Valerius Maximus. *Memorable Doings and Sayings.* Trans. D. R. Shackleton Bailey. Cambridge: Harvard UP, 2000.

DEMETRIUS OF PHALERON

(ca. 350s–283 BCE)

Lara O'Sullivan

Demetrius, son of Phanostratus from the Athenian deme of Phaleron, enjoyed illustrious careers both as rhetorician and statesman. He is reported to have entered political life at the time of the "Harpalus affair" in Athens in 324 BCE; this, combined with the fact that he survived into the 280s, suggests a birth date in the 350s. His family emerged from obscurity—Demetrius was, with his brother Himeraeus, of the first generation recorded to have been politically active—but there is no reason to credit the hostile tradition that the family had servile origins. Demetrius owed his rise to prominence largely to his association with the Macedonian house of Antipater, who had governed Greece and Macedonia on behalf of Alexander the Great. When Athens capitulated to Antipater in 322 after the Lamian war, Demetrius was one of the ambassadors who negotiated terms, and he was sufficiently implicated in the oligarchy that Antipater installed to be condemned to death when that regime was toppled in 318. He escaped execution by taking shelter in the Macedonian garrison that had occupied the Piraeus, and he was thus well placed to serve again as negotiator when, in early 317, Antipater's son Cassander regained control of the city. Under Cassander's settlement, Demetrius acted as the overseer (*epimeletes*) of an expanded oligarchy, a position he enjoyed for ten years; during this decade he enacted a program of legislation (probably under the title of *nomothetes*), and was archon in 309/8. When Demetrius Poliorcetes restored democracy to Athens in 307, Demetrius of Phaleron was forced to quit the city. He remained in Greece until Cassander's death in 297, and then turned to the court of Ptolemy Soter in Egypt, where he perhaps had a hand in formulating the idea for the library of Alexandria. His advocacy of the claims of Ptolemy's offspring by Eurydice precipitated his fall when the son of Berenice, Ptolemy Philadelphus, instead succeeded to the Egyptian throne in 283, and he died—allegedly of snakebite—shortly thereafter.

Throughout his life he maintained a close connection with Aristotle's Peripatos. A pupil of Theophrastus, he was a prolific scholar, and many have maintained that his legislative program was informed by his philosophical education. So closely was Demetrius associated with the philosophers that the backlash against his regime in 307 took the form of a legislative attempt to place philosophical schools under the control of the Athenian state.

DEMETRIUS'S RHETORICAL THEORY

The connection with the Peripatos is fundamental to Demetrius as a rhetorician. He taught rhetoric at the school, and the orator Dinarchus is said to have been one of his pupils. The influence of Theophrastus may be discerned in his ideas about rhetoric: he seems, for example, to have followed Theophrastus's interests in diction and delivery as aspects of the rhetorical art (see Fragments [FF] 134–39).[1]

A full appreciation of his style and of his significance to rhetorical theory is, however, hampered by the loss of his writings. Nothing remains of the collections of speeches that circulated in antiquity and were known to Cicero, upon whom we now depend for judgments on Demetrius's style. For his rhetorical ideas, we rely on reports of his *On Rhetoric* (*Peri Rhetorices*) in Philodemus's now fragmentary work of the same name. The surviving work *On Style* by a Demetrius (once commonly identified as Demetrius of Phaleron) is the product of a different author.

Despite the difficulty in isolating Demetrius's views, it is generally agreed that his importance lies in his attempt to reconcile the perceived divide between rhetoric and philosophy that had existed since Plato. There is a danger, however, that the emphasis by Philodemus and Cicero on this aspect of his theory is a reflection of their own interest in the argument raging between philosophy and rhetoric in the Rome of the second and first centuries BCE; Demetrius's reconciliation of the two fields may have been less daring to contemporaries than it was to Cicero. After all, even for Plato the separation between rhetoric and philosophy was not absolute: rather, the philosopher was to be deemed the only true orator (a view that may have found favor with Demetrius: F132). Moreover, Demetrius's own school apparently recognized a commonality between rhetorical training and philosophical investigation, with Diogenes Laertius (5.3) and Cicero (*Orator* 46) suggesting a rhetorical as well as dialectic purpose for the use, by Aristotle and Theophrastus, of *theses*—questions of a general nature that students were required to argue pro and contra. This Peripatetic application of dialectical training to rhetoric may have had a stylistic aspect (on which see below); it may have rested also on a belief that the methods of proof employed by philosophy were suited also to rhetoric.

The most significant record of Demetrius's own views concerns his classification of speeches (F130). To the commonly recognized deliberative and forensic branches of oratory, Demetrius added a category designated the *enteucticos logos*, or "conversational speech"; in this, he recalled a pre-Aristotelian categorization found in Plato's *Sophistes* (222c). The formulation of such an *enteucticos logos* stood to expand the realm of rhetoric (the discipline of continuous speech) to encompass dialogue. Philodemus understood enteuctic to include discourse with the ordinary people and ambassadorial dialogue with potentates. Most radically, it stood to ally with rhetoric the particular kind of dialogue and dialectic that characterized the investigations and writings of philosophical schools; this, at least, is the implication of Philodemus, who condemned Demetrius for what he saw as granting to rhetoric the "speech concerning conversation" (*logos peri homilias*) that was properly the domain of the philosophers (compare also F131 C).

Philosophical discourse had been kept distinct from rhetoric by a perceived gulf in the purposes of the two disciplines. Demetrius's own teacher, Theophrastus, had contrasted the need for philosophy to be directed primarily toward its subject matter, against that of rhetoric and its central concern for its audience. This distinction reflected a fundamental difference in the aims of philosophical and rhetorical speech: the former aimed to instruct, the latter to persuade. This difference of purpose is coupled by Cicero with a difference of style: real oratory demands "vigor" and "sting" to overwhelm its audience, but with their writings philosophers aim to "converse with scholars, whose minds they prefer to soothe rather than arouse; they converse [. . .] for the purpose of instructing rather than captivating" (see *Orator* 62ff.). It was this very division that Demetrius of Phaleron sought, to the distress of Philodemus, to blur, by "assigning to the rhetoricians" not just discourse that aimed to persuade but also those kinds of discourses that concerned "inquiries that require proof," thus bringing dialectic into the realm of oratory.

Just how Demetrius intended to incorporate his *enteucticos logos* within the established framework of rhetoric is unclear from Philodemus. The *enteucticos logos* may have been a fourth division to stand alongside the other categories of speech (forensic, deliberative, and epideictic/sophistic) recognized by Aristotle, or have been intended rather to replace epideictic; Philodemus does seem, however, to envisage some close relationship between sophistic and enteuctic, since he objects to Demetrius's belief that both forms of oration could be mastered by one and the same person.

RHETORICAL STYLE

The association of the *enteucticos logos*, or at least of philosophical discourse, with epideictic speech can be rationalized on grounds of style. For just as the *sermones* of the philosophers sought "to soothe rather than to arouse," so too did epideictic oratory aim "not to arouse the audience but to soothe it, not so much to persuade but to delight" (Cicero, *Orator* 65; cf. 63 where it is noted that philosophical writing too gives "pleasure" to its audience); as such, both epideictic and philosophical discourse could be permitted a greater degree of stylistic ornamentation (for example, through use of extended metaphors) than was deemed appropriate to forensic and deliberative oratory.

Cicero's pronouncements on Demetrius's own oratory resonate with these descriptions of both epideictic and philosophical writing, and also attest explicitly to his infusion of a philosophical style into rhetoric. At *De Officiis* 1.1.3, Demetrius's style is touched upon (he is "a subtle speaker, somewhat lacking in force but nonetheless charming"), and that style is attributed to the influence of Theophrastus.

Similarly, at *Orator* 91, Cicero, having delineated Demetrius's extensive use of ornamentation (metaphor and metonymy in particular), explains that this style is a frequent
product of training by philosophers and Sophists: indeed, Cicero claims in another
context (*Orator* 46) that Aristotle—and Theophrastus too according to *De Finibus*
(5.10)—employed *theses* in rhetorical training precisely with a view to encouraging
rhetorical abundance through the ornamentation of arguments. The effect of
Demetrius's style recalls that of both epideictic and philosophical writing: Demetrius
"entertained rather than stirred," and by relying on "charm rather than force" he did
not overwhelm his listeners (*Brutus* 36–37, where Demetrius's link with Theophrastus
is again noted).

In fostering this style, Demetrius was perceived to have marked a turning point
in Athenian oratory. Later schematizations of Greek rhetoric postulated that the
original, pure Attic style—that style exemplified by Aeschines and Demosthenes
among others—began to change under Demetrius of Phaleron (FF121, 122, 125);
styles of delivery may have undergone modification, too, to judge by Demetrius's
criticisms of Demosthenes (F137). The political circumstances of Athens at the time
may be important here: the curtailment of democracy will have undermined the
politically combative field of forensic oratory and encouraged instead a concentration
on other kinds of "encounters" as the context for rhetoric. In light of this, it is
perhaps unsurprising that the catalogue of Demetrius's works features no collection
of forensic speeches (only collections of public speeches and ambassadorial speeches
are listed). It may be noted too that one tradition ascribed to the period of Demetrius's rule the rise of fictitious forensic and deliberative speech writing.

NOTE

1. All fragment numbers refer to the William W. Fortenbaugh and Eckhart Schütrumpf
edition, listed in the bibliography.

BIBLIOGRAPHY

Primary Sources and Translations

Fortenbaugh, William W., and Eckhart Schütrumpf, eds. *Demetrius of Phalerum: Text, Trans-
   lation and Discussion*. Rutgers Studies in Classical Humanities 9. New Brunswick/London:
   Transaction Publishers, 2000.
Wehrli, Fritz. *Demetrios von Phaleron*. Die Schule des Aristoteles 4. Basel/Stuttgart: Schwabe, 1968.

Critical Sources

Dorandi, Tiziano. "Il Contributo dei Papiri alla Ricostruzione della Biographia e delle Idee
   sulla Retorica di Demetrio del Falero." Fortenbaugh and Schütrumpf 381–89.

————. "Senocrate nel giudizio di Demetrio del Falero." *Beiträge zur antiken Philosophie: Festschrift für Wolfgang Kullman.* Ed. Hans-Christian Günter and Antonios Rengakos. Stuttgart: Franz Steiner Verlag, 1997. 271–78.

Heldmann, Konrad. "'Hic primus inflexit orationem' und die gute alte Redenkunst." *Rheinisches Museum* 122 (1979): 317–25.

Kennedy, George. *The Art of Persuasion in Greece.* Princeton: Princeton UP, 1963.

van Ophuijsen, Jan M. "Where Have the Topics Gone?" *Peripatetic Rhetoric after Aristotle.* Ed. David C. Mirhady. Rutgers University Studies in Classical Humanities 6. New Brunswick/London: Transaction Publishers, 1994. 131–73.

"Demetrius," On Style

(ca. 275 BCE)

Scott G. Reed

On Style, a lengthy treatise designed to serve as a stylistic handbook for writers and rhetors in training, is a document sitting on the margins of history. Its authorship and date of origin have never been pinpointed to the satisfaction of the academic community, leaving the content of the piece to linger as disputed marginalia in the greater history of rhetoric. First, an author has never been attributed to the piece. Vague records once led manuscript scholars to attribute authorship to Demetrius of Phaleron, a move later "unanimously rejected" by scholars, citing among other things the fact that Demetrius of Phaleron is cited as a source within the text (Grube 22). Further investigations have demonstrated little other than the fact that our "Demetrius" lived some time after the third century BCE, had extensive knowledge of Aristotle's *Rhetoric*, and was likely a resident of Alexandria.

A second, and more fiercely contested, issue is the dating of the treatise itself. Two general schools of thought have coalesced on the subject. G. M. A. Grube works from historical and literary references in the work, along with certain post-sophistic notions embedded in the text's focus on style over virtue, to place *On Style* "around 270 BCE," following the Hellenistic expansion through the Mediterranean and Asia Minor, but predating the rhetorical advancement of Cicero, Quintilian, and other Roman rhetors by several hundred years. The second school, spear-headed primarily by early twentieth- and late-nineteenth-century scholars, have argued strenuously for a date running in line with the rhetorical explosion of the Second Sophistic age in Rome, from the mid-first century BCE to as late as the second century CE. Schenkeveld, drawing on the opinions of classical scholars Ludwig Radermacher and William Rhys Roberts, takes a more linguistic tack in his argument. His analysis of the Greek suggests a strong Attic influence, contrary to the more florid Asiatic style in vogue at the time suggested; these stylistic gestures reflect a later, non-Hellenic origin, perhaps even making our Demetrius an early contemporary of Cicero (137). Jeffrey Walker has recently argued that the original date of 270 BCE is still the best available, noting the tendency of Hellenistic rhetorical theorists to "subdivide" their subject matter (consistent with the structure of *On Style*). Walker also notes that the Asiatic style was still in development at this time, not reaching its greatest flourish until the latter half of the third century BCE. Furthermore, as Walker argues, the structure and focus of *On Style* represent a reflection and elaboration of the rhetorical theories of Theophrastus and the Peripatetic school (46–48). Ultimately, the treatise's focus on style over virtue and its references to Aristotle and the tradition of the Peripatetic school have led Walker and a majority of modern scholars to conclude that the date of 270 BCE is "hard to refute" (Conley 48n3). It is precisely this difficulty with locating *On Style* in the rhetorical tradition that I believe distracts many from a potentially profitable encounter with a work that provides interesting perspectives on the Sophists' notion of style, as well as a glimpse into the early tradition of rhetorical textbooks.

THE STRUCTURE OF THE WORK

On Style proceeds in two movements. In the first (sections 1–35), Demetrius provides a lengthy exposition on the mechanics of sentence grammar, addressing such tools as clause length and the uses of periods. The clause (*kola*) is for Demetrius the fundamental element of prose writing; it is the prosodic equivalent of poetic meter, within which the skillful stylist must learn to work. The uses for these grammatical elements are catalogued and discussed according to their usefulness in various situations. For modern purposes, this section is of little interest to those unfamiliar with the structure of Greek; it is clear from the discussion that the Greek notion of the period is quite different from our own.

With this foundation, Demetrius launches directly into his discussion of the four styles: the plain, the grand/impressive, the elegant, and the forceful. Each style is an accumulation of three primary elements: diction (word choice), arrangement, and subject matter. The usefulness of his initial exposition on sentence style is immediately useful here, as Demetrius provides meticulous instruction on composition techniques within each individual style. The grand or impressive style, for example, relies on long rhythms (sustained by long clauses), noble subject matter, and the strategic use of metaphor to achieve its effect. Its inverse, the plain style, is based on the lucidity of "natural" word arrangement, common to everyday speech. The elegant style, working from a basis in witty or charming subject matter, is most effective when elements in a sentence are arranged strategically to place emphasis on the end. Finally, the forceful or intense style uses shorter, brusque rhythms along with strategically placed euphemism and metaphor to drive home a point with minimal effort. To conclude the discussion of each style, Demetrius provides a brief exposition on the corresponding weakness of the style, although these sections are often vague, relying only on examples as illustrations.

The most frequently cited fault in the work is the author's tendency to digress. In the course of his discussion of the grand style, for example, he embarks on a long tangent on the nature and use of metaphor (sections 78–90). Most of his comments are related directly to stylistic concerns, but it is hard to fathom the usefulness of this particular paragraph in the context of the work: "parts of the body derive their names not from a metaphorical usage but from their physical resemblance to other objects" (section 88). In contrast, though, his brief advice on epistolary style (sections 223–35) is the treatise's most original and interesting point, which Walker notes as the author's most clear link to the exigent rhetorical practices of his day.

DEMETRIUS'S THEORY OF STYLE

On Style provides an impressively broad account of how writers may select and work within a variety of styles in order to achieve their goal, which is always assumed to be some sort of rhetorical persuasion, albeit persuasion based on the writer's stylistic eloquence. Indeed, an important facet of his legacy is the attention Demetrius, in following the historical developments of his time, pays to the nature of print. In his text, he draws on extensive examples from the Greek literary corpus, rarely, if ever, gesturing to the work of orators. His digression on letter-writing style removes him yet further from the realm of dikanic/forensic rhetoric of the sort practiced in the courts and government. His is a broad rhetorical training for literary life, the kind that provides opportunities for those capable of working within the still-malleable medium of print to influence people across long distances (appropriate enough for a writer who most likely was a resident of far-flung Alexandria).

Situated in the context of post-Aristotelian rhetoric, Demetrius's dual concerns with stylistic eloquence and print situate him in the context of "skilled, pragmatic rhetoric" that Walker sees as one of the defining features of rhetoric's evolution through the Hellenistic age (48). Furthermore, unlike Isocrates before him and Cicero after, Demetrius is not engaged in restoring rhetoric-as-philosophy. His rather bland directness in dealing with his own subject matter seems to indicate that he has no loftier goal in mind than providing a well-rounded education in rhetorical eloquence (the classical notion of *paideia*).

In presenting each of his four styles as a matrix of concerns, Demetrius assigns no particular importance to any of these three factors. Indeed, within the discussions of each style, he addresses them in different orders. His discussion of the plain style begins with the importance of simple and lucid word choice; the elegant style, on the other hand, requires a strong convergence with its topic, so subject matter is the first to be discussed. He adds to each style a discussion of the rhetorical figures suited to achieve the desired effect; even these overlap among the different styles in play. *Anaphora* (repetition), for example, can be used well within three of the four styles (saving plain style), and in each case Demetrius offers provisos and suggestions for the words and situations that would make best use of the device. For Demetrius, no rhetorical device is effective in itself; rather, its success is always determined by the care with which the writer manipulates its constituent stylistic elements. Perhaps the greatest measure of Demetrius's fluidity is the extent to which no stylistic mode is ever fixed or concretized. Unlike Cicero's later three-style model, in which elements are carefully sifted and divided, Demetrius's theory does not so much establish rigid stylistic categories (a move he deems "absurd") as it gestures toward the fundamental elements needed to perform within a broadly conceived style (cf. Grube 24).

"STYLE" IN THE PRESENT TENSE

Its rather intimidating aridity, combined with its historical displacement, has relegated *On Style* to the status of a relatively minor entry in the rhetorical canon. Indeed, as stylistics handbooks go, it does not even merit mention in Robert Connors's chapter on the subject, wherein the stylistic tradition follows a straight line from Cicero to Blair (260–61). Connors claims that the first textbook to relate style to sentence structure was Lindley Murray's *English Grammar* of 1795 (262). The well-known hegemony of Harvard College over writing instruction would later obliterate style from the composition agenda altogether, making Demetrius a disputed speck on the margins of history. This is not to impugn Connors's excellent history, but merely to suggest how Demetrius might play more of a part in the modern conversation by gesturing to the possibility of doing more with style. Unlike the *Elements of Style* (Strunk and White) so familiar to modern students today, Demetrius's theory is more a loose network of elements than a series of rules designed to promote one style, one whose primary virtue is clarity. With its dynamic, fluid approach, and steadfast attention to eloquence, teachers and theorists of writing may profit greatly from reclaiming Demetrius from the margins of history.

BIBLIOGRAPHY

Primary Sources and Translations

Demetrius. *On Style. A Greek Critic: Demetrius On Style.* Trans. G. M. A. Grube. Toronto: U of Toronto P, 1961. 60–129.

Critical Sources

Conley, Thomas M. *Rhetoric in the European Tradition.* Chicago: U of Chicago P, 1990.
Connors, Robert. *Composition-Rhetoric: Backgrounds, Theory, and Pedagogy.* Pittsburgh: U of Pittsburgh P, 1997.
Grube, G. M. A. *A Greek Critic: Demetrius On Style.* Toronto: U of Toronto P, 1961.
Schenkeveld, Dirk Marie. *Studies in Demetrius On Style.* Chicago: Argonaut Publishers, 1967.
Walker, Jeffrey. *Rhetoric and Poetics in Antiquity.* Oxford: Oxford UP, 2000.

DIO (CHRYSOSTOM) COCCEIANUS

(ca. 40–ca. 110 CE)

George Pullman

Dio Cocceianus, later nicknamed Chrysostom or "golden tongue," was born in Bithynia, Prusa (now northwestern Turkey) sometime between 40 and 50 CE. He died there sometime after 110, making him roughly contemporaneous with Plutarch and Quintilian. Dio's family was prominent. His father received proclamations of honor and his mother was posthumously granted a shrine and a sacred image (Jones 105). Dio most probably received a traditional education, studying Greek culture either at school or with a tutor and then, around age fifteen, studying rhetoric. We know that at Rome he was influenced by the Stoic philosopher Musonius Rufus. Certainly many of his orations approve Stoic virtues. We also know that Dio was banished from Rome and Italy generally as well as his home country during the reign of Domitian, probably in 82 (Cohoon 89) "on account of [his] reputed friendship with" (Oration 13) Flavius Sabinus, son-in-law of Domitian's brother Titus, who was emperor before Domitian and in whose shadow Domitian paled. During his exile, Dio traveled as far as Getae and continued to travel throughout Greece and the Balkans. He was recalled to Rome by Nerva sometime around 96. His most notable students were Favorinus and Polemo, whose rivalry is recounted by Maud Gleason.

RECEPTION

Two interpretations of Dio Chrysostom's intellectual life come to us from antiquity. The Christian Neoplatonist Synesius of Cyrene (370–413) argues that Dio began his adult life as a Sophist, using such diaphanous trifles as "Encomium of a Parrot" and "Encomium of a Gnat" as evidence. Both of these pieces are now lost. However, we do have a piece, "On Hair," that is reproduced in the midst of Synesius's piece "On Baldness" (Cohoon and Crosby, vol. 5 333–43), which suggests "sophistry" in the sense of trivial discourse designed to amuse and impress. Synesius also points to the fact that Dio wrote a piece, "Against the Philosophers," indicating that in the early part of his life he set himself up in opposition to philosophical thought and aligned himself with sophistic practice. But, Synesius asserts, orations written during and after his exile show a marked tendency toward philosophical thinking (381), the importance of free speech for philosophers, and the paramount importance of virtue for all people. Thus Synesius would have us believe that Dio underwent a sort of philosophical conversion as a result of exile, abandoning sophistic orations of the crowd-pleasing sort in favor of morally instructive speeches—homilies, almost. It certainly is true that discourses like "On Opinion" and "On Philosophy" promote ideas typically associated with philosophical rhetoric—the importance of knowledge in the pursuit of conviction, the fickleness of popular opinion, and so on. But there is no direct evidence of an actual "conversion."

Philostratus provides the other view that has been handed down to us from antiquity, arguing that Dio was never actually exiled (Wright 19), even though Dio himself says he was (Oration 13). Philostratus points to the "Encomium of the Parrot" and "all those writings in which he handled themes of no great importance," and concludes that, "we must not regard them as mere trifles, but rather as sophistic compositions; for it is characteristic of a sophist to devote serious study to themes even so slight as these" (19). Unlike Synesius, Philostratus held sophistry in high regard for combining engaging speech with engaging thought. He particularly admired Dio, whom he represents as having on one occasion quelled a rebellion with the mere force of his words, and of whom he asserts that Trajan said, "I do not understand what you are saying, but I love you as I love myself" (21). Much scholarly effort has been expended on trying to sort out who, Philostratus or Synesius, had it right about Dio (see Swain for a discussion of Dio's reception). In this brief space, it is probably worth saying nothing more about the argument except that it helps to perpetuate the rift between philosophy and rhetoric.

Orations

Regardless, Dio Chrysostom's speeches clearly indicate a gift for beautiful phrases as well as a wide range of intellectual and political interests. Some eighty pieces are attributed to him (two—37 and 64—were actually written by Favorinus, and Swain asserts that a third is also inauthentic [10]), some in the form of dialogues, ranging in themes from "On Beauty" and "On Personal Appearance" to pieces that dealt directly with the welfare of Prusa and Dio's own reputation as a political benefactor, to such philosophical pieces as "On Opinion," "On Virtue," and "On Trust." The portrait that emerges from all of these discourses is of a man deeply committed to traditional Greek *paideia*—an Atticist who emulated Demosthenes and Plato and who often spoke in the guise of classical figures like Diogenes and Socrates, with a gift for hiding acerbic social criticism beneath glittering phrases.

Although there is not space here to develop a treatment of many of the speeches, a quick look at several of the better known ones may give one a sense of what is to be admired and appreciated. Dio held closely to classical ideals in both diction and structure. In "Alexandria" and "Rhodes," for example, speeches ostensibly presented to the assembly in these towns respectively, Dio begins by praising the geography, the climate, the proximity to other great cities and places, and then talks about the people and their practices. But in each of these speeches, Dio has some biting criticism to offer. In the case of Rhodes, he admonishes the people there to abandon the practice of reinscribing existing statues with the names of currently prominent men, on the grounds that they are plundering their past and debasing those they would now honor. In the piece delivered to Alexandria, Dio admonishes the people to curb their zeal for chariot races and public music recitals, actually accusing them of behaving like criminals and drunks, causing arguments that turn into fights, and fights that turn into riots that last for days. In both speeches, Dio veils some of his more biting remarks in ironic pleasantries and prepares the way for his advice with careful compliments. Nevertheless, he is intent on making his audience feel his remarks. After praising Rhodes, for example, he offers this:

> perhaps these words of mine are pleasing to your ears and you fancy that you are being praised by me, as you are by all the rest who are always flattering you; but I was praising water and soil and harbours and places and everything except yourselves. For where have I said that you are sensible and temperate and just? [. . .] If a man speaks in praise of water, he is not praising men but wells; if he talks of good climate, he does not mean that the people are good [. . .] (207–08)

Although Dio castigates Cynic philosophers in some discourses, in "On Rhodes," for example, he was known as a proponent of Cynicism, and this is largely due to the fact that he clearly admired Diogenes. Dio wrote four discourses (Oration 6, 8–10) about Diogenes and his teaching, sometimes even speaking in the Cynic's voice. The sixth discourse, "On Tyranny," sets the tone well: "[Diogenes] used to ridicule the victims of conceit and folly, though it was against the sophists, who wanted to be looked up to and thought they knew more than other men, that he railed in particular" (Cohoon, vol. 1 263). It is perhaps for this reason, Diogenes' penchant for pricking puffs, that Dio takes such apparent delight in recounting how, at the end of a discourse on virtue, Diogenes made the Sophists cry out "like frogs in a pond when they do not see the water-snake" by ending his speech with a defecation instead of a peroration (Cohoon, vol. 1 399). Cohoon asserts that Dio wrote these pieces during his exile, at a time when he would have had a particular affinity for living close to the earth, as Diogenes did, and when using the mask of the dog philosopher would allow him to castigate Domitian and other powerful men without incurring their wrath.

While the encomia on animals and the invectives spat from beneath a dog's mask might lead us to see Dio as a crowd-pleasing moralist, another side of Dio's career is also extant in his orations. Dio was a significant political figure, a bene-factor who used his wealth and "pull" with Rome to bring empyreal concessions to Prusa and to beautify the city (Oration 44). Though he had some success, as several of his orations outline, he had enemies who were critical of his efforts, as his orations also make clear (Oration 47). He also incurred the fury of the commoners (Oration 46) when they presumed he had artificially inflated the price of grain. On that occasion, they would have razed his house if it were not so well protected. There was also a scandal involving the development of a portico, the money for which may have been misappropriated. Toward the later orations, a tone of bit-terness and resentment can be heard.

INFLUENCE ON RHETORICAL TRADITION

Dio Chrysostom Cocceianus's rhetorical legacy has perhaps yet to be fully under-stood. As Swain's admirable reception history shows, a great deal of effort has been spent trying to recruit Dio as either a Stoic-Cynic or a Sophist. Over the years, it has been noted that his prose was Atticist and that his rhetorical structures were highly conventional. It has also been duly noted that he loved to turn a phrase just so. Currently his rhetorical importance is that he melded wit and style with civic action and thus epitomized classical rhetoric six hundred years later.

BIBLIOGRAPHY

Primary Sources and Translations

Cohoon, J. W., trans. *Dio Chrysostom.* 5 vols. Vols. 1–3. Cambridge: Harvard UP, 1950.

Cohoon, J. W., and Lamar Crosby. *Dio Chrysostom.* 5 vols. Vols. 4–5. Cambridge: Harvard UP, 1932.

Russell, D. A., ed. *Dio Chrysostom: Orations VII, XII, XXXVI.* Cambridge: Cambridge UP, 1992.

Critical Sources

Gleason, Maud W. *Making Men: Sophists and Self-Presentation in Ancient Rome.* Princeton: Princeton UP, 1995.

Jones, C. P. *The Roman World of Dio Chrysostom.* Cambridge: Harvard UP, 1978.

Swain, Simon, ed. *Dio Chrysostom: Politics, Letters, and Philosophy.* Oxford: Oxford UP, 2000.

Wright, Wilmer C., trans. *Philostratus and Eunapius Lives of the Sophists.* Cambridge: Harvard UP, 1989.

Diogenes of Sinope

(ca. 404[?]–323 BCE)

D. Diane Davis and Victor J. Vitanza

Diogenes (aka the Dog) was born in Sinope during the last two decades of the fifth century BCE, probably between 413 and 404. What we know about him comes from doxagraphical anecdotes or Cynic *chreia*, which are frequently contradictory and/or historically improbable. Though Diogenes is credited with many written works—including dialogues, tragedies, and letters—it is not clear that he actually wrote anything at all. Nothing genuine seems to have survived, and most of the works attributed to him in antiquity were also occasionally ascribed to others. Even the letters, fifty-one of which survive, are now believed to be by unknown authors. We are therefore left to secondary sources, the most significant being Diogenes Laertius's *Lives of Eminent Philosophers*, which gathers a dizzying array of anecdotes and *chreia* from various, often nonextant ancient sources. Still, something of the force of Diogenes' cultural, political, and philosophical influence is revealed in the swirl of anecdotes he managed to provoke.

Little is known about Diogenes' early years, save that he was the son of the banker Hicesias, who was entrusted with the state's money, and that Diogenes was involved in an illegal manipulation of currency around 370 BCE. Apparently, either Diogenes or his father (or both) adulterated the state's coinage and was exiled; or Hicesias was imprisoned and Diogenes was exiled; or Diogenes committed the crime and fled to avoid punishment. A more imaginative account suggests that Diogenes was urged by the workers he supervised to deface the coinage, and he went to Delphi or to the Delian oracle in Sinope to ask Apollo for advice; when the god said he should "alter the political currency," Diogenes misunderstood and "adulterated the state coinage" (Laertius VI, 20). Another version—purely literary yet instructive—suggests that Diogenes had fled Sinope for Athens to avoid imprisonment and had traveled to Delphi to ask the oracle what he should do to "gain the greatest reputation." Apollo said he should "alter the political currency," so Diogenes "fell in with" the notorious Antisthenes, the father of Cynic philosophers, and spent the rest of his days challenging the political/cultural "currency" in Athens, where he lived until about 350 BCE, and then in Corinth (VI, 20–21).[1]

His relocation to Corinth may not have been by choice: Laertius tells us that while on a voyage to Aegina, Diogenes was captured by pirates who took him to Crete and sold him as a slave.[2] When the auctioneer asked about his talents, Diogenes replied that he was proficient "in ruling men," pointed to the Corinthian Xeniades, and said, "Sell me to this man; he needs a master" (VI, 74). Xeniades purchased Diogenes and put him in charge of educating his sons and managing his household. Except for his years with Xeniades, Diogenes apparently lived only in public spaces. In the *Orations*, Dio Chrysostom muses that "the whole earth was his abode" (quoted in Navia 22), and Laertius reports that Diogenes had lived in a tub in the Athenian Metroön, under the porticos of the Athenian temples, and in the Craneum, a public gymnasium located just outside Corinth's city walls. Diogenes died in the Craneum in 323 BCE, and Demetrius (for poetic effect) claimed it was on the same day that Alexander the Great died in Babylon (Laertius VI, 80). Diogenes was buried outside the gates of Corinth, and a statue of a dog made of Parian marble was placed on his grave. At his death, he was "said to have been nearly ninety years old" (VI, 76).

Diogenes did everything in public, including eating, sleeping, masturbating, urinating, and defecating. This scandalized the Athenian and Corinthian citizenry and eventually earned him the nickname "Dog." According to Laertius, Plato "styled him a dog" (VI, 40), and Aristotle in the *Rhetoric* refers to him not by name but simply as "the Dog," taking the association for granted (1411a). Though "dog!" was no doubt initially hurled as an insult, Diogenes embraced it, acknowledging that it captured the mode of life he so faithfully and scandalously practiced. This life mode came to be known as Cynicism, a derivation from the Greek term *kynikos*, meaning, literally, to be like a dog. Diogenes' philosophy took the form of a rigorously practiced doglike existence, a self-styled and extraordinarily "natural" mode of life that, as Foucault suggests, questioned all social norms, institutional rules, arbitrary standards of decency, and other "dependencies introduced by culture, society, civilization, opinion, and so on" (120). Whereas socialization grants one an identity in a culture, Diogenes held to an existential, cosmic identity. A proto-proponent of the cosmopolitan ethic, Diogenes refused all nationalism: "Asked where he came from, he said, 'I am a citizen of the world'" (Laertius VI, 63).

His resolute homelessness and spectacular poverty—Diogenes had no possession he could not carry—were not about self-sacrifice but about a lust for freedom, for the self-sufficiency gained through lack of need. Inasmuch as all societal institutions and normative presumptions introduce artificial needs, Diogenes pitted himself against them publicly, as Peter Sloterdijk observes, introducing "the original connection between happiness, lack of need, and intelligence into Western Philosophy" (158). Against the institution of marriage, for example, Diogenes asserted sexual independence by masturbating in the marketplace and then announcing that he "wished it were as easy to relieve hunger by rubbing an empty stomach" (Laertius VI, 46, 69). When Alexander the Great offered to grant him anything he wished—money, power, position—Diogenes, who was sunning himself, replied, "Stand out of my light" (Laertius VI, 38; cf. Dio I, 175), thereby affirming the natural pleasure of the sun over any artificial (political/cultural) ambition, and also reversing the "mythical genealogy whereby the king, as descended from god, was supposed to personify the sun" (Foucault 121). Still, Alexander greatly admired Diogenes, admitting, "Had I not been Alexander, I should have liked to be Diogenes" (VI, 32).

Diogenes had no patience for abstract philosophy nor for "so-called sophists" (Dio I, 185), practicing instead what Sloterdijk calls "dialectical materialism" (105), a cheeky form of resistance to idealism that countered the repression of material existence not through rhetorical eloquence nor through philosophical brilliance but through outrageous and strategically (*kairotically*) timed bodily "arguments"—the Diogenesean Cynic laughs, "farts, shits, pisses, masturbates on the street, before the eyes of the Athenian market" (103). Diogenes called "Plato's lectures a waste of time" (Laertius VI, 23) and consistently challenged abstract theory with materialist interventions, which could be what prompted Plato to call him "A Socrates gone mad" (VI, 53): "when somebody declared that there is no such thing as motion, he got up and walked about" (VI, 39); to Plato's "subtle theory of eros," he masturbated in the marketplace (Sloterdijk 101); when Plato offered an eloquent definition of "man" as "an animal, biped and featherless [. . .] Diogenes plucked a fowl and brought it into the lecture-room with the words, 'Here is Plato's man'" (Laertius VI, 40). What Diogenes offers rhetorical theory is not a theory but a mode of living that is "not satisfied with words," Sloterdijk observes, that "proceeds to a material argumentation that rehabilitates the body" (105). Diogenes does not "speak against idealism" but instead "lives against it," offering "a new twist to the question of how to *say* the truth" (104). According to Laertius, Diogenes held "freedom of speech" to be the most beautiful thing in the world (VI, 69), but here "speech" must be understood as an ethical saying, which may or may not be verbal(ized).

In his lectures on *parrhesia* (saying the truth), Foucault names Diogenes as an original *parrhesiastes*, as one who "said" the truth even when it endangered his life. Cynic *parrhesia*, Foucault notes, was "a public activity" that took three fundamental forms: critical preaching, scandalous behavior, and "provocative dialogue" (118–19). Diogenes is typically associated with scandalous behavior, but Foucault demonstrates that Dio Chrysostom's "Fourth Discourse on Kingship" also links Diogenes' truth-saying to a dangerous exchange that is not unlike Socratic dialogue. However, whereas Socrates shows his interlocutors they are ignorant of what they claim to know, Diogenes shows Alexander that he is not what he claims to be (126), that his devotion to wealth, physical pleasure, and political power indicate that he is a slave to socially constituted desires (132). Alexander becomes furious, but Diogenes holds his ground, telling Alexander to kill him if he has to, but that there will be no one left to tell him the truth: "for all are less honest than I am and more servile" (Dio I, 195–96; quoted in Foucault 128). Diogenes is depicted here as one who risks his life to say the truth, offering his interlocutor the chance to "internalize this *parrhesiastic* struggle" (Foucault 133) and so to open the path to independence, to freedom.

The figure of Diogenes—a doxagraphical yet compelling construction—offers the fields of oral and written rhetorics an ethico-political alternative to Enlightenment and Marxist thinking (as ideology critique or as cultural studies), which, according to Sloterdijk, lead to enlightened false consciousness or to modernist cynicism (5). In place of Enlightenment thinking, Sloterdijk reconstructs a lost Diogenesian "cheekiness," which he calls "Kynicism"; offers a "physiognomic main text," which he associates with the body politic (tongue, mouth, eyes, breasts, arses, and genitals); and provides a "cabinet of cynics," which function as Kynical exemplars (ancient and postmodern). The Kynic is a *parrhesiastes* who consistently counters sovereign, hegemonic power, affirming instead radical multiplicities, or excluded thirds, or what Davis calls "a kynical 'community'" (56; 47–56) and Vitanza calls "becoming dog" (50, cf. 36). Laertius tells us that Diogenes once "lit a lamp in broad daylight and said, as he went about, 'I am looking for a man'" (VI, 41)—looking, that is, for a dog, for a human being not mired in socially constituted needs and desires. Today, too, the values of Kynicism call for a lighting of the lamp in broad daylight to search for a community (without community) of dogs.

NOTES

1. Dio Chrysostom says Diogenes spent his winters in Athens and his summers in Corinth.

2. K. von Fritz traces this story to Menippus of Gadara's nonextant work *The Sale of Diogenes* and argues that it is purely fictional.

BIBLIOGRAPHY

Biographical Sources

Dio Chrysostom. "Fourth Discourse on Kingship." *Discourses I–IX.* Vol. I. Trans. J. W. Cohoon. Cambridge: Harvard UP, 1932. 168–233.

Laertius, Diogenes. *Lives of Eminent Philosophers.* Vol. 2. Trans. R. D. Hicks. Cambridge: Harvard UP, 1995.

Critical Sources

Branham, R. Bracht, and Marie-Odile Goulet-Caze. *The Cynics: The Cynic Movement in Antiquity and Its Legacy.* Berkeley: U of California P, 1996.

Davis, D. Diane. *Breaking Up [at] Totality: A Rhetoric of Laughter.* Carbondale: Southern Illinois UP, 2000.

Foucault, Michel. *Fearless Speech*. Ed. Joseph Pearson. Los Angeles: Semiotext(e), 2001.

Navia, Luis E. *Diogenes of Sinope: The Man in the Tub*. Westport: Greenwood P, 1998.

Sayer, F. *Diogenes of Sinope: A Study of Greek Cynicism*. Baltimore: J. H. Furst, 1938.

Sloterdijk, Peter. *Critique of Cynical Reason*. Trans. Michael Eldred. Minneapolis: U of Minnesota P, 1987.

Vitanza, Victor J. *Negation, Subjectivity, and the History of Rhetoric*. Albany: State U of New York P, 1997.

DIONYSIUS OF HALICARNASSUS

(ca. 55–ca. 7 BCE)

Jeffrey Walker

Aside from a few stray references in his own writings, little is known of the life of Dionysius of Halicarnassus. He was born in Halicarnassus (modern Bodrum, on the southwest coast of Turkey) probably sometime between 60 and 55 BCE; he thus came of age during the Roman civil wars that ended with the defeat of Antony and Cleopatra in 31 BCE, and saw the emergence of a new political order under the emperor Augustus. Dionysius went to Rome in 30 BCE, apparently to write his *Roman Antiquities* (*Rhōmaikē Archaiologia*), a history in Greek of the Roman state from its earliest beginnings, which he worked on until at least 8 BCE. Its main purpose was to reconcile an often-restive Greek audience to Roman rule, by demonstrating that the Romans had descended from ancient Greeks, and had evolved a civil society that embodied the best of the Greek character as enunciated by Isocrates in his *Panegyricus*: an identity based not on race or ethnicity, but on a shared civil culture (Gabba).

At Rome, Dionysius associated with an elite circle of (mostly Greek) men of letters, including the Roman historian Q. Aelius Tubero, and the Greek rhetorician Caecilius of Calacte (the author of the lost treatise to which Longinus's *On the Sublime* responds); and he taught rhetoric. As part of his teaching, he produced the works that have established his reputation as one of the foremost rhetorical (or "literary") critics of the ancient world. These include a series of critical essays *On the Ancient Orators*, of which the introduction and four essays on Lysias, Isocrates, Isaeus, and Demosthenes survive; a critical study of Thucydides; a treatise *On the Composition of Words* (*Peri Suntheseōs Onomatōn*), his most famous rhetorical work; a treatise *On Imitation* (*Peri Mimēseōs*), of which some fragments and a medieval "epitome" survive; *Dinarchus*, an essay on the authenticity of the speeches attributed to that Attic orator; and three letters on rhetorical-critical topics. Dionysius's lost works include a treatise *For Political Philosophy*; two more essays from *On the Ancient Orators* (which may never have been written); and three additional critical studies of Lysias, Isocrates, and Demosthenes.

Dionysius represents a strand of Isocratean rhetoric, which he calls "the old, philosophical rhetoric" and associates with Atticism in opposition to Asianism, and which he claims has long been in eclipse but recently has been restored (*On the Ancient Orators* 1–2). Thus he is an early representative, at the end of the Hellenistic period, of what will be the dominant rhetorical tradition during the Second Sophistic. His critical writings reflect an approach to "advanced" rhetorical instruction that, as with Isocrates, regards the purely technical rules and terminologies laid down in the standard manuals as useful but elementary and insufficient. (A similar view appears in Cicero's *De Oratore*.) Dionysius assumes a student who is familiar with that terminology, and now will engage in close critical study of major orators and writers, in order to identify their strengths and weaknesses, imitate their strengths (in composition and declamation exercises), and synthesize those strengths in a distinct, original voice that is the student's own.

DIONYSIUS'S RHETORICAL THEORY

Dionysius' basic definition of rhetoric, from *On Imitation*, is preserved as a quotation by the Byzantine commentator Syrianus: "Rhetoric is an artistic faculty of persuasive discourse on political matters, having the goal of speaking well" (*Rhētorikē esti dunamis technikē pithanou logou en pragmati politikōi, telos echousa to eu legein*); citations of this definition by later Byzantines suggest that it may have continued "according to what is possible" (*kata to endechomenon*, Usener-Radermacher vol. 2, 197–200). This definition has obvious Aristotelian resonances, since both "faculty" (*dunamis*) and "the possibilities" (*to endechomenon*) appear in Aristotle's famous definition (*Estō dē rhētorikē dunamis peri hekaston tou theōrēsai to endechomenon pithanon*, "Let rhetoric be a faculty of observing in each case the possible means of perusasion"). But Dionysius's placement of himself within an Isocratean tradition has certain implications. First, rhetoric is not simply the art of practical civic oratory that Aristotle describes. Rather, as with Isocrates, rhetoric is a general, political-philosophic discourse art that concerns itself primarily with questions in civics, ethics, justice, and public policy, and that manifests itself across the whole spectrum of practical, panegyric, and literary discursive genres, but preeminently the panegyric and literary (including history, philosophy, and poetry). Second, as an "artistic faculty," rhetoric cannot be merely a set of rules and recipes, but instead is a personal capacity cultivated over time through an educational process that resembles gymnastic training.

As Dionysius says in another fragment from *On Imitation*, the three requirements for "excellence in public discourse, and every art and branch of knowledge" are "a ready nature, careful study, and laborious exercise" (*phusis dexia, mathesis akribēs, askēsis epiponos*, Usener and Radermacher Vol. 2, 200). "Ready nature" means talent (and preparation), while "careful study" is the work of criticism. The meaning of "laborious exercise" is clarified in Dionysius's *Lysias* (11), where he says the special "grace" (*charis*) of Lysianic style cannot be described, but can be learned by "training one's nonrational sense-perception for a long time, through lengthy practice and nonrational felt experience" (*chronōi pollōi kai makrai tribēi kai alogōi pathei tēn alogon sunaskein aisthēsin*, translated very literally). Through prolonged immersion in the critical study of an author and continual writing and speaking practice with an eye to imitation, one can internalize the strengths of an author's discourse as part of one's intuitive linguistic and rhetorical competence. One gets the feel of it.

The essay *Lysias* provides the most straightforward example of Dionysius's Isocratean approach, which divides the analysis of discourse into the handling of subject matter (the *pragmatikos topos*) and style (the *lektikos topos*). In *Lysias*, he begins with style. He does not clearly follow the usual topics in Hellenistic style manuals—the four virtues of style (clarity, correctness, ornament, propriety), and the three types of style (plain, middle, grand)—but instead turns to a catalogue of the leading virtues or characteristics of Lysianic style: his pure Attic dialect, his use of "standard and common words" (the equivalent of "plain English"), his clarity, his vividness, his expression of character, his propriety, his persuasive naturalness, and the ultimate quality, his indescribable grace (*charis*), which arises from the combination of his other qualities and pervades the entirety of his discourse (2–11).

After a brief interlude, in which he talks about acquiring a feel for style (12–14), Dionysius turns to the characteristics of Lysias's handling of subject matter, or more specifically his invention and selection of arguments, his arrangement of material, and his development of arguments in the body of a speech: Lysias is good (and to be imitated) in his invention and selection, but somewhat weak in arrangement and development, especially where a strong emotional appeal is needed (15). These points are illustrated through the examination of several speeches (16–34): Dionysius gives the "hypothesis" (*hupothesis*) for each speech—a brief outline of the case, with some remarks on the rhetorical situation—and then he comments on Lysias's handling of the prologue, narration, proofs, and epilogue, quoting each part at length.

It is evident, in *Lysias* and in Dionysius's other essays, that his treatment of the *pragmatikos topos* is more or less conventional, though generally astute, while his treatment of the *lektikos topos* is quite original. Most notable is his focus on multiple characteristics such as clarity and vividness, and their combination in some overall quality such as grace. In *Demosthenes* and again in *On Composition*, he develops an exceptionally sophisticated analysis of prose rhythm, noting its close relation to (and important differences from) poetic rhythm and melody, and showing how particular combinations of words can produce through their prosody such qualities as "beauty," "pleasantness," "dignity," "impressiveness," and so forth. The result is a way of thinking about style that prefigures Hermogenes' extremely detailed analysis (nearly two centuries later) of twenty types of style arising from the synthesis of various features in different combinations, though Dionysius's approach is more impressionistic (Wooten); it also prefigures the sort of analysis we find in Longinus's *On the Sublime*. It is possible that Dionysius would reject Hermogenes' analysis as excessively mechanical, since Dionysius's goal is not an exhaustive, systematic description of stylistic types, but the identification of characteristics that are more appropriately felt and internalized, and that may not be describable at all. Longinus may be the true continuator.

One might ask whether Dionysius's interest in style prefigures a tendency in later classical rhetoric away from argumentation and toward stylistic rhetoric. Perhaps, but it seems unlikely. In the first place, a rhetoric merely of stylistic elaboration is what Dionysius associates with Asianism and criticizes as "mindless" (*On the Ancient Orators* 1–2). In the prologue of *On Composition*, he declares that the *pragmatikos topos* and the *lektikos topos* are equally important; but ability in thought, and the invention and judgment of arguments, require maturity and experience and are "difficult" (*chalepos*) for the young, whereas the attractions and powers of style are more accessible (1).

What we see in Dionysius, then, is an exemplary embodiment of Isocratean rhetoric and pedagogy at the end of the Hellenistic age, expressed in critical essays that are part of an advanced course of instruction for young men who have completed the basic course in rhetoric, but have not yet attained the fullness of experience, maturity, and knowledge. Along the way—and amid the business of writing his *Roman Antiquities*—he offers one of the most original and useful approaches to stylistics developed in the classical tradition.

BIBLIOGRAPHY

Primary Sources and Translations

Aujac, Germaine, trans. *Denys d'Halicarnasse: Opuscules Rhétoriques*. 6 vols. Paris: Société d'Édition "Les Belles Lettres," 1978–92.

Cary, Earnest, ed. and trans. *Dionysius of Halicarnassus: Roman Antiquities*. Loeb Classical Library (Greek and English). 7 vols. Cambridge: Harvard UP, 1937–50.

Jacoby, C., ed. *Dionysi Halicarnasensis Antiquitates Romanae*. 4 vols. Leipzig, 1885–1905. Rpt. Stuttgart: Teubner, 1967.

Usener, H., and L. Radermacher, eds. *Dionysii Halicarnasei Opusculorum*. 2 vols. Stuttgart: Teubner, 1965.

Usher, Stephen, trans. *Dionysius of Halicarnassus: The Critical Essays*. Loeb Classical Library (Greek and English). 2 vols. Cambridge: Harvard UP, 1974, 1985.

Critical Sources

Bonner, S. F. *The Literary Treatises of Dionysius of Halicarnassus: A Study in the Development of Critical Method*. Cambridge: Cambridge UP, 1939. Rpt. Amsterdam: Hakkert, 1969.

Cronjé, Jacobus Van Wyck. *Dionysius of Halicarnassus, De Demosthene: A Critical Appraisal of the Status Quaestionis*. New York: Olms, 1986.

Fox, Matthew. "History and Rhetoric in Dionysius of Halicarnassus." *Journal of Roman Studies* 83 (1993): 31–47.

Gabba, Emilio. *Dionysius and the History of Archaic Rome*. Berkeley: U of California P, 1991.

Grube, G. M. A. *The Greek and Roman Critics*. Toronto: Toronto UP, 1965. 207–30.

Kennedy, George A. *The Art of Rhetoric in the Roman World*. Princeton: Princeton UP, 1972. 342–63.

———. *A New History of Classical Rhetoric*. Princeton: Princeton UP, 1994. 161–66.

Reid, Robert S. "Dionysius of Halicarnassus' Compositional Style and the Theory of Literate Consciousness." *Rhetoric Review* 15 (1996): 46–64.

———. " 'Neither Oratory nor Dialogue': Dionysius of Halicarnassus and the Genre of Plato's *Apology*." *Rhetoric Society Quarterly* 27.4 (1997): 63–90.

Roberts, W. Rhys. *Dionysius of Halicarnassus: The Three Literary Letters*. Cambridge: Cambridge UP, 1901.

Schenkeveld, D. M. "Linguistic Theories in the Rhetorical Works of Dionysius of Halicarnassus." *Glotta* 61.1–2 (1981): 67–94.

Thompson, Wayne N. "Dionysius of Halicarnassus: A Reappraisal." *Quarterly Journal of Speech* 65 (1979): 303–10.

Vaahtera, J. "Phonetics and Euphony in Dionyius of Halicarnassus." *Menomosyne* 50.5 (1997): 586–95.

Wooten, Cecil. "Dionysius of Halicarnassus and Hermogenes on the Style of Demosthenes." *American Journal of Philology* 110 (1989): 576–88.

DIOTIMA OF MANTINEA

(ca. 460–420? BCE)

C. Jan Swearingen

Diotima appears in Plato's *Symposium*, where Socrates introduces her as a priestess from Mantinea who was invited to Athens in 440 BCE to avert plague. Within the dialogue, narratively placed in ca. 400 BCE, Diotima deems Socrates defective in the arts of love and discourse alike. His dialogue with Diotima differs from his consultations with other priests and priestesses reported in the dialogues; she speaks far longer than any of the other religious figures consulted by Socrates; and she is said to "speak like one of our best sophists" (*Symposium* 208c). Although bas reliefs dating to the second century BCE, and written testimony dating to the first century CE, depict Diotima as a historical figure and teacher of Socrates, Marsilio Ficino's 1485 *Oratio Septima II* presents Diotima as a literary invention (Waithe 105–06), and later historians and philologists increasingly assumed that Diotima is a fictional character, even though that would make her the only fictional character in Plato's dialogues. Revisionist historians of rhetoric are now reconsidering the historicity of Diotima and its implications for understanding Plato's, and later, views of rhetoric.

There are seveal reasons for considering Diotima as a significant figure in the history of rhetoric: her public presence in Athens, her role as a teacher of Socrates, and the rhetorical aspects of her teachings on discourse and love. Although it has long been claimed that she is a fictional character, her appearance in Plato's *Symposium* is given a historical setting that can be documented: the plague which afflicted Athens during the Peloponnesian war in 440 BCE, and which eventually caused Pericles' death. Athens regulated the public presence of women more strictly than other cities; priestesses were the only women allowed to speak in public without fear of rebuke or disgrace. It is therefore plausible that a priestess would have to be called from neighboring Mantinea. In real historical time, at the time of the writing of the *Symposium* in 385 BCE, Mantinea had recently been annexed by Athens. Like the Pythagorean women philosophers dispersed during the same period, the priestesses of Mantinea would not have celebrated the Athenian state deity, Athena, but more probably Aphrodite or her older counterpart, Demeter. Diotima presents herself as a teacher both of the mysteries and of the goddess of love, Aphrodite. Diotima, regardless of her historical status by modern standards, probably provides a reasonably accurate representation of the teachings of priestesses at that time; particularly the teachings regarding love that were entrusted to women celebrants in the mysteries. Even though an individual person named Diotima may never have existed, it is unlikely that Plato would have created a totally fictional character; the only counterpart is the "Elean Stranger" in the *Sophist*, chosen to represent views so radical that Plato dared not put them in the mouth of Socrates. There are no other candidates for totally fictional characters in Plato's dialogues. Plato took many liberties with his representation of characters, including Socrates. However, it is implausible that he created characters completely unrecognizable to his audiences. There are additional grounds for counting Diotima among the rhetorical figures represented by Plato. She is said to speak like "one of our best sophists" (208c). And she rebukes Socrates; she is presented as teaching him a few things about rhetoric and love, and about the relationships between the two. Diotima represents teachings about rhetoric, and about love, that are echoed in the much less questioned but also unreliably documented speech by Gorgias, the *Encomium on Helen*. Because by his own report she taught Socrates, and because she or priestesses like her were public presences in Athens, she is a firm candidate for inclusion in a revisionist history of classical rhetoric. Alongside Aspasia, Diotima is one of only two characters in the dialogues with whom Socrates adopts the role of student.

Putting aside the many facile dismissals of Diotima, let us turn to what, exactly, she has to say about rhetoric, and about love, and about the relationships between the two. When his turn comes in the *Symposium* to make a speech about love, Socrates instead recounts a dialogue with Diotima that took place twenty-five years earlier, in which discourse is likened to love; both are defined as intermediaries, as daimons or spirits that move back and forth between human individuals and between humans and gods. Like love, *logos* mediates between human and divine in two senses: as the link between human love and divine insight, and as a spirit that animates discursive as well as erotic desire. It has a higher and a lower aspect: Aphrodite *pandemos* is the god venerated by the common people as the patron, and cause, of erotic love and fertility. This love is the offspring of poverty and contrivance, born on Aphrodite's birthday, and thus easily confused with other kinds of love (*Symposium* 203). The higher Aphrodite, the aspect of Eros as desire for beauty, is taught in the mysteries through a process of transcending immediate desire for this beautiful thing or person in a gradual movement toward apprehension of beauty itself. Like the allegory of the charioteer in the *Phaedrus*, Diotima's teaching describes a ladder of ascent; but, challenging the rendering in the *Phaedrus*, Diotima chides Socrates. "You are wrong, Socrates, in supposing that love is of the beautiful" (206d). Man must beget virtue and beauty, and can do this only through seeing beauty in "that which makes it visible" (212a). Only then can the distinction between truth and illusion be determined, with the begetting and rearing of a true virtue through love. Compared with the speeches on love in the *Phaedrus*, Diotima's speech in the *Symposium* defines an ongoing, lifelong, dialectical relationship between visible, tangible "human" love and the divine spirit that both inspires and teaches the begetting of virtue, a drive as strong as the desire for reproduction. While some contemporary critics have seen in Diotima's teaching, and in the allegory of the charioteer, an appropriation of female reproductive birth-giving by male philosophers and philosophizing, the reverse can also be argued. Diotima chastizes the philosopher, Socrates, for his failure to embrace the human alongside the divine aspects of love. If his discourse and his interlocution avoid the tangibility of direct affection and exchange with other humans, he is then pursuing the ultimate illusion: that a mortal can "look upon essential beauty entire, pure and unalloyed" (212a). Comparison of Diotima's speech in the *Symposium* alongside Socrates' other discussions of rhetoric in the *Phaedrus* and *Gorgias* provide ample dialectical inquiries into the subjects of love, lack, desire, discourse, and rhetoric.

It is not difficult to define how Diotima challenges traditional histories of rhetoric and understandings of rhetoric. To include her in a history of rhetoric at all is to include a woman from classical times as a practitioner and teacher of rhetoric, a role that has been claimed for only a few others, and only recently. Because she has been deemed fictional by most classicists, including Diotima in a history of rhetoric opens up the larger question of the historical reliability of other accounts of classical figures. If Diotima is a fiction, what of Socrates? What of Gorgias? Plato's use of dramatic, literary, and rhetorical devices is increasingly acknowledged. In rereadings of the *Symposium*, Plato the alleged logocentrist can now be refigured as one of the poets, writers, and Sophists that he seems to rebuke. The debate between Socrates and Diotima in the *Symposium*, as recounted by Socrates, as recounted by Apollodorus, as recounted by Plato, throws all of these questions into high relief. Diotima's discourse on ascent and desire resembles the voice of Socrates, or Plato, in the myth of the charioteer in the *Phaedrus*, with Socrates as Diotima's student playing the role of the indolent youth more typical of one of his interlocutors. Is that why Socrates concludes the *Symposium* with a question that might be answered in the affirmative, for Plato: whether the same poet might win the prize for tragedy and comedy in the one work? Whether or not the *Symposium* is a joke on Socrates, or Diotima, or both, we must not forget that satire—comic as well as tragic—was a serious form of dramatic rhetoric for the Greeks. But what kind of satire, and what kind of irony, are represented in Plato's depiction of Diotima? As in so many other dialogues, he leaves that question for us to decide, dialectically.

BIBLIOGRAPHY

Biographical Sources

Henry, Madeleine. *Prisoner of History, Aspasia of Miletus and Her Biographical Tradition*. New York: Oxford UP, 1995.

Menage, Gilles. *The History of Women Philosophers* (1690, Latin; 1750, French). Trans. Beatrice Zedler. Lanham, MD: UP of America, 1984.

Nussbaum, Martha. *The Fragility of Goodness.* Cambridge: Cambridge UP, 1986.

Waithe, Mary Ellen. *A History of Women Philosophers, Vol. 1: 600 B.C.–500 A.D.* Boston: Nijhoff, 1987.

Critical Sources

Fantham, Elaine, et al. *Women in the Classical World.* New York: Oxford UP, 1994.

Halperin, Michael. "Why Is Diotima a Woman?" *Before Sexuality: The Construction of Erotic Experience in the Ancient World.* Ed. David M. Halperin, John Winkler, and Froma Zeitlin. Princeton: Princeton UP, 1990. 257–308.

Jahn, Otto. "Socrate et Diôtime, Bas-Relief de Bronze." *Annales de l'Institut Archéologique* 13 (1841): 3–4.

Mingazzini, Paolino. "Su Duo Oggetti in Terracotta Raffiguaranti Socrate." La Parole del Passato: *Rivista di Studi Antichi* 25 (1970): 351–58.

Morgan, Michael L. *Platonic Piety. Philosophy and Ritual in Fourth-Century Athens.* New Haven: Yale UP, 1990.

Plato. *Symposium.* 1925. Cambridge, MA: Loeb Classical Library, 1983.

Rosen, Stanley. *Plato's Symposium.* 2nd ed. New Haven: Yale UP, 1987.

Scott, Gary Allen. *Plato's Socrates As Educator.* Albany: State U of New York P, 2000.

Swearingen, C. Jan. "A Lover's Discourse: Diotima, Logos, and Desire." *Reclaiming Rhetorica: Women in the Rhetorical Tradition.* Ed. Andrea A. Lunsford. Pittsburgh: U of Pittsburgh P, 1995. 25–52.

———. "Plato's Feminine: Appropriation, Impersonation, and Metaphorical Polemic." *Rhetoric Society Quarterly* (Spring 1992): 109–23.

Wolf, Christa. *Cassandra.* Trans. Jan Van Huerck. New York: Farrar Straus Giroux, 1984.

DISSOI LOGOI

(ca. 400 BCE)

Edward Schiappa

Dissoi Logoi or *Twofold Arguments* (hereafter *DL*) is a problematic and interesting text. It is a problematic text because the authorship, date, state of completion, purpose, and even the original dialect are uncertain. Yet *DL* remains an interesting text because it is clearly influenced by what could be called the sophistic sensibilities of the late fifth century BCE.

Because there is a reasonably clear reference to the end of the Peloponnesian War in section 1.8 of *DL*, most (though not all) scholars agree that the text was probably written around 400 BCE. Such a dating also makes sense of the vocabulary that appears in section 8, which does not use such words as "rhetoric" or "dialectic" where one might expect them if the text had been written some decades later. A number of possible authors have been hypothesized, including representatives of Socratic, Stoic, and Pythagorean schools. In the late nineteenth century, attention turned to the older Sophists, and Protagoras, Gorgias, and Hippias have all been suggested as possible authors. T. M. Robinson's discussion of authorship remains the most thorough, and he suggests that the text is basically a compilation of notes influenced mostly by Protagoras and in smaller measure by such Sophists as Gorgias, Hippias, and Socrates.

The text begins with a series of chapters that present twofold arguments about various subjects that appear to illustrate Protagoras's claim that "there are two arguments (*logoi*) in opposition to each other about everything" (Schiappa 100). Section 1 is titled "On Good and Bad" and explores the idea that the same thing may be both good and bad: Illness is bad for the sick but good for the doctors, for example, or victory in competition is good for the winner but bad for the losers. Section 2 is titled "On Seemly and Shameful" and again provides a series of examples of how the same action can be viewed as either seemly or its opposite. Section 3 follows suit and is titled "On Just and Unjust," while section 4 is titled "On Truth and Falsehood."

The author not only provides illustrations in each chapter of how, for example, anything can be seen as either good or bad; the author also raises the metaphysical question of what the examples prove the status of "good" and "bad" may be. For example, in section 1.1 *DL* reads, "Some say that what is good and what is bad are two different things, others that they are the same thing, and that the same thing is good for some but bad for others, or at one time good and at another time bad for the same person." This pattern is repeated in sections 2, 3, and 4. What the author appears to be wrestling with can be explained in contemporary terms as the status of relational qualities. Today most people would readily understand the idea of a frame of reference; that is, we see no tension or even novelty to the notion that something, say nudity, may be socially appropriate in one context but inappropriate in another. With a clear notion of context, or frame of reference, we see no confusion either about nudity or about the ideas of "appropriate" and "inappropriate." But it was precisely such paradoxes as "X can be Y and not-Y" that fueled a good deal of debate in classical Greek philosophy. Parmenides, for example, sought to bar expressions of the form "X is not-Y," because pursuing the path of "is not" is described by Parmenides (B6) as leading to confusion and contradiction:

> First I bar you from this route of inquiry, but also from the one on which mortals wander, knowing nothing, double-headed. For helplessness in their breasts steers a mind set adrift. They are tossed about, as much deaf as blind, an undiscerning horde, by whom being and not-being are considered the same and not the same—and the route of all is backward-turning. (adapted from Austin 161)

Similarly, the dialogues of Plato collectively argue that if one believes some X is described as both Y and not-Y, we must not understand what Y really is. The syntax at work in *DL* makes it a small step to elevate "good" or "seemly" to *the* good and *the* seemly, the step that Plato's dialogues take to turn what we would call relational qualities into substantives represented in his theory of forms. Accordingly, the first four sections not only reflect Protagorean interest in what we would now call relativism, they also reflect an Eleatic and Socratic interest in the metaphysical status of qualities.

Section 5 is untitled and offers a refutation of the proposition that "the demented, the sane, the wise, and the ignorant both say and do the same things" (5.1). After illustrating the proposition with examples, the author argues that those who argue thusly are confusing general qualities with particulars, and they ignore the fact that while the wise and foolish say the same thing, the wise speak "at the right moment and the demented at moments when it is not proper" (5.9).

Section 6 explores the then-popular issue of whether wisdom (*sophia*) and excellence (*aretē*) can be taught. The author considers five arguments against the idea that they can be taught and offers refutations of each; the author concludes, "I am not saying that wisdom and excellence *are* teachable, but that the above mentioned proofs do not satisfy me" (6.13). Section 7, also untitled, offers a brief argument against assigning people to public offices by lot, arguing that people ought to be assigned jobs for which they are clearly suitable.

The untitled section 8 offers an interesting account of what sort of speaking skills are desirable to learn: "I believe it belongs to the same man and to the same skill to be able to hold dialogue succinctly, to understand the truth of things, to plead one's court-cases correctly, to be able to make popular speeches, to understand argument-skills, and to teach about the nature of all things—how they are [their condition] and how they came to be" (8.1). The section is interesting in two respects. First, the terminology is more appropriate to the fifth century BCE than the fourth, as it does not use the terms "rhetoric," "philosophy," or "dialectic" as later authors would. Second, no incompatibility is implied here between seeking truth versus political success. Far from it: success and true understanding are presented as two sides of the same coin.

The final section offers brief praise and practical advice for improving one's memory. It begins, "A very great and most attractive discovery that has been made for the way we live is memory; it is useful for all purposes, for both Inquiry and Wisdom" (*es philosophian te kai sophian*) (9.1). Again, it is noteworthy that the passage contains no explicit reference to the utility of memory specifically for public speakers.

DL's primary value today is that it provides historical insight concerning what can be described as early sophistic rhetorical and linguistic theory. Unraveling the sometimes convoluted arguments made could be a useful pedagogical exercise in understanding how we think about the relationship between words and their referents.

DL is sometimes referred to as *Dialexeis*. The best resource on *DL* remains T. M. Robinson's annotated edition. A translation is also available in Sprague, but Robinson's translation is a more accurate guide to the grammar and vocabulary of the text.

BIBLIOGRAPHY

Primary Sources and Translations

Robinson, Thomas M. *Contrasting Arguments: An Edition of the Dissoi Logoi*. Salem, NH: Ayer, 1979.
Sprague, Rosamond Kent, ed. *The Older Sophists*. Columbia: U of South Carolina P, 1972.

Critical Sources

Austin, Scott. *Parmenides: Being, Bounds, and Logic*. New Haven: Yale UP, 1986.
Schiappa, Edward. *Protagoras and Logos*, 2nd ed. Columbia: U of South Carolina P, 2003.

THE ELDER SENECA

(ca. 55 BCE–ca. 39 CE)

Beth S. Bennett

The Elder Seneca, so designated to avoid confusion with his identically named son,[1] is known for his collection of *controversiae* and *suasoriae* from the Augustan era of Rome titled *Oratorum et rhetorum sententiae, divisiones, colores.* He was born to a wealthy, equestrian family in Corduba (now Cordoba), "a deeply Romanized and cultured city in Southern Spain" (Sussman, *The Elder Seneca* 19). The cultural dominance of Rome had resulted from a long, continued presence of a standing army and military headquarters in this province, along with considerable immigration from Italy, and from the opportunities Rome provided native Spaniards for their support in military campaigns (Griffin 1). Though Seneca himself was born in Corduba, his family seems to have been Italian immigrants, either Etruscan or Illyrian, based on the family *nomen* Annaeus (Sussman, *The Elder Seneca* 20; cf. Griffin 4). What is known about his life comes chiefly from his own work, as well as from information found in extant works of his son, Seneca the Younger, 4 BCE–65 CE.

The Elder Seneca was born around 55 BCE,[2] when Cicero was still alive, but he never had the chance to hear the Roman orator-statesman speak, a deficiency for which he blamed the civil unrest of the time:

> I think I heard everyone of great repute in oratory, with the exception of Cicero; and even Cicero I was deprived of not by my age, but by the raging civil wars, which at that time were traversing the entire world, and which kept me behind the walls of my colony. (Winterbottom, *Contr. I* pr. 11)

As a young boy in Corduba, Seneca became friends with Porcius Latro (*Contr. I* pr. 13), and later both studied declamation at the school of a Spanish *rhetor* named Marullus (*Contr. I* pr. 22). Whether or not this school was in Rome, which is doubtful (see Fairweather 5; cf. Griffin 6), or in Spain, it provided Seneca with the opportunity to display his talent at memorization (*Contr. I* pr. 2) and to witness Latro's talent in declaiming (*Contr. I* pr. 22–24).

At the end of the civil unrest, sometime between 38 and 36 BCE, Seneca made his first trip to Rome, which resulted in a lengthy stay (see Sussman, *The Elder Seneca* 22; Griffin 7). During that and subsequent stays in Rome, Seneca occupied himself by attending the public declamations of his friend Latro and other professional *rhetores*, as well as performances by student declaimers and adult amateurs (Fairweather 6–8). Though sometimes referred to as Seneca Rhetor, there is no evidence that Seneca himself was ever a *rhetor* or even held political office (Edward x; Sussman, *The Elder Seneca* 25; Kennedy, *Art of Rhetoric* 323; Fairweather 8; Griffin 9). Rather, his family's wealth seems to have afforded him the opportunity to pursue his rhetorical and literary interests without requiring a career of public or political service.

Around the turn of the century, after being in Rome for some twenty years, Seneca returned to Spain and married a woman named Helvia, who was probably much younger than he (Sussman, *The Elder Seneca* 21; Griffin 7). Together, they had three sons: Novatus, Seneca, and Mela. Each son has received some distinction historically:

> Novatus was adopted by his father's friend [Junius] Gallio and is known to history as [Junius Gallio Annaeus] procounsul of Achaea at the time of St. Paul's ministry to Corinth (Acts 18:12), a second was the philosopher-dramatist-statesman bearing his father's identical name, Lucius Annaeus Seneca, and a third was Mela, father of the epic poet Lucan. (Kennedy, *Art of Rhetoric* 323; cf. Sussman, *The Elder Seneca* 24)

Seneca returned to Rome, with his young sons, and was to spend the major part of his later years there, with short visits back to Spain. His death, around 39 CE, seems likely to have been in Spain (Sussman, *The Elder Seneca* 23; Griffin 8).

In his work, *Oratorum et rhetorum sententiae, divisiones, colores*, Seneca provides a rich supply of detail not only of Roman declamatory practice, but also of the cultural and rhetorical tastes of an era that otherwise preserved not a single complete oration for study (Leeman 219). Lewis Sussman describes Seneca's collection of declamations as "our major source for understanding this unusual phenomenon and the profound effect it soon had on literary style [. . . as well as] for the sound, perceptive literary criticism contained in the works" (*The Elder Seneca* ix). As for Seneca's talents as a writer, George Kennedy comments, "There is no better witness than the elder Seneca to the importance which educated Romans of the early empire attached to rhetoric" (*Art of Rhetoric* 330).

Despite its historical significance as the main source of knowledge about Roman declamatory practice, Seneca's collection garnered limited scholarly attention until the 1970s (cf. Whitehorne 14), when first Michael Winterbottom published his translation of the collection for the Loeb series, in 1974, and then Lewis Sussman (1978) and Janet Fairweather (1981) published separate monograph studies on Seneca, overlapping in some subject areas but largely focusing on different aspects of Seneca's life and work (see Fairweather ix). Prior to Winterbottom, the most widely used translations of Seneca's work were that of Hermann J. Müller

(1887, 1963) and William A. Edward's English translation of the *suasoriae* (1928, 1996). The most often cited contemporary editions of the Latin text are those edited by Henri Bornecque (1902, 1932) and Adolf Kiessling (1872, 1967).

CONTRIBUTIONS TO THE RHETORICAL TRADITION

The original collection by the Elder Seneca seems to have consisted of ten books, each with its own prefatory remarks addressed to his sons, of extracts from *controversiae*, and at least two books of *suasoriae* extracts (Sussman, *The Elder Seneca* 34; Kennedy, *Art of Rhetoric* 324). Unfortunately, what remains are only five of the ten books on *controversiae*, two of which are missing prefaces, and only one book on suasoriae without a preface.[3] The books are organized around specific declamatory themes, illustrating how a theme was addressed by different declaimers, as well as providing evidence of the skills of individual declaimers of the day. In particular, Seneca arranged his treatment of a declamatory theme in terms of the *sententiae, divisiones,* and *colores* used by the declaimers, thereby emphasizing those features of Roman declamations. Seneca explains his purpose for writing such a work:

> [G]ladly will I comply with your request, making a present to the public of all the eloquent sayings of famous men that I can remember, so that they aren't mere private possessions of someone. [. . .] for in general there are no extant drafts from the pens of the greatest declaimers, or, what is worse, there are forged ones. So to prevent them being unknown, or known in the wrong light, I shall be scrupulous in giving each his due. (Winterbottom, *Contr. I* pr. 10–11)

Thus, Seneca aimed to make two kinds of contributions with this work: one, as an archivist or historian and two, as a critic of the chief declaimers of his day.

The historical significance of Seneca's efforts with this collection cannot be ignored; without it, we would have little evidence for understanding the rhetorical tradition of declamation. The excerpts Seneca gives us are not from school exercises but rather from rhetorical efforts made for public display. In his lengthy study on Roman declamation, Stanley F. Bonner comments that most of the Senecan *controversiae* "appear to have been based upon debates where rival professors used the school-subjects to exhibit their powers and win the plaudits [. . .] of their contemporaries" (39). As a historical collection, the work has been investigated by modern scholars to determine the reliability of Seneca's record and the accuracy of the words he attributes to the various declaimers. While stressing the need for a full *index verborum* to measure and to analyze the subtle differences in the language use recorded by Seneca, Janet Fairweather nonetheless has concluded, "Seneca recorded the words of the declaimers faithfully, though textual corruption has inevitably diminished the reliability of his record" (49).

Because of Seneca's record, we also have a better understanding of the characteristic differences between the *controversiae*, rhetorical exercises based upon legal conflicts, and the *suasoriae*, rhetorical exercises based upon historical or mythical events. Of the two, the *controversia* seems to have been regarded by Romans as the more challenging performance, both for its connection with Roman law and for its tradition of argumentation derived from the Hermagorean doctrine of *stasis*. But, the *suasoria* seems to have been popular among declaimers who enjoyed word play, rhetorical description, and poetic composition rather than argumentation. Seneca remarks that as a student, Ovid had been a good declaimer of *controversiae* but as a professional grew tired of argumentation and focused instead on *suasoriae* (*Contr.* II.2.9–12).

The chief element common to both forms of rhetorical display was the use of *sententiae*: "striking, brilliant, witty, elegant, pointed, or unusual remarks of the declaimers" (Kennedy, *Art of Rhetoric* 324). These witticisms could be inserted anywhere in the declamation, be universal or particular in relevance, and be in prose or poetic form. What they demonstrated was the value placed upon such linguistic skill, and modern scholars have suggested that Seneca's own writing displays that same fondness for "purple passages of declamations" (Kennedy, *Art of Rhetoric* 325). Furthermore, Fairweather cautions against accepting the "austere characterization" scholars have derived of Seneca from his son's portrait of him (see Edward xxviii) because the son's writing, too, follows the literary tastes of the era, valuing sententious discourse over factual description (20–21).

The other two elements emphasized in Seneca's collection are more pertinent to the *controversiae*. The first of these, the *divisio*, refers to the *rhetor*'s logical summary of the subject for the speech. In a *suasoria*, the *divisio* might essentially preview the main arguments to be presented, but in a *controversia*, it functioned to provide the analysis of the *stasis* of the legal case, including listing the main issues and their order of importance in the conflict. What is evident in Seneca is that declaimers commonly disputed between questions of law, *an liceat*, and questions of equity, *an debeat* (see Sussman, *The Elder Seneca* 38–41; Kennedy, *Art of Rhetoric* 325–26). The remaining element, the *color*, was the plea alleged by the accuser or the accused in the *controversia* to "color" or shade the disputed act rhetorically (see Sussman, *The Elder Seneca* 41–43). Seneca provides examples of *colores* in both the narration section of a speech (*Contr. VII.*1.20) and the section devoted to the main argument (*Contr.* I.1.16–19). The *color* enabled a declaimer to interpret the events of a case in an ingenious or novel way, which was important, Edward explains, because "as the subject was given, was hackneyed and had been handled scores of times, the interest of the declamation rested on the originality with which the ideas were expressed, on the novelty of the line of argument and of the *colores*" (xxxv–vi).

Seneca's structural arrangement of his collection may seem rather unsystematic and unlike typical rhetorical handbooks of the time, but Sussman argues that the format seems deliberate and reasonable (*The Elder Seneca* 44). Seneca's compilation of excerpts from the declamations, rather than whole speeches, and of *sententiae*, *divisiones*, and *colores* as the crucial elements for judging the merits of the declaimers seems well suited to his audience and his skills. Though it does not seem to be his intent, the format of Seneca's collection also made the work highly attractive for prospective declaimers to use in preparation for typical declamatory themes and probably explains its popularity and its survival in later centuries. Certainly, in the fourth or fifth century, Seneca's collection of *controversiae* was reduced to extracts for schoolroom use and became known simply as the *Excerpta.*

Importantly, though, beyond the historical preservation of excerpts from the Roman tradition of declamatory practice, Seneca has contributed to the rhetorical tradition through the critical commentary he provided for the practice he compiled. According to J. E. G. Whitehorne, "Seneca's primary function was that of the literary critic and there is general agreement among modern writers that, in this role, he acquitted himself exceedingly well" (16). After a close examination of Seneca's critical commentary (see *Roman Declamation* 133–48), Bonner concludes that the Elder Seneca should be regarded as "the Horace of Augustan prose criticism" (148).

Seneca's critical approach has been characterized as individualist because of his intuitive, unstudied critique of rhetorical practice (Fairweather 67; Sussman, *The Elder Seneca* 96, 107). Rather than arranging his subject matter according to traditional precepts from rhetorical handbooks or identifying elements with standard critical vocabulary, Seneca relies upon the use of a common historical-biographical motif, "pen-portraits," in his prefaces to provide descriptions of the declaimers (Fairweather 50–55). Throughout the collection of excerpts, his commentary is colorful and memorable, mixing examples and anecdotes with psychological and critical insights, resulting in a style that is warm and charming but not always refined (Fairweather 72). As Sussman notes, Seneca is a critic of "eloquence," how some achieve it and others do not, rather than strictly of "declamation" or "rhetoric" and thus is not constrained in his judgments by prevailing theory or rules (*The Elder Seneca* 94). Seneca admits, "I'm not one of those very rigid judges, determined to direct everything by a precise rule. I think that many concessions must be made to genius—but it is faults, not monstrosities that we must concede" (Winterbottom, *Contr. X.*10).

Nonetheless, Seneca assumes his descriptive criticism of declamatory practice will show that the state of eloquence had been declining since the days of Cicero (*Contr. I* pr. 6–7). A chief reason for this decline is that, since oratory is *vir bonus dicendi peritus*, he insists, moral character influences eloquence, and the depravity of Roman culture was self-evident (*Contr. I.*8–11). He also blames the decline on the change in the political system. Though he seems to have accepted the demise of the old Republic and to hold respect for Augustus, he ardently condemns the state-mandated book burning implemented by the imperial regime (Griffin 13–14). Yet a third reason he offers for this decline was a general law of nature promoted in Rome by Sallust: "*omnia orta occiduent et aucta senesceunt*" (Leeman 225).

Seneca's collection of extracts from over a hundred orators and declaimers (see Edward xl–xliv) shows that literary tastes of the early empire were changing toward a "new style" (Fairweather 301). Kennedy describes the features of this style:

> Sentences are much shorter than in Ciceronian Latin. There is a staccato effect from
> constant asyndeton, from the fondness of anaphora, from the tendency to seek

alliteration and Gorgianic figures, and above all from the repeated occurrences of
rhetorical questions and *sententiae*. The diction is quite pure and the prose rhythm often
Ciceronian. (*Art of Rhetoric* 328)

Despite the tendency to regard these features as a manifestation of Asianism (see
Leeman 220), characterizing the new declamatory style as Asianist is not supported
by Seneca. Seneca's infrequent use of the term *Asianus* suggests that, though the
conflict between Asianism and Atticism still existed, it was exceptional for a
rhetorician of that time to be regarded as "Asianist" (cf. *Contr.* X.5.21). He reveals
that many distinct *genera dicendi* were being practiced, not just one (Fairweather 296).
Fairweather argues that if either ancient stylistic label were appropriate to Roman
rhetoricians of this era, it was probably among those who saw themselves as Atticist
in the tradition of Demosthenes (262).

HISTORICAL SIGNIFICANCE

The *Oratorum et rhetorum sententiae, divisions, colores* of Seneca would have been significant historically if for no other reason than the fact that it managed to survive
and to influence subsequent declamatory practice for centuries afterward. Despite
its many detractors, declamation continued into the Middle Ages, both as a secular
link to classical rhetoric, as demonstrated in the *Rhetorimachia* of Anselm de Besate,
and as an instrument for the church, particularly the *suasoria*, to develop biblical
topics for the public (Edward xxxvi). The practice emerged again in the Renaissance, with the works of Erasmus and others, suggesting that the history of declamation may well be "one of the byways of humanism that has yet to be explored
fully" (Whitehorne 25). Even if preservation from antiquity was the result of
confusion about whether Seneca or his son the Younger wrote it (Edward xxxvi),
Seneca's collection became the primary source for declamatory examples and thus
became an important educational resource. The number of extant manuscripts of
the *Excerpta* and of medieval commentaries on the *Excerpta* indicates how popular
declamatory training was and the extent of Seneca's influence in the Middle Ages
(Whitehorne 15–16; cf. Sussman, *The Elder Seneca* 171–72).

But Seneca's influence is not explained by the mere survival of his collection.
His work represented the only major survivor of Ciceronian rhetoric in the Silver
Age of Rome until Quintilian; however, Quintilian, who was also Spanish and
shared many of the same Ciceronian ideals, never mentions him. Some personal
animosity Quintilian held toward Seneca's son the Younger, or perhaps Seneca
himself may explain the noticeable absence in Quintilian's otherwise encyclopedic
treatise (see Sussman, *The Elder Seneca* 162–66). Still, Seneca occupied a unique
position at the forefront of the ancient literary critical tradition. Sussman notes that
Seneca was the first to comment on the decline of eloquence and its causes, an issue
that would be debated for at least the next century, the first to call attention to
the stylistic abuses of declamation, and the first to express concern over the

dominance of declamation in the education system (154–55). Though he tells his son Mela that rhetoric is useful training even for a philosopher, Seneca also challenges the applicability of declamatory skill for legal pleading and public oration (cf. *Contr. II* pr. 3–4 and *Contr. III* pr. 1–2, 12–15).

In terms of literary influence, one of the most significant works indebted to Seneca was the *Gesta Romanorum*, a collection of romantic tales based on themes in his *controversiae* and widely circulated in the Middle Ages (Sussman, *The Elder Seneca* 169). In later European literature, his influence has been found amid such writers as Mlle. De Scudéry, *Ibrahim ou l'illustre Bassa*; Leonardo Bruni, *Antioco e Stratonica*; and Giovanni Boccaccio, *Decameron* (Sussman, *The Elder Seneca* 170). His prefatory pen portraits became popular models, particularly in the seventeenth century, for describing the literary characteristics of contemporary figures and were imitated by writers such as Montaigne and Abraham Cowley (Fairweather 50). Among these, most notable is the influence found in Ben Jonson's *Discoveries*. Jonson liberally used passages from Seneca's *controversiae*, for example Seneca's comments about Haterius (*Contr. IV* pr. 7–11), to describe Shakespeare's writing abilities (see Atkins 154; Fairweather 50–51; Sussman, *The Elder Seneca* 170–71).

NOTES

1. There has been some discrepancy as to the Elder Seneca's first name, whether it was Lucius or Marcus. According to Lewis Sussman, the confusion dates back to the Renaissance, when Raphael Volaterranus assumed Seneca's name would have conformed to a Roman custom that would make it the same as his grandfather's, Marcus. This assumption has not been accepted by modern scholars, who now agree that his name was Lucius, as was his son's (Sussman, *The Elder Seneca* 2, n. 6).

2. The dates of birth and death for Seneca the Elder are approximated from factual references to people and events within his work. The Library of Congress and Sussman (*The Elder Seneca*) both fix the dates as 55 BCE–39 CE. For discussion of these dates, see Sussman (20, 23–24); cf. Griffin 5.

3. For a discussion of the manuscript tradition, as well as the tradition of the *Excerpta* originating out of the fourth or fifth century CE, see Sussman, *The Elder Seneca* 34–35; cf. Whitehorne 15–16.

BIBLIOGRAPHY

Primary Sources and Translations

Bonaria, Mario, and Cesare Grassi, eds. and trans. *Seneca il Vecchio/Quintilliano.* By Lucius Annaeus Seneca and Quintiliano. Antologia della letteratura latina. Brescia: Paideia, 1971.

Bornecque, Henri, ed. and trans. *Sénèque le Rhéteur: Controverses et Suasoires.* 1902. Paris: Garnier Freres, 1932.

————, trans. *Les Déclamations et les Déclamateurs d'après Sénèque le Père.* Lille: Au siege de l'Université, 1902. Hildesheim: G. Olms, 1967.

————, trans. *Sentences, Divisions et Couleurs des Orateurs et des Rhéteurs: Controverses et Suasoires.* Paris: Aubier, 1992.

Bursian, Conrad, ed. *Oratorum et rhetorum sententiae, divisiones, colores.* Bibliotheca scriptorum Graecorum et romanorum Teubneriana. Liepzig: Teubner, 1857.

Chalvet, Mathieu de, trans. *Les controverses et suasoires de M. Annaeus Seneca rhéteur.* Rouen: M. de Preaulx, 1618.

Edward, William Alfred, ed. and trans. *Seneca the Elder: Suasoriae.* Cambridge: Cambridge UP, 1928. Rpt. London: Bristol Classical, 1996.

Håkanson, Lennart, ed. *Oratorum et Rhetorum Sententiae, Divisiones, Colores.* Bibliotheca scriptorum Graecorum et Romanorum Teubneriana. Leipzig: B. G. Teubner, 1989.

Kiessling, Adolf Gottlieb, ed. *Annaei Senecae: Oratorum et rhetorum sententiae divisiones colores.* Bibliotheca scriptorum Graecorum et Romanorum Teubneriana. Liepzig: B. G. Teubner, 1872. Rpt. Stuttgart: B. G. Teubner, 1967.

Müller, Hermann J., ed. *L. Annaei Senecae Oratorum et rhetorum sententiae, divisions, colores.* Bibliotheca Scriptorum Graecorum et Romanorum. Vienna: F. Tempsky, 1887. Rpt. Hildesheim: G. Olms, 1963.

Rieti, Alessandro da, supposed trans., and Fruttuoso Becchi, ed. *Il volgarizzamento delle Declamazioni di M. Anneo Seneca.* Florence: L. Pezzati, 1832.

Winterbottom, Michael, trans. *The Elder Seneca: Controversiae I-VI.* Loeb Classical Library, vol. 463. Cambridge: Harvard UP, 1974.

————. *The Elder Seneca: Controversiae VII-X; Suasoriae.* Loeb Classical Library, vol. 464. Cambridge: Harvard UP, 1974.

Zani, Christina, ed. *L. Anneus Seneca Rhetor.* Scriptorum Romanorum Quae Extant Omnia. Pisa: Giardini, 1976.

Biographical Sources

Fairweather, Janet. *Seneca the Elder.* Cambridge Classical Studies. Cambridge: Cambridge UP, 1981.

Ferrill, Arther Lee. *Seneca: The Rise to Power.* Diss. University of Illinois, Urbana, 1964.

Griffin, Miriam. "The Elder Seneca and Spain." *Journal of Roman Studies* 62 (1972): 1–19.

Grube, G. M. A. *The Greek and Roman Critics.* Toronto, 1965.

Kennedy, George A. *The Art of Persuasion in Greece.* Princeton: Princeton UP, 1963.

————. *The Art of Rhetoric in the Roman World.* Princeton: Princeton UP, 1972.

Simonds, Thomas Stanley. *The Themes Treated by the Elder Seneca.* Diss. Johns Hopkins University, 1896. Baltimore: Friedenwald, 1896.

Sussman, Lewis A. *The Elder Seneca.* Mnemosyne, bibliotheca classica Batava. Supplementum 51. Leiden: E. J. Brill, 1978.

————. "The Elder Seneca as a Critic of Rhetoric." Diss. University of North Carolina, 1969.

Critical Sources

Atkins, J. W. H. *Literary Criticism in Antiquity: A Sketch of Its Development.* Cambridge: Cambridge UP, 1934. Rpt. New York, 1952.

Bardon, Henry. *Le Vocabulaire de la Critique Littéraire chez Sénèque le Rhéteur*. Paris: Societé d'édition "Les Belles lettres," 1940.

Bonner, S[tanley] F. *Roman Declamation in the Late Republic and Early Empire*. Liverpool: UP of Liverpool, 1949. Rpt. 1969.

Clark, M. L. *Rhetoric at Rome: A Historical Survey*. London: Cohen and West, 1953. Rpt. 1962.

D'Alton, J. F. *Roman Literary Theory and Criticism*. London and New York: Russell and Russell, 1931. Rpt. 1962.

Leeman, A. D. *Orationis Ratio: The Stylistic Theories and Practice of the Roman Orators, Historians, and Philosophers*. Amsterdam: Adolf M. Kakkert, 1963.

Mendelson, Michael. "Declamation, Context, and Controversiality." *Rhetoric Review* 13 (1994): 92–107.

Norden, Eduard. *Die Antike Kunstprosa*. Leipzis and Berlin, 1923. Rpt. Stuttgart: B. J. Teubner, 1981.

Sochatoff, A. Fred. "Basic Rhetorical Theories of the Elder Seneca." *Classical Journal* 34 (1938–39): 345–54.

Sussman, Lewis A. "The Elder Seneca's Discussion of the Decline of Roman Eloquence." *California Studies in Classical Antiquity* 5 (1972): 195–210.

Whitehorne, J. E. G. "The Elder Seneca: A Review of Past Work." *Prudentia* 1 (1969): 14–27.

FAVORINUS

(ca. 80–150 CE)

Victor J. Vitanza

Favorinus records in an oration that he was born in a family of "equestrian rank" (Dio Chrysostom 25).[1] Philostratus, who provides an often quoted, brief background, reports that Favorinus was born during the latter part of the first century CE in Gaul in the city of Arelate (Arles) in the Rhone valley (*Lives* 23).[2] Philostratus writes that Favorinus's birth was marked with a paradox: Favorinus "was born double-sexed, a hermaphrodite" (*Lives* 23). Philostratus further describes him: "when [Favorinus] grew old he had no beard; it was evident too from his voice which sounded thin, shrill, and high-pitched, with the modulations that nature bestows on eunuchs also" (*Lives* 23). H. Mason suggests by way of modern medicine that Favorinus's disorder was Reifenstein's syndrome, or what has come to be known as hereditary male pseudo-hermaphroditism, which is an endocrineal disorder of undescended testicles. Philostratus recounts that Favorinus boasts "that there were in his life three paradoxes: Though he was a Gaul he led the life of a Hellene; [though] a eunuch, he had been tried for adultery; [though he] had quarrelled with an Emperor [he] was still alive" (*Lives* 23). This anecdote concerning the question of Favorinus's sexuality has become the primary way by which ancient and modern commentators have attempted to shape an understanding of Favorinus's life as textuality.

As a child, Favorinus most likely had teachers of both Latin and Greek grammar and rhetoric. Because of his proficiency in Greek, he was able upon adulthood to leave his native Arelate, rejecting the duties that he would inherit, and to travel broadly to Italy, Greece, and the East, often addressing his audiences in Greek. He was famous as a rhetor, as he suggests in his first paradox, in both Rome and Athens (*Lives* 29; Dio 25). Today, he is famous as a Sophist of the Second Sophistic (see *Lives* 7; cf. Kennedy 37–40). Favorinus's choice to leave home and not to follow in his family's footsteps as a member of the aristocracy testifies to his exuberance for life and hunger for fame. Wanting more education to prepare him to become famous in the world—perhaps even to have a statue raised in his

honor—he also studied philosophy with Dio Chrysostom (*Lives* 25) and became
friends with Plutarch (Gleason 5)[3] and Herodes Atticus (*Lives* 25).

But what we can know about Favorinus's life is problematic, for Favorinus
was, as Maud Gleason makes evident, a "performing artist" engaging in "self-
fashioning" and "multiple personae" (148); "his identity was entirely the product of
art" (168). Not only is Favorinus biologically a paradox but his self-representations
are just as rhetorically paradoxical. Perhaps Favorinus was overcompensating for
and capitalizing on his marked, androgynous birth. But as was the tradition among
the aristocracy, according to Gleason, "manliness was not a birthright" (159).
Favorinus had, therefore, to prove himself an aristocratic man by way of
performing his rhetorical-agnostic skills against another rhetor and philosopher or
even an emperor. Proving himself a man, however, was often realized by way of
a protean-paradoxical use of words. "But [Favorinus]," Gleason argues, "is not
merely playful. The sophist's 'word' is his 'work' and has all the seriousness of the
warrior's task, as it should in a society where rhetoric is the form of heroic combat
open to the public figure" (152). Combat for Favorinus was not at all limited to
discursive reason but fully open to flights and fugues of the imagination. Not unlike
the Sophist Gorgias, Favorinus's style of rebuttal was at times filled with literary
allusions and musical (chiming) seductions.

Hence, Favorinus's life—or lives—were his rhetorical and compositional
theories; his theories, his lives. As Gleason says, Favorinus was his own medium
and message (17).

FAVORINUS'S RHETORICAL THEORY

The primary exemplars of Favorinus's various personae that he displayed and
brandished in his battles to become a man (*becoming man*) are to be found and
experienced in his responses to the emperor Hadrian who threatened him with exile
or death, the Athenian and Corinthian magistrates that ordered statues of Favorinus
to be torn down, and his archrival M. Antonius Polemo (*Lives* 107–37) who ever
challenged Favorinus's image of manhood. To best understand Favorinus's
rhetorical theory of an *in propria persona* (or *ēthos*), it is best to see Favorinus's
responses—those that are extant or reported in doxagraphical form—to his
interlocutors.

Gleason has momentarily cornered the market on the Fab Favorinus. Specifically, her analysis and interpretation of Favorinus's extant "Corinthian Oration"
(Dio 1–47)—in which he responds to magistrates and citizens for having toppled
his statue—lays bare the rhetorical-sophistic, subtle strategies and tactics that
Favorinus uses against the Corinthians. In responding, Favorinus has to be cautious
about displaying any self-praise, and therefore, as Gleason points out, he at times
"pretends that his statue is on trial and plays the role of its advocate; at other times
he impersonates the statue itself. By speaking in multiple personae, he offsets the
dramatic limitations of the monologue, expanding the cast of characters involved"

(9). Exploiting his own ambiguous sexuality, Favorinus "cultivates grammatical ambiguity," Gleason tells us, "around the word *statue*. By avoiding the feminine noun *eikon*, and using instead the masculine alternative *andrias*, Favorinus manages to sprinkle his speech with masculine pronouns whose antecedents are ambiguous" (15). Favorinus was a shape-shifter. Gleason concludes, "it is naïve to ask the real Favorinus to please stand up" (148).

FAVORINUS'S CONTRIBUTION TO RHETORIC

What comes across strongly is that *becoming man* for Favorinus is fundamentally different from a masculine agonistics of brutally slaying one's opponent, of assassinating someone's character even in the self-defense of one's own. Favorinus does not pretend to be a gladiator. Nor does he pretend to be a male in drag with a flaming rhetoric. (He in his speeches is not a Liberace in Las Vegas.) Rather, I would suggest, to extend Gleason's discussion, that Favorinus is ever becoming a *third figure, or sex*, which is not to be confused with any biological notions of *man* or *masculine*, *woman* or *feminine*—a binary of two sexes—nor any parody of these, but can be seen as an expression of the potentialities of a third sex. Or as Giorgio Agamben might say, can be seen as "being engendered from *one's own* manner" or *habitus*. In this case "one's own" would refer to an *ēthos* in its *ēthea*, and a *manare* [manner] would refer to its own "rising forth," "enduring." Both would refer to a singularity rather than a subjectivity or objectivity that would be an individuality (29).

Favorinus—known as a *monstre*, a hermaphrodite, a eunuch—engendered *"hir"* own third-sex style of argumentation and persuasion. It is this very style—the style is the *third figure*—that Polemo as well as others attack as Favorinus's lack of manhood. Gleason claims, "Favorinus and Polemo represented opposing paradigms of masculinity" (xxvii). But these oppositions are not classic male versus female, or vice versa, or male versus failed manhood, or even genetic DNA forms contributing to what Anne Fausto-Sterling calls hermaphrodite, merm, ferm, and so on, but a disposition toward a third figure that is not a countable third and that is ever at the threshold or easement of the potentialities of sex and gender. In other words, what Favorinus's *ēthoi* in "hir" discourses and performances can be seen as *doing* and *making* is not determinable by a set theory of sex or gender, but by setless or radical multiplicities of *each is its own sex and gender in process*, if these incipient categories of sex and gender even matter any more.

Polemo's example of a man serves as a species in a genus, while Favorinus's, I would insist, lies not in a realm of being but in a relation of being against, but in the sense of *alongside*, or again at the threshold of potentialities (*dynamis, potenza*) that serves no sovereign power but "its own" (*Swedh*) in a community with other singularities. Favorinus is not active nor passive; rather, he can be seen as performing a third of radical passivity. Favorinus is an exemplar of an entity without the conditions of being an entity that does not, as Agamben might say, "befall" or "found" but instead "engenders" (29) "hir," and the discourse that speaks "hir."

I see (theorize) Favorinus as not necessarily a Sophist of the Second Sophistic but more as a Sophist of a Third Sophistic. I have posited this as such in terms of Favorinus's being "the most typical sophist" (Vitanza 51–55). He is not the paradigm of masculinity or femininity nor the paradigm of mixed, hybrid sexes such as a hermaphrodite. There is no reason in a Third Sophistic to read Favorinus, as Mason does, in terms of a "disorder" or a "syndrome." Rather he is *its own* sex and gender, which is its own third figure at the threshold of species-genus analytics. Favorinus can be productively seen, therefore, as forever engendering nonpositive affirmative sophistic rhetorics and kairotics of a radical finitude of discourses.

NOTES

1. The date is provided by the translators of Plutarch's *Moralia*, 9: 447.

2. Aulus Gellius in his multivolume *Attic Nights* has "jotted down" various anecdotes of Favorinus's sayings and travels (I: xxvii; see, e.g., I: 51, 133, 309–17; II: 143, 149, 353–61; III: 3–31, 81, 239–45, 251–53, 293–97, 319–25). These jottings range from discussions of grammar to breast-feeding. On the latter theme, see Gleason 141–42. Lucian often satirized Favorinus. ("Demonax" in I and "The Eunuch" in V. Gleason's discussions of these selections are helpful, 132–36.)

3. The translators of Plutarch's *Moralia* write that Plutarch "dedicated two books to" Favorinus and that Favorinus "wrote, in turn, a book entitled *Plutarch, or On the Academic Position*" (9: 205, note c).

BIBLIOGRAPHY

Primary Sources and Translations

Dio Chrysostom [Favorinus]. "The Corinthian Oration." *Discourses*. Trans. H. L. Crosby. Vol. 4 of 5. Cambridge: Harvard UP, 1946.

Biographical Sources

Gellius, Aulus. *Attic Nights*. Trans. John C. Rolfe. 3 vols. Cambridge: Harvard UP, 1927.
Mason, H. "Favorinus' Disorder: Reifenstein's Syndrome in Antiquity?" *Janus* 66 (1979): 1–13.
Philostratus and Eunapius. *Lives of the Sophists*. Trans. Wilmer C. Wright. Cambridge: Harvard UP, 1921.
Plutarch. *Moralia*. Trans. Edwin L. Minar et al. Vol. 9 of 15. Cambridge: Harvard UP, 1961.

Critical Sources

Agamben, Giorgio. *The Coming Community*. Trans. Michael Hardt. Stanford: Stanford UP.
Fausto-Sterling, Anne. "The Five Sexes: Why Male and Female Are Not Enough." *The Sciences* (March/April 1993): 20–25.

Gleason, Maud W. *Making Men: Sophists and Self-Presentation in Ancient Rome.* Princeton: Princeton UP, 1995.

Kennedy, George A. *Classical Rhetoric and Its Christian and Secular Tradition from Ancient to Modern Times.* Chapel Hill: U of North Carolina P, 1980.

Lucian. *Lucian.* Trans. A. M. Harmon. Vols. 1 and 5 of 8. Cambridge: Harvard UP, 1913.

Vitanza, Victor J. *Negation, Subjectivity, and the History of Rhetoric.* Albany: State U of New York P, 1996.

Marcus Cornelius Fronto

(ca. 95–167 CE)

Gary L. Hatch

Marcus Cornelius Fronto was a prominent orator, rhetorician, and grammarian, equal in reputation in his own time to Cato, Cicero, and Quintilian. However, because his works were lost for hundreds of years, his impact on the rhetorical tradition has been slight. Fronto was born ca. 90–95 in the Roman colony of Cirta, Numidia (now Constantine, Algeria) to T. Cornelius, a descendant of Roman colonists. Little is known of Fronto's youth. He was taught as a child by Aridelus, a Greek *paedagogus*, and furthered his education in Rome. After 120 CE, Fronto is mentioned, along with his brother, Q. Cornelius Quadratus, as a member of the Senate. He was quaestor of Sicily and praetor, but held no other position until he became consul suffectus (a substitute consul) for July and August of 143 CE. He was later offered the proconsulship of Asia, but was unable to accept because of his declining health. In his own time, Fronto had the reputation of being a competent lawyer and orator. The most significant time in Fronto's life occurred from 139 to 145 CE, when he served as tutor to Marcus Aurelius, who had been designated as the future successor to Antoninus Pius. Fronto tried to dissuade Marcus from his philosophical studies, but without success, and he was dismissed in 145, when Marcus married Pius's daughter and became coregent. Although Fronto corresponded with Marcus for several more years, their contact became less frequent. Fronto died "sick and disappointed" ca. 167 CE (van den Hout, *Commentary* vii).

Fronto's Reception

Fronto's fame among his contemporaries rested primarily on his orations, and his reputation as a speaker continued for nearly three hundred years after his death. In his introduction to his edition of Fronto's correspondence, C. R. Haines catalogues the references to Fronto's eloquence. Nearly a century after Fronto's death, Eumenius praised him as "not the second but the alternative glory of Roman eloquence." Writing in the fourth century, Macrobius identified Fronto as the exemplar of the plain style in contrast to the more florid style exemplified by Cicero. Jerome compares Fronto favorably with Quintilian, Cicero, and Pliny. Claudius Mamertus includes Fronto along with Plautus, Cato, Gracchus, Chrysippus, and Cicero in his list of authors worthy of imitation (ix–x). Unfortunately, only a few fragments remain of Fronto's orations, so it is impossible to determine whether his great reputation as an orator was deserved.

Fronto also had some reputation as a teacher; however, he left no systematic theory or manual on the art of rhetoric. His ideas on rhetoric, literature, and pedagogy must be derived from his only extant work, the collection of his correspondence with Antoninus Pius, Marcus Aurelius, and Lucius Verus. Unfortunately, these letters had little influence on the rhetorical tradition. Michel van den Hout concludes that Fronto had no intention of editing his letters himself, and they were not edited until the fourth century (*Commentary* x). Fronto's letters were later effaced and the leaves reused. As a result, the letters were hidden in palimpsest until 1815, when they were discovered by Angelo Mai, Roman cardinal, philologist, and prefect of the Ambrosian Library in Milan. Due to the poor state of the palimpsest and poor editing by later scholars, the letters are full of omissions. The standard modern edition of Fronto's correspondence was edited by Michel P. J. van den Hout (1954), and an English translation is available in the Loeb Classical Library, edited by C. R. Haines (1919). All quotations here come from Haines's translation.

Although Fronto's contemporaries and his successors praised him for his eloquence, later scholars have found little evidence in his correspondence to support Fronto's reputation. Early editors of his work found the letters insipid and lacking in literary quality. B. G. Niebuhr, who edited Fronto's letters in 1816, found the author "stupid, frivolous, and the very opposite of eloquent" (Champlin 2). S. A. Naber, who edited the letters in 1867, "expressed both dislike and contempt for an author whose works would have been better left buried in the palimpsest whence they had emerged" (Champlin 2). Michel van den Hout, Fronto's most recent editor (1954) and author of the only commentary on the letters (1999), is somewhat kinder in his criticism. He writes, "Since Niebuhr, modern literati have passed devastating judgement on Fronto's letters; not quite undeservedly, though Fronto was no simpleton, only a third-class writer" (*Commentary* x).

FRONTO'S RHETORICAL THEORY

Despite their literary shortcomings, Fronto's letters provide insight into the rhetorical culture of second-century Rome, particularly into the relationship between rhetoric and imperial leadership. Although Fronto's arguments about style will be of concern primarily to students of Latin, his ideas about rhetoric and governance may interest those concerned about the role of rhetoric in imperial Rome or more broadly about the relationship of rhetoric to power.

As the teacher of Marcus Aurelius, Fronto followed a familiar curriculum: study of the ancient poets and orators, verse composition, diligent practice in creating and using comparisons and *sententiae* (sayings), translations between Latin and Greek, and common rhetorical exercises. But in addition to this traditional curriculum, Fronto instructed Marcus Aurelius and Lucius Verus (Antoninus's son by adoption) in what an emperor should be. As Edward Champlin observes, Emperor Antoninus chose as tutors for his sons men who not only demonstrated ability in their chosen discipline but also exemplified by their lives and ideals the qualities of Roman leadership (119). In the first book of his *Meditations*, Marcus Aurelius lists no fewer than eighteen tutors. The four elementary teachers were not men of any particular rank, although as tutors to the future emperors, they were admitted to the equestrian rank. But most of the teachers of advanced subjects, including rhetoric and philosophy, were already men of rank, many of them senators and at least five of them consuls (Champlin 119). From this, Champlin argues, one may conclude that Antoninus chose for his sons tutors that would teach them how to govern from the perspective of their particular discipline (119). The tutor to have the greatest effect on Marcus Aurelius was no doubt the Stoic philosopher Junius Rusticus (consul, CE 162 and Roman prefect, CE 162–168). But Marcus certainly learned much from Fronto as well, although how much he learned from any one of his teachers is difficult to measure. In memory of Cornelius Fronto, Marcus summarizes what he learned from his teacher: "From Fronto: to observe how vile a thing is the malice and caprice and hypocrisy of absolutism; and generally speaking that those whom we entitle patricians are somehow rather wanting in natural affection" (quoted in Champlin 120).

Most of Fronto's ideas on rhetoric are found in five letters collected together under the title *De Eloquentia*, "On Eloquence." In these letters, Fronto argues that the study of rhetoric is the duty of an emperor. In response to the challenges of philosophy to the study of rhetoric, Fronto claims that rhetoric is necessary to the pursuit of wisdom—an essential quality for leadership. He argues that although a person does not live to eat, he must eat to live. So in order to possess wisdom—the goal of life—a person must eat. In a similar manner, although a leader should not study eloquence for its own sake, the study of rhetoric is necessary for leadership (Champlin 122–25). Rhetoric may not lead to wisdom, but it is necessary for wisdom. Fronto writes:

> For it falls to a Caesar to carry by persuasion necessary measures in the senate, to address the people in a harangue on many important matters, to correct the inequities of the law, to dispatch rescripts throughout the world, to take foreign kings to task, to repress by edicts disorders among the allies, to praise their services, to crush the rebellious and cow the proud. All these must assuredly be done by speech and writing. Will you not then cultivate an art, which you see must be of great use to you so often and in matters of such moment? Or do you imagine that it makes no difference with what words you bring about what can only be brought about by words? (*Eloq.* 2.7)

As Fronto explains to Marcus, rhetoric provides wisdom with *verborum lumina*, "the illumination of words" (*Eloq.* 4.4)

In a second set of letters collected under the title *De Orationibus*, "On Orations," Fronto continues his discussion of the relationship between rhetoric and imperial leadership. As Champlin observes, this set of letters is ostensibly an attack on what Fronto considered the rhetorical excesses of Seneca and his followers (126). Fronto discloses to Marcus that the only thing that could really detract from their friendship would be if Marcus were to completely neglect his study of eloquence. But what would be even worse, he confesses, would be for Marcus to follow a false rhetoric, such as that exemplified by Seneca. But for Fronto, Seneca's extravagance is not just an aesthetic or stylistic concern; it is a matter of proper governance. For Fronto, clarity and directness are not just virtues of style, they are virtues of leadership as well. To illustrate the problems with the Senecan influence, Fronto analyzes an imperial edict, showing how it is too full of circumlocutions and digressions, implying that this edict is not just poor writing, but also poor legislation (Champlin 126).

In his letters to Lucius Verus, Fronto's other famous student, he continues upon a similar theme. In one letter in particular, Champlin describes how Fronto responds to the eloquence displayed by Lucius in his report of his victory in the Parthian Wars. In his excessive praise of Lucius, Fronto writes that now he may die in peace, having left behind in Lucius a great monument and eternal glory (127). Returning to his theme of the relationship between rhetoric and leadership, Fronto instructs Lucius to "rule all with oratory." He writes, "Therefore, if you seek a veritable sovereign of the human race, it is your eloquence that sways men's minds. It inspires fear, wins love, is a spur to effort, puts shame to silence, exhorts to virtue, exposes vice, urges, soothes, teaches, consoles" (*Ver. Imp.* II.1.7). For Marcus Aurelius, Fronto argued that rhetoric is a necessary precondition to wisdom. For Lucius Verus, he argued that rhetoric is necessary for exercising imperial might. He writes, "Now *imperium* is a word that connotes not only power but also speech, since the exercise of *imperium* practically exists in bidding and forbidding. If he did not praise good actions, if he did not blame evil doings, if he did not exhort to virtue, if he did not warn off from vice, a ruler would belie his name and be called *imperator* to no purpose" (*Ver. Imp.* II.1.10).

Cornelius Fronto's letters focus ostensibly on issues of style, but considered in a broader context, this teacher of future emperors is discussing the relationship between rhetoric and leadership, between words and power. For Fronto, the study of rhetoric is not just a pastime but a necessary part of the training of a leader, and Fronto concerns himself with the application of the "good man skilled in speaking" to the practical art of governance. It is likely for this reason, Champlain remarks, that Marcus remembered Fronto more for what he taught about politics than about oratory. As Fronto expressed in a letter to Marcus Aurelius, "You and your father, moreover, who are bound to wear purple and crimson, must on occasion clothe your words too in the same dress" (*M. Caes.* I.9.3).

BIBLIOGRAPHY

Primary Sources and Translations

Haines, C. R., ed. *The Correspondence of Marcus Cornelius Fronto*. Loeb Classical Library 113. Cambridge: Harvard UP, 1919.

van den Hout, Michel P. J., ed. *M. Cornelii Frontonis Epistulae*. Leiden: E. J. Brill, 1954. Rpt. New York: Arno P, 1975.

Biographical Sources

Champlin, Edward. *Fronto and Antonine Rome*. Cambridge: Harvard UP, 1980.

Critical Sources

Astarita, Maria Laura. *Frontone Oratore*. Catania: Università di Catania, 1997.

Brock, M. Dorothy. *Studies in Fronto and His Age*. Cambridge: Cambridge UP, 1911.

Cawley, Elizabeth Mary. *The Literary Theory and Style of Marcus Cornelius Fronto*. Diss. Tufts University, 1972.

Fontanella, Ruggero. *Index Verborum mit Statistischen Aufstellungen zu De Nepote Amisso, De Feriis Alsiensibus, Arion, Laudes Fumi et Pulveris, Laudes Neglegentiae von M.C. Fronto*. Hildesheim: Olms, 1981.

Marache, René. *La Critique Littéraire de Langue Latine et le Développement du Gout Archaïsant au IIe Siècle de Notre Ere*. Rennes: Plihon, 1952.

Pennacini, Adriano. *Lessico del De Orationibus e del De Eloquentia di M. C. Frontone*. Hildesheim: Olms, 1976.

Portalupi, Felicita. *Marco Cornelio Frontone*. Torino: G. Giappichelli, 1961.

Schmitt, Anni. *Das Bild als Stilmittel Frontos*. Diss. U. of Munich, 1933. München: Druck der Salesianischen Offizin, 1934.

van den, Hout, Michel P. J. ed. *A Commentary on the Letters of M. Cornelius Fronto*. Leiden: E. J. Brill, 1999.

GORGIAS

(ca. 480s–380s BCE)

John Poulakos

Gorgias lived from the 480s to the 380s BCE. A native of Leontini, he is reported to have gone to Athens for the first time as an ambassador around 427, and to have made several visits afterward. During his first visit, he impressed the Athenians with his eloquence. Eventually he acquired a considerable following as a prominent figure of the sophistic movement, an accomplished orator, and a teacher of rhetoric. His following included the statesman Pericles, the historian Thucydides, the tragic poet Agathon, and the Sophist Critias. He is said to have been a student of the Pythagorean philosopher Empedocles and a teacher of Isocrates, Polus of Acragas, and Alcidamas of Elaea. Ancient sources credit him with significant contributions to rhetoric, said to rival those of Aeschylus to tragedy. They also credit him with various innovations in rhetorical practice, including the use of poetical language in civic prose and the frequent employment of elaborate figures and tropes as well as improvisation in speaking. He is said to have spoken at the Olympic and Pythian Games, written a handbook of rhetoric, and charged high fees for his instruction. He spent the last years of his life in Thessaly, making important contributions to the intellectual culture of that region. A golden statue of himself was erected near the temple of Delphi. He died at over 105 years old.

Gorgias's preserved works, which can be found in Rosamond K. Sprague's edited volume *The Older Sophists*, include a philosophical treatise (*On Non-Being or On Nature*), two rhetorical compositions (*The Encomium of Helen, The Defense of Palamedes*), and a fragment of a speech (*Funeral Oration*). These works constitute the basis of his rhetorical theory. Three other speeches attributed to him (*Speech at the Olympic Games, Speech at the Pythian Games,* and *Encomium for the People of Elis*) are not preserved. Beyond these works, Gorgias is also believed to have maintained various notions, the following of which are of particular relevance to rhetoric: the art of persuading differs a great deal from all other arts—for all things under it are made slaves willingly, not through violence; tragedy produces a deception in which the deceiver is more justly esteemed than the nondeceiver and the deceived is wiser than the undeceived; reality is not manifest if it does not involve appearance, and appearance is unreliable if it does not involve reality; the opposition's seriousness is to be demolished by laughter and laughter by seriousness. These notions are for the most part consistent with what he says in his works.

GORGIAS'S RHETORICAL THEORY

Gorgias's rhetorical theory advances several stipulations about human perception, language, thought, and action. To begin with, Gorgias asserts that there is a difference between the world in its actuality and the world as perceived. He further asserts that the primary access that humans have to the physical world is perceptual, based on their senses. Even though he acknowledges that things have their own nature, not the one we wish them to have, he posits that such a nature falls outside the domain of human knowledge—what humans can know is not things in themselves but their own perceptions of things. But knowledge of one's perceptions is far from certain, given that perceptions are often unreliable and subject to change. But if this is so, perceptions are important for rhetoric not because they contribute to knowledge but because they impact and elicit emotional reactions from those who hold them. In this regard, Gorgias's point is that humans are vulnerable to and affected by their sensory perceptions. In their encounter with what they see, hear, or taste, they often feel intense emotions (e.g., fear, joy, pain, pleasure), which, in turn, determine their thought processes and dictate their actions. As he observes in the *Helen*, "people, after having seen frightening sights, have lost presence of mind for the present moment" (17). Similarly, "whenever pictures perfectly create a single figure and form from many colors and shapes, they delight the sight, while the creation of statues and the production of works of art furnish a pleasant sight to the eyes" (18). Gorgias further observes that the result of fear is often indifference to such habitually pursued goals as honor and victory. When feeling fearful, people run away from that which appears dangerous. On the other end of the emotional continuum, pleasure often leads to longing and desire for the object of perception. When feeling pleasure, people set out to pursue that which appears pleasant. The conclusion of these observations is that the senses affect the human psyche by engraving upon it images of the things that have been perceived. When thus engraved, the psyche experiences powerful feelings, which become the forces behind actions. Actions, in other words, are not always determined by thought. When they are in an emotional state, humans are not entirely in control of their actions. What they do in such instances is the result of passion, not rational deliberation. Gorgias refers to the specific case of fear, stating that it often "extinguishes and excludes thought" (*Helen* 17).

This theory of perception applies to both natural and cultural objects—although the two sets of objects are different, the process is the same. This means that humans can engender certain kinds of perceptions in each other by virtue of their own appearance as well as objects that they make. Thus any craftsman or artist is, for Gorgias, not only a maker of objects but also of perceptions. But insofar as humans entertain several perceptions at any given time, and inasmuch as all perceptions are not consistent with one another, perceptions compete with one another for prominence at any one moment. Those perceptions prevail which are stronger.

In addition to their psychological impact, perceptions are of interest to the student of rhetoric because they lead to language. For Gorgias, language arises from our sensory encounter with external things (*On Non-Being* 85). Precisely how this happens he does not explain; he only says that certain perceptions linger, and what lingers is analogous to what is spoken (*Helen* 18). As in the case of objects as they are and our perceptions of them, words and the things they name are not identical; on the contrary, they are very different. Accordingly, Gorgias observes in *On Non-Being*, when we communicate with others we do so through language (*logos*), seemingly revealing to them what and how things are either in themselves or in the way we perceive them. In actuality, however, what we do reveal to our listeners is neither the nature of things nor our perception of them—strictly speaking, we only reveal words. In effect, Gorgias suggests that words may have little, if anything at all, to do with the objects to which we make them refer. We may believe that language corresponds or is directly related to the things it names, but this is a belief borne out of repeated experience and tacit agreements. In actuality, there is no such correspondence. To support this point, Gorgias reminds the reader that language can and does name things that do not exist empirically. For example, Scylla and Chimera, a man flying, or chariots racing in the sea are, empirically speaking, nonexistent things; yet they exist in language (*On Non-Being* 79–80). In fact, the whole treatise *On Non-Being or On Nature* is a logically strict discussion of the problem of being and nothingness vis-à-vis the instrumentality of language. In this treatise, Gorgias explores the word "nothing," showing that although it refers to what does not exist, it grants existence to nothingness just the same. His exploration presents the reader with the paradox of the existence of nothingness and the nothingness of existence. Insofar as what exists cannot be accessed without the mediations of perception or language, its status borders on the nonexistent. And insofar as what does not exist can manifest itself in language or perception, its status borders on the real.

In addition to his theoretical remarks on the origin of language and its relation to what it names, Gorgias addresses the impact that language has on its listeners. Specifically, he posits that words affect people emotionally, in the same way that their perceptions do, and with similar results. Accordingly, he assigns language the power to elicit emotions in the audience or allay them altogether. In his words, "Speech is a powerful lord, which by means of the finest and most invisible body effects the divinest works: it can stop fear and banish grief and create joy and nurture pity" (*Helen* 8). Gorgias illustrates this general statement by pointing to two specific forms of oral language, tragic poetry and sacred incantations, both of which have discernible effects on an audience. About poetry he says, "Fearful shuddering and tearful pity and grievous longing come upon its hearers, and at the actions and physical sufferings of others in good fortunes and in evil fortunes, through the agency of words, the soul is wont to experience a suffering of its own" (*Helen* 9). In the case of incantations, the interaction between words and psyche is no different: "Sacred incantations sung with words are bearers of pleasure and banishers of pain, for, merging with opinion in the soul, the power of the incantation is wont to beguile it and persuade it and alter it by witchcraft" (*Helen* 10). Gorgias concludes his discussion of the power of words by likening them to drugs. In so doing, he underscores their potential to confer either harm or benefit to their recipients. As he puts it:

> The effect of speech upon the condition of the soul is comparable to the power of drugs over the nature of bodies. For just as different drugs dispel different secretions from the body, and some bring an end to disease and others to life, so also in the case of speeches, some distress, others delight, some cause fear, others make the hearers bold, and some drug and bewitch the soul with a kind of evil persuasion. (*Helen* 14)

Precisely how persuasion works Gorgias does not say. His discussion points more to the results of persuasion and less to the process. Even so, he offers some insight when he claims that persuasion "has the form of necessity but it does not have the same power" (*Helen* 12). In fact, he goes as far as to say that persuasion "is wont to impress the soul as it wishes" (*Helen* 13), suggesting that people cannot easily resist its influence. To make his case, Gorgias points the reader to three ways in which belief, the basis of persuasion, is shaped. First, the discourse of scientists does nothing more for the lay public than "make what is incredible and unclear seem true to the eyes of opinion." Scientists (more exactly, astronomers) do this not by proffering true knowledge of the way things are in actuality but by "substituting opinion for opinion, taking away one but creating another." Second, single speeches that one usually hears in public debates often persuade great crowds, owing their effectiveness to art rather than truth. Third, philosophical debates, which are typically fast and furious, generally make the opinions of the audience "subject to easy change" (*Helen* 13). In all three cases, Gorgias observes, persuasion has the character of a compelling force. All discourses, be they scientific, political, or philosophical, work similarly and have the same goal: they manipulate the opinions of the audience, and they aim to have the perspective of the speaker espoused.

Clearly, Gorgias's rhetorical theory is predicated on the power of language (more accurately, speech), the emotional excitability of the psyche, and the impressionability of the human mind. A correlate to this perspective is that the cognitive capacities of most humans are not especially adept—their reasoning generally takes place by means of opinion, not knowledge. Gorgias speculates that if people had the ability to recall the past accurately, consider the present adequately, and predict the future precisely, rhetoric would not function the way it does. In so doing, he seems to suggest that whereas reality and knowledge would make persuasion unnecessary, appearances and opinions make it possible. Persuasion, in other words, is possible because opinion is the order of the day in every given case. As Gorgias puts it, "on most subjects most men take opinion as counselor to their soul, but since opinion is slippery and insecure it casts those employing it into slippery and insecure successes" (*Helen* 11). In effect, Gorgias acknowledges the unreliability of opinion as a guide to action but maintains that there is no better substitute; this is the ordinary state of human affairs—people cannot know and they cannot be certain; still, they are under the imperative to act. When they do act, they do so on the basis of the emotions that the perceptions and the words to which they are exposed engender.

It should be evident from the above that Gorgias's rhetorical theory is speaker oriented. For him, the orator is an artist of words who can manipulate existing perceptions or create new ones, and in so doing evoke in listeners the kinds of emotions that can lead to actions that the orator deems desirable. In effect, Gorgias suggests that the orator creates in the audience virtual perceptions by means of language. In this regard, language re-creates the listeners' perceptions of things, thus making them respond to language as if they were responding to the objects of their perception.

RECEPTIONS OF GORGIAS

The reception of Gorgias goes as far back as Plato. In his dialogue *Gorgias*, Plato has Socrates interrogate the character Gorgias about the nature of rhetoric, its status as an art, its power, its capacity to instruct rather than persuade, and its contributions to the moral advancement of the citizens. Given Plato's hostility toward the Sophists, it comes as no surprise that Gorgias fares poorly in the dialogue that bears his name. He is shown to be unable to define rhetoric properly and unconcerned with its inability to discover the truth of any given matter or to ensure justice in the courts. Plato's major complaint is that Gorgias teaches techniques of eloquence without also teaching their ethical uses. In doing so, Plato maintains, Gorgias values probability more than the truth, rhetoric more than philosophy, and action more than contemplation. In a marked contrast, Scott Consigny, a recent commentator on Gorgias's texts, portrays Gorgias as "a sophisticated thinker and an accomplished artist" whose work is "logically consistent, thematically coherent, and stylistically purposive" (203). The historical and intellectual distance between Plato and Consigny is covered by a host of readings, which shed light not only on Gorgias's preserved texts but also on the epochal concerns and intellectual orientation of their authors.

Many of these readings revolve around the difference between philosophy and rhetoric and depend on the author's relative understanding or valuation of these two areas of human endeavor. Among the most definitive readings, one can point to Hegel's, which, reversing Plato's long-standing criticism, discusses Gorgias as a philosopher. As part of his effort to include for the first time the Greek Sophists in the history of philosophy, Hegel saw in Gorgias the attempt to come to terms with the difficulties of realism and subjectivism. In his words:

> Gorgias on the one hand pronounces a just polemic against absolute realism, which, because it represents, thinks to possess the very thing itself, when it only has a relative [awareness], but falls, on the other hand, into the false idealism of modern times,

according to which thought is always subjective only, and thus not the existent, since through thought an existent is transformed into what is thought. (383)

Another very influential reading is George Grote's, which views Plato's treatment of Gorgias as fundamentally unfair. Grote sees Plato as a reformer and Gorgias and his sophistic colleagues as professors of rhetoric working in the light of the socially accepted practices and standards of their times. Despite his sociocultural perspective, Grote focuses primarily on Gorgias's philosophical treatise, *On Non-Being or On Nature*, underscoring the plausibility of his three theses and depicting the whole treatise as a negative example, an example of what to avoid:

the first negation [nothing exists] was neither more untenable nor less untenable than that of those philosophers who before him had argued for the affirmative: on the two last points [nothing can be known and nothing can be described] his conclusions were neither paradoxical nor improperly sceptical, but perfectly just and have been ratified by the gradual abandonment, either avowed or implied, of such ultra-phenomenal researches among the major part of philosophers. It may fairly be presumed that these doctrines were urged by Gorgias for the purpose of diverting his disciples from studies which he considered as unpromising and fruitless. (52)

Eduard Zeller, following Hegel's lead, discusses Gorgias in philosophical terms, placing Gorgias in the tradition of scepticism: "No other Sophist seems to have taken such pains about the complete justification of scepticism" (455). Like Grote, Zeller concentrates on *On Non-Being or On Nature*, concluding that Gorgias's "arguments are in part purely sophistical; but, at the same time, real difficulties are touched by them, especially in respect to the third proposition [even if something can be known, it cannot be communicated]: and the whole might well have been regarded at that period as a formidable attempt to establish doubt as to the possibility of knowledge" (455).

Opting for a middle ground between Hegel and Grote, Theodor Gomperz portrays Gorgias as possessing "a sparkling wit, [and] a fertile and powerful imagination." He sees in him a "reformer of Greek style" (480), and a founder of Greek prose. When reading Gorgias's rhetorical compositions, Gomperz is impressed by the style, which he finds "brilliant, exalted, stately, flowery, and full of color" (477). When reading his philosophical treatise, he is impressed by the reasoning, which he finds "remarkable" (482). Gomperz concludes that Gorgias must be considered a hybrid thinker, "half a rhetorician and half a philosopher" (481), responsible for pioneering innovations in both fields.

Following Gomperz, Mario Untersteiner views Gorgias as both philosopher and rhetorician. Going beyond Gomperz, however, he attributes to Gorgias an elaborate philosophy consisting of an ontology and an epistemology, an ethic and an aesthetic, and founded on a tragic view of the world. In Untersteiner's words:

Gorgias is to be regarded as a mind of profound human intuition which has felt a great truth—the "tragic element," original discovery of the Greeks—and has translated it into philosophical terms without forgetting its literary origin. Therefore he is both philosopher and man of letters together. [...] But even in his two-fold extremism, speculative and literary, there emerges the harmonious unity of a man who has known how to infuse all the experiences of the soul with a great idea. (202)

Perhaps the most comprehensive philological study of Gorgias is Charles Segal's. He shows that Gorgias applied a rationalistic method to that part of rhetoric which concerns itself with the audience's emotional responses to art. For Segal, Gorgias's research anticipated later developments in Plato and Aristotle's more systematic approach to rhetoric. Summarizing his estimation of Gorgias's contribution to early rhetorical theory, Segal states:

It is Gorgias' achievement to have perceived and formulated as a *techne* that the formal structuring of the *logos* [...] evokes emotional forces, and to have generalized this formulation [...] to include both the linguistic and the visual arts. At the same time he attempts a scientific definition of the process by seeking an analogy in the most exact empirical science which the late fifth century could offer, medicine. In so doing, he treats the psyche as a tangible reality and places its functions on a level of reasonable explicability coordinate with other physical phenomena. (133)

By most standards of judgment, Gorgias is an important figure in the history of rhetoric. And if one judges the significance of historical figures by the volume of critical scholarship devoted to them, Gorgias figures very prominently in the field of rhetoric during the last fifty years. The attention he has received during this period bespeaks not only an ongoing interest in the early days of rhetoric but, more important, a coincidence of sensibilities, his and ours.

BIBLIOGRAPHY

Primary Sources and Translations

Diels, Hermann, and Walther Kranz. *Die Fragmente der Vorsokratiker.* 3 vols. Berlin: Weid-
    mannsche Verlagsbuchhandlung, 1952.
Plato. *Lysis, Symposium, Gorgias.* Trans. W. R. M. Lamb. Cambridge: Harvard UP, 1975.
Sprague, Rosamond K., ed. *The Older Sophists.* Columbia: U of South Carolina P, 1972.

Biographical Sources

Philostratus and Eunapius. *Lives of the Sophists.* Trans. Wilmer C. Wright. Cambridge: Harvard
    UP, 1989.

Critical Sources

Consigny, Scott. *Gorgias: Sophist and Artist.* Columbia: U of South Carolina P, 2001.
Gomperz, Theodor. *Greek Thinkers: A History of Ancient Philosophy.* Vol. 1. Trans. Laurie
    Magnus. New York: Humanities P, 1964.

Grote, George. *A History of Greece*. Vol. 7. London: John Murray, 1888.

Guthrie, W. K. C. *The Sophists*. Cambridge: Cambridge UP, 1971.

Hegel, G. F. *Lectures on the History of Philosophy*. Vol. 1. Trans. E. S. Haldane. New York: Humanities P, 1963.

Segal, Charles. "Gorgias and the Psychology of the Logos." *Harvard Studies in Classical Philology* 66 (1962): 99–155.

Untersteiner, Mario. *The Sophists*. Trans. Kathleen Freeman. New York: Philosophical Library, 1954.

Zeller, Eduard. *A History of Philosophy*. Vol. 2. Trans. S. F. Alleyne. London: Longmans, Green, 1881.

GREGORY OF NAZIANZUS

(ca. 329–389 CE)

Roxanne Mountford

Gregory of Nazianzus, also known as Saint Gregory the Theologian, was born around 329 CE in a Roman province of Asia Minor (now Turkey).[1] He is the least well known of the Eastern Orthodox Church's Three Holy Hierarchs (Basil of Caesarea and John Chrysostom are the others). He served as a presbyter (elder or priest) under his father, who was bishop of Nazianzus, and later was named bishop of both Sasima (a position he never accepted) and Constantinople. Honored as a saint in both the Roman Catholic and Eastern Orthodox churches, Gregory was a prolific writer: forty-four orations, sixteen of which are part of the Byzantine liturgy; 250 letters; and 17,000 lines of poetry are extant (Demoen 20–21). Throughout his lifetime, Gregory was swayed by eremitic practices and thought from within both secular and Christian philosophy and believed that action in the world—including preaching and leading fellow believers—was inferior to a life of self-examination and prayer. Nevertheless, Gregory studied rhetoric in Athens, which he applied briefly as a teacher and later as a celebrated preacher after he reluctantly agreed to forego the contemplative life.

The son of wealthy Christians, Gregory and Nonna, who held estates near Nazianzos in Cappadocia, Gregory was born in the village of Arianzus. Gregory's family believed in the importance of a classical education, and so both he and his brother, Caesarios, were sent away to larger cities of the Hellenistic world for their secular training. Gregory attended grammar school in nearby Nazianzus and then traveled to Caesarea, which was then the capital of Cappadocia, for his next level of education. Seeking deeper knowledge of rhetoric and philosophy, Gregory traveled to Palestine, site of a famous school where Origen had once taught. From Palestine, Gregory traveled to Alexandria, where he encountered intellectual traditions that were both classical and Christian. According to Rosemary Radford Ruether, "Gregory's studies in Palestine and in Alexandria undoubtedly [...] shaped his predilection for Platonism and for Origenist theology and exegesis" (19). After two or three years in Palestine and Alexandria, Gregory traveled to Athens, a diminished but still renowned center of learning, where he stayed for ten years, focusing his study on rhetoric and philosophy (Ruether 18–19). After a long career serving in Christian leadership, Gregory retired in his native Nazianzus in 383 CE, his last five years spent in the peaceful contemplative life he preferred. One third of his extant letters were written during this period and many poems. He died around 389 CE. Gregory is an important figure in the history of rhetoric because while he professed an open contempt (after his conversion) for politics and rhetoric, he is perhaps one of the greatest preachers of the Second Sophistic period (Conley 367). While Gregory does not contribute new theory to the history of rhetoric, his rhetorical practices and biography are noteworthy examples of the dynamic mingling of the Christian and secular at the beginning of the Byzantine Empire.

GREGORY AND THE SECOND SOPHISTIC

Gregory had the good fortune of learning rhetoric at a rare moment when Christian and secular scholars were on an equal footing in the classical world. During the fourth century CE, Sophists once again attracted students from all around the region, and oratory was marked by highly ornate language, an abundance of tropes and figures, and elaborate prose rhythms. The chair of sophistry in Athens and Gregory's teacher of rhetoric, Prohaeresius, attracted students from throughout Asia Minor. Although Prohaeresius was a Christian, he taught a traditional classical curriculum that was indistinguishable from his secular counterparts'. "Indeed, if Euanpius [...] had not told us that Prohaeresius was a Christian, we would have had no reason to suspect it, for in every other way he was typical of the contemporary sophist" (Ruether 20). Prohaeresius was also a student of philosophy; Euanpius reports that his lifestyle was ascetic, as befitting a philosopher (McGuckin 62).

While Sophists were established as chairs throughout the Roman empire, philosophers did not enjoy such popularity. Marcus Aurelius established several chairs of philosophy during his reign, but philosophical schools were in decline in Athens when Gregory was there. While he undoubtedly studied Plato and Aristotle as part of his training as an orator, it is unclear whether or not Gregory trained directly with philosophers when he was in Athens. Nevertheless, scholars agree that Gregory was influenced by Neoplatonic ideas, including the dualism of body and mind (converted by Christians into body and spirit) and the asceticism that accompanied this belief (Ruether 15; McGuckin 57). McGuckin writes, "The combination of an ascetic lifestyle as an essential accompaniment to the philosophic quest was a principle the early Church shared with the Neoplatonists" (62). Gregory's melding of these traditions is clearly stated in his poem *De Rebus Suis*: "Long ago I cut myself off from this world / My soul was melded with radiant spirits of heaven, / and my spiritual intellect carried me aloft, / setting me down from the flesh [...]" (quoted in McGuckin 66). Tellingly, Gregory as well as Gregory of Nyssa refer to the ascetic life as the "philosophic life" (Ruether 15 n. 2).

Throughout his life, Gregory wavered between a life of the world in service of the church, which he ultimately chose, and the life of a monk (or "philosophic life"), which he favored. Gregory's lifelong friend Basil established a monastery in Annesoi, Cappadocia, and Gregory joined him there for a time after leaving Athens. While serving as bishop of Nazianzus, his father coerced him into the priesthood in 361 or 362, but Gregory fled back to Annesoi and remained there in seclusion for several months before taking up the ministry beside his father. After Basil became bishop of Caesarea, he ordained Gregory bishop of the town of Sasima, and Gregory again fled into seclusion. But ultimately Gregory embraced a life in the world, even though his longing for the ascetic life is a major theme of his writing (Sterk). Theologically, he was an important member of the Nicene party and instrumental in the establishment of the doctrine of the Trinity, which some scholars attribute to Neoplatonic influences (Wolfson 141–232). He defended this doctrine against rival groups, most notably the Arians, using his considerable skill as a rhetor. He is credited with building the foundation for the Eastern Orthodox Church by reestablishing orthodoxy in Constantinople.

Although Gregory was frequently and openly contemptuous of pagan[2] Greek culture and even of sophistry, he did not shy away from quoting pagan authors and displaying the eloquence he learned in Athens. In an oration preached in Constantinople, he says, "Let us leave such jesting to the legends and the Greeks, who think but little of truth and enchant ear and mind by the charm of their fictions and the daintiness of their style" (quoted in Ruether 159). When Gregory of Nyssa decided to teach rhetoric, Gregory angrily denounced him in a letter, imploring him to "return to sobriety and your true character" and to stop being an "empty-headed fool" (Ruether 160–61). Nevertheless, when his Athenian classmate Julian closed the schools to Christians on the grounds that one could not both scorn the gods and teach Greek culture, Gregory bitterly condemned his policies in several orations. Privately, he wrote to Basil a protean theory of Christian education: "we know that neither fire nor food nor iron nor any other of the elements is of itself most useful or most harmful except according to the will of those who use it" and "so from secular literature we have received principles of inquiry and speculation while we have rejected their idolatry [. . .]" (quoted in Ruether 165). He goes further in *Carmina ad Seleucum* and in the poem *Nicobuli filii ad patrem*, praising the study of pagan Greek literature, history, rhetoric, and philosophy for the education of Christian students. He does not go as far as Augustine would later in *De doctrina Christiana*, but the merging of pagan and Christian perspectives on rhetoric are clearly underway in Gregory's thinking.

In his writing and oratory, Gregory freely mingled both pagan and Christian sources. Gregory quoted widely from pagan Greek philosophers, including Homer, Hesiod, Euripides, Herodotus, Demosthenes, Heraclitus, Aristotle, and, of course, Plato (the most frequently quoted pagan writer in his work), to name just a few. He borrowed not only maxims from these writers, but also exempla—stories and mythology, which he used to illustrate his sermons (Demoen 209–31). From a contemporary perspective, given Gregory's stated contempt for pagan cosmology, these borrowings of Greek literature and culture are curious. However, when we consider the style of the Second Sophistic with its display of elaborate figures, Gregory's choices seem to fall fully within the requirements of the rhetorical style he had mastered. In describing the principles upon which Gregory's orations are based, Ruether writes,

> An idea is never stated in just one way. It is stated in numerous different ways. One does not just use one metaphor or example; one uses numerous metaphors or examples. One aims at virtually overwhelming the listener with the richness of thought, the myriad images and nuances of language which tumbled out in rapid succession. (59)

Stylistically, Gregory's use of such figures of language is so elaborate and poetic that it is sometimes called "Gregory's hymnic style." Perhaps the best example of Gregory's elaborate style occurs in Oration 40, *On Baptism*, in which he includes a remarkable sentence made up of twelve alliterative words in a row (Ruether 62). In addition to these stylistic choices, Gregory also emulated traditional genres of rhetoric along with topics traditionally associated with these forms, including epideictic, as in his funeral oration for Gorgonia, his sister (Ruether 115). He also is widely praised for his panegyric sermons (Kennedy; Milovanovic-Barham 23–24).

Despite his contempt for Hellenistic language and literature (which may have driven him to order the burning of Sappho's poetry), Gregory is in many ways more pagan in both style and substance than the next generation of Christian philosopher-rhetors would be. In this way, he is noteworthy as a "bridging" figure in the history of rhetoric. Through study of Gregory of Nazianzus, it is clear that Augustine (who came later), while perhaps the first to articulate a fully Christian theory of oratory, was not the only patrician to lay claim to pagan rhetorical practices in the name of Christianity. Indeed, though a celebrated Christian theologian, Gregory also was a master rhetorician and Neoplatonic philosopher who borrowed freely from pagan sources and practices and insisted on the importance of pagan training in philosophy and rhetoric.

SCHOLARSHIP ON GREGORY

The most complete study of Gregory of Nazianzus's rhetoric in English occurs in Ruether's *Gregory of Nazianzus*.[3] A more recent study of Gregory's exempla occurs in Demoen's *Pagan and Biblical Exempla in Gregory Nazianzen*. The best biography available to date is McGuckin's *St. Gregory of Nazianzus*. Important treatments of Gregory's rhetoric occur in Kennedy's *Greek Rhetoric under Christian Emperors* and *Classical Rhetoric*. Scholars will find Conley's treatment of Byzantine rhetoric helpful for understanding the rhetorical tradition in Byzantium after the Second Sophistic.

Scholars who are interested in the study of Gregory of Nazianzus will be challenged by the lack of a proper critical edition of his works, which has been underway for over fifty years (McGuckin 403).[4] Few English translations exist.

Scholarship on Gregory in English is somewhat more promising, with important new secondary works published recently (in addition to the works above, see Daley, Elm, and Sterk). As Conley notes, Byzantine rhetoric after Gregory remained devoted to the study of figures, a development that may reflect Gregory's legacy in the Byzantine world (367). Scholars such as Milovanovic-Barham who explore Gregory's oratory to build a broader context for understanding rhetorical theory in late antiquity illustrate the fruitfulness of looking beyond the well-traveled roads to Rome when studying classical rhetoric.

NOTES

1. The date of Gregory's birth is in dispute. Classical sources suggest his birth was in 301; however, Gregory's own writing would suggest 329 (see Ullmann).

2. While "pagan" is a word commonly used by scholars to refer to non-Christian religions in antiquity, it tends to render homogenous what were diverse local rituals and beliefs that existed throughout antiquity (see Limberis 373–74, n.1).

3. For a complete list of Gregory of Nazianzus's oratory and letters and selected examples of his poetry, see Ruether, 178–80.

4. Bernard Coulie's *Corpus Nazianzenum* is a multivolume series of Gregory of Nazianzus's edited corpus, with commentaries; volumes in this series continue to be published. The *Patrologia Graeca* is the only series that includes all the extant writing and oratory of Gregory of Nazianzus.

BIBLIOGRAPHY

Primary Sources and Translations

Coulie, Bernard, ed. *Corpus Nazianzenum, vol. 1–*. Corpus Christianorum, Series Graeca. Turnhout, Belgium: Brepols, 1988–.

Gilbert, Peter, trans. *On God and Man: The Theological Poetry of St. Gregory of Nazianzus.* Crestwood, NY: St. Vladimir's Seminary P, 2001.

King, Charles W., trans. *Julian the Emperor, Containing Gregory Nazianzen's Two* Invectives *and Libanius' Monody with Julian's Extant Theosophical Works.* London: G. Bell, 1888.

Madison, Arthur James, ed. *The Five Theological Orations of Gregory of Nazianzus.* Cambridge: Cambridge UP, 1899.

McGuire, Martin R. P., trans. *Funeral Orations by Saint Gregory Nazianzen and Saint Ambrose.* New York: Fathers of the Church, 1953.

Migne, Jacques-Paul, ed. *Patrologia Graeca*, vols. 35–38. Paris: Migne, 1857–66.

Moreschini, Claudio, and D. A. Sykes, trans. *Poetmata Arcana.* Oxford Theological Monographs. Oxford: Oxford UP, 1997.

Vinson, Martha Pollard, trans. *Select Orations.* Fathers of the Church 107. Washington, DC: Catholic U of America P, 2003.

White, Carolinne, trans. *Gregory of Nazianzus, Autobiographical Poems.* Cambridge Medieval Classics 6. Cambridge: Cambridge UP, 1996.

Biographical Sources

McGuckin, John A. *St. Gregory of Nazianzus: An Intellectual Biography.* Crestwood, NY: St. Vladimir's Seminary P, 2001.

Meredith, Anthony. *The Cappadocians.* London: Geoffrey Chapman, 1995.

Ullmann, Carl. *Gregory of Nazianzum, Ho Theologos, "The Divine": A Contribution to the Ecclesiastical History of the Fourth Century.* Trans. George V. Cox. London: John W. Parker, 1851.

Critical Sources

Conley, Thomas. "Byzantine Teaching on Figures and Tropes." *Rhetorica* 4.4 (1986): 335–74.

Daley, Brian E. "Building a New City: The Cappadocian Fathers and the Rhetoric of Philanthropy." *Journal of Early Christian Studies* 7 (Fall 1999): 431–61.

Demoen, Kristoffel. *Pagan and Biblical Exempla in Gregory Nazianzen: A Study in Rhetoric and Hermeneutics.* Turnhout, Belgium: Brepols, 1996.

Elm, Susanna. "Hellenism and Historiography: Gregory of Nazianzus and Julian in Dialogue." *Journal of Medieval and Early Modern Studies* 33.3 (2003): 493–515.

———. "A Programmatic Life: Gregory of Nazianzus' Orations 42 and 43 and the Constantinopolitan Elites." *Arethusa* 33.3 (2000): 411–27.

Harrison, Verna E. F. "Male and Female in Cappadocian Theology." *Journal of Theological Studies* 41 (October 1990): 441–71.

Kennedy, George A. *Classical Rhetoric and Its Christian and Secular Tradition from Ancient to Modern Times.* 2nd ed. Chapel Hill: U of North Carolina P, 1999.

———. *Greek Rhetoric under Christian Emperors.* History of Rhetoric, vol. 3. Princeton: Princeton UP, 1983.

Limberis, Vasiliki. " 'Religion' as the Cipher for Identity: The Cases of Emperor Julian, Libanius, and Gregory Nazianzus." *Harvard Theological Review* 93.4 (2000): 373–400.

Milovanovic-Barham, Celica. "Three Levels of Style in Augustine of Hippo and Gregory of Nazianzus." *Rhetorica* 11.1 (1993): 1–25.

Ruether, Rosemary Radford. *Gregory of Nazianzus: Rhetor and Philosopher.* London: Oxford UP, 1969.

Sterk, Andrea. *Renouncing the World Yet Leading the Church: The Monk-Bishop in Late Antiquity.* Cambridge: Harvard UP, 2004.

Wolfson, Harry A. *The Philosophy of the Church Fathers.* Cambridge: Harvard UP, 1956.

HERACLITUS

(floruit ca. 500 BCE)

John T. Kirby

Heraclitus (Greek *Hērakleitos*, "famed of Hera," a name similar in meaning to that of Heracles) was born in Asia Minor (modern-day Turkey) in Ephesus, an important Ionian city between Smyrna and Miletus. Little is known of his personal life except, possibly, the name of his father (Bloson? Heracon?) and a story that he ceded to a younger brother his hereditary claim to a (basically honorary) kingship (*basileia*). The latter, if true, means that he could probably trace his lineage back to the ancient kings of Athens. He is one of our earliest written sources for Greek prose, though his work survives only in fragments.

His book, titled (like so many ancient philosophical treatises) *Peri phuseōs*, "On Nature," is said to have been composed in three sections: one on the universe ("on the all," says Diogenes Laertius 9.1.5), one on politics, and one on theology. We are told that he deposited this book in the temple of Ephesian Artemis as an offering, and that he purposely wrote in an obscure style so that it would not be comprehensible to ordinary readers. One of his epithets, indeed, was "The Obscure" (*ho skoteinos*), and the aptness of this label is readily underscored by the difficult and riddling quality of the extant fragments of his writing. Diogenes Laertius (2.22) reports that, when Euripides gave Socrates a copy of Heraclitus's book, Socrates remarked, "The parts I've grasped are splendid, as doubtless are the parts I have not grasped; but it would take a Delian diver to get to the bottom of it."

HERACLITUS AND EARLY GREEK PHILOSOPHY

Heraclitus is traditionally said to have reached the height of his powers during the sixty-ninth Olympiad, which would put his floruit at about 500 BCE. This would also make him the heir to a century or so of philosophical thinking by a number of men from neighboring cities, including Xenophanes of Colophon, Pythagoras from the nearby island of Samos, and such figures as Thales, Anaximander, and Anaximenes, who hailed from the city of Miletus, south of Ephesus. Each of these three Milesian thinkers had sought the origin or first principle (*arkhē*) of the universe in some substance or notion: for Thales, it appears to have been water; for Anaximenes, air. Anaximander posited something he called the *apeiron*, that is, "indefinite" or "undetermined"—though what he meant by that is not entirely clear. For Heraclitus, if we may believe Aristotle, the *arkhē* of the universe was fire. The extant fragments (all cited here in the still-standard numeration of Diels and Kranz) call it "ever-living" fire (*aeizōōn*, fr. 22 B 30) and an exchange for all things that exist (*antamoibē hapantōn*, fr. 22 B 90). What would it mean for all things to come from fire in this fashion? If Diogenes Laertius is right, the process is one of condensation and rarefaction—of the elements becoming more and then less densely packed. (As Diogenes himself remarks, however, Heraclitus "expresses nothing clearly"; and Diogenes may have had access to the entire work, not just fragments, although it is possible that he was depending on the summary in the *Phusikōn doxai* of Theophrastus.) This proposed common source of the entire phenomenal universe, as we have remarked, harmonizes Heraclitus's approach to some extent with that of the Milesian philosophers, but it also enables us to make sense of some other doctrines that he appears to propound: for example, that "all things are one" (22 B 50)—and, more specifically, that even opposites share an essential unity: the sea, for example, is both the purest and the most polluted of waters (22 B 61); immortals are mortals (22 B 62); the movement of a carding comb (or, depending on your reading of the Greek, of producing written letters) is both straight and crooked (22 B 59); the path upward is identical to the path down (22 B 60). Moreover, he tells us, God is both day and night, winter and summer, war and peace, satiety and famine (22 B 67). This notion of the unity of opposites (cf. fr. 22 B 10) may be at the core of his mysterious but famous saying that "they do not understand how, while differing, it agrees with itself [literally, 'how, being carried in different directions, it is brought back together']—a backward-turning [or 'back-stretched'] connection, like that of a bow and of a lyre" (22 B 51). It may also give us a way of linking all these sayings with his equally famous assertion that everything is in constant flux (the oft-cited formula *panta rhei*, "everything flows," comes from the sixth-century CE commentary on Aristotle's *Physics* by Simplicius, and may be a summary rather than a verbatim citation): according to Heraclitus, it is impossible to step twice into the "same" river (22 B 91), or rather, we both do and do not step into the same rivers (22 B 49a); upon those who enter the "same" rivers, different waters flow (22 B 12). In his insistence upon unity, he seems to be a forerunner of the monism of Parmenides; in his reference to the "strife" (*eris*, 22 B 8, 80) that fuels change in the universe, he appears to be one of the basic sources for the system of Empedocles (cf. also fr. 22 B 30, 31, 90).

HERACLITEAN THEMES

What is it, then, that unifies opposites, directs change in the universe, and holds everything together in an architectonic unity? Heraclitus's answer appears to be: *logos*.

This notoriously slippery (because polysemous) word is the more difficult because it may, in his extant fragments, sometimes have the rather ordinary meaning of "account" in the sense of "narrative" or "explanation." But there is strong indication that it has a more cosmic meaning, at least sometimes in Heraclitus's thought: what Kirk, Raven, and Schofield call "the unifying formula or proportionate method of arrangement of things, what might almost be termed their structural plan both individual and in sum" (187). Moreover, this *logos* turns out to be, in many respects, "co-extensive with the primary cosmic constituent, fire" (188, 199–200); thus "natural changes of all kinds are regular and balanced, and [...] the cause of this balance is fire, the common constituent of things that was also termed their Logos" (212). The *logos* governs everything that happens (fr. 22 B 1); it is "common," which apparently means it is shared by all people, whether or not they all understand it in the same way (22 B 2).

Another prominent theme in the writing of Heraclitus is that the truth is difficult to grasp—or at least that most people have not grasped it. (As we have seen, he himself is said to have written purposely in order to obfuscate, although this may be a post hoc explanation of his opacity.) People do not, he tells us, comprehend the *logos* (22 B 1); some of them are just inexperienced, while others are quite oblivious of what they themselves are doing (22 B 1). Their incomprehension is like a deaf person's not hearing (22 B 34). They prefer their own imaginings to an understanding of the information they take in (22 B 17). Even their daily experiences seem strange to them (22 B 72). This rather jaundiced view of human intellection extends to a spirited criticism of such illustrious Greek authors as Hesiod, Archilochus, Pythagoras, Xenophanes, and even the mighty Homer himself (22 B 40, 42, 56, 57, 106, 129, and perhaps 81). Opinions, he tells us, are like children's toys (22 B 70); sensory intake should be the basis of thought, especially sight and hearing (22 B 55), but sight even more than hearing (22 B 101a); even so, the eyes and ears of one with a "foreign psyche"—whatever that may mean—are not reliable witnesses (22 B 107). Some just do not know how to listen (22 B 19). Nonetheless, the capacity to think (*phronein*) is common to all humans (22 B 113), as is also to think soberly, moderately, and with self-restraint (*sōphronein*, 22 B 116, if that fragment may be considered authentic); *sōphronein* is identified as the greatest excellence and wisdom (22 B 112, following the punctuation of Kahn [42], though Marcovich [96] and others do not regard this as an actual citation from Heraclitus); *sōphronein* appears to be glossed here as "to say and do true things and to perceive things according to [their] nature." To understand the world around us is inherently difficult; nature, says Heraclitus, likes to hide itself (22 B 123). But that he does not despair a priori of the potential power of thought is shown by the fact that he himself made such philosophic inquiry, beginning (it would seem) with himself: "I enquired into myself" (22 B 101), he says, in a statement quoted both by Diogenes Laertius and by Plutarch. The former takes it to mean that he was thereby able to teach himself everything; the latter refers it to the Delphic precept "know thyself." But in any case, for Heraclitus the psyche itself is limitless: "if you travel every path you will not find the limits

of the psyche, so deep is its *logos*" (22 B 45). And those who love wisdom
(*philosophoi*) must inquire into very many things (22 B 35), beginning with themselves (22 B 116).

TOWARD A HERACLITEAN RHETORIC

It is not clear, from the extant fragments, what the implications are of this psychology for an understanding of rhetoric. The only passage that may have specifically to do with rhetoric, considered as a set of elementary teachings or even
possibly an introductory handbook (*eisaōgē*) for public speakers (*rhētores*), is cited in a
treatise on rhetoric by Philodemus, a first-century BCE writer whose writings are
themselves still in great editorial disrepair. The fragment (22 B 81) reads as follows,
in the translation of Jonathan Barnes (*Philosophy* 111): "The orators' *Introduction* [*hē
tōn rhētorōn eisagōgē*] bends all its theorems to this end [sc. deception] and is,
according to Heraclitus, the leader of cheats [*kopidōn . . . arkhēgos*]." Kahn (41 n.)
aptly glosses *arkhēgos* as "prince, initiator, founder, ring-leader." The problem,
textually, is that *arkhēgos* may not in fact be the predicate of *hē tōn rhētorōn eisagōgē*
here: there is some indication that Heraclitus's "prince of liars" in this sentence is
actually Pythagoras (cf., e.g., Kahn 41, 114; Marcovich 67–73). In that case, the
negative comments in the sentence about *hē tōn rhētorōn eisagōgē* must strictly be
imputed to Philodemus himself.

What else, then, might be said—or surmised—about Heraclitus's thoughts on
communication? What can we draw from the extant fragments that will illuminate
Heraclitus's importance for the twenty-first-century rhetorician? Taking the fragments at their face values, we may say that he appears to have a moralistic notion of
the value of telling the truth (22 B 28b), and to acknowledge that untrustworthiness
(*apistiē*, if this may be so translated) is difficult to recognize (22 B 86). He feels it is,
or should be, possible to arrive at a commonly shared account of the way things
actually are in the universe (22 B 1, 2, 89, 116) based on a common cognitive
experience thereof (22 B 55, 101a, 113). He values self-knowledge (22 B 101, 116)
but does not assume that education will automatically lead to profound thought (22
B 40, 57, 104, 129, and perhaps also 107). Indeed, his psychology and/or sociology
appears to be somewhat elitist in nature, not egalitarian (22 B 25, 29, 49, 104; and
we should probably also include here, if they are to be considered as beast fables,
the animal illustrations in 22 B 9, 11, 13, 82–83, and 97). In the public sphere,
Heraclitus stresses the fundamental importance of justice (22 B 23, 28b, 80); despite
his somewhat progressive religious views, his insistence upon the importance of the
rule of law in society (22 B 43, 44)—a notion promulgated a century earlier in
Athens by Solon—seems (for Heraclitus) to be rooted in the dependence of human
law upon divine law (22 B 114). And in view of the importance, almost two
centuries later, of the word *ēthos* (personal character as perceived by the audience) in
Aristotle's *Rhetoric*, it is worth noting that for Heraclitus, one's *ēthos* is one's destiny
(literally, one's *daimōn*, i.e., "god," 22 B 119).

BIBLIOGRAPHY

Primary Sources and Translations

Diels, Hermann, and Walther Kranz, eds. *Die Fragmente der Vorsokratiker*. 1910. 6th ed.
    Dublin/Zurich: Weidmann, 1951–52.
Freeman, Kathleen. *Ancilla to the Pre-Socratic Philosophers*. Cambridge: Harvard UP, 1978.

Critical Sources

Barnes, Jonathan. *The Presocratic Philosophers*. 1979. 2nd ed. London: Routledge, 1982.
———, ed. *Early Greek Philosophy*. New York: Penguin, 1987.
Guthrie, W. K. C. *A History of Greek Philosophy*. 6 vols. Vol. 1. *The Earlier Presocratics and the
    Pythagoreans*. Cambridge: Cambridge UP, 1962.
Kahn, Charles H. *The Art and Thought of Heraclitus*. Cambridge: Cambridge UP, 1979.
Kirk, G. S. *Heraclitus: The Cosmic Fragments*. 1954. 2nd ed. Cambridge: Cambridge UP, 1962.
Kirk, G. S., J. E. Raven, and M. Schofield. *The Presocratic Philosophers*. 1957. 2nd ed. Cam-
    bridge: Cambridge UP, 1983.
Marcovich, Miroslav. *Heraclitus*. Merida: Los Andes UP, 1967.
Wheelwright, Philip. *Heraclitus*. Princeton: Princeton UP, 1959.

HERMAGORAS OF TEMNOS

(late second century BCE)

Beth S. Bennett

Historians of rhetoric have called Hermagoras of Temnos "the most important single Greek rhetorician" of the Hellenistic era, 323–390 BCE (Murphy 131). Yet, we have little biographical information about him, except that he was a professional teacher of rhetoric who lived sometime during the second century (see Matthes, *Testimonia et fragmenta* v; cf. Kennedy 303 n. 73). Hermagoras's importance in the history of rhetoric is based upon textual evidence of his rhetorical doctrine and its influence among ancient authors of his own era and subsequent ones.

According to ancient sources, Hermagoras produced a systematic treatise on rhetoric, *Technai rhētorikai*, which may have contained as many as six parts (Matthes, *Testimonia et fragmenta* vi). The treatise was reported to have covered all five *erga* (*officia*) of rhetoric, though style (*lexis*) and arrangement (*taxis*) were both subsumed under a general rubric of *oikonomia* (management), usually translated as prose economy (Matthes, "Hermagoras von Temnos" 60–61; cf. Quintilian 3.3.9). From this work by Hermagoras, the inventional doctrine of *stasis* seems to have had the most far-reaching influence, particularly as it was transmitted in the Latin rhetorical treatises of Cicero and Quintilian and in the doctrine of the Greek rhetorician, Hermogenes of Tarsus, in the second century CE. Because the treatise itself is lost, discussion of Hermagorean doctrine has been based upon textual fragments attributed to him by ancient sources.

References to Hermagoras are found throughout many ancient texts. The most substantive Latin sources are Cicero's *De inventione*, the anonymous *Rhetorica ad Herennium*, Quintilian's *Institutio oratoria*, and the work perhaps most faithful to Hermagorean doctrine, Aurelius Augustine's *De rhetorica* (see Dieter and Kurth 93–95). These ancient authors all seemed to have recognized the importance of Hermagorean influence on rhetorical doctrine, while acknowledging that Hermagoras himself had been confronted by harsh criticism from among his contemporaries.

Throughout the *De rhetorica*, Hermagoras is cited specifically as the chief authority of rhetorical doctrine but often in what appears to be a defensive tone against alleged "disparagers of Hermagoras" (Dieter and Kurth 96, 3). For example, in explaining the function of the orator, the author states, "Hermagoras, to avoid all malicious misinterpretations added a clause to the statement and left it behind in writing in this form: The end of the office of the orator is to persuade, to the extent that the condition of things and persons permits" (Dieter and Kurth 96, 2). In the *De inventione*, a young Cicero issues his own criticism of Hermagoras, whose ability Cicero describes as "such that one will more readily deny him the power of rhetoric than grant him acquaintance with philosophy" (1.6.8). Regardless, Cicero admits that some have been unfair in their criticism of Hermagorean doctrine, motivated "by a spirit of envy and a desire to disparage a rival" (1.11.16).

Modern scholarship on Hermagoras began with early efforts by Karl Wilhelm Piderit, in 1839, and then, in 1893, with Georg Thiele's *Hermagoras; ein Beitrag zur Geschichte der Rhetorik*. In the twentieth century, serious efforts at reconstructing Hermagorean rhetorical doctrine, based upon Thiele's edition of the fragments, were made by Otto Alvin Loeb Dieter and Ray Nadeau and by Louis Maxime Sirois, in an unpublished master's thesis. Then, in 1962, Dieter Matthes published a new critical edition of Hermagoras, which remains the authoritative source of these textual fragments. In the early 1960s, Karl Barwick also did significant work on reconstructing the rhetorical doctrine of Hermagoras. Nonetheless, despite this scholarly attention, Hermagorean doctrine remains somewhat uncertain in its details. As Dieter and Kurth noted, in their introductory comments, in 1968:

> Barwick was frank to admit that in his day there was no agreement among scholars concerning the general structure, the main divisions, and numerous details of the Hermagorean system, but he hoped that he had made some progress in that direction. A thought which he left with us was that whoever undertakes some day to write a history of ancient rhetoric worthy of its name will have to devote much time and attention to Hermagoras of Temnos and his rhetoric. (95)

Thus, while modern scholarship has established the importance of Hermagoras in the history of rhetorical theory, it has not been able to resolve the discrepancies in the specific details found amid the various sources of his doctrine. What follows is a summary of what has been generally accepted as attributable to Hermagoras of Temnos.

COMPONENTS OF HERMAGORAS'S RHETORICAL DOCTRINE

Hermagoras is credited with defining rhetorical action as investigation into civic affairs (Sirois 54). Specifically, he used the phrase *zētēmata politika*, political questions, to define the activity of the orator (Matthes, *Testimonia et fragmenta* viii). The orator's task was defined as "to discuss capably those matters which law and custom have fixed for the uses of citizenship, and to secure as far as possible the agreement of his hearers" (*Ad Her.* 1.2.1).

Somewhat controversially, at the time, Hermagoras considered general or in-definite questions of inquiry, *theses*, as well as specific or definite questions of inquiry, *hypotheses*, as appropriate for rhetorical investigation, thereby blurring any material distinction between philosophical and rhetorical inquiry (Quintilian 3.5.5; Dieter and Kurth 98, 5). The term *thesis* referred to an inquiry confronting a legal or abstract philosophical problem apart from specific people or circumstances. The term *hypothesis* referred to an inquiry into a specific set of circumstances, which usually constituted court action or a particular forensic case.

Within the Hermagorean conceptual framework, what defines a rhetorical dispute, *amphisbētēsis*, is not the material but the form of the action, "an actual individual two-way movement in thought and speech of some one specific thing by opposite or contrary-minded speakers," a controversy (Dieter 351). Nonethe-less, since pursuing abstract controversies was less profitable than pursuing spe-cific ones for professional orators (Quintilian 3.5.12), many criticized Hermagoras for assigning to rhetoric material they regarded as more properly suited to phi-losophy (Cicero 1.6.8). Although Hermagoras apparently considered the process of rhetorical investigation as appropriate and useful for philosophical problems, what we know of his specific doctrine of rhetorical investigation pertains to the *hypothesis* (Sirois 56; cf. Thiele).

Unlike the *thesis*, the essential elements of a *hypothesis* were concrete, not ab-stract; the orator had to consider the set of particular circumstances, *moria peristaseōs*, out of which the particular controversy had come into being. In *De rhetorica*, seven attributes of *peristasis* are identified: "Who? (*quis*), What? (*quid*), When? (*quando*), Where? (*ubi*), How? (*cur*), In what manner? (*quem ad modum*), By what means? (*quibus adminiculis*)" (Dieter and Kurth 99, 7). The answers to these questions would reveal the nature of the controversy and the contrary information being disputed. Un-derstanding the opposing or the contrary positions was vital to analyzing the rhetorical dispute. As Dieter explains the process:

> [T]he "start," or the beginning of every rhetorical *pragma*, [...] or real existing controversy is a Charge (*Kataphasis, Intentio*) and an Answer (*Apophasis, Depulsio,* or *Abnuentia*), or an Accusation and a Denial of the Charge. As opposites, or contraries, these declarations [...] make *stasis* with, or block one another, or effect the consti-tution of a conflict. (366)

Thus, the charge of "You did it" is answered with "I did not" and generates the central question, "Did the defendant do what is charged?" The function of the rhetorical dispute, then, was to enable a judgment (*to krinomenon*) to be rendered about the question of the charge (*zētēma*).

Ancient sources of Hermagorean fragments agree that he recognized these parts of a rhetorical dispute and how they constituted the *prima conflictio* to be judged. Unfortunately, sources do not agree about the how the secondary parts of the controversy functioned to render judgment about justification, rather than denial, of the charge. Modern scholars have offered different views. Hermagorean sources do agree that, in such controversies, a motive or cause (*aition*) is given as well as a refutation (*synechon*) that leads to a *secunda controversia* over the legitimacy of the justification.

Central to the analysis of the dispute, and thus to Hermagorean rhetorical doctrine, is the concept of *stasis*. The term itself derives from the root *sta*, to stand, and in ancient Greek culture represented "a temporary standing in conflict, undecided and unwavering, between contrary impulses" (Dieter 350). Based upon Quintilian's account of its use by rhetoricians (3.6.21), the concept of *stasis* appears to have functioned in two ways for Hermagoras, both as the principle for *noesis*, intellectually grasping the nature of the matter, and for *poiesis*, rhetorically handling or managing the dispute (Dieter 368). Initially, the orator had to eliminate matters that were asystatic, too indefinite to be investigated. Sources credit Hermagoras with identifying four types of indefinite matters: deficient or omitted evidence (*ellipse*), balanced evidence (*isotēta*), one-sided evidence (*heteromerian*), and inconclusive evidence (*aporon*) (Matthes, *Testimonia et fragmenta* viii–ix; Nadeau, "Classical Systems" 61, "Hermogenes" 378).

Focusing on matters that were static and therefore suitable for rhetorical investigation, Hermagoras developed two sets of questions for identifying the type of *stasis* applicable in a given controversy. First, and best known in the rhetorical tradition, is his set of logical questions that were derived, scholars have argued, from methods used by both the Stoics and the Peripatetics for systematic inquiry: (1) did an act take place, (2) what is the essential nature of the act, and (3) what is the nature of the nonessential qualities of the act? (Nadeau, "Hermogenes" 371). Along with the conjectural *stasis* (*stochasmos*) and the two *stases* of justification, definition (*horos*) and quality (*poiotēs*), is a fourth *stasis*, one of objection to the charge, *metalēpsis*. Cicero reports that Hermagoras was credited with inventing that fourth *stasis*, which applies "when the question arises as to who ought to bring the action or against whom, or in what manner or before what court or under what law or at what time, and in general when there is some argument about changing or invalidating the form of procedure" (1.11.16). The second set of questions pertains to legal issues or questions about that which is written (Quintilian 3.5.4). The legal questions include letter of the law and its intent, conflicting contrary laws, ambiguity, and inference (cf. Matthes, *Testimonia et fragmenta* viii).

Once the dispute had been analyzed to identify the applicable *stasis*, orators in forensic situations could use the Hermagorean system of *stasis* to prepare the relevant proof for their cases. The system provided a set of inventional topics (*heuresis*) for each *stasis*, which could generate arguments for either the prosecution or the defense. Matthes constructed an outline of these topics, which was translated by Nadeau (see "Hermogenes" 375; cf. Matthes, *Testimonia et fragmenta*).

The remainder of Hermagorean rhetorical doctrine, pertaining to the preparation of the orators for disputation, is referred to as prose economy (*oikonomia*). According to Quintilian, this term is the heading Hermagoras used for judgment, division into parts, order, and "*quaeque sunt elocutionis*," everything related to eloquence (3.3.9). Unfortunately, there is scarce specific textual evidence from

Hermagorean fragments either to elucidate or to validate Quintilian's claim (refer to Matthes, "Hermagoras von Temnos" 187–211). Scholars seem to have accepted a brief reference to Hermagoras in *De rhetorica* as evidence that he distinguished among four kinds of introductions, depending on the type of audience one faced (*Ad Her.* 1.3.5, n.c). What is stated in that treatise is that Hermagoras argued against the necessity of an introduction when the audience already holds the speaker in high regard: "For, he [Hermagoras] declares, if it is for the sake of gaining good will that we usually make introductions, on a theme which is in good repute [. . .] when those to whom we are about to speak are well disposed, nothing is gained by making provisions for what has already been provided" (Dieter and Kurth 106, 19). For the most part, the rest of the rhetorical doctrine attributed to this technical tradition has been reconstructed from the extant treatises that claim Hermagoras as a source, such as Cicero's *De inventione* and the *Rhetorica ad Herennium*.

HISTORICAL SIGNIFICANCE

The Hermagorean *stasis* system was made popular by those Greek rhetoricians who valued a technical approach to the teaching of rhetoric, and consequently, it proved to be well suited to the type of advanced rhetorical training sought by Romans. As the Roman declamatory practice of *controversia* became popular, both in the classroom and for public display, Hermagoras's *stasis* system (in Latin, *constitutio*, later *status*) was the system used for rhetorical invention and remained so for centuries. According to Quintilian's explanation, Hermagoras "carved out a path of his own, which many have followed," despite competition from rivals such as Athenaeus, Apollodorus of Pergamus, and Theodorus of Gadara (3.1.16–17). George Kennedy has provided this comment on Hermagoras's historical significance:

> With him [Hermagoras] the rhetorical handbook and the traditional system of ancient rhetoric achieved almost its full development. The dullness and sterility of the system were recognized by such men as Cicero (*Brutus* 263 and 271) and Tacitus (*Dialogus* 19), but the system was not rejected for that reason, for the rhetorical mind, of which Hermagoras' was an exceedingly neat example, had been fond of categories from the start. In fact, Hermagoras was very influential, certainly on the rhetoricians and perhaps also on Roman law. (318)

The fact that *stasis* theory remained at the center of rhetorical doctrine on invention for centuries beyond antiquity, until the end of the Renaissance, is due not only to the dominant influence of Cicero and Quintilian in the western part of the Roman Empire, but also to the influence of Hermogenes of Tarsus and his work, *Peri Staseōn*, in the Byzantine Empire. Ray Nadeau calls Hermogenes' treatise "the most thorough exposition" on *stasis* to have survived from antiquity ("Hermogenes" 66). Although his treatment of *stasis* is often viewed merely as a "practical 'revised edition' of Hermagoras," written for classroom instruction, Hermogenes preserved, explicated, and codified *stasis* theory and was the dominant influence in the Greek rhetorical tradition in the East for almost fifteen hundred years (Nadeau, "Hermogenes" 66–71).

In the fifteenth century, Hermogenean doctrine was reintroduced to the West in the treatise *Rhetoricorum libri quinque*, by George Trebizond (1395–ca. 1472), perhaps the most comprehensive treatment of rhetoric in the Renaissance. Trebizond's translation and paraphrasing of Hermogenes helped the Greek tradition of *stasis* theory be assimilated into the Latin rhetorical tradition. As late as the sixteenth century, evidence of this tradition appears in the early work of Philipp Melanchthon (1521) and in the first rhetorical handbook in English, the *Arte or Crafte of Rhethoryke* by Leonard Cox (1530). Cox, who names both Cicero's *De inventione* and Trebizond's work as his sources, includes Hermagoras's original divisions of invention, judgment, disposition, and style as the main parts of rhetoric.

Of course, by the end of the sixteenth century, in an attempt to simplify disciplinary boundaries, educators had largely accepted Ramistic doctrine that would assign invention, judgment, and arrangement to dialectic and leave only style and delivery as proper to rhetoric. The effect of Ramism, reducing the art of rhetoric to the study of artificial techniques for presenting the knowledge of others, severely restricted the traditional role of the rhetorician as it had been understood by Hermagoras and his followers. As contemporary scholar Malcolm Heath states, "The concept of rhetoric as *tekhnē* [...] implies a quest for understanding; the attempts of Hermagoras and his successors to work out a formal Model for the analysis of rhetorical problems, and so to provide a theoretical underpinning for practical work with *stasis*, were part of that quest" ("The Substructure of *Stasis*-Theory" 129).

BIBLIOGRAPHY

Primary Sources and Translations

Auctor. *Ad C. Herennium: De ratione dicendi (Rhetorica ad Herennium)*. 1954. Trans. Harry Caplan. Cambridge: Harvard UP, 1977.

Cicero, Marcus Tullius. *De inventione*. 1949. Trans. H. M. Hubbell. Cambridge: Harvard UP, 1976.

Matthes, Dieter, ed. *Testimonia et fragmenta, adiunctis et Hermagorae cuisdam discipuli Theodori Gadarei et Hermagorae Minoris fragmentis*. Leipzig: B. G. Teubner, 1962.

Quintilian, Marcus Fabius. *Institutio oratoria*. Vol. 1. 1920. Trans. H. E. Butler. Cambridge: Harvard UP, 1969.

Critical Sources

Barwick, Karl. "Augustins Schrift *De rhetorica* und Hermagoras von Temnos." *Philologus* 105 (1961): 97–110.

———. "Zur Erklärung und Geschichte der Stasislehre des Hermagoras von Temnos." *Philologus* 108 (1964): 80–101.

————. "Zur Rekonstruktion der Rhetorik des Hermagoras von Temnos." *Philologus* 109 (1965): 186–218.

Braet, Antoine. "The Classical Doctrine of *Status* and the Rhetorical Theory of Argumentation." *Philosophy and Rhetoric* 20.2 (1987): 79–80.

Dearin, Ray D. "The Fourth *Stasis* in Greek Rhetoric." *Rhetoric and Communication*. Ed. Jane Blankenship and Hermann G. Stelzner. Urbana: U of Illinois P, 1976. 3–16.

Dieter, Otto Alvin Loeb. "*Stasis*." *Speech Monographs* 17 (1950): 345–69.

Dieter, Otto Alvin Loeb, and William Charles Kurth. "The *De Rhetorica* of Aurelius Augustine." *Speech Monographs* 35 (1968): 90–108.

Heath, Malcolm. *Hermogenes on Issues*. Oxford: Clarendon, 1995.

————. "The Substructure of *Stasis*-Theory from Hermagoras to Hermogenes." *Classical Quarterly* 44 (1994): 114–29.

Jaeneke, Walther. *De statuum doctrina ab Hermogene tradita*. Leipzig: Robert Noske, 1904.

Kennedy, George. *The Art of Persuasion in Greece*. Princeton: Princeton UP, 1963. 303–21.

Kroll, Wilhelm. "Rhetorica VI: Die πραγματική στάσις des Hermagoras." *Philologus* 91 (1936–37): 197–205.

Matthes, Dieter. "Hermagoras von Temnos, 1904–1955." *Lustrum* 3 (1958): 58–214.

Murphy, James J. "The Codification of Roman Rhetoric: With a Synopsis of the *Rhetorica ad Herennium*." *A Synoptic History of Classical Rhetoric*. 3rd ed. Ed. James J. Murphy and Richard A. Katula with Forbes I. Hill and Donavan J. Ochs. Mahwah, NJ: Lawrence Erlbaum, 2003. 127–49.

Nadeau, Ray. "Classical Systems of *Stases* in Greek: Hermagoras to Hermogenes." *Greek, Roman, and Byzantine Studies* 2 (1959): 51–71.

————. "Hermogenes' *On Stases*: A Translation with an Introduction." *Speech Monographs* 31 (1964): 361–424.

————. "Some Aristotelian and Stoic Influences on the Theory of *Stases*." *Speech Monographs* 26 (1959): 248–54.

Netzker, Hermann. *Hermagoras, Cicero, Cornificius: Quae docuerint de "statibus."* Kiliae: C. F. Mohr, 1879.

Piderit, Karl Wilhelm. *Commentatio de Hermagore rhetore*. Hersfeld: F. Schuster, 1839.

Reid, Robert S. "Hermagoras' Theory of Prose *Oikonomia* in Dionysius of Halicarnassus." *Advances in the History of Rhetoric* 1 (1996): 9–24.

Schütrumpf, Eckart. "Hermagoras of Temnos and the Classification of Aristotle's Works in the Neoplatonic Commentaries." *Mnemosyne* 44 (1991): 96–105.

Sirois, Louis Maxime. "The Rhetoric of Hermagoras: A Translation and Editing, with an Introduction." Thesis. University of Denver, 1957.

Thiele, Georg. *Hermagoras; ein Beitrag zur Geschichte der Rhetorik*. Strassburg: K. J. Trübner, 1893.

Volkmann, Richard von. *Hermagoras: oder Elemente der Rhetorik*. Stettin: Nahmer, 1965.

HERMOGENES OF TARSUS

(160–ca. 225 CE)

Janet B. Davis

Hermogenes was a Greek-speaking professional rhetor who won fame as a youthful prodigy aged about fifteen, in 175–176 CE. In that year, the emperor Marcus Aurelius went to hear him perform, and the emperor was impressed. During a brief, brilliant career, Hermogenes also wrote some monographs on rhetorical theory; but while still in early manhood he suffered a breakdown from which he never recovered. He lived to be an old man and died in obscurity. Tentatively, therefore, an estimate of his lifetime puts his birth in 160 and his death around 225.

The earliest and most reliable source for Hermogenes' biography is Philostratus, who was a member of the empress Julia Domna's intellectual circle early in the third century. The period was called "the Second Sophistic" on account of a resurgence of widespread interest in, and influence of, rhetoric as a professional practice. Philostratus published a work titled *Lives of the Sophists* in about 230; but he was mainly interested in success stories, so he did not give much space to Hermogenes, whose meteoric career had been disappointingly short. The account given by Philostratus reads as follows:

> Hermogenes, who was born at Tarsus, by the time he was fifteen had attained such a reputation as a sophist that even the Emperor Marcus became eager to hear him. At any rate Marcus made the journey to hear him declaim, and was delighted with his formal discourse, but marveled at him when he declaimed extempore, and gave him splendid presents. But when Hermogenes arrived at manhood his powers suddenly deserted him, though this was not due to any apparent disease, and this provided the envious with an occasion for their wit. For they declared that his words were in very truth "winged," as Homer says, and that Hermogenes had moulted them, like wing-feathers. And once Antiochus the sophist, jesting at his expense, said: "Lo, here is that fellow Hermogenes, who among boys was an old man, but among the old is a boy." The following will show the kind of eloquence that he affected. In a speech that he was delivering before Marcus, he said, "You see before you, Emperor, an orator who still needs an attendant to take him to school, an orator who still looks to come of

age." He said much more of this sort and in the same facetious vein. He died at a ripe
old age, but accounted as one of the rank and file, for he became despised when his
skill in his art deserted him. (205–07)

Various sources confirm that Marcus Aurelius toured cities in the eastern Empire,
including Tarsus, in 175–176. The anecdote of his going to hear Hermogenes
perform is repeated by the historian Cassius Dio (LXXI.1).

Philostratus makes no mention of Hermogenes as an author, but allows for a
period of a few years, between the emperor's visit and the sudden breakdown,
when he was in full possession of his powers. For the assumption that he did some
writing on rhetoric during that time, we rely, first, on the existence of commentaries
on various parts of a text referred to as "Hermogenes' Art of Rhetoric" beginning
with that by Syrianus in the fifth century, and second, on the tenth-century
Byzantine encyclopedic compilation known as the Suda. The Suda item, in part,
reads:

> Hermogenes of Tarsus, nicknamed Xyster (a rasp or plane), sophist. The philosopher
> Musonios attended his classes. . . . [A]ged about 18 or 20 he wrote these books, laden
> with marvels: Art of Rhetoric, which is in everyone's hands; On Issues (1 book); On
> Types of Style (2 books); On Coele Syria (2 books). [Here the Suda inserts Philostratus'
> text, then continues:] This is also said about him by some people: after his death he was
> cut open, and his heart was found to be covered in hair, and far to exceed in size the
> human nature. These are the stories that are told about him. (*Suda On Line*)

While the Suda account, and other Byzantine references collected by Hugo Rabe,
add color to the short, sad story told by Philostratus, they lack reliability (for
example, Musonios lived more than a century before Hermogenes, and there is no
trace of material about Syria in the extant Hermogenic corpus).

What the Byzantine references do unequivocally show is that Hermogenes'
fame survived and grew for many centuries after his death. This is because what
seems to have been the standard text for teaching rhetoric in the Greek-speaking
world of later antiquity was attributed to his authorship. The work was known as
Hermogenes' Art of Rhetoric (Hermogenous technē rhētorikē), and had five parts, two of
which were most likely treatises that Hermogenes wrote in his late teens or early
twenties. Throughout the Byzantine era, the teaching of language arts was linguis-
tically and culturally conservative; one goal of teachers of both grammar and rhetoric
was the preservation of classical Attic Greek and its canonical literature. *The Art of
Rhetoric* served this objective in that it presented Demosthenes (384–322 BCE) as the
ideal orator, quoting extensively from his speeches, and drew its examples from
Demosthenes and from others whom Hermogenes called "the ancients" (*hoi arch-
aioi*), including Homer, Herodotus, Thucydides, Plato, Xenophon, Isocrates, and the
writers of Greek tragedy and comedy. Given this background, it is not surprising that
a collection of treatises attributed to a young declaimer famous in antiquity became
established as a standard textbook in the Byzantine schools of rhetoric.

CONTENTS OF *HERMOGENES' ART OF RHETORIC*

At least two works on rhetoric by that historical Hermogenes seem to have formed the nucleus of a multipart teaching text dating probably from the fifth century. To assess the significance of first the "authentic" parts and then the work as a whole, it will be helpful to describe the contents and attribution of each part of *Hermogenes' Art of Rhetoric*. Listed in the order in which they appear in the Teubner volume edited by Rabe, the five treatises are as follows.

Progymnasmata

This series of twelve preliminary exercises would have come at the beginning of the course in rhetoric. They start with a simple task (compose a fable) and conclude with quite a difficult one (propose a law). For each exercise, the author specifies a format to be used for the composition and gives an example of its application. Most scholars agree that these exercises were not written by Hermogenes, and they are missing from many of the codices. However, a graded sequence of exercises like these was a standard part of the rhetorical curriculum.

Peri Tōn Staseōn (On Issues)

The treatise that appears second in the *Art* explains how to identify and argue the central point at issue in a dispute. It divides the possible issues in legal or political disputes into thirteen categories (these are the *stases*), for each of which it presents a set sequence of heads under which any question of that type can be argued. Since early in the twentieth century, the scholarly consensus, on grounds of manuscript tradition as well as writing style, has been that Hermogenes of Tarsus was most likely the author of "On Issues" (see, for example, Rabe, *Opera* iii; Radermacher 870–71). It certainly preceded "On Types of Style" if the author heeded his own prescription, for he writes:

> It is impossible [. . .] for anyone who has not yet studied the pure division of questions into their so-called heads, or who is unfamiliar with what are known as the issues of problems, to have a sound grasp of [appropriate styles of discourse]. So it is completely senseless to teach the theory of types of styles before these subjects. [. . .] The theory of styles of discourse and their respective use is the subject of a separate and far from trivial treatise. (Heath 35)

The author's voice here—confident, opinionated, dismissive of other approaches— sounds very much like that of the author of "On Types of Style."

Peri Heureseōs (On Invention)

There are four parts to "On Invention." The first instructs students on how to compose speech introductions; its longest chapter shows how to adapt introductions to the assumptions (or prejudices) held by various parties to a case. The second part is about narration, or setting forth the facts of a case. Part 3 deals with argumentation. It addresses such technical topics as preliminary division, heads of argument, confirmation and refutation, epicheiremes, the enthymeme, definition, and arrangement. Part 4 deals with details of style such as figures of speech and the construction of lexical units such as the period. The treatise concludes with discussion of certain advanced rhetorical exercises.

Probably Hermogenes did write a treatise on invention. He says he did in "Style" 378.18, and alludes to such a work in "Issues" 53.12 (page references to Rabe). However, the four-part text that has come down to us in the *Art of Rhetoric* is almost certainly not that work. Problems with the text include its not being all about invention (book 4 is about style) and its never addressing an important element of invention, how to compose conclusions. In some places the text does not follow its own previews, suggesting serious mutilation at the very least. More generally, the writing style of the author of "On Invention" differs greatly from that of the author of "On Style" and "On Issues." Who, then, wrote the text we have? He is an experienced Sophist who claims to have created some rhetorical exercises and written a commentary on Demosthenes. He dedicates part of the treatise to a man named Julius Marcus with whom he has discussed some fine rhetorical points. His tone is didactic and mature; he is less insistent on thrusting his own personality forward than is the author of "On Style" and "On Issues." Ian Rutherford plausibly suggests he could have been a teacher in the school associated with Hermogenes, and possibly a generation older than he (*Canons* 114), but no such identification is sure. The text as we have it appears in the majority of documentary sources consulted by Rabe.

Peri Ideōn Logou (On Types of Style)

Like "On Issues," the treatise on style is generally accepted as the work of Hermogenes of Tarsus, and it appears in nearly all the codices. Its tone is similar—C. W. Wooten, its translator into English, says it is "filled with all the self-assurance, overstatement, and exuberance that one often associates with a high-school essay" (xviii). Its author has taken material from many predecessors and made of it a comprehensive system with a distinctive terminology, which would be quite easy to grasp and to memorize. He names nineteen types and subtypes of style, and gives instructions for how to achieve them, with numerous illustrations from classical Greek literature. The treatise has come down to us divided into two books, the same format that was known to the compilers of the Suda.

Peri Methodou Deinotētos (On the Method of Forcefulness)

Hermogenes did intend to write a book on this subject. When in "On Style" he came to the type he named *deinotēs*, he found the material too extensive for one chapter and announced his intention to deal with it in a separate treatise (Wooten

107–08). "On Style," however, defines *deinotēs* as what some scholars call "deco-rum" (Patterson; Conley), and what might less technically be named "mastery." It seems to refer to a fully informed competence in all aspects of technical rhetoric, the ability to choose among available strategies of arrangement and argumentation, and the skill to put all the parts together in a speech that has forceful effects. Covering such topics would indeed form an appropriate conclusion to the pre-ceding parts of the *Art*. But they are not addressed in the text we have, which, after an interesting introduction, comprises thirty-six brief chapters about details of style or strategy in rhetorical competition. It is a practical manual rather than a work of theory. However, Syrianus mentions *Peri methodou deinotētos* and cites details that correspond with details in our text, so it had already been incorporated within the *Art* by the fifth century. One cannot discount the possibility that Hermogenes wrote the introduction but failed to follow up on it, leaving the remaining chapters to be supplied from a handbook in use at the school associated with his name.

IMPORTANCE OF HERMOGENES TO THE RHETORICAL TRADITION

Hermogenes' Art of Rhetoric is important because it is the text that connects us most securely to the Greco-Roman tradition of technical, rule-based rhetoric. Byzantine rhetoricians knew little of Aristotle; Hermogenes was their authority. To get an idea of what they found in his work, consider the material covered by the two texts thought to be authentically Hermogenean, beginning with "On Issues."

Stasis theory was not new with Hermogenes. It had practical application in legal pleading, and Aristotle briefly explored the subject in his *Rhetoric* (1373b38–1374a17; 1417b21–7). Later authorities credited Hermagoras of Temnos with presenting the first fully developed terminology for it. From Hermagoras's frag-mentary surviving work, it appears he divided the *stases* into the following four coordinate categories:

1. Conjecture: Is there a factual basis for the dispute?
2. Definition: If the parties agree on the act that is in dispute, can they define it?
3. Quality: If they agree on definition, can arguments for mitigating circumstances be discovered?
4. Objection: Have all procedures been properly followed?

By Hermogenes' time, three or four centuries after Hermagoras, rhetoric was taught more as an academic discipline than a vocational skill for lawyers. Other rhetori-cians of the Second Sophistic, such as Minucianus, may have preceded him in expanding the old fourfold system, but Hermogenes' succinct though complex version lent itself to school use and learning by rote.

Hermogenes first identified cases that would be invalid (or lack issue) for such reasons as being insoluble or impossible, or lacking sufficient circumstantial evidence. Then he named thirteen *stases*, with a list of heads accompanying each. This is a subordinating system, in which at each stage one makes a yes/no decision leading to either another decision or a set of applicable arguments. Conjecture, definition, and objection remain much as in the fourfold system, but the *stasis* of quality has been subdivided. The analyst must decide whether the dispute focuses on features of an act or on application of a law, and whether the dispute concerns a past or future act. Depending on the outcome of those decisions, Hermogenes lists the *stases* named counterplea, counterposition, counterstatement, counteraccusation, transference, mitigation, letter and intent, assimilation, conflict of law, and ambiguity (Heath 31–35). For each *stasis*, he offers a checklist of heads to be used for the discovery of arguments. Not all will be relevant in any given case, but the trained rhetor must know them all and understand how to apply them. Under conjecture, for example, Hermogenes lists these possible heads of argument: making an exception; demanding evidence; raising questions of motive, capacity, or sequence of events; making counterplea or objection; and transposition of cause, an instance of which would be defending burial of a corpse in a remote place on grounds that it is always right to bury the unburied.

"On Issues" thus amplified an established system and made the amplified version comprehensible. "On Style" similarly presents an elaborate system labeled by a specialized terminology. Both treatises give definitions of these technical terms and illustrate them with quotations or examples. Both multiply existing sets of categories established by earlier rhetoricians.

The canon of style covers the many ways in which verbal choices can be made to yield rhetorical effects. Aristotle's observations on style in *Rhetoric* book 3, as further developed by his successor Theophrastus, apparently informed the pronouncements of such Roman authorities on the subject as Cicero and Quintilian. These predecessors identified three types of style: plain, for instructing an audience; middle, for pleasing and entertaining; and grand, for moving audiences to change opinions or behavior. In the first century BCE, Dionysius of Halicarnassus had presented a more complex list of "elements" of style, which has some similarities with Hermogenes' version. In his treatise, Hermogenes specified seven types (*ideai*) of style—clarity, grandeur, beauty, rapidity, character, sincerity, and force (Wooten xi)—asserting that these elements characterized the style of Demosthenes. Some types comprise several subtypes, giving a grand total of nineteen categories. For example, clarity comprises the subtypes purity (achieved by straightforward narration and everyday vocabulary) and distinctness (to achieve which an orator uses linear arrangement, effective transitions, and repetition).

Both "On Issues" and "On Style" were well adapted to ancient pedagogy. Selecting from six centuries of rhetorical tradition, which by the Second Sophistic was a sprawling accumulation of lore, their author fashioned concise bodies of knowledge that could be memorized and applied in traditional exercises grounded in classical literature. Furthermore, their insistence on guiding students to follow a method of division into categories (or ideal types) would have recommended them to Neoplatonist teachers in the centuries following Hermogenes' lifetime.

Neoplatonism was a highly influential school of thought (and Syrianus, the earliest extant commentator on Hermogenes, became head of the Academy at Athens in 431–432).

Someone, perhaps a Neoplatonist editor, completed the *Art of Rhetoric* early in the fifth century by adding the texts that are now considered spurious. They supplied material on subjects that Hermogenes referred to but perhaps had not written up or completed when his career ended. Though demonstrably different in style, they are broadly similar to "On Style" and "On Issues" in method; that is, they are made up of many short chapters, each of which defines and illustrates a rhetorical term or technique. They are practical texts. Their contents lend themselves to memorization, and "On Invention" in particular includes numerous themes for exercises in speech composition.

Though they did not always include "Progymnasmata," the other four parts of the *Art of Rhetoric* share a remarkably stable manuscript tradition, and any inconsistencies and contradictions among them hardly troubled their many Byzantine commentators. The whole work served as an authoritative teaching text for more than a millennium; it set the standards for Byzantine rhetoric; and after it reached the West, it influenced humanists and teachers forging new rhetorics in the Renaissance. It is worth inquiring what distinctive qualities assured its survival, and whether those qualities have relevance for contemporary rhetorical theory.

Previous paragraphs have argued that the work is comprehensive, knowledgeably eclectic regarding the rhetorical tradition, and well adapted to school use. Another characteristic promoting longevity is its flexibility. The formulas it presents can be applied to rhetoric in any medium. Different parts have served the interests of different eras. Syrianus, for example, made extensive comments about "On Issues." Centuries later, Michael Psellos, the tutor to a future emperor around 1060, wrote a synopsis in verse of the whole *Art* that mentions "On Issues" and "On Style" only cursorily, but gives detailed attention to "On Invention." Jeffrey Walker, who has translated Psellos's synopsis into English, suggests that "On Invention" may have seemed most useful and relevant in teaching "the actual practice of deliberative rhetoric where real political power was transacted" (18).

Hermogenes' name and precepts of technical rhetoric began reaching the West before the fall of Constantinople in 1453. Thomas Conley has shown that the *Art of Rhetoric* was frequently drawn on (though seldom cited) in a work in Latin by George of Trebizond known as *Rhetoricorum Libri V* and published in Venice around 1434 (117). Aldus Manutius brought out the first printed edition of *Hermogenes' Art of Rhetoric* in Greek in a volume titled *Rhetores graeci* in 1508. As humanists in the West grew familiar with the work, it became a resource for scholars who were trying to forge rhetorics for Italian, French, and other vernaculars. Numerous editions and translations came out in the sixteenth century, and Renaissance theorists were specially interested in "On Style." (For example, Johannes Sturm published an edition of "On Style" in 1571 as well as a Latin translation of the whole *Art*, with commentary.) Patterson, noting the inclusion of Hermogenes in educational programs proposed by English writers such as Thomas Elyot in 1531 and John Milton in 1644, has argued that the flexibility and implicit Platonism of the *Art*—and of "On Style" in particular—made it useful in times when new literary genres were being developed (20–35).

After the Renaissance, *Hermogenes' Art of Rhetoric* settled into relative obscurity until recently, in part perhaps because the authenticity and integrity of the text were questioned. However, interest in the work may be reviving in the postmodern age, as reissue of the Teubner text and recent translations seem to show. Parts have been translated into English by Wooten and M. Heath, and M. Patillon published a translation of the complete work in French. Work on a translation of "On Invention" into English is in progress.

Two scholars who have found Hermogenes relevant to their current interests are Rutherford and Patillon. Rutherford addressed the issue of canonicity by suggesting that the epilogue to "On Style"—a reading list of mostly prose writers—may represent an effort to restructure the ancient canon that privileged writers of verse (355–78). Patillon has for some years been exploring points of intersection between Hermogenes and contemporary discourse theory (notes to his 1997 translation pursue the same interest). Patillon's comments suggest that the introduction to "On the Method of Forcefulness"—whoever wrote it—offers an example of how the insights of *Hermogenes' Art of Rhetoric* may have presaged the current distinction between performance and competence by nearly two millennia. Here is a translation: "Every unit of speech is chosen to designate some matter, yet it occurs within a particular circumstance. The circumstance, with the addition of the element of usage, creates a unique meaning—and not just one meaning, but another that differs from it; and not just one difference, but many; and not just differences, but opposites" (Rabe, *Hermogenis* 414: 1–6).

BIBLIOGRAPHY

Primary Sources and Translations

Baldwin, Charles S. *Medieval Rhetoric and Poetic.* New York. Macmillan, 1928.

Davis, Janet B. "Hermogenes' On the Method of Forcefulness: A Translation and Critical Commentary." Diss., University of Iowa, 1993.

Heath, Malcolm. *Hermogenes On Issues: Strategies of Argument in Later Greek Rhetoric.* Oxford: Clarendon, 1995.

Kennedy, George A. "Preliminary Exercises Attributed to Hermogenes." *Progymnasmata: Greek Textbooks of Prose Composition and Rhetoric.* Atlanta Society of Biblical Literature, 2003. 73–88.

Patillon, Michel. *Hermogène: L'Art Rhétorique.* Lausanne: L'Age d'Homme, 1997.

Rabe, Hugo, ed. *Hermogenis Opera.* 1913. Stuttgart: Teubner, 1985.

Wooten, Cecil W. *Hermogenes' On Types of Style.* Chapel Hill: U of North Carolina P, 1987.

Biographical Sources

Philostratus. *Lives of the Sophists*. Trans. W. C. Wright. Cambridge: Harvard UP, 1921.

Rabe, Hugo. "Aus Rhetoren-Handschriften: Nachrichten über das Leben des Hermogenes." *Rheinisches Museum fur Philologie* 62 (1907): 247–64.

Radermacher, Ludwig. "Hermogenes, Rhetor aus Tarsos." *Pauly's Real-Encyclopaedie der classischen Altertumswissenchaft*. Ed. G. Wissowa and W. Kroll. Stuttgart: Metzler, 1913.

Suda On Line s.v. Hermogenes. Trans. M. Heath. 2001 <www.stoa.org/sol/>.

Critical Sources

Conley, Thomas. *Rhetoric in the European Tradition*. New York: Longman, 1990.

Nadeau, Ray. "Hermogenes' On Stases: A Translation with an Introduction and Notes." *Speech Monographs* 31.4 (1964): 361–424.

Patillon, Michel. *La théorie du discours chez Hermogène le Rhéteur*. Paris: Les Belles Lettres, 1988.

Patterson, Annabel. *Hermogenes and the Renaissance: Seven Ideas of Style*. Princeton: Princeton UP, 1970.

Russell, D. A., and M. Winterbottom. "Hermogenes." *Ancient Literary Criticism*. Oxford: Clarendon, 1972: 561–79.

Rutherford, Ian. *Canons of Style in the Antonine Age*. Oxford: Clarendon, 1998.

———. "Inverting the Canon: Hermogenes on Literature." *Harvard Studies in Classical Philology* 94 (1992): 355–78.

Walker, Jeffrey. "Michael Psellos on Rhetoric: A Translation and Commentary on Psellos' Synopsis of Hermogenes." *Rhetoric Society Quarterly* 31.1 (2001): 5–40.

HERODES ATTICUS

(ca. 101–177 CE)

Angela Mitchell Miss

Hailed as one of the Ten Attic Orators, Herodes Atticus was one of the most celebrated Sophists of the second-century Roman Empire. Much of what we know about Herodes comes to us through Philostratus in *Lives of the Sophists*, written between the years 230 and 238, approximately fifty years after Herodes' death in 177. Philostratus devotes a great deal of space in *Lives of the Sophists* to praising Herodes. This praise, however, is suspect because Philostratus's patron, Antonius Gordian, was a descendant of Herodes.[1] While Philostratus spends a great deal of time justifying the controversial events of Herodes' life, he does not provide much detail about Herodes' skill as a rhetorician.[2] Herodes, therefore, remains an ambiguous figure, one whose fame appears to be derived from his monumental wealth and influence, not from enduring rhetorical contributions.

Born in Marathon to a wealthy Athenian family, Herodes received his formal education in Athens and was educated by the most important teachers of his time, including Polemo, Favorinus, and Scopelia. Herodes also attended the lectures of Secundus the Athenian, nicknamed "Wooden Peg," studied oratory with Theagenes of Cnidos and Munatius of Tralles and Platonic philosophy with Lucius Calvenus Taurus of Tyre (Philostratus 135). Because of the wealth and influence of his family, Herodes held most of the important political offices in Athens at an early age (Tobin 25). Significantly, he was also the tutor for the emperor Marcus Aurelius, and in later years, he may have also been appointed to one of the priestly colleges in Rome (Tobin 65). Like many wealthy Sophists of this period, Herodes exhibited a great deal of patronage, improving the water supply of many cities, building monuments and stadiums, and commissioning numerous statues. Although Sophists during Herodes' lifetime generally emerged from wealthy families and were expected to provide benefactions for public works, Herodes' extensive philanthropy seems to have gone beyond mere obligation; however, whether his patronage can be attributed to benevolence, as Philostratus claims, or to extreme political ambition is unclear.

Herodes is buried in the Panathenaic Stadium that he built, his tomb inscribed with the epitaph, "Here lies all that remains of Herodes, son of Atticus, of Marathon, but his glory is world-wide" (Philostratus 183). However, his epitaph did not prove to be prophetic: Herodes' glory as a Sophist, at least, was not to survive the fall of the Roman Empire.

HERODES ATTICUS'S RHETORICAL CONTRIBUTION

Although his fame as Sophist barely survived antiquity, Herodes was one of the most celebrated rhetors of the Second Sophistic. While most Sophists traveled throughout the major cities of the Roman world earning money for speeches, Herodes' popularity was such that scholars would usually travel to Athens to study with him (Tobin 65). Philostratus's description of Herodes' rhetorical abilities reads like a checklist of all the best qualities of a Roman orator, and he compares Herodes' eloquence to "gold dust shining beneath the waters of a silvery eddying river" (179). Although Philostratus reports that in his day, "there are extant by Herodes very many letters, discourses and diaries, handbooks and collections of suitable passages in which the flowers of antique erudition have been collected," none have survived (179). Philostratus fails to provide any specific details about Herodes' actual speeches, noting only the themes of three speeches: two dealing with the Peloponnesian War and one on the "Golden Mean" (Tobin 49). One speech, "On the State," has been attributed to Herodes, but not without controversy (see Anderson, *Philostratus* 119). Although Herodes' reputation as a speaker and a teacher was well-established during his lifetime, what we actually know of Herodes as a Sophist is based on vague allusions and doubtful attributions. Indeed, even Herodes' reputed skill as a rhetor seems doubtful as most of the actual accounts of Herodes' speeches reveal him as a notoriously overly emotional prima donna, who appears to have preserved his reputation only with the aid of influential friends such as Marcus Aurelius (Anderson, *The Second Sophistic* 21).

Although Sophists are often ambiguous figures, Herodes' ambiguity lies in an uncertain legacy, one that appears to be founded more on wealth and patronage than on any lasting rhetorical contributions. Significantly, however, a study of Herodes' life reveals the way in which rhetoric, and, in particular, sophism, was strongly tied to wealth and social eminence in the second-century Roman Empire, supporting G. W. Bowersock's claims in *Greek Sophists in the Roman Empire* that the Second Sophistic was more defined by politics than by rhetoric (58). Herodes' legacy is more valuable in showing how such powerful and wealthy rhetoricians enabled Greek rhetoric to thrive in the Roman Empire of the second century.

NOTES

1. G. W. Bowersock in *Greek Sophists in the Roman Empire* questions that Gordian really was a descendent of Herodes. For a more complete analysis, see Bowersock 7–8.

2. Herodes was accused twice of murder and once of treason against the emperor, his friend, Marcus Aurelius.

BIBLIOGRAPHY

Biographical Sources

Fronto, Marcus C. *The Correspondence of Marcus Cornelius Fronto*. Trans. C. R. Haines. Cambridge: Harvard UP, 1919.

Philostratus. *Lives of the Sophists*. Trans. W. C. Wright. Cambridge: Harvard UP, 1952.

Tobin, Jennifer. *Herodes Attikos and the City of Athens: Patronage and Conflict under the Antonines*. Amsterdam: J. C. Gieben, 1997.

Critical Sources

Anderson, Graham. *Philostratus: Biography and Belles Lettres in the Third Century A.D.* London: Croom Helm, 1986.

———. *The Second Sophistic: A Cultural Phenomenon in the Roman Empire*. New York: Routledge, 1993.

Bowersock, G. W. *Greek Sophists in the Roman Empire*. Oxford: Clarendon, 1969.

———, ed. *Approaches to the Second Sophistic*. University Park: American Philological Association, 1974.

Bowie, E. L. "The Importance of the Sophists." *Yale Classical Studies* 27 (1982): 29–50.

Goldhill, Simon, ed. *Being Greek under Rome*. Cambridge: Cambridge UP, 2001.

Oliver, J. H. *Marcus Aurelius: Aspects of Civic and Cultural Policy in the East*. Princeton: American School of Classical Studies at Athens, 1970.

Woloch, Michael. *Roman Citizenship and the Athenian Elite A.D. 96–161*. Amsterdam: Adolf M. Hakkert, 1973.

HIMERIUS

(ca. 320–ca. 396 CE)

Charles Platter

Himerius was one of the most important Sophists of the fourth century CE, with a distinguished roster of students, including the future emperor Julian, and the brothers Basil of Caesarea and Gregory Nazianzus. Originally from Bithynia, Himerius taught rhetoric in Athens and Constantinople. He was also associated with the imperial court in Constantinople during the brief reign of Julian (361–363 CE). Twenty-four of his speeches remain out of a total of eighty, with fragments of another ten.[1] The speeches cover a variety of types, from declamations on historical topics to ceremonial panegyrics and occasional oratory of various sorts. He was not a composer of deliberative oratory, and his speeches are not directed at persuasion (beyond the inherent orientation of imperial panegyric) as much as at the production of pleasure, through the deployment of his repertoire of rhythmic cadences, mythical allusions, quotations, and rhetorical tropes. His style is ornate and often obscure, qualities that have not favored his reputation in recent times.

Himerius was born in Prusias in the province of Bithynia (northwestern Turkey) around 320 CE, the son of the rhetor Ameinias (Barnes). He was educated in Athens and came to Constantinople in 343, where he taught rhetoric until 352 when he moved his teaching activities to Athens. There he became a citizen and married an Athenian woman, with whom he had two children. He remained in Athens until 361. On the accession of Julian, however, who for a brief time had probably been his student in Athens, he was invited to join the imperial court in Constantinople. He was an enthusiastic supporter of the new emperor, particularly Julian's attempts to reestablish the pagan cults. In Constantinople he delivered a panegyric of Julian (lost) and was initiated into the mysteries of Mithras. After the emperor's death in 363, Himerius remained in the East, although his movements are not well known. In 366 he gave a speech in honor of the city prefect, and on the basis of references in his speeches he is thought by some to have traveled to Egypt. He returned to Athens in 369 and resumed his former occupations, teaching rhetoric and delivering occasional oratory. In 370–371 he gave a speech in praise of

Hermogenes, who was serving as proconsul to the province of Achaea. His last datable speech is from 383. The date of his death is unknown, but he seems to have died prior to Eunapius's *Lives of the Philosophers* (c. 396).

Himerius was not a theoretician of rhetoric, but his involvement in the production of speeches gave him an intense practical familiarity with the requirements entailed by different sorts of compositions. Two of his orations (9, 10), are prefaced by *protheōriai* (preserved by the Byzantine scholar Photius), short commentaries on the rhetorical tactics that the compositions employ.[2] These emphasize both the attention to stylistic detail required for excellence in composition and reliance on the models of Greek antiquity, both poetic and philosophical. Content is assumed to be unproblematic from a rhetorical point of view. Therefore, the writer's primary interest is the elaboration of the various conceits, allusions, and tropes that contribute to the esthetic impact of the speech. In addition, Oration 68, a protreptic speech for students of oratory, urges them to seek variety (*poikilia*) in composition. The speech itself dramatizes this point by comparing the practice of the Sophist to the various parts of the shield of Achilles in the *Iliad*, to the sea god Proteus, and to the demiurge, the creator of the world, described in Plato's *Republic* as a "wondrous sophist" (596d). As George Kennedy aptly remarks, this latter comparison not only displays Himerius's rhetorical *poikilia* but also pays tribute to the rhetorical profession in general by characterizing rhetorical creation as "a microcosm of the universe" (*Greek Rhetoric* 149).

Himerius was well known in the fourth century. His contemporary Eunapius discusses him in *Lives of the Philosophers*, although he claims familiarity with him only through his writings. Eunapius describes his oratory as "agreeable and harmonious" (*eukolos* [. . .] *kai sunērmosmenos*), and adds that his style had the sound of political oratory. He also alludes to a rivalry with the Sophist Prohaeresias, holder of the chair of rhetoric in the school of Julian at Athens, and to this he attributes Himerius's association with the court of the emperor (who, he says, disliked Prohaeresias). Eunapius attributes Himerius's decision to remain in Asia Minor after the death of Julian to a desire to await the death of Prohaeresias before returning to Athens (516–518). Another contemporary, Libanius, alludes to Himerius in uncomplimentary terms in a letter, but elsewhere attempts to intercede with an official on the rhetorician's behalf (Letters 442, 15, quoted in Barnes 212).

The style of Himerius is focused, above all, on the display of eloquence. It is highly imagistic, employing elaborate periphrases, allegorical language, and complex euphony. These features have not endeared Himerius to modern readers, who remark, for example, his ability "to say nothing gracefully and at length" (Browning 707). This is certainly a misleading judgment, motivated in part, no doubt, by modern distaste for panegyric. Most important, it fails to explain Himerius's evident success and the fact that the oratory that he produced had avid audiences, as well as imitators. Fourth-century oratory was a special type of artistic performance, just as it was for many Athenians in the classical period. This type of social setting inevitably highlighted the oral features of Himerius's works, and his own performance of them. Such features (rhythm, euphony, speaking style, etc.) do not translate well to the printed page, however, and it is unsurprising that few modern readers have found the style of Himerius congenial, beyond the difficulties caused by his frequent obscurity. Nevertheless, these aspects of oral performance were important to Himerius's contemporaries. Nor does even a hostile critic like Eunapius, who gives Himerius faint praise, remark the verbose indirectness that modern authors find so exasperating. Himerius deserves to be seen instead as an extremely successful composer and public performer of oratory, whose long career implies that his talents and achievements were well attuned to the demands of his age, and even beyond, as his speeches continued to be read with interest as late as the ninth century by Photius and his associates.

NOTES

1. There is no complete English translation of Himerius. The text is that of Collona.
2. Translations of the *protheōriai* can be found in Walden (Oration 9, 238–39) and Kennedy (Oration 10, 247–48).

BIBLIOGRAPHY

Primary Sources and Translations

Collona, Aristides. *Himerii declamationes et orationes cum deperditarum fragmentis.* Rome: Typis Publicae Officinae Polygraphicae, 1951.

Biographical Sources

Browning, Robert. "Himerius." *The Oxford Classical Dictionary.* 3rd ed. Ed. Simon Hornblower and Antony Spawforth. Oxford: Oxford UP, 1996.

Critical Sources

Barnes, T. D. "Himerius and the Fourth Century." *Classical Philology* 82 (1987): 206–25.
Kennedy, George. *Greek Rhetoric under Christian Emperors.* Princeton: Princeton UP, 1983.
———. *A New History of Classical Rhetoric.* Princeton: Princeton UP, 1994.
Philostratus and Eunapius. *Lives of the Sophists.* Trans. Wilmer Cave Wright. London and New York: Heinemann and Harvard UP, 1952.
Walden, John. *Universities of Ancient Greece.* Freeport, NY: Books for Libraries P, 1970.

HIPPIAS OF ELIS

(ca. 460–400 BCE)

Jane Sutton

Although the dates have not been fixed exactly, Hippias is believed to have been born about 460 BCE in Elis, Peloponnese, Greece and to have died about 400 BCE. What is known about the life and work of Hippias comes from other sources, primarily Plato's *Greater Hippias* (285b–286d), *Protagoras* (318d–e, 337c–338a), and *Lesser Hippias* (368b–9), which is also mentioned in Aristotle's *Metaphysics* 1025a.6–9. What few writings are ascribed to Hippias exist as either fragments or titles to works (DK 86B 1–4).[1] Mario Untersteiner is one among a few commentators who links the identity of Hippias to other writings, including the *Anonymus Iamblichi* (273–303; "A Survey of Recent Work" 181; Hoerber 123n.5).

Hippias traveled from place to place and lectured on poetry, grammar, history, politics, archaeology, mathematics, and astronomy. Specifically, he is known for his interest in speech, its letters, syllables, rhymes, and harmonies, for perfecting the mnemonic system, for supporting nature (*physis*) over and against human legislation (*nomos*), and for discovering a curve, later called the "quadratrix," to assist in the trisection of an angle but did not use it for squaring the circle, to which the name "quadratrix" refers. It is not clear whether Hippias himself recognized that the quadratrix could be used to square the circle; the first to explicitly note that seems to have been Dinostratus, who is much later (O'Connor and Robertson). The curve is still mentioned in calculus texts, but mostly for historical reasons.

As an official ambassador, Hippias traveled more frequently to Sparta than to Athens. He claimed to have gone to Sicily when Protagoras was there. Hippias appeared in Athens during the years of the peace of Nicias and on special occasions (Zeller 85; Freeman 370). Hippias is most known for attending the games at Olympia. One performance he regularly gave at the games was a type of speech called an *epideixis*, a public display speech. He offered to speak on anything that anyone chose from the subjects that he had prepared for the exhibition and to answer any questions (Plato, *Lesser Hippias* 363c–d). He once brought to Olympia "only the things he had made," including sandals, the ring he wore, and an oil flask.

By bringing to Olympia only the things he had made, Hippias, in effect, brought his craft of "speaking" as one of the many things he made. In addition to the games in Athens, Hippias appears (in Plato's *Protagoras*) in the wealthy home of Callias seated in a raised chair. The seated figure of Hippias replying to questions and speaking "of celestial matters" is not meant to portray a specialist in astronomy. By the fifth century, celestial matters had widened to include ethical matters, which involved rhetoric. Thus, the raised chair signifies rhetoric and teaching people about how to get on in life (Romilly 3–4; Kerferd 26).

As for rhetoric, the significance of Hippias to the tradition may be delineated through his epithet of "Polymath" (Plato, *Lesser Hippias* 368b–d; Hoerber 124–25). All the aspects of his life—from making the ring he wore to Olympia, to hearing fifty names once and reciting them from memory, to rejecting the notion that human laws are natural—combined with what he said and what he did can offer a way to view Hippias's sense of rhetoric. In this manner, Hippias's rhetoric may be examined topically as "crafty," "versatile," and "clever." In what follows, I discuss the contributions of Hippias topically, inventorying craftiness through the theme of education, versatility through the theme of culture, and finally cleverness through the canon of memory.

HIPPIAS'S RHETORICAL THEORY

The word "crafty" links Hippias to the trade and retail of the products of his own manufacture (Oscanyan). He made and traded in not only the kinds of goods he brought to Olympia, but also is reported (in Pseudo-Aristotle's *Economics* 1347a) to have called in "the existing currency" and issued "coins with the head of Athena and the owl of a new denomination for a fee using the same silver" (Williams 13). In terms of learning and thinking, Plato dealt with the question of production and exchange of money as a bad method closely related to sophistry. Specifically, Plato's Socrates clashes with Hippias's craft on the grounds that production and exchange of goods reduce learning and thinking to reception and recall of information and training.

But the motif of intercity trade animating Hippias's sense of rhetoric need not be reduced to rote learning and stereotypical methods typified as sophistical. The notion of "exchange" also points to rhetoric as a "*technē/epistēmē*." So conjoined, rhetoric is committed to personal attainment, self-sufficiency, and responsibility to the collective order. With respect to retailing goodness, Hippias appears to make no distinction in rhetoric between art and knowledge, for they are disposed in the shape of collective interests. That collective interest is, in turn, shared among inhabitants because it is distributed through the exchange of words whether in making/buying speeches or teaching/selling arguments.

That Hippias's craft of rhetoric makes no distinction between *technē/epistēmē* indicates versatility and a shift in values in terms of human laws and institutions. Insofar as laws of humans differ in their origin of ware, like goods or commodities they are manufactured or produced. In Plato's *Protagoras* (337d), Hippias declares that human custom or "law" (*nomos*) is a tyrant that constrains us against nature (*physis*). Unlike "laws of nature," the social is a transitory institution and not all of its changes are good. However, some aspects of the social are comparable to the laws of nature and might serve as a template for questions of legislation. Xenophon's *Memorabilia* records a lengthy conversation in book 4 between Socrates and Hippias in which the two interlocutors explore the question of legislation. In this debate, Hippias understands *nomos* as custom or arbitrary law which he opposes to unwritten laws of nature (*physis*). Part of the context for this debate features incest. Citing problems with offspring, Hippias regards incest as a violation of *physis*. According to Hippias, it follows that if human law (*nomos*) does not restrict incest, then human law violates nature or *physis*. Taken to its logical conclusion, *nomos*, rather than nature, is a tyrant or despot that must be corrected (Plato, *Protagoras* 337c6e2).

Finally, Hippias is regarded as clever through his displays of memory, especially the recitation of names. Hippias did not invent "memory" but is said to have perfected the mnemonic system. In rhetoric, memory is one of the five canons. It all but disappeared from rhetoric by the end of the nineteenth century. In rhetorical theory and pedagogy of the twentieth century, Hippias has been revived through work seeking to recover the "lost" canon of memory. After being lost or dropped from the canon by the British rhetoricians Hugh Blair and George Campbell in the eighteenth century, Bromley Smith reintroduced memory through the figure of Hippias.

With the reintroduction of memory, debates on knowing and learning again came into focus. In these debates, the retrieval and storage of information, particularly in the context of computers, is contrasted with the ability to apply generalizations to individual decisions and judgments (Brumbaugh and Lawrence). Also related to the theme of education is the teaching of public speaking with an emphasis on delivery. Calling upon Hippias for pedagogical purposes, writers of public-speaking textbooks feature memory primarily in relation to memorized and extemporaneous styles of delivery. In 1928, Earl W. Wells detailed methods of memorization through organization and outlines. Wells's view that "training in memory" is "training in thinking" indicates indebtedness to Hippias's views on memory and education (64).

In the years that followed the discovery of the lost canon, memory has had wide applicability in the field of rhetoric (Hoogestraat). Although his name is rarely mentioned, Hippias comes into focus in topics of memory as it relates to cultural criticism, historiography, and political agency. Since 1926, it would be fair to say that, in the main, the scope of Hippias's influence in rhetoric ranges from delivery of speeches (Wells; Hennessey) to theories of education (Brumbaugh and Lawrence; Lentz) to critical rhetoric.

However, critical rhetoric and memory do not stem from a loss of the canon of memory but rather from an attack on rhetoric. In the 1960s, Richard Weaver put forward the view that memory was something attacked, as opposed to something lost or dropped from rhetoric. In the chapter "The Attack on Memory," Weaver claimed that any disparagement of memory was a disparagement of rhetoric (40–54). In this vein, scholars are turning to questions concerning memory in an effort to articulate a critical theory and/or to write about feminisms and rhetorics (Cox; Irwin; Jarratt). Ironically, as scholars bring memory back to the study of rhetoric, the figure of Hippias, like the canon of memory before him, becomes lost.

NOTE

1. I use Sprague's translation and system of reference. Thus, DK 86A 3 refers to author (86), section (A), and fragment (3).

BIBLIOGRAPHY

Primary Sources and Translations

Plato. *Greater Hippias*. Trans. H. N. Fowler. Vol. 4. 12 vols. Cambridge: Harvard UP, 1926.
————. *Lesser Hippias*. Trans. H. N. Fowler. Vol. 4. 12 vols. Cambridge: Harvard UP, 1926.
————. *Protagoras*. Trans. W. R. M. Lamb. Vol. 2. 12 vols. Cambridge: Harvard UP, 1924.
Sprague, Rosamond Kent, ed. *The Older Sophists: A Complete Translation by Several Hands of the Fragments in* Die Fragmente der Vorsokratiker, *Edited by Diels-Kranz*. Columbia: U of South Carolina P, 1972.
Xenophon, *Memorabilia*. Trans. Amy L. Bonnette. Ithaca: Cornell UP, 1994.

Biographical Sources

Freeman, Kathleen. *The Pre-Socratic Philosophers*. Oxford: Oxford UP, 1949.
Kerferd, G. B. *The Sophistic Movement*. Cambridge: Cambridge UP, 1981.
O'Connor, J. J., and E. F. Robertson. *Hippias of Elis*. Jan. 1999. School of Mathematics and Statistics, University of St. Andrews, Scotland. Available: <http://www-gap.dcs.st=and.ac.uk/~history/Mathematicians/Hippias.html>. 2001.
Romilly, Jacqueline de. *The Great Sophists in Periclean Athens*. Trans. Janet Lloyd. Oxford: Clarendon, 1992.
Untersteiner, Mario. *The Sophists*. Trans. Kathleen Freeman. Oxford: B. Blackwell, 1954.

Critical Sources

Brumbaugh, Robert S., and Nathaniel M. Lawrence. "Knowledge as Skill and Used Information; Hippias." *Philosophical Themes in Modern Education*. Ed. Robert S. Brumbaugh and Nathaniel M. Lawrence. Boston: Houghton Mifflin, 1973. 25–35.
Cox, J. Robert. "Memory, Critical Theory, and the Argument from History." *Argumentation and Advocacy* 27 (1990): 1–13.

Hennessey, Joseph B. "A Theory of Memory as Applied to Speech." *Today's Speech* 7 (1959): 15–19.

Hoerber, Robert G. "Plato's *Lesser Hippias*." *Phronesis* 7 (1962): 121–31.

Hoogestraat, Wayne E. "Memory: The Lost Canon?" *Quarterly Journal of Speech* 46 (1960): 141–47.

Irwin, Clark T. "Rhetoric Remembers: Richard Weaver on Memory and Culture." *Today's Speech* 21 (1973): 21–26.

Jarratt, Susan C. "Sappho's Memory." *Rhetoric Society Quarterly* 32 (2002): 11–43.

Kerferd, G. B. *The Sophistic Movement*. Cambridge: Cambridge UP, 1981.

Lentz, Tony M. "From Recitation to Memory." *Southern Speech Communication Journal* 51 (1985): 49–70.

Minar, Edwin L., Jr. "A Survey of Recent Work in Pre-Socratic Philosophy (Concluded)." *Classical Weekly* 47.12 (1954): 177–82.

Oscanyan, Frederick S. "On Six Definitions of the Sophists: *Sophist 221 c–231 e*." *Philosophical Forum* 4 (1973): 241–59.

Poulakos, John. *Sophistical Rhetoric in Classical Greece*. Columbia: U of South Carolina P, 1995.

Smith, Bromley. "Hippias and the Lost Canon of Rhetoric." *Quarterly Journal of Speech Education* 12.3 (1926): 129–45.

Taylor, Alfred Edward. *Plato: The Man and His Work*. London: Methuen, 1949.

Weaver, Richard. *Visions of Order*. Baton Rouge: Louisiana State UP, 1964.

Wells, Earl W. "Methods of Memorization for the Speaker and the Reader." *Quarterly Journal of Speech* 14 (1928): 39–64.

Williams, Roderick T. "The 'Owls' and Hippias." *Numismatic Chronicle* 6 (1966): 9–13.

Zeller, Eduard. *Outlines of the History of Greek Philosophy*. Trans. L. R. Palmer. 13th ed. New York: Dover, 1980.

HOMER

(eighth century BCE?)

Patrick O'Sullivan

Nothing certain is known about the life of Homer—the name under which *Iliad* and *Odyssey* have come down to us—so the question of his identity necessarily involves the methods of composition of the two epics. Here this can be given only in the barest outline. Nearly all Greeks of the archaic and classical periods were convinced that these epics (and the whole epic cycle on the Trojan war overall, as well as the Theban saga concerning the doomed house of Oedipus) were the work of one man. Later scholars of the Alexandrian period cast doubt on the unity of authorship of the *Iliad* and *Odyssey* and deleted passages they found problematic. Some modern scholarship, especially since the late eighteenth century, has continued these trends, arguing for multiple authorship of the poems, seeing them as littered with interpolations, so that we can barely talk of a fixed text much before the third century BCE. Others have maintained that the epics were essentially composed in the sixth century BCE when committed to writing under Peisistratos, the tyrant of Athens from 546 to 527 BCE. But a more influential scholarly consensus has emerged that sees the two epics reaching a largely coherent final form in the mid to late eighth century BCE.

Taking into account a complex series of linguistic, archaeological, and historical factors, much scholarship has established that the epics are the result of a tradition of heroic poetry orally composed through formulaic, metrical language over some centuries. Some elements of the epics may stretch back to the Mycenaean age of which Homer sings (thirteenth century BCE and earlier); but the epics also allude to practices of the dark ages (eleventh to ninth centuries BCE), as well as objects and practices known from the eighth century BCE onward. The artificial, traditional nature of the epics is evident in their being composed in a linguistic amalgam of different periods and regions: predominantly Ionian dialect with some Aeolic and Attic elements. Indeed, cities such as Chios and Smyrna made the most persistent claims in antiquity to be the poet's birthplace. Many, then, would argue that "Homer" was active in Ionia from about 750 to 700 BCE, emerged at the end of an oral tradition, and constructed two monumental epics, which were based on memorized, repetitive phrases, but combined into a coherent and improvised poetic whole. As our understanding of the conditions of oral poetry has increased due to the pioneering work of Milman Parry in the 1920s and 1930s, this view has gained considerable ground in recent decades.

To explain the brilliant artistic design of the epics, which together amount to nearly 28,000 hexameter verses, it has been suggested that Homer composed with the aid of writing, which emerged in the eighth century BCE, or that he may have dictated the poems. But there is no scholarly unanimity on all these issues, known as the "Homeric Question." The ancient biographies of Homer, such as those of Pseudo-Herodotus and Pseudo-Plutarch, contain more than their fair share of fantasy and fabrication, affording no real help in identifying the figure behind the name or the date and place of the poems' composition. Whether we choose to believe in an individual called Homer or not, we do have the two epics themselves, which remain among the very greatest and most influential poems of all time.

RHETORIC IN THE HOMERIC EPICS

The powers of direct speech and attempts at persuasion work on a number of important levels throughout the Homeric epics, even in the absence of a consciously stated theory of rhetoric. Direct speech comprises around fifty percent of each epic, and in the *Iliad* alone there about six hundred speeches. These take many forms, including commands, exhortations, boasts, prayers, insults, and supplications, many of which occur already in book 1 of the *Iliad*. Eloquence in both epics is accorded considerable prestige. The battlefield, as one might expect in the *Iliad*, is described as a place "where men win glory" (*Il.* 6.124, etc.); but so, too, is the agora, the assembly place of the army for counsel and debate (*Il.* 1.490). Indeed, the central components of the ideal Homeric warrior involve ability with words and martial prowess. In Phoenix's address to Achilles—the self-professed "best of the Achaeans"—the older man tells the young hero that he taught him "to be a speaker of words and a doer of deeds" (*Il.* 9.443). This is expressed in a chiasmus (a symmetrical expression made up of two mirroring halves) and involves the word "*rhētēr*," an early cognate of the Greek word "rhetoric" itself. The importance of this ideal is underlined in the difficulty of achieving it, even for such mighty warriors as Achilles (*Il.* 18.104–06) and Hector (*Il.* 18.251–52). In the *Odyssey*, too, speech-making abilities indicate a man's worth, and are, of course, a notable feature of Odysseus, himself a great talker (and liar). When upbraided by the handsome but boorish Euryalos in Phaeacia, Odysseus pointedly asserts the superiority of eloquence, and its inseparability from intelligence, over mere good looks (*Od.* 8.166–77). Abilities at public speaking displayed by the young Telemachus, Odysseus's son, are interestingly presented as signs of his oncoming maturity and heroic valour. He not only speaks with authority to his mother, who is amazed at his words (*Od.* 1.345–61), but confronts the suitors, who "wonder" at his boldness and attribute it to the gods (*Od.* 1.368–87; and cf. *Od.* 1.320–24). Similarly, the impact of public address in the *Iliad* is often presented as powerful and impressive (*Il.* 3.95, 9.431–32, 9.693–94, etc.), again indicating its effective role within the world of Homeric heroes. Public speech making is a conspicuous feature of the civic life of the poet and his audience. The many images depicting typical scenes from life on the divinely crafted shield of Achilles include a detailed description of a dispute between two litigants, requiring the sound judgment of an elder, all of which is eagerly watched by a large crowd (*Il.* 18.497–508).

Lengthy episodes are taken up with speeches in the *Iliad*, which propel the narrative, beginning with the clash between Achilles and Agamemnon before the assembly. Book 2 contains another assembly scene where Thersites argues for abandoning the war and heading home. The inferiority of this character—the "worst of the Acheans"—is manifest not only in his being obnoxious and the ugliest man at Troy, detested by Achilles and Odysseus, but also in his method of speaking; he rants in a totally disordered, uncontrolled fashion (*Il.* 2.211–21). The "embassy scene" of book 9 includes important speeches by Odysseus, Phoenix, and Ajax, who each try different techniques at persuading Achilles to return to battle. The hero's famous refusal has long been considered a rhetorical tour de force, in which the very language he uses is seen as something that sets him apart from all the Greeks (*Il.* 9.308–429). One of the most powerful moments in all Homeric epic involves Priam's supplication gesture and speech to Achilles to return Hector's corpse. The moving eloquence of the Trojan king's speech is crucial to the overall *pathos* and reconciliation that emerges in this justly famous scene (*Il.* 24.477–506; cf. *Il.* 24.628–34). Another significant feature of Homeric speech making is its stylistic quality, evident in certain similes and descriptions of certain speakers. In the *Iliad*, Nestor, a man past his fighting age but held in high esteem by all, is singled out for his eloquence "which flowed sweeter than honey" (*Il.* 1.247–49), as he tries to resolve the quarrel between Achilles and Agamemnon. The Trojan Antenor (*Il.* 3.204–24) recalls that, during a visit to Troy, Menelaus spoke clearly and plainly, not wasting his words, while Odysseus's own "words and mighty voice were like the wintry snows," making him an invincible speaker. Such passages left a profound impression on later ages, becoming reappropriated in more fully fledged theories of rhetorical style.

RECEPTION OF HOMER, ANCIENT AND MODERN

As Homer has almost come to mean all things to all people at one stage or another, only a very brief sketch of the Homeric legacy can be offered here. In antiquity he was imagined as a blind, divinely inspired bard, much like Demodokos in book 8 of the *Odyssey*, whose song was seen to come directly from the Muses, patron goddesses of poetry, song, and dance (*Od.* 8.44–45, 487–08, 499). Professional reciters of Homer, called rhapsodes, performed at major Greek festivals from at least the sixth century BCE, adding to Homer's early prestige, which made him a source for the Greeks' history, religion, and culture. Herodotos in the fifth century BCE suggests this role for Homer and epic poet Hesiod (2.53), as does the sixth-century BCE philosopher Xenophanes, even though he criticizes both poets (FF B10, B11, B12 D–K). Despite Plato's objections to Homer in his *Republic*, the Homeric epics were not only treated as guides for military affairs and ethical insights (e.g., Xenophon, *Symposium* 3.5), but also provided ancient rhetoricians with rich material for their own flights of fancy and stylistic theories. Sophists of the fifth and fourth centuries BCE such as Gorgias in his *Palamedes* and *Encomium of Helen*, Alcidamas in his *Odysseus*, and Antisthenes in his *Judgement on the Arms of Achilles* incorporated Homeric characters and episodes into their own rhetorical display pieces, often alluding to specific passages from the great epics. Homeric figures were also often invoked as model speakers or embodiments of rhetorical style, as in Aristophanes (*Clouds* 1055–57) and Plato (*Phaedrus* 261 b–c). Later rhetorical works of Quintilian (10.1.46; 12.10.64–65), Aulus Gellius (6.14.7), and Pseudo-Plutarch (*de Vit. Hom.* 74, 161, 172), among others, develop these tendencies. These later writers saw in the epics the origins of the rhetorical interests of their own time (first and second centuries CE) and linked figures such as Nestor, Menelaus, and Odysseus with major stylistic categories of their day. It would be anachronistic to go as far as these later ancient critics in seeing a developed theory of rhetoric in the *Iliad* or *Odyssey*. Yet these later appropriations further testify to the importance of direct speech and its effects in the poems, which comprise another significant strand in Homer's overall influence in antiquity and beyond.

Homer's prestige among the Romans from an early date is evident in the poetry of Ennius (239–169 BCE), who imagined himself to be Homer's reincarnation (F 1.2–10). Above all, Vergil (70–19 BCE) reveals a profound debt to Homer in making his epic, the *Aeneid*, to some extent a Roman counterpart to both the *Iliad* and *Odyssey*. While during the Middle Ages and Renaissance Vergil seemed to eclipse Homer as Europe's great poet par excellence, as Dante's *Divine Comedy* shows, Homer's position as the first poet of the Western tradition has by and large remained secure. For centuries, English translations have continued to be made, with the versions by Alexander Pope proving something of a watershed, notwithstanding the great classicist Richard Bentley's reservations about their accuracy. In the next century, numerous influential writings on Homer were penned by public figures such as Matthew Arnold and English prime minister William Gladstone. Into the twentieth century, Homer inspired the works of writers and poets, from James Joyce's *Ulysses* to Derek Walcott's *Omeros*; and filmmakers still draw more or less explicitly on Homeric themes (A. Konchalovski's *The Odyssey*; the Coens' *O Brother, Where Art Thou?*; Wolfgang Petersen's *Troy*). The rich and varied reception of the Homeric epics demonstrates the enduring qualities of the poems, whose murky origins and cultural and chronological distance have never precluded their appeal to subsequent generations. At their best, we find in them a vividness of imagery, a mastery of narrative sophistication, an emotional intensity, and an overall grandeur of vision—at once heroic and deeply human—that have deservedly remained paradigmatic in Western culture for well over two and half millennia.

BIBLIOGRAPHY

Primary Sources and Translations

Allen, Thomas, ed. *Homeri Opera: Ilias*. 3rd ed. Vols. 1–2. Oxford: Clarendon, 1920.
———. *Homeri Opera: Odyssea*. 2nd ed. Vols. 3–4. Oxford: Clarendon, 1917.
Radermacher, Ludwig, ed. *Artium Scriptores. Reste der voraristotelischen Rhetorik*. Vienna: Rudolf
    M. Rohrer, 1951.
Lattimore, Richmond. *The Iliad of Homer*. Chicago: U of Chicago P, 1951.
———. *The Odyssey of Homer*. New York: Harper Collins, 1965.

Biographical Sources

Allen, Thomas, ed. *Homeri Opera*. Vol. 5. Oxford: Clarendon, 1912.
Keaney, John J., and Robert Lamberton, eds. [Plutarch] *Essay on the Life and Poetry of Homer*.
    Atlanta: Scholars P, 1996.
Lefkowitz, Mary. *The Lives of the Greek Poets*. Baltimore: Johns Hopkins UP, 1981.

Critical Sources

Kennedy, George. "The Ancient Dispute over Rhetoric in Homer." *AJPh* 78 (1957): 23–35.
———. *The Art of Persuasion in Greece*. London: Routledge and Kegan Paul, 1963.
Martin, Richard P. *The Language of Heroes: Speech and Performance in the Iliad*. Ithaca and London:
    Cornell UP, 1989.
Morris, Ian, and Barry Powell, eds. *A New Companion to Homer*. Leiden and New York: Brill,
    1997.
Pernot, Laurent. *La Rhétorique dans l'Antiquité*. Paris: Librairie Générale Française, 2000.
Solmsen, Friedrich. "The 'Gift' of Speech in Homer and Hesiod." *TAPhA* 85 (1954): 1–15.
Thalmann, William. *Conventions of Form and Thought in Early Greek Poetry*. Baltimore and
    London: Johns Hopkins UP, 1984.
Walker, Jeffrey. *Rhetoric and Poetics in Antiquity*. Oxford: Oxford UP, 2000.

HORTENSIA

(ca. 70s–10s BCE)

D. Alexis Hart

Born in the first century BCE, Hortensia was the daughter of the famous court orator and rival of Cicero, Quintus Hortensius. She had the advantage of a wealthy upbringing, one consequence of which was a thorough education in language and literature. She seems to have learned the conventions of public oratory from her father. Like her father, Hortensia became renowned as an orator, although her public speaking career was apparently limited to a single performance. Little else is known about her personal life.

HORTENSIA'S RHETORICAL PRACTICE

In 42 BCE, civil war broke out in Rome after the murder of Julius Caesar. During the power struggle that followed, the triumvirs Octavian, Antony, and Lepidus attempted to levy a tax on fourteen hundred of the wealthiest Roman women. Unwilling to finance a war between Roman citizens, the women initially attempted to appeal privately to the female family members of the triumvirs, in the hopes that these women could persuade their sons and husbands to repeal the tax. They successfully rallied Octavian's sister and Antony's mother to their cause, but failed to persuade Fulvia, Antony's wife. Next, the women sought a male advocate willing to argue their case for them, but to no avail. Left with no other recourse, the women selected Hortensia to be their spokesperson and to plead their case publicly before the tribunal in the forum. Once she and her followers made their way before the triumvirs, Hortensia addressed them as follows:

> As befitted women of our rank addressing a petition to you, we had recourse to the ladies of your households; but having been treated as did not befit us, at the hands of Fulvia, we have been driven by her to the forum. You have already deprived us of our fathers, our sons, our husbands, and our brothers, whom you accused of having

wronged you; if you take away our property also, you reduce us to a condition unbecoming our birth, our manners, our sex. If we have done you wrong, as you say our husbands have, proscribe us as you do them. But if we women have not voted any of you public enemies, have not torn down your houses, destroyed your army, or led another one against you; if we have not hindered you in obtaining offices and honours,—why do we share the penalty when we do not share the guilt?

Why should we pay taxes when we have no part in the honours, the commands, the state-craft? (Appian 4.4.32–33)

The triumvirs were furious that a woman should dare to speak against them publicly, so they drove Hortensia and her fellow women from the forum, but the crowds of male citizens in attendance supported Hortensia's no-taxation-without-representation argument and consequently the triumvirs agreed to reduce the number of women to be taxed to four hundred.

Hortensia's address to the triumvirs was remarkable. According to Richard Bauman, "[t]here almost certainly were no public orations [by women] before Hortensia's single, but significant, contribution" (78). She stands out not only as a woman who broke tradition by speaking in public and against male authority figures but also as a woman who was lauded by men for doing so, although most often in the context of displaying her father's talents or carrying on the example of her father. For instance, Valerius Maximus praises Hortensia for "reviving her father's eloquence" and claims that her father "lived again in his female progeny and inspired his daughter's words" (VIII.3). What such acclamations suggest is that Hortensia was recognized for contributing to the male tradition of public oratory only insofar as she carried on her father's heritage of eloquence—something his sons, shamefully, had not managed to do. The historical evidence from Valerius Maximus seems to support this argument. Two other women are included with Hortensia in his record of "Women Who Pleaded Before Magistrates for Themselves or for Others." The first, Maesia of Sentinum, who in one instance pleaded her own case before the praetor, is described as bearing "a man's spirit under the form of a woman" and is known thereafter as "Androgyne" (VIII.3). The second, Carfania, defended herself on multiple occasions and is condemned even more harshly as "a notorious example of female litigiousness" and a "monster" (VIII.3). Hortensia appears to have escaped such condemnations because her speech could be regarded as a demonstration and advancement of the oratorical reputation of her father and because she was speaking before the tribunal not solely on her own behalf, but to support the cause of numerous Roman women.

However, other scholars have argued that Hortensia actually may have earned a reputation as an orator in her own right. For example, Quintilian states that "the speech delivered before the triumvirs by Hortensia, the daughter of Quintus Hortensius, is still read—and not just because it is by a woman" (1.1.16). As Robert Cape explains, the distribution of Hortensia's testimony as a model suggests that she "is credited with a public speech, an *oratio*" which is read "not as an aberration but, it seems, with genuine respect for it as an oration" (117). She argues in a manner appropriate to her social position and audience, and she skillfully utilizes recognizable standard elements of forensic address such as stating what has driven her to seek recourse before the forum, asking rhetorical questions, and citing historical and legal precedents. She also makes a point of proclaiming her dedication to and concern for the future of the Republic. While these features may be considered to constitute a traditionally masculine argumentative style, Hortensia's successful deployment of them should not be diminished as a consequence.

HORTENSIA'S CONTRIBUTION

Although Hortensia clearly fashioned her speech within the customs of an otherwise predominantly "male" argumentative style and therefore cannot be regarded as developing a distinct and praiseworthy "female" or "feminist" rhetoric, and although her record of public speaking seems confined to this single episode, she deserves recognition as an important figure in the rhetorical tradition because her speech provides compelling evidence that women were capable of learning and successfully applying the standardized elements of eloquence and persuasion just as well as men. The other women's choice of Hortensia as their spokesperson surely suggests that she was known, at least among the circle of wealthy and literate women, as an educated, persuasive, and eloquent speaker even prior to her public address. Although no mention is made of who spoke to the triumvir's female relatives, it is certainly likely that Hortensia was selected by her peers for that task as well. Unfortunately, we have no record of Hortensia's speech before these women. Furthermore, the women's choice not to confine their voices to the private sphere (with the appeal to the triumvirs' female relations) and not to give up in the absence of a male advocate illustrated the possibility of public petitions by female advocates and allowed other women to consider that possibility themselves. Finally, Hortensia can also be regarded as an early feminist due to her extraordinary public advancement of women's rights, albeit in a "manly" style. Her eloquence, bravery, intelligence, and willingness to break from her traditionally assigned role serve as an inspiration to other women to use their education and training to stand up for their rights, even in the face of threats of physical violence.

BIBLIOGRAPHY

Primary Sources and Translations

Appian. "Protest of Hortensia." Trans. Horace White. *Appian's Roman History*. Cambridge: Harvard UP, 1913.

Biographical Sources

"Hortensia." *Biographical Dictionary of Ancient Greek and Roman Women: Women from Sappho to Helena.* Ed. Majorie Lightman and Benjamin Lightman. New York: Facts on File, 2000. 116–17.

"Hortensia." *Encyclopedia of Women in the Ancient World.* Ed. Joyce E. Salisbury. Santa Barbara: ABC CLIO, 2001. 161–62.

Critical Sources

Bauman, Richard A. *Women and Politics in Ancient Rome.* London: Routledge, 1992.

Best, Edward E. "Cicero, Livy and Educated Roman Women." *The Classical Journal* 65.5 (1970): 199–204.

Cape, Robert W., Jr. "Roman Women in the History of Rhetoric and Oratory." *Listening to Their Voices: The Rhetorical Activities of Historical Women.* Ed. Molly Meijer Wertheimer. Columbia: U of South Carolina P, 1997. 112–32.

Fantham, Elaine, Helene Peet Foley, Natalie Boymel Kampen, Sarah B. Pomeroy, and H. A. Shapiro. *Women in the Classical World: Image and Text.* New York: Oxford University Press, 1994.

Fraschetti, Augusto. *Roman Women.* Trans. Linda Lappin. Chicago: U of Chicago P, 2001.

Glenn, Cheryl. *Rhetoric Retold: Regendering the Tradition from Antiquity through the Renaissance.* Carbondale: Southern Illinois UP, 1997.

Pomeroy, Sarah B. *Goddesses, Whores, Wives, and Slaves: Women in Classical Antiquity.* New York: Schocken Books, 1975.

Quintilian. *Institutio Oratoria.* Trans. Donald A. Russell. *Quintilian: The Orator's Education.* Cambridge: Harvard UP, 2001.

Valerius Maximus. *Memorable Doings and Sayings.* Trans. D. R. Shackleton Bailey. Cambridge: Harvard UP, 2000.

Hypatia

(355[?]–415 CE)

Elizabeth Ervin

The life of Hypatia has been fictionalized and mythologized for centuries and is therefore difficult to reconstruct definitively. Although she was generally thought to have been born around 370 CE in the city of Alexandria, Maria Dzielska has recently put the date at 355, making her sixty years old—an elderly woman—at the time of her death in 415. While little is known of Hypatia's mother, much more is known about her father, Theon, a respected teacher and mathematician at the Alexandrian Museum. Legend has it that Theon was determined that his daughter develop into "a perfect human being" (Osen 23). Toward that end, he arranged for Hypatia to receive a comprehensive liberal education; she was tutored in mathematics, philosophy, literature, religion, rhetoric, science, and the arts by some of the most eminent scholars of the day. She also practiced a regimen of physical exercise and may have traveled abroad. The personal and intellectual independence Hypatia experienced in this environment continued throughout her life.

By the year 390, Hypatia had become a renowned and popular teacher, delivering public lectures on mathematics, science, and Neoplatonist philosophy and accepting private pupils from the most privileged families of Alexandria; she received many civic honors and her counsel was regularly sought by both secular and ecclesiastical leaders. Alexandrians admired Hypatia for her *sophrosyne*—a virtue that encompassed moderation, integrity, discipline, and sexual abstinence. These qualities were integrally linked to the principles of mathematics and astronomy that she espoused—"divine geometry" in the words of one of her students—functioning not only as the foundations of higher philosophy but also as components of a broader ethical and cosmological framework. In short, they implied "a way of life," not simply an approach to academic study (Waithe 5). Hypatia distrusted dogma of any kind, including organized religions; she was not a practitioner of the pagan cult mysteries or Greek polytheism that she absorbed into her philosophy, and she refused to convert to Christianity even when many of her contemporaries did so for reasons of personal safety. Moreover, she appears not to have actively participated in the religious conflicts of the time, reportedly accepting students from all religions at a time of increasing rancor among pagans, Jews, and Christians. This has led scholars like Elbert Hubbard and polemicists like John Toland to conclude, somewhat controversially, that she was branded a heretic and persecuted by fanatical Christians.

Although fifth-century Alexandria was a cosmopolitan city and considered the greatest seat of learning in the world, its vital intellectual and religious climate was increasingly imperiled by the Roman Empire's conversion to Christianity. Initially, and for the most part amicably, civil and ecclasiastical authorities cooperated in their management of the city, and Hypatia and her students reportedly enjoyed full intellectual autonomy during this period. In 412, however, Cyril was named bishop of Alexandria and began aggressively to extend episcopal authority to municipal affairs previously accepted as secular. Quickly realizing the power that Hypatia held among the Alexandrian elite—and noting as well her friendship with Orestes, the prefect of Egypt and Cyril's chief political rival— Cyril and his followers began spreading rumors among the uneducated and volatile Alexandrian masses (with whom Hypatia had no contact or influence) that Hypatia was a witch casting satanic spells on the people of the city. The contemporary historian Socrates Scholasticus records this version of the events that followed: a mob pulled Hypatia from her chariot as she made her way home; after dragging her into a nearby church, they stripped her naked, beat her to death (and possibly raped her), ripped her flesh from her bones, and quartered and burned her body. Although it is unclear whether Cyril personally ordered Hypatia's murder, most scholars agree that he instigated the defamation campaign against her and more generally created a climate that allowed such a brutal act to take place (see Alic 46; Dzielska 97–98). The murder was never investigated, Hypatia's ally Orestes fled Alexandria, and Cyril ordered that Hypatia's writings be destroyed; he was later canonized.

The historical significance of Hypatia's death is contested. Edward Gibbon goes so far as to assert that it accelerated the decline of the Roman Empire, thus marking the effective conclusion of a long period of intellectual advancement in Europe (though Greek science would flourish in Byzantium and the Arab world during the so-called Dark Ages that ensued). Dzielska and others, however, argue that she was simply the victim of political expediency, and that efforts to transform her into a symbol of intellectual persecution serve mainly to obscure her legitimate intellectual legacy. Clearly, the sensational circumstances of Hypatia's murder at a transitional point in history have invited interpretations that serve a variety of ideological motives. As a result, she has too often emerged from literary and historical sources less as a human being than as a series of deeply entrenched tropes. Dzielska expresses the hope that, as the facts of Hypatia's life are separated from myth, she will emerge "as a scholar known not only by the titles of her works"—or, presumably, the ideological interests of her commentators—"but also by their contents" (72).

Hypatia's Legacy

It was long believed that none of Hypatia's writing survived intact; however, many scholars now believe that her work can be found in texts attributed to her father and certain editions of Ptolemy and Diophantus that she probably prepared (see, e.g., Alic 42–44; Waithe 6–7). Hypatia is also credited with writing three major treatises on geometry and algebra and one on planetary movement, of which only fragments remain; besides popularizing and explicating the work of ancient scholars such as Euclid, she identified several new mathematical problems and alternative solutions to existing problems. Other direct evidence of Hypatia's teaching and intellectual contributions has been gleaned primarily from correspondence with and among her students, most notably Synesius of Cyrene, who later became the powerful Bishop of Ptolemais and whose letters reveal an abiding respect and affection for Hypatia, his time spent under her tutelage, and his fellow students. In addition to references to her lectures in philosophy and mathematics, these letters contain Hypatia's designs for several scientific instruments, including tools for distilling water and studying astronomy, thus hinting at her interest in practical technology.

Strictly speaking, Hypatia was not a rhetorician, though she is frequently described as eloquent and scholars allude to her rhetorical education and to rhetors in her intellectual circle. Dzielska infers from the letters of Synesius that Hypatia "urged her students to be conscientious about form in speech and in writing" (30), but Mary Ellen Waithe asserts that she "makes no attempt at rhetorical innovation," focusing on the beauty and symmetry of her proofs, not of her language (8). Lynn Osen claims that Hypatia's father cautioned her against using language to manipulate her impressionable pupils, suggesting that rhetoric contributed to the ethical praxis for which Hypatia was so esteemed—a praxis that depended upon the Platonic distinction between truth and artifice as well as Pythagorean notions of *harmonia*, balance, and reciprocity.

Thus Hypatia's contributions to rhetorical theory mainly derive from her reputation as a conscientious teacher and the historical affiliation of rhetoric with other disciplines in the sciences and humanities as well as with politics and civic life. Nevertheless, Hypatia remains a relevant figure within classical rhetoric for several reasons. Perhaps most important, Hypatia was one of the first female scholars whose life and intellectual legacy is thoroughly documented. Even during Hypatia's own lifetime, her name was synonymous with women unusually interested or gifted in science and philosophy, and more recently it has inspired the titles of two scholarly journals: *Hypatia: A Journal of Feminist Philosophy*, published in the United States by the Society for Women in Philosophy since 1983, and *Hypatia: Feminist Studies*, published in Greece since 1984.

Despite these accolades, Hypatia's status as the "mother of women's philosophy" is problematic. For one thing, she had many predecessors. Plato's Academy admitted women, and several women during the classical period distinguished themselves as students, teachers, orators, and political advisors. There is, moreover, little in the surviving historical record to suggest that Hypatia was particularly sensitive to women's perspectives, and she is not believed to have accepted female students. The sixth-century historian Damascius relates the following story: one of Hypatia's students fell in love with her, but when he confessed his love, Hypatia showed him her sanitary napkin, reportedly saying, "This is what you really love, my young man, but you do not love beauty for its own sake" (quoted in Dzielska 50). Although the story may be apocryphal, Dzielska interprets it as an illustration of Hypatia's profoundly Platonic worldview, which manifests itself in a "repugnance toward the human body and sensuality" (51). Arens, by contrast, suggest that the story depicts Hypatia's commitment to the purportedly "disembodied" discourses of philosophy and science as a means of achieving a rhetorical authority that operated outside the constraints of gender.

Even if we separate her accomplishments from her gender, this fact remains: Hypatia successfully negotiated conflicting institutional discourses during a time when the stakes were particularly high—a feat of considerable rhetorical skill, and one which recommends two additional reasons why Hypatia remains a vital figure for rhetorical study. First, Hypatia's particular version of Neoplatonism gives us insight into the ways in which classical Greek philosophies have been appropriated by the narratives and epistemologies of other historical contexts, in this case emergent Christianity. Second, Hypatia's personal and professional life exemplifies the ways in which rhetoric fits into a comprehensive ethical framework and how this ethical framework can secure tolerance for unpopular ideas even in a violent world.

BIBLIOGRAPHY

Primary Sources and Translations

Fitzgerald, A. *The Letters of Synesius*. London: Oxford UP, 1926.
Knorr, Wilbur. *Textual Studies in Ancient and Medieval Geometry*. Boston: Birkhauser, 1989.

Biographical Sources

Deakin, Michael A. B. *Mathematician and Martyr: A Biography of Hypatia of Alexandria*. Clayton: Monash UP, 1996.
Dzielska, Maria. *Hypatia of Alexandria*. Trans. F. Lyra. Cambridge: Harvard UP, 1996.
Hubbard, Elbert. *Hypatia*. New York: Roycrofters, 1908.
Kingsley, Charles. *Hypatia, or New Foes with an Old Face*. 1853. London: Macmillan, 1920.
Mauthner, Fritz. *Hypatia: Roman aus dem Altertum*. 1892. Stuttgart: Deutsche Verlags-Anstalt, 1919.
Toland, John. "Hypatia; or, the History of a Most Beautiful, Most Virtuous, Most Learned and in Every Way Accomplished Lady; Who Was Torn to Pieces by the Clergy of Alexandria, to Gratify the Pride, Emulation, and Cruelty of the Archbiship, Commonly but Undeservedly Titled St. Cyril. *Tetradymus*. 1720. London: Brotherton, 1921.

Critical Sources

Alic, Margaret. *Hypatia's Heritage: A History of Women in Science from Antiquity through the Nineteenth Century.* Boston: Beacon, 1986.

Arens, Katherine. "Between Hypatia and Beauvoir: Philosophy as Discourse." *Hypatia* 10.4 (1995): 46–75.

Gibbon, Edward. *The Decline and Fall of the Roman Empire.* New York: Modern, 1932.

Molinaro, Ursule. "A Christian Martyr in Reverse, Hypatia: 370–415 A.D." *Hypatia's Daughters: Fifteen Hundred Years of Women Philosophers.* Ed. Linda Lopez McAlister. Bloomington: Indiana UP, 1996. 1–3.

Osen, Lynn M. "Hypatia." *Women in Mathematics.* 1974. Cambridge: MIT P, 1994. 21–32.

Waithe, Mary Ellen. "Finding Bits and Pieces of Hypatia." *Hypatia's Daughters: Fifteen Hundred Years of Women Philosophers.* Ed. Linda Lopez McAlister. Bloomington: Indiana UP, 1996. 4–15.

ISOCRATES

(436–338 BCE)

Takis Poulakos

Isocrates had a prolific career as a writer. He started writing in his early thirties and published his last work, *Panathenaicus*, at the age of ninety-seven, one year before his death. His long life covered the period from the Peloponnesian War and the death of Pericles to the reconstruction years of Athens and Philip's final victory over the Athenians. He was born about eight years before Plato and died about ten years after Plato's death. Though his origins were nonaristocratic, he received a good education thanks to his father's wealth, which came from the manufacturing of flutes. Not much is known about his formal training, except that he is said to have been a student of Gorgias and to have probably studied under Socrates. It is widely accepted that he made himself available to several educators and that he acquainted himself with and was influenced by a variety of intellectual currents in his day.

Isocrates started his career as a logographer, a writer of speeches for the courts. He earned his living by selling his craft of language to his fellow citizens who, having to represent themselves as litigants or defendants, could afford to hire specialists in public oratory. Like other orators with nonaristocratic origins, Isocrates took his craft to a sphere of public activity where the demand for oratory was at its heaviest, and carved his professional identity next to the second generation of Sophists. Like them, he adapted his expertise in the art of speaking to the requirements of legal self-representation, whose demand became exacerbated by the ongoing changes of Athenian laws. His career as logographer, which lasted about ten years, seems to have been lucrative enough to afford him the pursuit of a different career. Changing his profession to teacher of rhetoric, he opened his own school around 390, about four years before Plato founded the Academy. Soon, he grew wealthy from fees and gifts he received from his students, some of whom were prominent men within and outside Athens. Having reached financial independence, Isocrates never again returned to his former profession and, eventually, came to deny that he ever wrote speeches for the courts. With Isocrates' school, the study of rhetoric ceased to be thought solely in terms of a tutorial education and to be associated exclusively with visitors.

As an educator, Isocrates sought to cultivate the art of rhetoric outside the domain of its established uses and beyond its mainstream applications in the court and the assembly. His own works, which he used as models for rhetorical instruction, attest to his lifelong ambition to give rhetoric a new direction, a direction that would bring it closer to the collective concerns of citizens and the general welfare of the *polis*. Taking issue with other contemporary educators, and especially with the second generation of Sophists, whose rhetorical instruction he considered mechanical, opportunistic, and immoral, he explored the potential of rhetoric to promote public welfare and improve the polity. Under his instruction, rhetoric was treated as an art well equipped to address ongoing concerns of the city-state and to deal with general issues of importance to everyone, not merely ephemeral issues of policy in the assembly. As he put it in *Antidosis* 285, it is the affairs of the *polis* that should be the object of our toil, our study, and our every act. Some of the major themes persisting throughout his writings include building a community-minded rather than an individualistically centered citizenry; approaching rhetorical education as a means for creating caring citizens rather than experts in specialized knowledge; applying one's rhetorical training to the service of the community rather than to one's own gain; employing the resources of rhetoric to convince Athenians and their allies to launch a preemptive expedition against their common enemy, Persia, under the leadership of Athens; finally, following his failure to persuade the Athenian demos, convincing Philip to assume the leadership of a similar expedition on behalf of Athens.

Isocrates' efforts to attach the art of rhetoric to the general concerns of the *polis* gave a distinctly political and moral trajectory to the tradition of rhetoric he had inherited. Unlike the Sophists before him, who had cultivated the art by applying its principles to a wide range of particular situations, Isocrates applied the known principles of the art only to general situations in whose outcome the entire community had a stake. By foregrounding rhetoric's potential to address politically broad issues that would promote common interests and secure communal benefits, Isocrates hoped to place rhetoric beyond the charge of immoral opportunism levied against it by several intellectuals and especially by Plato. Committed to a version of rhetoric that would have the improvement of the *polis* as its principal goal, Isocrates joined Plato in delivering scathing attacks against practices of oratory catering to an orator's personal gain or to a demagogue's private ambition. His pragmatic view of morality, which distinguished moral from immoral uses of rhetoric solely on the criterion of the collective good, gave rhetoric a new place in the *polis*, somewhere between the two extreme positions it had been assigned to by the Sophists and Plato. The place of Isocrates in the history of rhetoric, then, depends to a large extent on how we position him in relation to the Sophists and Plato.

RHETORICAL TRADITION AND RHETORICAL THEORY

Isocrates' rhetorical theory, as described in his rhetorical treatises and as embodied in his political writings, attests to the combined influence that the Sophists and Plato had on him as an intellectual. His own crafting of rhetoric into an art of political deliberation, or *logos politikos*, shows his ability to channel intellectual influences to a practical domain and to use the art of rhetoric as a means of providing responses to problems encountered by his city. Past this instrumental view of rhetoric, Isocrates experimented with ways of blending political and epideictic discourses together, demonstrating his inclination to view rhetoric also as identification and to explore its constitutive possibilities. In addition to crafting political deliberation artistically, Isocrates sought to infuse it with cultural norms of practical wisdom. Exhibiting practical wisdom as an integral part of political deliberation, his *logos politikos* earns him a distinguished place in the history of rhetoric as the precursor to Aristotle's conception of *phronēsis*, even though Isocrates approached *phronēsis* performatively, not conceptually.

Isocrates' conception of rhetoric is based on the typically Greek premise that the interests of citizens are inextricably bound to the welfare of the *polis*: what is good for the *polis* is good for the citizens. It is also based on the premise, equally typical in Greek notions of political deliberation, that, though the good of the *polis* is ultimately self-evident, varying situations and changing circumstances make the task of arriving at it difficult and elusive. Starting with these two premises, Isocrates approached rhetoric as a resource for arriving at the best course of action, that is, the best way of realizing concretely the good of the *polis* and advancing tangibly the collective interests of all citizens. This approach committed orators under his instruction to address each new situation encountered by the city-state in its particularity, as a unique occasion to discern the right course of action in the face of uncertainty. In the *Meno*, Plato had addressed the problem of arriving at the correct solution for the city as a problem haunting every statesman. Even though the good statesman of the *Meno* wants to make the right decision for his people every time, he is inevitably caught up in a situation where, with only opinion as his guide, he sometimes hits and sometimes misses the mark. For Isocrates, this was a problem facing statesmen and orators alike and, indeed, anyone who cared to become involved in the affairs of the city. It was in response to the specific problem of discovering sound courses of action when the welfare of the *polis* was at stake, and to the challenges this problem presented to concerned statesmen, orators, and citizens, that Isocrates crafted his conception of rhetoric and erected his entire program of rhetorical education.

Like Plato, Isocrates understood the problem of making decisions for the *polis* as a problem of rendering judgments without recourse to a definitive standard. Because opinion, or *doxa*, offers an unstable guide, decision makers relying on opinion alone involve themselves in a hit-and-miss quandary, and even the best decisions made in this way are nothing more than lucky guesses. But he did not agree with Plato's view that an objective way of knowing could be attained, made accessible, and provide a definitive standard that would lead to definitive solutions and would do away with the deficiencies of opinion. He rejected Plato's characterization of knowledge, expressed in the *Meno*, as a resource with the potential to provide decision makers what opinion could not: "he who has knowledge will always hit on the right way, whereas he who has right opinion will sometimes do so, but sometimes not" (97c). The strength of Isocrates' outright rejection of Plato's view of knowledge as *epistēmē* stems from his practical outlook on the problem he was addressing. In occasions of decision making about the future welfare of the *polis*, he would have reasoned, certainty can only come from an ability to predict the future, not from a theoretical grasp of knowledge or a scientific insight of some sort. As he put it in the *Antidosis*, "no system of knowledge can possibly cover these occasions, since in all cases they elude our science" (184). In this he echoes Gorgias's dictum in the *Encomium of Helen* that, since humans cannot predict the future, they are obliged to "take opinion as counselor to their soul," even though opinion is slippery and oftentimes deceptive (11).

Although Isocrates shared Gorgias's worldview of human beings burdened by the need to act against chance and circumstance but having no sufficient knowledge on which to base their judgments or any secure ground on which to anchor their beliefs, he sought nevertheless to develop his students' judgments. In this endeavor he was influenced by Plato—whose project of arriving gradually at an epistemic view of knowledge necessitated the intermediary step of correct opinion, between ignorance and knowledge. The distinction made by Plato between, on the one hand, ordinary or false beliefs and, on the other hand, correct but rationally inexplicable beliefs must have appealed to Isocrates as a commonsense criterion for distinguishing uninformed, unreliable, and irresponsible opinions from informed, responsible, and sound ones. For the history of Athens, from the earliest times of democracy through the golden age of Pericles to the bleak years of the postwar era, attested to the likelihood of beneficial and harmful decisions alike, decisions that led the city and its citizens sometimes to the heights of glory and other times to the brink of catastrophe. Caught between the sharply contrasting positions advanced by Plato and the Sophists, which held human judgments either to be secured on a stable foundation or to be unsustainable and groundless, Isocrates looked to the history of the community's decision-making practices as offering some degree of certainty. Carving an intermediary position between Plato and the Sophists, he banked on the possibility that a close study of wise decisions in the past could provide a guide for decision making in the present. To the extent that this guide could offer no guarantee for success, Isocrates remained very much aligned with the Sophists, who regarded the task of making decisions as an endeavor predicated on insufficient knowledge and lack of certainty. To the extent that this guide could offer some possibility for improving the quality of one's decisions, Isocrates became somewhat aligned with Plato, who regarded human judgments as amenable to improvement through education. Turning to the lessons of history as a way of resolving the dilemma between indeterminacy and certainty, Isocrates placed an emphasis on the possibility of arriving at sound decisions more often than not. Even though there is no room for certainty in occasions of decision making, he remarked, "those who apply their minds to them and are able to discern the consequences which for the most part grow out of them, will most often meet these occasions in the right way" (*Antidosis* 184).

This was, then, Isocrates' educational program in a nutshell. It was a program designed to educate students, be they orators, citizens, or future statesmen, on how to improve their judgments with regard to the affairs of the *polis* so that, when they found themselves in the position of deliberating, they would be able to discern the best option available most of the time. In other words, they would be able to identify more often than not those judgments that best advanced the collective welfare of their fellow citizens and secured the good of the *polis*. Clearly, what drives this educational program is both a great deal of confidence in the power of *paideia* to wrest the grip of luck on human affairs, and a good dose of humility before *tuchē* and the unpredictable ways through which the workings of chance manage to frustrate human control. Even as he champions the great accomplishments that education makes possible, he considers the humbling lessons of chance and luck to be indispensable, even to the best-educated people. "In dealing with matters about which they take counsel," he remarked, men of intelligence "ought not to think that they have exact knowledge of what the result will be, but to be minded toward these contingencies as men who indeed exercise their best judgment, but are not sure what the future may hold in store" (*Peace* 8).

Why would Isocrates give to his educational program, which focused generally on political deliberation and specifically on the question of how to discern the best course of action for the good of the *polis*, the label "philosophy"? Is this label, as some scholars are inclined to think, a rhetorical ploy on Isocrates' part, a clever way of distancing his instruction from the bad reputation that the term "rhetoric" had acquired in his day (Cahn)? Or is it, as other scholars point out, a justified label given that the practices of philosophy at the time, far from having been crystallized into a set discipline, still pointed to a fairly open-ended activity (Nehamas)? Are we to understand his claim to teach philosophy as an indication that his rivalry with Plato extended, beyond a competition between rhetoric and philosophy, to questions about the very nature of philosophical activity or to a debate over whether theoretical or practical pursuits ought to constitute the ends of philosophy proper? Did he have Plato in mind when he prefaced his own views about philosophy with the provocative remark that "what some people call philosophy is not entitled to that name" (*Antidosis* 270)? While these questions cannot be answered definitively, a close reading of *Antidosis* supports the view that, even as Isocrates considered the act of discerning the best course of action to be a problem of rhetoric, he regarded the process of improving one's ability to discern the best course of action to be a problem of philosophy. That he makes a distinction between reaching sound decisions and preparing one's ability to make sound decisions becomes apparent in *Antidosis* (270–71), where he concludes a discussion about his own understanding of wisdom and philosophy: "For since it is not in the nature of man to attain a science by the possession of which we can know positively what we should do or what we should say, in the next resort I hold those men to be wise (σοφοὺς) who are able by the power of conjecture to arrive generally at the best course, and philosophers (φιλοσόφους) those occupying themselves with the studies from which they gain most quickly that kind of insight (φρόνησιν)."

This passage uses the terms "wisdom" and "philosophy" to separate the domain of action from the realm of contemplation. Wise people are men of action, blessed with practical wisdom and the power to make correct conjectures or, translated more literally, to arrive at successful opinions (ταῖς δόξαις ἐπιτυγχάνειν), as much as that is possible. Philosophers are those who study the decisions of wise men, who turn the wise decisions of the past into an object of study, and who contemplate manifestations of wisdom in order to cultivate their own ability with practical wisdom, or *phronēsis*. *Phronēsis* ties together the domain of action with that of contemplation. Great statesmen of the past, who were also excellent orators, exhibit *phronēsis* in concrete action, through their judgments as to the best course, while philosophers seek to improve *phronēsis* by studying the ways it has manifested itself in past decisions. Accordingly, what the label "philosophy" might have conveyed to Isocrates' contemporaries is a program focused on the kind of mental preparation one would need to go through to be able to make an entrance into the domain of action as a person capable of making sound decisions. As requisite preparation for a successful life in politics, a philosophical inquiry into past instances of *phronēsis* would endow statesmen, orators, and citizens with the greatest ability possible to reach sound judgments in their own political deliberations at present.

The difficulty in deciphering the exact process of learning he had in mind stems from the fact that in his time, *phronēsis* had yet to be distinguished from *sophia* and, like Plato, Isocrates used the two terms interchangeably. This makes it unclear whether *phronēsis* in Isocrates' works demarcates, as in Aristotle, a particular form of intelligence that provides a standard for *doxa*, or indexes a sense for proper conjecture, a knack for hitting the right course of action, and a talent for making educated guesses. The difference is a crucial one. For if Isocrates could not grasp practical wisdom as qualitatively different from the power of conjecture, then his claim to have been able to improve *doxa* through education would not have been taken seriously. Without a form of reasoning that operates at a higher level of intelligence than clever opinion, Isocrates would have had no real way to distinguish himself from the Sophists, or to escape the relative domain of *doxa*, a domain in which one's opinion appears to be as good as another's. If, on the other hand, practical wisdom designated for him a qualitatively different activity from conjectural intelligence, then Isocrates' notion of *phronēsis* would have to be understood as a significant innovation in rhetorical theory, one that paved the way toward, and bore some important similarities to, Aristotle's theoretical conception of *phronēsis*.

One clue to this interpretive problem is provided by Isocrates' discussion about the great Athenian statesmen of the past (*Antidosis* 231–36). Through a lengthy exaltation of such men as Solon, Cleisthenes, Themistocles, and Pericles, Isocrates draws a composite portrait of practical wisdom in actions past. These men, he remarks, had acted decisively, spoken eloquently, and advocated courses of action that conferred the greatest benefits on their fellow Athenians. Throughout this discussion, Isocrates does not attempt to designate practical wisdom as a particular form of intelligence possessed by great statesmen; nor does he seek to demonstrate the ways in which this type of intelligence might have guided their process of decision making. He merely notes their sound decisions and calls these men "the best statesmen ever to have come before the rostrum," "the most reputable orators among the ancients," and "the cause of most blessings for the city" (231). Thus, even as he does not use *phronēsis* to indicate—as Aristotle did—a specific cognitive capacity, he does employ the term to refer to the ineffable workings of an activity that can only be known after the fact. All this points to the possibility that Isocrates might have understood *phronēsis* less in terms of a phenomenon to be grasped conceptually and more in terms of an event to be understood and recognized after its occurrence and only by means of its effects on others. For him, the claim that practical wisdom guided the decision of a given statesman could only be ascertained after the fact, after the consequences of that decision had become self-evident to the members of the polis.

This ex post facto validation of *phronēsis* enables Isocrates to do two things. First, he is able to press the point about uncertainty in decision making and to account for situations, well known to his contemporaries, in which not even the wisest statesman in the past had been able to make the right decision. This places a limit on *phronēsis* and signals yet another reminder that his rhetorical training is not promising any miracles: the best his students can hope for is an education that may enable them to discern the right course of action most of the time. However powerful, *paideia* cannot always overcome chance. As he puts it in *Panathenaicus*, it is not too infrequent that "those who are reputed to be the wisest sometimes miss the expedient course of action, whereas now and then some chance person from the ranks of men who are deemed of no account and are regarded with contempt hits upon the right course and is thought to give the best advice" (248). Second, he is able to assess *phronēsis* extrinsically, on the basis of the kinds of benefits conferred on citizens and the degree of reputation earned in the *polis* by the decision-making statesman. This places *phronēsis* not inside a person's mind but outside, in the public space, between deliberating agents pronouncing a given decision and fellow citizens feeling the effects of that decision. Clearly, Isocrates did not share with Aristotle an interest in *phronēsis* as an intrinsic good, an excellence for its own sake. Nor did he see any need to explore its workings rationally, since *phronēsis* for him was to be determined by the rulings of the Athenian people, not by the verdicts of reason.

Nevertheless, by situating *phronēsis* in the past and by making its study a requisite for reaching sound judgments, Isocrates does anticipate Aristotle somewhat. To make a wise decision about a given case at present, Aristotle remarked, one needs to consult a past precedent—a case in which *phronimoi* exercised a wise decision—and to use this precedent as a guide for sizing up a situation at present.

While Aristotle approached *phronēsis* formally, as a self-sufficient event, Isocrates approached *phronēsis* as an open-ended activity signaling a rare convergence of excellence in political deliberation, in oratorical eloquence, and in wise statesmanship. This is perhaps the reason why Isocrates saw *phronēsis* as facilitating a dialectical exchange not, as Aristotle held, between past principles and present contingencies, but between the manifestation of and possibility for excellence in deliberation: just as the *phronimoi* reached the heights of excellence in their deliberating practices, so will it be possible for citizens to reach similar heights of excellence in their future deliberations. By witnessing, marveling in, and studying past cases of wise decision making in the history of their community, citizens and orators could aspire to inform their own political activities at present with a similar spirit of excellence. For Isocrates, past cases of practical wisdom in deliberation provided students of oratory not so much with a source of imitation as much as with a space for habituation. A student of philosophy, Isocrates remarked, will select "those examples which are the most illustrious and the most edifying" and, after "habituating himself to contemplate and appraise such examples, he will feel their influence not only in the preparation of a given discourse but in all the actions of his life" (*Antidosis* 277).

Like Plato and Aristotle, then, Isocrates sought to improve judgments in political deliberation by discriminating one *doxa* from another. Unlike them, he believed he could improve his students' judgments without escaping communal norms through the imposition of an external standard—be it Plato's theoretical knowledge of the divine, or Aristotle's esoteric knowledge of the cognitive operations of the *phronimoi*. Like the Sophists, Isocrates remained anchored within the community and understood the impossibility of arriving at some definitive standard from within, amid competing norms and conflicting values. Unlike them, he regarded the community as a single entity unified by a shared knowledge, a history of collective experiences, and a common language. Far more conservative than the Sophists, he placed his faith in the prevailing conventions of the community and took for granted the truth-value of its time-honored traditions. Yet this conservatism was tempered, and at times even contradicted, by a rhetorical sensibility that often led him to recognize the constitutive capacity of language and to conceive speech as a maker of culture (*Nicocles* 5–9). His monolithic perspective on the community, in other words, did not prevent him from also ascertaining the power of *logos* to reconstitute established norms. It is this recognition, that communal norms may after all be the outcome of the most rhetorically effective constructions of *doxai*, which guided Isocrates' notion of *phronēsis* and shaped his conviction that his students' opinions could be improved through the study of wise judgments in the past.

This is also made evident in the *Panegyricus*, a work in which Isocrates assumes the persona of a wise member of the community and undertakes the explicit task of improving the judgments of his fellow citizens. Since he relied on his own works to train his students, Isocrates may have used the *Panegyricus* as a case study of how an orator can engage the community's conventional *doxai* rhetorically. Indeed, the lengthy section in praise of Athenian traditions demonstrates how an orator's strategic exaltation of the city's cherished traditions and celebrated myths may provide audiences with a new way of perceiving their community's past and a novel manner of understanding their own history. Articulated as a culturally viable history that gives audiences a new sense of self-understanding in preparation for the challenges of a changing world at present, Isocrates' *doxa*—vying against conventional *doxai*—constitutes audiences not only as proud citizens of the *polis* but also as leading members of a potentially unified nation. More than that, Isocrates may have also regarded the *Panegyricus* as a rhetorical performance of his own *phronēsis*. For he presents himself in this work as a statesman proposing a course of action for the common good, and providing audiences with a new identity as political subjects; a philosopher guiding audiences to reflect on their cultural heritage and to refashion their history in a way that will give their new identity a sense of continuity with the past; an orator providing audiences with the necessary means for identifying with and linking together their refashioned history, their reconstituted identities, and their sense of urgency to face the demands of a changing world; a public servant enacting his civic duty by giving advice to his fellow citizens and staking his reputation on the verdict they will eventually reach as to whether or not his *doxa*, and its effects on their welfare, had in fact been a wise decision and a manifestation of his *phronēsis*.

Our own students of rhetoric can benefit from the study of Isocrates today, provided they relinquish universalizing attitudes about their community and grand narratives about their history. At the local level, the same issues Isocrates raised about civic responsibility pertain to our own times, and the manner in which he confronted these issues can offer a guide to our students. Following Isocrates, for example, students can learn to display the traditional values of our democracy artistically, in a manner that sheds light on new possibilities for equality and opportunity for all, and in a way that gives local communities new directions for realizing these values through concrete action. In other words, students can explore how the very process of linking traditional values with new, more democratic visions of the community can lead to important challenges to conventional thought. Abandoning preconceived notions about classical rhetoric as an instrument of symbolic influence with the sole end of winning over auditors in particular situations, students can join Isocrates in exploring the constitutive possibilities of rhetoric and in discovering how these possibilities may be realized through identification rather than persuasion. With Isocrates, students of rhetoric can explore how their own efforts to intervene in the conventional language we use to exalt our values may lead them not only to meet their societal responsibility but also to realize themselves as civic agents.

CURRENT SCHOLARLY TRENDS

In the mid-twentieth century, an interest in Isocrates' educational program became the focal point of research for a number of scholars. Following Werner Jaeger, who aligned Isocrates' educational views with the ideals of Greek *paideia*, Henri Marrou, George Kennedy, and Frederick Beck provided valuable insights on Isocrates' pedagogy and detailed information about his school. These scholars helped establish Isocrates' hierarchical approach to education, comprising many fields of knowledge, with rhetoric being placed at the top, since the study of rhetoric entailed not just the knowledge of the art but also the experience of applying all fields of knowledge to the concerns of the *polis*. Through these scholars, Isocrates' school came to be understood as the earliest instance of a humanities education and his reputation as the father of humanities came to be widely accepted.

With the ideological turn spreading through the academy in the 1960s and 1970s, studies of Isocrates followed the general critique of values in ancient Greek culture and exposed Isocrates as an elitist promoting aristocratic ideals. M. I. Finley provided a sweeping history of elitist education whose roots he placed with Isocrates' school, and Norman Baynes critiqued Isocrates' Cyprian Orations as speeches in defense of the institution of monarchy. Gunther Heilbrunn argued that Isocrates' educational views were driven by his own elitist and oligarchic tendencies, and that his pursuit of Panhellenic politics under the leadership of Philip completely disregarded the democratic processes of the polis. The ideological critique of Isocrates continued in the next two decades and through such prominent studies as Nicole Loraux's work on funeral orations, in which Isocrates was placed next to fourth-century orators as one more apologist for aristocratic values. It culminated in Victor Vitanza, who, based on Samuel Isseling's study of the affinities between Isocrates and Heidegger on *logos*, saw in Isocrates' politics the seeds of Nazi values. With Yun Lee Too, whose work extended Heilbrunn's thesis, ideological critique receded into the background, with an emphasis now being placed on the formation of civic identity and on Isocrates' efforts to establish a political-cultural identity for the citizen that, according to Too, was both hegemonically Greek and Athenian. In this process of identity formation, through which Isocrates sought to alter pupils' and readers' views of the relationship between politics and culture by integrating Panhellenic and Athenian perspectives, writing was seen by Too as playing a far more important role than speaking, and Isocrates' self-presentation as a weak orator was taken as a deliberate effort to construct a literate persona that replaces orality.

In the last two decades, scholars have sought to identify the relevance that the study of Isocrates may have for us at present, by confronting rather than avoiding the constraints posed by the vast difference in values separating our society and culture from that of classical Greece. My *Speaking for the Polis: Isocrates' Rhetorical Education* argued that a relevance to our own democratic politics lies in the space opened up by Isocrates' rhetorical instruction in how to speak for the collective interests and common concerns of the *polis*. Norman Clark saw an additional relevance in the affinities between Isocrates' rhetorical theory and critical rhetorical studies today, and especially in the role that an orator/critic plays in serving his or her community. Kathleen Welch placed the present significance of Isocrates on his educational principle that the study of rhetoric should lead not to a technical expertise, but to an ability to address the affairs of the community. Using that principle,

Welch recuperated Isocrates' rhetorical education for current studies in critical pedagogy.

More recently, scholarly interest in Isocrates diverged into a number of different inquiries, including the nature of his *philosophia*, the constitutive dimension of his rhetoric as well as its artistic and performative character. Following Alexander Nehamas, David Timmerman and Edward Schiappa explored the possibility that Isocrates might have practiced a legitimate predisciplinary form of philosophy. Andrew Ford and Ekaterina Haskins examined the artistic dimension of Isocrates' rhetoric as a craft shaped, respectively, by the socioeconomic conditions of the times and by the aesthetic impulses of a still oral culture. Josiah Ober and Steve Schwarze placed the performative character of Isocrates' rhetoric at the center of their studies, arguing for an essentially democratic spirit that informed Isocrates' relation to the *demos* and the process of political deliberation. Haskins also examined the performative quality of Isocrates' rhetoric, which she saw as being predicated on a constitutive rather than instrumental view of rhetoric—a view also explored by me (Poulakos, "Isocrates' Use of *doxa*").

These recent lines of inquiry are explored further in *Isocrates and Civic Education*, edited by Takis Poulakos and David Depew, a collection of essays whose authors look to Isocrates as a unique case that, more than Plato and Aristotle, resists the perspective assumed by the far right that has nearly monopolized the study of civic education in classical Greece. By examining Isocrates' program in civic education next to that by the Sophists, Plato, and Aristotle, as well as next to our own models of humanities education today, contributors draw a portrait of Isocrates as a critic of the Athenian *demos* who nevertheless took an essentially democratic stance (Ober), a non-Sophist who nevertheless shared with the Sophists the performative tradition of Greek *paideia* (J. Poulakos; Haskins "Rhetoric between Orality and Literacy"), an elitist who inhabited the contradictions of taking pride in democracy while admiring other nondemocratic institutions (Konstan; Morgan), an educator who placed the autonomy of public deliberation in the traditions of the community (T. Poulakos, "Isocrates' Civic Education"; Depew), and someone we could readily follow today in our efforts to support practices that contribute to the sustainability of public culture as well as to our struggles to promote civic virtue within the context of modern democracy (Hariman; Leff).

BIBLIOGRAPHY

Primary Sources and Translations

Mirhady, David, and Yun Lee Too, trans. *Isocrates I*. Oratory of Classical Greece, Vol. 4. Austin: U of Texas P, 2000.

Norlin, George, trans. *Isocrates*. Vols. 1–2. London: William Heinemann and Cambridge: Harvard UP, 1928, 1929.

Papillon, Terry, trans. *Isocrates II*. Oratory of Classical Greece, Vol. 7. Austin: U of Texas P, 2004.

Van Hook, Larue, trans. *Isocrates*. Vol. 3. London: William Heinemann and Cambridge: Harvard UP, 1945.

Biographical Sources

Jebb, R. C. *The Attic Orators*. Vol 2. London: Macmillan, 1893.

Critical Sources

Baynes, Norman. *Byzantine Studies and Other Essays*. London: Athlone, 1960.

Beck, Frederick, *Greek Education 450–350 BC*. New York: Barnes and Noble, 1964.

Cahn, Michael. "Reading Rhetoric Rhetorically: Isocrates and the Marketing of Insight." *Rhetorica* 7 (1989): 121–44.

Clark, Norman. "The Critical Servant: An Isocratean Contribution to Critical Rhetoric." *Quarterly Journal of Speech* 82 (1996): 111–24.

Depew, David. "The Inscription of Isocrates into Aristotle's Practical Philosophy." Poulakos and Depew. 157–85.

Finley, M. I. *Use and Abuse of History*. New York: Penguin, 1975.

Ford, Andrew. "The Price of Art in Isocrates: Formalism and the Escape from Politics." *Rethinking the History of Rhetoric*. Ed. Takis Poulakos. Boulder: Westview, 1993. 31–52.

Hariman, Robert. "Civic Education, Classical Imitation, and Democratic Polity." Poulakos and Depew. 217–34.

Haskins, Ekaterina. "*Logos* and Power in Sophistical and Isocratean Rhetoric." Poulakos and Depew. 84–103.

———. "Rhetoric between Orality and Literacy: Cultural Memory and Performance in Isocrates and Aristotle." *Quarterly Journal of Speech* 87 (2001): 158–78.

Heilbrunn, Gunther. "Isocrates on Rhetoric and Power." *Hermes* 103 (1975): 154–78.

Ijsseling, Samuel. *Rhetoric and Philosophy in Conflict*. Hague: Martinus Nijhoff, 1976.

Jaeger, Werner. *Paideia: The Ideals of Greek Culture*. Vol. 3. Trans. G. Highet. New York: Oxford UP, 1965.

Leff, Michael. "Isocrates, Tradition, and the Rhetorical Version of Civic Education." Poulakos and Depew. 235–54.

Loraux, Nicole. *The Invention of Athens*. Trans. Alan Sheridan. Cambridge: Harvard UP, 1986.

Kennedy, George. *The Art of Persuasion in Greece*. Princeton: Princeton UP, 1963.

Konstan, David. "Isocrates' 'Republic.'" Poulakos and Depew. 107–24.

Marrou, Henri. *A History of Education in Antiquity*. New York: Sheed and Ward, 1956.

Morgan, Kathryn. "The Education of Athens: Politics and Rhetoric in Isocrates (and Plato)." Poulakos and Depew. 125–54.

Nehamas, Alexander. "Eristic, Antilogic, Sophistic, Dialectic: Plato's Demarcation of Philosophy from Sophistry." *History of Philosophy Quarterly* 7 (1990): 3–16.

Ober, Josiah. "I, Socrates . . . The Performative Audacity of Isocrates' *Antidosis*." Poulakos and Depew. 21–43.

Poulakos, John. "Rhetoric and Civic Education: From the Sophists to Isocrates." Poulakos and Depew. 69–83.

Poulakos, Takis. "Isocrates' Civic Education and the Question of *doxa*." Poulakos and Depew. 44–65.

————. "Isocrates' Use of *doxa*." *Philosophy and Rhetoric* 34 (2001): 61–78.

————. *Speaking for the Polis*. Columbia: U of South Carolina P, 1997.

Poulakos, Takis, and David Depew, eds. *Isocrates and Civic Education*. Austin: U of Texas P, 2004.

Schiappa, Edward. "Isocrates' *Philosophia* and Contemporary Pragmatism." *Rhetoric, Sophistry, Pragmatism*. Ed. S. Mailloux. Cambridge: Cambridge UP, 1995. 33–60.

Schwarze, Steve. "Performing *Phronesis*: The Case of Isocrates' *Helen*." *Philosophy and Rhetoric* 32 (1999): 79–96.

Timmerman, David. "Isocrates' Competing Conceptualization of Philosophy." *Philosophy and Rhetoric* 31 (1998): 145–59.

Too, Yun Lee. *The Rhetoric of Identity in Isocrates*. Cambridge: Cambridge UP, 1995.

Vitanza, Victor. *Negation, Subjectivity, and the History of Rhetoric*. Albany: State U of New York P, 1997.

Welch, Kathleen. *Electric Rhetoric: Classical Rhetoric, Oralism, and a New Literacy*. Cambridge: MIT P, 1999.

LIBANIUS

(314–395 CE)

George Pullman

Libanius was born in 314 CE at Antioch, what is now part of western Syria. His family had been members of the ruling elite for several generations, but the emperor Diocletian impoverished them ten years before Libanius was born. His father died when Libanius was ten. His uncles acted as his guardians and saw that he was educated in the traditional *paideia*. At fifteen he rejected Christianity in favor of classical theology, a decision that would profoundly influence the trajectory of his life. Against the wishes of his family and at an age (twenty-two) when most young men had already completed their education, Libanius went to Athens to study rhetoric. According to his autobiography, his experience in Athens was underwhelming. He found his fellow students more interested in intrigue and rivalry than rhetoric, while he himself was viewed as officious and aloof. In 340 he was in Constantinople teaching rhetoric privately. He was forced to flee the city during the riots of 342. Two years later he was ensconced as the municipal Sophist in Nicomedia. There, through his oratory, Libanius developed connections among members of the empyreal court. Because of the success of his panegyric on the reigning emperors, he was recalled to Constantinople in 349 to take up the chair of rhetoric. In 352 or 353 he was offered the chair of rhetoric in Athens, but he refused—citing a story about a non-Athenian chair who was kidnapped and hung upside down over a well until he promised to abandon his post and leave Athens forever. What Libanius wanted was the position of municipal Sophist at Antioch, an ambition that he finally realized in 354. Despite his professional successes, Libanius suffered numerous personal disasters, the death of a fiancé, the early death of his father and later his mother and his uncle and mentor, and the death of his only child, not to mention being struck by lightning (Or. 1.91; Ep. 727). His pagan faith placed him at odds with the Christian elite, and his favor and power rose and sank as the Christians' power sank and rose.

Libanius's professional high point coincided with the reign of the Emperor Julian, a pagan and Neoplatonist whose religious reforms had educational ramifications, tied so closely together as education and religion were. In particular, the study of rhetoric as it existed within the rhetorical tradition meant not only studying the classical texts, Homer through Aeschylus through Plato through Demosthenes, but also embracing the classical religion: paganism. Conversely, embracing Christianity meant rejecting rhetoric and classical education. As translator A. F. Norman puts it, "The choice for such teachers was quite clear— their religion or their profession" (*Selected Works* 1, xxi). Julian's enactment of laws that protected pagan practices and attempted to reduce religious bigotry made the world safe for the study of rhetoric, and Libanius's strict observance of pagan practices and rituals made him a favorite of the emperor, though he scrupulously rejected all empyreal favors and even championed the Andochenes (citizens of Antioch) when their religious convictions conflicted with Julian's reforms. Conversely, Libanius also wrote defending the emperor to the Andochenes (Or. 16), thus showing his willingness to support unpopular causes in the name of what he thought was right, irrespective of political considerations. As he says in Oration 16, "I am perfectly well aware that I shall displease all or most of you by my frankness, but it is far better for you to find my remarks disagreeable and yet be pleased with their consequences, than for you to listen to something you like and, for the sake of some paltry pleasure, suffer much severe punishment" (Norman, *Selected Works* 213). It is worth pointing out that this oration was apparently never given, and thus despite the radical political stance, no political considerations were truly at stake. Nevertheless, the speeches left by Libanius, published and unpublished, show a man concerned with the issues of his day: forced labor, religious freedom, distribution of wealth, causes of civic unrest, prison reform, education, justice, and so on.

LIBANIUS'S RHETORICAL THEORY

As a Sophist working within the rhetorical tradition, Libanius was profoundly conservative, sticking close to the rules as defined by such people as Menander Rhetor. The speech in praise of Antioch, for example, follows the presentation of topics for speeches in honor of a city completely and in order. Libanius was not a theorist, but rather a conservative practitioner, a champion of Atticism and a preserver of all things traditional. This fact is best observed in the oration "To Those Who Called Him Tiresome" (Or. 2, Norman, *Selected Works*, Vol. 2). The premise of this speech is that a friend, Andromachus, has told him that others are saying he is "Tiresome and overbearing" (Or. 2; 1). He responds by first trying to locate the source of this criticism, ultimately lighting on the idea that it is inspired by his constant critique of contemporary beliefs and practices. "The complaint is that I am constantly praising and longing for what is dead and done, denouncing the present day, harping on the past prosperity and the present misery of the cities, and that this is my tale everywhere every day" (26). He counters this claim by saying that those who make it are those "who benefited from the present situation," and therefore the true accusation ought to be that Libanius is tiresome to the nouveaux riches and those who "batten on the misery of the majority" (28). There follows a series of vituperations against various members of society, the *honorati*, the soldiers, tax collectors, even the horses of the cavalry. On the subject of education, he observes, "Rhetoric, that in the past used to flash like lightning, is now under a cloud" (43). Instead of studying Greek rhetoric and literature, the students are preoccupied with Latin law (45) and shorthand (46). Ultimately Libanius complains that the new social order has impoverished those members of society who had once been hereditarily (and therefore deservedly) rich while improperly enriching people who were "only recently hawkers of meat, bread or vegetables" (54); some of whom, "just by the size of their houses, are a nuisance to their neighbors, for they do not allow them the enjoyment of full clear daylight" (55). Libanius may or may not have been tiresome, but he certainly was pedagogically and socially conservative.

Libanius made his views known to audiences of various sizes, from attendees at Olympic games to intimate gatherings (see letters 64 and 76 for references to publication practices). Sometimes he circulated written copies of his work and sometimes shorthand copyists circulated unauthorized versions (this was apparently the case with his autobiography). Because he did not hold a political office and because his occupation depended on the good graces of politicians, Libanius's political influence was for the most part indirect. He would make his position clear to a small circle of influential friends and then expect them to disseminate his ideas. On some occasions, however, he spoke directly to the council.

One such occasion affords a glimpse of the lives of contemporary rhetoric teachers. Libanius was forced to plead for money on behalf of his four assistants who together received only what the one head Sophist before Libanius had received. Libanius's suggestion that the four men receive the interest from publicly held farmlands seems reasonable enough, given that other teachers were paid by public money at the time. Certainly the picture Libanius paints of his beleaguered underlings suggests that the life of a rhetor could be onerous. From this oration on behalf of his underlings, we can gather that while the municipal Sophist taught and gave public speeches, both political and ceremonial, and received both a salary and special financial considerations (many of which Libanius eschewed), rhetoricians of the time spent their days in the classroom with students of all ages, a system not unlike the contemporary system of tenured professors and temporary lecturers.

RHETORICAL LEGACY

A remarkable amount of Libanius's work has survived, over fifteen hundred letters and sixty-four orations as well as the autobiography. For this reason alone, he is important to contemporary scholars and students of rhetoric. But the way he lived makes Libanius important because he acts as a counterweight to the prevalent notion that the Second Sophistic was a low point in the rhetorical tradition. While it is true that Libanius held a merely political appointment and rarely engaged in actual politics, it is nevertheless also true that he did exert some influence. When Julian was emperor, Libanius was offered awards and offices which he declined, even going so far in his efforts to avoid the appearance of favoritism as to risk offending the emperor. This scrupulous avoidance of political favoritism afforded Libanius the privilege of the trusted outsider, allowing him to speak his mind, albeit in small circles of influential people, and thus provide a moral influence without actually engaging in politics directly. While this is certainly a diminished participation by traditional standards, it is also a far cry from sterile exercises about rape and abduction and encomia on parrots.

If we can say that the classical rhetorical tradition was that of the civically significant rhetor, where the emphasis on instruction was to train statesmen, and that the trajectory of the tradition from Plato on was increasingly toward instruction and performance and away from civic practice, culminating ultimately during the Second Sophistic with its emphasis on artistic display for the sake of instruction and indirect civic influence, then Libanius, with his conservative pedagogy and meticulous attention to rhetorical formalism and attic Greek, is an exemplar of what classical rhetoric was like just before it left the agora for the pulpit.

BIBLIOGRAPHY

Primary Sources and Translations

Norman, A. F., trans. *Antioch As a Centre of Hellenic Culture As Observed by Libanius*. Pittsburgh: U of Pennsylvania P, 2001.

———. *Libanius: Selected Works with an Introduction and Notes*. 3 vols. Cambridge: Harvard UP, 1969.

Biographical Sources

Norman, A. F., trans. *Libanius: Autobiography and Selected Letters*. 2 vols. Cambridge: Harvard UP, 1992.

Critical Sources

Anderson, Graham. *The Second Sophistic: A Cultural Phenomenon in the Roman Empire*. London: Routledge, 1993.

Bonner, Stanley F. *Education in Ancient Rome*. Berkeley: U of California P, 1977.

Gleason, Maud W. *Making Men: Sophists and Self-Presentation in Ancient Rome*. Princeton: Princeton UP, 1995.

Russell, D. A. *Greek Declamation*. Cambridge: Cambridge UP, 1983.

Walden, John W. H. *The Universities of Ancient Greece*. 1909. Freeport: Books for Libraries P, 1970.

Longinus, On the Sublime

(first–third centuries BCE)

Hans Kellner

Although it is a straightforward and coherent work, the *Peri Hypsos* of Longinus presents us with several enigmas and misunderstandings. Its date, authorship, and principal concept are all open to dispute. The author is traditionally called Longinus because the oldest manuscript, the tenth-century Paris Greek codex, lists as the author "Dionysion he Longion" ("Dionysos or Longinus"); elsewhere in the manuscript he is named Dionysus Longinus. Thus he has been called Dionysus or Pseudo-Longinus as well. (This essay follows the conventional name.) Theories associating the author of *Peri Hypsos* with others named Longinus or Dionysus have not proven persuasive, and the issue seems insoluble. Because there is no other mention of him or this work in the ancient world, all further evidence is internal. A Greek writer living in the eastern Roman Empire, he is familiar with both the rhetorical tradition and the Hebrew Scriptures, and expresses sharp criticism of current rhetorical practice. The date of the work has also been variously given. Some suggest the first century BCE because of the rebuke to Caecilius of Calacte and the sense of rhetorical decline; others have associated the work with Cassius Longinus of the third century. In the absence of any definitive evidence, we must conclude that the work appeared between the first and third centuries. About two thirds of it have survived.

On Grandeur of Thought and Expression

The title *Peri Hypsos* is traditionally translated *On the Sublime*, a quite misleading and anachronistic phrase. Certainly, "On Grandeur of Thought and Expression" better describes the work's content than does "sublime," a word that made its appearance with sixteenth-century Latin translations, and was taken up by Boileau's epochal version. In any case, the word "sublime," as inevitable if imperfect as the attribution to a Longinus, remains, erroneously burdening *Peri Hypsos* with the weight of centuries of later usage and anachronistic meanings. For *hypsos* is a flexible term as Longinus uses it. The greatness he celebrates takes many forms; he is inclusive and open about the topic of greatness.

Longinus identifies five sources of *hypsos*. The first two derive from nature; the rest can be learned. The first source of elevation in language is greatness of thought or conception; it is the product of a great soul. Selections from Homer, Sappho, and the book of Genesis are mentioned as examples. Amplification, which is an important and teachable part of grandeur in the classical rhetorical tradition, is separate from the sublime, which aims at elevation rather than quantity. Longinus cites Demosthenes and his rugged, lightning-like grandeur, as distinct from the more diffuse wildfire of Cicero. Rhetorically, the former style is best for amazing an audience, the latter for overwhelming one. Although greatness of soul is the original source, imitation is a means of attaining sublimity if one imitates greatness. Plato, among others, is sublime because he imitates Homer. One must, therefore, imagine how a Homer, Demosthenes, or Thucydides would have expressed a thought, and one must write with an eye to posterity. Visualizations are important devices in both poetry and oratory. In poetry, visual images bring forth reality and truth, but in oratory they exceed mere persuasion and master the audience.

As later commentators would regretfully note, the second source of the sublime, *pathos*, is not discussed. Although the whole work breaks off with the announcement of a discussion of *pathos*, it is assumed that the lacuna after the discussion of greatness of conception was a treatment of the subject. Nevertheless, Longinus insists throughout that both great thoughts and strong emotion are attributes of the soul. Although imitation can open us to them, the ethical import of the sublime comes from its origin in a certain kind of person.

The other three sources of the sublime are given by art, and thus are technical. The third source, figures, is discussed in sections 16 through 29. The natural suspicion that figuration evokes, the feeling that the audience is being condescended to or manipulated can be overcome if the figure accompanies a sublime thought and emotional intensity. Demosthenes' Marathon oath from the First Philippic serves to illustrate how the power of the situation can lend itself to the ideal—the figuration that conceals its figurality. Longinus emphasizes that emotion is the best guarantee that the figures he describes will not prove frigid. He notes that critics have disapprovingly cited Plato's words in the *Laws*, "let not silvern treasure nor golden settle and make a home in a city" (sec. 29). If sheep were to be banned, the critics joked, he might have said "ovine and bovine treasure" (sec. 29). Feeling is the key to this aspect of the sublime.

This discussion of figures causes Longinus to attack Caecilius, who had stated that no more than three metaphors should be used together. Longinus opposes not only this rule-bound approach, but also the cautious use of phrases ("as if," "as it were," etc.) that soften the boldness of figural language. Any problem arising from lofty language must be solved by strong emotion which sweeps everything along with it and transfers the feelings of the speaker to his audience. Similarly, hyperbole is best when it conceals its status as hyperbole by being uttered in a moment of high emotion. He writes, "As I am never tired of saying, to atone for a daring phrase the universal specific is found in actions and feelings that almost make one beside oneself" (sec. 38).

Caecilius's pedantic attack on Plato and his assertion of Lysias's superiority here bring forth from Longinus an important digression on genius and its relation to formal perfection. It is greatness that counts, he asserts, not correctness. The faults of Homer or Demosthenes are many, but who, he asks, would not be Homer rather than Apollonius? The lesser, correct, writers "do not trouble the peace of the audience" as the great do (sec. 34). Longinus praises the human imagination, which must strive to surpass its limits; we were born for an admiration of the great and extraordinary. Like our wonder at the Nile or the ocean, we admire the genius of the great through all ages.

The fifth and last source of the sublime is word arrangement, about which Longinus states that he has written two other books. Using musical images, Longinus maintains that the sound of word rhythms can capture the mind and raise it to the heights. Like the human body, in which no member has value apart from the others, the effects of grandeur must be united by the ties of rhythm.

After this discussion of the sources of *hypsos* and the digression on genius, the work concludes with a political and ethical argument to explain the decline of grandeur in Longinus's time. An unnamed "philosopher" friend is quoted to the effect that the absence of transcendent natures and the dearth of literature in an age that has produced many competent public orators is due to the decline of democracy, which fostered greatness by encouraging competitiveness and optimistic spirit of freedom. Instead, he said, a dull servility rules an imprisoned oratory. To this Longinus replies that it is not, perhaps, peace in the world that prevents greatness as much as the inner strife that comes from the love of money and pleasure. To make a god of wealth is to breed arrogance and luxury, insolence and shamelessness. Greatness of soul, the ability to transport an audience or to be swept away by grandeur of thought and language, withers as men care for their mortal part. Because of this widespread corruption of soul, Longinus writes, it is better perhaps to live in servitude, or else greed would prevail. The rest of the work is missing.

LONGINUS'S INFLUENCE

Peri Hypsos left no mark on ancient discourse, a fact that makes the identity of its author less crucial. It enters European literary discourse in the mid-sixteenth century; but it was with Boileau's French translation in 1674 ("Du Sublime") that the work exploded onto the scene. It soon became a defining force in cultural history; the next century and a half cannot be grasped without taking into account the notion of the sublime in many areas of European culture. Its place today is largely based upon the accumulated discourse on the sublime that it inspired and continues to inspire.

Although *Peri Hypsos* is not the first work on affective poetics or reader response—before it, Aristotle's theory of catharsis in tragedy had suggested in a limited way how certain techniques can produce a reaction in an audience—it is the first to suggest that a nobility of spirit may emerge in literature and carry away the reader or listener. Longinus's sliding, overlapping categories differ from Aristotle's strict definitions and draw a more subtle picture of the emotions stimulated by literature. Because of his belief that strict adherence to rules can lead to mediocrity and that outbursts that exceed or violate the canons of proper practice may transport the listener or reader to spiritual heights, Longinus has an ambiguous position with regard to classical rhetoric. He is clearly a rhetorician by trade, and his work has been called the great treatise on style. Yet it is misleading to see, as Kennedy does, his first source of the sublime as a study of invention; the greatness of soul and theme that drive it go far beyond any boundaries set by invention theories that derive from the subject at hand.

Some question the importance of Longinus's ethical appeal near the end of *Peri Hypsos*. It is not clear whether the "good friend" philosopher at the end is a person, or simply Longinus offering a counterargument in another voice. There is, however, another political aspect to the work that speaks for the sincerity of the ethics of the sublime. Many of Longinus's examples contrast Greek and Latin writers, an implied politics in which the conquered Greek has the elevation of spirit, while the imperial Roman can merely produce figures. Here the challenge to the rhetoric of the schools is made pragmatically clear. *Hypsos*, greatness of spirit, cannot be produced or contained by structures. Something will break forth for a moment from the writer or the topic, and because this greatness or sublimity will work a change, however momentary, in the reader or listener, interpretation will never be a settled matter, but rather always open.

BIBLIOGRAPHY

Primary Sources and Translations

Aristotle, *Poetics*; Longinus, *On the Sublime*; Demetrius, *On Style*. Loeb Classical Library. Cambridge and London: Harvard UP and William Heinemann, 1925.

Ashfield, Andrew, and Peter de Bolla. *The Sublime: A Reader in British Eighteenth-Century Aesthetic Theory*. Cambridge: Cambridge UP, 1996.

Dorsch, T. D. *Aristotle/Horace/Longinus: Classical Literary Criticism*. London: Penguin, 1965.

Grube, G. M. A. Introduction. *On Great Writing (On the Sublime)*. New York: Library of Liberal Arts, 1957.

Critical Sources

Doyle, Laura. "Sublime Barbarians in the Narrative of Empire; Or, Longinus at Sea in *The Waves*." *Modern Fiction Studies* 42 (1996): 323–47.

Johnson, William Bruce. "Introduction." *Longinus On the Sublime: The Pero Hupsous in Translations by Nicolas Boileau-Despreaux (1674) and William Smith (1739)*. Delmar, NY: Scholars Facsimiles and Reprints, 1975.

Kennedy, George A. *Classical Rhetoric and Its Christian and Secular Traditions from Ancient to Modern Times.* Chapel Hill: U of North Carolina P, 1980.

Macksey, Richard. "Longinus Reconsidered." *MLN 108* (1993): 913–34.

Russell, Donald A. F. M. "Longinus." *Oxford Classical Dictionary.* 2nd ed. Ed. N. G. L. Hammond and H. H. Scullard. Oxford: Oxford UP, 1970. 619.

Smith, Rebekah. "Two Fragments of 'Longinus' in Photius." *Classical Quarterly* 44 (1994): 525–29.

Wooten, Cecil W. "Abruptness in Demetrius, Longinus, and Demosthenes." *American Journal of Philology* 112 (1991): 493–505.

Menander of Laodicea

(third century CE)

Martin M. Jacobsen

Greek rhetorician Menander of Laodicea (or Menander Rhetor) lived during the third century CE and "was a native of Laodicea-on-Lycus," where he seems to have been a teacher of rhetoric (Gascó 3111). His classroom practices appear to have contributed substantially to his theoretical arguments (Heath, "True Story"). Other facts about his life appear to be lost. This essay first examines the two treatises on epideictic oratory attributed to Menander, examines arguments regarding their attribution, and then details the growing interest in Menander by surveying current scholarship.

Menander's Rhetorical Theory

Commonalities exist between the two treatises. Both are Aristotelian in presentation, carefully defining the purpose of epideictic oratory, dividing and subdividing the speeches into their parts, and using copious examples. Both treatises focus entirely on praise, except for the assertion in *Treatise I* that "blame has no subdivision" (3). Both draw examples from classical authors from many disciplines (literature, philosophy, history, the Sophists, classical rhetoricians). The reliance on these sources creates a didactic tone in both works, which are essentially formularies supported with received texts. These commonalities influence rhetorical theory by privileging the Aristotelian approach to rhetorical analysis. Moreover, the academic tendencies reflected by Menander's affiliation with Aristotelian rhetorical principles and classical texts support the assertion that Menander was a teacher of rhetoric. These practices, along with Menander's status as the authoritative source for epideictic oratory through the Middle Ages, supports the modern conceptualization of Aristotle's rhetoric as the foundation of the Western rhetorical tradition.

Treatise I subdivides praise into two categories: gods and mortal objects. Hymns to the gods take eight forms: cletic, apopemptic, scientific, mythical, genealogical, fictitious, precatory, and deprecatory. Poetic language is used for gods, prose for mortal things. Plato is cited as an author who uses "practically all these forms" (9). Menander then delineates how to praise countries, cities, bays, harbors, and citadels based on their nature, position (both geographic and in relation to other like entities), pleasure, utility, virtues, and accomplishments.

Treatise II serves as a formulary for fifteen different forms of oration:

1. The encomium of the emperor
2. The speech of arrival
3. The talk, the propemptic talk (a speech that marks a person's departure on a journey)
4. The epithalamium (wedding speech)
5. The bedroom speech
6. The birthday speech
7. The consolatory speech
8. The address (praise of deeds)
9. The funeral speech
10. The crown speech
11. The ambassador's speech
12. The speech of invitation
13. The leavetaking
14. The monody (expression of pity)
15. The Sminthiac oration

An effective means of analysis for the more comprehensive and complex *Treatise II* lies in Aristotle's means of persuasion and five rhetorical canons. In terms of *logos*, Menander advocates recounting facts such as place of birth, lists of accomplishments, and so forth; in terms of *pathos*, he implies a natural need to sway the audience to accept the feeling the speech is to convey. However, Menander privileges *ēthos* above the other two. This is in keeping with the epideictic purpose, especially considering Menander's references to the way in which the speaker should appear to feel about his subject. His reliance on the canons to guide composition obviates the need for elaborate proofs, and distinct purposes tend to produce the feeling epideictic oratory actually confirms. Since the other means of persuasion are accomplished by the formula and purpose for the addresses, the speaker's primary responsibility becomes projecting a sincere persona. For instance, in book 9, Menander states that the consolatory speech need not "preserve the sequence of the encomia" because the speaker should appear to be "out of his mind and distracted by emotion" (161).

The five canons of rhetoric heuristically detail the remainder of Menander's contribution to the theory of epideictic oratory. Invention derives entirely from the subject of the address: once the subject is determined, the type of speech and proofs needed are assumed. Arrangement—without question Menander's primary methodology—follows the pattern for the encomium. Menander lists the elements of that pattern in his discussion of the imperial speech in book 1:

1. Prooemia
2. Native country
3. Family status
4. Birth
5. Nature
6. Nurture/education
7. Accomplishments
8. Actions
9. Cardinal virtues
10. Fortune
11. His reign
12. Epilogue

The entire treatise then bases the designs for the fifteen speeches on which elements to emphasize or how the structure may differ in a given case.

Style varies with purpose and is based heavily on literary borrowings. Menander goes to great lengths to dictate the actual language of any given division of a speech, often suggesting how formal the language should be, and occasionally suggesting an optimum length. He says nothing about memory, probably because the speeches are composed. Delivery lies in the use of exhaustive descriptions, literary allusions, and quotations, and is largely governed by merging arrangement and style.

MENANDER'S INFLUENCE

Thus, Menander's contribution to rhetorical theory based on *Two Treatises* lies largely in the preservation of classical models. Modern studies of Menander argue that his influence is greater and expands into both deliberative and forensic rhetoric. The loci of current scholarly attention to Menander lie primarily in four scholars: D. A. Russell, N. G. Wilson, Fernando Gascó, and Malcolm Heath. A chronological survey of their work, along with implications present in other Menander scholarship, demonstrates Menander's current status in modern rhetorical theory. Russell and Wilson's 1981 volume *Menander Rhetor* stands as the foundation for the study of *Two Treatises*. This detailed and thorough work places the Greek text and English translation on facing pages (the former on the verso, the latter on the recto). The introduction and commentary (arranged in endnote format) are trenchant and exhaustive. Bibliographies for subsequent scholarship on Menander confirm that this volume is the necessary first step for any scholarly examination. Ironically, current scholarship suggests only one of these treatises, the second, is actually Menander's.

The best current scholarship in print on *Two Treatises* is an excellent survey by Fernando Gascó of the University of Seville, who argues the treatises were the authoritative texts regarding epideictic oratory well into the Middle Ages (Gascó 3117). He shows the striking differences between the two works. *Treatise I*, he argues, offers a primarily theoretical view of epideictic rhetoric grounded in the principles of the Second Sophistic. After citing Aristotle's divisions of rhetoric, the author of *Treatise I* discusses hymns to the gods, praise of territories, and praise of cities. Sources other than Aristotle cited in this work include Isocrates, Plato, and second-century authors (Gascó 3126–29). All in all, *Treatise I* is a theoretical work grounded in the epideictic principles of the Second Sophistic.

Treatise II, a formulary for various encomia, differs somewhat from the first and is the treatise that most scholars agree is actually Menander's. This work dispenses with theoretical considerations and begins immediately with the desultory delineation of the sixteen speeches. Sources also differ. While Isocrates is cited with some frequency (as he was in *Treatise I*), Plato's importance gives way to that of more literary figures such as Homer, Herodotus, Xenophon, and other classical writers (Gascó 3132–37). Finally, *Treatise II* takes a more didactic approach to encomia than *Treatise I* does, offering much more specific and detailed structures for its discourses.

University of Leeds classics professor Malcolm Heath agrees that only *Treatise II* is Menander's, a conclusion shared by Gascó (3115). However, Heath argues that Menander's influence on rhetorical theory lies not only in the *Two Treatises* but also in his *Commentary on Demosthenes* ("True Story"). Although the text of the *Commentary on Demosthenes* has not survived, references to it abound in the scholia on Demosthenes and other figures. In his 1996 address to the Classical Association, Heath asseverates that "the perception of Menander as a specialist in epideictic is a misperception" and that examining "the whole range of testimonia to Menander's work" will lead to a "different picture" ("True Story"). The scholia, Heath shows, refer to Menander via two grammatical forms: one implying quotation of references to Menander, the other suggesting direct citation of Menander's writing. Heath then offers an extended example "that may help to fill out our sense of Menander as a teacher" ("True Story"). This example exhibits Menander's command of *stasis* theory—derived in part from Demosthenes—as part of an address to advanced students. *Stasis* theory is an element of forensic rhetoric; therefore, Menander's influence does appear to extend beyond epideictic rhetoric. Finally, Heath demonstrates that Menander's teaching is both theoretically based and rhetorical in its delivery, stating that "Menander is not just talking *about* rhetoric: he is actually *using* rhetoric" ("True Story").

Heath's work culminates in the book *Menander: A Rhetor in Context*. Heath's Web site associated with the research for this book suggests that Menander influences all three Aristotelian rhetorical divisions, and that his theoretical and pedagogical prowess contribute more to the rhetorical tradition of late antiquity than the record currently reflects. Further, he argues that classroom teaching may actually underlie Menander's theoretical acumen (Heath, *Third-Century Rhetor*).

Heath's book is a logical reexamination of Menander's influence based on the discovery of new data and the increase in critical attention.

Also intriguing is the scope of interest in Menander. Bibliographic citations show that critical attention to Menander began in the late eighteenth century and appears in most major European languages. In fact, German scholar M. R. Dilts's *Scholia Demosthenica* made Heath's work viable (Heath, *Third-Century Rhetor*). In 2001, an article on Menander in English appeared in the Danish journal *CIMAGL* by University of Copenhagen philologist Pernille Harsting. Thus, Menander's contribution to contemporary rhetorical theory lies in both his contested position in the Second Sophistic and in the methodological principles of modern rhetorical studies. Clearly, a lively critical enterprise surrounds the theory, practice, and influence of both Menander and the modern scholars who study him. The changing view of Menander's record confirms that rhetorical study possesses the needed methodological depth to address historical, linguistic, and rhetorical puzzles.

BIBLIOGRAPHY

Primary Sources and Translations

Dilts, Mervin R., ed. *Scholia Demosthenica*. Leipzig: Teubner, 1983.
————. *Scholia Demosthenica*. Vol. 2 Munich: Saur KG, 1986.
Russell, D. A., and N. G. Wilson. *Menander Rhetor*. New York: Oxford UP, 1981.

Critical Sources

Cairns, Francis. "A Note on the *Editio Princeps* of Menandor Rhetor." *Eranos* 85 (1987): 138–39.
Gascó, Fernando. "Menander Rhetor and the Works Attributed to Him." *Aufstieg und Niedergang der römischen Welt* II.34.4 (1998): 3110–46.
Harsting, Pernille. "More Evidence of Menander Rhetor on the Epithalamium: Angelo Poliziano's Transcription in the Statius Commentary (1480–81)." *CIMAGL* 72 (2001): 11–34.
Heath, Malcolm. *Menander: A Rhetor in Context*. New York: Oxford UP, 2004.
————. *Menander of Laodicea: A Third-Century Rhetor in His Cultural and Social Context*. December 2000. University of Leeds. 14 June 2002 <http://www.leeds.ac.uk/classics/heath/Menander.htm>.
————. "Menander Rhetor: The True Story." Annual General Meeting of the Classics Society. Nottingham, England. April 1996. University of Leeds. 22 June 2002 <http://www.leeds.ac.uk/classics/heath/q-menand.html>.

PERICLES

(ca. 500–429 BCE)

David M. Timmerman

A prominent fifth-century Athenian politician, rhetor, and military general, Pericles came from the Alcmaeonid, a prestigious Athenian family. His father, Xanthippus, played a prominent role in the defeat of the Persians by the Athenians in the early fifth century. In his early days, Pericles was a leader in the state action against Cimon and the negotiation of the thirty years' peace with Sparta. His power derived from leadership in battle, political activities, and abilities as a persuasive orator. Pericles supported the statesman Ephialtes in his reorganization of the Areopagus, which shifted power to the assembly and court juries. Pericles continued the trend by instituting pay for jurors. This, along with pay for those who attended the assembly, significantly broadened participation in the Athenian democracy. Pericles led Athens in an aggressive building campaign that included the Parthenon, Propylaea, Odeon, the Long Wall that stretched from Athens to the port at Piraeus, and many other public buildings.

The leadership accomplishments of Pericles are all the more impressive because he did not formally enjoy the powers of a ruler or monarch but rather led through the Athenian democratic structure. He won reelection as strategos fifteen years in a row—an unequaled record. Athens elected ten of these military and political leaders each year, but Thucydides emphasizes the prominence of Pericles by stating that during these years "what was nominally a democracy was becoming in his hands government by the first citizen" (4.65.9 in Strassler). Pericles was married, but also maintained a relationship with the rhetorician and philosopher Aspasia. His appreciation for intellectual pursuits was also evidenced by his relationship with the historian Herodotus, several Sophists, the playwright Sophocles, and the sculptor Pheidias. In his *Life of Pericles*, Plutarch gives the most complete early recounting of Pericles' life, written four centuries after his death. Plutarch recounts many events from the political life of Pericles, highlighting the idea that Pericles favored the interests of the masses over those of the elites. The enduring significance of Pericles in the rhetorical tradition resides in his accomplishments as a highly prominent and successful political orator and his close association with and encouragement of the humanistic tradition.

RHETORICAL PRAXIS AND THE DEVELOPMENT OF DEMOCRACY

Rhetorical scholars who wish to assess the rhetorical legacy of Pericles are presented with a paradox. On the one hand, we know a great deal about Pericles as a political and historical figure, the historical context in which he lived, and even several of the significant decisions, actions, and speeches that he gave. On the other hand, as many have noted, we do not possess the words he spoke. What we have are Thucydides' accounts of several of his speeches, carried through a three-decade-long oral tradition, and as constructed by Thucydides for the purpose of supporting his account of the Peloponnesian war.

Thus, a rhetorical perspective on Pericles raises interesting questions about the presentation of Pericles by Thucydides. Such questions revolve around how the Periclean speeches function rhetorically in the narrative itself, as well as how Thucydides' presentation has functioned rhetorically over the subsequent millennia in terms of our understanding of Pericles, deliberative and epideictic rhetoric, and the Athenian democracy. Scholars have taken up this task with renewed interest in recent years. For example, Harvey Yunis seeks to reveal "how Thucydides exploited Pericles' indistinct rhetorical legacy in order to create the account of Periclean rhetoric that has dominated ever since" (63). That account, according to Yunis, is dominated by Thucydides' intent to demonstrate that Pericles was able to use a rhetoric characterized by authority and instruction in a manner that supported the democracy in ways that his predecessors did not. The fault for Athens's loss of the Peloponnesian War and thus the fault for her fall from dominance, therefore, lay not with democracy, but with the particular leaders who followed Pericles.

THE ENDURING SIGNIFICANCE OF PERICLES THE RHETOR AND DEMOCRATIC PERSONA

Particularly intriguing for rhetorical scholars is the fact that the two primary sources that discuss Pericles, Thucydides and Plutarch, make transparent arguments concerning the rhetorical legacy of Pericles. Many of those who have examined the speeches by Pericles have noted that Thucydides presents Pericles as an extremely authoritative, powerful speaker who argued for the supremacy of Athens in comparison to Sparta. Plutarch frames an argument concerning Pericles' impact on rhetorical theory by linking his success not merely to his words but also to his actions and his imperviousness to bribes.

The significance of Pericles is also located in the Athenian funeral oration recorded by Thucydides. That funeral oration is the most complete and extensive example we have of this genre. Nicole Loraux contends that by means of the funeral oration, Pericles and others were able to subsume and sublimate the powerful tensions that ripped other city-states apart. In the case of Athens, then, a complete understanding of the democracy rests to a significant degree on an understanding of the role played by public discourses such as the funeral oration. Recent scholars have mined this example to demonstrate how such ceremonial speeches functioned to construct, reconstruct, support, and strengthen the civic identity of the Athenians (Loraux; Mackin; Ober, *Political*; Yunis).

BIBLIOGRAPHY

Primary Sources and Translations

Strassler, Robert B., ed. *The Landmark Thucydides: A Comprehensive Guide to the Peloponnesian War*. Trans. Richard Crawley. New York: Simon and Schuster, 1996.

Thucydides. *History of the Peloponnesian War*. Trans. Charles Forster Smith. Loeb Classical Library. Cambridge: Harvard UP, 1928.

Thucydides. *Historiae*. Oxford Classical Text. H. Stuart-Jones with revised critical apparatus by J. E. Powell. Oxford: Clarendon, 1942.

Biographical Sources

Bowra, Cecil Maurice. *Periclean Athens*. London: Weidenfeld and Nicolson, 1971.

Burn, Andrew R. *Pericles and Athens*. London: English UP, 1949.

Conner, Walter R. *Thucydides*. Princeton: Princeton UP, 1984.

Hornblower, Simon. *Thucydides*. Baltimore: Johns Hopkins UP, 1987.

Kagan, Donald. *Pericles of Athens and the Birth of Democracy*. New York: Free Press, 1991.

Plutarch. *Life of Pericles*. Trans. Bernadotte Perrin. London: William Heinemann, 1966.

Critical Sources

Bosworth, A. B. "The Historical Context of Thucydides' Funeral Oration." *Journal of Hellenic Studies* 120 (2000): 1–17.

de Romilly, Jacqueline. *Thucydides and Athenian Imperialism*. Trans. P. Thody. Oxford: Blackwell, 1963.

Gomme, Andrew W., Anthony Andrewes, and Kenneth J. Dover. *A Historical Commentary on Thucydides*. 5 vols. Oxford: Clarendon, 1945–81.

Harris, Edward M. "Pericles' Praise of Athenian Democracy: Thucydides 2.37.1." *Harvard Studies in Classical Philology* 94 (1992): 157–67.

Hornblower, Simon. *A Commentary on Thucydides*. Oxford: Oxford UP, 1991.

Hudson-Williams, H. L. "Thucydides, Isocrates, and the Rhetorical Method of Composition." *Classical Quarterly* 42 (1948): 76–81.

Loraux, Nicole. *The Invention of Athens: The Funeral Oration in the Classical City*. Trans. Alan Sheridan. Cambridge: Harvard UP, 1986.

Mackin, James A. "Schismogenesis and Community: Pericles' Funeral Oration." *Quarterly Journal of Speech* 77 (1991): 251–62.

Ober, Josiah. *Mass and Elite in Democratic Athens: Rhetoric, Ideology, and the Power of the People.* Princeton: Princeton UP, 1989.

———. *Political Dissent in Democratic Athens: Intellectual Critics of Popular Rule.* Princeton: Princeton UP, 1998.

Poulakos, Takis. "Historiographies of the Tradition of Rhetoric: A Brief History of Classical Funeral Orations." *Western Journal of Speech Communication* 54 (1990): 172–88.

Stadter, Philip A. *The Speeches in Thucydides: A Collection of Original Studies with a Bibliography.* Chapel Hill: U of North Carolina P, 1973.

Yunis, Harvey. *Taming Democracy: Models of Political Rhetoric in Classical Athens.* Ithaca: Cornell UP, 1996.

PHILODEMUS

(ca. 110–ca. 40 BCE)

Robert N. Gaines

Philodemus was an Epicurean philosopher and epigrammatic poet. He was born around 110 BCE in the ancient Syrian town of Gadara (Strabo, *Geographica* 16.2.29) and studied under Zeno of Sidon (Angeli), while Zeno was head of the Epicurean School in Athens (ca. 110/105–ca. 79/78 BCE, Angeli and Colaizzo). During the seventies, Philodemus migrated to Italy, and about 70 BCE he secured patronage of L. Calpurnius Piso Caesoninus, a Roman senator (Cicero, *In Pisonem* 68–70, Asconius, *In Pisonianam* 68; Philippson). The latest reference in Philodemus's writings may be dated 40 BCE, and he probably died around this date (Gigante, *Filodemo*).

After arriving in Italy, Philodemus's intellectual activities were evidently centered in the region around Herculaneum and Neapolis. The former connection is suggested by the significant presence of philosophical works by Philodemus in a library of Greek book rolls discovered at Herculaneum during 1752–54 (Capasso). Without these Herculanean papyri, nearly all of Philodemus's philosophical works would be unknown; accordingly, most scholars believe that Philodemus was associated with the book collection and the residence in which it was found. Philodemus's Neapolitan connection is confirmed by his friendship and presumed collaboration with Siro, who led an Epicurean philosophical community in Neapolis (Gigante, "Virgilio"; Cicero, *De Finibus* 2.35).

Most of Philodemus's literary activity may be assigned to his time in Italy. Of his numerous epigrammatic poems (Parsons, "List"), about thirty-six survive in the traditional sources of the *Greek Anthology* (Sider). Most of these poems are erotic; the rest are dedicatory, eulogistic, epideictic, protreptic, convivial, and satirical. Philodemus's poetry received favorable recognition as early as 55 BCE (Cicero, *In Pisonem* 70). Along with his participation in the Neapolitan Epicurean community, Philodemus's reputation as a poet brought him personal contact with the finest literary minds in Italy, including Virgil, Plotius Tucca, Varius Rufus, and Quintilius Varus (Gigante and Capasso). Outside his personal relationships, Philodemus's poetic practice influenced a number of writers, including Catullus, Horace, Tibullus, Propertius, and Martial (Tait).

Philodemus's philosophical prose corpus was extensive—at least thirty-five treatises—and prosecuted upon many subjects, including history of philosophy, aesthetics, ethics, theology, and logic (see Janko; Gigante, *Catalogo*). Among the aesthetic works is Philodemus's *On Rhetoric*. A reconstruction of this work was first attempted by Siegfried Sudhaus, whose edition presented *On Rhetoric* in seven books. Sudhaus's reconstruction was subsequently reorganized and much extended by Tiziano Dorandi ("Per una ricomposizione"), who used a different seven-book scheme. Recently, however, Francesca Longo Auricchio ("New Elements") discovered that among the papyri that constitute *On Rhetoric, P. Herc.* 832/1015 contains in its title page the book number "H" (*oktō* = 8); she also observed that *P. Herc.* 1669 bears traces of what may be the book number "I" (*deka* = 10). In consequence of these findings, *On Rhetoric* must have contained at least eight books and may have contained as many as ten. The date of *On Rhetoric* was formerly assigned to the seventies BCE, because the work refers to Zeno in the present tense in book 2; however, Jakob Wisse has recently shown that the present tense need not signify that Zeno was alive at the time of reference. An alternative dating scheme has been proposed by Guglielmo Cavallo based on paleographical evidence; within this scheme, books 1 through 3 are assigned to 75–50 BCE, while subsequent books are assigned to 50–25 BCE. This proposal is attractive, but some scholars advise caution in its application (Parsons, Rev. of *Libri*). Consistent with the foregoing, the structure and dating of *On Rhetoric* remain uncertain. Nonetheless, *On Rhetoric* constitutes a rich and unique source for our understanding of rhetoric in relation to the Hellenistic schools of philosophy, especially Epicureanism; it likewise discloses Philodemus's participation in the developments characteristic to rhetorical theory around the mid-first century BCE.

PHILODEMUS'S RHETORICAL THOUGHT

The contents of Philodemus's *On Rhetoric*—as we now know it—may be summarized as follows. Book 1 addresses the artistic status of rhetoric and generally characterizes philosophical responses to the problem, not least by certain Epicureans who contradict, so Philodemus says, the position of Epicurean leaders (Epicurus, Metrodorus, and Hermarchus) that sophistic rhetoric is an art (text = Longo Auricchio, *Philodēmou*; Blank). Book 2 provides detailed critique of various philosophical arguments for and against the artistic status of rhetoric (text = Longo Auricchio, *Philodēmou*; Blank). Especially featured is Philodemus's defense of Zeno's position that sophistic rhetoric is an art in some sense acceptable to leaders of the Epicurean School. Essential to argumentation in this book is a distinction of "art" into exact and conjectural types. Philodemus apparently exploits this distinction to assign conjectural artistic status to persuasive forms of rhetoric (*P. Herc.* 1674 cols. 5.31–6.19; cf. Cicero, *De Oratore.* 1.107–09). Book 3 opposes the Stoic position of Diogenes of Babylon regarding philosophy, rhetoric, and statesmanship; otherwise, it refutes the view that rhetoric, especially sophistic rhetoric, creates expertise in statesmanship (text = Sudhaus; Arnim; Hammerstaedt; Dorandi, "Appunti"). Book 4 disputes claims by rhetoricians and Sophists concerning rhetorical style, delivery, arrangement, and invention, as well as forensic, deliberative, and epideictic speaking (text = Sudhaus; Longo Auricchio "Frammenti"; Gaines, "Textual Notes," "Philodemus and Cicero"; Dorandi, "Fragmenta," "Due 'edizioni'"). Philodemus's discussion emphasizes style and delivery over arrangement and invention (cf. Cicero *Orator* 43–50, 51–236). Regarding style, he prefers naturally beautiful expression, rejecting expression conceived as beautiful according to an arbitrary determination. Delivery, arrangement, and invention all depend in part on other disciplines, especially invention, since rhetors—as practitioners of rhetoric—are incapable of finding or judging arguments on subjects other than rhetoric (Gaines, "Philodemus"; cf. Cicero *De Oratore* 1.20, 48–50, 53, 60). Philodemus's comments on forensic and deliberative speaking are cursory; however, he vigorously critiques sophistic theory and practice of epideictic speaking, insisting that Sophists do not have the moral knowledge or practical insight to praise and blame successfully. Book 8 discusses the rhetorical theories of Nausiphanes and Aristotle (text = Sudhaus; Longo Auricchio, "Nuove letture nei frammenti," "Nuove letture nel *PHerc.* 1015"). Philodemus criticizes Nausiphanes' claim that training in natural philosophy creates good speakers. He also denounces Aristotle for teaching rhetoric and admitting politics into philosophy. Of the books with uncertain numbers, that constituted by *P. Herc.* 1004 offers criticism of the view that rhetoric is useful and treats several positions that compare rhetoric with philosophy (text = Sudhaus; Cappelluzzo). One position belongs to an Ariston (his identity is uncertain), another to Diogenes of Babylon, and a third position may represent a Peripatetic philosopher (cf. Hubbell). The remaining book—possibly numbered 10—comprises *P. Herc.* 220, 473, 1078/1080, 1118, 1669, 1693 (Dorandi, "Per una ricomposizione") and offers further comparisons of rhetoric with philosophy (text = Sudhaus; Ferrario, "Verso una nuova edizione," "Frammenti," "Per una nuova edizione"). Philodemus pursues these comparisons in response to multiple arguments that elevate rhetoric and denigrate philosophy. Ultimately Philodemus says that while many evils arise from rhetorical persuasion, philosophy teaches everything that contributes to happiness.

Cicero used Philodemus's *On Piety* in composing his own *De Natura Deorum*; among later writers, Philodemus's philosophical corpus is cited by Diogenes Laertius and perhaps by St. Ambrose (Philippson, Obbink).

BIBLIOGRAPHY

Primary Sources and Translations

Angeli, Anna. *Filodemo. Agli amici di scuola (PHerc. 1005)*. La scuola di Epicuro 7. Napoli: Bibliopolis, 1988.

Angeli, Anna, and Maria Colaizzoa. "I frammenti di Zenone Sidonio." *Cronache Ercolanesi* 9 (1979): 47–133.

Arnim, Ioannes ab, ed. *Stoicorum Veterum Fragmenta.* Vol. 3. Lipsiae: Teubner, 1903. 240–43.

Cappelluzzo, Maria Giustina. "Per una nuova edizione di un libri della Retorica Filodemea (PHerc. 1004)." *Cronache Ercolanesi* 6 (1976): 69–76.

Dorandi, Tiziano. "Appunti sul PHerc. 468." *Zeitschrift für Papyrologie und Epigraphik* 91 (1992): 47–49.

————. "Due 'edizioni' del IV libro della Retorica di Filodemo." *Zeitschrift für Papyrologie und Epigraphik* 81 (1990): 33–35.

————. "Fragmenta Herculanensia inedita." *Zeitschrift für Papyrologie und Epigraphik* 71 (1988): 43–46.

Ferrario, Matilde. "Per una nuova edizione del quinto libro della 'Retorica' di Filodemo." *Proceedings of the XVIII International Congress of Papyrology: Athens, 25–31 May 1986.* Ed. Basil G. Mandilaras. Athens: Greek Papyrological Society, 1988. 167–84.

————. "Frammenti del quinto libro della Retorica di Filodemo (PHerc. 1669)." *Cronache Ercolanesi* 10 (1980): 55–124.

————. "Verso una nuova edizione del quinto libro della 'Retorica' di Filodemo." *Cronache Ercolanesi* 4 (1974): 93–96.

Gaines, Robert N. "Textual Notes on Philodemus, *Peri rhētorikēs*, Book IV." *Hermes* 113 (1985): 380–81.

Hammerstaedt, Jürgen. "Der Schlußteil von Philodems drittem Buch über Rhetorik." *Cronache Ercolanesi* 22 (1992): 9–117.

Hubbell, Harry M., trans. *The Rhetorica of Philodemus. Transactions of the Connecticut Academy of Arts and Sciences* 23 (1920): 243–382.

Janko, Richard, ed., comm., and trans. *Philodemus, On Poems, Book 1.* Oxford: Oxford UP, 2000.

Longo Auricchio, Francesca. "Frammenti inediti di un libro della Retorica di Filodemo (PHerc. 463)." *Cronache Ercolanesi* 12 (1982): 67–83.

————. "Nuove letture nei frammenti del *PHerc.* 1015 (Filodemo, *Retorica*, libro incerto)." *Cronache Ercolanesi* 23 (1993): 93–98.

————. "Nuove letture nei *PHerc.* 1015 (Filodemo, *Retorica*, libro incerto)." *Cronache Ercolanesi* 24 (1994): 109–10.

————, ed. and trans. *Philodēmou Peri rhētorikēs, Libros primum et secundum.* Ricerche sui Papiri Ercolanesi 3. Napoli: Giannini, 1977.

Obbink, Dirk, ed., comm., and trans. *Philodemus, On Piety, Part 1.* Oxford: Clarendon, 1996.

Parsons, P. J. "List of Epigrams." *Oxyrhynchus Papyri* 54 (1987) no. 3724.

Sider, David. *The Epigrams of Philodemus.* New York: Oxford UP, 1997.

Sudhaus, Siegfried, ed. *Philodemi Volumina Rhetorica.* 2 vols. and Supplementum. Lipsiae: Teubner, 1892–96.

Biographical Sources

Philippson, Robert. "Philodemos (5)." *Paulys Real-Encyclopädie der classischen Altertumswissenschaft* 19.2 (1938): cols. 2444–82.

Tait, Jane Isabella Marion. *Philodemus' Influence on the Latin Poets.* Ann Arbor: Edwards, 1941.

Critical Sources

Blank, David. "La philologie comme arme philosophique." *Cicéron et Philodème: La polémique en philosophie.* Études de littérature ancienne 12. Ed. Clara Auvray-Assayas and Daniel Delattre. Paris: Éditions Rue d'Ulm/Presses l'École normale supérieure, 2001. 241–57.

Capasso, Mario. *Manuale di Papirologia Ercolanese.* Galatina: Congedo, 1991.

Cavallo, Guglielmo. *Libri scritture scribi a Ercolano.* Primo supplemento a *Cronache Ercolanesi* 13. Napoli: Macchiaroli, 1983.

Dorandi, Tiziano. "Per una ricomposizione dello scritto di Filodemo sulla Retorica." *Zeitschrift für Papyrologie und Epigraphik* 82 (1990): 59–87.

Gaines, Robert N. "Philodemus and Cicero on Models of Rhetorical Expression." *Cicéron et Philodème: La polémique en philosophie.* Études de littérature ancienne 12. Ed. Clara Auvray-Assayas and Daniel Delattre. Paris: Éditions Rue d'Ulm/Presses l'École normale supérieure, 2001. 259–72.

———. "Philodemus on the Three Activities of Rhetorical Invention." *Rhetorica* 3 (1985): 155–63.

Gigante, Marcello. *Filodemo in Italia.* Bibliotechina del saggiatore 49. Firenze: Felice Le Monnier, 1990.

———. "Virgilio fra Ercolano e Pompei." *Atene e Roma* 28 (1983): 31–50.

———, ed. *Catalogo dei Papiri Ercolanesi.* Napoli: Bibliopolis, 1979.

Gigante, Marcello, and Mario Capasso. "Il ritorno di Virgilio a Ercolano." *Studi Italiani di Filologia Classica,* 3rd ser. 7 (1989): 3–6.

Longo Auricchio, Francesca. "New Elements for the Reconstruction of Philodemus' Rhetorica." *Akten des 21. Internationalen Papyrologenkongresses, Berlin 1995. Archiv für Papyrusforschung,* Beiheft 3 (1997): 631–35.

Parsons, P. J. Rev. of *Libri scritture scribi a Ercolano* by G. Cavallo. *Classical Review* 39 (1989): 358–60.

Wisse, Jakob. "The presence of Zeno: The date of Philodemus' *On Rhetoric* and the use of the 'citative' and 'reproducing' present in Latin and Greek." *On Latin: Linguistic and Literary Studies in Honour of Harm Pinkster.* Ed. Rodie Risselada, Jan R. De Jong, and A. Machtelt Bolkestein. Amsterdam: Gieben, 1996. 173–202.

PHILOSTRATUS

(ca. 170–244/249 CE)

Jerry L. Miller and Raymie McKerrow

The Sophist Philostratus, also known as Lucius Flavius Philostratus or Philostratus II, was one of four prominent relatives in the Philostratus family to achieve literary recognition. The number of relatives named and referred to simply as Philostratus contributes to some confusion and difficulty in accurately identifying the specific contributions of Lucius Flavius Philostratus to the field of rhetoric. The threefold name of Lucius Flavius Philostratus suggests Roman citizenship. It is believed that he was born on the isle of Lemnos, an overseas territory of Athens, because of references he makes to himself as a Lemnian (Philostratus the Lemnian is the son-in-law of Lucius Flavius Philostratus) (Lendering, par. 10). Lucius Flavius Philostratus is identified as Philostratus the Athenian, as well. It is suggested that the name Philostratus the Athenian is the result of his father's decision to send him to Athens to study under Proclus of Naucratis. Philostratus later studied with unknown teachers in Asia Minor, and it is believed that it was during this time that he developed his skills of sophistry. Much of what is known about Lucius Flavius Philostratus comes from his own writings. The Sophist married Aurelia Melitene and together they had one son, Capitolinus, and a daughter. The daughter married Philostratus III, referred to as Philostratus of Lemnos, who, like his father-in-law, is known for his literary contributions (Lendering, par. 15).

Early in the third century, Philostratus lived in Athens and became the hoplite general, an important function in charge of heavy infantry and citizen-soldiers. Moving to Rome, he embarked on the practice of sophistry. Between June 203 and 208, Philostratus was introduced to Emperor Septimius Severus (193–211), his wife, Julia Domna, and sons, Geta and Caracalla. It is during this period that Philostratus's contributions to rhetoric begin. Included among his writings are eight books including *The Life of Apollonius, Lives of the Sophists (two books), Gymnasticus,* and a collection of fictional letters known as *Love Letter* (Lendering, par. 9; "Philostratus, Flavius, the Athenian" 388). It is suggested that Lucius Flavius Philostratus wrote other notable works, including *Heroicus,* a dialogue on the heroes of the Trojan War, and two books called *Imagines*, a rhetorical description of a visual art known as *ekphrasis* that was popular during the Second Sophistic (Shaffer 303); however, there is disagreement among scholars as to which Philostratus actually wrote these texts, including speculation that *Imagines* and *Heroicus* were written by his son-in-law, Philostratus III (Lendering, par. 9; "Philostratus, Flavius, the Athenian" 388; "Philostratus, the Lemnian" 388).

In addition to the rhetorical style expressed through Apollonius, Philostratus's *Life* includes a detailed account of some of his real-life experiences as he accompanied the royal family to Britain, where they engaged in a war against the Picts, people of uncertain origin who inhabited parts of northern Britain, fought against the Romans, and in the ninth century CE united with the Scots. In *Life*, Philostratus describes the ocean waves as he and the royal family sailed to Britain. While at war with the Picts, Septimius Severus fell ill and died and was succeeded by his sons Geta (211–212) and Caracalla (211–217). Philostratus remained with the imperial court and observed the murder of Geta by his brother, Caracalla, another story he details in *Life of Apollonius* (Lendering, par. 15).

PHILOSTRATUS'S RHETORICAL THEORY

Julia Domna commissioned *The Life of Apollonius*, written by Lucius Flavius Philostratus after 217. *Life* introduces the reader to a charismatic teacher and Pythagorean philosopher, Apollonius of Tyana. Apollonius is described as an "assiduous traveler, speaker, and miracle worker" (Billault 227). Philostratus, through his character, Apollonius, criticizes the rhetorical tradition of the time and, instead, practices rhetoric of authority and truth, a rhetoric whose philosophical roots imply concepts such as teaching, morals, and metaphysics (Billault 231). At an early age, Apollonius regarded rhetoric as an inferior subject. Much of the traditional rivalry of rhetoric and philosophy that began with Socrates' debate with the Sophists, as described in Plato's dialogues, is paralleled in *Life*, as Apollonius reveres philosophy and derogates rhetoric. Apollonius denounces rhetoric that is void of any references to a hierarchy of values. Such rhetoric without thought as its base is a mere self-centered display of technique with no relation to reality. Rather than this futile and absurd form of rhetoric, Apollonius advocates a form of rhetoric with responsibility at its core. The originality of this rhetoric arises from a fundamental difference that implies that one should speak pertinently about what one knows (Billault 229). Interestingly, Apollonius's *ēthos* is measured by his relationship with the gods. This divine acquaintance is fundamental to Apollonius's life and the development of the rhetoric of sovereign speech. Sovereign speech is based on self-sufficiency, existing outside the deliberative-forensic-epideictic triad. What Apollonius reveres in sovereign speech is truth that is free from persuasion (deliberative), argumentative rebuttal (forensic), and praise (epideictic), as the audience assumes a passive attitude and simply accepts the sovereign speech. This rhetoric implies a natural dominance of some persons over others because those who possess the truth have the power and duty to inculcate it in others who benefit by it (Billault 231). Based on divine acquaintance, this philosophy is reinforced in Philostratus's *Life* when Apollonius compares *mimesis*, a Platonic theory of imitation used to explain artists' conception of divinity in order to create statues of Greek gods, to *phantasia*, which claims to produce what the senses may have never experienced, but is a production of perfect reality. Where *mimesis* is wrought with distractions due to an artist's mental capacity, *phantasia*, Apollonius argues, is another mental capacity that is free from such disturbances (Benediktson, 185–88; Flory 150).

From a rhetorical perspective, the other important work by Philostratus is *Lives of the Sophists* (*Bioi Sophiston*), written after 231 and finished in 237. This work is a collection of biographies that describes both the classical Greek Sophists of the fifth century BCE and later philosophers and rhetoricians. In *Lives*, Philostratus writes of the famous Sophists of the day, distinguishing between the two ages of the "art of speaking": the First Sophistic, founded in the fifth century BCE by Gorgias, and the Second Sophistic, a term coined by Philostratus that describes the second age of the "art of speaking" founded in the fourth century by Aeschines (Swain 160). *Lives* does not provide a complete description of sophistic practices of the day, but provides anecdotes, literary criticisms, and general gossip about prominent Sophists, specifically, Polemo of Laodicea (90–145) and Herodes Atticus (101–177) (Lendering, par. 27). Written at a time when declamatory speaking was at its height, the account concentrates more on matters of style and eloquence than on matters of invention. As Thonssen and Baird state, "The standards of excellence that Philostratus sets up presuppose the all-sufficiency of style as the measure of speaking. Unless speaking well is accepted as an absolute standard, which cannot be properly granted, the *Lives* affords a type of criticism that is unmistakeably capricious" (203). Philostratus could be complimentary and harsh in his dismissals. Of one Sophist he wrote, "he both Atticized and employed an ornate style of eloquence" (Philostratus the Athenian, *Lives of the Sophists* 246). Of another Sophist he argued, "Let those who think Varus of Laodices worthy of mention receive no mention themselves. For he was trivial, vain and fatuous [...]" (Philostratus the Athenian, *Lives of the Sophists* 297). As W. C. Wright has observed, "Without Philostratus we should have a very incomplete idea of the predominant influence of Sophistic in the educational, social, and political life of the empire in the second and third Christian centuries" (Philostratus the Athenian, *Philostratus* xvi).

Bibliography

Primary Sources and Translations

Alciphron. *The Letters of Alciphron, Aelian and Philostratus.* 1949. Trans. Allen Rogers Benner and Francis H. Fobes. Cambridge: Harvard UP, 1979.

Philostratus the Athenian. *Life and times of Apollonius of Tyana.* Trans. Charles P. Eells. New York: AMS Press, 1967.

————. *The Life of Apollonius of Tyana, the Epistles of Apollonius and the Treatise of Eusebius.* Trans. F. C. Conybeare. Cambridge: Harvard UP, 1969.

————. *Philostratus and Eunapius: The Lives of the Sophists.* Trans. Wilmer Cave Wright. Cambridge: Harvard UP, 1968.

Philostratus the Elder. "Imagines." *Philostratus Imagines: Callistratus Description.* Trans. Arther Fairbanks. Ed. T. E. Page, E. Capps, and W. H. D. Rouse. New York: Putnam's Sons, 1931. XV, 1–274.

Biographical Sources

Lendering, Jona. "Philostratus." *The Columbia Encyclopedia.* 6th ed. 13 Aug. 2001. <http://www.livius.org/phi-php/philostratus/philostratus.htm>.

"Philostratus, Flavius, the Athenian." *The New Encyclopedia Britannica I.* 4th ed. 2002.

"Philostratus, the Lemnian." *The New Encyclopedia Britannica I.* 4th ed. 2002.

Critical Sources

"Ancient Greek and Roman Philosophy." *The New Encyclopedia Britannica.* 15th ed. 2002.

Anderson, Graham. *The Second Sophistic: A Cultural Phenomenon in the Roman Empire.* New York: Routledge, 1993.

Benediktson, D. Thomas. *Literature and the Visual Arts in Ancient Greece and Rome.* Norman: U of Oklahoma P, 2000.

Billault, Alain. "The Rhetoric of a 'Devine Man': Apollonius of Tyana as Critic of Oratory and as Orator According to Philostratus." *Philosophy and Rhetoric* 26.3 (1993): 227–35.

Bowersock, G. W. *Fiction as History: Nero to Julian.* Berkeley: U of California P, 1994.

Flory, Dan. "Stoic Psychology, Classical Rhetoric, and Theories of Imagination in Western Philisophy." *Philosophy and Rhetoric* 29.2 (1996): 147–67.

Jarratt, Susan C. "The Role of the Sophists in Histories of Consciousness." *Philosophy and Rhetoric* 23.2 (1990): 85–95.

Poulakos, John. "Hegel's Reception of the Sophists." *Western Journal of Speech Communication* 54.2 (1990): 160–71.

————. "Rhetoric, the Sophists, and the Possible." *Communication Monographs* 51.3 (1984): 215–26.

Romilly, Jacqueline de. 1988. *The Great Sophists in Periclean Athens.* Trans. Janet Lloyd. Oxford: Oxford UP, 1992.

Shaffer, Diana. "Ekphrasis and the Rhetoric of Viewing in Philostratus's Imaginary Museum." *Philosophy and Rhetoric* 31.4 (1998): 303–16.

Swain, Simon. "Defending Hellenism: Philostratus, *In honour of Apollonius.*" *Apologetics in the Roman Empire: Pagans, Jews, and Christian.* Ed. Mark Edwards, Martin Goodman, and Simon Price. Oxford: Oxford UP, 1999. 157–96.

Thonssen, Lester, and Albert Craig Baird. *Speech Criticism: The Development of Standards for Rhetorical Appraisal.* New York: Ronald P, 1948.

PLATO

(429/7–347 BCE)

Yun Lee Too

Plato has become in many ways a representative figure of classical Athens. He is best known to us as a philosopher, indeed as the philosopher par excellence of the Western tradition, such that all subsequent philosophy has been regarded as mere "footnotes" to Plato (Whitehead 63). But what it meant to be a philosopher in ancient Athens and in Plato's own terms requires qualification for the contemporary reader, for philosophy was not simply abstract thought disengaged from the rest of life, even though Plato himself and later Aristotle presented contemplation as the highest of human activities. Philosophy, for Plato, had among its concerns the formation of the ideal community. Between 387 and 370 he opened the Academy, an institution where young men would come to talk and be instructed in mathematics, law, and politics with the aim of helping the government of their states. His writings, such as the *Republic* and *Laws*, certainly address what the philosophical city-state should and could be, while the *Critias* treats the lost civilization of Atlantis, possibly using this ancient state as an allegory for the city-state of the philosopher's own time. Furthermore, Plato's own political activities demonstrate a concern to reform historical societies after his own ideals. In 367 he accepted from the tyrant Dion an invitation to oversee the education of the new tyrant of Syracuse, Dionysius II, and although his efforts bore little fruit, Plato maintained his contact with the politics of Syracuse until the murder of Dion in 354.

It is with regard to Plato's political concerns that we should understand his concern with rhetoric. Rhetoric was an essential part of the culture of fourth-century Athens, offering the means of political engagement in the city-state. It determined public opinion and action on public matters, as orators would stand up to speak in the Assembly in response to the invitation *ho boulomenos*, "he who wishes [to speak]," and in the law courts to plead their own cases. But public discourse was open to criticism from a variety of writers in classical Athens, including Plato. The agents of public speech did not seek to speak the truth, but they appealed to what the people knew, opinion or *doxa*, and what they felt, and this created an environment in which the city as a whole might act irrationally, as in the case of the condemnation of the generals at Arginusae for abandoning their men to drown (406 BCE) or as in the decision to destroy Mytilene for its disobedience and then the change of heart over this matter (Thucydides 3.36–49). Furthermore, orators furthered their political agendas by accusing opponents in the law courts on made-up charges, and they made speeches that appealed to the emotions and desires of the popular mob (the *demos*), as Thucydides (3.36–40) and Isocrates (*On the Peace* 9), among others, complain.

If Plato has been regarded as the great enemy of rhetoric, it is because his significance for the history of rhetoric has been misunderstood. The philosopher is the enemy of the conventional rhetoric of his society, but that is not the same as saying that he is the opponent of rhetoric *toto caelo*. Plato is someone who re-envisions rhetoric and its place in society, which he also reimagines, and it is precisely society that offers the all-important context for understanding the philosopher's contribution to the history of rhetoric. Plato is a critic of rhetoric because of what rhetoric does in his world, and Plato's world is one that needs to be transformed. For him, rhetoric is no longer to be a means of public address, as it was in fourth-century Athens, but a discourse by which individuals achieve greater knowledge of themselves and their world.

PLATO'S REJECTION OF CONVENTIONAL RHETORIC

Plato paid significant and critical attention to the role of public speech in society. He addresses rhetoric most directly in one dialogue of the early period and in the dialogues of his middle period, presenting rhetoric as a discourse which, in view of the way that people use and manipulate it, does evident and notable harm to the well-being of the community. The earliest of the dialogues to deal with rhetoric is the *Apology*, a work in which the author presents Socrates' self-defense against the charges that he corrupted the city's youth and worshipped other gods. This text is one that situates Socrates in an obviously rhetorical scenario as a defendant in the law court, and it is also one that has the philosopher subvert all the norms of conventional rhetoric as he eschews the language and strategies of the orators in favor of truth in a manner that is paradigmatic for the later dialogues. Indeed, he opens the speech by privileging truth (*aletheia*), observing that his accusers have not spoken it when they claim that Socrates is a "clever speaker" (*deinos legein*) (17b3). The defendant points to the fact that he is not adept at manipulating the methods and devices of the men who stand up and harangue the *demos* in the law courts and the Assembly with popular opinion and their deceptive representations; rather, his concern is to speak the truth. As Socrates himself declares, "but you shall hear from me the whole truth, not, however, by Zeus, O Athenian men, words that have been made beautiful by some of them, with verbs and nouns nor words which are ordered but you will hear words randomly spoken with the words as they come" (17b7–c2). He insists later that the "virtue of the orator is to speak the truth" (18a5–6), privileging the content over the form of the speech, although it is the case that the content of conventional rhetoric is also depicted as perverted. It is because the words of Socrates' accusers, Anytus and Meletus, are a deceptive and misrepresentative discourse that they are dangerous (18b1–8). It is important to realize that the orators are not particularly dangerous. They are harmful just like others who manufacture language for the public sphere, as, for instance, the tragic poets or the comic poet Aristophanes, who in his play *The Clouds* caricatured the philosopher as a wise man who thought about the affairs in the heavens, investigated the things under the earth, and made the weaker speech the stronger speech (18b6–8).

PLATO AND THE SOPHISTS

The *Apology* offers other more specific criticisms of the culture of rhetoric. Socrates takes to task the Sophists, the professional and itinerant educators who claimed to teach, among other skills and knowledges, the ability to speak (19e). He rehearses the familiar complaints against the Sophists. They—such individuals as Gorgias, Prodicus, Hippias, and Evenus—teach for vast sums of money; however, they do not provide a just return for what they receive from their students (see Blank). The representation of the Sophists is set starkly against the philosopher's own self-representation as someone who does not receive a fee for the education that he provides to his pupils. The Sophists come in for further disparagement when the philosopher recounts how, after learning from the Delphic oracle that no one is wiser than himself, he went out to test the validity of this statement by questioning those who had a general reputation for wisdom. Statesmen are the public speakers of the city-state, and Socrates reports that he finds them lacking in wisdom and knowledge (21c1–d3), like the poets and the craftsmen he also investigates. Thus rhetoric is one of the activities in which the city places an undeserved regard.

Yet if Socrates presents himself as ignorant of the conventions and forms of rhetoric, Plato presents him, nonetheless, as someone who is able to invoke and to manipulate this language and its forms with great skill. He declares that he has never spoken previously in a public place, a claim that the fourth-century rhetorician Isocrates would emulate (see Isocrates 15.9–10), and which serves to garner sympathy from the audience, assuring the listeners that the speaker is not a political meddler. Furthermore, Socrates closes his defense speech with a nod to another rhetorical commonplace, the convention of the condemned man bringing out his children and his household in an unspoken plea for pity (34c). Yet the philosopher cites this device in order to disavow it for his own defense, something that Isocrates would again copy (cf. Isocrates 15.321). What the *Apology* demonstrates is Plato using the structures of rhetoric in order to dismantle rhetoric: Socrates disavows rhetorical technique despite displaying an adeptness at using it.

The strategy of employing rhetoric against rhetoric is indeed central to Plato's posture toward this discipline, and it has been unrecognized or underplayed by scholars (for one exception, see Neel). The Platonic dialogue is itself an essentially rhetorical structure. The dialogues have been regarded as a form of drama (Nightingale 4); however, Platonic drama draws on a central device of rhetoric, namely *ethopoeia*, or the construction of a plausible speaking voice. Plato makes his characters, including and especially Socrates, speak as his contemporary audience would have expected them to, albeit now speaking to the end of philosophy rather than of rhetoric. One dialogue where characterization is pronounced is the *Menexenus*, in which Socrates reproduces an *epitaphios logos*, or funeral oration, as supposedly uttered by Aspasia, the mistress of the general Pericles, for the benefit of Menexenus. This work, as Nicole Loraux rightly observes, is "disturbing" since it offers a rhetorical staging at one remove where the speaker is a foreign woman— and the genre requires that the orator be an Athenian man—and its audience, Socrates, is not politically engaged (9). This perversely Platonic framing of the rhetorical scenario, somewhat corrected in the dialogue by Socrates' role as rapporteur, has caused the work's authenticity to be doubted (Loraux 9), although the delivered speech presents the commonplaces of the genre, namely, praise of the city's past wars and its ancestors, and an appeal to the present citizens to emulate their forebears. But all this serves to stand as a critique of a form of public discourse that has been so key to Athenian identity and ideology, for Socrates declares that the *epitaphios logos* casts a spell on its audience (235a2–3; Loraux 264), enabling it to be deceived; furthermore, it confuses reality with fantasy (Loraux 267). What Plato does in the *Menexenus* is to present rhetoric in order to show that a mode of speech which is so central to Athens's sense of identity is harmful because discourse is divorced from the truth and thus from the goals of philosophy.

Ethopoeia is also a key strategy of the *Gorgias*, one of the middle dialogues to deal prominently with rhetoric, and here what the characters say serves in the end to undermine the authority of public address (Vickers 84). This dialogue is one in which Socrates discourses with Gorgias, the noted Sicilian Sophist and author of such works as *Encomium of Helen*, *Palamedes*, *On Not Being*; Polus, a younger teacher of rhetoric; and Callicles, an antidemocrat who believed in using the spoken word to gain power, to highlight the epistemological shortcomings of conventional rhetoric. The work begins with Socrates making Gorgias admit that he is a rhetorician (449a), and continuing with the admission that rhetoric is such an art as can make others rhetoricians by giving them knowledge concerning speeches (449c9–d3; 449e1), and that it enables its practitioners to persuade jurists in the law court, councilmen in the council, assemblymen in the assembly and indeed in every assembly (452d1–5). In fact, Gorgias proceeds to declare that the rhetorician is more able to persuade than the specialist on any topic, so that this individual is more credible when he speaks on the topic of health than even a doctor (459a1–3). The rhetorician in effect asserts that knowledge and its transmission are anything but the concern of rhetoric.

The conversation with Gorgias is one in which the interlocutor is far from forthcoming, and Socrates then turns to speak with Polus. In this segment of the dialogue, the philosopher makes his famous claim that rhetoric is a "knack" (*empeiria*) rather than a skill, and in this respect it is like cooking, makeup, and sophistry (462d3–4; 463b4–6). The discourse with Polus reveals, furthermore, that rhetoric also resembles cookery in being a form of flattery that also seems to be concerned with the body (465b–e): rhetoric is a deceptive and fraudulent activity. But the characterization of rhetoric degenerates in Socrates' account of it, for the philosopher observes that orators kill and expel from the city whomsoever they wish, just as tyrants do even though they do not have any power (466d). The discussion continues with Polus on the topic of justice and turns to Callicles at 481b6. Callicles takes recourse to nature (*phusis*) to argue why some people should have more power than others, that is, they are by nature stronger (483d1–4). He goes on to criticize individuals who spend their lives doing philosophy, for this is an activity suited only to the young who are beginning their educations (484c4–485e3). Socrates undermines Callicles' understanding of power, claiming that men must first be rulers of themselves, and specifically of their appetites, rather than of other people (492d1–9). Later, when the conversation returns to deal directly with rhetoric, the philosopher observes that there are two kinds of rhetoric. In one, orators do not seek to improve people so that they become as good as they can be but only to gratify them, surrendering the common good and interest for private gain (502d9–e8); in the other kind, orators do strive to make their listeners good and to say the best possible thing (503a7–b3). Socrates then declares that it is important for the soul to be orderly and to have structure (504b4–5), and this is something that conventional rhetoric does not aid and thus for this reason it can have no place in society.

PLATO'S RHETORICAL THEORY

Having mentioned the possibility of a good rhetoric, Socrates sets out in the final part of the *Gorgias* his requirements for a what true rhetoric must be. First, it is necessary that the rhetorician be a good and just man who benefits the city (507b5–e3). It is on this basis that the philosopher is critical of Pericles, for he left the citizens in a worse state than he found them in (515d4–516d2), and of the Sophists, whose own students behave unjustly to them and refuse to pay them their fees (519c3–d7)—sophistry and rhetoric resemble one another, the reader learns at 520a. Socrates continues with the claim that he alone practices the true politics (521d6–8), and provides a prophecy of his own trial and death, foreseeing that it will be upsetting to be put to death due to ignorance of the flattering rhetoric but that he will, nonetheless, be at peace (522b3–e6). Plato closes the *Gorgias* with an eschatology that justifies the need to be good and for rhetoric to be ethical: there is a judgment and only the souls of the good, namely of philosophers, go to the Isles of the Blessed (526b5–c7). The important point with which Socrates closes the dialogue is that one must be, not merely seem, good (527b5–6).

Plato condemns rhetoric and some of its foremost practitioners in the *Gorgias* while offering a model for what an ideal rhetoric might be in the context of his philosophy. Two other dialogues of the middle period, the *Symposium* and the

Phaedrus, continue with the project of criticizing contemporary rhetoric, but they also dramatize what Plato envisions as a philosophical rhetoric. The *Symposium* presents a dialogue in which two speakers, Apollodorus and an unnamed individual, discuss a drinking party that took place some years previously. The participants of the party include Socrates and a number of Athens's leading political and intellectual figures: Phaedrus, who would later become a tyrant and is the featured interlocutor of the *Phaedrus*; Pausanias, who is present as the lover of another of the guests, Agathon; the doctor Eryximachus; the comic poet Aristophanes; and the prize-winning tragedian Agathon. The symposiasts decide that the emphasis at the gathering should not be on drink but on discourse. So they give speeches in praise of Eros, and the party becomes a friendly rivalry of *epideixis*, of the rhetoric of praise and blame performed in public scenarios or more intimate gatherings such as the present one. The speakers each rehearse the commonplaces of *epideixis*: they articulate the genealogy of the subject being praised, its education where relevant, its virtues, and its benefits for humankind. Each of the speakers also presents a speech that characterizes who he is, so that Pausanias characterizes an Eros in keeping with his homosexuality, Eryximachus an Eros who bespeaks his medical knowledge, Aristophanes, one which demonstrates aspects of his comic genius, and Agathon, an Eros who typifies his own identity as a delicate sophisticate.

When it comes to Socrates' turn to speak at the drinking party, Plato subverts all the norms of *epideixis* and assimilates this rhetorical form to his larger philosophical goals, using this form of public discourse to communicate his teachings. Plato has Socrates recall a speech on the topic of Eros that he once heard from the prophetess Diotima of Mantinea. A woman, like Aspasia to whom a funeral oration is attributed in the *Menexenus*,[1] undermines the normally all-male scene of rhetoric and is thus Plato's means to redefine and transform conventional rhetoric. According to Diotima, Eros is himself neither good nor ugly but something in between; furthermore, he is also neither a god nor a mortal but something in between, a *daimon*, who mediates between gods and men (202b1–203a8). Being himself neither wise nor entirely ignorant, Eros is indeed like a philosopher because such an individual needs to know that he does not possess knowledge and this piece of knowledge makes possible the pursuit of knowledge; absolute ignorance would enable such an individual to remain ignorant because he does not know he is such (204a1–7).

Socrates' characterization of Eros is significant for understanding philosophical rhetoric. The *daimon* himself bears a notable resemblance to Socrates, the unshod and apparently ugly philospher, who has the capacity to weave verbal spells over his audiences (cf. *Meno* 80a). Diotima concludes her speech on Eros, in effect Plato's redefinition of *epideixis* in the context of his philosophy, with the observation that contemplation of beauty will give birth to many beautiful and magnificent speeches and thoughts through philosophy, which is an activity that proceeds from Desire (210d4–6). The mysteries of Eros—recall that Diotima is a prophetess—entail that one begins by contemplating beauty in one or two individuals, then in all individuals, then in beautiful practices and pursuits, then in beautiful learnings until at last one sees Beauty itself, an abstract, because pure and unmixed, principle (211b7–4). This philosophical discourse on desire and knowledge is the speech that Socrates offers in praise of Eros to subvert current rhetorical practice, to make up for rhetoric's epistemological deficiency.

After Socrates' speech, the general Alcibiades crashes the drinking party, uninvited and in a drunken state, and he offers a further characterization of Socratic-Platonic rhetoric. Alcibiades is an admirer of Socrates, an individual who has been trying to seduce the philosopher and, as such behavior demonstrates, someone who has not progressed very far on the path of philosophy. He offers an encomium to the philosopher, which is nevertheless an encomium of philosophical rhetoric and, because Socrates is like Eros, also an encomium of Eros. According to him, Socrates bewitches his listeners with bare words (215c7). Bewitching is, of course, the effect that the rhetorician has on his listener (de Romilly 4–37); Plato now conceives of Socratic discourse as the ideal, philosophical rhetoric. Alcibiades reveals in addition that he has glimpsed divine, gold statues inside Socrates (216e6–217a2). The simile is important because it makes the point that exteriors—Socrates is ugly—do not always signify the interior and so contradicts rhetoric's emphasis on appearance and mere form at the expense of content and meaning. The speech as a whole makes the overall point that as well as being a representative of the ideal rhetoric, Socrates is also a human counterpart of Eros, for Alcibiades states that conversation with the philosopher is after all like the lover conversing with his beloved in solitude (217b4–5).

Redefining Rhetoric as Philosophy

If the *Symposium* uses the drinking party as a site for the redefinition of rhetoric, the *Phaedrus* is a dialogue that takes place out of the obvious rhetorical scenario. Socrates encounters Phaedrus, who also appeared in the *Symposium*, as he is going on a walk outside the walls of Athens and so away from conventional settings for public speech. The two strike up a conversation and come to rest under a plane tree, where Boreas is said to have snatched off Oreithyia (229a7–b6). Socrates initiates the discourse on rhetoric when he imagines that Phaedrus is such an admirer of the orator Lysias that he repeatedly listens to the latter's speech—one in which a nonlover urges a younger partner to gratify him (cf. 230e6–234c6), and furthermore, that he borrows the book in which this speech was written so that he can study and memorize it from morning until evening (228a5–c5). Socrates urges Phaedrus to perform the speech, an example of protreptic rhetoric, so that he may criticize conventional rhetorical pedagogy, which has pupils imitate and memorize discourses so that they speak the words of someone else rather than their own words. But the philosopher also specifically rejects rhetoric as speech writing, which the Lysianic speech, handled and revered as a static object by Phaedrus, exemplifies, making an objection that Jacques Derrida has seen to be the grounds for a most disturbing paradox, namely a critique of writing as a medium of philosophical inquiry in a written text (see especially the myth of Theuth, where writing is presented as a drug for forgetting [274c5–275b2]).

To accept Derrida's reading, I would suggest, is to fail to notice that Plato offers a philosophical rhetoric, represented by Socrates' second speech, intended as a palinode or refutation of the Lysianic *Eroticus*, commonly known as the "central myth." Here Plato radically redefines conventional rhetoric, showing that textual order is something other than a formal arrangement of a "plot," for the central myth starts from a beginning, here the topic of the soul, specifically termed the *archē*. The soul is the first principle (*archē*) of all living beings and the origin of motion in itself and in other beings (cf. 245c10, 245d7; *Republic* 511b6–7). It is immortal and dwells in the celestial heaven. The myth explains the relationship of the soul to the living being or *zōion*, picking up the idea that the well-formed speech should be like a living being. Living beings are terrestrial bodies with souls that have fallen to the earth (246c4). What causes the soul to plummet to the ground is psychological disorder and lack of contact with reality, namely what is divinely beautiful (*kalon*), wise (*sophon*), and good (*agathon*) (246e1), which nourishes the soul's wings (246e1–2; 247c6ff.).

What constitutes philosophical rhetoric, furthermore, is the relation of the *archē* to reality. According to Socrates, the soul is like a chariot team composed of one good and obedient horse and one bad and unruly one. The chariot is driven by a charioteer around the heavenly vault (246a6–b1). The charioteer and his team try to follow the gods, who are arranged and arrayed in eleven companies with Zeus at the head (247a1–4). Those which most closely follow the gods (248a1–2) are able to participate in the banquet of reality to some degree. The souls affected by disorder travel in the lower region of the heavenly sphere and depart from the vault with only the "food of appearance" (248a4–b6). Deprived of proper nourishment, the wings of these souls waste away and the souls themselves descend to the earth where they take on a body. The fallen soul with the greatest knowledge of reality is planted in a lover of wisdom, beauty, or the Muses (248d2–4); that with the second least amount of knowledge becomes a Sophist or demagogue; and that with the least experience of truth becomes a tyrant (248e3); while that without any knowledge of reality ends up as a brute animal, perhaps a wild beast.

After addressing the myth of Eros, the *Phaedrus* patently turns to rhetorical concerns. Socrates observes that the rhetorician is obliged to appeal to the false, deceptive images that he and the audience commonly believe to be true, appealing to *doxa* or opinion (259c7–260a4). For instance, an orator who wishes to praise a horse may mistakenly produce an encomium on a donkey, being led astray and leading astray by the similarity between these creatures, that is, their large ears (262a6, a10, b3, b6). Furthermore, speaking and writing badly is shameful (258d5–6), as is the Lysianic *Eroticus* because it has no real order; words and lines are thrown together randomly (264b3–11). According to the philosopher, a speech must observe a "logographic necessity" (*anagkē logographikē*) so that its beginning (head), middle (body), and end (feet) are suited and resemble a living being (*zōion*) (264c2–5).[2] The Lysianic *Eroticus* starts not from its beginning (*ap' archēs*) but from its end, swimming upon its "back" (264a5–6). Order determines that a speech must be like a living being, but not in the sense that rhetoric normally is. The *zōion* metaphor significantly recurs at 275d4–e4, where the philosopher draws an analogy between the drawing or painting of living creatures (*zōgraphia*) and written discourse. Pictorial representations—drawing or writing—appears to be the very live animal itself but it is nonetheless a bad imitation because it cannot answer when questioned and says the same thing to anyone it address. As such, writing resembles children who require the aid of their father, namely the author (275a4–6).

The central myth foregrounds the soul for rhetoric, and later, at 271d1–3, Socrates sets out what seems to be a second rhetorical necessity when he declares that a speech maker needs to learn the different kinds and numbers of souls and speeches. He elaborates this psychological "necessity" at 277b5ff. In the latter passage, the philosopher explains that the speech maker must understand the various types of souls and speeches so that he can apply like speeches to like souls: he is to achieve a symmetry of speech to soul—complex to complex, simple to simple, and so on. Socrates assumes a methodology for determining the different types of souls and speeches, and the methodology that he assumes is the process he names "division and collection" (266b4). Socrates speaks of "arranging" and "ordering" a speech by fitting it to an appropriate soul (277c1–2). Because the speech maker's knowledge of souls informs both the content and form of his oration, his speech is "ensouled" (cf. *logon . . . empsuchon*, 276a8–9). The speech maker composes such a work to the extent that he can, for Socrates admits that it is beyond human means to give a complete account of the soul (246a4–6). The "texts" produced by the new rhetoric are its author's legitimate sons (278a6), and they in turn father "texts" in the souls of others, producing their own offspring and foster brothers (278b1).[3]

Platonic rhetoric is characterized as a *psuchagōgia* (261a8; 271c10), as a driving of the soul toward knowledge of reality. If the Platonic art of speech is to differentiate itself from conventional civic rhetoric and to satisfy the requirement that it be concerned with the soul, it has to represent its audience's soul by reflecting an awareness and responsiveness of it in its topics and arguments. What this means is that the speech maker is to be engaged in producing an *ad hominem* or, more accurately, an *ad animam* rhetoric (*pace* Kennedy 79). Philosophical rhetoric will no longer be the discourse of the public sphere, but rather, ideally, a Platonic dialogue that takes place between two interlocutors, for the speechwriter can now address only one soul at any time, ideally only the soul suited to philosophy, for at 276e6–7 Socrates says that the speech maker should plant and sow speeches with knowledge in a suitable soul. This is the realization that shows the philosopher to be someone who seeks the radical remaking of rhetoric in the classical world, rather than its abolition, and so Thomas Cole is quite correct to declare, "the *Phaedrus* is the most striking testimony to the breadth of the gap separating [Platonic] rhetoric from its antecedents" (153).

NOTES

1. See McClure on the assimilation of rhetoric to the female in the *Menexenus*.

2. Aristotle picks up Plato's metaphor for literary unity in his discussion of the structure of a tragic plot in the *Poetics*. According to Aristotle, the plot of a tragedy needs to have a beginning, middle, and end (1450b26–27)—Plato's head, middle and feet—so as to be like a living creature, again ζῷον (1450b34). While this passage of the *Poetics* offers a gloss that may seem to clarify the meaning of Plato's metaphor, it should not be permitted to constrain and limit the significances of the Platonic text.

3. For πατὴρ τοῦ λόγου used with reference to Lysias, see 257b2, and with reference to Phaedrus, see *Symposium* 177d5.

BIBLIOGRAPHY

Primary Sources and Translations

Plato. *Plantonis Opera*. 5 vols. Ed. John Burnet. Oxford: Oxford UP, 1900–01.
———. *Symposium*. Ed. K. J. Dover. Cambridge: Cambridge UP, 1980.

Biographical Sources

Annas, J. "Plato." *Greek Thought: A Guide to Classical Knowledge*. Ed. J. Brunschwig, G. E. R. Lloyd, and P. Pelligrin. Cambridge: Belknap, 2000. 672–92.

Critical Sources

Blank, D. "Socratics versus Sophists on Payment for Teaching." *Classical Antiquity* 4 (1985): 2–6.
Cole, Thomas. *The Origins of Rhetoric in Ancient Greece*. Baltimore: Johns Hopkins UP, 1991.
de Romilly, Jacqueline. *Magic and Rhetoric in Ancient Greece*. Cambridge and London: Harvard, UP, 1975.
Derrida, Jacques. "Plato's Pharmacy." *Dissemination*. Trans. Barbara Johnson. Chicago: U of Chicago P, 1981. 63–171.
de Vries, Gerrit Jacob. *A Commentary on the Phaedrus of Plato*. Amsterdam: Hakkert, 1969.
Ferrari, Giovanni. *Listening to the Cicadas: A Study of Plato's Phaedrus*. Cambridge: Cambridge UP, 1987.
Kennedy, George. *The Art of Persuasion in Greece*. London: Routledge and Kegan Paul, 1963.
Loraux, Nicole. *The Invention of Athens: The Funeral Oration in the Classical City*. Trans. A. Sheridan. Cambridge: Harvard UP, 1986.
McClure, Laura. "Introduction." *Making Silence Speak: Women's Voices in Greek Literature and Society*. Ed. André Lardinois and Laura McClure. Princeton: Princeton UP, 2001.
Neel, Jasper. *Plato, Derrida, and Writing*. Carbondale: Southern Illinois UP, 1988.
Nightingale, Andrea. *Genres in Dialogue: Plato and the Construct of Philosophy*. Cambridge: Cambridge UP, 1995.
Vickers, Brian. *In Defence of Rhetoric*. Oxford: Oxford UP, 1988.
Whitehead, Alfred North. 1929. *Process and Reality*. New York: Free P, 1978.

PLINY THE YOUNGER

(ca. 61–ca. 112 CE)

Joy Connolly

Born in 62 CE to a wealthy family in Comum, Italy (present-day Como), Gaius Caecilius Secundus traveled to Rome as a youth to study with Nicetes Sacerdos, a Greek rhetorician of the ornate Asianic school, and the Roman teacher Quintilian, holder of the first imperially funded teaching post in rhetoric (q.v.). He took the name Plinius from his maternal uncle, the prolific writer and natural historian known to later ages as Pliny the Elder, whose death in the eruption of Vesuvius the younger Pliny described years later in a famous letter to his close friend, the historian Tacitus (*Epistles* 6.16). Adopted under the terms of his uncle's will, the younger Pliny embarked at the age of eighteen on what was to be a celebrated career in literature, politics, and oratory.

Pliny first achieved prominence in the Roman centumviral court, which settled inheritance and property disputes. After a stint as military tribune in Syria, he climbed the ladder of political offices known as the *cursus honorum*, attaining the praetorship in 93 by permission of the emperor Domitian, who excepted Pliny from the rule mandating an extended time interval between political offices. This mark of favor suggests that Pliny enjoyed cordial relations with the increasingly malevolent emperor, but in fact he remained detached from Domitian's inner circle and even associated with those opposing him. In 93, for example, Pliny prosecuted one Baebius Massa for corruption. Convicted and bankrupt, Massa brought charges against Pliny's fellow prosecutor, a member of a group of Romans sharing an interest in Stoicism who had begun to attract Domitian's suspicions (*Ep.* 3.11). Indignant, Pliny successfully intervened on behalf of his colleague, though the man was executed on other grounds before the year was out (*Ep.* 7.33). Recollections of the terror and oppression of Domitian's reign lent energy and authority to Pliny's famous exhortation of the emperor Trajan in the *Panegyricus*, the speech on which his reputation as an orator is built.

Having weathered Domitian's overthrow, Pliny remained in government service, and in 100 CE the emperor Trajan granted him the suffect consulship, the highest office in Roman imperial government. It was on the occasion of his assumption of office at the new year that Pliny publicly performed the *Panegyricus*. Other civil duties in Rome followed; in 111, Trajan sent him to govern Bithynia (northwest Turkey), a post he held until 113. Throughout these years, following the model of Cicero, Pliny composed eloquent letters to his friends and colleagues, including Trajan, which are collected in ten books, the *Epistles*. He died abroad.

PLINY'S CONTRIBUTIONS TO RHETORIC

It is commonplace even for modern critical histories of Roman literature and culture to echo ancient complaints that Roman rhetoric experienced a fatal decline after the fall of the Republic. The younger Pliny's significance for the history of rhetoric is the corrective he offers to this view. His writing is an important reminder of the platitudinous nature of Roman lamentations of cultural decline, which appear as early as the second century BCE. Writing under the emperors Augustus and Tiberius early in the first century CE, the elder Seneca suggested three causes driving the decline: the enervating effects of imperial luxury, the lack of substantial material or political reward for oratory, and the naturally cyclical nature of human achievement (*Controversiae* 1, preface). Pliny's teacher Quintilian wrote a treatise, now lost, on the causes underlying the corruption of eloquence, and his famous handbook of rhetoric, the *Institutio Oratoria*, suggests that the state of contemporary oratory betokens the general decay of ancestral Roman virtues. The Roman historian Tacitus adopts this approach in his influential *Dialogue on Orators (Dialogus de Oratoribus)*, in which the main character forcefully argues that "great and famous eloquence is the child of license [...] it does not flourish in a peaceful state" (40.2–3). Without the dynamic competition for power fostered under a republican constitution, Tacitus claims, oratory grows artificial, unmanly, prettified, and weak.

Pliny, by contrast, offers a relatively optimistic assessment of oratorical activity in Rome a century after the founding of the Julio-Claudian imperial dynasty. This is not to deny that oratorical activity in Rome assumed a new character in what scholars generally call "the shift from Republic to Empire." Traditional venues for deliberative oratory, the Senate and the public assemblies, radically declined in real significance after the reign of Augustus (27 BCE–14 CE), as the emperors assumed responsibility for decision making at the highest levels. The imperial law courts, the customary site of elite contests for political power and symbolic capital under the Republic, tended to showcase trials involving conspiracy or disloyalty to the emperor. While Pliny recognizes the significant changes in the oratory of his era, his letters reveal a lively scene of forensic and ceremonial (epideictic) speech making, alongside an extrapolitical civic culture based on rhetorical practices of various kinds: declamatory competition inside and outside the rhetorical schools, debates over pedagogical method, and keen appreciation of the relationship between literary genres, especially history, epic poetry, and oratory (*Ep.* 6.11, 7.17, 9.23). The evidence of Pliny's own speeches, too, demands a more sophisticated approach to the nature of Roman rhetoric under autocracy.

Pliny's epistolary style in his *Epistles*—which inspired Montaigne, Walpole, Cowper, and others—is elegant but unaffected, featuring emphatic anaphoras, neologisms, and witty epigrams or *sententiae* (e.g., "many fear gossip, few conscience,"*multi famam, conscientiam pauci verentur, Ep.* 3.20.8). In his letters, the rotund and digressive Ciceronian period is trimmed down to sleek, descriptive, and often entertaining prose. The *Panegyricus* is the only surviving example of Pliny's rhetorical style. Not a reliable representative of the original performance, having been much embellished in later rewritings, the speech for Trajan is considerably more ornate and lofty in tone than the *Epistles*. It does not follow the current oratorical fashions as Pliny himself trenchantly describes them—featuring rhythmic phrasing, musical vocalizing, and extravagant flights of fancy (*Ep.* 1.5, 2.3)—though these criticisms are familiar from Cicero's rhetorical treatises written a century earlier, and are not entirely reliable evaluations of contemporary rhetoric. Nor, however, does the *Panegyricus* slavishly obey Quintilian's conservative advice on panegyric structure. Like Cicero, Pliny viewed the future of Roman oratory with optimism, and as an opportunity for risk taking and innovation (*Ep.* 1.2, 4.16, 9.26). The oratorical battles of the Republic might be a thing of the past, but new arenas for virtuous rhetoric remained open for those who sought them.

In the *Panegyricus*, Pliny pioneered a new development in Roman rhetoric, which was to exert great influence in centuries to come: the didactic speech of praise. It became the benchmark for the pagan and Christian encomiastic orators of later imperial antiquity, eleven of whose speeches survive with Pliny's in the *Panegyrici Veteres*, a codex rediscovered in 1433. The first extant genuine prose panegyric in Latin, the speech draws on several traditions: the Greek encomium (e.g., Isocrates' *Evagoras*); the traditional Roman funeral laudation, dating back to the middle Republic (*laudatio funebris*); Cicero's so-called Caesarian speeches, given before the dictator in 46 and 45 BCE, especially the *Pro Marcello*; the short speeches of thanks given to the emperor by Roman senators taking office (*gratiarum actio*); and the long tradition of poetic encomia in Latin and Greek.

As a window on Roman politics in the early second century, the speech provides a useful study of the ways in which traditional republican virtues could be reconceived in an imperial context. It begins with a powerful appeal to Roman political tradition, a theme elaborated in Pliny's repeated entreaties that Trajan take up a third consulship. That most emperors (notably Domitian) regularly occupied the consulship for several consecutive terms is a fact of early imperial politics that probably appeared with clockwork regularity in the senators' yearly speeches of thanks. But in a twist typical of the oration, Pliny turns what might have remained a mere encomiastic formula into an assertive reiteration of his own and the Senate's traditional authority. He suggests that it is by holding the office of consul that Trajan maintains his supremacy in the empire—a canny argument that seeks to restore the dignity and power of political office to the Roman elite.

Later writers tend to imitate the three strategies from Pliny's speech: his coupling of a claim of sincerity with a strong disavowal of flattery, his assumption of an authoritative didactic voice, and his use of the emperor as a moral exemplar for himself and the audience. The last is Pliny's most important achievement: to combine praise of Trajan with a general exhortation to virtue on a much larger scale. As in the case of the emperor's consulship, Trajan's moral exemplarity is an obvious topic for a panegyrist to address (it is recommended by Cicero and Quintilian), but Pliny transforms his praise of the emperor from a simple "mirror for princes" into a "mirror for all." His speech adroitly blends recognition of Trajan as the ideal emperor into a call for the Senate and the people of Rome to embrace their ancestral virtues of courage and liberty. Pliny's deference to Trajan, to a degree, becomes an affirmation of Pliny's own value as a judge of virtue.

Panegyrics have a long history of mistreatment at the hands of their critics. In the body of the *Panegyricus* and in his *Epistles* (*Ep.* 2.19, 7.17), Pliny himself acknowledges that oratorical acts of praise are easily misinterpreted as false acts of flattery; and the *Panegyricus* is certainly extravagant with praise and pompous verbosity. Late antique writers such as Isidore of Seville attacked panegyric as a pandering genre, morally corrupt and out of keeping with Roman dignity (*Libri Etymologiarum* 6.8.7). Renaissance court writers, however, especially in Italy and England, found in Pliny a useful model of the ideal courtier, who praised the supreme authority of prince or God while asserting his own dignity and learning. Erasmus used Pliny as the model for his *Panegyricus* to Philip of Burgundy (1504); he was one of a series of humanists, poets, and orators who praised and instructed rulers in a Plinian mode to the end of the eighteenth century, including Ermolao Barbaro, Thomas More, and John Dryden. In the early modern period, Thomas Hobbes revived the ancient criticism of panegyric in *Leviathan* that "in Orations of Prayse... the designe is not truth" (I.8.33). Recent studies of the *Panegyricus* have successfully moved beyond Hobbes's blanket dismissal to focus on the intricate ways in which Pliny negotiates and even ironizes the task of praising a prince.

BIBLIOGRAPHY

Primary Sources and Translations

Pliny. *Letters and Panegyricus*. Trans. Betty Radice. 2 vols. Cambridge: Harvard UP, 1969.
——. *Letters I-X*. Ed. R. A. B. Mynors. Oxford: Oxford UP, 1963.
——. *XII Panegyrici Latini*. Ed. R. A. B. Mynors. Oxford: Oxford UP, 1964.

Critical Sources

Bartsch, Shadi. *Actors in the Audience: Theatricality and Doublespeak from Nero to Hadrian*. Cambridge: Harvard UP, 1994.

Braund, Susanna Morton. "Praise and Protreptic in Early Imperial Panegyric: Cicero, Seneca, Pliny." *The Propaganda of Power.* Ed. Mary Whitby. Leiden: Brill, 1998. 53–76.

MacCormack, Sabine. "Latin Prose Panegyrics." *Empire and Aftermath: Silver Latin II.* Ed. T. A. Dorey. London: Routledge and Kegan Paul, 1975. 143–205.

Radice, Betty. "Pliny and the *Panegyricus.*" *Greece and Rome* 15 (1968): 166–74.

PLUTARCH

(ca. 46–ca. 120 CE)

Hans Kellner

The Greek moralist and biographer Plutarch was born about 46 CE in the Boeotian town of Chaeronea during the reign of Claudius. He was educated in Athens in a broad curriculum of humanistic studies. After travel in Greece, Asia Minor, and Egypt, Plutarch returned to Chaeronea to teach and to represent the town before the Roman governor. During official visits to Rome, he met important people and began a lecture tour of Italy, speaking in Greek on philosophical and moral matters. These lectures apparently provided the materials for a series of essays, the *Moralia.* Somewhat later, he undertook a second series of lectures, which made him a celebrated figure in Rome, with the support of a pro-Hellenic series of emperors. About 99 CE, Plutarch returned to Chaeronea, where he served in a number of official posts. For the last two decades of his life, he was the head priest at Delphi, improving the condition of the temple and maintaining the prestige of the oracle. It was during the final period of his life that Plutarch wrote his famous *Parallel Lives of the Noble Greeks and Romans.* He died about 120 CE.

Plutarch had a wide knowledge of Greek philosophy, poetry, and history, as well as considerable knowledge of Latin work, although he was modest on the latter subject. His relation to rhetoric is complex. He wrote little that can be described as directly contributing to the discourse of rhetoric. Historians of ancient rhetoric cite him principally as a source of biographical information about famous rhetors. Yet, using indirect evidence, C. P. Jones has concluded that Plutarch went through a youthful rhetorical phase before his conversion to the philosophy of the Academy and its hostility to sophistics. This phase, during the late reign of Nero, may have taken Plutarch to Smyrna, where the Second Sophistic was in its early stages. Works such as a declamation on the fortune of Rome show Plutarch as a highly trained rhetor, but his Athenian studies with the Egyptian Platonist Ammonius led him in another direction.

The *Parallel Lives* consisted of some fifty-odd biographies, most of which are presented in pairs, a Greek and a Roman, followed by a brief comparison. Of these, twenty-three pairs remain, with eighteen comparisons. There are as well four single lives and traces of twelve missing lives. Thus, Theseus and Romulus, Alcibiades and Coriolanus, Demetrius and Anthony, and Demosthenes and Cicero are paired and compared. (Alexander and Caesar are paired but lack a comparison.) The "Comparison of Demosthenes and Cicero" contrasts these famous speakers by noting the seriousness and lack of embellishment in the ever-anxious Greek, while the cheerful Roman loved to display his learning and develop elaborate jests and paradoxes. Demosthenes, however, was disgraced and banished for bribery, while Cicero's exile was an honorable one, caused by his ridding his country of villains.

Plutarch's *Parallel Lives* was a reconceptualization of the Greek past that placed Athens at the center of Greek history, and endorsed the Virgilian idea that Greece was the teacher of Rome. The *Lives* remove their subjects from any historical background, foreground moral issues at the expense of all others, and equate very different people and historical situations. The comparisons are often built from rhetorical topics, such as factors that show alternately the superiority of Caesar over Alexander and of Alexander over Caesar. The pairing of lives is sometimes peculiar or random, apparently the product of Plutarch's own imagination. Neither the Greek style nor the structure of the biographies can be called outstanding, yet the *Lives*, ostensibly of no direct value to rhetorical theory and frequently critical of rhetorical excess, have contributed to the tradition in at least five ways: (1) the *Lives* have served as a generic model for biography and argumentation; (2) they have provided information about the lives of the great orators of antiquity; (3) they have provided examples of speeches and dialogues; (4) they have provided an encyclopedic catalogue of ethical types; and (5) they have provided raw materials for many different kinds of *topoi* and *exempla*. These factors have led one commentator to call the *Lives* "a huge, hybrid textbook to complement rhetorical training" (Lamberton 145).

In the essays and miscellaneous work called the *Moralia*, Plutarch examines a wide range of topics, some of which deal with oratory, poetics, and education. The "Lives of the Ten Orators" (Antiphon, Andocides, Lysias, Isocrates, Isaeus, Aeschines, Lycurgus, Demosthenes, Hypereides, Deinarchus), long thought to be by Plutarch but probably spurious, relate the largely political involvements of his subjects, occasionally describing their talents. Antiphon, for instance, was clever in invention, attacked his opponent unexpectedly, and argued from both laws and emotions. Demosthenes, we are told, when asked to name the three most important aspects of oratory, replied: "Delivery, delivery, and delivery." The essay "On Listening to Lectures" is addressed to a youth who has studied how to speak, but not how to listen. The goal is to become philosophical, rejecting both sophistry and the mere acquisition of information. Plutarch advises that one listen in silence, avoiding quick criticisms and pleasure at the speaker's weaknesses. One's attention should rather be on oneself and the avoidance of error.

An example of Plutarch's educational writings is his essay "How the Young Should Listen to Poetry." Because of the dangers attributed to poetry, youths must be trained to resist what is bad and develop in themselves the hermeneutic abilities that poetry can foster. Poets lie and use figurative language to mislead and seduce the listener. Consequently, the youth must be trained in aesthetic judgment: to judge a work not on its imitation of reality but on its qualities as art. Symbols of the divine are open to multiple interpretations because they can reveal only fragments of ultimate truth. He rejects far-fetched allegories and licentious verse. The dangers of poetry can be overcome if the listener resists treating the poets as lawgivers, but rather sees them as figures to be questioned and rationally examined.

Although a Greek, Plutarch was a Roman citizen and spent his life in the culture of the early Roman Empire. Twelve years younger than Quintilian and eight years older than Tacitus, he benefited from the high respect afforded to Greek language and culture. Through his *Parallel Lives*, he educated the Roman world about Greek culture. In doing so, he became one of the most influential writers of antiquity. Shakespeare drew plot and speeches for his Roman plays from Plutarch; even the monster in Mary Shelley's *Frankenstein* learned about human greatness from reading Plutarch's *Lives*. In both his miscellaneous essays (the *Moralia*) and his *Lives*, Plutarch cared most about moral instruction; his works are not always reliable historical records. Character, rather than politics, was his theme, as he himself recognized. This is, perhaps, the reason for the enduring popularity of the work.

BIBLIOGRAPHY

Primary Sources and Translations

Plutarch. *The Lives of the Noble Greeks and Romans*. Trans. John Dryden. Rev. Arthur Hugh Clough. New York: Modern Library, 2001.
———. *Plutarch's Moralia*. Loeb Classical Library. Cambridge: Harvard UP, 1927.

Biographical Sources

Barrow, R. H. *Plutarch and His Times*. Bloomington: Indiana UP, 1967.
Gianakaris, C. J. *Plutarch*. New York: Twayne, 1970.
Jones, C. P. *Plutarch and Rome*. Oxford: Clarendon, 1971.
Lamberton, Robert. *Plutarch*. New Haven: Yale UP, 2001.

Critical Sources

Scardigli, Barbara, ed. *Essays on Plutarch's Lives*. Oxford: Clarendon, 1995.

MARCUS ANTONIUS POLEMO

(ca. 88–144 CE)

Grant M. Boswell

Marcus Antonius Polemo was born in Laodicea ca. 88 CE while Laodicea belonged to Phrygia. Thus in Philostratus's *Lives of the Sophists*, Polemo is referred to as the "Phrygian." Polemo has a distinguished pedigree. He was grandson to Polemo II, the last king of Pontus (38–63 CE), whose dynasty was established by the triumvir Mark Antony. Zeno, the famous rhetorician (first century BCE), was the direct ancestor of the Polemo family. During the Empire, Rome pressured the Polemos to abdicate their claim to kingship, and they moved to Smyrna in Laodicea, where Marcus Antonius Polemo was born (Reader 7–8). Polemo had a distinguished career but later in life suffered from crippling arthritis and chose voluntary death over prolonged suffering. About 144 CE at age fifty-six, he was taken to Laodicea where he could be buried at his ancestral home. In the presence of family and friends, he was buried alive while urging those laying the bricks to hurry lest the sun see him reduced to silence. And as the last hole was being closed, he uttered, "Give me a body and I will declaim!" (Philostratus 543–44).

POLEMO'S RHETORICAL PRACTICE

In addition to his lineage, Polemo benefited from an exceptional sophistic heritage. Smyrna was a center of sophistical schools and activity. In Smyrna, Polemo attended the school of the famous Sophist Scopelianus of Clazomenae. Scopelianus was renowned in his day for his eloquence and, according to Philostratus, attracted students from all over Asia Minor, from Achaea and Athens, and from as far away as Assyria and Egypt (518). In Smyrna, Polemo also studied four years with Timocrates of Heraclea, who regarded himself more a philosopher than a Sophist. Nevertheless, Polemo said that Timocrates was the father of his eloquence. Philostratus observes that Timocrates' style was "fluent, vigorous, and ready," and as a result, "Polemo, who loved this headlong style of oratory, valued him so highly" (536). Polemo also went to Bithynia to study with Dio Chrysostom.

In his twenties, Polemo became an independent Sophist and was elected as Smyrna's representative to the emperor Trajan, replacing his aging teacher Scopelianus. Polemo considered Demosthenes the model of Greek eloquence and even erected a statue of Demosthenes, claiming that Demosthenes had come to him in his dreams. Polemo said that "the works of prose writers should be brought out by the armfuls, but the works of the poets should be brought out by the wagon loads," implying that for the student of rhetoric the poets were more important for his education than the prose writers (Philostratus 539). There is little evidence, however, that Polemo actually used the writings of poets or prose writers in his teaching or in his declamations. Moreover, Polemo apparently did not require the rhetorical training exercises of his students (progymnasmata). Instead, Polemo seemed to favor a quick wit and practice in declamations (*meletai*) (Reader 10). These declamations would have been assigned both by him and by the audience gathered to hear the students. Polemo undoubtedly provided numerous examples for his students.

Polemo did not write a rhetorical treatise. There survive records of ten of his declamations, all on typically Greek themes. But only two declamations are extant. These two speeches fall under the genre *controversiae*. There were two kinds of declamations: the *suasoriae* and the *controversiae*. *Suasoriae* were advice speeches exhorting a prominent figure from Greek history to take some course of action. Although ceremonial in nature, the *suasoriae* were deliberative in force. The *controversiae* were speeches given on a single issue by two speakers as if they were adversaries in a legal suit. The *controversiae* were considered the more difficult genre of declamations. Polemo's speeches are *controversiae* (Reader 26–30). The theme of Polemo's extant speeches is the Battle of Marathon, at which the Greek hoplites routed a superior force of Persians, sustaining light casualties for themselves while inflicting heavy casualties on the Persians. The setting for Polemo's speeches is the ceremony honoring the dead of the Battle of Marathon, at which the fathers of the fallen soldiers could argue why their sons were to be considered the most valorous of the fallen heroes (Reader 30–40).

Traditionally the speeches on this topic pitted the father of Cynegirus the foot soldier against the father of Callimachus the commander. Cynegirus followed the fleeing Persians to their ships, hewing them down as they fled, and tried to restrain the ships from sailing away with his bare hands. In so doing, he lost his hand (in some accounts both hands), as the Persians, desperately trying to escape the Greek onslaught, hacked it off. Callimachus led his army against the Persians and pursued them as they fled. Callimachus was shot with so many arrows that he would not fall down, and so he fought on, propped up by the many arrows piercing his body. Polemo's rhetorical strategy in these speeches is to offer a barrage of arguments on both sides of the issue and to rely on the overwhelming effect of both the many arguments and the vivid descriptions of the heroic deeds.

In form, both speeches reflect a typical structure: exordium, narration, argument, and conclusion. The text of both speeches is of respectable length, about

6,040 words and, for the modern reader's comparison, is longer than Hebrews (4,942 words), but shorter than 1 Corinthians (6,807 words). The first speech arguing the case for Cynegirus is shorter than the one for Callimachas, and as a result, contrary to custom, both speeches were probably given on the same day. Polemo's style reflects many features of classical Greek, and it falls between Atticist and Asianist exemplars. Polemo employs many grammatical and rhetorical figures, but seems to prefer chiasm and pleonasm, although polysyndeton, asyndeton, paronamasia, and parachesis are also common. Although difficult to date with certainty, these speeches can be assumed to represent Polemo's abilities after he had become well known, if not at the height of his reputation (Reader 40–46).

POLEMO'S SOPHISTIC CAREER

Polemo was extremely well known and respected as a Sophist. And to be a Sophist during the period of the Second Sophistic (50–390 CE) meant more than simply being a proficient public speaker. A Sophist was something of an ambassador, an ombudsman, and, if successful, an asset for his city. A well-respected Sophist would attract students from other places. The students and the public performances sponsored by the students and the Sophists were entertainment and a cause for festivals that could be quite lucrative to cities and their merchants. Sophists were often engaged in public works and public interests. For example, Polemo won fame and respect in Smyrna for resolving long-standing disputes between residents of the shore and the hills. He held many public offices. He arbitrated economic disputes, keeping matters within the jurisdiction of the city, and thus kept Roman interference to a minimum. When necessary, as in cases of adultery, murder, or temple desecration, he saw that offenders were handed over to Roman justice. In all, Polemo was known in Smyrna for his "government free from faction" (Philostratus 531). Moreover, Polemo represented Smyrna well on embassies to the emperor. Hadrian had been inclined to favor Ephesus, but after Polemo's embassy, Hadrian was persuaded to favor Smyrna and gave Smyrna ten million drachmae with which Smyrna built a corn market, a splendid gymnasium, and a spectacular temple. On civic matters generally, Polemo gave the city officials wise advice, curing them of "arrogance and every kind of insolence" (Philostratus 531–32).

On several occasions, Polemo represented Smyrna to the emperor on matters of legal, economic, and political significance. His first embassy was to the emperor Trajan (113 CE), after which Hadrian bestowed on Polemo the right of *libera legatio*, or the privilege of traveling throughout the empire on land or sea with all expenses paid. Polemo took great advantage of this right and always traveled in style, for which he was both criticized by some for his lavish tastes and defended by others for the great stature and the prestige he brought to Smyrna. Later Hadrian extended this same privilege to all of Polemo's descendants, and when some residents of Smyrna complained to the emperor that Polemo was taking too great advantage of the *libera legatio*, Hadrian defended Polemo in a letter to the city. Polemo also served as ambassador to Hadrian (118, 123–124, 133 CE) and to Antonius Pius (143 CE) (Reader 12). When the temple of Olympian Zeus was finally completed at Athens after hundreds of years of construction, Hadrian invited Polemo to make the oration at the sacrifice consecrating the temple. This invitation gave Polemo pride of place among the Sophists of the day. In his final days, Polemo was again appointed as ambassador to the emperor Antonius Pius to represent Smyrna on behalf of its temples and their rights. Polemo, however, died before he could plead the case to the emperor, and the task was assigned to other advocates. The suit did not go well, and the emperor asked the city officials if Polemo had not been assigned to plead the suit. When they answered that he had, the emperor suggested that perhaps Polemo had written down some notes that could be procured for the occasion. The Smyrna council was unaware of any text Polemo had prepared, so the emperor adjourned the proceedings until they could discover whether Polemo had written a speech. When the council found such a speech and returned with it and read it to the emperor, he decided in favor of Smyrna, and the council went back rejoicing that Polemo had come back to life to help them (Philostratus 539–40).

Polemo was influential in his own time among other Sophists and to later Sophists of the second phase of the Second Sophistic (330–390 CE). Among these latter Sophists on whom Polemo had a great influence was the Christian bishop Gregory of Nazianzus. It was not unusual for Christians to study pagan Sophists at this time (Reuther 20), and Gregory developed a penchant for imitating Polemo's style, a penchant that, according to Jerome, was obvious to anyone who perused Gregory's orations. Polemo's declamations were first published by the famous Estienne Press, along with the declamations of others, in 1567.

BIBLIOGRAPHY

Primary Sources and Translations

Polemo, Marcus Antonius. *Polemonos Imeriou, kai allon tinon meletai: Polemonis, Himerii, and aliorum quorundam declamationes, nunc primum editae.* Geneva, 1567.

Reader, William W. *The Severed Hand and the Upright Corpse: The Declamations of Marcus Antonius Polemo.* Atlanta, GA: Scholars P, 1996.

Critical Sources

Bowersock, G. W. *Greek Sophists in the Roman Empire.* Oxford: Clarendon, 1969.

Gleason, Maud W. *Making Men: Sophists and Self-Presentation in Ancient Rome.* Princeton: Princeton UP, 1995.

Juttner, Hugo. *De polemonis Rhetoris vita operibus arte.* Hildesheim: Georg Olms Verlagsbuch-
    handlung, 1967.
Philostratus. *Lives of the Sophists.* Trans. W. C. Wright. Loeb Classical Library. Cambridge:
    Harvard UP, 1968.
Reuther, Rosemary Radford. *Gregory of Nazianzus: Rhetor and Philosopher.* Oxford: Clarendon,
    1969.

Prodicus of Ceos

(fifth century BCE)

Neil O'Sullivan

Prodicus was born in Ioulis, on the Cycladic island of Ceos (A1 Diels and Kranz). Although he is described as a contemporary of Democritus and Gorgias, and a pupil of Protagoras, we have no firmly datable events in his life; for what it is worth, he appears as a prominent participant in Plato's *Protagoras*, a report of a (perhaps imaginary) conversation set in Athens around 433 BCE; but the anachronisms of Plato's dialogues attracted comment already in the ancient world. That dialogue also seems to be the source of various reports of his exceptionally deep voice and his ill health, which was apparently not due to his age at the time (A2; cf. A1a; Plutarch, *Moralia* 791e). Prodicus, like other Sophists, used his talents to represent his homeland on diplomatic missions on a number of occasions (A1a, A3), but according to the hostile tradition (traceable back to Plato and Xenophon) he was able to combine this with his main interest of traveling around and making money through teaching (A1a, A3, A4, A4a). This interest seems further attested in the careful demarcation between his "50 drachma" and "1 drachma" lectures (A11), although he was not above including some elements of the former in the cheaper course to gain the audience's attention (A12). Ancient testimony suggests that, like other Sophists, he spent much of his time in Athens, the financial and political power of which ensured its position as the leading intellectual city in the fifth-century Greek world. Active rivalry with other Sophists in this environment is to have been expected and is attested between Prodicus and Gorgias (A20; cf. Gorgias A24). It is reported that his pupils included the historian Xenophon (A1a), the politician Theramenes (A6), the playwright Euripides (A8), and the orator Isocrates (A7); his influence on the historian Thucydides was also detected (A9). Even Plato's Socrates refers—how ironically is not clear—to attending his lectures (A11) and to sending on unpromising pupils to him (A3a). Like other teachers of the time—including, of course, Socrates himself—Prodicus was accused of corrupting his students (A4b, A5); indeed, one ancient source confuses his fate with Socrates' and reports that he was executed by hemlock in Athens for corrupting the youth (A1). The date and real cause of his death remain unknown.

WRITINGS

The earliest references to Prodicus, from Aristophanes' comedies, suggest a strong interest in natural science, especially in the heavens and the origins of the universe (references in A5); a fragmentary reference, virtually comparing him to a book, may indicate that he was known for his reading or writing of books at a time when this was unusual. Indeed, Gorgias's criticism of him (see above) does seem to be based on his devotion to the written word in preference to the extemporaneous speech that was the other's hallmark. Devotion to natural science is also indicated by a work, *On Nature*, which, it seems, was chiefly concerned with the nature of man (B4 Diels and Kranz), although, as we will see, its one surviving fragment indicates what for us would be a philological rather than physiological concern.

The only other work of his we know was the *Seasons* (*Hōrai*) (B1–2), although the title may not have been Prodicus's own. There has been much speculation about its contents, but we know only that the famous myth of the Choice of Hercules belonged to it. The story is related at length by Xenophon (*Memorabilia* 2.1.21–34 = B2); in terms of content (although not the style, which Xenophon indicates that he has not preserved), it represents one of the largest surviving pieces of the thought of the First Sophistic. In brief, the myth runs like this: Hercules as a young man sits hesitating at a fork in the road of his life's journey, and is approached by two women. The first to address him is brazen and immodestly dressed, and promises him a life full of pleasure; at this point Hercules asks the woman her name (*onoma*), to which she replies that her friends call her Happiness and her enemies call her Vice. Then the second woman (who is not named but who is obviously Virtue) refutes her claims and makes clear to Hercules that the world is so arranged that everything truly desirable can only be obtained through hard work. The paraphrase from Xenophon ends at this point, but another report of the piece (B1) indicates that Hercules chooses the path of Virtue, as we would indeed expect from our knowledge of the career of Greece's greatest hero.

Prodicus's decision to write such a self-conscious allegory of education has many points of interest, not least in the light of his theory of the development of religion. According to our reports (B5), he claimed that "things nourishing and benefiting us were first considered gods and honoured as such, and after these the discoverers of food and shelter and other practical arts, such as Demeter and Dionysus." The allegory with its personification of Virtue may be seen an example of this theory in action, as something that helps human life becomes mythologized. The view described in the second stage ("and after these") is known as euhemerism, after the Hellenistic writer who maintained that the traditional gods were only humans whose memories had been immortalized because of the benefits they had procured for mortals; but (and it must be admitted that the reliability of our source has been questioned) here we seem to have Prodicus maintaining the same position, more than a century before Euhemerus. Indeed, Prodicus may well have had reasons based on his linguistic doctrines for supporting this theory (see further below).

Of various pieces attributed to Prodicus by ancient sources but doubted by modern scholars, perhaps the most interesting and least dubious is the speech enumerating the evils of life reported from him in the pseudo-Platonic *Axiochus* (A9 contains the introduction, but not the full text).

RHETORICAL DOCTRINES

A topic of some controversy among ancient scholars was whether Prodicus should be classified as a philosopher or a rhetorician: Callimachus, who compiled the catalogue of the great library at Alexandria, regarded him as the latter, but others disagreed (A10); perhaps the whole question is anachronistic for the time in which Prodicus lived, and the linguistic underpinning of his "philosophical" ideas demonstrates how thoroughly fused the two categories were in the pre-Platonic Greek world.

In numerous passages (collected in A13–18), Plato refers to and gives examples of Prodicus's habit of distinguishing apparent synonyms. In *Protagoras* 337a–c, for instance, he is shown as distinguishing in rapid sequence *koinos* ("impartial") from *isos* ("equal"), *amphisbētein* ("dispute") from *erizein* ("quarrel"), *eudokimein* ("be esteemed") from *epaineisthai* ("be praised"), and finally *euphrainesthai* ("be pleased") from *hēdesthai* ("take pleasure"). This careful distinction was called by Prodicus *orthotēs onomatōn*, "correctness of words" (A16), and it is also attributed to him by authors who seem to have further knowledge independent of the Platonic evidence (A19, B4). It seems clear that most of Prodicus's distinctions were not based on normal usage (A15), but rather on an a priori conviction that different words must of necessity convey different ideas. Not surprisingly, Aristotle accused him of confusing words with things (A19).

At the same time, there is evidence that Prodicus's distinctions were not simply arbitrary. The medical writer Galen (B4) reports from *On Nature* that what we normally call "phlegm" was called *blenna* by Prodicus, because etymologically *phlegma* should be related to *phlegō*, "burn," and phlegm, being cold and wet, is nothing like something burned. A scholion on *Iliad* 16.594 also indicates that he assumed an etymological basis for a name, and his euhemeristic doctrine on the origins of religion outlined above would also seem to be based on observed linguistic change: in this case, the metonymic use of divinities' names for objects (e.g., "Hephaestus" for "fire") found in old poets seems to have suggested to him that these names were originally the common nouns denoting things. By a process very similar to that of the "disease of language" imagined by nineteenth-century scholars of mythology like Max Müller, these common nouns became imaginary proper nouns. Finally, the explicit concern which his Choice of Hercules has with names (Greek *onoma*, "word [esp. noun]" as well as "name") would seem to be an expression of the emphasis he placed on the correct naming of things for one's preparation for life; it can be no coincidence that it is the personification of Vice who claims that (contrary to true linguistic doctrine) she has two names. In short, then, it is possible that there was greater depth to his linguistic ideas than would appear from the generally dismissive attitude of Plato.

The fairly austere figure who emerges from this outline of his linguistic interest seems to be at odds with another report of his rhetorical studies, namely that he was among the first to discuss emotions in a rhetorical context (A10). The report is vague, however, and it may be that even here the analysis was essentially based on definitions; indeed, it may even have included the fragment which tells us that "desire (*epithumia*) doubled is love (*erōs*), and love doubled is madness (*mania*)" (B7).

INFLUENCE AND IMPORTANCE

The ancient reports, mentioned above, of Prodicus's pupils are, in all likelihood, based on merely the influences perceived by ancient readers, and do not establish personal contact. But even in this light the list is impressive, and it cannot be doubted that Prodicus's instruction must have had considerable impact for him to have been able to make a career as an expensive peripatetic teacher. Modern research has in fact independently shown how widespread was Prodicus's influence on the literature of the fifth and fourth centuries. The first known attempt to give precise definitions to words is certainly worthy of admiration, however much it may have seemed overdone to later generations. Even on the very limited evidence we have, it would seem that Plato did Prodicus less than justice—similarities have been shown between Prodicean doctrine and the concern for definition which the Platonic Socrates exhibits (see esp. Guthrie 222–23, 275–76)—and the pioneer's work is explicitly linked to the linguistic ideas of the later Stoics in one ancient testimony (A19).

BIBLIOGRAPHY

Primary Sources and Translations

Diels, H., and Kranz, W., eds. *Die Fragmente der Vorsokratiker.* 6th ed. Berlin: Weidmann, 1951–52.
Radermacher, L., ed. *Artium scriptores (Reste der voraristotelischen Rhetorik).* Wien: Rudolf M. Rohrer, 1951.
Sprague, R. K., ed. *The Older Sophists.* Columbia: U of South Carolina P, 1972.

Critical Sources

Guthrie, W. K. C. *A History of Greek Philosophy*. Vol. 3. Cambridge: Cambridge UP, 1969. 274–80.

Kuntz, M. "The Prodikean 'Choice of Herakles.' A Reshaping of Myth." *Classical Journal* 89 (1994): 163–81.

Mayer, H. "Prodikos von Keos und die Anfänge der Synonymik bei den Griechen." Diss., München, 1913.

PROGYMNASMATA

(first–fifth centuries CE)

Christy Desmet

The Greco-Roman progymnasmata are graduated exercises in speaking and writing designed for boys before they take up the formal study of rhetoric. Most writers distinguish the progymnasmata from the declamations in terms of length and complexity; they distinguish the progymnasmata from hypotheses—orations in real courtroom or political contexts—by the fact that progymnasmata deal more generally with issues while hypotheses must adapt themselves to the circumstances of particular cases.

While the term "progymnasmata" appears first in the sophistic *Rhetoric for Alexander* (fourth century BCE), the pedagogical treatises we have appear relatively late in Greco-Roman culture. The earliest is attributed to Aelius Theon (first century CE), usually identified as a Sophist schoolmaster from Alexandria. A second, attributed to Hermogenes of Tarsus (who may or may not be the author), appeared in the second century CE. Both of these writers are credited, as well, with other rhetorical treatises. Nicolaus, a Byzantine Sophist influenced by Neoplatonism (fifth century CE), is the author of another Greek set of progymnasmata that is known only from a fifteenth-century manuscript in the British Museum. It was Aphthonius, a teacher of rhetoric in Antioch (fifth century CE), who produced the most complete and detailed set of exercises. Aphthonius probably studied with the Sophist Libanius in Antioch, and the Byzantine encyclopedia Suda reports that he wrote a commentary on Hermogenes, now lost. Aphthonius's *Progymnasmata* survive in Greek manuscripts of Hermogenes, sometimes with scholia or marginalia; the most important commentary on Aphthonius's *Progymnasmata* is by John of Sardis (ninth century CE). Aphthonius added only one exercise to Hermogenes' list of twelve, but offered a model oration to exemplify each type. His definitions and ordering of the exercises set the standard for late antiquity and after.

In Europe during the Middle Ages and Renaissance, both Hermogenes and Aphthonius were known and used through Greek editions, Latin translations, and finally through a few English adaptations. The grammarian Priscian of Caesarea, teaching in Constantinople around 515 CE, translated Hermogenes' *Progymnasmata* into Latin as the *Praeexercitamentis*. Aphthonius's *Progymnasmata* were made available in Latin first by Johannes Maria Catanaeus (1507) and then by Reinhard Lorich (1542), who added scholia, model themes, and quotations derived primarily from Hermogenes (via Priscian) and Quintilian.

Aphthonius remained popular in Europe, judging from the number of versions published, until around 1650. William Shakespeare and John Milton were trained in the progymnasmata, and the mature poetry and prose of both show evidence of their facility with these exercises. In seventeenth-century America, the progymnasmata were assigned at Harvard College. Either because of the rise of the "plain style" associated with John Locke, the Royal Society, and the Enlightenment or because of the decline of Latin language education, or both, the use of the progymnasmata both in the schools and in literary production came to an end after 1650 (Clark, "Rise and Fall" 263). Recently, a small but growing population in the rhetoric and composition community has reintroduced the progymnasmata as staged and sequenced heuristics to help student writers with invention and arrangement. In the United States, the progymnasmata have also been revived as part of the classical, Christian classical education, and home schooling movements.

PEDAGOGY: FROM INVENTION TO DELIVERY

In the classical period, the progymnasmata provided young speakers with prompts for invention, arranged in order of increasing difficulty from narration to argumentation; each exercise built on knowledge from previous ones, but added something new. The progymnasmata also provided civic, or ethical, training to young orators. Theon suggests, perhaps optimistically, that the exercises will promote not only facility in speaking, but also "honest morals" through exposure to the sayings of wise men. Because they are oriented toward the past, the progymnasmata tended to be culturally conservative rather than progressive. Yet the exercises also encouraged the practice of refutation and suggested, in the manner of the Sophists, that equal arguments can be made on both sides of any issue. Finally, the progymnasmata served to train boys in both oratory and written prose composition.

The earliest treatise, Theon's *Exercises* (first century CE), includes valuable information about pedagogy. In Theon's system, students should read aloud, listen to the teacher read and comment on texts, and then paraphrase those texts; original composition and argument from opposing sides come later (Kennedy, *Greek Rhetoric* 57). Paraphrase can work by rearrangement, addition, substitution, and subtraction—on the level of the word, of grammatical forms, and even of narrative elements. Theon's practice is humane: he advises that in the early stages, teachers should not correct all mistakes, just the most conspicuous ones, so that the students will not "be discouraged and lose hope about future progress" (Kennedy, *Progymnasmata* 14). At the same time, the teacher and exemplary authors that the students studied functioned as intellectual and moral role models.

Not all student rhetors achieved the oratorical heights imagined by Theon's *Exercises* or demonstrated in Aphthonius's model speeches. Examining student narratives on papyrus, Teresa Morgan found that most condensed rather than elaborated on their models, were simple in substance and diction, and showed little attempt to imitate literary sources. Morgan concludes that most students were destined not to produce persuasive rhetoric in the public sphere, but to be good bureaucrats (225 and passim). Such evidence notwithstanding, this same educational system produced both Cicero and Shakespeare, *The Aeneid* and *Paradise Lost.*

THE EXERCISES AND THEIR SEQUENCE

Since the form and sequence of the progymnasmata are set early on and show little variation over time, I shall describe the most popular and durable version, that of Aphthonius. An anonymous "Prolegomenon" to Aphthonius's *Progymnasmata* indicates that different exercises prepare students for the different branches of Ciceronian oratory and offer them an opportunity to practice all three levels of Ciceronian style (Kennedy, *Progymnasmata* 94–95). Finally, performing the exercises aloud helps the student learn to speak properly and to use gestures effectively (Clark, *Rhetoric* 110). Thus, the progymnasmata provide young students with the "building blocks" necessary for further rhetorical training.

First and simplest among the progymnasmata is the fable (*mythos*), a fictitious tale that teaches moral lessons by attributing human thoughts, ethics, and emotions to animals and inanimate objects. Aphthonius recommends the Fables of Aesop— short, monitory stories such as the ant and the grasshopper—as models. Aphthonius also subdivides fables into two groups: those that feature humans and those that feature talking animals. Sharon Crowley and Debra Hawhee remark that contemporary comic strips qualify as fables of both kinds (322).

The second exercise is the narrative or tale (*diēgēma*), whose subject matter comes primarily from poetry and history. Narratives can be descriptive, dramatic, or mixed, and in general answer the newspaper writer's basic questions of who, what, when, where, how, and why. The example that Aphthonius gives is mythological, concerning how the white rose became red. When Adonis, the beloved of Venus, insisted on hunting the boar and was gored to death, Venus rushed to his aid; she stepped on the rosebush's thorns and her blood colored the flower red, commemorating Venus's sorrow at the loss of her beloved (Kennedy, *Progymnasmata* 97). Both Ovid (in the *Metamorphoses*) and Shakespeare (in his long poem *Venus and Adonis*) composed more elaborate and sophisticated verse forms of this progymnasma. In *Hamlet*, to give a second Shakespearean example, the ghost of the prince's father relates succinctly, under time pressure, the story of his death by poisoning at the hands of his brother Claudius.

The *chreia* or anecdote, "a brief recollection, referring to some person in a pointed way" (Kennedy, *Progymnasmata* 97), combines the method of narrative with the fable's moralizing framework. Young speakers or writers could begin with either a famous event or a saying; alternatively, they could produce a "mixed *chreia*" that addresses both words and deeds of a famous person. Aphthonius's example of a *chreia* based on action, which is much cited in other textbooks, describes an imaginary scene in which Diogenes, seeing an ill-behaved young boy, beat not the child but his schoolmaster. His example of a verbal *chreia* addresses Isocrates' saying that "the root of education is bitter, but the fruits are sweet" (Kennedy, *Progymnasmata* 98–99).

At this point in the curriculum, students begin to amplify their material within a more complex arrangement. Aphthonius describes the set pattern for a *chreia*, dividing the exercise according to the following headings: To use the example of the proverb "the roots of education are bitter, but the fruits are sweet," the speech begins with praise for the speaker (Isocrates); paraphrase of the saying or deed; discussion of causes of education's "bitterness" (students are afraid of teachers); an argument from the contrary (students who flee education never learn to speak fluently, a second bitter occurrence); comparison (educational toil is like sowing seeds and then reaping the fruits of labor); example (Demosthenes, the most glorious of orators, also worked the hardest); testimony of the ancients (in this case, Hesiod on the roughness of the road to virtue); and an epilogue that praises once again Isocrates' wisdom on the subject of education. Hamlet's dissection of his own inaction in the soliloquy that begins, "O what a rogue and peasant slave am I," can be seen as a *chreia* based on an action rather than a saying.

Aphthonius defines the next exercise, the proverb, maxim, or saying (*gnōmē*), as a "summary statement, in declarative sentences, urging or dissuading something" (Kennedy, *Progymnasmata* 99). The proverb follows the *chreia*, according to Nicolaus's logic, because it is more abstract, offers advice rather than merely analysis, and deals more directly with questions of good and evil (Kennedy, *Progymnasmata* 142–43). In this exercise, the initial saying is explained through paraphrase, analysis of causes, comparisons, testimony from the ancients, examples from classical literature, argument from the contrary, and, at last, a conclusion. John Milton, as a schoolboy, wrote a proverb on the saying "It is most healthy to rise at break of day" (Clark, *John Milton* 235–37) that actually quotes material from Aphthonius's model composition. In *Hamlet*, to return to our principal example, Polonius's litany of proverbial wisdom functions as a mnemonic treasure trove, each piece of which might be developed into a "proverb" by someone with more focus or substance. Claudius's long speech to Hamlet, counseling the prince that "to persevere in obstinate condolement is a course/Of impious stubbornness," is an expanded maxim that explains, albeit disingenuously, why Hamlet should not mourn his dead father beyond the proper time limit.

From this point on in Aphthonius's sequence, the exercises become more complex and the examples more like full-scale declamation. They deal with issues that are credible, rather than those commonly accepted as true or false, and admit argument from both sides of the question. Thus, there is more logic, less exposition. The example of refutation that Aphthonius offers is from Ovid's *Metamorphoses*, a refutation detailing the improbability of the myth of Daphne, who was turned into a laurel tree to protect her from Apollo's romantic advances. Confirmation (*kataskuē*) or "the corroboration of some matter at hand" (Kennedy, *Progymnasmata* 103) works in exactly the opposite way, establishing the credibility, certainty, possibility, and so forth, of an event or action. Aphthonius's example involves defending the credibility of the myth about Daphne.

Next in the sequence of Aphthonius's exercises comes the "common-place" (*koinos topos*), "a speech amplifying evils" (Kennedy, *Progymnasmata* 105), in which the student expands on a moral platitude. The exercise can praise virtue or excoriate vice, but more frequently addresses vice. The common-place also provides a "warm up" for courtroom rhetoric in that it allows student-advocates to proceed to judgment without having to address the facts of the case (Clark, *Rhetoric* 192). Aphthonius offers as an example a common-place against a tyrant. Hamlet himself works out a common-place on the topic "Frailty, thy name is woman," using his mother's remarriage as evidence.

In Aphthonius's chronology, the student then moves into encomium (*enkōmion*) and vituperation (*psogos*), speeches in praise or dispraise of a specific person. For the encomium, students must not only take a strong ethical stand but also marshal details from biography (or, in the absence of such details, probable deeds and actions). The orator should consider the person's national and family origins, education, habits and skills, achievements, spiritual and physical qualities, moral status compared with others around them and in history, and finally end with an epilogue. Aphthonius offers as his example "An Encomium to Wisdom." In *Hamlet*, perhaps not surprisingly, praise is in short supply. The only encomium to be found in that play is a brief one produced by Ophelia after the nunnery scene, when she thinks that Hamlet has lost his wits; in it, a distraught Ophelia details the social markers and inner features of Hamlet's virtue and laments their destruction.

Invective (*psogos*) is the opposite of praise. Aphthonius distinguishes vituperation, which attacks a particular person, from the common-place, which attacks vice more generally and has punishment as its goal (Kennedy, *Progymnasmata* 111). As his example, Aphthonius provides a speech in dispraise of Philip of Macedon. The play *Hamlet*, surprisingly, contains no sustained invective. In the closet scene, Hamlet attempts to influence his mother with a spirited invective against Claudius. But ironically, just as Hamlet begins to excoriate Claudius as "a murderer and a villain," "a cutpurse of the empire and the rule," and a "king of shreds and patches," the ghost himself interrupts the diatribe.

Synkrisis, or the "comparison," compares two entities according to common criteria. Aphthonius describes the exercise as a speech that "doubles" praise and invective or combines them (Kennedy, *Progymnasmata* 113–14). Hermogenes compares Odysseus with Herakles, Aphthonius the war heroes Achilles and Hector (Kennedy, *Progymnasmata* 84, 114–15; Crowley and Hawhee 347–48). Hamlet is less generous; using his mother in her closet as a captive audience, he embarks on a scathing comparison between his dead father (a "Hyperion" or human sun god) and his uncle Claudius (a "satyr").

The *ethopoeia* involves impersonation of a character from history or poetry. Aphthonius uses the term *"ēthos"* as Aristotle did, to mean the character of a speaker as demonstrated through moral choice and words (Kennedy, *Greek Rhetoric* 64). He subdivides the exercise into the categories of *ethopoeia* (description of inner moral character); *prosōpopoeia* (imitation of a real, fictional, or deceased person by word and deed); and *eidolopoeia* (a visual image or spirit of a person). Hermogenes, in a slightly different vein, distinguishes the speeches by subject; in *ethopoeia* we imagine words for a real person, in *prosōpopoeia* a nonexistent person; in *eidolopoeia* we attribute words to the dead. The success of *ethopoeia* in general depends on the fledgling orator's ability to identify with others—that is, to put himself in the "place" of persons, real or imagined, who are remote from him in space and time. He must also, as Quintilian notes, adapt his style to the character he impersonates (Quintilian, *Institutes* 9.1.8–42; Clark, *Rhetoric* 103).

Aphthonius offers as an example "what words Hecuba," the Trojan queen who lost both husband and multiple sons to the Greek invasion, "might say when Troy was destroyed" (Kennedy, *Progymnasmata* 116). Interestingly, the Player's speech, which spurs Hamlet to produce his Mousetrap play and "catch the conscience of" his enemy Claudius, describes a Hecuba in agony whose cries, if the gods could hear her, would make them drop tears like milk. But instead, the gods turn a deaf ear. In *Hamlet*, the empathy that makes possible impersonation is denied to its hero; while a common Player can produce- a successful *ethopoeia*, Hamlet is merely haunted and disabled by the ghost, or *prosōpopoeia*, of his deceased father.

The goal of description (*ekphrasis*) is vividness or *enargeia*—"bringing things clearly before the eyes" of auditors. These descriptions, found frequently in classical and later literature, follow a natural order and are organized by simple criteria such as time or space. Descriptions of persons, for instance, proceed from head to toe, as do the erotic anatomies of English Renaissance love poetry. Shakespeare's most famous *ekphrasis*, which he paraphrases in verse from Plutarch's "Life of Mark Antony," is the extended description of how Cleopatra, seated in her barge in the guise of Isis, both outdid Antony with her grandeur and, at the same time, stole his heart.

Most complex among the progymnasmata is the thesis or argument, which Aphthonius defines rather unhelpfully as "a logical examination of any matter under inspection" (Kennedy, *Progymnasmata* 120). Of all the exercises, the thesis comes closest to our contemporary understanding of argument as a performance that involves both defense of one position and an attack on the opposition. Aphthonius divides the thesis into two types: the theoretical (involving specific fields of knowledge and particularly philosophy) and the political (involving actions, even domestic ones, that can affect the *polis*).

Crowley and Hawhee wrongly identify Hamlet's "To be or not to be" speech, the most rhetorical of all his utterances, as an *ethopoeia*. When considered as an oration rather than as a meditation about suicide, however, the "To be or not to be" speech is a thesis that argues the issue of whether existence ("to be") or nonexistence ("not to be") is preferable. Hamlet also begins, but then abandons, another thesis when, in the nunnery scene that follows, he tells Ophelia, "There will be no more marrying." Although not explicitly, Hamlet alludes to Aphthonius's model thesis, which addresses the question of "whether one should marry." In the speech, Aphthonius argues that marriage does not create widows and orphans when husbands die, but instead, creates new families when the mothers remarry. This is not an argument that Hamlet finds persuasive.

Finally, there is the exercise called the "introduction of a law" (*nomou eisphora*). Because this progymnasma brought the child orator into the judicial realm, Aphthonius assigned it to the rhetorician rather than the grammarian. The "introduction of a law" is a "double exercise" that asks orators to speak both for (*synēgoria*) and against (*katēgoria*) the law. The sample exercise offered by Aphthonius, "A Speech in Opposition to a Law Requiring the Killing of an Adulterer When Taken in the Act," defines precisely Hamlet's situation while denying him a much-desired narrative certainty, since Hamlet cannot establish definitively the fact of his mother's adultery.

CONCLUSION

The larger cultural role played by the progymnasmata has changed over time, even though the exercises themselves have not. Rhetoric, as taught in the Greco-Roman schools, prepared boys for professional careers as advocates, for debate in legislative assemblies, and for public, ceremonial occasions. In the Byzantine period, rhetorical training lost its vocational function as legal power was transferred almost exclusively to the magistrates. But up through the sixteenth century, the progymnasmata prepared boys for public life by teaching logical analysis and verbal polish. At the same time, rhetorical education has always provided a foundation for literature. Without the progymnasmata, there would be no *Aeneid*, no *Paradise Lost*, no sonnets by Shakespeare. Perhaps in a new pedagogy of composition, the progymnasmata can once again stimulate the imagination and technical skill of writers at all levels.

BIBLIOGRAPHY

Primary Sources and Translations

Collections

Hock, Ronald F., and Edward N. O'Neil. *The Chreia in Ancient Rhetoric. Vol. 1: The Progymnasmata*. Atlanta, GA: Scholars P, 1986.
Kennedy, George A., trans. *Progymnasmata: Greek Textbooks of Prose Composition and Rhetoric.* Atlanta: Society of Biblical Literature, 2003.

Murphy, James J. *Renaissance Rhetoric: A Short Title Catalogue of Works on Rhetorical Theory from the Beginning of Printing to A. D. 1700.* New York and London: Garland, 1981.

Aphthonius, Progymnasmata

Aphthonius. *Aphthonii Progymnasta.* Ed. Hugo Rabe. *Rhetores Graeci.* Leipzig: Teubner, 1926. 9:1–51.

————. *Progymnasmata.* Trans. Ray Nadeau. *Speech Monographs* 19 (1952): 264–85. Rpt. in *Readings from Classical Rhetoric.* Ed. Patricia P. Matsen, Phillip Rollinson, and Marion Sousa. Carbondale: Southern Illinois UP, 1990. 267–88.

John of Sardis. *Ioannis Sardiani Commentarium in Aphthoinii Progymnasmata.* Ed. Hugo Rabe. Leipzig: Teubner, 1928.

Rainolde, Richard. *Foundacion of Rhetorike.* 1563: Rpt. with an introduction by Francis R. Johnson. New York: Scholars' Reprints and Facsimiles, 1945.

Hermogenes, Progymnasmata

Baldwin, Charles Sears. "The Elementary Exercises of Hermogenes." *Medieval Rhetoric and Poetic.* New York: Macmillan, 1928. 23–38.

Priscian, *De pre-exercitamentis rhetoricis.* Ed. Heinrich Keil. *Grammatici latini.* Leipzig: Teubner, 1959. 3:430–40.

————. *Fundamentals Adopted from Hermogenes.* Trans. Joseph M. Miller. *Readings in Medieval Rhetoric.* Ed. Joseph M. Miller, Michael H. Prosser, and Thomas W. Benson. Bloomington: Indiana UP, 1973. 52–68.

————. *Rhetores latini minores.* Ed. Carolus Halm. Leipzig, 1863; rpt. Hildesheim, 1981. 551–60.

Nicolaus, Progymnasmata

Felton, Joseph, ed. *Nicolai Progymnasmata.* Leipzig: Teubner, 1913.

Nicolaus. *Progymnasmata.* Trans. Patricia P. Matsen. *Readings from Classical Rhetoric.* Ed. Patricia P. Matsen, Phillip Rollinson, and Marion Sousa. Carbondale: Southern Illinois UP, 1990. 264–65 (Preface only).

Theon, Exercises

Butts, John R. *The "Progymnasmata" of Theon: A New Text with Translation and Commentary.* Diss., Claremont Graduate School, 1986.

Theon, Aelius. *Progymnasmata.* Trans. Patricia P. Matsen. *Readings from Classical Rhetoric.* Ed. Patricia P. Matsen, Phillip Rollinson, and Marion Sousa. Carbondale: Southern Illinois UP, 1990. 253–62.

————. *Progymnasmata.* Ed. Michel Patillon and Giancarlo Bolognesi. Edition Budé. Paris: Les Belles Lettres, 1997.

————. *Progymnasmata.* Ed. Leonard Spengel. *Rhetores Graeci.* Leipzig: Teubner, 1926. 2:59–130.

Biographical Sources

Kennedy, George A., trans. *Progymnasmata: Greek Textbooks of Prose Composition and Rhetoric.*
Atlanta: Society of Biblical Literature, 2003.

Critical Sources

Bonner, Stanley F. *Education in Ancient Rome from the Elder Cato to the Younger Pliny.* Berkeley:
U of California P, 1977. 250–76.

Clark, Donald Lemen. *John Milton at St. Paul's School: A Study of Ancient Rhetoric in English
Renaissance Education.* New York: Columbia UP, 1948. 230–49.

———. "Rhetoric and the Literature of the English Middle Ages." *Quarterly Journal of Speech*
45 (1959): 19–28.

———. *Rhetoric in Greco-Roman Education.* Morningside Heights, NY: Columbia UP, 1957.
177–261.

———. "The Rise and Fall of the Progymnasmata in Sixteenth and Seventeenth Century
Grammar Schools." *Speech Monographs* 19 (1952): 259–63.

Comprone, Joseph J., and Katharine J. Ronald. "Expressive Writing: Exercises in a New
Progymnasmata." *Journal of Teaching Writing* 4.1 (1985): 31–53.

Crowley, Sharon, and Debra Hawhee. *Ancient Rhetorics for Contemporary Students.* 2nd ed.
Boston: Allyn and Bacon, 1999. 320–66.

Hageman, John. "Modern Use of the Progymnasmata in Teaching Rhetorical Invention."
Rhetoric Review 5 (1986): 22–29.

Henderson, Ian H. "Quintilian and the *Progymnasmata.*" *Antike und Abelund* 37 (1991): 82–99.

Johnson, Francis R. "Two Renaissance Textbooks of Rhetoric: Aphthonius' *Progymnasmata*
and Rainolde's *A book called the Foundacion of Rhetorike.*" *Huntington Library Quarterly* 6
(1942–43): 427–44.

Kennedy, George A. *Classical Rhetoric and Its Christian and Secular Tradition from Ancient to Modern
Times.* Chapel Hill: U of North Carolina P, 1980.

———. *Greek Rhetoric under Christian Emperors.* Princeton: Princeton UP, 1983. 54–73.

———. *A New History of Classical Rhetoric.* Princeton: Princeton UP, 1994. 202–08.

Morgan, Teresa. *Literate Education in the Hellenistic and Roman Worlds.* Cambridge: Cambridge
UP, 1998. 198–226.

Murphy, James J. "The Modern Value of Ancient Roman Methods of Teaching Writing, with
Answers to Twelve Current Fallacies." *Writing on the Edge* 1 (1989): 28–37.

———. "Roman Writing Instruction as Described by Quintilian." *A Short History of Writing
Instruction from Ancient Greece to Twentieth-Century America.* Ed. James J. Murphy. Davis,
CA: Hermagoras P, 1990. 53–61.

Prill, Paul E. "Rhetoric and Poetics in the Early Middle Ages." *Rhetorica* 2 (1987): 129–47.

Viljanaa, Toivo. "First Exercises in Composition According to Quintilian, Inst. 1.9." *Arctos*
22 (1988): 179–201.

Protagoras

(490–420 BCE)

Edward Schiappa

Protagoras of Abdera is generally regarded as the first and most famous of the Older Sophists. Only a handful of fragments survive of his writings, though the so-called Great Speech featured in Plato's *Protagoras* is considered by many to be a reasonably faithful recreation of an authentic Protagorean text. His fragments are preserved in several collections (Diels and Kranz; Sprague; Untersteiner) and have been the subject of two books (Loenen; Schiappa) and articles too numerous to list by scholars in philosophy, classics, communication, political science, education, and English.

Little is known of the details of Protagoras's life. We know that he spent time in Athens and apparently was known to Pericles. It is commonly believed, partly based on the Great Speech, that Protagoras provided Pericles with a philosophical rationale for a democratic form of government. Diogenes Laertius claims that Pericles appointed Protagoras to draft the legal code for the important Greek colony of Thurii. Plutarch reports that a young man, Epitimus of Pharsalus, was killed accidentally with a javelin. Pericles and Protagoras supposedly spent an entire day trying to decide whether one should regard the cause of death as the javelin, the man who threw it, or the supervisor in charge of the grounds. Regardless of the veracity of such historical details, there is little doubt that Protagoras was an influential thinker whose human-as-measure tenet was at the heart of what we now consider the sophistic movement. His influence has been claimed to extend to fifth-century playwrights and historians, and his arguments were treated seriously by philosophers of the fifth and fourth centuries BCE.

The Major Fragments of Protagoras

The most famous of Protagoras's sayings is his human-as-measure tenet. Reported to be the opening sentence of a treatise titled *Truth*, the tenet holds that "Of All

Things the Measure is Human(ity): Of that which is, that it is the case, of that which is not, that it is not the case" (Diels and Kranz 80 B1). *Pantōn anthrōpos metron* is often glossed as "Man is the Measure of All Things," where *anthrōpos* can refer either to individuals or to humanity in general. The tenet is typically understood as a response to Parmenides, who claimed that contradictory claims of the form "X is Y" and "X is not-Y" were impossible since a thing ("X") could not both be and not be. As Charles Kahn has argued, the meaning of "to be" (*einai*) in the fifth century was far from clear, and only those we now regard as philosophers ever used a negative construction such as found in Protagoras's saying. For Eleatic philosophers, such as Parmenides and his follower Melissus, the populace believed what is impossible, namely, that the same thing could both be and not be. In Melissus's words, the masses believed that "what is warm becomes cold, and what is cold warm; that what is hard turns soft, and what is soft hard, that what is living dies, and that things are born from what lives not; and that all those things are changed" (Diels and Kranz 30 B8).

In spite of the Eleatics' distrust of the expression "not-be" (*ouk esti*), Protagoras explicitly stated that people determine what is not the case (*hōs ouk estin*) as well as what is the case. The Eleatics had declared that people were "two-headed," allowing that things could both be and not be, and that the senses were not to be trusted since people perceive change and becoming. In contrast, Protagoras openly embraced the evidence of the senses as well as claims involving what is not the case. Although the evidence is indirect, it appears that Protagoras answered the Eleatic challenge with an incipient relativistic notion of frame of reference. To return to the discussion between Pericles and Protagoras about the javelin incident, there can be no single correct response to the question of cause: To a doctor the correct account (*orthos logos*) would be the javelin; to a law court the correct account would be the person who threw the javelin; and to an administrator the correct account would be the supervisor. Each frame of reference could be the measure of what was or was not the case. Similarly, in the dialogues of Plato there are numerous discussions of Protagoras in which different measures (or frames of reference) yield different assessments of what is or is not the case. For example, in Plato's *Theaetetus* (152b), the wind may be cold for one person and not-cold for another. Later in the dialogue, Socrates describes Protagoras's position as follows: "The object, when it becomes sweet or sour and so on, must become so *to someone*: it cannot become sweet and yet sweet to nobody" (160b). Thus, the attributes of things *are* or *are the case* only for those who "measure" them. Thus, while Parmenides sought to deny the reality of contrary attributes, and Plato would later elevate many attributes to Forms with their own independent essences, Protagoras seems to suggest that attributes are directly experienced by humans and "are the case" not in an abstract sense but "are the case" relative to people. The measure of what is or is not the case is not philosophy, as Parmenides suggests, or God, as Plato speculates in the *Theaetetus*, but all human beings. It should be apparent why many consider Protagoras an early example of a secular humanist, and in a contemporary sense can be described as antiessentialist because he appears to deny the value of hypothesizing about "things-in-themselves."

Almost as famous as his human-as-measure tenet is Protagoras's claim that "There are two opposing accounts (*logoi*) concerning everything (*pragmata*)" (Schiappa 100). This slogan has been translated in a variety of ways that can be grouped as the subjective and the Heraclitean interpretations. The subjective interpretation emphasizes the pragmatic notion that opposing arguments or speeches can be given on any topic. This notion survives in such expressions as "there are two sides to every issue" or "something can be said on both sides of every question." Such a sentiment lives on in the practices of contemporary debate pedagogy as well as in the way parliamentary rules guide discussions in venues as diverse as faculty meetings or the deliberations of the U.S. Congress. The Heraclitean interpretation is not necessarily in conflict with the subjective interpretation, but builds upon the idea that Protagoras was extending on Heraclitus's way of describing the world.

A number of pre-Socratics were concerned with opposites, including Anaximander, Anaximenes, Heraclitus, Parmenides, Empedocles, and Melissus. It is not too much of an exaggeration to say that the "problem of opposites" drove a good deal of pre-Socratic philosophy. To these thinkers, the world seemed full of opposites—night and day, life and death, hot and cold, wet and dry, up and down, just and unjust, mortal and immortal, and so forth. Furthermore, the things of the world appear to many to change from one opposite condition to the other. But how is this possible? According to Parmenides and the Eleatics, it was not possible: The appearance of change is an illusion since it allows a thing to both be and not be. Heraclitus, by contrast, embraced opposites, which he claimed exist in a unity. An exemplary fragment reads, "The teacher of most is Hesiod. It is him they know as knowing most, who did not recognize day and night: they are one" (fr. 19, quoted in Kahn, *Art* 37). Aristotle interpreted Heraclitus's unity of opposites thesis in broad terms: "The doctrine of Heraclitus is that all things are and are not" (*Metaphysics* 1012a). And Sextus understood Heraclitus as claiming that the "same thing" is the subject of "opposite realities" (*Outlines of Pyrrhonism* 1.210).

The leap from Heraclitus's unity of opposites thesis to Protagoras's claim that all things (*pragmata*) have two opposing *logoi* about them is not far, especially if we read this Protagorean slogan next to his human-as-measure tenet. To the extent that humans can experience any and all things in a contradictory manner (what is or is not the case), then it would follow that two contrary accounts (*logoi*) are possible about such things. But such a claim is not merely an observation of the human ability to argue about anything, for it is closely linked to an understanding about the way the world is experienced. Protagoras's extension of Heraclitus's thesis is noteworthy as it pushes Heraclitean thought into the direction of linguistic theory and the exploration of the relationship between language and reality.

Perhaps Protagoras's most infamous saying is the promise, reported by Aristotle, "to make the weaker argument stronger" (*Rhetoric* 1402a). No other surviving fragment of Protagoras has suffered more at the hands of translators than this one. For example, Lane Cooper's translation of Aristotle's *Rhetoric* translates the phrase as "making the worse appear the better cause" (177). The Greek here is important: *ton hēttō de logon kreittō poiein.* The word "appear" is not in the Greek, "cause" is a misleading translation of *logos*, there is no definite article before "stronger," and *hēttōn* and *kreittōn* mean "weaker" and "stronger." Cooper is not alone in his rather perverse interpretation, however, as other translators of Aristotle also tend to insert "appear" or "seem" and use "worse" and "better" instead of the more obvious translation of "weaker" and "stronger."

The weaker/stronger fragment can be read as echoing the many Greek writers who understood the idea of change as the shifting or swapping of opposites. Heraclitus, for example, wrote, "cold warms up, warm cools off, moist parches, dry dampens" (quoted in Kahn, *Art* 165). The medical writers of the late fifth century BCE often described opposites as cures for opposites—counteracting cold with hot, moist with dry, and so forth. The notion of change as a swapping of opposite conditions reaches its clearest expression in Aristotle, who describes the process in more abstract terms as a shift from potential to actual, such that both moist and dry are both potential qualities of a thing, but only one can be actualized at a given point in time. Protagoras's weaker/stronger fragment amplifies the meaning of the two opposing *logoi* slogan; not only are there two contrary qualities possible to describe about any thing, but at any given time one is weaker and the other stronger.

A passage in Plato's *Theaetetus* suggests that Protagoras saw the role of *logos* as trying to promote change from a weaker to stronger condition: "To a sick man his food appears sour and is so, to the healthy man it is and appears the opposite. [. . .] What is wanted is a change to the opposite condition, because the other state is better. [. . .] Whereas the physician produces a change by means of drugs, the Sophist does it by discourse (*logoi*)" (166d). The careful reader may realize that *logos* is being described in Protagoras's fragments and subsequent discussions as both a process and an outcome. That is, *logos* is both the means of change and the result of change. This ambiguity is a function of the multivocal character of the Greek word *logos*, which was used to describe language, accounts, and arguments as well as nonlinguistic events and courses of action. So, for example, war and peace are described as competing *logoi* in Euripides' *Suppliants* (486), and Prodicus's "Choice of Heracles" describes two competing *logoi* that are linked to two competing ways of life. This conflation of means and ends is nowhere clearer than in Aristophanes' *Clouds*, which portrays a debate between two personifications of *logoi* named, in Protagorean fashion, "Weaker" and "Stronger." The characters not only give contrasting speeches, they also represent two competing ways of life. The Stronger *logos* represents tradition, religious piety, and respect for elders, while the Weaker *logos* represents what Aristophanes thought were the threats of a sophistic education— a challenge to tradition, agnosticism, and moral nihilism. In the play, the Weaker *logos* "wins" (at least until the Sophists' "Thinkery" is burned down), which may be why some commentators have equated "weaker" with "morally inferior," despite the fact that there is no evidence that Protagoras would have done so.

A curious slogan translated as "[It is] impossible to contradict" (*ouk estin antilegein*) is also attributed to Protagoras (Diels and Kranz 80 A1, A19). Most discussions of this phrase take place in the texts of Plato and Aristotle where they appear to be engaging the uses to which the phrase was put in the fourth, rather than the fifth, century BCE. The idea is simple enough: If two people appear to contradict each other, they must be talking about different things, since the same thing would result in the same, not contradictory, *logoi*. Different *logoi* suggest that different things are being talked about, not that there is a contradiction. Such a position can be reconciled with Protagoras's human-as-measure tenet. The same thing, such as the wind, can be experienced (or "measured") in different ways: as cold or not-cold. To each person experiencing or measuring the wind it may be a different thing—a cold wind or a not-cold wind. Such things-as-experienced do not contradict; they are simply different. Understood thusly, *ouk estin antilegein* can be seen as another facet of Protagoras's response to the Eleatic charge that people are "two-headed." While disagreement in the form "X is Y" and "X is not-Y" was viewed by Parmenides and his followers as a sign of error and confusion, Protagoras saw no contradiction once the idea of a frame of reference was added. After all, there is no contradiction between the propositions "X is Y to A" and "X is not-Y to B."

The last Protagorean fragment to be discussed here is his famous "concerning the gods" statement, which is believed to have been the first sentence of a speech or pamphlet titled *On the Gods*: "Concerning the gods I am unable to know whether they exist or whether they do not exist, or what they are like in form; for there are many hindrances to knowledge, the obscurity of the subject and the brevity of human life" (Schiappa 141). This statement can be viewed as a sort of manifesto for agnosticism and what we would now call secular humanism, and it is part of the reason that authors see Protagoras and other Sophists as precursors to later humanist movements. Protagoras does not claim there are no gods; he simply states the matter is impossible to know. But if the sentence was only the first in a speech or publication titled *On the Gods*, what else might Protagoras have said? Unfortunately, we have no way of knowing. It has been conjectured that Protagoras urged a turn away from theological disputes over the existence and form of the gods and toward what we would call an anthropological investigation of the origins, evolution, and functions of belief in divinity. Such a conjecture gains plausibility from a passage in Plato's *Theaetetus* (162d) where Protagoras takes neither a theistic nor atheistic position by explicitly refusing to discuss the existence or nonexistence of the gods.

There is a tradition in the classical literature that Protagoras was tried and sentenced to death for impiety as a result of his professed agnosticism. In some versions, Protagoras's books were burned and he was executed, while in other accounts, he was simply banished. Such accounts are probably later fabrications, however, since the alleged trial and sentence are never mentioned by any fifth- or fourth-century author, and there is no mention at all of any book burnings of any sort. Given Protagoras's prominence, it is hard to imagine that no author would mention such a fate, particularly if it would add fuel to their criticism of Protagoras and his doctrines. It may be the case that the book-burning story was inspired by the burning of the Thinkery in Aristophanes' *Clouds*, given the play's critique of sophistic, and especially Protagoras's, teaching.

THE GREAT SPEECH OF PROTAGORAS

In the dialogue named after Protagoras, Plato provides a generally positive portrayal of the famous Sophist and treats him with great respect, compared to most of Socrates' interlocutors. Most commentators now agree that the so-called Great Speech presented in the dialogue *Protagoras* (320c–328d) is a reasonably faithful reproduction by Plato of a genuine speech or text by Protagoras, and some have speculated that it may even be inserted into the dialogue intact. Protagoras is asked to defend his thesis that excellence (*aretē*) can be taught. Protagoras agrees, and begins with a story (*mythos*) that can be summarized as follows.

Once there were gods but no mortal creatures. When the time came for the gods to create mortals, Prometheus and Epimetheus were charged with equipping the creatures and giving each suitable power for survival. Different creatures received different skills, sizes, foods, and means of protection from the elements and from each other. However, Epimetheus had overlooked humans, whom Prometheus discovered naked and unready for survival. So from Hephaestus and Athena, Prometheus stole wisdom in the arts together with fire and gave them to humanity. Because humans had received a share of the gods' gifts, they alone of all creatures worshipped the gods. Further, through their skills, humans discovered speech and names and provided themselves with life's necessities.

Nonetheless, humanity was nearly wiped out by wild animals because they lacked the art of politics (*politikē technē*). Zeus, fearing their total destruction, sent Hermes to impart to humans respect for others (*aidōs*) and for justice (*dikē*). Anyone incapable of acquiring *aidōs* and *dikē* must be put to death as a plague to the city.

Protagoras then shifted from *mythos* to a reasoned account (*logos*) for the teachability of *aretē*. In matters of political wisdom, when individual virtues such as justice (*dikaiosunē*) and moderation (*sōphrosunē*) are involved, all are expected to partake in the discussion. Without such skills, the city could not long endure. The city's practices demonstrate that all agree that these skills are acquired by instruction. One such practice is punishment, which is not undertaken for the sake of revenge, but to deter future wrongdoing. If some one lacks *dikaiosunē* or *sōphrosunē* and cannot be taught, that person must be expelled or executed.

The process of education occurs throughout life. The family teaches the child to excel, then the schools do the same, then the state itself does through its laws. Those with sufficient wealth continue their children's education as long as possible, which proves they believe *aretē* is teachable. It is true that some parents turn out worthless children, but that fact does not deny the teachability of *aretē*. Such children would still show more justice than savages without comparable training. Everyone in the city is a teacher of *aretē*, just as everyone is a teacher of the Greek language. Protagoras proclaimed himself as better than many at helping men become noble and excellent, and thus had earned for himself the career of Sophist.

There are three respects in which the Great Speech is regarded as genuinely Protagorean. The first is the defense of the teachability of *aretē*. The defense itself is ingenious, since it both affirms the democratic notion that all citizens possess political virtue and a sense of justice and also leaves room for the improvement that education (including sophistic education) can provide. The analogy to learning Greek is also interesting. All Greek speakers both learn from each other and teach each other, but that does not deny the possibility that some people can use and teach the language better than others.

The second authentic Protagorean thesis of the Great Speech is his theory of punishment. Prior to Protagoras, punishment was seen as retribution or revenge for harmful acts. Protagoras's highly original contribution was to argue that the more important social role of punishment is to deter future harms, and that punishment practices are evidence of the belief that citizens can be educated not to do harm. Protagoras's position was quite innovative for its time, as the traditional understanding of justice involved injury for injury ("an eye for an eye") and the belief that crime was the result of inherited guilt or god-sent sins.

The third important Protagorean thesis found in the Great Speech concerns the role of *logos* in politics. In four different passages of the *Protagoras*, the means of discursive participation by many citizens is linked to the intended end of good judgment. Coming to a good decision is not, in Protagoras's view, a function of divine inspiration or guidance, nor is it an ability limited only to the wealthy and noble born. Rather, all citizens possess the political virtues appropriate for making a collective and reasoned judgment. As Aristotle would make explicit in his *Rhetoric*, "the use of persuasive speech is to lead to judgment" (1391b). Arguably, Protagoras was expressing a notion that we would now recognize as political speech contributing to improved decision making by fostering a "marketplace of ideas." Reaching a consensus or common mind (*homonoia*) through a shared *logos* is what we might now call the intersubjective function of discourse.

Protagoras is rightly credited with providing the first theoretical basis for participatory democracy. It should be acknowledged that political participation was denied to a majority of the adult population, including women, noncitizens, and slaves. Nonetheless, the scope of Athenian democracy exceeded anything seen before in Western history. Athenian democracy has been described as the parent of all democracies, and Protagoras was its first reasoned defender.

PROTAGORAS'S LEGACY TO RHETORICAL THEORY AND PEDAGOGY

In recent decades, attention has been given to the influence of growing literacy in classical Greece during the fifth and fourth centuries BCE. Prior to the fifth century, very few Greeks could read. All composition was done with an ear toward oral delivery and easy memorization, and theistic myths penetrated most preserved discourse. Even Parmenides' proto-philosophical treatise was written in epic hexameters and was framed as teachings from a goddess, and Heraclitus wrote in highly memorable aphorisms. What we would call prose texts were very rare prior to the last third of the fifth century when the prevalence of literacy, and the variety of its uses, grew considerably.

Most scholars agree that the Older Sophists, including Protagoras, are best understood as transitional figures that played a significant role in expanding and exploring the uses of written prose. In the texts of intellectuals such as the Sophists, written discourse began to move away from the mythic-poetic mind-set dominant in the early fifth century toward a more humanistic and analytical approach to exploring and expressing ideas. It is important not to overstate the situation by declaring a "great divide" between oral and literate mind-sets, but at the same time it is important not to understate the Sophists' contributions to pedagogy and compositional practices. As Aristophanes' *Clouds* suggests (although in the form of parody), both the form and content of Greek pedagogy were being changed significantly by the Sophists.

The form of Protagoras's preserved fragments is instructive. Almost all of his extant sayings are crafted in the form of easily memorized aphorisms. In the case of the human-as-measure tenet, for example, memorization is encouraged through the use of antithesis, rhythm, and balanced phrasing—obvious in the English translation as well as in the original Greek—yet his use of the unconventional *ouk estin* marks a clear departure from oral-poetic semantics. The "concerning the gods" statement is preserved in nearly identical fashion by a number of sources. It has a rhythmic quality typical of an oral culture, yet its content is propositional and logical. While one must be careful not to impute an overly narrow sense to the term "rational," it is fair to say that Protagoras advanced a form of humanistic rationalism that can be contrasted to a religious belief in divine truth, to pious faith to tradition, as in Aristophanes, or to the mysticism of Pythagoras and (arguably) Parmenides.

Part of Protagoras's distinctive contribution to humanistic rationalism is that he was among the first to provide what can be called a *logos* of *logos*, or a reasoned account of language. For example, Protagoras is traditionally credited with analyzing and criticizing aspects of epic poetry, which would have been considered to be Greek culture's storehouse of received wisdom. Protagoras's observations about *logos*, the gender of words, and the moods and modes of language are noteworthy. They contributed to the formulation of a metalanguage—a set of terms appropriate for the analysis of language. Such a language is obvious in the writings of Plato and Aristotle, but their technical vocabulary did not spring into place overnight. Plato's account of Protagoras analyzing epic poetry is the earliest recorded instance of what we would call textual criticism, and it apparently began a practice that was continued by other Sophists at least through Isocrates' time.

Ancient commentators credit Protagoras with a host of "firsts," including the invention of what would later be called the Socratic method, originating the practice of arguing by questions, and inventing competitive debate (*antilogikē*). He is also one of several pre-Socratics credited with an interest in *orthos logos*, or "correct language." Some scholars believe that Protagoras may have written a text titled *Orthoepeia*, from which the various quotations from Protagoras about epic poetry and language may have been derived. It is unlikely that the Greek word for rhetoric, *rhētorikē*, was in use during Protagoras's lifetime, and it would be a mistake to assume that Protagoras's interest in language was *purely* rhetorical—if by "rhetorical" we exclude what we would call a philosophical interest. For Protagoras and other writers interested in *orthos logos*, such as Prodicus, the correct use of language is a reflection of an accurate understanding of the world. It may be worthwhile to quote a passage from the text known as *Dissoi Logoi*, which most scholars agree is heavily influenced by Protagoras: "I believe it belongs to the same man and to the same skill to be able to hold dialogue succinctly, to understand the truth of things, to plead one's court-cases correctly, to be able to make popular speeches, to understand argument-skills, and to teach about the nature of all things—how they are [their condition] and how they came to be" (8.1). This passage, dated about 400 BCE, suggests quite a different sophistic approach to understanding and discourse than one finds portrayed a decade or so later in Plato's *Gorgias*. In Plato's text, successful persuasion is divorced from truthful understanding. No such division is ever evident in the surviving texts by and about Protagoras.

There is no persuasive evidence to suggest that Protagoras ever authored an "Art of Rhetoric." Rather, he conceptualized the functions of *logos* in a way that, in retrospect, can be viewed as an incipient philosophy of discourse. His teaching methods probably included a formal expository lecture style, verbal exchange in small, informal discussion groups to "hold dialogue" (*dialegesthai*), and antithetical formulations of public positions (*antilogoi*). These methods cumulatively represent a significant contribution to new fifth-century pedagogical practices. The purpose of Protagoras's theory and practice was to change people for the better. An important analogy is found in descriptions of Protagoras that suggests he saw the role of the Sophist's art as analogous to that of medicine. Just as the doctor attempts to improve the physical health of a patient, the pedagogical promise to make the weaker *logos* stronger was to make the best case for the best course of action possible. The thesis that people can be improved and made more excellent marked a significant departure from the traditional belief that *aretē* was a function purely of wealth and noble birth.

Protagoras's teachings functioned ideologically to advance the precepts of Periclean democracy and to oppose the aristocratic implications of Eleatic monism. For Protagoras, *logos* was the means through which citizens deliberated and came to collective judgments. Protagoras contributed to the theoretical defense of consensual decision making, and he may have contributed rules concerning the orderly conduct of debate and discussion.

Compared to Aristotle's conceptualization of rhetoric, Protagoras's approach to *logos* was undifferentiated and precategorical; that is, it was independent of context and did not distinguish sharply between types of discourse on the basis of distinctive principles or degrees of certainty. Plato's explicit and Aristophanes' implicit description of Protagoras's educational activities did not limit him to the training of orators in the sense *rhētorikē* was used by the mid-fourth century. Protagoras probably would have agreed with Isocrates' description of *logon paideia*, or education in discourse, as training for the mind as physical training is for the body (*Antidosis* 181). His faith in democracy, his pragmatism, his antifoundationalist humanism, and his belief in the importance of public discourse and collaborative decision making have made Protagoras an inspiration for many scholars over the past century (Mailloux). He will continue to be a source of inspiration as long as scholars value the connections between theory and pedagogy.

BIBLIOGRAPHY

Primary Sources and Translations

Diels, Hermann, and Walther Kranz. *Die Fragmente der Vorsokratiker.* 6th ed. Dublin/Zurich: Weidmann, 1951–52.

Sprague, Rosamond Kent, ed. *The Older Sophists.* Columbia: U of South Carolina P, 1972.

Untersteiner, Mario. *Sofisti: testimonianze e frammenti.* 4 vols. Firenze: La Nuova Italia, 1949–62.

Biographical Sources

Loenen, D. *Protagoras and the Greek Community.* Amsterdam: V Noord-Hollandsche, 1940.

Schiappa, Edward. *Protagoras and* Logos: *A Study in Greek Philosophy and Rhetoric.* 2nd ed. Columbia: U of South Carolina P, 2003.

Critical Sources

Barnes, Jonathan, ed. *The Complete Works of Aristotle.* Princeton: Princeton UP, 1984.

Cooper, Lane. *The Rhetoric of Aristotle.* Englewood Cliffs: Prentice-Hall, 1932.

Hamilton, Edith, and Huntington Cairns. *The Collected Dialogues of Plato.* Princeton: Princeton UP, 1961.

Kahn, Charles H. *The Art and Thought of Heraclitus.* Cambridge: Cambridge UP, 1979.

———. *The Verb "Be" in Ancient Greek.* Dordrecht: D. Reidel, 1973.

Mailloux, Steven. *Rhetoric, Sophistry, Pragmatism.* Cambridge: Cambridge UP, 1995.

Robinson, Thomas M. *Contrasting Arguments: An Edition of the Dissoi Logoi.* Salem, NH: Ayer, 1979.

PYTHAGOREAN WOMEN

(late sixth century BCE–third century CE)

Ekaterina Haskins

Pythagoreanism flourished from the late sixth century BCE to approximately the third century CE. Scholars typically distinguish three periods within Pythagoreanism: early Pythagoreanism (late sixth–fifth centuries BCE), late Pythagoreanism (fourth–third centuries BCE), and neo-Pythagoreanism (first–third centuries CE). Most writings attributed to Pythagorean women come from a collection dubbed "pseudoepigrapha Pythagorica," compiled by members of neo-Pythagorean schools during the first and second centuries CE. Several fragments bear the names of women who belonged to the original school of Pythagoras, but the bulk of writings attributed to women Pythagoreans dates back to the fourth and third centuries BCE (Waithe 59–74).

The early Pythagoreans included immediate disciples of Pythagoras as well as his followers throughout Greece and southern Italy. Most of what we know about them comes from scholars and biographers who lived centuries after Pythagoras of Samos founded his community in Croton, southern Italy, around 630 BCE. Although embellishment and simplification are to be expected from later sources, modern scholars were able to reconstruct some tenets of early Pythagoreanism. Early Pythagorean sects, in Croton and throughout Magna Graecia, espoused the rigorous life of the intellect combined with asceticism in diet, clothing, and behavior. Their dietary restrictions and specific burial rites were apparently tied to the belief in the immortality of the soul and metempsychosis, or reincarnation, which dictated respect for animal life (Burkert 120–65). Central to the Pythagorean worldview and teaching was the notion of *harmonia*, a principle of "cosmic union," whose function was "to produce unity out of multiplicity by bringing diverse and discordant elements into an agreement with one another" (Kahn 24–25). Although in Pythagorean teachings *harmonia* was conceived in terms of numerical ratios and musical scales, the so-called Pythagorean way of life cannot be identified with speculative science alone; rather, it was an amalgamation of religious and mystical traditions, speculative cosmology, and ethico-political practices.

Many ancient sources agree on the importance of women in the Pythagorean circle. For instance, in Plato's *Meno*, Socrates introduces the doctrine of reincarnation by describing what he has "heard from both men and women who are wise about divine matters" (81a, quoted in Kingsley 160). Original Pythagorean sects were closed societies, yet their selectivity was based on merit and discipline, rather than gender or socioeconomic status. According to ancient biographers, a five-year initiation period of listening to the teacher's voice in silence was followed by a test that determined whether the initiate would become one of the "esoterics," members of the inner circle, or leave the community altogether. The content of the teachings (*akousmata*) was protected by the vow of silence, so it is perhaps after the breakup of the original communities that Pythagorean teachings became more widely known in the Greek world. *Akousmata* were treated by the later tradition either as ritual injunctions that must be believed and obeyed without questioning or as riddles in need of symbolic interpretation (Burkert 166–92).

The place of women Pythagoreans within the history of philosophy has been established at least since the late seventeenth century (e.g., Menage). However, their contribution to the rhetorical tradition has not yet been recognized. This silence is due, in part, to the association of ancient Greek "rhetoric" with public speech of the Athenian democracy of the fifth and fourth centuries BCE (Kennedy 3). As a consequence, women's discourses belonging to other speech genres have been typically excluded from the canonical list of practitioners and theorists of rhetoric (see Glenn). In addition, the scarcity of extant texts and the difficulty in authenticating them allow for little beyond informed speculation. Still, it is evident from ancient biographies and surviving writings that women were not simply permitted to engage in religious rites and educational practices associated with Pythagoreanism; indeed, they took an active part in them as priestesses and teachers. Their contribution to the rhetorical tradition, then, consists not in formalizing norms of eloquent public speech, but in speaking and writing as authorities endowed with divine insight and human wisdom.

MAJOR FIGURES

Theano of Croton (Theano I) is often mentioned as one of the major figures of the early Pythagoreanism; she is usually identified as Pythagoras's wife who became the leader of the school after his death. In contrast with the lore surrounding the legendary wife of Pythagoras, little is known about the identity of Pythagoreans of the late period besides the texts that bear their names. The late Pythagoreans include Perictione I, Perictione II, Aesara of Lucania, Phintys of Sparta, and Theano II. Philological analysis suggests that Perictione I, whose discourse *On the Harmony of Woman* was written in Ionic, was an Athenian and a contemporary of Plato. Perictione I uses the same terms for virtues (*andreia, sophrosyne, dikaiosyne,* and *sophia*) as does Plato in the *Republic*. Phyntis is believed to be a daughter of a Spartan admiral, Kallikratidas, who died in the battle of the Arginusae in 406 BCE. Fragments by

Perictione II, Aesara, and Phyntis are in Doric, which indicates that they were probably written in the second half of the fourth century, after Archytas of Tarentum popularized inscripted Doric in western Greece (Waithe 68). Although scholars continue to disagree about the precise dating of these texts, they display many substantive and stylistic similarities to warrant dating them between the early fourth and early third centuries BCE (Waithe 59–73).

WRITINGS

Several fragments are attributed to Theano I, among them a fragment from *On Piety* and a number of apothegms. Although the authenticity of these texts is suspect, given the early Pythagoreans' reliance on the oral method of teaching, the very fact of attributing them to a woman is noteworthy. *On Piety*, for example, invokes Theano's authority to authenticate an exegesis of the notion of number against what "many of the Greeks believe Pythagoras [had] said" (Thesleff, *The Pythagorean Texts* 195). A testimony of Theano, an Orphic priestess and the person closest to Pythagoras, is thus used in a much later polemic between rival traditions of interpretation (Burkert 61). Theano's reported apothegms also combine exegesis and moral authority; some explain Pythagorean doctrines of immortality and metempsychosis, others comment on the role of women as moral agents whose wisdom and temperance are key to the harmony within the home (Waithe 13–15). These statements can be "best understood in the light of the writings of the later Pythagorean [women] philosophers," who stress women's "responsibility for creating the conditions under which harmony and order, and law and justice can exist in the state" (Waithe 14).

The major commonality among the writings of late Pythagoreans is the articulation of the normative principle of *harmonia*. Some of the writings follow discursive conventions of speculative philosophical treatises, while others take the form of advice given by one woman to another. *On Wisdom* by Perictione II and Aesara's *On Human Nature* belong to the former type. Perictione II asserts that "humankind came into being and exists in order to contemplate the principle of the nature of the whole" (Waithe 56). Aesara's discourse posits an analogy between the tripartite hierarchical structure of the soul and social order, proclaiming that "justice is the orderly arrangement of the soul" (Waithe 20). On their face, these pronouncements resemble the idealist moral philosophy of Plato and the Academy. However, because the author's gender alone can add layers of meaning to an otherwise unmarked discourse (or a discourse typically linked to a male tradition), female authorship implicitly suggests women's equal share in metaphysical and political theorizing.

Fragments by Perictione I, Phyntis of Sparta, and Theano II, on the other hand, vividly portray social constraints faced by a philosophically minded woman. However, rather than seeking to transcend their gendered position, these authors adopt a pragmatic stance by integrating the principle of *harmonia* into women's lives as wives, mothers, and managers of households. In Waithe's words, these writings "specify what it takes for a woman to be morally praiseworthy in an actual society, not what the role of women might be in some hypothetical, ideal, and vastly different society" (37).

On the Harmony of Women by Perictione I sets forth the conditions that enable a woman to nurture wisdom (*phronesis*) and self-control (*sophrosyne*), the virtues that will bring "worthwhile things" for "herself, her husband, her children and household, perhaps even for a city—if, at any rate, such a woman should govern cities and tribes" (Waithe 32). These conditions involve moderation in diet and dress, avoidance of cosmetics and jewelry, and selfless devotion to one's husband regardless of his behavior. Although admittedly conservative, this advice can be viewed as a "pragmatic response to the question of moral responsibility in the face of an entrenched *status quo*" (Waithe 35). Similarly, in her *Moderation of Women*, Phyntis of Sparta assigns the virtue of moderation to women, but asserts that "courage and justice and wisdom are common to both" genders (Waithe 27). Phyntis accepts the custom that circumscribes the range of women's social roles, yet defends the right of women to philosophize. Although women's appearance in public is limited to shopping errands and participation in religious rituals, their moral agency exceeds the household. The letters written by Theano II display how a woman's moral responsibility toward her children, her husband, and her servants underlies both domestic and social justice. If a woman brings up her children with a view to temperance (*To Eubole*), acts justly toward her husband even if he is unjust to her (*To Nikostrate*), and treats her slaves as human beings whose souls are no less than her own (*To Kallisto*), she will not only keep a moral high ground, but also produce harmony within and without the household.

Unlike their male contemporaries, whose moral philosophy dwells on the public sphere and ignores the private, Perictione I, Phyntis and Theano II shed light on the continuity and interdependence between the public and the private. By showing how women can exercise their capacity to reason about a variety of ethical issues, their writings affirm women's deliberative rationality as a key to the harmonious functioning of the social whole.

Bibliography

Primary Sources and Translations

Guthrie, Kenneth Sylvan, ed. *The Pythagorean Sourcebook and Library: An Anthology of Ancient Writings Which Relate to Pythagoras and Pythagorean Philosophy.* Grand Rapids, MI: Phanes, 1987.

Thesleff, Holger, ed. *The Pythagorean Texts of the Hellenistic Period.* Abo: Abo Academi, 1965.

Waithe, Mary Ellen, ed. *A History of Women Philosophers. Volume 1: 600 BC–500 AD.* Dordrecht: Martinus Nijhoff, 1987.

Biographical Sources

Kahn, Charles H. *Pythagoras and Pythagoreans: A Brief History*. Indianapolis: Hackett, 2001.

Kersey, Ethel M. *Women Philosophers: A Bio-Critical Source Book*. New York: Greenwood, 1989.

Menage, Gilles. *The History of Women Philosophers*. Trans. Beatrice H. Zedler. Lanham, MD: UP of America, 1984.

Critical Sources

Burkert, Walter. *Lore and Science in Ancient Pythagoreanism*. Trans. E. L. Minar. Cambridge: Harvard UP, 1972.

Glenn, Cheryl. *Rhetoric Retold: Regendering the Tradition from Antiquity through the Renaissance*. Carbondale: Southern Illinois UP, 1997.

Kennedy, George A. *A New History of Classical Rhetoric*. Princeton: Princeton UP, 1994.

Kingsley, Peter. *Ancient Philosophy, Mystery, and Magic*. Oxford: Clarendon, 1995.

Navia, Luis E. *Pythagoras: An Annotated Bibliography*. New York and London: Garland, 1990.

Thesleff, Holger. *An Introduction to the Pythagorean Texts of the Hellenistic Period*. Abo: Abo Academi, 1961.

FABIUS QUINTILIANUS

(ca. 40–ca. 100 CE)

Joy Connolly

Fabius Quintilianus, commonly known as, and hereafter referred to as, Quintilian, was born between 30 and 40 CE to an affluent family in Calagurris, Spain, and completed his education in the rhetorical schools of Rome. According to the common practice of Roman adolescents since the second century BCE, known as the *tirocinium fori* or "apprenticeship of the forum," he formed a connection with an experienced orator whom he accompanied to work in the law courts, in his case the well-known Domitius Afer. The historian Tacitus attacks Afer as a greedy and sycophantic prosecutor who was responsible for the downfall of wealthy citizens suspected by the emperor Nero of treason and conspiracy. Quintilian, by contrast—characteristically silent regarding the stormy political atmosphere of the early imperial period—says nothing about his mentor beyond praising his comparatively restrained mode of speech, which seems to have influenced his own relatively conservative oratorical style. After Afer's death in 59, Quintilian returned to Spain, where he probably pleaded cases in the provincial courts. Within a decade he was again living in Rome, building a successful career as a forensic orator by 71 CE, when he received an official post teaching rhetoric at the state's expense. The first such position in Roman history, it was funded by the emperor Vespasian, who modeled his patronage on the activity of the monarchs of the post-Alexandrian Greek kingdoms, particularly the Ptolemies in Egypt. That Quintilian was chosen attests to his reputation as an orator and his known interest in teaching; it is likely that he had launched a school of his own sometime before taking up the imperial post. Among his many students were Pliny the Younger (q.v.) and possibly the satirist Juvenal.

Quintilian retired from his public career around 90 CE, as the emperor Domitian's rule collapsed into a reign of terror. Almost immediately he published a short treatise on the causes of the decline of eloquence (*De Causis Corruptae Eloquentiae*), now lost, and the only surviving work that is attributed to him with certainty, the magisterial *Institutio Oratoria* or *Education of the Orator*. The circumstances of his death are not known; the younger Pliny suggests a date before 100 CE.

QUINTILIAN'S CONTRIBUTIONS TO RHETORIC

In terms of intellectual significance for the Renaissance and early modernity, Quintilian's treatise on rhetorical education in twelve books is one of the most important works produced in classical antiquity. For rhetoricians, it stands with Aristotle's *Rhetoric* at the ancient center of the discipline. Distilling a tradition of Greek and Roman rhetorical theory and practice already over four centuries old in Quintilian's lifetime, the *Institutio Oratoria* combines abstract discussion of grammatical and rhetorical theory with the practical prescriptions of a deportment handbook. Over a century earlier, in his three-book dialogue *De Oratore* (*On the Orator*) and two shorter works, Cicero had interwoven the material traditionally included in a standard rhetorical treatise with an innovative discussion of the philosophical properties of speech and the political and moral responsibilities of the ideal orator. In the tradition of Cicero's ambitious scope and specifically his belief that the art of persuasion should embrace all the knowledge appropriate to free men, the *liberales artes*, Quintilian links his analyses of the cardinal elements of rhetoric, such as the structure of language and the psychology of emotions, to broader questions of logic, ethics, and the literary canon. The result is much more than a collection of maxims for teachers of public speaking; it is a guide to organizing intellectual thought and moral values on a broad scale.

What is rhetoric? Is it an art or a craft, a faculty, or a power? Is it a product of nature or of culture? These questions were energetically disputed by writers in Athens and Rome whose urban and urbane world was organized around public speech making, and whose literature was thoroughly influenced by the tactics of oratorical performance. Quintilian's importance lies partly in his belief in the inalienable ethical component of the spoken and written word, which unfolds in his study of the debate over the definition of rhetoric in the first two books of the *Institutio*. In the fourth century BCE, as he acknowledges, Plato framed what was to become the central philosophical challenge to rhetoric in the dialogue *Gorgias*, where, in an effort to differentiate sophistic rhetoric from his own brand of philosophical dialectic, Socrates defines rhetoric as speech that communicates conviction rather than knowledge and, worse, as a kind of flattery based on ignorance instead of truth. Some Greek and Latin rhetoricians writing after Plato sought to evade this argument and its ethical and epistemological implications by suggesting that the term "rhetoric" refers to the power of persuasion, pure and simple—a stance Quintilian rejects on the ground that many things have the capacity to persuade, from money to a beautiful woman, like the Greek courtesan Phryne, who famously undressed in court to sway a jury (2.15.9). "The art of deception" or "the art of giving pleasure through speech" he discards as biased and excessively simplistic notions of a practice essential to maintaining legal and political order in the ancient city-state.

Aristotle's influential description of rhetoric as the "power of discovering every means of persuasion in speech" has flaws more interesting to the Roman rhetorician. In Quintilian's reading, Aristotle's definition is accurate but crucially incomplete, due to its ethical emptiness. In eliminating the moral component of persuasion, Aristotle eviscerates rhetoric's force as the virtue Quintilian believes it to be. In keeping with this view, he finally defines rhetoric as the *bene dicendi scientia*, the "science of speaking well"—for, in Quintilian's famous Ciceronian formulation, "no man can speak well who is not himself a good man" (2.15.34). To put it in the elder Cato's terms, the good orator is a *vir bonus dicendi peritus*, a "good man skilled in speaking" (12.1.1). Key to this definition are the words *vir*—"man," as opposed to the broader (though still sexist) Latin term for human, *homo*—and *bonus*, "good," which implies membership in the Roman propertied class and even, in some contexts, adherence to conservative politics. In his prescriptive stress on the essential moral goodness of properly trained speech, which is closely bound up with the values of Rome's male elite, Quintilian may be seen as fulfilling Aristotle's identification of rhetoric as a branch of ethics, in a way the Greek philosopher himself did not seek to do.

The deep significance of rhetoric for Quintilian emerges in the prefatory argument of the second book of the *Institutio*, where rhetorical training is claimed to yoke the knowledge of how to persuade with the knowledge of whom to persuade, for what reasons, and to what end. True eloquence entails a grasp of the honorable and the dishonorable, the just and the unjust, and the good and the bad, correct knowledge of which, in his view, belongs only to virtuous men. To be a man of eloquence is perforce to be a man of virtue. As a discourse that teaches men how to live well—the goal of many an intellectual enterprise of the Hellenistic Greek and Roman era, from medicine to didactic poetry—rhetoric thus represents a genuine alternative to, and even an improvement upon, the speculative and meditative practices of philosophy. It combines an abstract grasp of justice and prudence with the practical virtues of courage and self-restraint. No less important, in Quintilian's estimation, is the fact that in the course of his training, the eloquent man develops the charisma and air of nobility that make him attractive to his fellow citizens, enabling him, as a leader of social and political opinion, to put his virtues into practice for the good of the community.

As for the hairsplitting over the codification of speech that is commonly associated with the discipline of rhetoric in his time—the kind of obsession with syntax, tropes, and figures that Roland Barthes calls "taxonomic frenzy"—Quintilian dismisses it as a minor science. True, a degree of formal analysis of language and logical reasoning is necessary in order to train the student systematically in the complex and fluctuating sphere that constitutes human communications; and the *Institutio* itself devotes several books to the meticulous explication of these matters. But Quintilian condemns rhetoricians whose devotion to fine-tuning grammar or logic blinds them to the true nature of eloquence, a virtue embracing other virtues.

This is essentially a Stoic position, insofar as the Stoics considered all virtues to form a single unity. But in Quintilian's hands (with help from Cicero, from whom he draws his inspiration), the doctrine of virtuous eloquence cleared the ground for the refinement and justification of what were to become during the early modern period "the humanities." Modernity's greatest ideological inheritance from Quintilian is the enduring belief that the study of the humanities, especially literature, represents a clear if intangible good, and that learning to read, write, and speak with propriety and grace effectively inculcates virtue. It is a belief for which there is, unfortunately, no truly convincing argument unless one resorts to a Platonic view of knowledge as the exclusive property of the virtuous: as Richard Lanham points out in a trenchant essay on rhetoric and virtue, there are plenty of well-read criminals. Quintilian's value to defenders of the humanities is his ability to camouflage the weakness of the equation between education and virtue with a thick layer of sensible advice and enlightened insights into the civilizing potential of eloquence.

QUINTILIAN ON EDUCATION

In light of the scanty but disturbing descriptions of teachers in the literature of the early Roman empire, Quintilian stands out as a patient and humane educator, with a sanguine view of children's natural intellectual capacity and eagerness to learn. At the same time, his account reveals just how the beliefs and values of the first-century male Roman elite shape pedagogical ideals—not only of his period but our own. The genius of any effective educational system, as the sociologist Pierre Bourdieu has noted in *The Logic of Practice*, lies precisely in the way it "extorts what is essential while seeming to demand the insignificant," instilling a "whole cosmology through injunctions as insignificant as 'sit up straight'" (69). Just as feminists like Simone de Beauvoir see that womanhood is an attribute acquired through careful training in posture, gesture, grooming, and mental attitude, so Quintilian and his fellow Romans take it for granted that manliness is not a quality formed spontaneously in the growing boy. Becoming a proper man, which is to say developing the right mixture of authority, vigor, refinement, and wit, involves extensive and highly specialized training. This rhetoric is uniquely positioned to provide. A discipline that involves the exercise of both mental and physical faculties, rhetoric prepares the youth to move successfully in a community filled with exacting eyes and ears, to whom a nervous tic, an affected slouch, or a shaky voice is proof of an unstable, effeminate character. The *Institutio* furnishes the reader with a detailed map of the ideal elite Roman male body and its behaviors in private and public, with long lists of actions that appear authoritative and manly (squared shoulders, restrained gestures, a masterful gaze) and those that connote weakness and vice (shifting feet, swaying hips, lewd expressions, a timid glance).

To be successful, such a program must begin in very early childhood. Quintilian's pedagogical program, outlined in book 1 of the *Institutio*, begins in infancy and continues through retirement, offering advice for mature men on memory training and extempore speaking. Unlike his predecessors (with the possible exception of the elder Pliny, whose rhetorical writings are lost), Quintilian gives careful thought to what the Romans called *educatio*. By contrast with *institutio*, which refers to the inculcation of knowledge at a more advanced level, *educatio* is the literal "upbringing" of the young child, from the Latin words *e-* (up or out) and *ducere* (to lead or bring). Beginning from the stage at which babies cannot speak (the literal meaning of the Latin *infans*, infant), through childhood, when children acquire their native language and the first outlines of their moral character, to adolescence, when they begin advanced schooling, the first book of the *Institutio* describes the ideal regimen of physical and mental nurture. It is worth noting that fathers are clearly the intended readers of this book; very little is said of mothers, whose sole responsibility rests in giving birth, and whose influence Quintilian mistrusts nearly as much as slaves'. He warns the fathers of young children to keep a close watch on the wet-nurse and the pedagogue (the child's constant guardian and companion). In spite of their slave status, a normal condition in the households Quintilian has in mind, these figures are expected to behave like Phoenix, the loving and upright tutor of Achilles (2.3.12). Ideally, like all the other household attendants who come into contact with the small child, they should maintain a standard of personal hygiene and behavior that equals the perfect purity of their Latin. Throughout this description of the child's earliest instructors, certain values emerge—intellegibility, honesty, and self-control—that mark the character of the ideal orator Quintilian seeks to form. In this context, Quintilian famously condemns corporal punishment as ineffective and dangerous, transforming children into servile cowards (1.3.13).

A child undertaking Quintilian's ideal education remains at home until about the age of seven, learning to read, write, and do basic arithmetic under the tutelage of a trained pedagogue. At that point, he or she goes to study with other children in the school of a *grammaticus*, or teacher of grammar. Gymnastics are recommended to increase the child's confidence, physical strength, and grace, especially useful for the boy who plans to continue his studies with a rhetorician (a stage girls did not reach). Quintilian never mentions the possibility of learning how to read and write outside the home in a small school led by an alphabet teacher (*litterator*), or a schoolmaster (*magister ludi*), though these were popular inside and outside Rome in the imperial period. His apparent dislike of the practice arises from his quintes-sentially Roman suspicion of the professionalization of education, the traditional responsibility of the family circle, and his belief in the dangers facing the morally unformed child outside the secure and familiar surroundings of the home.

When the adolescent pupil advances to the rhetorical school, he studies logic, history, and philosophy; and he begins to practice declamation. This is a topic about which much was being written at Rome in the first century CE, most of it critical. Declamation is the performance of practice speeches that in the Roman rhetorical system fall into two categories: the court case or *controversia*, and the address to a particular figure or group, known as the *suasoria*. Quintilian's name is attached to two collections of such speeches, known as the *Major* and *Minor Declamations*. All nineteen of the *Major Declamations* are *controversiae*, and like all speeches of this type, they argue fictional cases based on laws that are the stuff of imagination or legend. By contrast to their full length *Major* counterparts, the collection of 145 *Minor Declamations* (those that survive of the original 388) consists of very brief speeches and selections from longer treatments. Quintilian's authorship of the books is extremely unlikely for historical and stylistic reasons, though there is some overlap between the declamatory topics recorded in the *Institutio* and those included in them, but he clearly considers declamation useful preparation for the budding orator. Consideration of the topics involved explains why.

A typical *controversia* of the first century BCE (its earlier history was debated even among ancient historians of rhetoric and education) involves a civil case with a melodramatic plot rivaling modern soap operas. Certain motifs and figures predominate—there are Suspicious Husbands and Adulterous Wives, Clinging Mothers, Envious Fathers and Evil Stepmothers, Vicious Tyrants and Virtuous Prostitutes. A student in a school like Quintilian's would defend or prosecute one side of the case, relying not on case precedent, as a modern law student might, but on *ēthos*, the moral character of the figures involved in the dispute. For example, in one *controversia* in the *Major Declamations*, a wealthy widower had a blind son, whom he subjected to bad treatment after his second marriage. One night, the man is murdered while in bed with his new wife; the next morning, bloody palm prints are discovered on the walls leading to his son's rooms. The son and the stepmother accuse one another of the crime. The student arguing one side or the other of this case required the ability to gauge his hearers' prejudices, the emotional probability-values they would attach to the characters in the case. The *controversiae* did not exactly ignore the ever-growing body of Roman civil law, then, but its usefulness as a teaching tool largely lay outside the legal arena. What it unquestionably provided was deep training in Roman values. Through their adolescence, students learned to balance the ties of blood and the state, the competing claims of friends and fathers, husbands and wives; they absorbed the traditional Roman suspicion of political tyranny (an interesting wrinkle to the politics of rhetorical training, given the autocratic extremism of some Roman emperors); and they acquired an ethics that privileged the interests of the dominant social class, which must have seemed all the more persuasive for having been put to the test. Along the way, they learned to construct logical arguments, appeals to emotion, and proper delivery. About these things, Quintilian also has much to say.

RHETORICAL THEORY IN THE *INSTITUTIO ORATORIA*

Quintilian is not an innovator in the area of language systematization. His contribution is twofold: the clarity of his extended discussion, and his synthesis of the traditional methods of dividing and labeling elements of language, argument, and delivery into the ethical scheme described above. Underlying the *Institutio*'s long commentary on the elements, parts, figures, and tropes of speech is his belief that "a man speaks just as he lives" (11.1.30): based on this, Quintilian encourages flexibility and naturalness in the orator's preparation and final performance. If Quintilian's discussion of the codification and regulation of language at first appears constricting, even oppressive, he is markedly more appreciative than most ancient rhetoricians of variation among speakers, and even, within limits, innovation. He agrees with Cicero that the orator's adoption of a style far removed from the common language of his listeners leads inevitably to failure. This humane quality in the *Institutio* makes it possible to grasp its importance for early modern readers frustrated with what they saw as the sterile disconnection of medieval scholastic discourse from the civic speech of the Italian republics and the English Parliament.

The division of oratory into three types—deliberative speeches that advocate or criticize a course of action, usually in a political assembly; demonstrative or epideictic speeches of praise or celebration; and Quintilian's favorite, forensic or judicial speeches for the law court—he draws directly from Aristotle (3.4.12). From the influential (lost) work of Theophrastus, Aristotle's student, Quintilian appropriates the threefold division of style into grand, low, and middle, providing examples in Greek and Latin oratory (12.10.58–76). True to Quintilian's expansive view of rhetoric, his discussions of the five formal parts of the speech agreed upon by most ancient rhetoricians (3.9.1) address topics of broader significance for ethics and psychology. The opening of the speech, or *prooemium*, brings Quintilian in book 4 to issues familiar to modern students of communications, especially the relationship between speaker and audience. His investigation of the proper narration of the facts of the case (*narratio*) includes a culturally value-laden account of the Hellenistic oratorical ideals of clarity, brevity, and credibility, which turn out to capture what Quintilian sees as the essential moral strengths of the Latin language. Long, technically intricate, and occasionally inconsistent chapters in book 5 on proof and refutation (*probatio* and *refutatio*) explore logic and legal theory; analysis of the peroration (*peroratio*) includes an extended digression into psychology, particularly Quintilian's theories of emotion and humor (book 6).

Following traditional approaches as usual, Quintilian describes the process of composing a speech before he can examine its parts. The steps in the rhetorical process, often called the "five parts of rhetoric" as opposed to the five parts of the speech, begin with invention (*inventio*), the literal "discovery" of the parts of the speech that is necessary before they may be arranged or "disposed" in the second stage (*dispositio*), according to the speaker's characteristic style (*elocutio*), the signs of which are woven into the speech in the advanced stages of its verbal composition. Once the speech is committed to memory (*memoria*), it is finally prepared for delivery (*actio*). Books 2 through 7 take up invention and arrangement; 8 through 11 treat the remaining three parts, including a long and famous excursus in book 10 on literature and literary criticism.

A complicated and much studied topic, invention involves defining the main topic of a case (the *quaestio*). This dictates the required speech genre (deliberative, demonstrative, or forensic), and further, its *status*, the system by which the question would be handled. By Quintilian's lifetime, numerous systems of determining *status* were available. He adapts the system of the influential Hellenistic Greek rhetorician Hermagoras, outlining a fairly straightforward, flexible, and nondogmatic set of recommendations that focus on the most challenging and complicated area of *status* theory, the law court speech. The forensic orator begins by asking the following questions: does his case involve a legal question, such as the correct interpretation of the law, or not? Either answer leads to further questions narrowing down the path of reasoning to be undertaken in the speech: is the case a dispute over facts ("he said, she said"), definition ("what I said was not illegal"), or quality ("I said it, and I was right to say it")? For example, a man is charged with murder. Did he do it or not? Does the accuser have the legal right to bring charges? Are there extenuating circumstances? These are a selection of the many potential *status* questions that could be brought to bear on a murder case.

As with *status*, the *Institutio*'s examination of argumentative proof and refutation rests on an extensive body of earlier work, particularly Aristotle's analysis of the *enthymeme*, a logical argument whose premises are probabilities rather than certainties. Books 5 and 6, of interest to modern scholars of semiotics as well as logic and Roman law, draw clear if not always rigorous distinctions among different types of evidence, circumstantial, documentary, oral (from witnesses, tortured and otherwise), and from supernatural sources such as omens or oracles. Book 7 covers points of law (including the distinction between the letter of the law and its intention, and advice on handling contradictory laws), the appropriate presentation of facts and conjectures, and the treatment of ambiguity of word or deed in a court action.

Quintilian's discussion of style is the bedrock for compositional theory and rhetorical speech analysis even today. He promotes four values: linguistic accuracy and purity, clarity, ornament, and propriety (8.preface.31). Working from Theophrastus's systematic discussion of the virtues of speech (now lost) and Cicero's *De Oratore*, Quintilian adds a distinctive treatment of the principle of imitation and the importance of wide reading, especially in poetry and history. All of this material, while geared to the active pedagogical goal of training orators, was and is useful for the literary critic. In his discussion of ornament, Quintilian distinguishes three types of words: proper, neologisms, and metaphors. Proper diction includes both common and archaic language—the latter, like neologisms, to be used in moderation; metaphors turn out to be part of the larger category of tropes, the substitution of one word or words for others (9.1.4–6). From metonymy, synecdoche, and onomatopoeia to other terms less familiar to modern readers, tropes are the topic of an ambitious but somewhat arbitrary analysis at the end of book 8. Most important here is Quintilian's sensitivity to the effect of ornamented language on the audience's psyche, his extensive use of examples from literature, and his commitment to transforming what had been a discourse of poetic criticism to prose. The treatment of figures of speech and thought in book 9—Quintilian discusses over one hundred of them, including irony, impersonation, emphasis, and ellipse—is more enlightening and has exerted heavy influence on later composition theory. His evaluations of poetry, history, and oratory in book 10 are strictly utilitarian: their lucidity may be the reason why his assessments of so many Latin writers have defined their reception in later periods. His comments on Senecan prose and the Roman elegists, in particular, are still quoted in literary histories today; and his habit of recording long passages of Cicero and Vergil, the writers most often quoted in the *Institutio*, helped make them central parts of the rhetorical curriculum, not only in ancient Roman schools, but in modernity up through the nineteenth century.

Book 11's account of oratorical delivery is the fullest discussion of the ancient body to be found in antiquity outside of medical discourse. Face, hair, head, neck, upper torso, arms, hands, fingers, spine, hips, legs, and feet are all subjected to Quintilian's scrutiny. His descriptive strategy exploits existing prejudices against women, non-Romans, slaves, and other culturally marginalized groups such as actors and eunuchs to create a negative template by which his readers may judge their own practice. Proper oratorical performance becomes a matter of avoiding the ungovernable—and deceptive—deportment and speech of those groups, in favor of employing the "naturally" honest and noble speech of good men. Roman courts did not normally permit women to speak, though Quintilian records that a speech was given in the mid-first century BCE by Hortensia, the daughter of Cicero's famous rival. The speech of women and effeminate men was therefore available as a useful model for images of oratorical vice.

George Kennedy, the author of several magisterial histories of rhetoric, remarks that "no concept is more dear to Quintilian than nature" (34). His comment is not inaccurate, but it simplifies a highly complicated tension at the heart of the *Institutio*, and indeed all Roman rhetoric, which is related to the Roman suspicion of professionalized scholarship. As an artificial discourse of culture—in fact one that enables the survival of culture, as Quintilian might say in the best Ciceronian tradition—rhetoric occupies an uneasy position vis-à-vis nature. Quintilian's habit of representing the artificial techniques he teaches as natural or a product of nature cannot conceal that they are learned and learnable tricks. When he advises his readers to avoid gestures used by Asiatic Greeks or slaves, for example, in favor of the "naturally" manly stance of a good Roman, he is, in a sense, admitting that identity is rooted in the pretense of well-trained appearances. What then remains of Quintilian's most important claim on behalf of oratory, that the good orator is a good man? Is it based merely on effective deception, as Plato had claimed in the *Gorgias*? In his discussion of style and delivery in books 8 through 11, Quintilian sets out to dispel anxieties on that score by arguing that the tropes and figures of speech he exhaustively enumerates are unequivocally natural outgrowths of verbal practice, and that the physical conditions for virtuous delivery are accessible only to men, and a limited number of men at that.

In the *Institutio*'s preface, Quintilian ascribes his decision to compose the work to the insistence of his friends. This is not a trivial point; it heralds an important matter troubling nearly all Latin studies of rhetoric. The Romans traditionally disdained interest in scholarly topics that were the province of professionals, especially those originating with the Greeks; and the Greeks (so the Romans liked to repeat) were the inventors of eloquence and the masters of the more technical aspects of persuasion. In social terms, the teaching of rhetoric particularly suffered under prejudice that had peaked in the second century BCE, when thousands of recently enslaved Greeks entered the Italian peninsula as grammarians and rhetoricians. The censors, high Roman magistrates responsible for the ethical oversight of the wealthy senatorial and equestrian classes, expelled all the teachers of Latin rhetoric in

97 BCE. Whether their reasons derived from political or moral concerns, the censors' decision reflects the willful unwillingness of Roman elites to acknowledge the central importance of rhetoric in their systems of pedagogy and politics—an attitude that persists today. In antiquity and early modernity, the *Institutio* helped define the purpose of the professional teaching of language and literature.

But Quintilian cannot be called a progressive. He was a provincial from Spain, writing a handbook of civic and cultural Romanization for other provincials. As such, it is likely that his discussion of the ideal orator in book 12, the influential and often-excerpted conclusion to the *Institutio* that reiterates his interest in maintaining strict standards of manly behavior, pure Latinity, and correct grammar, is tempered by what linguists call the "archaism of the periphery"—that is, as a relative outsider seeking to blaze a path for others like him, he adopted relatively conservative attitudes for his age.

Read only rarely in the decades following Quintilian's death, the *Institutio Oratoria* was passed down by the early Christian fathers in the fourth and fifth centuries to the Italian humanists: a complete manuscript was rediscovered in St. Gall by Poggio in 1416. Among its more famous devotees are Petrarch, Lorenzo Valla, Erasmus, Peter Ramus, Martin Luther, Montaigne, La Fontaine, Racine, Lessing, and John Stuart Mill. Evidence of Quintilian's pedagogical influence is to be found everywhere from Italian manuals of courtly behavior like Baldesar Castiglione's 1512 *Book of the Courtier* (*Il Libro del Cortegiano*) to the eighteenth-century lectures of Adam Smith and John Quincy Adams on rhetoric and belles lettres. In the early twentieth century, John Dewey's call for a reformed educational system focused on training in civic values and practices found its origins in the *Institutio.*

Today Quintilian is studied primarily by rhetoricians and by historians of Roman culture, especially education. New areas of research are currently being mapped by scholars interested in cultural studies and gender studies, who find in the *Institutio* a wealth of sophisticated information about the intellectual and ideological making of elite Roman men. Also rediscovering Quintilian are political theorists interested in techniques of persuasion and public deliberation, and in the historical interrelationship between rhetoric and political thought. Quentin Skinner, for instance, argues that Roman theories of rhetoric and pedagogy play a central role in the evolution of early modern English thought on the citizen, the state, and public speech. Scholars of early American culture have begun to examine the impact of Quintilian's work on the debates over the nature of political discourse and literary culture in the early United States.

BIBLIOGRAPHY

Primary Sources and Translations

Quintilian. *Institutio Oratoria*. Trans. H. E. Butler. 4 vols. Cambridge: Harvard UP, 1920–22.
———. *Institutio Oratoria*. Ed. Michael Winterbottom. Oxford: Oxford UP, 1970.

————. *The Major Declamations Ascribed to Quintilian*. Trans. Lewis A. Sussman. Frankfurt and New York: Peter Lang, 1987.

Critical Sources

Barthes, Roland. "The Old Rhetoric: An Aide-mémoire." *The Semiotic Challenge*. New York: Noonday, 1988.

Bonner, Stanley A. *Education in Ancient Rome*. London: Campus, 1977.

Bourdieu, Pierre. *The Logic of Practice*. Trans. Richard Nice. Stanford: Stanford UP, 1990.

Connolly, Joy. "Mastering Corruption: Constructions of Identity in Roman Oratory." *Women and Slaves in Greco-Roman Culture: Differential Equations*. Ed. Sandra Joshel and Sheila Murnaghan. London: Routledge, 1998. 130–51.

Fantham, Elaine. "The Concept of Nature and Human Nature in Quintilian's Psychology and Theory of Human Instruction." *Rhetorica* 13 (1995): 125–36.

Fliegelman, Jay. *Declaring Independence: Jefferson, Natural Language, and the Culture of Performance*. Stanford: Stanford UP, 1993.

Grafton, Anthony, and Lisa Jardine. *From Humanism to the Humanities: Education and the Liberal Arts in Fifteenth and Sixteenth Century Europe*. Cambridge: Harvard UP, 1986.

Gunderson, Eric. "Discovering the Body in Roman Rhetoric." *Parchments of Gender*. Ed. Maria Wyke. London: Oxford UP, 1998. 169–89.

Kennedy, George A. *Quintilian*. New York: Twayne, 1969.

Lanham, Richard. "The 'Q' Question." *South Atlantic Quarterly* 87 (1988): 653–700.

Leeman, A. D. *Orationis Ratio: The Stylistic Theories and Practice of the Roman Orators, Historians, and Philosophers*. 2 vols. Amsterdam: A. M. Hakkert, 1963.

Monfasani, John. "Episodes of Anti-Quintilianism in the Italian Renaissance: Quarrels on the Orator as a *Vir Bonus* and Rhetoric as the *Scientia Bene Dicendi*." *Rhetorica* 10 (1992): 119–28.

Morgan, Teresa. "A Good Man Skilled in Politics: Quintilian's Political Theory." *Pedagogy and Power: Rhetorics of Classical Learning*. Ed. Yun Lee Too and Niall Livingstone. Cambridge: Cambridge UP, 1998. 245–62.

Ramus, Peter. *Arguments in Rhetoric against Quintilian*. Trans. Carole Newlands. Ed. James J. Murphy. DeKalb: U of Illinois P, 1986.

Skinner, Quentin. *Reason and Rhetoric in the Philosophy of Hobbes*. Cambridge: Cambridge UP, 1994.

Winterbottom, Michael. "Quintilian and the *Vir Bonus*." *Journal of Roman Studies* 54 (1964): 90–97.

RHETORICA AD HERENNIUM

(ca. 86–82 BCE)

Richard Leo Enos

THE DATE, AUTHORSHIP, AND RHETORICAL SITUATION OF THE *RHETORICA AD HERENNIUM*

Our knowledge of the *Rhetorica ad Herennium* undeniably would be enhanced if we were certain of its exact date and authorship, but there is still a great deal to be learned from this work without such knowledge. The best estimates of the date of the *Rhetorica ad Herennium* come from the scholarship of Harry Caplan, who fixes its composition within the range of 86–82 BCE (xxvi).[1] Some of the reasons for these dates come directly from the text itself. The author of the *Rhetorica ad Herennium* makes reference to the Social War in Italy as a theme for declamation (3.2.2), which would fix the date of the *Rhetorica ad Herennium* sometime after 90 BCE. We also have a reasonable knowledge of when Marcus Tullius Cicero began to write his own *Rhetorica*, and his earliest work, *De Inventione*, appears after the mid-eighties. As Caplan indicates (xxvi), there is a possibility that *De Inventione* could have been written prior to the *Rhetorica ad Herennium*. Yet, we should bear in mind that *De Inventione* is not only incomplete but, more important, that it was written by a very youthful Cicero, and the remains of his fragmentary efforts, while admirable for his age, do not yet compare with the synthesis and scope of rhetorical education that is evident in the *Rhetorica ad Herennium*. What is important, however, is not so much fixing the exact year but the general frame of time in which the *Rhetorica ad Herennium* was produced, for it is through an understanding of the social context of the time that we can appreciate the importance of the *Rhetorica ad Herennium*.

There is very clear evidence that rhetoric was introduced into Rome from three principle sources (Enos, *Roman Rhetoric*).[2] The first source of exposure was the introduction of Greek culture, including arts and letters, from Greek cities that had been colonies in southern Italy or *Magna Graeca*. The second avenue of exposure to rhetoric came from Roman citizens who traveled to Greece (often for study) and brought back to Rome the fruits of their education. Cicero's experiences as a young man studying in Greece and Asia Minor (79–77 BCE) are a good illustration of this type of introduction to rhetoric. Finally, Romans were exposed to rhetoric by Greek Sophists coming to Rome before the date of the *Rhetorica ad Herennium*. The influence of Greek rhetoricians from Rhodes was so pervasive that it led Harry Caplan to believe that the *Rhetorica ad Herennium* drew much of its material from the rhetoric that was practiced on the island of Rhodes (xv). Recent research on Rhodian rhetoric reinforces Caplan's views, providing further evidence of an earlier and long-lasting relationship in rhetoric between Rome and Rhodes (Enos, "Art of Rhetoric").

What we also can appreciate from the date of the *Rhetorica ad Herennium* are the social and cultural forces that nurtured the work into existence. It is an understatement to say that Romans had mixed reactions to Greek culture. On the one hand, the years of exposure to Greek and Etruscan civilizations had given the Romans unmistakable evidence of their own cultural shortcomings, particularly in arts and letters. Yet, Romans had an innate pride in their own heritage and language, and an equally strong desire to establish their own identity in the arts and education; in fact, Cicero stresses this very point repeatedly in his *De Oratore*, *Brutus*, and *Orator*. The desire to elevate the dignity and sophistication of their own *Humanitas* is particularly evident in how Romans approached their native language: Latin. Romans recognized the merits of Greek rhetoric and literature but wished to have a "Roman" rhetoric through "proper Latin" or *Latinitas* (4.12.17). This attitude is clearly apparent in their policies. Romans passed various acts that initially were done to outlaw rhetoric at Rome, which they felt was an undesirable Hellenic intrusion on their culture and incompatible with their values (Enos, *Roman Rhetoric*). Yet, the benefits of effective persuasion that came from the study of "Greek" rhetoric were undeniable and were soon recognized as a source of power in the Roman Republic (Enos, *Literate Mode*). Unable to thwart the growing popularity of the study of rhetoric, conservative Romans tried to restrict the Greek schools of rhetoric and encourage "Roman" schools, where rhetoric was studied, taught, and practiced in Latin with Roman themes. From this perspective, we can see why the *Rhetorica ad Herennium* would have significance, for it clearly appears to be a Roman rhetoric in many respects. Yet, as we shall see, it is heavily indebted to Greek rhetoric and thus provides a clue to the sources from which the author drew his or her material.

Exhaustive efforts have been made to determine the author of the *Rhetorica ad Herennium*, particularly by Harry Caplan. Since the time of Jerome, Caplan argues, this treatise was credited to Cicero, which most likely influenced its later popularity and even preservation (vii–viii). Inferences from Quintilian led later scholars to believe that the author may have been a (otherwise unheralded) rhetorician named Cornificius. In the introduction to his translation, however, Caplan argues convincingly that Cornificius lived at a time later than the author of the *Rhetorica ad Herennium* (ix–xiv). Caplan lays out the possibilities for authorship in the introduction to his translation and comes to the conclusion that the author must remain uncertain (xiv, i.e., "*auctor incertus*"). Despite this uncertainty, we still know a great deal about the author, who was clearly exposed to Hellenistic education, demonstrating both a thorough and a sophisticated knowledge of the Greek tenets of classical rhetoric. Yet, the knowledge of Roman history and social themes and the sophistication of the use of Latin all encourage us to think that the author is a native speaker of Latin and a Roman. This perspective encourages us to qualify the common attributions given to the *Rhetorica ad Herennium*. While it is clearly a "Roman" rhetoric in many respects, the treatise is also a transitional work. That is, the *Rhetorica ad Herennium* assimilates, translates, and modifies established Greek themes and precepts to Roman culture and Roman tastes (e.g., 4.7.10). For example, to illustrate a point of style, the author will use both the Greek hero Alexander and the Roman hero Tiberius Gracchus (4.22.31). For students of the history of rhetoric, this phenomenon of assimilation and adaptation is not new. St. Augustine's *De Doctrina Christiana*, the Venerable Bede's work on schemes and tropes, and numerous Renaissance manuals of rhetoric all exhibit (for various purposes) adaptation of other cultures to meet current social, religious, and political needs. In fact, one of the reasons why rhetoric has endured and prospered for so long is its ability to be modified and adapted to meet contemporary social exigencies. What we can say about the *Rhetorica ad Herennium*, however, is that this work may well be the first detailed illustration of such a process of assimilation and adaptation that led to the creation of a new, Roman rhetoric.

PROMINENT FEATURES AND THEMES OF
THE *RHETORICA AD HERENNIUM*

The author of the *Rhetorica ad Herennium* makes the purpose and orientation of the work clear from the introduction: this work on rhetoric is intended to enhance individual expression for the purpose of effective citizenship (1.1.1.). Mastery of the art of effective rhetoric cannot come about, the author asserts, without the self-discipline necessary for continued practice. Readers of the history of rhetoric will see the tripartite relationship of art, imitation, and practice (1.2.3) as harmonious with the views expressed in Isocrates' "Against the Sophists" and "Antidosis" and echoed later in Cicero's *De Inventione* and *De Oratore*. The explicit emphasis on the practical functions of rhetoric are important to note, but so also is the belief that the mastery of this art will serve not only the individual but the society as well. Although the Greek (Isocratean) antecedents are obvious, it is this theme—the development of the individual as a basis for the development of the Republic—that will become an identifiable trait of Roman rhetoric. The *Rhetorica ad Herennium* also demonstrates that the author has a thorough understanding of the three "causes" of rhetoric: demonstrative (epideictic), deliberative (political), and judicial (forensic). Further, the author believes that these causes can only be understood through the five canons of rhetoric: invention, arrangement, style, memory, and delivery. Such an orientation makes it clear that the author is familiar with the conventions of

Hellenistic rhetoric, but the notion that rhetoric is an art devoted to civic service helps us to understand the priorities that determine both the orientation and the sequence of his or her presentation of material.

Of the four books of the *Rhetorica ad Herennium*, no less than the first two are devoted to judicial rhetoric and invention. The author of the *Rhetorica ad Herennium* sees judicial rhetoric as immensely important to the Republic and the invention of arguments difficult (but essential) to master. Legal argumentation was a sanctioned system in the Republic, a process that served both a normative and regulatory social function. That is, through rhetoric individuals had the power to persuade listeners in matters of civic virtue, justice, and policy. Legal causes afforded Romans the opportunity to praise "proper" conduct as well as to condemn and correct vice (Enos, *Literate Mode*). Unlike the nascent procedures of forensic rhetoric in classical Athens, Roman legal procedure was much more complex and established. Every part of the arrangement of a rhetorical argument—from introduction to conclusion—was the subject of invention, since each aspect of the argument dictated the protocol for appropriate modes and methods of argument. In order to facilitate the process of localized invention, the author stresses the importance of mastering *constitutio* (1.11.18). The heuristic of *constitutio* is the Latin equivalent of *stasis*, a well-established process in Greek rhetoric for determining the point at issue in a rhetorical argument. *Stasis* was firmly established in Greek schools of declamation by the Hellenistic period, and its Latin equivalent is introduced to Romans in the *Rhetorica ad Herennium*. Similar to its Greek counterpart, *constitutio* enabled the rhetor to make a choice of the "issue" to be argued and how that issue could be presented at different points in the argument. Determining the issue, however, is only one feature of invention, for the rhetor must find effective ways of laying out the proofs and counterarguments for the audience. To facilitate this evidentiary process, the author of the *Rhetorica ad Herennium* again draws from Greek rhetoric and introduces the epicheireme, a five-part rhetorical syllogism (2.2.2) that assists the audience in reasoning with the rhetor. The attention that the *Rhetorica ad Herennium* gives to jurisprudential reasoning is clearly predicated on the needs of, and responsive to, the importance of law in the Roman Republic.

The author of the *Rhetorica ad Herennium* believes that mastery of judicial rhetoric and invention must take place before the remaining causes of rhetoric can be covered. In the third book, the author turns to deliberative and epideictic rhetoric and three of the last four canons of rhetoric: arrangement, delivery, and memory. Style is left to be treated extensively in the fourth and final book. Despite the fact that the *Rhetorica ad Herennium* implies (almost) algorithmic prescriptions for composition and expression, the theme of the third book is that precepts and guidelines can, and should, be modified to the situation. As mentioned earlier, it is clear that the importance of arrangement has been underscored by its close relationship with invention and, based on that understanding, we can see why the disposition of discourse is never removed from the creation of lines of proof and refutation (3.9.16–17). Yet despite the apparent regimentation of arrangement, the author of the *Rhetorica ad Herennium* underscores the value of creative adaptation. The rhetorical situation, the author notes, may well encourage a modification and even departure from conventional patterns of arrangement, if such deviations help to secure a favorable audience judgment (3.9–10.17). The flexibility that the author encourages in arrangement is apparent in delivery. The popularity of declamation makes delivery an important topic, and the author rigorously and systematically details the appropriate modes of presentation in the performance of one's argument. Yet in the conclusion of this topic, the author encourages the reader to remember that effective delivery is predicated on a sincere spirit (3.15.27), which implies a genuine sensitivity to the context of the situation and the audience.

The importance of adaptation and creativity is further underscored in the discussion of memory. There is little doubt that memory is extremely practical in an oral society where the assimilation of knowledge provides individuals with a repository of social wisdom (3.24.39). Various exercises for memory training are discussed in the third book, even including the importance of writing as an aid to memory (3.17.30). Equally important, however, is that such expansive, accumulated wisdom provides an array of possibilities of responding to various rhetorical situations. It is this ability to adapt to circumstances that links memory with creativity and underscores the value of practice and exercise.

As mentioned above, the fourth and final book is devoted to style. Here we see the detail and explication of style that has earned the *Rhetorica ad Herennium* both its fame and its reputation for tedious, exaggerated detail. The discussion of style, to which much of the treatise is devoted, is categorized into three levels (*gravis*, *mediocris*, and *adtenuata*) and the treatment of tropes and figures provides a comprehensive presentation of terms and precepts (4.8.11, 4.11.16). Given the perspective taken in this study, however, we can now look at the meticulous study of levels of style and figures from a far different perspective. The fact that the discussion of style, and many of the examples on style, are drawn from Latin sources and illustrations makes it clear that the author wishes to establish and affirm that this is to be a Roman rhetoric. There is no doubt that Greek precepts have been used throughout the *Rhetorica ad Herennium*, and the discussion of style, in this respect, is no different from the Hellenistic undertones of the previous three books. Yet the constant and continued explication of the particulars of the Latin language is (at the least) an indirect statement that rhetoric is being adapted to have a Roman identity through Latin artistry in rhetoric (e.g., 4.12.17). The concluding remarks of the *Rhetorica ad Herennium* tell us not only a great deal about the author's views on style but the importance of the work as a whole. For the author of the *Rhetorica ad Herennium*, a command of Latin style will not only refine diction but also bring out the best of all the remaining four canons of rhetoric. That is, invention, arrangement, delivery, and memory will all attain their best versions through a mastery of style. This mastery of style, and in turn the other canons of rhetoric, can only come about, the author stresses, if the art of rhetoric is complemented with diligent practice.

THE HISTORICAL SIGNIFICANCE OF THE
RHETORICA AD HERENNIUM

The *Rhetorica ad Herennium* is regarded by historians of rhetoric as an invaluable artifact in our discipline's history. The primary reason for the preservation and prestige of this work is believed to be the fact that the *Rhetorica ad Herennium* is the earliest and most complete manual of Roman rhetoric. Efforts to collect early examples of Roman rhetoric have been limited and unable to bring to light any other comparable work. Early in the twentieth century, Henrica Malcovati collected fragments of Roman rhetoric and oratory, but the relatively few extant fragments of manuals in no way provide the thorough explication of rhetoric that is contained in the *Rhetorica ad Herennium*. Yet the very thoroughness and detail of the *Rhetorica ad Herennium* also has been a constraint on scholarship. Because of its meticulous and exhaustive explication of the technical features of rhetoric, the *Rhetorica ad Herennium* has lacked the attention given to other, more engaging specimens of Roman rhetoric. The *Rhetorica ad Herennium*, for example, lacks the charm and urbanity of Cicero's *De Oratore*, which uses a dialogue format to discuss the place of rhetoric and oratory in the Republic. Nor does the *Rhetorica ad Herennium* offer the pedagogical flavor and personality of Quintilian's *Institutio Oratoria*, a work that grew out of the imperial period and became a cornerstone of Roman education. Some scholars even believe that the *Rhetorica ad Herennium* may well have not survived at all had it not been for the fact that this *ratio* was mistakenly attributed to Marcus Tullius Cicero and, therefore, preserved within the corpus of that famous Roman's *Rhetorica*.

The value of the *Rhetorica ad Herennium*, however, extends far beyond the fact that it is both a complete and early illustration of a Roman handbook. The *Rhetorica ad Herennium* is a victim of stereotyping: few of its qualities are discussed outside of its fixed categorization as a Roman manual of rhetoric. A close examination of the topics, intention, and themes of the *Rhetorica ad Herennium* tell a great deal about Roman rhetoric and the environment within which it existed. What may be more important to historians of rhetoric is not so much that the *Rhetorica ad Herennium* is identifiable as a homogenous "Roman" rhetoric but rather, as is argued here, that it is better understood (and appreciated) as a transitional work that synthesizes Greek rhetoric into Roman education. In this respect, the *Rhetorica ad Herennium* provides numerous clues that help historians of rhetoric to better understand not only the emergence of rhetoric in Rome but how rhetoric was introduced to that society's culture.

In the next generation, Cicero would adopt the Isocratean principle of uniting wisdom and eloquence for the benefit of the Republic. His testimony to the value of rhetoric would be lived out in both his theory and his career in politics. We can appreciate the influence of not only Isocrates but also other Greek rhetoricians as a basis of departure in the evolution of Cicero's rhetoric and the general acceptance and assimilation of rhetoric into Roman culture. Yet we also should recognize the *Rhetorica ad Herennium* as a transitional document in the history of rhetoric. The

Rhetorica ad Herennium did synthesize what were most likely the precepts of the Rhodian school of Hellenistic rhetoric, but did so in a manner and with an intent to create a rhetoric in its own right, one brought into existence to facilitate effective and engaged citizenship in the Republic.

The mere survival of the *Rhetorica ad Herennium* is testimony that this extensive treatment of rhetoric served Roman society long and well. The various editions, translations, and commentaries of the *Rhetorica ad Herennium* provide indirect testimony to how this work also was treasured throughout the Middle Ages and Renaissance. Yet as Caplan points out in his own edition, the influence of the *Rhetorica ad Herennium* has yet to be chronicled by historians of rhetoric (xxxv). In addition to its historical significance, there is much that the *Rhetorica ad Herennium* can contribute to contemporary rhetorical practices. For example, it should give us pause to reflect on the nature and impact of modern handbooks. More than mere prescriptive advice, such works help us unlock the relationship between cognition and expression in social interaction. That is, the *Rhetorica ad Herennium* provides a blueprint of how the relationship between thought and expression was seen by people from another culture and period. Its endurance also tells us that the benefits of this work were acknowledged and (to some degree) were passed along diachronically to other periods and cultures. As Caplan notes, the more than one hundred manuscript copies that are known today "is in itself an index of its popularity" (xxv). The *Rhetorica ad Herennium* is a detailed illustration of how rhetorical manuals shape not only our expression but also our very mentalities. By examining the epistemic presumptions grounding the *Rhetorica ad Herennium*, we can not only unlock prescribed rhetorical practices but have a paradigm that will help us to better understand our present-day presumptions about effective expression.

NOTES

I wish to express my appreciation to the rare book librarians at the Biblioteca Reale Di Torino who allowed me to examine a fourteenth-century copy of the *Rhetorica ad Herennium* in July 2000. Special thanks are also given to Paola Banchio, who facilitated all operations, arrangements, and permission forms in Torino, Italy.

1. Harry Caplan's translation of the *Rhetorica ad Herennium* in the Loeb Classical Library edition by Harvard University Press (1964) offers an excellent English translation facing the Latin text as well as a comprehensive introduction both to the work and classical rhetoric generally. Caplan's introduction is reprinted in *Of Eloquence: Studies in Ancient and Medieval Rhetoric by Harry Caplan*, edited by Anne King and Helen North (Cornell UP, 1970). Augustus S. Wilkins also offers a thorough (but dated) analysis of the *Rhetorica ad Herennium* in his introduction to Cicero's *De Oratore*. Ray Nadeau's translation and commentary of book I of the *Rhetorica ad Herennium* (*Speech Monographs*, 1949) is the only other substantial scholarship on the topic.

2. For general works on Roman rhetoric, readers are encouraged to consult the research on Roman rhetoric by George Kennedy and Richard Leo Enos that are also listed in the bibliography.

BIBLIOGRAPHY

Primary Sources and Translations

Cicero. *Ad C. Herennium de Ratione Dicendi (Rhetorica ad Herennium)*. Trans. with an introduction by Harry Caplan. Loeb Classical Library. Cambridge: Harvard UP, 1964.

Malcovati, Henrica, ed. *Oratorvm Romanorvm Fragmenta Liberae Rei Pvblicae, I: Textvs*. Torino: G. B. Paravia, 1953.

Nadeau, Ray. "*Rhetorica ad Herennium*, Commentary and Translation of Book I." *Speech Monograhs* (now *Communication Monographs*) 16 (1949): 57–68.

Critical Sources

Caplan, Harry. "Introduction to the *Rhetorica ad Herennium*" and "A Medieval Commentary on the *Rhetorica ad Herennium*." *Of Eloquence: Studies in Ancient and Medieval Rhetoric by Harry Caplan*. Ed. Anne King and Helen North. Ithaca and London: Cornell UP, 1970. 1–25, 247–70.

Enos, Richard Leo. "The Art of Rhetoric at Rhodes: An Eastern Rival to the Athenian Representation of Classical Rhetoric." *Rhetoric Before and Beyond the Greeks*. Ed. Carol S. Lipson and Roberta A. Binkley. Albany: State U of New York P, 2004. 183–96.

———. *The Literate Mode of Cicero's Legal Rhetoric*. Carbondale and Edwardsville: Southern Illinois UP, 1988.

———. *Roman Rhetoric: Revolution and the Greek Influence*. Prospect Heights, IL: Waveland, 1995.

Kennedy, George A. *The Art of Rhetoric in the Roman World: 330 B.C.–A.D. 300*. Princeton: Princeton UP, 1972.

Wilkins, Augustus S. "Introduction: 5. Analysis of the Treatise *Ad Herennium De Arte Rhetorica*." *M. Tulli Ciceronis De Oratore Libri Tres*. Hildesheim: Georg Olms Verlangsbuch-handlung, 1965. 56–64.

SAPPHO

(ca. 612–580 BCE)

David M. Timmerman

The earliest image of the poet Sappho is found on a late sixth-century vase drawing, playing the lyre. An examination of the received biography of Sappho produces a series of claims of greater or lesser probability beyond the fact that she wrote lyric poetry. It may be best, as many have suggested, to take the position that we actually know nothing of the historical Sappho and move directly, and solely, to the fragments. This seems needlessly cautious. However, the following biographical sketch is included with a more than healthy dose of caution. Sappho was married to a wealthy man, had a daughter (Cleis), and maintained a school which, according to at least one ancient commentary, was composed of the daughters of the most noble in Lesbos and Ionia. Her father was a wealthy wine seller named Scamandronymus and she had three brothers, one of whom (Charaxus) ran off with a courtesan. Sappho was exiled to Sicily due to political intrigue ca. 600. Finally, and most dramatically, she died as the result of leaping off a cliff at Leucas, after her love for a ferryman went unreciprocated.

The island of Lesbos produced a number of famous poets, none more so than Sappho. Even during the classical period her work was highly regarded; Plato referred to her as the tenth muse and we know of six plays that take her as their subject. Her life and work were lampooned by playwrights and condemned as morally corrupt by later Christian writers. In 1073, Pope Gregory VII called for the public burning of her poetry in both Rome and Constantinople. It was not until the Renaissance that Sappho and her work were once again valued and studied.

The age of Greek lyric poetry began in the age of orality in ancient Greece in the seventh century and continued through the fifth century BCE (Ong). The merging of the music of the lyre with the words of the poet resulted in a powerful rhetorical form that scholars are still examining (Cole). Sappho is the most prominent of the Greek lyricists and because her work stands on a par with that of Homer, her significance in the history of rhetoric would be hard to overstate. However, her poetic expression strays from the traditional rhetorical subject matter of war and politics, as Cheryl Glenn notes: "She moves the lyric from an expression of masculine heroism, political dominance, and male individuality to the ardor and nobility of the feminine soul, thereby contributing to literary rhetoric (poetics) and disrupting the continuum of male-dominated poetics" (27). As such, the persona and poetry of Sappho reside at the very foundation of the feminist revision of the rhetorical tradition.

THE ORIGIN OF LYRIC POETRY IN RITUAL AND PUBLIC PERFORMANCE

Sappho deserves greater attention from rhetorical scholars for the beauty and passion of her poetry as well as the important themes she addresses. Her poetry was recorded after her death, from oral tradition, as writing took hold in ancient Greece. Most commentators operate on the assumption that her poems were originally utilized in exclusively female gatherings and celebrations, possibly in connection with her school and perhaps as part of religious celebrations in honor of female deities such as Aphrodite, Athena, Artemis, or Hera. While performed in public, Sappho's poetry does not address typically public issues. Rather, her focus is the experiences of women from girlhood to adulthood.

Sadly, we possess just one complete poem, the *Ode to Aphrodite*. It survived in the writings of Dionysius of Halicarnassus, who quoted it in its entirety. It is prized as the earliest expression of sexual desire and eroticism in the Western tradition. Several fragments are considered by scholars to be wedding songs, which lament the separation of female companions upon marriage. The beauty and attractiveness of the bride are praised even as the loss of companionship is mourned. In addition, there are thirty fragments long enough to make some sense of their context and many additional fragments that range from several lines to one or two words. The dominant meter in the poems that survive involves three lines of equal length and rhythm, followed by a shorter fourth line. This is known as Sapphic meter.

THE ENDURING LEGACY OF SAPPHO: THE POET AND SYMBOL

Sappho gives us an important window into the lives of ancient women and continues to draw the admiration and attention of scholars to this day. Her wedding choruses in particular are important as they highlight the loss of identity, freedom, and female companionship that accompanied marriage for ancient women. She celebrates love and addresses issues such as jealousy, the loss of love, and rivalry. Her poetry raises the constructs of both heterosexual and homosexual female sexuality. The women of Lesbos were apparently known for sexual activity generally, and homosexual behavior more particularly. Care must be taken with this connection, however, because current understandings of sexuality differ from those of ancient times. In particular, in ancient times the central feature may not have been the gender of the two participants but the role each played (active or passive, the pursuer or the one pursued). Related to this is the idea that in the ancient world, a person's sexual "orientation" (a contemporary term) was not considered as central to the personality as it is sometimes taken to be today. The use of the term "lesbian" to refer to a female homosexual began in the nineteenth century (Blundell 83).

Sappho is also worthy of greater examination as an enduring symbol. The manner in which she has been handled by scholars over the last three centuries has varied dramatically, and these various appropriations and interpretations reveal a good deal about the scholarly perspectives as well as the historical and social context. Precisely because both Sappho the person and her poetry are so rhetorically powerful, these texts have generated both passionate and varied lines of interpretation (DeJean; Snyder). To cite one example, Mary Lefkowitz documents the heterosexual bias with which Sappho's treatment of female friendship has historically been received by her commentators ("Critical Stereotypes"). This bias extends to the translation of her poems themselves. Nevertheless, for rhetorical scholars, these multiple interpretations and uses of Sappho serve as the indisputable markings of a rhetorically powerful and highly significant figure.

BIBLIOGRAPHY

Primary Sources and Translations

Bernard, Mary, trans. *Sappho: A New Translation.* Berkeley: U of California P, 1958.
Campbell, David A., ed. *Greek Lyric I: Sappho and Alcaeus.* Cambridge: Harvard UP, 1982.
Lobel, Edgar, and Denys Page. *Poetarum Lesbiorum Fragmenta.* Oxford: Oxford UP, 1955.
Voigt, Eva-Maria, ed. *Sappho et Alcaeus: Fragmenta.* Amsterdam: Polak and Van Gennep, 1971.

Biographical Sources

Lefkowitz, Mary R. "Critical Stereotypes and the Poetry of Sappho." *Heroines and Hysterics.* New York: St. Martin's, 1981. 59–68.
———. *The Lives of the Greek Poets.* Baltimore: Johns Hopkins UP, 1981.
Page, Denys. *Sappho and Alcaeus: An Introduction to the Study of Ancient Lesbian Poetry.* Oxford: Oxford UP, 1955.
Parker, Holt N. "Sappho Schoolmistress." *Transactions of the American Philological Association* 123 (1993): 309–51.

Critical Sources

Blundell, Sue. *Women in Ancient Greece.* Cambridge: Harvard UP, 1995.
Cole, Thomas. *The Origins of Rhetoric in Ancient Greece.* Baltimore: Johns Hopkins UP, 1991.
DeJean, Joan. *Fictions of Sappho 1546–1937.* Chicago: U of Chicago P, 1989.

DuBois, Page. *Sappho Is Burning*. Chicago: U of Chicago P, 1995.

Glenn, Cheryl. *Rhetoric Retold: Regendering the Tradition from Antiquity through the Renaissance*. Carbondale: Southern Illinois UP, 1997.

Greene, Ellen, ed. *Rereading Sappho*. Berkeley: U of California P, 1996.

Lardinois, Andre. "Keening Sappho." *Women's Voices in Greek Literature and Society*. Ed. Andre Lardinois and Laura McClure. Princeton: Princeton UP, 2001. 75–92.

Ong, Walter. *Orality and Literacy: The Technologizing of the Word*. London: Methuen, 1982.

Reynolds, Margaret, ed. *The Sappho Companion*. New York: Palgrave, 2001.

Snyder, Jane McIntosh. *Lesbian Desire in the Lyrics of Sappho*. New York: Columbia UP, 1997.

Stehle, E. *Performance and Gender in Ancient Greece: Nondramatic Poetry in Its Setting*. Princeton: Princeton UP, 1997.

———. "Sappho's Gaze: Fantasies of a Goddess and Young Man." *Reading Sappho: Contemporary Approaches*. Ed. Ellen Greene. Berkeley: U of California P, 1996. 193–225.

Williamson, Margaret. *Sappho's Immortal Daughters*. Cambridge: Harvard UP, 1995.

Seneca the Younger

(4 BCE–65 CE)

Michael G. Moran

Lawyer, orator, teacher, courtier, philosopher, scientist, dramatist, essayist—Lucius Annaeus Seneca was one of the great intellectuals of Rome in the Silver Age. Known as Seneca the younger because he was the son of Annaeus Seneca, author of books on declamation, the younger Seneca was born in Spain but raised in Rome, where he enjoyed the best education available to a child of wealth and privilege. Since his father was fascinated with rhetoric, young Seneca studied this discipline with some of Rome's best teachers. Unlike his father, however, the son rejected traditional rhetoric, turned to philosophy, and became one of antiquity's important Stoic philosophers, personalizing Stoicism to develop an ethical code designed to guide one's life according to the dictates of reason.

Seneca began his career in the law courts, then entered politics, and began a long, painful association with three emperors. Under Caligula, Seneca gained the office of quaestor but fell out of favor when the unstable emperor became jealous of his brilliant oratory. The next emperor, Claudius, banished Seneca in 41 CE to Corsica for a purported adulterous affair with the emperor's niece. Seven lonely but productive years later, Claudius's fourth wife, Agrippina, convinced her husband to end the banishment so that Seneca could return to Rome as her son Nero's tutor. When Nero became emperor, Seneca, along with Burrus the praetorian, served as his principal advisor and worked to liberalize many Roman laws that ushered in the *Quinquenniam Neronis*, the golden age of Nero (Baker and Baker 177). During this period, he wrote philosophical dialogues and was active in the theater, writing some of his best tragedies (Boyle 284). Seneca eventually fell out of favor with the erratic emperor, who wanted to confiscate Seneca's wealth. In 62 CE Seneca withdrew from public life and wrote many of his important works, including *Ad Lucilium Epistulae Morales* (ca. 62–65) (Motto 13), his collection of letters to an old friend and student in which his reflections on rhetoric appear. In 65 Seneca was linked, perhaps unfairly, with the Pisonian conspiracy against Nero, and the emperor seized this opportunity to destroy his advisor. An imperial messenger arrived at Seneca's villa with a choice: commit suicide or suffer execution. Seneca chose the former and met a stoic end, talking with his friends as he slowly bled to death.

The purpose of the *Epistulae*, consisting of 124 extant letters, was not to set forth a theory of rhetoric; it was to enunciate a set of Stoic values to teach correct understanding and proper action (Sorensen 190–91). Written to Lucilius, a longtime pupil of Seneca's in philosophy, the letters respond to the student's questions and objections as if the two were in conversation. While not about rhetoric, the letters often address questions of rhetoric as Seneca attempts to articulate a theory of appropriate language use consistent with Stoic principles (Kennedy, *New* 176). Seneca criticizes traditional views of rhetoric, which he argues emphasize superficial study of words rather than the mastery of knowledge, and states his own views of the subject, advocating philosophical discourse aspiring to conversation spoken and written in a plain, natural style that reflects an ordered mind and character.

SENECA'S RHETORICAL THEORY

Seneca writes little about traditional rhetoric in the *Epistles*, and what little system he presents is truncated. That Seneca offered such an abridged system was not due to ignorance. He was trained in Roman rhetoric and oratory, and he himself was an orator in the courts. As he comments in Epistle 49, however, he soon "lost the desire to plead, [. . . and then] lost the ability" (49.3), as his interests turned to philosophy. His slighting of formal rhetoric resulted from his suspicion of many assumptions of the discipline as then practiced. In Epistle 89, "On the Parts of Philosophy," for instance, he limits rhetoric to style and arrangement when he defines its concerns as "words, and meanings, and arrangements" (89.17); he ignores delivery, which he mentions in other letters, and invention, which he dismisses in its traditional Aristotelian form. His rejection of invention is centrally important to his view of rhetoric. He repudiates superficial methods of accumulating information and calls regularly throughout the *Epistles* for thoroughly mastering systems of thought. In this sense, he is more Platonic than Aristotelian.

One form of invention that Seneca flatly rejects for mature thinkers is the memorizing of maxims. For Aristotle, maxims can function as the premises for enthymemes, but Seneca thought that maxims discouraged original thought. While maxims might be appropriate for youthful minds, Seneca rejects them for mature thinkers, scornfully calling the results of such study "note-book knowledge" (33.7). To become educated means mastering systems of thought as a whole; to learn only parts of a masterpiece distorts the work (33.5). The depth of understanding that Seneca values must go beyond memorizing facts; wisdom requires that knowledge be integrated into the reader's intellectual system. Seneca therefore distinguishes between remembering and knowing: "Remembering is merely safeguarding something entrusted to the memory; knowing, however, means making everything your own; it means not depending upon the copy and not all the time glancing back at the master" (33.9). Such collections, Seneca claims, encourage the regurgitation of the thought of others and therefore prevent original reflection. Truly educated thinkers must strike out on their own investigations, follow their own paths, draw their own conclusions (38.10–11). They "should make such maxims [themselves] and not memorize" those of others (33.7), Seneca argues.

Seneca therefore rejects all superficial learning and calls for broader knowledge. One of his primary themes is the importance of reading to develop a "well ordered mind" (2.2–3). But Seneca rejects perfunctory reading and argues that reading too widely leads to trouble. Like the traveler who "has many acquaintances, but no friends," the "same thing must hold true of men who seek intimate acquaintance with no single author, but visit all in a hasty and hurried manner" (2.2). The person who hopes to develop a well-stocked mind must read deeply the works of a few "master-thinkers" (2.2–3) and return to these works regularly to reflect more deeply on their contents. Lucilius is advised to follow Seneca's own method of reading. He should read each day to fortify himself against misfortunes such as poverty or death—basic Stoic advice—and then select one thought to thoroughly digest. By concentrating on that thought, Seneca makes something from his reading his own (2.5). He can then draw on this knowledge when discoursing with others.

Seneca rejects ostentatious uses of language, and he sometimes identifies such ostentation with oratory. In Epistle 75, "On the Diseases of the Soul," for instance, he rejects showy communication that draws attention to itself. "Even if I were arguing a point," he comments, "I should not stamp my foot, or toss my arms about, or raise my voice; but I should leave that sort of thing to the orator, and should be content to have conveyed my feelings to you without having either embellished them or lowered their dignity" (75.3). In place of such demonstrative presentations, Seneca argues for a simpler delivery. Rather than using ostentatious methods to communicate, speakers should quietly express only those thoughts that they are "wedded to" and believe in deeply (75.3). As Seneca puts it, "Let this be the kernel of my idea: let us say what we feel, and feel what we say; let speech harmonize with life" (75.4–5). In contrast to the Aristotelian tradition, which emphasized finding ways to persuade in any situation, Seneca places his primary emphasis on the character of the speaker. Discourse must suit the speaker's character and be unadorned and direct. He criticizes those who strain to be eloquent but recognizes the importance of eloquence, if it is held within its proper bounds. Speakers who are naturally eloquent and achieve that eloquence "at slight cost" should "make the most of it and apply it to the noblest of uses" (75.6). But language should be used to "display facts rather than itself" (75.6). Seneca values a language that expresses the writer's ideas clearly and directly.

One fault that can destroy clarity is a too-rapid delivery, which is often the sign of an immature or a manipulative orator. Seneca points to Homer's orators for examples of younger men who speak like a "snow-squall" compared with the mature speakers, whose "eloquence flows [. . .] gently, sweeter than honey" (40.2). Mountebanks often speak rapidly and copiously to confuse listeners (40.3). Such rapid speech rushes by like a bird on the wing and is not designed to "sink in," to make us understand; it is used instead to "impress the common herd, to ravish heedless ears" (40.4). These "word-gymnasts" use linguistic tricks that might seem interesting at first but soon tire the audience (40.6–7). A speaker who wishes to communicate to an intelligent listener should use a conversational speech with "unadorned and plain" language designed to impart truth (40.4). But even orators who must speak to "inexperienced and untrained jurors" should not speak rapidly because the listeners will not be able to follow a disordered speech (40.8).

Epistle 75 addresses a related principle of delivery. Lucilius had complained that Seneca's letters are "carelessly written" (75.1), and the philosopher retorts that he wants his letters to aspire to the quality of friendly conversation—informal, spontaneous, easy. This point resonates with a similar contention of an earlier letter, number 38, "On Quiet Conversation." There Seneca had pointed to the benefits of conversation as opposed to lectures, harangues, or formal speeches. These are loud but lack intimacy and do not encourage learning. Conversation, on the other hand, is quieter, and words spoken "enter more easily, and stick in the memory" (38.1). While conversation, with its give and take, resembles in some ways dialectic, Seneca appears to distinguish between the two methods. He identifies the latter with defining terms and negotiating meanings; conversation, on the other hand, is less formal, freer. Its purpose is to stimulate thought, for the thoughts that friends share take root and grow (38.2). Seneca therefore advocates philosophical conversation designed to explore ideas and encourage their growth.

The canon of rhetoric that Seneca explores most thoroughly is style. One of Seneca's central arguments is the psychological assertion that words reflect the nature of the mind, character, and soul of the speaker or writer. A person who uses language carefully has a well-ordered mind, whereas a person who uses language badly reflects a disordered mind (59.4–5). As Seneca writes in Epistle 114, "On Style as a Mirror of Character," "When the mind is sound and healthy, style of speech too is forceful, firm and virile. If the mind has given way the rest follows in collapse" (114.22). Rapid and disorganized speech mirrors the speaker's soul—both are disordered (40.7). And state of mind influences character (114.3): "from [our mind] our thoughts and our words proceed, from there we derive our dress, our demeanor, our gait" (114.22). It therefore follows that language use reflects the state of both mind and character. Seneca gives the negative example of Maecenas, a Roman patron of literature who was sloppy, self-indulgent, and careless in both his character and his literary style. Consequently, "his eloquence is that of a drunkard, complex, rambling and wanton" (114.4). To improve his style Maecenus would have to improve both his mind and character.

Seneca takes his argument to the sociological level. If immorality in the individual perverts style, the same phenomenon occurs in societies, and Seneca argues that style and morality are linked. Just as individuals can have stylistic faults, so can ages, which are often corrupted stylistically by the introduction of luxury and opulence. As a society grows wealthy, opulence progresses from fancy clothes, to elaborate furniture and houses, to extravagant food (14.10–11). As Seneca argues, "So whenever you see a corrupt style is popular there you can be sure that morality had gone astray," and a psychological component exists because the spread of luxury "reveals the degeneracy of the minds from which the words proceed" (114.11–12). Once corruption sets in, it influences not only the average person but the intelligentsia, especially the critics, who accept the faulty taste (114.12). Seneca's views of the role immorality plays in the corruption of style reflects the times in which he lived. The simplicity of life in the mythical Golden Age must have seemed to him far away from the corruptions of imperial Rome, in which Seneca could find degeneracy and vice wherever he looked (Motto 49).

CONCLUSION

The principles of Stoicism pervade Seneca's discussion of rhetoric. He argued throughout his works that humans must follow reason and use this faculty to help them live in harmony with nature. Language is the tool through which humans can exercise reason, and he rejects all rhetoric that de-emphasizes a quiet, philosophical search for truth. This tool can easily be dulled by misuse if humans allow themselves to succumb to immorality, which means that mind, character, language, and morality have degenerated.

BIBLIOGRAPHY

Primary Sources and Translations

Seneca. *Letters from a Stoic.* Ed. and trans. Robin Campbell. Hammondsworth: Penguin, 1969.
———. *Ad Lucilium Epistulae Morales.* Ed. R. M. Gummere. 3 vols. Cambridge: Harvard UP, 1917–25.
———. *17 Letters.* Ed. and trans. C. D. N. Costa. Warminister, UK: Aris and Phillips, 1988.

Biographical Sources

Baker, Rosalie, and Charles F. Baker III. *Ancient Romans: Expanding the Classical Tradition.* New York: Oxford UP, 1998. 175–78.
Boyle, A. J. "Seneca the Younger." *Ancient Roman Writers. Dictionary of Literary Biography.* Vol. 211. Ed. Ward W. Biggs. Detroit: Gale, 1999. 281–90.

Critical Sources

Kennedy, George A. *The Art of Rhetoric in the Roman World 300 B.C.–A.D. 300.* Princeton: Princeton UP, 1972. 465–81.
———. *A New History of Classical Rhetoric.* Princeton: Princeton UP, 1994. 176–77.
Motto, Anna Lydia. *Seneca.* New York: Twayne, 1973.
Russell, D. D. "Letters to Lucilius." In *Seneca.* Ed. C. D. N. Costa. London: Routledge and Kegan Paul. 1974. 70–95.
Sorensen, Villy. *Seneca: The Humanist in the Court of Nero.* Trans. W. Glyn Jones. Chicago: U of Chicago P, 1976.

SEXTUS EMPIRICUS

(second–third century CE)

Robert N. Gaines

Sextus Empiricus was a skeptical philosopher and physician. We have no reliable indication of his birthplace or locus of professional activity (despite his association with Chaeronea according to the Suda [*sigma* 235]). His intellectual relations are sketched by Diogenes Laertius, who mentions Herodotus of Tarsus as his teacher and Saturninus as his student (9.116). But Diogenes' accuracy on the succession of skeptical philosophers has been questioned (Glucker), and the dates of Sextus's purported teacher and student are insecure (House). Thus, we have little help in dating Sextus and can conclude only that he lived in the period between the early second and early third century CE (House).

Three works survive in whole or part from Sextus's literary corpus, and they provide our only detailed information regarding Pyrrhonian skepticism. *Outlines of Pyrrhonism* (P) summarizes skeptical thought (1.1–241), then applies skepticism to the branches of dogmatic philosophy (logic 2.13–259; physics 3.1–167; ethics 3.168–278). A second work, incompletely preserved, was apparently titled *Skeptical Treatises* (Blomqvist), but its surviving contents are traditionally known as the last five books of *Against the Professors* (M 7–11). These books cover the same ground as P 2–3, though at greater length (logic M 7–8; physics M 9–10; ethics M 11). The third work, *Against the Professors*, contains one book in opposition to each of six encyclopedic arts: grammar, rhetoric, geometry, arithmetic, astrology, and music (M 1–6). Various sequences have been proposed for these works, but the standard view is that they appeared in the order given here (Floridi).

In *Against the Professors*, Sextus opposes dogmatic claims for the arts with general and special arguments. The general critique appears at M 1.9–38. For all the arts, he insists, there is no such thing as a subject taught, a teacher, a learner, or a method of learning; therefore, none of the arts is a subject of learning. The special critiques are previewed at M 1.39–40. Sextus says that he will not refute all claims made on behalf of each art; rather; he will refute only foundational claims upon which all other claims depend. Regarding rhetoric, the special critique arises in *M 2*, *Against the Rhetoricians*. Here Sextus provides the Pyrrhonist perspective on rhetoric, preserves much of the ancient dispute between rhetoric and the philosophical schools, and poses questions that endure to the present day for the rhetorical discipline (Barnes).

SEXTUS'S CRITIQUE OF RHETORIC

At the beginning of *M 2*, Sextus obtains assertions from Plato, Xenocrates, Stoic philosophers, and Aristotle that rhetoric "is an art" concerned with "speeches" or "speaking well," the end of which is "persuasion" (2.1–9). In response, Sextus argues that rhetoric is not an art (2.10–47), that rhetoric has no subject matter (2.48–59), that rhetoric has no end (2.60–88), and that the parts of rhetoric cannot achieve their respective ends (2.89–112).

Sextus begins his critique by citing a Stoic definition of "art," namely, "a system of apprehensions organized towards an end useful for life" (2.10). Rhetoric, he says, contains false principles which cannot be apprehended; therefore, rhetoric does not exist—at least as an art (2.11–12). He next summarizes earlier arguments against the artistic status of rhetoric, emphasizing Peripatetic contributions at 2.12–20 and Academic contributions at 2.20–43 (see Karadimas). He concludes on the art problem by responding to apologists for rhetoric (2.43–47).

Concerning the subject matter of rhetoric, Sextus argues that its supposed subject, speech, does not exist, because words and their combinations do not exist (2.48). But even if speech existed, it would be artistic only if it were beneficial, yet rhetorical speech is not beneficial, since it opposes laws and depraves the audience (2.49–50). Neither does rhetoric have a special claim to speech, since speech is common to many arts; thus rhetoric has no subject of its own (2.51). Finally, Sextus argues that the subject of rhetoric cannot be speaking well, because rhetoric is incapable of producing either fine expression or good speaking (2.52–59).

On the end of rhetoric, Sextus offers skeptical opposition to the typical view that the end of rhetoric is persuasion. What is persuasive, he says, must be credible insofar as it is true, false, or partakes of both; yet rhetoric can have none of these as its object; therefore persuasion is not its end (2.60–71). He then rehearses others' arguments on the end. Two arguments conclude that persuasion is not the end, because persuasion does not belong to the rhetor alone, and because persuasion is not the ultimate objective of the rhetor (2.72–73). Four arguments maintain that rhetorical speech does not persuade: it is overwrought, which offends; it is unclear, which fails to persuade; it is knavish, which arouses suspicion; and it appeals to emotions, which perverts rather than persuades the judge (2.74–78). Sextus does not disclose sources for these arguments, but Epicurean influence seems almost certain (Karadimas). Sextus concludes arguments on the end by refuting ends other than persuasion that have been proposed; thus, he resists views that the end of rhetoric is discovering possible arguments (2.80–83), implanting opinion in judges (2.84), what is advantageous (2.85), or victory (2.86–87).

Sextus next turns to the parts of rhetoric, judicial, deliberative, and encomiastic. Because these have distinctive ends—justice, advantage, and nobility respectively—it follows that the ends of the parts are inconsistent with one another and with the supposed end of rhetoric, persuasion (2.89–92). Moreover, Sextus argues that the parts cannot achieve their ends (2.93–105). Parts of rhetoric must succeed with speeches that are either consistent, inconsistent, or indifferent with regard to their respective ends. But in each of these conditions, the speeches are ineffectual, unrhetorical, or impossible. Again, if speech pursuant to an end is evident, then it is unrhetorical; but if it is doubtful, then conflicting speeches frustrate the end by confusing the judges. Finally, he reasons that the ends of all speeches are established by proof, but proof is nothing (2.105–12).

Reception

Sextus's skeptical works exerted little influence from late antiquity through the fourteenth century; skepticism was not well suited for the advancement of religion, and European readers preferred Latin sources. However, beginning in the fifteenth century Sextus received increasing attention from humanists, who recovered his works (e.g., Stephanus), as well as philosophers, who applied his skeptical methods to apologetics, science, and epistemology (e.g., Montaigne). By the second quarter of the seventeenth century, Sextus had become established alongside Gianfrancesco Pico della Mirandola, Henricus Cornelius Agrippa, and Francisco Sánchez as a figure central to the understanding of contemporary skepticism (Naudé). In this connection, Sextus's skeptical works should be recognized as forming an integral part of modern philosophy (Floridi).

Bibliography

Primary Sources and Translations

Bury, R. G., trans. *Sextus Empiricus*. 4 vols. Cambridge: Harvard UP, 1933–49.

Janáček, Karel. *Sexti Empirici indices*. 3rd ed. Studi (Accademia toscana di scienze e lettere La Colombaria). Firenze: Olschki, 2000.

Mau, J., ed. *Sexti Empirici Opera*. Vol. 3. Leipzig: Teubner, 1961.

Mutschmann, H., ed. *Sexti Empirici Opera*. Vol. 2. Leipzig: Teubner, 1914.

———, ed., rev. J. Mau. *Sexti Empirici Opera*. Vol. 1. Leipzig: Teubner, 1958.

Biographical Sources

House, D. K. "The Life of Sextus Empiricus." *Classical Quarterly* N.S. 30 (1980): 227–38.

Critical Sources

Barnes, Jonathan. "Is Rhetoric an Art?" *D[iscourse] A[nalysis] R[esearch] G[roup] Newsletter* 2:2 (1986): 2–22.

Blomqvist, Jerker. "Die Skeptica des Sextus Empiricus." *Grazer Beiträge* 2 (1974): 7–14.

Floridi, Luciano. *Sextus Empiricus: The Transmission and Recovery of Pyrrhonism.* American Classical Studies 46. Oxford: Oxford UP, 2002.

Glucker, John. *Antiochus and the Late Academy.* Hypomnemata 56. Göttingen: Vandenhoeck and Ruprecht, 1978.

Karadimas, Dimitrios. *Sextus Empiricus against Aelius Aristides: The Conflict between Philosophy and Rhetoric in the Second Century A.D.* Studia Graeca et Latina Lundensia 5. Lund: Lund UP, 1996.

Naudé, Gabriel. *Advis pour dresser une bibliotheque.* Paris: Targa, 1627.

SOCRATES

(ca. 469–399 BCE)

Christopher Lyle Johnstone

Socrates lived through the rise, decline, and resurgence of democracy in Periclean and post-Periclean Athens. At his birth, Athens was still the city of those who had defeated the Persians at Marathon, Salamis, and Plateia. The prime of his life saw Athenian supremacy under the leadership of Pericles and the first years of the Peloponnesian War. During his last decade, Socrates witnessed the defeat of Athens by Sparta and its allies, the brutal rule of the Thirty Tyrants, and restoration of a democracy that ultimately tried and executed him.

Socrates was born the son of Sophroniscus and Phaenarete, Athenian citizens of the deme of Alopeke. His father was said to have been a stonemason or a sculptor, and was apparently reasonably well-off. Socrates, in any event, was able to afford the armor of a hoplite (infantryman) and served with some distinction in the Peloponnesian War.[1] His mother, whose name literally means "she who brings virtue to light," was reportedly a midwife, a fact which, if true, may have inspired Socrates to compare his method of philosophical interrogation to the midwife's art (Plato, *Theaetetus* 149a). Late in life he married Xanthippe (who was notoriously bad tempered) and had three sons, the youngest of whom seems to have been a child at the time of Socrates' death.

Socrates' youth came during the first decades of Athens's ascendancy as the cultural, political, and economic center of the Greek world. During his childhood and adolescence, the philosopher Anaxagoras was teaching in Athens and the Sophist Protagoras first settled there. Tradition holds that Socrates was a student of the nature philosopher Archelaus (himself a pupil of Anaxagoras), and he was roughly contemporary with the Atomists Leucippus and Democritus, with whose works he may have been familiar. Initially Socrates took a serious interest in natural philosophy, but he abandoned this when he became convinced that the philosophers could not explain what, for him, are the most important matters a person can consider—ethical and moral ideas and the conduct of life.

The decades of the Periclean "Golden Age" coincided with Socrates' twenties and thirties, when he turned away from natural philosophy and pursued the study of human affairs. It is this study for which Socrates is now chiefly remembered, and it emerged during a time when he had numerous opportunities to converse with intellectuals from throughout the Greek world. Gorgias, for example, first visited Athens in 427, when Socrates was entering middle age, and such other Sophists as Prodicus, Hippias, Antiphon, and Thrasymachus spent time in the city during the remainder of his life. The events that dominated his last three decades—war, demagoguery, treachery, tyranny—doubtless affected Socrates' views of virtue, rhetoric, and "the life worth living." It was a time of great turmoil, when traditional beliefs were challenged and ancient customs were violated, when both collective and personal violence tore at the social fabric, and when intellectual debate and inquiry focused on moral questions.

In 399, following what some scholars view as a politically motivated trial,[2] Socrates was found guilty of refusing to acknowledge the gods recognized by the city, of introducing new divinities, and of corrupting the young. He refused to take advantage of a plan for his escape, made by some of his friends, and after a month's imprisonment he was executed by being made to drink hemlock, dying in the company of friends and followers.

SOCRATES AND THE SOPHISTS

Because he wrote nothing of his own, our understanding of Socrates' beliefs depends on the writings of those who knew him or his teachings. Most prominent among these writers is Plato, but additional information can be found in the works of Xenophon and Aristotle. None of these portraits is complete or unbiased, and we must be cautious in imputing to the historical Socrates the views that are attributed to him by any of these writers. Nonetheless, we can construct at least a tentative representation of his philosophical contributions to early rhetorical theorizing.

Socrates' views of rhetoric are portrayed solely in the dialogues of Plato. Xenophon's portraits reveal the character and personality of the real man, and they show something of his philosophical beliefs. However, they generally shed little light on his thoughts concerning the speaker's art. Unlike Plato and Xenophon, Aristotle did not have a personal acquaintance with Socrates, but his long association with Plato's Academy gave him an unparalleled opportunity to know the relation between the philosophies of Plato and Socrates. Thus, he is an important source for understanding the latter's distinctive contributions to philosophical inquiry. However, as with Xenophon, Aristotle's representation of Socratic teachings tells us little about his views of rhetoric. Consequently, the present discussion will draw exclusively on Plato's portrayal of these views.

Socrates is not generally regarded as a theorist of rhetoric. Even so, his views concerning the significance and origins of moral knowledge and its role in public debate and decision have important implications for both Greek and contemporary rhetorical theory. For the Greeks themselves, Socrates represented a watershed in the development of philosophical thought. At a more speculative level than did the Sophists, who were principally concerned with the practical effectiveness of speech in the courtroom and the assembly, he turned intellectual inquiry away from the concerns of the nature philosophers—about the origin and composition of the universe, the composition and motions of the heavenly bodies, and the causes of natural growth and decay—and concentrated instead on what it meant to be a human being and on the moral purposes of human existence.

Socrates' thinking concerning the goals and techniques of a genuine "art" of rhetoric cannot be understood except in comparison with the views of the fifth-century Sophists, and most particularly with those of Protagoras and Gorgias. Although it would be a mistake to say that Socrates' interest in moral philosophy was merely a reaction to the moral skepticism and relativism of some of his contemporaries, it would also be erroneous to conclude that his thought was not shaped to some extent by the formidable opposition these views presented. He sought to make ethics and politics the subjects of a systematic, scientific inquiry that would disclose universal laws or truths, in contrast to the skepticism and relativism that had turned all moral, judicial, and political questions into matters of opinion and had left personal conviction at the mercy of the persuader with the smoothest tongue.

Sophists such as Protagoras and Gorgias based their instruction on the belief that *aretē* or virtue could be taught. Socrates accepted this idea, and so concluded that therefore virtue must be a kind of knowledge. His philosophy was essentially a search for this sort of moral knowledge—that is, for stable, logically coherent moral principles that could guide human conduct. While he did not claim to have discovered any such principles himself, Socrates did develop and employ a discursive technique of inquiry by means of which he thought they could be discovered—the method of question and answer that came to be called dialectic.

SOCRATES' INFLUENCE ON RHETORICAL THEORIZING

Socrates' views concerning rhetoric are portrayed most vividly in Plato's two dialogues, the *Gorgias* and the *Phaedrus*. Although we must be careful in attributing to the historical Socrates all the doctrines that Plato has him profess, these two dialogues are generally regarded as representing accurately Socrates' criticisms of the "speaker's art" as it was taught in his day and his thinking about the preconditions of a "true art" of persuasion.[3] In the *Gorgias*, Socrates engages in an extended conversation with the old Sophist (and some of his followers) about the relationship between moral knowledge and the duties of one who teaches others how to persuade (449–61). Socrates then states his own view that rhetoric is not a true art, but instead is a "pseudo-art" of "pandering," akin to the knack of cookery, because it is concerned with mere appearance rather than with the "truth" of moral concepts (463–67). He says at one point, "I maintain that it [rhetoric] is merely a knack and not an art because it has no rational account to give of the nature of the various things which it offers. I refuse to give the title of art to anything irrational" (465a). How can one teach or practice an "art" of persuasion, Socrates would ask, if one cannot give a coherent explanation of the moral ideas upon which this art focuses its attention: Justice, Virtue, the Good, and so on?

Similarly, in the *Phaedrus* the title character observes, "I have heard it said that it is not necessary for the person who plans to be an orator to learn what is really just and true, but only what seems so to the crowd who will pass judgment; and in the same way he may neglect what is really good or beautiful and concentrate on what will seem so; for it is from what seems to be true that persuasion comes, not from the real truth" (260a). In the face of such a view, Socrates maintains that, "if a speech is to be well and fairly spoken, must not the mind of the speaker know the truth about the matters he intends to discuss" (259e)? Since this is so, Socrates concludes, "if he doesn't give enough attention to philosophy, [a person] will never become a competent speaker on any subject" (261a). His own presumed rhetorical practice, at any rate, reflects his commitment to the idea that "telling the truth about the subject" under discussion is more important in persuasion than are the artifices and techniques of the trained orator.[4]

THE SOCRATIC LEGACY

Socrates' contributions to rhetorical theorizing center on the relationship between persuasion and moral knowledge, and thus on the relationship between rhetoric and philosophy. It is upon this relationship that his student Plato also concentrated (see "Plato," this volume) and that became a matter of primary importance for succeeding generations of rhetorical theorists from Isocrates and Aristotle, Cicero and Quintilian, to Giambattista Vico and George Campbell, Lloyd Bitzer and Henry Johnstone, Jr. Most particularly, Socrates insisted that the would-be persuader must examine the meanings of the moral terms upon which his or her arguments turn—such terms as Justice, Goodness, Piety, Courage, Virtue—before he or she is competent to speak. Although the precise significance of Socrates' contribution to philosophical and rhetorical inquiry has been a matter of considerable debate, his influence on later thought is indisputable.

NOTES

1. Moreover, though he avoided taking an active part in politics, Socrates did serve in 406 as a member of the *prytaneis*, the fifty-member "committee" that managed Athens's day-to-day business.

2. Following the overthrow of the Thirty Tyrants and the restoration of Athenian democracy in 403, Socrates' earlier association with the tyrant Critias, the traitor Alkibiades,

and other antidemocratic figures induced three of his fellow citizens to bring charges against him. Moreover, he was notorious for having said things that seemed incompatible with the democratic form of government as it was practiced in Athens. On Socrates' trial, see Brickhouse and Smith, *Socrates*; Guthrie; Phillipson; Taylor.

3. Most modern scholars agree that Plato's aims in the early dialogues, which include the *Gorgias*, were to defend Socrates' reputation and to preserve his teachings. In the early and transitional dialogues, Socrates is concerned almost exclusively with moral issues, such as the nature of justice, courage, or piety, and not with the metaphysical and epistemological doctrines that are taken up in the middle and later dialogues. Indeed, the early dialogues provide a compelling portrait of Socrates' character as well as giving some insight into his thinking. In any event, we may feel somewhat secure in drawing conclusions about these matters from the early works, even as some of the middle dialogues (such as the *Phaedrus*) provide additional insight. See Vlastos; Guthrie; Brickhouse and Smith, *Philosophy*; Santas.

4. See, for example, Socrates' lead-up to his eulogy of Eros in Plato's *Symposium* (198b–199b), and his opening comments when he spoke in his own defense at his trial (*Apology* 17a–18a).

BIBLIOGRAPHY

Primary Sources and Translations

Aristotle. *Metaphysics*. Trans. Hugh Tredennick. Cambridge: Harvard UP, 1980.
Plato. *Apology*. Trans. Benjamin Jowett. Buffalo, NY: Prometheus, 1988.
———. *Gorgias*. Trans. Walter Hamilton. London: Penguin, 1960.
———. *Phaedrus*. Trans. W. C. Helmbold and W. G. Rabinowitz. Indianapolis: Bobbs-Merrill, 1956.
———. *Protagoras*. Trans. W. K. C. Guthrie. London: Penguin, 1956.
Xenophon. *Apology*. Trans. O. J. Todd. Cambridge: Harvard UP, 1923.
———. *Memorabilia*. Trans. E. C. Marchant. Cambridge: Harvard UP, 1923.
———. *Oeconomicus*. Trans. E. C. Marchant. Cambridge: Harvard UP, 1923.
———. *Symposium*. Trans. O. J. Todd. Cambridge: Harvard UP, 1923.

Biographical Sources

Brickhouse, Thomas C., and Nicholas D. Smith. *Socrates on Trial*. Princeton: Princeton UP, 1989.
Phillipson, Coleman. *The Trial of Socrates*. London: Stevens, 1928.
Taylor, A. E. *Socrates: The Man and His Thought*. Garden City, NY: Doubleday Anchor, 1953.

Critical Sources

Benson, Hugh H., ed. *Essays on the Philosophy of Socrates*. Oxford: Oxford UP, 1992.
Brickhouse, Thomas C., and Nicholas D. Smith. *The Philosophy of Socrates*. Boulder, CO: Westview, 2000.
Guthrie, W. K. C. *Socrates*. Cambridge: Cambridge UP, 1971.

Matthews, Gareth B. *Socratic Perplexity and the Nature of Philosophy*. Oxford: Oxford UP, 1999.

Santas, Gerasimos Xenophon. *Socrates: Philosophy in Plato's Early Dialogues*. London: Routledge and Kegan Paul, 1979.

Scott, Robert L. "On Viewing Rhetoric as Epistemic." *Central States Speech Journal* 18 (1967): 9–17.

Vlastos, Gregory. *Socratic Studies*. Ed. Myles Burnyeat. Cambridge: Cambridge UP, 1994.

CORNELIUS TACITUS

(ca. 55–117 CE)

Elizabeth Ervin

Cornelius Tacitus was born around 55 to 57 CE, probably in a province of northern Italy. He was not part of the Roman aristocracy but rather what Ronald Syme calls a *novus homo*: a member of the provincial nobility who had found avenues for advancement through service to the empire (566–84). Tacitus reveals little about himself in his own writing; there are large gaps in our knowledge of his life and much of what we do know comes from his correspondence with the younger Pliny, a close friend whose career paralleled his own.

As a youth Tacitus moved to Rome, where he presumably studied rhetoric, possibly with Quintilian, the premier rhetoric teacher at the time. Gaston Boissier describes Tacitus as "a singularly independent pupil": his work demonstrates little allegiance to any single teacher and it is likely that he did not pursue his studies beyond what he considered useful for his political career (3). It is difficult to speculate about Tacitus's skills as an orator, since none of his speeches survive; Pliny, however, describes him as being "in the prime of glory and renown" even as a young man (VII.20), a reputation he earned in part from his funeral oration for the celebrated general Lucius Verginius Rufus and from his successful prosecution of Marius Priscus, former governor of Africa, on charges of extortion. His professional performance earned the recognition of Agricola, the governor of Aquitania, whose daughter Tacitus married in 77. Tacitus held a quaestorship in 81 or 82, was praetor in 88, then spent four years away from Rome, likely as a legionary commander under a consular governor. The culmination of his senatorial career came in the years 112 to 113, when he served as governor of the province of Asia. When his term ended, Tacitus essentially disappeared from the political arena in order to devote himself to the study of history. He died in 117.

During the classical period, most credible histories were written by men who had been intimately involved in public life and thus had access not only to state documents but also to individuals who could provide firsthand accounts of events.

Tacitus epitomized this tradition. He published two monographs in 98: *Agricola*, a biography of his father-in-law, and *Germania*, an ethnological survey of the land and people of Germany, whose culture Tacitus deeply admired. He later wrote fourteen *Histories* (published around 112) and sixteen *Annals* (published in 116). Taken together, these works compose a narrative of Rome's first two imperial dynasties: the *Histories* cover the years 69 to 96, during which the Roman Empire struggled for survival at the end of the Julio-Claudian dynasty, and the *Annals* detail the years 14 to 68, beginning with the death of Augustus.

Although Tacitus's rhetorical skills can be inferred from his historiographical writings, the *Dialogue on Orators* is his only work to consider the subject of rhetoric explicitly. It remains one of the few critical statements documenting the shifting status of rhetoric during this period.

TACITUS'S RHETORICAL THEORY: *DIALOGUE ON ORATORS*

For centuries scholars attributed the *Dialogue* to Pliny, Suetonius, or even Quintilian, since Tacitus's name does not appear on the manuscript and it differs stylistically from his other work. Today, however, the *Dialogue* is almost always credited to Tacitus, owing to meticulous scholarship comparing the language and intellectual themes of the *Dialogue* to those of Tacitus's other works (see, e.g., Bennett; Gudeman). The publication date of the *Dialogue* is more difficult to determine definitively. Bennett and Moses Hadas, for example, place its date of composition at 81, when Tacitus would have been around twenty-five years old and before he had developed his later, distinctive style. Herbert W. Benario, George Kennedy, and Syme, on the other hand, believe it to have been written around 102 to 107, for several reasons: first, the work is dedicated to Fabius Justus, a friend of Tacitus who was consul in 102, and it was common at this time to dedicate literary works to friends upon the occasion of significant events; second, references to the *Dialogue* appear in the writings of Pliny published during those years; and finally, a man of mature age and secure reputation would be more likely to make a pronouncement on the condition of oratory.

Written in Ciceronian dramatic form, the *Dialogue on Orators* is structured as Tacitus's response to Fabius Justus, who asks why "our age is so forlorn and so destitute of the glory of eloquence that it scarce retains the name of orator" (1). Declining to answer the question himself, Tacitus instead purports to reconstruct a conversation he overheard as a youth, in the year 75, during which four eminent men discussed the very same issue. The setting for the *Dialogue* is the home of Curiatius Maternus, an acclaimed tragic poet and former advocate, who is reviewing his manuscript of the drama *Cato*, the subject of much talk among the people of Rome after a controversial public recitation the day before. The action opens with the visit of Marcus Aper and Julius Secundus, leading barristers of the day, who tease Maternus about writing a "safer" version of the play. When Maternus rebuffs their suggestion, Aper chides him for abandoning the study of oratory in favor of poetry, and the characters commence a debate regarding whether oratory was in fact in decline and if so what was the cause.

The first speaker, Aper, declares the continued vitality of oratory, a "manly" and practical art that acts as "both a shield and a weapon," "bring[ing] aid to friends, succour to strangers, deliverance to the imperilled." Oratory, he asserts, not only gives pleasure to audiences but offers to the orator the thrill of genius, the consciousness of "superhuman power," and a kind of prestige not conferred by the emperor (5–8). To this, Maternus responds that poetry—no less a manifestation of eloquence than oratory—is a delight in itself, harms no one, and promises a greater security of fame. While oratory may indeed be a potent weapon, he maintains, it is preferable to rely upon the protections of virtue and good conscience rather than the flattery, avarice, and intrigue that characterize "the harassing and anxious life of the orator" and rob him of his freedom (13).

At this point, the young senator Vipstanus Messalla joins the group, lamenting the paucity of great orators like Cicero and Demosthenes. Aper accuses Messalla of "sneering at and disparaging the culture of our own day" and argues that it is unreasonable to judge orators by the criteria of another age (15). Messalla, however, contends that the difference is not style but substance—the diminishment of oratory to rhetorical exercises that no longer depend on a passion for philosophical understanding and a commitment to public service. In short, rhetoricians with their "cunning tricks of flattery" have replaced the learned, virtuous orators, and Messalla blames "the indolence of the young, the carelessness of parents, the ignorance of teachers, and neglect of the old discipline" for this state of affairs (27–29). A lacuna in the *Dialogue* leaves Messalla's speech unfinished; some scholars believe that a speech by Secundus may also have been lost, since he plays an otherwise minimal role in the dialogue (see, e.g., Syme 106). In any case, the manuscript resumes with Maternus making his final point: that oratory thrives in times of war and corruption and declines in times of prosperity and peace, and that to bemoan the diminishment of oratory is to wish for an end to tranquility. Maternus concludes by assuring his friends that "had you been born in the past [. . .] the highest fame and glory of eloquence would have been yours" (41). The *Dialogue* ends with the four men parting amicably, agreeing to continue the discussion another time.

While all of the characters in the *Dialogue* were well-known public figures during Tacitus's youth, critics disagree on which of them most closely represents Tacitus's own views. Boissier, for example, believes that it is Messalla (9), while Benario (39) and Kennedy claim that it is Maternus; Kennedy notes, for example, that "Maternus is presented as an orator of great ability who has recently decided to abandon oratory, as Tacitus himself seems to have done" when he turned to history (518). Syme suggests that Tacitus's views can be found in those expressed by both Aper and Maternus, whom the author has equipped "with two conflicting portions of his own personality" (109n). Scholarly conjecture notwithstanding, it is more useful to regard the issue itself as evidence of the contested state of rhetoric during Tacitus's life. The *Dialogue* takes place during the early Roman empire, after a painful transition from the violence and political turmoil of the late Republic to a more stable but less democratic government composed of the emperor, Senate, and principate. Rhetoric continued to be the centerpiece of Roman education, but increasingly it emphasized declamations—formulaic performances that dealt with hypothetical and fantastical subject matter rather than traditional questions of politics and philosophy, which were seen as too volatile to treat directly. These trends mark the beginning of the period known as the Second Sophistic.

Tacitus is often described as a difficult writer for his digressive style and tendency toward what Boissier calls "counter debates" (73). However, translations of his work are highly accessible and offer relevant insights into the ways in which bold and meaningful public discourse may be circumscribed not only by tyrannical governments but also by a complacent citizenry.

BIBLIOGRAPHY

Primary Sources and Translations

Pliny the Younger. *Letters*. Trans. William Melmouth. 2 vols. Cambridge: Harvard UP, 1961–63.
Tacitus, Cornelius. *The Annals of Tacitus*. Trans. Donald R. Dudley. New York: New American Library, 1966.
———. *Histories*. Trans. K. Wellesley. New York: Penguin, 1995.
———. *Tacitus' Agricola, Germany, and Dialogue on Orators*. Ed. Herbert W. Benario. Norman: U of Oklahoma P, 1991.

Biographical Sources

Dudley, Donald R. *The World of Tacitus*. Boston: Little, 1969.

Critical Sources

Benario, Herbert W. *An Introduction to Tacitus*. Athens: U of Georgia P, 1975.
Bennett, Charles Edwin. "Introduction." *Dialogus de Oratoribus*. Tacitus. Boston: Ginn, 1894. vii–xxviii.
Boissier, Gaston, and William G. Hutchinson. *Tacitus: And Other Roman Studies*. New York: Constable, 1906.
Gudeman, Alfred. "Introduction." *Dialogus de Oratoribus*. Tacitus. Boston: Allyn and Bacon, 1898. v–xxxiii.
Hadas, Moses. *A History of Latin Literature*. New York: Columbia UP, 1952.
Kennedy, George. *The Art of Rhetoric in the Roman World, 300 B.C.–A.D. 300*. Princeton: Princeton UP, 1972.
Luce, T. James, and A. J. Woodman. *Tacitus and the Tacitean Tradition*. Princeton: Princeton UP, 1993.
Mellor, Ronald, ed. *Tacitus: The Classical Heritage*. New York: Garland, 1995.
O'Gorman, Ellen. *Irony and Misreading in the Annals of Tacitus*. Cambridge: Cambridge UP, 2000.

Sinclair, Patrick. *Tacitus the Sententious Historian: A Sociology of Rhetoric in Annales 1–6*. College Park: Pennsylvania State UP, 1995.

Syme, Ronald. *Tacitus*. 2 vols. New York: Oxford UP, 1997.

Woodman, Anthony J. *Rhetoric in Classical Historiography: Four Studies*. London: Areopagitica, 1988.

———. *Tacitus Reviewed*. New York: Oxford UP, 1998.

THEOPHRASTUS

(ca. 371–287 BCE)

Christy Desmet

In ancient Greece, Theophrastus was well known as a biologist, a philosopher of the Peripatetic school, and a rhetorician. Diogenes Laertius writes that he came from Eresus in Lesbos and was the son of Melantus, a cloth fuller. Theophrastus was a member of Plato's Academy; he also accompanied Aristotle to the court of Philip of Macedon and later, in his role as biologist, worked with Aristotle on the island of Lesbos. Originally named Tyrtamus, it is said, he was renamed Theophrastus, or "divine speaker," by Aristotle. During his career, Theophrastus was indicted for impiety but acquitted and also spent a brief time in exile. In his will, Aristotle named Theophrastus as the next director of his school, the Lyceum, and bequeathed to him his library and manuscripts. Heading the Lyceum for about thirty-five years, Theophrastus may have taught as many as two thousand students and received notice from the kings Philippus, Cassander, and Ptolemy. The Suda reports that Theophrastus died from days of continual writing followed by celebration of a student's marriage. In the *Tusculan Disputations*, Cicero also says that when Theophrastus was dying, he reproached nature for giving men such a short life because at the point of death, he had just begun to understand the arts (Fortenbaugh et al. 21–88, passim). Theophrastus died in Athens, asking in his will that he be buried at home in some convenient place in the garden.

As head of the Lyceum, Theophrastus produced an impressive number of treatises on philosophy and the natural sciences. According to extant references, Theophrastus also wrote extensively on rhetoric, discussing the topics, enthymemes, delivery, and style; a treatise *On Lexis* was especially influential (see Fortenbaugh, "Theophrastus on Delivery" 15). Altogether, Diogenes Laertius lists 213 works by Theophrastus, which he says amounts to about 232,850 lines (in Fortenbaugh et al. 41); unfortunately, all but two long studies on botany and the *Characters* are lost. Given the range of Theophrastus's expertise, he probably would be surprised to find himself remembered as the father of literary character. The *Characters* themselves probably were written within three years of the time Theophrastus took up his post as director of the Lyceum; he may have begun the sketches in 321 and worked on them for the next six years (Anderson xii). In his collection, Theophrastus offers thirty vignettes, exclusively of men, that represent unattractive social types.

In the Byzantine period, Theophrastus's *Characters* found their way into collections of rhetorical writings by Hermogenes and Aphthonius, probably as aids to character description (Fortenbaugh, "Theophrastus, the *Characters*" 18; Rusten et al. 29). In the process, they were sometimes shortened, sometimes made longer, and moralizing epilogues were added. Theophrastus had little direct influence in the medieval period, but he became known in England after 1592, when Isaac Casaubon printed the Greek text of the *Characters* with a Latin translation and commentary. In the history of European letters, Theophrastus is known primarily as the father of the character sketch, which enjoyed brief popularity as a minor literary genre in seventeenth- and eighteenth-century England and France (see Boyce; Smeed). Although the fad for character sketches waned, character portraiture as a rhetorical exercise was absorbed into other literary genres. Renaissance dramatist Ben Jonson included, in his published plays, descriptions of their social and humoral "characters." In the nineteenth century, Charles Dickens's *Sketches by Boz* and the novels of Anthony Trollope offer variations on the Theophrastan character (Rusten et al. 39).

THE CHARACTER'S RHETORICAL FUNCTION

The word "character," at the time when these sketches were written, was an agent noun, indicating someone who makes on a flat surface a mark or "character," usually the outline of a stamp (as on a coin) or an engraved line or shape (such as an alphabetic character). In time, the term "character" became passive rather than active, indicating the mark itself rather than the activity of engraving. Because coins were stamped in batches, not as unique items, a "character" designates a series of identical shapes rather than a unique one (see Anderson xv). Hence, written characters, like engraved ones, are things rather than acts, typical rather than individual.

What functions did the Theophrastan *Characters* serve? Some scholars speculate that Theophrastus offered the *Characters* to his student, the dramatist Menander, as a taxonomy of dramatic types (Anderson xiii) or that he added them as an appendix to his own lost work on comedy (Anderson xiv; Vellacott 9). Others consider the sketches as models for character description that could be incorporated into longer speeches (Fortenbaugh, "Theophrastus, the *Characters*" 18 ff.). The *Characters* have been linked particularly to 1.9 of Aristotle's *Rhetoric*, which discusses virtue and vice, and to Aristotle's later discussion of audiences according to age and other cultural contingencies (2.12–19; Fortenbaugh, "Theophrastus, the *Characters*" 29 ff.). In this light, they help orators to assess their audiences. Alternatively, the *Characters* may be no more than witty literary entertainment.

A more complex argument links Theophrastus's sketches with Aristotle's theory of identity. In the *Nicomachean Ethics*, Aristotle discusses the way in which ethical character develops through action in the public sphere. A person acquires character not by random activity, but by repeated actions that are governed by active choice and by ethical knowledge. As companion pieces to Aristotle's writings on ethics, Theophrastus's *Characters* represent as "product" the ethical identities that people achieve by the "practice" of virtuous and vicious behavior. While the *Ethics* describes the process by which we become who we are, the *Characters* record its results, providing snapshots of society's less savory products. As William Fortenbaugh points out, in the *Nicomachean Ethics* Aristotle focuses on the choices that turn scattered acts into habitual behavior and then into a settled tendency toward particular virtues and vices. Theophrastus's illustrations, by contrast, do not deal with underlying causes. He tells us what a character will probably say and do, but not why (Fortenbaugh, "Theophrastus, the *Characters*" 30-31). Fortenbaugh concludes that Theophrastus's interest in iterative but superficial behaviors rather than in choice represents a shift in Aristotle's thought between the *Nicomachean* and *Eudemian Ethics* that continued, after Aristotle's death, as a general trend in Peripatetic philosophy.

CONSTRUCTING CHARACTERS: STYLE, FORM, AND CONTENT

As literary set pieces, Theophrastus's *Characters* lack the rhetorical consistency and polish that defined the performances of his European heirs. Theophrastus's style can be awkward and obscure. He strings together details by polysyndeton, relying often on the weak connective "and." Theophrastus also uses formulas, such as "he is likely to say . . . ," and stresses the repetitive flavor of his subject's actions by using a tense that translates best into English as the future ("he will go to bed . . ."), but carries with it the present-tense force of habit or repetition. Theophrastus also flavors his style with extravagant metaphors. At least one editor speculates that the sketches were either lecture notes or a sketchbook and therefore not intended for publication (Rusten et al. 9).

Each of Theophrastus's portraits follows the same loose principle of organization: A general observation about the character type is followed by sample details of appearance, activity, and speech that follow the wandering trajectory of the portrait painter's eye. "The Flatterer," a type that was popular with Theophrastus's seventeenth-century imitators, pulls loose threads from his patron's cloak and looks toward him even when his attention should be elsewhere: "He tells everybody else to keep quiet while you are speaking, too, and he praises you in your hearing; or if you stop talking for a moment he puts in a 'Well said!' And when you try some feeble joke he will burst out laughing at it, with his coat stuffed against his mouth as if he had tried to hold back but couldn't" (Anderson 11).

Some of the characters are merely grotesque. "The Repulsive Man," for instance, will appear in public with "swollen fingernails and a loathsome skin disease";

he "is apt to have open sores on his shins or fingers," "wipes his nose with the back of his hand at the table and scratches himself while sacrificing." Worst of all, he will join his wife in bed without first washing himself (all from Anderson 81). But even in the case of the obviously Repulsive Man, the reader finds himself thrust into an uncomfortable rhetorical proximity to the figure's sores and smells. By focusing on expressions and gesture, the *Characters* recall Theophrastus's belief in the importance of delivery for oratorical performance (see Fortenbaugh, "Theophrastus on Delivery"). In other words, a character is an "anti-orator" whose appearance, behavior, and words are met with derision from the knowing audience. The *Characters* also provide an occasion for broader social commentary. While the caricaturist mocks the Flatterer openly, for instance, he also subjects to irony the vanity of that "Great-one" on whom the Flatterer fawns, exposing the defects of both society's outcasts and its respectable members.

CONCLUSION

Theophrastus's *Characters* are not merely a storehouse of types for orators or specimens in a scientific taxonomy of human nature. Neither are they simply deficient efforts at rhetorical description. As a genre, the character creates insight and pleasure by relying on narrative twists and turns illuminated by sharply-etched details. At the same time, the character keeps audiences engaged and off-balance. As potential dupes of the characters themselves and as potential subjects for the satiric portraitist, we too are subjected to the robust irony that marks the character as a genre.

BIBLIOGRAPHY

Primary Sources and Translations

Anderson, Warren, trans. *Theophrastus: The Character Sketches*. With notes and introduction by Warren Anderson. Kent: Kent State UP, 1970.
Rusten, Jeffrey, I. C. Cunningham, and A. D. Knox, ed. and trans. *Theophrastus, "Characters"; Herodas, "Mimes"; Cercidas and the Choliambic Poets*. Loeb Classical Library. Cambridge: Harvard UP, 1993.
Ussher, Robert G., ed. and introduction. *The Characters of Theophrastus*. London: Macmillan; New York: St. Martin's, 1960.
Vellacott, Philip, trans. *Theophrastus, "The Characters"; Menander, "Plays and Fragments."* Baltimore: Penguin, 1967.

Biographical Sources

Fortenbaugh, William W., et al., ed. and trans. *Theophrastus of Eresus: Sources for His Life, Writings, Thought, and Influence*. Leiden and New York: E. J. Brill, 1992. Part 1.

Critical Sources

Boyce, Benjamin. *The Theophrastan Character in England to 1642*. Cambridge: Harvard UP, 1947.

Bush, Douglas. "Characters." *Oxford History of English Literature (English Literature in the Earlier Seventeenth Century, 1600-1660)*. 2nd ed., rev. New York: Oxford UP, 1962. 5:208–219.

Fortenbaugh, William W. "Theophrastus on Delivery." *Rutgers University Studies in Classical Humanities*, 2 (1990): 269–88.

———. "Theophrastus, the *Characters* and Rhetoric." *Rutgers University Studies* 6 (1994): 15–35.

Greenough, Chester N. *A Bibliography of the Theophrastan Character in English*. Cambridge: Harvard UP, 1947.

Innes, Doreen C. "Theophrastus and the Theory of Style." *Rutgers University Studies* 2 (1990): 251–67.

Smeed, J. W. *The Theophrastan "Character": The History of a Genre*. Oxford: Clarendon, 1985.

THRASYMACHUS

(ca. 470–400 BCE)

Patrick O'Sullivan

Thrasymachus was a native of Chalcedon in Bithynia, who, like so many Sophists, was a professional orator and made his way to Athens. There he was well-known enough by 427 BCE to rate a mention in Aristophanes' *Banqueters* (fr. 205 K–A), produced that year. He wrote forensic rhetoric, on various aspects of deliberative rhetoric, rhetorical technique, exercises, and subjects for speeches. Titles of his lost works include: *The Big Textbook (Megale Techne)* (B3), *Overthrowing Arguments (Hyperballontes)* (B7), and *Techniques for Arousing Pity (Eleoi)* (B5). He also wrote political speeches such as the *Politeia (Constitution,* fr. B1 D–K) and a speech for the people of Larisa against Archelaus of Macedon, who ruled 413–399 BCE (fr. B2 D–K). Thrasymachus's forensic oratory seems to have all but disappeared by the first century BCE. Cicero (*De Orat.* 3.22.128) tells us that, like other Sophists such as Protagoras and Prodicus, Thrasymachus speculated on the physical world. He appears in Plato's *Republic* (dramatic date, ca. 420 BCE) as a fierce-tempered but incisive interlocutor of Socrates, espouses the view that justice is nothing more than the interests of the stronger party (*Rep.* 338c), and goes on to say that injustice is more profitable than justice. Elsewhere he calls justice "the greatest of goods for mortals" (fr. B 8 D–K), whose neglect by the human race indicates the gods' indifference to human affairs; the concept here clearly seems to embrace higher ideals for him, rather than simply being an instrument wielded by those in power. Details of his death are unknown. The tradition that he suicided, based on a scholiast's reading of a disputed passage of Juvenal (7.204), seems unlikely to have much foundation. His greatest legacy to ancient rhetoric involves pioneering developments of prose style—which earned him the praise of critics in antiquity—as well as devising techniques for imbuing speeches with considerable emotional power.

THRASYMACHUS'S CONTRIBUTIONS TO RHETORIC

No rhetorical theory of Thrasymachus survives. His handbooks probably involved some treatment of rhetorical principles, illustrated by specific examples. That Thrasymachus focused on the emotional content of a speech can be gleaned from Plato's *Phaedrus*, which mentions his great ability to enrage his audience, beguile them with his enchantments, and dish out and dispel slander (267c–d). He was especially noted for his capacity to arouse pity in his audience and for teaching speakers to bewail their lot, be it the problems of old age, poverty, or their children. Thrasymachus, then, shares an interest in the emotive and psychological powers of speech with Gorgias, who famously outlined these features in his *Encomium of Helen* (8–14). Such rhetorical interests of Thrasymachus are likely to find full expression in his *Eleoi*, and would be well suited to a range of speeches: judicial, epideictic (display), or deliberative. Thrasymachus's *Hyperballontes* may have been a counterpart or even response to Protagoras's *Kataballontes* (*Knock-Down Arguments*), suitable for scoring points in adversarial contexts.

Thrasymachus made stylistic contributions to prose, including work on clause and sentence structure, and especially prose rhythms. Aristotle (*Rhet.* 1409a1–3) associates his prose style with the paean, which involved the groupings of one long syllable followed by three shorts or vice versa. These devices, periodically applied, would have the advantage of adding some variety to the delivery of speeches, as well as avoiding the strict regularity of poetic meters. Thrasymachus's attempt at developing artistic prose in this way underlines just how much more fifth-century Greeks were attuned to the importance of euphonics than we are. The one piece of his writing of any significant length to survive is a fragment of the *Politeia*. Here is found a general avoidance of hiatus, which becomes a marked feature of the later prose of Plato, and less obvious antithesis than is found in Gorgias's writings. But how representative this fragment is of Thrasymachus's overall style is hard to gauge in the absence of his other works. Particularly noteworthy, however, is its political content. Thrasymachus would not have delivered it in Athens himself, due to his status as a foreigner, so the speech was either a pamphlet for distribution or written for an Athenian client to be delivered before the assembly. While we cannot say to what extent it reflects Thrasymachus's own political views, it contains much of interest. The speaker begins by announcing his wish to belong to a time when the elders held sway and it was not necessary for a younger man to address the assembly, and finishes with a plea to defer to these elders in matters beyond the experience and understanding of others. A key point made along the way is the critique of those who seek power without thinking, and who fail to see how the arguments of their opponents are embodied in their own policies. This plea for unity, while ostensibly conservative, rests on a subtle and paradoxical reading of the situation, consistent with many sophistic speculations. It seems here that Thrasymachus is invoking the insights afforded by sophistic training to make a telling political point.

RECEPTION OF THRASYMACHUS, ANCIENT AND MODERN

While noted in antiquity for his developing prose structure and rhythms, Thrasymachus also embodied the "middle" or "mixed" style for critics such as Theophrastus (Dionys. Hal. *Lysias* 6), a pupil of Aristotle, and Dionysius of Halicarnassus, a critic of the first century BCE. This style was seen to combine "austere" and "light" elements, and Dionysius finds it in the *Politeia* (*Demosthenes* 3). In fact, this fragment was preserved by Dionysius specifically for its stylistic interest, which so preoccupied ancient literary criticism. Elsewhere Dionysius admired Thrasymachus for his neatness of expression and his stylistic refinement and purity, as well as his powers of invention (*Isaeus* 20). He also praised Thrasymachus for his "condensed thought and expression," and found his style appropriate for law courts and all agonistic types of rhetoric (*Lysias* 6).

Due to the bullish character and definition of justice ascribed to him in *Republic* 1, Thrasymachus has often been considered an ethical nihilist—a view held by such influential thinkers as Sir Karl Popper, among others. But Plato's portrait of him may be due more to a desire to construct a dramatic foil for his Socrates than to give us the real Thrasymachus. We need to bear in mind his other views on justice (fr. B 8 D–K) and his observations on the problems caused by faction fighting and power-hungry politicians in the *Politeia*. Thrasymachus need not be endorsing the view Plato attributes to him, but conceivably is speaking about what is hypocritically announced as justice in an age of power politics and internecine strife that gripped the Greek world in the late fifth century BCE. If so, his concerns would be not so far removed from those of another observer of the same conflict, the historian Thucydides, especially in his devastating account of the *stasis* in Corcyra (3.81–83). There the combatants are described as manipulating language to invert the appalling reality they have created around them. As for his view on justice in Plato's *Republic*, Thrasymachus may perhaps be better understood as a disillusioned moralist, or unflinching iconoclast, rather than a simple advocate of "might is right."

BIBLIOGRAPHY

Primary Sources and Translations

Diels, Hermann, and Walther Kranz. *Die Fragmente der Vorsokratiker*. Vol. 2. 8th ed. Berlin: Weidmann, 1956.
Sprague, Rosamond, ed. *The Older Sophists*. Columbia: U of South Carolina P, 1972.

Critical Sources

Dover, Kenneth. *The Evolution of Greek Prose Style*. Oxford: Clarendon; New York: Oxford UP, 1997.

Guthrie, W[illiam] K[eith] C[hambers]. *The Sophists*. Cambridge: Cambridge UP, 1971.

Kennedy, George. *The Art of Persuasion in Greece*. London: Routledge and Kegan Paul, 1963.

Kerferd, George B. *The Sophistic Movement*. Cambridge: Cambridge UP, 1981.

Popper, Sir Karl. *The Open Society and Its Enemies: The Spell of Plato*. Vol. 1. 5th ed. London: Routledge and Kegan Paul, 1966.

Rankin, Herbert. *Sophists, Socratics and Cynics*. London: Croom Helm; Totowa, NJ: Barnes and Noble, 1983.

VERGINIUS FLAVUS

(floruit 49 CE)

Daniel R. Fredrick

Verginius Flavus is one of many, perhaps thousands, of figures in the history of Roman rhetoric with a terribly slim biography. There is neither a known date of birth nor death for the man, no record of parents, siblings, wives, nor children. However, history was kind enough to mark Flavus in Rome in 49 CE as the rhetoric teacher for the poet Persius; and Flavus was competent enough as a writer of rhetorical precepts that he received, albeit mixed with some sharp criticism, much praise from Quintilian. Until his own works surface, we can only reconstruct a small part of Flavus's career through second-hand references. What is certain is that Flavus promoted pragmatic/forensic rhetoric as outlined in the *ars rhetorica* (rhetorical precepts originating from Greek manuals that were studied in Roman schools), yet he assented to growing changes in Roman education, specifically the shift in emphasis from pragmatic/forensic rhetoric to artistic/epideictic.

In 1416, Paggio discovered a long-lost, complete copy of Quintilian's *Institutio Oratoria*, a treatise that extended the list of Roman rhetoricians, filling in the first century with important names between Cicero and Quintilian. Flavus was one of these important rhetoricians whom Quintilian esteems: "But Gallio's predecessors, Celsus and Laenas, and in our own day Verginius [. . .] have treated rhetoric with greater accuracy" (1:381). What exactly can we know about Flavus's treatment of rhetoric?

FLAVUS'S RHETORICAL THEORY

Flavus's treatment of rhetoric was to a large extent influenced by the values of the Silver Age, an era which experienced a major paradigm shift in rhetorical education. Rhetoricians after the death of Augustus in 14 CE, an event that marked the beginning of the Silver Age, lived in a vastly different society compared to Cicero's late Republic where pragmatic rhetoric flourished in the Roman Forum. In what

Richard Enos calls the "institutionalized *kairos*" of the Roman Forum, teams of advocates verbally battled the innocence or guilt of a client, influencing the judgment of jurors and the popular assembly (17). During the Republic, rhetoric education was designed primarily to prepare the young Roman to plead cases in the Forum. However, after the Republic, the need for legal advocates became only a facade under the emperor's rule (Kennedy 430). The "institutionalized *kairos*" crumbled. Consequently, during the empire, artistic/epideictic rhetoric—politically less threatening—subordinated pragmatic/forensic rhetoric in the schools. As a result, other elements besides legal exercises became dominant, such as *elocutio* (style), which fostered the creation of polished, literary stylists. Thus, the orator in the Silver Age was less a practicing lawyer and more an entertainer or poet.

Taking into account this major shift in rhetorical education that occurred during the Silver Age, we can note that a rhetorician such as Flavus faced two major challenges as a teacher of rhetoric: (1) How could rhetoric be made useful when pragmatic rhetoric, the staple of rhetorical education for hundreds of years, was no longer a social necessity? (2) How could students receive a complete education in the *ars rhetorica* when they found parts of it irrelevant to their personal aspirations?

The teaching career of Flavus best underscores this dilemma, for Flavus desired to teach the whole of the *ars rhetorica* even though some of his students found elements of it irrelevant. One such student was the famous Persius, a satirical poet so effective that Nero, perturbed by Persius's attacks against the wealthy, indulgent Roman elite, exiled him. Persius's penchant for satire most likely led him to criticize Flavus's pedagogy, particularly those elements that trained legal advocates, such as *declamatio*. The extent of Persius's prickly relationship with Flavus is unknown, but Persius "clearly did not enjoy declamation" (Kennedy 462). His distaste for declamation, we can infer, was not merely the quirk of an eccentric satirist. Numerous educators, such as Petronius (see the opening passages of *Satyricon*), disapproved of declamation, believing the exercises to be too far removed from reality to be useful. Persius most likely represents a typical view of the growing number of Roman students who were not studying rhetoric for its ability to make one upwardly mobile in law and politics, but rather for its intensive, literary value. As declamation was more for legal training, Persius did not find it valuable for learning poetry. Thus, Persius may have found some of Flavus's curriculum unimportant if not irritating to his own poetic pursuits. What then would compel a student with the talent and potential of Persius to continue his education with Flavus or any Silver Age rhetoric teacher who persistently taught the *ars rhetorica* in its entirety?

One possible answer is that declamation was only one feature in an art that, according to Cicero, put such great demands on the student that being accomplished in any of its canons—invention, arrangement, style, memory or delivery—was a great intellectual feat in itself (15–17). The *ars rhetorica* not only helped prepare legal orators, but poets could prepare their skills with the canon of style, which offered hundreds of stylistic choices useful for all genres of writing. Persius therefore could develop best as a poet by studying the canon of style. In short, Flavus's adherence to teaching all of the *ars rhetorica* ensured something practical for all of his students. Though rhetoric students in the Silver Age may have found legal training unnecessary to their interests, they undoubtedly found *elocutio* useful. Flavus's contribution to the history of rhetoric, minor yet perhaps of greater interest to those researching Roman rhetoric in the early years of the empire, is that he carried on the full tradition of the *ars rhetorica*, never diminishing a student's experience in that tradition despite the shift away from pragmatic/forensic rhetoric.

Although Flavus was a reputable teacher, his writing of rhetorical precepts did not escape Quintilian's criticism. Quintilian believed Flavus to be one of the best of his era, and many of Flavus's contributions Quintilian approved of—his ability to preserve the *ars rhetorica* with accuracy, his coining of many new words for the Latin language (3: 229), and his great wit (4: 311). However, Quintilian found weaknesses in Flavus's understanding of the legal heuristic *stasis* theory (3: 121). Quintilian seems to be criticizing Flavus for not accounting for the wide legal application and complexity of *stasis* theory and for his possible pandering to popular school topics of declamation. Quintilian's criticism reemphasizes what little can be deduced given the absence of Flavus's works: Although Flavus carried on the full tradition of the *ars rhetorica*, he may have been retooling the tradition to meet the new demands of a society that saw artistic/epideictic rhetoric as more suited to its own interests.

BIBLIOGRAPHY

Primary Sources

Cicero, Marcus Tullius. *De Oratore, Books I-II.* Trans. E. W. Sutton. Cambridge: Harvard UP, 1942.

Quintilian, Marcus Fabius. *Institutio Oratoria.* Trans. H. E. Butler. 4 vols. Cambridge: Harvard UP, 1958.

Critical Sources

Enos, Richard Leo. *Roman Rhetoric: Revolution and the Greek Influence.* Prospect Heights: Waveland, 1995.

Kennedy, George A. *The Art of Rhetoric in the Roman World.* Princeton: Princeton UP, 1972.

BIBLIOGRAPHIC ESSAY

Michelle Ballif and Michael G. Moran

James J. Murphy, in his "Open Letter" ("Conducting Research," 1997), offers (future) historians of rhetoric pragmatic advice for how to conduct research; Richard Leo Enos and Ann M. Blakeslee, in their report on the state of research in "The Classical Period" (1990), encourage future research, and indeed identify needed areas for such research. To aid the (future) historian and student of classical rhetoric, we offer the following range of sources—mostly contemporary, mostly book-length, from primary to secondary, from studies in classics, speech communications, and rhetoric and composition, in order to provide a paper trail for the reader interested in learning more about classical rhetoric.

Several important overviews of classical rhetoric are available. The most detailed scholarly study covering all of classical rhetoric is George A. Kennedy's *A New History of Classical Rhetoric* (1994). This book both abridges and revises his three previous histories listed in our bibliography and offers an overview of the classical tradition from its beginnings in ancient Greece to its decline in the Middle Ages. A shorter introduction is available in the first three chapters of Thomas Conley's *Rhetoric in the European Tradition* (1990) and in the early sections of Patricia Bizzell and Bruce Herzberg's *The Rhetorical Tradition* (second edition, 2001), which includes excellent bibliographies. James J. Murphy and Richard A. Katula, *A Synoptic History of Classical Rhetoric* (third edition, 2003) contains detailed summaries of the major statements, including those of Aristotle, Cicero, and Quintilian. Briefer overviews such as Edward P. J. Corbett and Robert J. Connors's "A Survey of Rhetoric" (1999), Roland Barthes's "The Old Rhetoric" (1988), and Kennedy's "Classical Rhetoric" (2001), as well as his "Historical Survey of Rhetoric" (1997), the first chapter of Brian Vickers's *In Defence of Rhetoric* (1988), and the first three chapters of Renato Barilli's *Rhetoric* (1989) provide readers with a solid framework on which to build further study. More specific and detailed analyses are available in the resources below, as well as in the bibliographies listed at the conclusion of each figure's entry in the collection.

Several general bibliographies, anthologies, and reference books for the field have been compiled. A good bibliography with an introductory discussion is Richard Leo Enos and Anne M. Blakeslee's "The Classical Period" (1990). (This updates Enos's "The Classical Period" [1980, 1983]). Murphy and Katula's *Synoptic History* contains an unannotated but resourceful list, "A Basic Library for the Study of Classical Rhetoric" (1994). Thomas O. Sloane's impressive *Encyclopedia of Rhetoric* (2001) as well as Teresa Enos's *Encyclopedia of Rhetoric and Composition* (1996) include many entries relevant to classical rhetoric, as do the following reference sources edited by Simon Hornblower and Antony Spawforth: *The Oxford Classical Dictionary* (third edition, 2003), *Oxford Companion to Classical Civilization* (1998), and *Who's Who in the Classical World* (2000). Stanley E. Porter's *Handbook of Classical Rhetoric in the Hellenistic Period* (1997) is a rich compilation of rhetorical *topoi*: from the genres and canons of rhetoric to the various rhetorical practices and individuals of Hellenistic rhetoric. Philip B. Rollinson and Richard Geckle's *A Guide to Classical Rhetoric* (1998) is a handbook that provides detailed summaries from Greek and Latin rhetoric written before the fifth century CE. Although not limited to rhetoricians, Luci Berkowitz and Karl A. Squitier's *Thesaurus Linguae Graecae: Canon of Greek Authors and Works* (1986) proves useful as a bibliographic guide for ancient authors. And Donald C. Bryant et al.'s edited *Ancient Greek and Roman Rhetoricans* (1968) briefly identifies the major figures and works of classical rhetoric. A *Glossary of Greek Rhetorical Terms* (2000), prepared by R. Dean Anderson, Jr., provides a rich resource for specifically classical terminology. Richard A. Lanham's *A Handlist of Rhetorical Terms* (1991), although extending beyond the purview of classical times, catalogues and defines the parts of rhetoric as well as its figures of speech and thought. The aforementioned Bizzell and Herzberg collection, *The Rhetorical Tradition* (2001), anthologizes classical rhetoricians from Gorgias to Quintilian, and Patricia P. Matsen et al.'s *Readings from Classical Rhetoric* (1990) ranges from Homer to Augustine. Additional anthologies such as *The Presocratic Philosophers*, edited by G. S. Kirk, J. E. Raven, and M. Schofield (1983), Kathleen Freeman's *Ancilla to the Pre-Socratic Philosophers* (1983), Rosamond Kent Sprague's translation of the Diels-Kranz compilation of the work of the Sophists, *The Older Sophists* (1972, rpt. 1990), John Dillion and Tania Gergel's *The Greek Sophists* (2003), and Michael Gagarin and Paul Woodruff's *Early Greek Political Thought from Homer to the Sophists* (1995) provide readers access to primary works in translation. Resources for investigating women's contributions can be found in Mary Ellen Waithe's edited *A History of Women Philosphers* (1987), as well as Ethel M. Kersey and Calvin O. Schrag's *Women Philosophers* (1989), which contains an introductory overview of women in antiquity, alphabetized entries of such, and an appendix that lists women by historical period as well as discipline, rhetoricans included. Additionally, *The History of Women Philosophers* (1984)—a translation of a seventeenth-century compendium by Gilles Ménage—provides primary references to as well as commentary on female dialecticians, Peripatetics, and Pythagoreans, for example. And, although the scope of this bibliographic essay is to report on contemporary print sources, particularly book-length studies, we did want to recommend two rich resources, databases of primary and secondary materials available electronically; the inspired Perseus Digital Library (www.perseus.tufts.edu/) and L'Année Philologique (www.annee-philologique.com).

Given classical rhetoric's historical connection to pedagogy, many histories of rhetoric have focused on educational concerns and practices of the classical period, such as James J. Murphy's edited *A Short History of Writing Instruction* (second edition, 2001), which contains two chapters on Greek and Roman writing pedagogy. Donald Leman Clark in *Rhetoric in Greco-Roman Education* (1957) explores the many ways that Greek and Roman instructors taught their students to speak and write effectively, and Henri Irenee Marrou in *A History of Education in Antiquity* (1982) analyzes many of the rhetorical components of the classical education system. Werner Jaeger's three-volume *Paideia: The Ideals of Greek Culture* (1943–45) provides a foundational understanding of how education served to perpetuate Greek culture. Contemporary speech communication and composition pedagogues have appropriated and reclaimed classical rhetoric's pedagogical precepts. Kathleen E. Welch in *Contemporary Reception of Classical Rhetoric* (1990) explores this appropriation, analyzing how classical rhetoric has been received since the last half of the twentieth century. Part I of *Rhetoric and Pedagogy* (1995), edited by Winifred Bryan Horner and Michael Leff, examines classical rhetoric and its (potential) relationship to contemporary pedagogical practices. *Essays on Classical Rhetoric and Modern Discourse* (1984), edited by Robert J. Connors, Lisa S. Ede, and Andrea A. Lunsford, contains essays that explore the influence of classical rhetoric on modern composition studies. While many composition textbooks draw on the classical tradition, several are based almost entirely on it. The oldest, Corbett and Connors's *Classical Rhetoric for the Modern Student* (fourth edition, 1999), makes classical theory available to contemporary students and includes, as mentioned above, an excellent short essay on the history of rhetoric and a useful bibliography. John H. Mackin's *Classical Rhetoric for Modern Discourse* (1969) teaches contemporary students to apply the principles of classical rhetoric to their speaking and writing. Other similar books include Winifred Bryan Horner's *Rhetoric in the Classical Tradition* (1988), Sharon Crowley and Debra Hawhee's *Ancient Rhetorics for Contemporary Students* (third edition, 2004), and Frank D'Angelo's *Composition in the Classical Tradition* (2000).

In addition to appropriating and reclaiming classical rhetoric, contemporary scholars have attempted to revise it historically, as the following recent titles demonstrate: Susan C. Jarratt's *Rereading the Sophists* (1991), Cheryl Glenn's *Rhetoric Retold* (1997), Janet M. Atwill's *Rhetoric Reclaimed* (1998), and James L. Kastely's *Rethinking the Rhetorical Tradition* (1997). Scholars, acknowledging the ideological nature of histories and history writing, have addressed revisionary concerns and practices in the historiography of classical rhetoric. Two edited collections provide readers with an understanding of various methodologies of history writing, including reconstructive, monumental, revisionary, critical, and even subversive: Takis Poulakos's *Rethinking the History of Rhetoric* (1993) and Victor J. Vitanza's *Writing Histories of Rhetoric* (1994). In addition, a special issue of the journal *Pre/Text* (edited by Victor J. Vitanza, 1987) addresses historiographical concerns.

A particular revisionary concern for contemporary historiographers of rhetoric is to regender the rhetorical tradition by including non-canonical women in that tradition, such as the three entries found in Andrea A. Lunsford's collection, *Reclaiming Rhetorica* (1995), or by, in addition, redefining rhetorical practices to include the discourses of women, including silence, which Cheryl Glenn's *Rhetoric Retold* (1997) attempts. Two special issues of the journal *Rhetoric Society Quarterly*, one guest edited by Jarratt (1992) and the other by Bizzell (2002) offer feminist rereadings in the history of rhetoric, and Andrea Nye's *Words of Power: A Feminist Reading of the History of Logic* (1990) demonstrates how philosophy (and philosophic rhetoric) excludes the feminine from its practices. Jane Donawerth's introduction to *Rhetorical Theory by Women before 1900* (2002) and Bizzell's "Opportunities for Feminist Research in the History of Rhetoric" (1992–93) offer overviews of the various methodologies and presuppositions of such revisionary historiography. Scholars have also examined the rhetorical tradition and how it has informed the construction of masculinity. Maud Gleason's *Making Men* (1995), Lin Foxhall and John Salmon's edited *Thinking Men* (1998), and Eric Gunderson's *Staging Masculinity* (2000) reread classical rhetoric to interrogate the relationship between rhetoric, performance, and masculinity.

RHETORIC IN ANCIENT GREECE

Several recent books have attempted to complicate our understanding of the beginnings of rhetoric in ancient Greece. Richard Leo Enos's *Greek Rhetoric before Aristotle* (1993) examines the evidence of rhetoric's beginnings before Aristotle and supports in general the traditional view that rhetoric emerged from Sicily. Two other books question the old saw that Sicily's Corax and Tisias invented rhetoric to argue cases in court over land disputes. Thomas Cole's *The Origins of Rhetoric in Ancient Greece* (1991) rejects notions that rhetoric gradually developed from earlier ideas or that a group of intellectuals created it in the late fifth century. Instead, he argues, rhetoric was a "typically fourth-century phenomenon" that Plato and Aristotle were the first to recognize and put to use (x). The two philosophers made possible the self-conscious awareness of written eloquence that was required for rhetoric to develop. Edward Schiappa in *The Beginnings of Rhetorical Theory in Classical Greece* (1999) also argues for a later development by pointing to the fact that the Greek term for rhetoric did not achieve widespread usage until the early fourth century, when the discipline of rhetoric began to be formulated.

Many scholars argue that rhetoric—as a discipline—emerged at this time as a result of the transition from a largely oral and mythic culture to an increasingly literate and rational one. The development of literacy enabled, according to Eric A. Havelock, a form of subjectivity that constructed the sort of self-consciousness that made possible the kind of rhetorical practice of which Cole speaks (Havelock, *Preface to Plato* [1963], "The Linguistic Task of the Presocratics" [1983], *The Muse Learns to Write* [1986]). Jacqueline de Romilly's *Magic and Rhetoric in Ancient Greece*

(1975), E. R. Dodds's *The Greeks and the Irrational* (1957), Marcel Detienne's *The Masters of Truth in Archaic Greece* (1996), Arthur W. H. Adkins's *From the Many to the One* (1970), Tony Lentz's *Orality and Literacy in Hellenic Greece* (1989), and Connors's "Greek Rhetoric and the Transition from Orality" (1986) provide the contextual background to understand the shift from oral, poetic eloquence or "protorhetoric" to rhetoric, as a disciplined set of practices. Jeffrey Walker, in *Rhetoric and Poetics in Antiquity* (2000), challenges the assumption that rhetoric—to be rhetoric—needed to divorce itself from poetry; on the contrary, he argues, and reinterprets classical rhetoric to make epideictic rhetoric more central to the classical system. C. Jan Swearingen's *Rhetoric and Irony* (1991) provides a historically conditioned examination of the relationship between rhetorical theory, rhetorical practice, and literacy training. Deborah Steiner's *The Tyrant's Writ: Myths and Images of Writing in Ancient Greece* (1994) offers an impressive historical, political, and cultural account of literacy. And in *Electric Rhetoric* (1999), Kathleen E. Welch traces the "new literacy" of our current age back to classical rhetoric.

Other scholars attribute the "invention" of rhetoric to the rise of democracy in classical Athens. Despite its origination, most historians of rhetoric assume a connection between rhetoric and politics, if not rhetoric and democracy. Harvey Yunis's *Taming Democracy* (1996) explores this relationship by demonstrating how political theorists in classical Athens theorized rhetoric as political discourse. The aforementioned collection *Early Greek Political Thought from Homer to the Sophists* (1995), edited by Gagarin and Woodruff, documents primary sources on the subject. Ekaterina V. Haskins's *Logos and Power in Isocrates and Aristotle* (2004) examines rhetoric's relationship to politics as theorized by these two rhetoricians; Haskins does so with the aim of addressing the future of democratic education. Susan C. Jarratt's *Rereading the Sophists* (1991) is motivated by similar concerns.

The best single overview of classical Greek rhetoric is George Kennedy's *The Art of Persuasion in Greece* (1963). Written primarily for students of the classics and speech, this book begins with persuasion in early Greek literature and then discusses all the major Greek theorists and important issues, including the influence of Greek theory on Rome, the quarrel between rhetoric and philosophy, and the tension between Asianism and Atticism. Other books have examined more narrowly focused issues in Greek rhetoric. Michael Edwards's *The Attic Orators* examines these ten early orators by briefly discussing each one's life, style, and works. Ian Worthington's collection, *Persuasion: Greek Rhetoric in Action* (1994), examines the complex relationships among rhetoric, oratory, and literature. Robert W. Smith in *The Art of Rhetoric in Alexandria* (1974) discusses the roles that rhetoric played in this Egyptian city founded by Alexander the Great in 330 BCE. *Greek Oratory: Tradition and Originality* by Stephen Usher (1999) provides treatments of speeches, particularly forensic, of individual orators.

John Poulakos and Takis Poulakos's *Classical Rhetorical Theory* (1999), as well as Christopher Johnstone's edited collection, *Theory, Text, Context: Issues in Greek Rhetoric and Oratory* (1996), offer thematic discussions that address not only traditional concerns (such as rhetoric and politics) but also various theoretical stakes involved in the development of rhetoric. Edward Schiappa's edited *Landmark Essays on Classical Greek Rhetoric* (1994) arranges a variety of sources, addressing issues from rhetoric's pre-Socratic origins to the post-Aristotelian age and offering a variety of theoretical approaches ranging from traditional historical reconstruction to more modern historical appropriations. Although traversing beyond the classical period, *Rhetoric and Kairos: Essays in History, Theory, and Praxis* (2002), edited by Phillip Sipiora and James S. Baumlin, offers various discussions of the rhetorical concept of *kairos*. And *Ethos: New Essays in Rhetorical and Critical Theory* (1994), edited by Baumlin and Tita French Baumlin, comes at the classical, rhetorical conception of *ēthos* back- ward: from contemporary theoretical thought.

Substantive discussions of the Sophists—the thematics of their practice as well as the particularities of individual Sophists—can be found in Harold Barrett's *The Sophists* (1987), G. B. Kerferd's *The Sophistic Movement* (1981), W. K. C. Guthrie's *The Sophists* (1971), and Mario Untersteiner's *The Sophists* (1954). More current research on the Sophists includes John Poulakos's *Sophistical Rhetoric in Classical Greece* (1995), which features discussions of how contemporaries of the Sophists received them, and Jacqueline de Romilly's *The Great Sophists in Periclean Athens* (1992), whose goal is to recover the Sophists in their own context, to create a broad "history of ideas" rather than to read the Sophists (either individually or collectively) through a par- ticular critical or philosophical lens. Much of the current research on the Sophists debates, however, whether a historian of the Sophists can, indeed, recover the Sophists on their own terms, and tends to recover the Sophists for contemporary concerns, such as Bruce McComiskey's *Gorgias and the New Sophistic Rhetoric* (2002), Susan C. Jarratt's *Rereading the Sophists* (1991), and Jasper Neel's *Plato, Derrida, and Writing* (1988). The following references provide the reader with an understand- ing of the methodological debate, as well as the stakes of the controversy: Scott Consigny's "Seeking the Sophist" (2001), Victor J. Vitanza's "The Sophists?" (1997), Edward Schiappa's "Neo-Sophistic Rhetorical Criticism or the Historical Reconstruction of Sophistic Doctrines?" (1990), and John Poulakos's "Interpreting Sophistical Rhetoric: A Response to Schiappa" (1990).

RHETORIC IN ANCIENT ROME

Roman rhetoric continues to receive scholarly attention. Kennedy's *The Art of Rhetoric in the Roman World, 300 B.C.–A.D. 300* (1972) remains the standard history of rhetoric in ancient Rome. M. L. Clarke's earlier *Rhetoric at Rome* (1953) empha- sizes both theory and practice of rhetoric in that city. Enos's *Roman Rhetoric* (1996) supplements earlier histories by focusing on the cultural upheavals of the first century BCE that influenced the development of a distinctive Roman rhetoric. William J. Dominik's collection titled *Roman Eloquence* (1997) examines rhetoric as a cultural phenomenon in Rome, focusing on its contributions to Roman literature, education, and oratory. Robert Morstein-Marx in *Mass Oratory and Political Power in the Late Roman Republic* (2004) examines the roles of political discourse and how this discourse distributed power between the masses and the Senate during the final years of the Roman Republic. In a more specialized work, Gregory S. Aldrete in *Gestures and Acclamation in Ancient Rome* (1999) studies the two-way communication that took place between Roman speakers and their audiences. The book focuses primarily on the "rules and patterns of behavior" that formed the basis of verbal, as well as nonverbal, communication.

Discussions of the so-called Second Sophistic include G. W. Bowersock's *Greek Sophists in the Roman Empire* (1969), which features a chapter on the contribution of Julia Domna to the rhetoric of this time, and Graham Anderson's *The Second Sophistic* (1993). Much of the current research on the Second Sophistic attempts to complicate and to challenge the "standard" story of rhetoric's decline during this period by investigating sophistic practices from a variety of fresh angles. Jeffrey Walker's *Rhetoric and Poetics in Antiquity* (2000) demonstrates that the prevailing, traditional assumption that rhetoric is "originally, primarily, essentially an art of pragmatic oratory whose paradigmatic scenes are the civil forums of a democratic polity" (45) is responsible for the narrative of decline. On the contrary, Walker argues, if one challenges this presumption, this delimiting definition of rhetoric, one can see the Second Sophistic as a time of "astonishing cultural vitality in which rhetoric, rhetoricians, and rhetorical literature seem highly prominent, prolific, and influencial" (45). Maud Gleason's aforementioned *Making Men* (1995) also offers an interesting *apologia*, hoping to ameliorate the "gloomy picture of this period," by focusing on the "social dynamics of rhetoric as an instrument of self-presentation, and in the process refine our appreciation of the functional aesthetics of a profoundly traditional performance genre" (xx). Her examination of two "star performers" of the Second Sophistic—Favorinus and Polemo—reveals how rhetorical practices engendered the voices and bodies of the orators. Simon Goldhill's edited *Being Greek under Rome* (2001) examines the cultural conflicts of the era, "the tensions, clashes and conservative strands of Empire society" (15), and how cultural identity of the Greek and/as the Roman was constructed and negotiated.

Declamation, a rhetorical exercise practiced by the Romans, has received some scholarly attention. The system was described by The Elder Seneca in two books, *Controversiae* and *Suasoriae*. As Michael Winterbottom argues in *Roman Declamation* (1980), declamation entered Rome by means of Greek teachers, was used to educate the young men of wealthy and influential families, and remained established as an instructional method for six centuries.

The standard work on declamation remains S. F. Bonner's *Roman Declamation in the Late Republic and Early Empire* (1949), which traces the early history of declamation from the Greek *thesis*, through the Ciceronian *causae*, to its final forms as *controversiae*. Bonner also explores the characteristics, styles, and ancient critics of declamation. In *Education in Ancient Rome* (1977), he presents a summary of his views. In "The Thesis in the Roman Rhetorical Schools of the Republic" (1951), Clarke questions Bonner's claim that there was a simple movement from the Greek *thesis* to the Roman *controversia*, arguing that the *thesis* continued to play a small role in Roman education (165). But, as Gaston Boissier argues in *Tacitus and Other Roman*

Studies (1906), Romans rejected the theoretical emphasis of the Greeks and replaced it with a practical one. Hence the development of *controversiae* and rejection of the more abstract *thesis*. Good short, recent discussions are found in Kennedy's *The Art of Rhetoric in the Roman World* (1972) and *A New History of Classical Rhetoric* (1994). Not all scholars view declamation positively. Clarke in *Rhetoric at Rome* (1953) and Harry Caplan in "Decay of Eloquence" (1970) argue that with the fall of the Republic, rhetoric disappeared from the legislature, and declamation came to emphasize "ingenuity, not serious argument" (163).

Declamation influenced Roman literature, and some scholars have studied that connection. G. O. Hutchinson in *Latin Literature from Seneca to Juvenal* (1993) argues that declamation was one of the sources for wit in the poetry of the age. Sander M. Goldberg in "Melpomene's Declamation" (1997) demonstrates that declamation influenced Roman tragedy, especially that of Seneca, by placing less emphasis on spectacle and more on language. And Susanna Morton Braund in "Declamation and Contestation Satire" (1997) claims that declamation provided the idiom for Juvenal's satire.

RHETORIC AND ORATORY IN LATE ANTIQUITY

The standard introduction to Greek rhetoric and oratory in late antiquity is Kennedy's *Greek Rhetoric under Christian Emperors* (1983). Kennedy argues that rhetorical education came to emphasize a variety of functions, including public address, literary composition, and training for bureaucrats, philosophers, preachers, and controversialists. The book discusses a variety of important figures, schools, and movements. A second seminal study of this period is James J. Murphy's *Rhetoric in the Middle Ages* (1974), which examines how the writers of late antiquity and the early medieval period continued the traditions of classical rhetoric. Other studies have examined more narrowly focused concerns. Mary Whitby's collection, *The Propaganda of Power* (1998), studies in detail the complex uses of panegyric in the ancient world from the first to the early seventh century CE, and Roger Rees's *Layers of Loyalty* (2002) studies in depth five short panegyrics delivered in Gaul in late antiquity. A significant amount of work has been completed recently on rhetorical strategies from ancient rhetoric used by the early church fathers and in the New Testament. Steven M. Oberhelman's *Rhetoric and Homiletics in Fourth-Century Christian Literature* (1991) examines the rhetorical strategies in the sermons of Ambrose, Jerome, and Augustine. Peter Auski's *Christian Plain Style* (1995) devotes a chapter to the classical discussion of the plain style and its influence on Christian discourse. Carl Joachim Classen's *Rhetorical Criticism and the New Testament* (2000) applies various principles of classical theory to the four gospels and Paul's epistles. St. Paul's use of rhetoric has received considerable recent attention. Duane Litfin's *St. Paul's Theology of Persuasion* (1994) shows the extent to which St. Paul in his preaching drew on classical theory, especially the principles of audience adaptation, and L. L. Welborn in *Politics and Rhetoric in the Corinthian Epistles* (1997) argues that Paul had a thorough familiarity with the rhetorical tactics of his time. Other books, such as Brian K. Peterson's *Eloquence and Proclamation of the Gospel in Corinth* (1994) and Kieran J. Mahony's *Pauline Persuasion* (2000), also examine Paul's rhetorical prowess. Bruce Winter's *Philo and Paul among the Sophists* (1997) interprets Pauline epistles as a rhetorical response to the Sophists, whom Paul mistrusted. Some recent work has been done on rhetoric later in the early Christian period. Carol Dana Lanham's *Latin Grammar and Rhetoric* (2002) provides an interesting collection of essays that explores many connections between ancient rhetoric and the Latin Middle Ages.

The scholars represented in this bibliographic essay, as well as others—including the authors of the entries in this volume—are contributing to the historiography of the evolving tradition of classical rhetoric. Perhaps they, as does Murphy when concluding his advice to the (future) historian, would remark: "Writing about the history of rhetoric [. . .] depends on the expanding knowledge base of the writer to identify the known and to go beyond that to the as-yet unknown" ("Conducting Research" 194). In this sense, all historians of rhetoric are future historians in that they contribute to the invention of the as-yet history of classical rhetoric. It is to these future historians that we dedicate this work.

BIBLIOGRAPHY

Adkins, Arthur W. H. *From the Many to the One.* Ithaca: Cornell UP, 1970.

Aldrete, Gregory S. *Gestures and Acclamation in Ancient Rome.* Baltimore: Johns Hopkins UP, 1999.

Anderson, Graham. *The Second Sophistic: A Cultural Phenomenon in the Roman Empire.* New York: Routledge, 1993.

Anderson, R. Dean, Jr. *Glossary of Greek Rhetorical Terms Connected to Methods of Argumentation, Figures and Tropes from Anaximenes to Quintilian.* Leuven: Peeters, 2000.

Atwill, Janet M. *Rhetoric Reclaimed: Aristotle and the Liberal Arts Tradition.* Ithaca: Cornell UP, 1998.

Auski, Peter. *Christian Plain Style: The Evolution of a Spiritual Ideal.* Montreal: McGill-Queen's UP, 1995.

Barilli, Renato. *Rhetoric.* Trans. Giuliana Menozzi. Minneapolis: U of Minnesota P, 1989.

Barrett, Harold. *The Sophists: Rhetoric, Democracy, and Plato's Idea of Sophistry.* Novato, CA: Chandler and Sharp, 1987.

Barthes, Roland. "The Old Rhetoric: An Aide Mémoire." *The Semiotic Challenge.* Trans. Richard Howard. New York: Hill and Wang, 1988. 11–93.

Baumlin, James S., and Tita French Baumlin, eds. *Ethos: New Essays in Rhetorical and Critical Theory.* Dallas: Southern Methodist UP, 1994.

Berkowitz, Luci, and Karl A. Squitier, eds. *Thesaurus Linguae Graecae: Canon of Greek Authors and Works.* 2nd ed. New York: Oxford UP, 1986.

Bizzell, Patricia. "Opportunities for Feminist Research in the History of Rhetoric." *Rhetoric Review* 11.1 (1992–93): 50–58.

———, ed. Special Issue: "Feminist Historiography in Rhetoric." *Rhetoric Society Quarterly* 32.1 (2002).

Bizzell, Patricia, and Bruce Herzberg, eds. *The Rhetorical Tradition: Readings from Classical Times to the Present.* 2nd ed. Boston: Bedford, 2001.

Boissier, Gaston. *Tacitus and Other Roman Studies*. Trans. W. G. Hutchinson. London: Constable, 1906.

Bonner, Stanley F. *Education in Ancient Rome*. Berkeley: U of California P, 1977.

———. *Roman Declamation in the Late Republic and Early Empire*. Liverpool: UP of Liverpool, 1949.

Bowersock, G. W. *Greek Sophists in the Roman Empire*. Oxford: Clarendon, 1969.

Braund, Susanna Morton. "Declamation and Contestation Satire." *Roman Eloquence: Rhetoric in Society and Literature*. Ed. William J. Deminik. London: Routledge, 1997.

Bryant, Donald C., Robert W. Smith, Peter D. Arnott, Erling B. Holtsmark, and Galen O. Rowe, eds. *Ancient Greek and Roman Rhetoricians*. Columbia, MS: Artcraft, 1968.

Caplan, Harry. "Decay of Eloquence." *Of Eloquence: Studies in Ancient and Medieval Rhetoric*. Ed. Anne King and Helen North. Ithaca: Cornell UP, 1970. 160–95.

Clark, Donald Leman. *Rhetoric in Greco-Roman Education*. Morningside Heights, NY: Columbia UP, 1957.

Clarke, M. L. *Rhetoric at Rome: A Historical Survey*. London: Cohen and West, 1953.

———. "The Thesis in the Roman Rhetorical Schools of the Republic." *Classical Quarterly* 45.3 (1951): 159–66.

Classen, Carl Joachim. *Rhetorical Criticism and the New Testament*. Tübingen: Mohr Sieback, 2000.

Cole, Thomas. *The Origins of Rhetoric in Ancient Greece*. Baltimore: Johns Hopkins UP, 1991.

Conley, Thomas. *Rhetoric in the European Tradition*. New York: Longman, 1990.

Connors, Robert J. "Greek Rhetoric and the Transition from Orality." *Philosophy and Rhetoric* 19.1 (1986): 38–65.

Connors, Robert J., Lisa S. Ede, and Andrea Lunsford, eds. *Essays on Classical Rhetoric and Modern Discourse*. Carbondale: Southern Illinois UP, 1984.

Consigny, Scott. "Seeking the Sophist." *Gorgias: Sophist and Artist*. Columbia: U of South Carolina P, 2001. 1–34.

Corbett, Edward P. J., and Robert J. Connors. *Classical Rhetoric for the Modern Student*. 4th ed. New York: Oxford UP, 1999.

———. "A Survey of Rhetoric." *Classical Rhetoric for the Modern Student*. 4th ed. New York: Oxford UP, 1999. 489–543.

Crowley, Sharon, and Debra Hawhee. *Ancient Rhetorics for Contemporary Students*. 3rd ed. New York: Pearson/Longman, 2004.

D'Angelo, Frank J. *Composition in the Classical Tradition*. Boston: Allyn and Bacon, 2000.

de Romilly, Jacqueline. *The Great Sophists in Periclean Athens*. Oxford: Clarendon, 1992.

———. *Magic and Rhetoric in Ancient Greece*. Cambridge: Harvard UP, 1975.

Derrida, Jacques. *Dissemination*. Trans. Barbara Johnson. Chicago: U of Chicago P, 1981.

Detienne, Marcel. *The Masters of Truth in Archaic Greece*. Trans. Janet Lloyd. New York: Zone, 1996.

Dillion, John, and Tania Gergel, trans. *The Greek Sophists*. New York: Penguin, 2003.

Dodds, E. R. *The Greeks and the Irrational*. Boston: Beacon, 1957.

Dominik, William J., ed. *Roman Eloquence: Rhetoric in Society and Literature*. London: Routledge, 1997.

Donawerth, Jane, ed. *Rhetorical Theory by Women before 1900: An Anthology*. New York: Rowman and Littlefield, 2002.

Edwards, Michael. *The Attic Orators*. London: Bristol Classical, 1994.

Enos, Richard Leo. "The Classical Period." *Historical and Contemporary Rhetoric.* Ed. Winifred Bryan Horner. Columbia: U of Missouri P, 1983. 10–39.

————. "The Classical Period." *Historical Rhetoric: An Annotated Bibliography of Selected Sources in English.* Ed. Winifred Bryan Horner. Boston: G. K. Hall, 1980. 1–41.

————. *Greek Rhetoric before Aristotle.* Prospect Heights, IL: Waveland, 1993.

————. *Roman Rhetoric: Revolution and the Greek Influence.* Prospect Heights, IL: Waveland, 1996.

Enos, Richard Leo, and Ann M. Blakeslee. "The Classical Period." *The Present State of Scholarship in Historical and Contemporary Rhetoric.* Rev. ed. Ed. Winifred Bryan Horner. Columbia: U of Missouri P, 1990. 10–39.

Enos, Theresa, ed. *Encyclopedia of Rhetoric and Composition: Communication from Ancient Times to the Information Age.* New York: Garland, 1996.

Foxhall, Lin, and John Salmon, eds. *Thinking Men: Masculinity and Its Self-Representation in the Classical Tradition.* New York: Routledge, 1998.

Freeman, Kathleen. *Ancilla to the Pre-Socratic Philosophers.* 1948. Cambridge: Harvard UP, 1983.

Gagarin, Michael, and Paul Woodruff, trans. and eds. *Early Greek Political Thought from Homer to the Sophists.* Cambridge UP, 1995.

Gleason, Maud. *Making Men: Sophists and Self-Presentation in Ancient Rome.* Princeton: Princeton UP, 1995.

Glenn, Cheryl. *Rhetoric Retold: Regendering the Tradition from Antiquity through the Renaissance.* Carbondale: Southern Illinois UP, 1997.

Goldberg, Sander M. "Melpomene's Declamation (Rhetoric and Tragedy)." *Roman Eloquence: Rhetoric in Society and Literature.* Ed. William J. Deminik. London: Routledge, 1997. 166–81.

Goldhill, Simon, ed. *Being Greek under Rome: Cultural Identity, the Second Sophistic, and the Development of Empire.* Cambridge: Cambridge UP, 2001.

Gross, Nicolas P. *Amatory Persuasion in Antiquity.* Newark: U of Delaware P, 1985.

Gunderson, Erik. *Staging Masculinity: The Rhetoric of Performance in the Roman World.* Ann Arbor: U of Michigan P, 2000.

Guthrie, W. K. C. *The Sophists.* Cambridge: Cambridge UP, 1971.

Haskins, Ekaterina V. *Logos and Power in Isocrates and Aristotle.* Columbia: U of South Carolina P, 2004.

Havelock, Eric A. "The Linguistic Task of the Presocratics." *Language and Thought in Early Greek Philosophy.* Ed. Kevin Robb. La Salle: Monist, 1983.

————. *The Muse Learns to Write: Reflections on Orality and Literacy from Antiquity to the Present.* New Haven: Yale UP, 1986.

————. *Preface to Plato.* Cambridge: Harvard UP, 1963.

Hornblower, Simon, and Antony Spawforth, eds. *The Oxford Classical Dictionary.* 3rd ed. Oxford: Oxford UP, 2003.

————, eds. *Oxford Companion to Classical Civilization.* Oxford: Oxford UP, 1998.

————, eds. *Who's Who in the Classical World.* Oxford: Oxford UP, 2000.

Horner, Winifred Bryan. *Rhetoric in the Classical Tradition.* New York: St. Martin's, 1988.

Horner, Winifred Bryan, and Michael Leff, ed. *Rhetoric and Pedagogy: Its History, Philosophy, and Practice.* Mahwah, NJ: Erlbaum, 1995.

Hutchinson, G. O. *Latin Literature from Seneca to Juvenal.* Oxford: Clarendon, 1993.

Ijsseling, Samuel. *Rhetoric and Philosophy in Conflict.* The Hague: Martinus Nijhoff, 1976.

Jaeger, Werner. *Paideia: The Ideals of Greek Culture.* 3 vols. Trans. Gilbert Highet. New York: Oxford UP, 1943–45.

Jarratt, Susan C. *Rereading the Sophists*. Carbondale: Southern Illinois UP, 1991.

———, ed. Special Issue: "Feminist Rereadings in the History of Rhetoric." *Rhetoric Society Quarterly* 22.1 (1992).

Johnstone, Christopher L., ed. *Theory, Text, Context: Issues in Greek Rhetoric and Oratory*. Albany: State U of New York P, 1996.

Kastely, James L. *Rethinking the Rhetorical Tradition: From Plato to Postmodernism*. New Haven: Yale UP, 1997.

Kennedy, George A. *The Art of Persuasion in Greece*. Princeton: Princeton UP, 1963.

———. *The Art of Rhetoric in the Roman World, 300 B.C.–A.D. 300*. Princeton: Princeton UP, 1972.

———. "Classical Rhetoric." *Encyclopedia of Rhetoric*. Ed. Thomas O. Sloane. New York: Oxford UP, 2001. 92–115.

———. *Greek Rhetoric under Christian Emperors*. Princeton: Princeton UP, 1983.

———. "Historical Survey of Rhetoric." *Handbook of Classical Rhetoric in the Hellenistic Period*. Ed. Stanley E. Porter. New York: Brill, 1997. 3–42.

———. *A New History of Classical Rhetoric*. Princeton: Princeton UP, 1994.

Kerferd, G. B. *The Sophistic Movement*. Cambridge: Cambridge UP, 1981.

Kersey, Ethel M. *Women Philosophers: A Bio-Critical Source Book*. Ed. Calvin O. Schrag. Westport, CT: Greenwood, 1989.

Kirk, G. S., J. E. Raven, and M. Schofield. *The Presocratic Philosophers: A Critical History with a Selection of Texts*. 3rd ed. New York: Cambridge UP, 1983.

Lanham, Carol Dana, ed. *Latin Grammar and Rhetoric: From Classical Theory to Medieval Practice*. London: Continuum, 2002.

Lanham, Richard A. *A Handlist of Rhetorical Terms*. 2nd ed. Berkeley: U of California P, 1991.

Lentz, Tony M. *Orality and Literacy in Hellenic Greece*. Carbondale: Southern Illinois UP, 1989.

Litfin, Duane. *St. Paul's Theology of Persuasion*. Cambridge: Cambridge UP, 1994.

Lunsford, Andrea A., ed. *Reclaiming Rhetorica: Women in the Rhetorical Tradition*. Pittsburgh: U of Pittsburgh P, 1995.

Mackin, John H. *Classical Rhetoric for Modern Discourse*. New York: Free P, 1969.

Mahony, Kieran J. *Pauline Persuasion*. Shefield: Sheffield Academic P, 2000.

Marrou, Henri Irenee. *A History of Education in Antiquity*. Trans. George Lamb. Madison: U of Wisconsin P, 1982.

Matsen, Patricia P., Philip Rollinson, and Marion Sousa, eds. *Readings from Classical Rhetoric*. Carbondale: Southern Illinois UP, 1990.

McComiskey, Bruce. *Gorgias and the New Sophistic Rhetoric*. Carbondale: Southern Illinois UP, 2002.

Ménage, Gilles. *The History of Women Philosophers*. Trans. Beatrice Zedler. Lanham, MD: UP of America, 1984.

Morstein-Marx, Robert. *Mass Oratory and Political Power in the Late Roman Republic*. New York: Cambridge UP, 2004.

Murphy, James J. "Conducting Research in the History of Rhetoric: An Open Letter to a Future Historian of Rhetoric." *Publishing in Rhetoric and Composition*. Ed. Gary A. Olson and Todd Taylor. Albany: State U of New York P, 1997. 187–95.

———. *Rhetoric in the Middle Ages: A History of Rhetorical Theory from St. Augustine to the Renaissance*. Berkeley: U of California P, 1974.

———, ed. *A Short History of Writing Instruction from Ancient Greece to Modern America*. 2nd ed. Mahwah, NJ: Erlbaum, 2001.

Murphy, James J., and Richard A. Katula, with Forbes Hill and Donovan J. Ochs, eds. *A Synoptic History of Classical Rhetoric*. 3rd ed. Mahwah, NJ: Hermagoras, 2003.

Neel, Jasper. *Plato, Derrida, and Writing*. Carbondale: Southern Illinois UP, 1988.

Nye, Andrea. *Words of Power: A Feminist Reading of the History of Logic*. New York: Routledge, 1990.

Oberhelman, Steven M. *Rhetoric and Homiletics in Fourth-Century Christian Literature*. Atlanta, GA: Scholars, 1991.

Peterson, Brian K. *Eloquence and Proclamation of the Gospel in Corinth*. Atlanta, GA: Scholars, 1994.

Porter, Stanley E., ed. *Handbook of Classical Rhetoric in the Hellenistic Period*. New York: Brill, 1997.

Poulakos, John. "Interpreting Sophistical Rhetoric: A Response to Schiappa." *Philosophy and Rhetoric* 23.3 (1990): 218–28.

———. *Sophistical Rhetoric in Classical Greece*. Columbia: U of South Carolina P, 1995.

Poulakos, John, and Takis Poulakos. *Classical Rhetorical Theory*. Boston: Houghton Mifflin, 1999.

Poulakos, Takis, ed. *Rethinking the History of Rhetoric*. Boulder, CO: Westview, 1993.

Rees, Roger. *Layers of Loyalty in Latin Panegyric: AD 289–307*. Oxford: Oxford UP, 2002.

Rollinson, Philip B., and Richard Geckle. *A Guide to Classical Rhetoric*. Signal Mountain, TN: Summertown, 1998.

Schiappa, Edward. *The Beginnings of Rhetorical Theory in Classical Greece*. New Haven: Yale UP, 1999.

———, ed. *Landmark Essays on Classical Greek Rhetoric*. Davis, CA: Hermagoras, 1994.

———. "Neo-Sophistic Rhetorical Criticism or the Historical Reconstruction of Sophistic Doctrines?" *Philosophy and Rhetoric* 23.3 (1990): 192–217.

Sipiora, Phillip, and James S. Baumlin, eds. *Rhetoric and Kairos: Essays in History, Theory, and Praxis*. Albany: State U of New York P, 2002.

Sloane, Thomas O., ed. *Encyclopedia of Rhetoric*. Oxford: Oxford UP, 2001.

Smith, Robert W. *The Art of Rhetoric in Alexandria*. The Hague: Martinus Nijhoff, 1974.

Sprague, Rosamond Kent, ed. *The Older Sophists*. Columbia: U of South Carolina P, 1972.

Steiner, Deborah Tarn. *The Tyrant's Writ: Myths and Images of Writing in Ancient Greece*. Princeton: Princeton UP, 1994.

Swearingen, C. Jan. *Rhetoric and Irony: Western Literacy and Western Lies*. Oxford UP, 1991.

Untersteiner, Mario. *The Sophists*. Trans. Kathleen Freeman. Oxford: Blackwell, 1954.

Usher, Stephen. *Greek Oratory: Tradition and Originality*. Oxford UP, 1999.

Vickers, Brian. *In Defence of Rhetoric*. 1988. Oxford: Clarendon, 1997.

Vitanza, Victor J. *Negation, Subjectivity, and the History of Rhetoric*. Albany: State U of New York P, 1997.

———, ed. Special Issue: "Historiography and the Histories of Rhetorics I: Revisionary Histories." *Pre/Text* 8.1–2 (1987).

———. "The Sophists?" *Negation, Subjectivity, and the History of Rhetoric*. Albany: State U of New York P, 1997. 27–56.

———, ed. *Writing Histories of Rhetoric*. Carbondale: Southern Illinois UP, 1994.

Waithe, Mary Ellen, ed. *A History of Women Philosophers*. Vol. 1. Dordrecht: Martinus Nijhoff, 1987.

Walker, Jeffrey. *Rhetoric and Poetics in Antiquity*. New York: Oxford UP, 2000.

Welborn, L. L. *Politics and Rhetoric in the Corinthian Epistles*. Macon: Mercer UP, 1997.

Welch, Kathleen E. *Contemporary Reception of Classical Rhetoric: Appropriations of Ancient Discourse.*
        Hillsdale, NJ: Erlbaum, 1990.
————. *Electric Rhetoric: Classical Rhetoric, Oralism, and a New Literacy.* Cambridge, MA: MIT P,
        1999.
Whitby, Mary, ed. *The Propaganda of Power: The Role of Panegyric in Late Antiquity.* Boston: Brill,
        1998.
Winter, Bruce W. *Philo and Paul among the Sophists.* Cambridge: Cambridge UP, 1997.
Winterbottom, Michael. *Roman Declamation.* Bristol: Bristol Classical, 1980.
Worthington, Ian, ed. *Persuasion: Greek Rhetoric in Action.* London: Routledge, 1994.
Yunis, Harvey. *Taming Democracy: Models of Political Rhetoric in Classical Athens.* Cornell UP,
        1996.

INDEX

About the Editors
and the Contributors

Editors

MICHELLE BALLIF is Associate Professor in the Department of English at the University of Georgia, where she teaches courses in rhetorical theory, the history of rhetoric, writing theory, and literary theory. With research interests in the relations between classical rhetoric and contemporary theory, she is the author of *Seduction, Sophistry, and the Woman with the Rhetorical Figure* and the coeditor (with Michael G. Moran) of *Twentieth-Century Rhetorics and Rhetoricians*.

MICHAEL G. MORAN is Associate Professor of English and Graduate Coordinator at the University of Georgia, where he teaches courses in writing, rhetorical theory, the history of rhetoric, and eighteenth-century British literature. His most recent edited volumes are *Eighteenth-Century British and American Rhetorics and Rhetoricians* and, with Michelle Ballif, *Twentieth-Century Rhetorics and Rhetoricians*. His research interests include the history of composition theory and practice and the history of technical communication.

Contributors

JANET M. ATWILL is Professor of English at the University of Tennessee. She is the author of *Rhetoric Reclaimed: Aristotle and the Liberal Arts* and coeditor of *Perspectives on Rhetorical Invention* and *The Viability of the Rhetorical Tradition*. She is the 2005 president of the American Society for the History of Rhetoric and serves on numerous editorial boards. She is presently completing a book titled *New Civic Rhetorics*.

BETH S. BENNETT is Associate Professor of Rhetorical Studies at the University of Alabama, where she teaches various undergraduate and graduate courses in rhetorical studies for the Department of Communication Studies. She studies the historical development of rhetorical theory and practice, from the classical period to the present, specifically publishing work in the area of medieval rhetoric. She also is interested in the critical application of rhetorical principles to contemporary issues affecting human communication, in both traditional and new media.

GRANT M. BOSWELL is Associate Professor of English at Brigham Young University, where he teaches composition, language, rhetoric, and theory. His research interests and publications focus on rhetorical theory and the history of rhetoric, specifically rhetoric in the seventeenth century, including rhetoric and religious disputes, rhetoric and Christian meditation, and rhetoric and education.

JOY CONNOLLY is Assistant Professor of Classics at New York University. She is the author of *Citizens and Subjects*, a book on rhetoric and political theory in ancient Rome forthcoming from Princeton University Press. Her interests include the history of political thought, feminist theory, and Latin literature. She holds degrees from Princeton and the University of Pennsylvania, and has previously taught at the University of Washington and Stanford University.

D. DIANE DAVIS is Assistant Professor in the Division of Rhetoric and the Department of English at the University of Texas at Austin, where she teaches graduate courses in rhetoric and writing theory and undergraduate courses in cyberculture. She is the author of *Breaking Up [at] Totality: A Rhetoric of Laughter* and the editor of *The UberReader: Selected Works of Avital Ronell* (forthcoming from the University of Illinois Press). She is currently completing a collaborative book with Michelle Ballif and Roxanne Mountford titled *Women's Ways of Making It . . . In Rhetoric and Composition* (forthcoming from Erlbaum), and a second single-authored book titled *Inessential Solidarity*, which addresses the intersections of rhetoric and community after humanism.

JANET B. DAVIS is Emerita Professor of Communication at Truman State University in Kirksville, Missouri. She was trained as a classicist, receiving the BA in Latin and Greek with First Class Honours from the University of Bristol, England. She earned an MA in Communication from the University of Nebraska at Omaha and a PhD in Communication Studies from the University of Iowa. She is currently at work on a translation into English of Hermogenes' *On Invention*.

CHRISTY DESMET is Associate Professor and Director of First-Year Composition at the University of Georgia. She is the author of *Reading Shakespeare's Characters: Rhetoric, Ethics, and Identity* (1992) and of essays on rhetoric and computers and composition. With Robert Sawyer, she has edited *Shakespeare and Appropriation* (1999) and *Harold Bloom's Shakespeare* (2001).

RICHARD LEO ENOS received his PhD from Indiana University (1973) and is Professor and holder of the Lillian Radford Chair of Rhetoric and Composition at

Texas Christian University. He has studied with the Vergilian Society in Italy and at the American School of Classical Studies at Athens. His area of research is in classical rhetoric with an emphasis on the relationship between thought and expression in antiquity. He is the recipient of the Karl R. Wallace Award (1976) and the Richard E. Young Award (1992) for research in classical rhetoric.

ELIZABETH ERVIN is Associate Professor of English and former director of the Women's Resource Center at the University of North Carolina at Wilmington. She has taught writing at all levels, composition theory and pedagogy for K–12 teachers, rhetorical theory at the graduate and undergraduate levels, and women's studies. Her primary research focus is public writing: the circumstances that inspire it among people who normally do not think of themselves as writers, the ways in which it is circulated and mediated in the present, and the ways in which it supports or fails to support political ideals. She is currently working on a book project that explores the rhetorical concept of *copia*.

DANIEL R. FREDRICK studied with Richard Leo Enos at Texas Christian University while working on his dissertation, "Helmsmen of the State: An Explication of Cicero's Rhetorical Theory" (2003). He is Assistant Professor at the American University of Bulgaria in Blagoevgrad. His research interests include classical rhetoric, orality and literacy, and classical rhetoric pedagogy.

MICHAEL GAGARIN is the James R. Dougherty, Jr., Centennial Professor of Classics at the University of Texas. He has written widely in the areas of Greek law, rhetoric, literature, and philosophy, with works including *Drakon and Early Athenian Homicide Law* (New Haven, 1981), *Early Greek Law* (Berkeley, 1986), *The Murder of Herodes* (Frankfurt, 1989), and *Antiphon the Athenian: Oratory, Law and Justice in the Age of the Sophists* (Austin, 2002).

ROBERT N. GAINES is Director of Honors Humanities and Associate Professor of Communication at the University of Maryland, College Park. His recent research explores the interactions of rhetoric with philosophy in ancient times—particularly in relation to the works of Cicero and Philodemus. He is currently composing a critical edition and translation of Philodemus's *On Rhetoric*, book 4.

D. ALEXIS HART is Assistant Professor of Rhetoric and Composition at the Virginia Military Institute. Her research interests include Isocrates, civic rhetoric, digital citizenship, computers and writing, and markup languages.

EKATERINA HASKINS is the author of *Logos and Power in Isocrates and Aristotle* (University of South Carolina Press, 2004). Her research on classical and contemporary rhetoric has been published in the *Quarterly Journal of Speech*, *Rhetoric Society Quarterly*, *Philosophy and Rhetoric*, *Space and Culture*, *Journal of Communication Inquiry*, and *American Communication Journal* as well as in a number of edited collections. She is president of the American Society for the History of Rhetoric and book review editor for the *Rhetoric Society Quarterly*. Haskins teaches in the Department of Language, Literature, and Communication at the Rensselaer Polytechnic Institute.

GARY L. HATCH is Associate Dean of Undergraduate Education at Brigham Young University and oversees the University Writing Program. His current research focuses on the influence of the classical rhetorical tradition on the teaching of composition.

MARTIN M. JACOBSEN, Assistant Professor of English at West Texas A&M University, won the WTAMU 2001–2002 Excellence in Teaching Award. His book, *Transformations of Literacy in Computer-Mediated Communication: Orality, Literacy, Cyberdiscursivity*, was published by the Edwin Mellen Press in 2002. He has also published several articles, online articles, and reviews. He earned his PhD in Discourse Studies at Texas A&M University in 1999.

KAREN D. JOBE is a PhD student in Composition, Rhetoric, and Literacy at the University of Oklahoma, currently working on her dissertation. She also is an Instructor of English at Oklahoma State University in Oklahoma City.

CHRISTOPHER LYLE JOHNSTONE is Associate Professor of Rhetoric and Basic Course Director in the Department of Communication Arts and Sciences at the Pennsylvania State University. His teaching and research interests focus on Greek rhetoric and philosophy, the history of rhetorical theory and practice, and communication ethics. His essays in these areas have appeared in such journals as *The Quarterly Journal of Speech* and *Philosophy and Rhetoric*, and in several edited books. His current research investigates the connections between speech and wisdom in early Greek thought.

HANS KELLNER is Professor of English at North Carolina State University. He is the author of *Language and Historical Representation: Getting the Story Crooked*, coeditor (with F. R. Ankersmit) of *A New Philosophy of History*, and of essays on rhetorical and historical theory.

JUSTIN KILLIAN is currently a graduate student in the Department of Speech Communication at the University of Georgia. His research interests include classical rhetorical theory, political and campaign communication, and issues related to gender.

JOHN T. KIRBY is Professor of Classics at Purdue University, where he has chaired the programs in Classical Studies and in Comparative Literature. His books include *The Rhetoric of Cicero's Pro Cluentio* (Gieben, 1990), *The Comparative Reader* (Chancery Press, 1998), *Secret of the Muses Retold* (University of Chicago Press, 2000), *Classical Greek Civilization* (Gale, 2001), and *The Roman Republic* (Gale, 2001).

WILFRED E. MAJOR has published on ancient Greek stage comedy, from Aristophanes to Menander, and is continuing his research into the development of rhetoric in ancient Greece. Currently he teaches at Louisiana State University.

RAYMIE MCKERROW is Professor in the School of Communication Studies at Ohio University and Director of the McNair Scholars Program. He teaches courses in argument at the undergraduate level and in feminist rhetorical theory, Foucault and social change, and rhetoric and culture at the graduate level. His current research is centered on issues of civility in the public sphere.

J. E. PARKER MIDDLETON is Assistant Director of the Franklin College Writing Intensive Program at the University of Georgia and an academic advisor for students entering the Grady College of Journalism and Mass Communication. Her teaching and research involve writing productivity, writing and task engagement, advertising and media rhetoric, and the scholarship of teaching and learning.

JERRY L. MILLER is Associate Professor and Cassese Director of Forensics at Ohio University. His research interests include political communication (specifically, political advertising and gender) and argumentation. His teaching interests include argumentation, forensics pedagogy, and gender communication. He has published articles in journals such as *Political Communication* and *Contemporary Argumentation and Debate*.

ANGELA MITCHELL MISS graduated with her PhD in English from the University of Georgia in the spring of 2004. Her research interests include examining connections between classical rhetoric and digital technologies.

ROXANNE MOUNTFORD is Associate Professor of English at the University of Arizona, where she teaches history and theory of rhetoric, religious rhetoric, gender and communication, and ethnographic methods. She is the author of *The Gendered Pulpit: Preaching in American Protestant Spaces* and numerous essays in edited volumes and such journals as *JAC*, *Rhetoric Review*, and *Rhetoric Society Quarterly*. She is currently coauthoring a book on issues affecting women faculty in rhetoric and composition.

SEAN PATRICK O'ROURKE is Associate Professor of Rhetoric in the Department of Communication Studies at Furman University. A former president of the American Society for the History of Rhetoric, he writes on rhetoric, law, and civil rights.

LARA O'SULLIVAN is a graduate of the University of Western Australia, where she also teaches in Classics and Ancient History. Her doctoral dissertation was on Demetrius of Phaleron, and she has published several articles on early Hellenistic political and intellectual history.

NEIL O'SULLIVAN is Senior Lecturer in Classics and Ancient History at the University of Western Australia. A graduate of the universities of Melbourne and Cambridge, he has research interests in Greek literature of the fifth and fourth centuries BCE. His publications include *Alcidamas, Aristophanes and the Beginnings of Greek Stylistic Theory* (Stuttgart, 1992).

PATRICK O'SULLIVAN received his BA and MA from Melbourne University and his PhD from Cambridge, and is Lecturer in the Department of Classics at the University of Canterbury (New Zealand). He has published on Greek drama, lyric poetry, and rhetoric as well as Greek and Roman art. Currently he is working on a book on Euripides' *Cyclops* and major fragments of satiric drama, to be published by Aris and Phillips.

CHARLES PLATTER is Associate Professor of Classics at the University of Georgia. He is the coeditor of *Rethinking Sexuality: Foucault and Classical Antiquity*. His most recent work is *Aristophanes and the Carnival of Genres*.

JOHN POULAKOS is Associate Professor in the Communication Department at the University of Pittsburgh, where he teaches rhetorical theory, philosophy and rhetoric, and history of rhetoric. He is the author of *Sophistical Rhetoric in Classical Greece* and coauthor of *Classical Rhetorical Theory*. He is currently working on a book about rhetoric and aesthetics.

TAKIS POULAKOS was born and grew up in Nafplion, Greece. He has taught at the University of Pittsburgh and is now Associate Professor of Rhetoric at the University of Iowa. He is the author of *Speaking for the Polis*, the editor of *Rethinking the History of Rhetoric*, and the coeditor of *Isocrates' Civic Education*.

GEORGE PULLMAN is Associate Professor in the English Department at Georgia State University where he teaches history of rhetoric and digital information design. He has published articles in such journals as *Rhetoric Society Quarterly, Rhetoric Review,* and *JAC*.

SCOTT G. REED is a PhD student at the University of Georgia concentrating in new media and rhetoric and composition studies. His current projects focus on imagistic and algorithmic approaches to composition, and critical intersections between aesthetic and rhetorical theories.

DAVID CHRISTOPHER RYAN is Assistant Professor of Communication Studies at the University of San Francisco. His research and teaching interests relate the proto-pedagogy and civic rhetoric of Isocrates to modern composition theories and practices. His teaching, research, and publishing interests include classical rhetoric, theories of orality and literacy, and rhetorical pedagogy. He has published in *Rhetoric Review* and has published articles on Renaissance poetry.

EDWARD SCHIAPPA holds the Paul W. Frenzel Chair of Liberal Arts at the University of Minnesota, where he is Professor and Director of Graduate Studies in the Department of Communication Studies. His books include *Defining Reality: Definitions and the Politics of Meaning*, *Protagoras and Logos: A Study in Greek Philosophy and Rhetoric*, and *The Beginnings of Greek Rhetorical Theory*.

JANE SUTTON is Associate Professor in the Department of Communication Arts and Sciences at Penn State University, York campus, where she coordinates the undergraduate degree in CAS and teaches rhetorical theory, rhetorical criticism, and courses in communication and culture and public speaking. She is currently completing a book-length manuscript titled "In the House of Rhetoric." She is past president of the American Society for the History of Rhetoric and the author of numerous articles, book chapters, and review essays on the history of rhetoric, sophistical rhetoric, and feminist studies of rhetoric. Her work has appeared in *Rhetorica, Philosophy and Rhetoric, The Canadian Journal of Rhetorical Studies, Argumentation, Southern Communication Journal, The Canadian Journal of Rhetorical Studies, PRE/TEXT: A Journal of Rhetorical Theory, Tidskrift för Littaturvetenskap, Rhetoric Society Quarterly, Quarterly Journal of Speech*, and *Rhetoric Review*.

C. JAN SWEARINGEN is Professor of English at Texas A&M University and a past president of the Rhetoric Society of America (1998–2000). Her book *Rhetoric and Irony: Western Literacy and Western Lies* (Oxford University Press, 1991) shared the W. Ross Winterowd Award in 1992, and has been translated into Chinese (2004). She has published numerous articles and chapters on the history of rhetoric, women in the history of rhetoric, rhetoric and religion, and literacy-orality studies. Her edited collection, *Rhetoric, the Polis, and the Global Village*, brings together ancient and modern rhetorical studies of the relations among rhetoric, community, and democracy.

DAVID M. TIMMERMAN is Associate Professor and Chair of the Speech Department at Wabash College in Crawfordsville, Indiana. He teaches courses in classical rhetoric as well as rhetorical theory, African American rhetoric, legal debate, and political debate. His work on classical rhetoric has appeared in *Rhetoric Society Quarterly, Argumentation and Advocacy, Advances in the History of Rhetoric, Philosophy and Rhetoric*, and the *Encyclopedia of Rhetoric*.

YUN LEE TOO has published seven books including *The Idea of Ancient Literary Criticism* (Oxford University Press, 1998) and the edited work *Education in Greek and Roman Antiquity* (EJ Brill, Leiden, 2001).

VICTOR J. VITANZA is Professor of Rhetoric at the University of Texas at Arlington, where he teaches the history of rhetoric, multimedia authoring, and film theory. He is the author of *Negation, Subjectivity, and the History of Rhetoric* and the editor of *The CyberReader, Writing Histories of Rhetoric*, and *PRE/TEXT: The First*

Decade. He is the editor and publisher of both the journal *PRE/TEXT* and of its online cousin, *PRE/TEXT: Electra(Lite).* He has just completed the sequel to *Negation,* titled *Chaste Rape,* which concerns ways of thinking, reading, and writing about sexual violence and specifically suggests ways of thinking about the proximities among "rape," "pedagogy," and "canon/ization."

JEFFREY WALKER received his PhD in Rhetoric from the University of California, Berkeley (1985), and is Professor of Rhetoric and Composition at the University of Texas, Austin. He is the author of *Bardic Ethos and the American Epic Poem* (1989), *Rhetoric and Poetics in Antiquity* (2000), and numerous articles and essays on ancient rhetoric and rhetorical theory.

KATHLEEN ETHEL WELCH, Samuel Roberts Noble Family Foundation Presidential Professor of English at the University of Oklahoma, is the author of *Electric Rhetoric: Classical Rhetoric, Oralism, and a New Literacy, The Contemporary Reception of Classical Rhetoric: Appropriations of Ancient Discourse,* and numerous essays in *College Composition and Communication, Rhetoric Review, Written Communication, Into the Blogosphere* (ed. Laura Gurak et al.), *Rhetoric Society Quarterly,* and other scholarly journals. She is founding president of the Coalition of Women Scholars in the History of Rhetoric and Composition and past president of the Rhetoric Society of America and of the Association of Teachers of Advanced Composition. Her in-progress book is *Power Surge: Computers and Writing.* She teaches writing at all levels, including technical writing and writing in the digital realm.